RHODE ISLAND

MICHAEL BLANDING & ALEXANDRA HALL

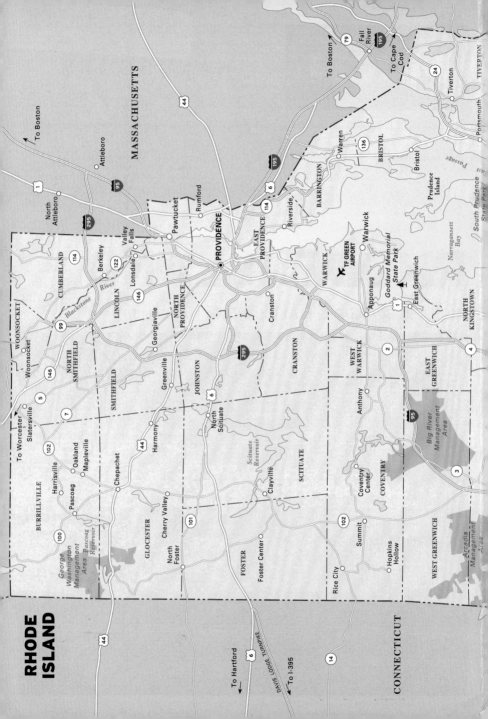

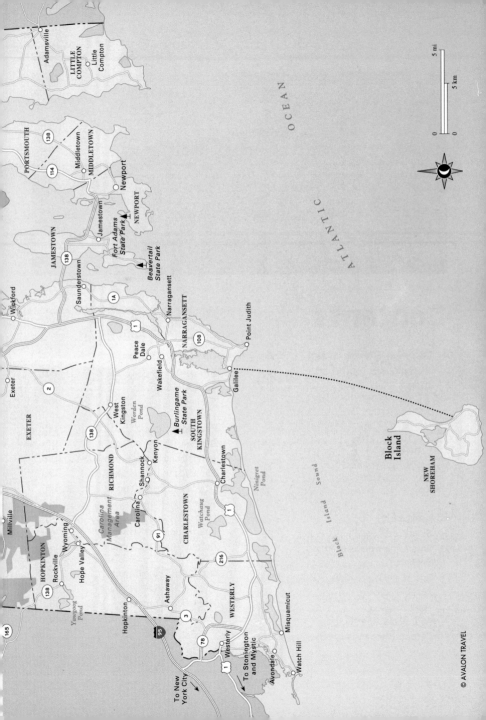

Contents

Discover Rhode Island

The nickname "Ocean State" may sound like a slight exaggeration for Rhode Island – its 42 miles of ocean frontage, after all, is less than virtually every other state. And yet, no state has been so dramatically shaped by the ocean in its economy, history, and landscape. Whether it's the soaring seaside cliffs of Block Island, the yachting anchorages of Newport and Bristol, or the miles of sunny beaches of South County, the constant scenic interplay of land and wave dominates the memories of many visitors.

But the ocean has had a more subtle influence on the character of the people. The second-smallest state in the union, Rhode Island maintains a low profile compared to its louder New England neighbors. Its historic connection to the sea, however – through shipbuilding, fishing, and trade – has given it a broad, independent outlook since it was first founded by religious heretics seeking a better, more tolerant life. "Little Rhody" was the first state in the union to declare its independence, two months before that first Fourth of July. It was the first to outlaw the slave trade. And it was the state where the fast-running rivers and Yankee ingenuity first gave rise to the industrial revolution that transformed the United States from agrarian backwater to industrial powerhouse.

That spirit of independence and ingenuity has continued to the present day. Rhode Island's capital city, Providence, has become a model of urban renaissance, building on its artsy, student-oriented population to

revive a downtown that charms visitors with upscale restaurants and art galleries even while maintaining its youthful, funky edge. Perhaps it's being in touch with the rhythms of the sea that has made Rhode Islanders throughout the state more laid-back and low-key than their tightly wound Northeastern cousins. The state's small size makes it feel like everyone knows everyone else – and once you are invited into the club, it make them feel uncommonly gregarious and welcoming for New Englanders (especially once you learn the native patois of coffee milk, stuffies, and of course, Buddy).

Sure, Rhode Island can be tacked onto a trip to the rest of the region, but it takes spending a few days or a week here to really get into the state's unique spirit. And, of course, it takes getting out onto the water. While the ocean is still important to Rhode Island's fishing industry, these days it's even more important as the center of tourism. Days of vacationing here can be a blur of sails and sun, sand and surf, broken only by visions of the awesome mansions and grand hotels that still exist from the Victorian days when Rhode Island was first "discovered" as a vacation mecca. Then, as now, it brings its visitors back like the tide.

Planning Your Trip

▶ WHERE TO GO

From the perspective of tourism, little Rhode Island is a land of separate communities. You don't so much vacation in Rhode Island as you do in Newport, Providence, South County, the East Bay, or Block Island. That being said, if you spend time in any one part of Rhode Island, you'll find it quite simple to venture over to virtually any other town in the state, which is just a short drive away.

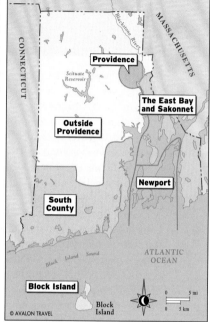

Newport

Newport offers the sophistication and luxury as well as lodging and dining variety you might expect of much larger East Coast cities, and yet it's a fairly small place that's easy to navigate. It's both a well-preserved colonial seaport community and a living history museum of the Gilded Age, with stunning mansions situated on rocky cliffs. It's an adult-oriented city, with few attractions and accommodations geared to kids; this makes it an ideal getaway for a romantic weekend.

The East Bay and Sakonnet

East Bay is a great weekend destination: Warren is an antiques hub while stately Bristol features charming inns and good museums. Sakonnet makes a great day trip as it's laced with country roads and contains a handful of fun shops, cafés, roadside farm stands, and a bit of beach access. Alas, there are hardly any accommodations in Sakonnet's two towns, Little Compton and Tiverton, but it's a short drive from either Aquidneck Island or Bristol.

Providence

Providence offers the gastronomical experience you might expect of a city several times its size, and it feels like the coolest college town and the most genuine blue-collar enclave at the same time.

The presence of several colleges—Brown University, the Rhode Island School of Design (RISD), Johnson and Wales, and Providence College—give the city a youthful, alternative edge and a thriving music, fine arts, and club scene.

Outside Providence

Greater Providence encapsulates a diversity of environments that reward day-trips, drive-throughs, and even longer stays. The Blackstone River Valley features

WaterPlace Park in Providence is a great spot for a stroll.

recreational opportunities thanks to its fast-running river.

More outdoor activities can be found west of the city in Glocester, Burrillville, and Scituate, which abound with opportunities for biking, hiking, and boating as well as back-country drives through picturesque villages.

South County

This part of Rhode Island offers a mix of lively beach villages studded with condos, motels, and guesthouses along with quieter interior communities known for lush forests, rippling ponds and rivers, and great hiking and golfing. The coastal area tends to be seasonal and is best visited from spring through summer. This is the most family-friendly part of Rhode Island, owing to its busy beaches with kid-oriented diversions, from miniature golf to water sports.

Block Island

Block Island is both beautiful and accessible, thanks to a conservancy that preserves more than a quarter of the island's open spaces. You'll find historic bed-and-breakfasts and inns here, including several mammoth Victorian hotels.

▶ WHEN TO GO

Rhode Island is a year-round destination. If you're planning to take advantage of the Ocean State's vast access to the water, focus your visit around the warmest months, generally from mid-May through mid-October and especially from mid-June through Labor Day. Keep in mind, however, that in Newport, Block Island, and South County, you'll be competing with throngs of other sea-lovers for space and parking at the beach,

IF YOU HAVE . . .

- **A WEEKEND:** Visit Newport, with one day to tour the mansions and another to stroll the waterfront and take a sail.

- **5 DAYS:** Add a trip to Providence, stopping on the way to explore the East Bay towns of Warren and Bristol.

- **A WEEK:** Add a day at a South County beach and an overnight to Block Island.

- **10 DAYS:** Add side trips to the Sakonnet Peninsula, the Blackstone River Valley, and a drive around the villages west of Providence.

in restaurants, and at hotels. Newport and parts of South County have made an effort to attract off-season visitors; museums have begun keeping longer winter hours, and many hotels offer special rates in the off-season. Block Island has few hotel options and even fewer dining options in winter. The best compromise might be visiting in shoulder season—in May before Memorial Day, when the days are often warm and sunny, or in September after Labor Day, when the ocean is at its warmest.

Because the colleges in Providence infuse downtown and College Hill with energy when the schools are in session, some visitors prefer fall, spring, and even winter in the state capital, which can seem empty in summer when there aren't as many students. Providence can also be uncomfortably hot and muggy in July and August. Winters are not brutal, but the state does get socked with the occasional snow- or ice storm, and the wind and frigidity can be uncomfortable from December through March.

The most bewitching and scenic seasons in Rhode Island are spring, when the entire state is abloom with greenery and flowers, and fall, when the foliage changes color, the woods lighting up with brilliant swamp maples and the fields with cherry-red cranberry bogs.

▶ BEFORE YOU GO

Planning a trip to Rhode Island is not unlike planning for a trip to any city or town with a four-season climate and an oceanfront setting. This is a small, somewhat industrialized state without a great many opportunities for true wilderness hiking and camping, so unless you're planning a very specific adventure of this kind, it's not necessary to think much in terms of advanced camping gear. Also, virtually nowhere in the state are you very far from almost any kind of household, clothing, food, or travel supply—distances in Rhode Island between gas stations, grocery stores, and department stores are very short.

Winters are not as brutally cold here as they are in northern New England, but it can snow as early as November and as late as April, or rarely even in early May, so especially when visiting during the spring or fall, prepare for a wide range of weather. You could need shorts and short-sleeved shirts in October or April, or you might want to bundle up at these times.

If you're headed toward the shore, as so many vacationers in Rhode Island are, bring your sandals, swimwear, and a windbreaker, even in summer, as it can be very cool if you're out on the water sailing. Also, while it's easy to find sunscreen and other conveniences at shops throughout the shore towns, it's more economical to bring these supplies yourself.

Explore Rhode Island

▶ THE BEST OF RHODE ISLAND

With a week to explore Rhode Island, you can easily see the state's key towns and cities and enjoy a sampling of its major attractions. This approach begins in Providence and then steers you down through the state's coastal hubs, ending in Bristol, just an hour's drive from Providence. It's not difficult to manage this tour in just five to six days by using Providence and Newport as your bases and spending one night instead of two on Block Island, but to fully soak up the region's appeal, plan to take seven full days to get around.

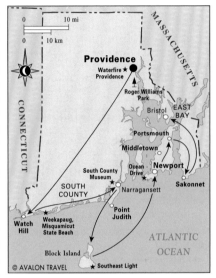

Days 1-2: Providence

Providence's renaissance has occurred largely around its downtown riverfront, so spend your first day getting acquainted with WaterPlace Park, perhaps taking a ride on a gondola during the warmer months. On many Saturdays from March through November you can also watch the dazzling Waterfire Providence, a dramatic display of bonfires set in cauldrons along the river.

In the same day, you can cross the river to College Hill, home to Brown University and the Rhode Island School of Design as well as several attractions, some of them related to the neighborhood's academic institutions: must-sees include the John Brown House, the RISD Art Museum, and the Providence Athenaeum. Be sure to stroll along Benefit Street, which is lined with stunning Colonial and Victorian homes, and check out the funky shopping, gallery-hopping, and inexpensive dining along both Thayer and Wickenden Streets.

On your second day, make a point of getting out of town, either to Roger Williams Park, which is four miles south of downtown (either drive or take the bus). This sprawling green park contains Roger Williams Park Zoo and the excellent Museum of Natural History, making it an especially enjoyable attraction if you have kids in tow. Alternatively, make a day trip north of the city to Slater Mill Historic Site, in downtown Pawtucket, a 15-minute drive north of Providence. Finish off the day with dinner and a stroll through Federal Hill, Providence's mecca for Italian food and culture.

Day 3: South County

Laid-back South County contains some of Rhode Island's best beaches as well as copious opportunities for hiking, boating, golfing, and getting outside. It's also where you

SHACKING UP

Rhode Island is chockfull of that time-honored institution, the classic New England clam shack. Almost all of them claim to fry up the best clam around, but each also boasts slightly different specialties and unique traits. For those who aren't fans of the clam, there are almost always other options: lobster rolls, fish-and-chips, mussels, clam cakes, peel-and-eat shrimp, and other options, usually served simply on paper plates (and with plenty of napkins, of course). Here are the local favorites:

- **Flo's Clam Shack** (4 Wave Ave., Middleton, 401/847-8141) is loved for its clam cakes and fried oysters, but the raw bar is worth digging into too.

- **The Starboard Galley** (1 Charlestown Beach Rd., Charlestown, 401/364-7100) is all about

the chowder (or "chowdah," as it's more regularly called).

- **Hammerhead Grill** (1230 Ocean Rd., Narragansett, 401/789-6159) churns out ultra-fresh fish-and-chips and serves them on an open-air deck overlooking the sea.

- **Iggy's Doughboys & Chowder House** (1157 Point Judith Rd., Narragansett, 401/783-5608) is as popular for its nonseafood offerings (sausage-and-peppers lovers line up nightly) as for its fried calamari and clams.

- **Champlin's Seafood Deck** (256 Great Island Rd., Narragansett, 401/783-3152) is about as fresh as they come: It's situated on a fishing dock and is part restaurant, part fish market. Go for the lobster roll; you won't regret it.

catch the ferry to the next place on this tour, Block Island.

A great way to make the most of a day in South County is to drive along the shore, beginning in the quaint Victorian seaside town of Watch Hill and continuing along Route 1A and U.S. 1 (and some side roads) through such charming seaside communities as Weekapaug, Misquamicut State Beach (the best spot for a stroll along the sand or some saltwater taffy), Charlestown, Jerusalem, Galilee, and Point Judith. A bit north, Narragansett is home to the county's top attractions, South County Museum, which preserves the legacy of a gentleman's farm, and the Gilbert Stuart Museum, the home of George Washington's foremost portraitist. Don't feel like you have to spend the day sightseeing, however—when you find the beach that matches your personality, whether that's kid-friendly Watch Hill, pristine Charlestown, or raucous Misquamicut, feel free to pull out that towel and sunbathe.

Day 4: Block Island

Beautiful and isolated Block Island, just 10 miles or so south of the mainland, feels a world away from the rest of the state. Far less developed than other New England island retreats, such as Martha's Vineyard and Nantucket, Block Island is home to numerous nature preserves as well as some of the grandest Victorian seaside resorts in the country. While it's possible to go for an afternoon, you'll need an overnight stay to really get the feel of the island. Go for a bike ride, hike along the grounds of Southeast Light or through Rodman's Hollow preserve, grab an ice-cream cone at Aldo's, or simply laze away your time reading in a lawn chair at your hotel.

Days 5-6: Newport

You should not visit Newport without taking a road trip along winding Ocean Drive, which meanders along the waterfront and affords close-up views of some of this small city's prettiest homes. Spend the rest of your

SAILING, FISHING, AND KAYAKING

They don't call it the Ocean State for nothing – Rhode Islanders live on the water, especially in summertime, hitting the waves for a variety of water sports. Opportunities span the state and range from adventurous to relaxing. Here are some spots to enjoy them.

SAILING

Newport is the undisputed center for sailing on the Eastern Seaboard, and one of the best places in the world to harness the wind and the waves with a charter or a personal lesson. A combination of stunning natural beauty and experienced yachters means you won't have a hard time putting together the perfect sailing experience. Try the **Newport Yacht Charter Association** (28 Church St., 401/849-3340, www.newportcharters.com) to find a captain, or **Sail Newport** (60 Fort Adams Dr., 401/846-1983 or 401/849-8385, www.sailnewport.org) to book a lesson.

yachting in Newport

DEEP-SEA FISHING

The waters of Block Island Sound run with the bluefish and striped bass, making it a perfect place to experience a deep-sea fishing expedition. Despite the decline of the New England fishing industry, little Galilee is still one of the top 20 fishing ports in the country, and it teems with experienced anglers who can take you out to enact your own personal Hemingway novel. Try **Frances Fleet** (33 State St., Galilee, 401/783-4988, www.francesfleet.com), which charters bluefish, striped bass, and tuna trips.

JET SKIING AND PARASAILING

Who says all water sports have to be relaxing? Nothing is as thrilling as jumping on a Jet Ski and launching yourself into the waves. You'll find a lot of company on Rhode Island's designated party beach, Misquamicut Beach, in South County. For rentals, stop by **Purple Ape** (401/596-9518, www.purpleape.com). If you'd rather fly above the waves than on them, parasailing is just as much an adrenaline rush with the added thrill of sightseeing from a completely different vantage point. Take a trip out to Block Island and strap yourself in with **Block Island Parasail** (401/864-2472, www.blockislandparasail.com) for one of the most dramatic ways to experience the island's famous clay bluffs.

CANOEING AND KAYAKING

Not all of the water-sports action in the state occurs offshore. Rhode Island's network of pristine rivers, especially in the Western and Southern sections of the state, makes for some heady kayaking and canoeing. One of the best spots is the crystalline **Wood River** in the state's southwest corner. Traveling its full length is an all-day affair through 14 miles of pristine woodland, with some good rapids along the way. Several good put-ins, however, offer shorter trips, including the relatively smooth six-mile run from Hope Valley Road Landing to Alton Dam. To plan the best trip, contact the **Kayak Centre** (562 Charlestown Beach Rd., Charlestown, 401/364-8000, www.kayakcentre.com).

EATING YOUR WAY THROUGH THE OCEAN STATE

Rhode Island may be tiny, but it has a big appetite. Most people know about quahogs, the local clam that's featured in just about everything, but clams just skim the surface of the state's unique palate.

Jonnycakes have a loyal following among fans of hearty breakfast fare. The cornmeal cakes are cooked on a griddle and carry considerably more flavor than their wheat-based cousins, pancakes. Typically served silver-dollar size, they come in a variety of styles, from thick and eggy cakes to thinner, almost crepe-like wafers. Try some at **Commons Lunch**.

Coffee cabinets, awful-awfuls, coffee milks, or frappés – whatever you call them, milk drinks flavored with coffee syrup and sometimes coffee ice cream have been a local favorite at diners and beach stands since the 1920s. **Newport Creamery** makes the, ahem, cream of the crop, but every mom-and-pop lunch counter makes a version, usually with Autocrat brand coffee syrup.

New York System wieners may have originated in Coney Island, but Rhode Island has adopted them as its favorite fast-food snack. Now sometimes just called "hot wieners," they are smaller than traditional hot dogs and stuffed with veal and pork. They are often smothered in hamburg sauce (a seasoned blend of finely ground hamburger meat) along with onions, celery salt, chili sauce, and mustard. For the full effect, order your wiener "all the way" at **Peter's Coney Island System**.

Rhode Island–style clam chowder differs from New England chowder (which has heavy or light cream) and Manhattan clam chowder (which has a tomato-based broth). Here the chowder has a clear broth and either no cream or just a touch of it. Clam juice is the main component of the broth, supplemented with chopped potatoes, diced celery, onions,

Ye Olde English Fish and Chips

and other seasonings. You can't go wrong with the chowder at the **Hitching Post**.

Clam cakes (or clam fritters) are not unlike their counterpart, crab cakes, but have more the look and consistency of Southern hushpuppies – they consist of chopped clams rolled into small cakes with a batter of beaten eggs, milk, flour, baking powder, and salt and pepper; these are then deep-fried to a golden brown and served with tartar sauce, Portuguese hot sauce, or just a squeeze of lemon. **Iggy's Doughboys** serves some of the best cakes in the state.

Last but not least, Rhode Island's state specialty, stuffed quahogs, are universally referred to as simply "stuffies." To make them, cooks take the biggest and juiciest quahogs they can find, steam them, chop them, and mix them with minced sautéed onions, bread crumbs, bell peppers, garlic, cayenne pepper or Tabasco sauce, parsley, saffron, and other spices. Once stuffed into the shell, they are baked for around 15 minutes. Eat a few from **Ye Olde English Fish and Chips** and you'll be stuffed as well.

the gardens at Blithewold Mansion

first day becoming acquainted with the compact and highly walkable downtown, making stops at the city's two most engaging attractions, the Museum of Newport History and the 18th-century Hunter House, in the colonial Point District.

Save your second day in Newport for touring the massive summer homes of the Gilded Age, along Bellevue Avenue, the most famous of which is The Breakers. After the imposing Breakers, if you have time to see only one other mansion, your best bet is The Elms. Also pay a visit to the International Tennis Hall of Fame and its museum.

Or, if mansions aren't your thing, head north to visit the towns of Portsmouth and Middletown, where sightseeing highlights include the Norman Bird Sanctuary and Green Animals Topiary Garden, as well as the best sandy beaches in the state.

Day 7: East Bay

End your tour of Rhode Island with a visit to the relatively unheralded East Bay area, which you can reach from Newport more scenically by making a short detour through Sakonnet, a small patch of villages bordering Massachusetts and the ocean, and home to the state's best winery, Sakonnet Vineyards.

Head north to reach the East Bay, whose main towns are Bristol and Warren. Bristol may be relatively small, but it's home to some superb attractions, including Blithewold Mansion and Arboretum and the Herreshoff Marine Museum.

► CAMPUS PROVIDENCE

With its profusion of colleges—Brown, the Rhode Island School of Design (RISD), Johnson & Wales Culinary Institute—sometimes the city of Providence seems like one big university campus. The city's student population keeps the city young and artsy, infusing its neighborhoods with a funky, energetic vibe. The various districts of the city, however, are far from homogenous, each imbued with a different feel depending on which school is closest and which students call it home. When you are done touring the city's attractions, do as the students do and check out these hangout spots.

College Hill

Brown University's stomping grounds, the streets of College Hill teem with insouciant preppies and trust-fund hipsters skirting the intersection of privilege and bohemia. That's reflected in the character of the shopping district of Thayer Street, where the genuine thrift stores intermix with trendy boutiques that sell thrift store–inspired fashion with significantly higher price tags. Brown students line the alfresco tables at Greek restaurant Andreas (268 Thayer St., 401/331-7879, www.andreasri.com) to see and be seen for brunch, and trendier nightspots for weekend nights, especially Paragon/Viva (234 Thayer St., 401/331-6200, www.paragonandviva.com) for tapas and Kartabar (284 Thayer St., 401/331-8111, www.kartabar.com) for martinis.

Downcity

Perhaps it's in part the presence of Johnson & Wales, with all its creative, culinary energy, that has made Providence's downtown neighborhood such a foodie mecca. Students save their pennies for flawless French cuisine at Pot au Feu (44 Custom House St.,

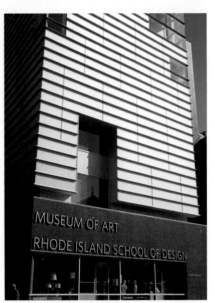
Take a look at RISD's art exhibits.

401/273-8953, www.potaufeuri.com) or the farm-to-table tasting menu at Gracie's (194 Washington St., 401/272-7811, graciesprovidence.com). For more day-to-day dining, they slide into booths at Downcity Food and Cocktails (50 Weybosset St., 401/331-9217, www.downcityfood.com) for a creative new take on diner cuisine with a cocktail on the side (and a popular, if quirky, "drag brunch"). And when Johnson & Wales students are looking for that hard-to-find ingredient for their culinary creations, they stop in at Gourmet Heaven (173 Weybosset St., 401/787-4533, www.gourmetheaven.com), which also has some of the best on-the-go lunch options at its extensive deli bar.

Wickenden Street

While RISD may be located a few blocks from Brown on College Hill, many of its students

FAMILY MATTERS

Traveling with kids isn't always as easy as the guidebooks make it sound, but Rhode Island is, in fact, as ideal a place to do it as any, thanks to its balance of education and fun. For every historical town, there is an aquarium or well-run zoo; for every carousel or arcade, there's an equally fun beach or baseball game. There is no bad time to pack up the minivan either: Spring is wonderful for outside strolls in the parks; summer begs for cooling dips at the beach; fall is foliage and festival time; and winter is when you can head for the indoor museums. These are the top sights and activities for kids:

- **Ryan Family Amusements** (268 Thames St., Newport, 401/846-5774) is a blinking, beeping extravaganza of an arcade that keeps the family happy for hours, rain or shine.

- **Green Animals Topiary Garden** (380 Cory's Lane, Portsmouth, 401/847-1000) is a seven-acre estate overlooking Narragansett Bay where 21 of the 80 trees have been sculpted into giant animals.

- **Gray's Ice Cream** (16 East Rd., Tiverton, 401/624-4500) is a famed fixture of Rhode Island as much for its history (it has been around for 80-plus years) as for its rum-raisin.

- **Save the Bay Exploration Center and Aquarium** (175 Memorial Blvd., Newport, 401/272-3540) is where wee ones can check out rare calico lobsters, among other sea creatures.

- **PawSox** (1 Columbus Ave., Pawtucket, 401/724-7300) are the minor-league affiliates of the Boston Red Sox, and they're every bit as much fun as their big-time version, minus the crowds and expensive tickets.

- **Roger Williams Park Zoo** (1000 Elmwood Ave., Providence, 401/785-3510) is world-class, housing more than 957 species, a children's farmyard exhibit, a carousel, and a playground.

- **Flying Horse Carousel** (Bay St., Westerly, 401/348-6007) brings smiles (and dizziness) to thousands of just-from-the-beach kids every summer.

snow leopards at Roger Williams Park Zoo

The Coffee Exchange is a great place to relax.

make their homes at the bottom of the hill along the waterfront around funky   Street. The neighborhood's unofficial meeting place is The Coffee Exchange (207 Wickenden St., 401/273-1198, www.sustainablecoffee.com), which overflows with fair-trade coffee, artwork, and creative energy. The flavors of the area's eateries are invariably ethnic, with some of the city's best Indian to be found at Taste of India (230 Wickenden St., 401/421-4355, www.tasteofindiaprovri.com) and sushi without attitude at Sakura (231 Wickenden St., 401/331-6861, www.eatinri.com/sakura). When students celebrate after a successful art show, it's at cozy pan-Asian boîte O-cha (221 Wickenden St., 401/421-4699) before heading out to shake a tail in the neighboring Jewelry District at warehouses turned dance clubs such as the popular Ultra (172 Pine St., 401/454-LIVE—401/454-5483).

▶ A LONG WEEKEND IN NEWPORT

Newport ranks among the most appealing long-weekend destinations in New England—it's within an afternoon's drive of several major cities, and it's small yet culturally rich enough to satisfy the appetites of all types of travelers without overwhelming them. Although this is a particularly popular place for boaters and sailors and thus is much visited from late spring through early autumn, Newport still makes for a terrific long-weekend retreat in the off-season, when most attractions remain open and hotels drop their rates, sometimes tremendously.

Saturday

Today's suggested itinerary is best enjoyed when there's good weather, so check the forecast before deciding on which day to pursue it; the itinerary suggested for Sunday is somewhat more indoor-oriented.

Assuming the weather is good, plan to spend your first day making a full drive of Greater Newport, from the sea to some neighboring towns, with a couple of tours of summer cottages thrown in. Note that there aren't a lot of dining options along this route, so pack a picnic lunch (grab supplies at Portabella).

Begin on Ocean Drive, the famously scenic road that loops around for about 10 miles edging the sea and passing dramatic summer homes. Then continue onto tree-shaded Bellevue Avenue, the main thoroughfare of Newport's Gilded Age, studded with palatial mansions that have been converted into house-museums. Both The Breakers and The Elms are among the best mansions to tour. As you continue along Bellevue, pay a visit to the International Tennis Hall of Fame and its museum.

Play a match at the International Tennis Hall of Fame.

Several lanes headed east from Bellevue provide access to Cliff Walk, a rocky path that runs along a bluff and affords exceptional views of Rhode Island Sound as well as the backyards of several waterfront estates; definitely plan to hike along at least a section of this path. Finally, end the day by heading over the massive bridge to Jamestown, where you can watch the sunset at dramatic Beavertail State Park, or just catch a table for alfresco oysters and steamers at a quaint bistro.

Sunday

On your second full day, you don't need a car at all. This is your chance to explore downtown Newport, which abounds with impressive historic sites and museums and overlooks a busy and scenic harbor. Kick things off in one of New England's best-preserved early colonial neighborhoods, the Point District, near the Newport Visitor Information Center. Here you can learn a bit about the city's history with a tour of the 18th-century Hunter House. From here, head south along Thames Street, planning a visit to downtown's superb Museum of Newport History. Then walk by some of the most famous historic sites downtown, such as Touro Synagogue and, a few blocks farther down, Trinity Church.

Later in the day, head to the marina at Newport Harbor, and take a water taxi across to Fort Adams State Park, home to the Museum of Yachting, a fascinating place. In winter, when the taxi isn't running, you'll have to drive out to Fort Adams—it's only a 10-minute jaunt by car.

Return at dinnertime to downtown Newport, where you can grab a memorable meal on Bowen's Wharf. Also keep in mind that Broadway, just northeast of downtown but still within walking distance, has two of

breaking waves off the Cliff Walk

the city's best dinner options, Salvation Cafe and Tucker's Bistro.

Monday

If you're headed west toward Connecticut or up to the T. F. Green Airport near Providence, you'll follow Route 138 out of town, which affords you another chance to tour Jamestown and Beavertail State Park. If you're headed east into Massachusetts, follow Route 114 north through Middletown and Portsmouth, stopping either at Prescott Farm or Green Animals Topiary Garden, both right off the main road. Remember that distances aren't extensive in Rhode Island, so it's not hard to enjoy a little more of the state's magnificent scenery or see a few more cultural attractions on your way back home from Newport.

NEWPORT

But for historical happenstance, Newport might easily have become the largest city in New England. It's hard to imagine this elegant, sometimes almost quaint peninsula of colonial homes and lavish mansions instead studded with glass-and-steel skyscrapers, but Newport was headed in that direction until the Revolutionary War, and even for a time afterward. Originally one of the most successful ports in the New World, Newport saw its fortunes dashed by the war, in which most of its residents fled from the occupying British, and its star was quickly eclipsed by the thriving ports of Boston and New York.

Newport's resurgence began in the 19th century, when it became a favored destination for the Victorian moneyed class, who built enormous mansions on its cliffs, each more opulent than the last. Those mansions are still one of Newport's—and Rhode Island's—main draws for visitors, but the city has many other historical and recreational sites to recommend it as well.

Befitting its reputation as a yachting hub, Newport remains fairly preppy and conservative in its demeanor, though not its politics. This is a tolerant, socially progressive city with a relatively democratic (with a small *d*) edge. Sure, it's still scattered with seaside mansions once owned by eminent families with names like Duke and Astor, and certainly it still draws plenty of modern-day celebrities, CEOs, and astoundingly preppy families. But it also welcomes a salad of others: artists, college students, mansion gawkers, and bona fide sailors, all of whom congregate on Thames Street and

COURTESY OF PRESERVATION SOCIETY OF NEWPORT

HIGHLIGHTS

LOOK FOR ◖ TO FIND RECOMMENDED SIGHTS, ACTIVITIES, DINING, AND LODGING.

◖ **Touro Synagogue:** The oldest Jewish house of worship in the United States dates to 1763 and serves a congregation that started in the 1650s (page 28).

◖ **The Point District:** Newport's most notable colonial neighborhood has enjoyed an astounding renaissance in recent years. Today it has the finest concentration of colonial architecture in New England (page 33).

◖ **Ocean Drive:** Arguably the most stunning shore drive on the East Coast, Ocean Drive reveals one gorgeous photo op after another (page 34).

◖ **Rough Point:** The former summer home of heiress Doris Duke, this late Victorian mansion on a rocky point overlooking the ocean has been left furnished almost exactly as when Duke lived in it. Guests are welcome to relax on the gracious grounds for as long as they'd like after their tour (page 35).

◖ **The Breakers:** Cornelius Vanderbilt's little summer cottage is simply the most stunning of all Newport's mansions – and that's saying a lot (page 43).

◖ **Cliff Walk:** You can enjoy a memorable 3.5-mile stroll along this fabled oceanfront path that fringes some of Newport's most expensive and famous mansions, including The Breakers and Rough Point. It's Newport's best free activity (page 46).

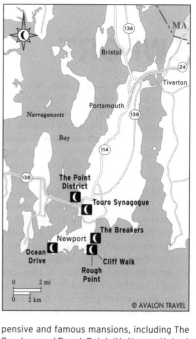

the waterfront to create an unparalleled people-watching experience.

Looking around this busy but small-scale city today, with its stunning parks and green spaces, its fine homes of all styles, and diversions that include sailing charters, romantic inns, and posh boutiques, it's easy to guess that most of the city's residents and visitors are happy that fate chose not to turn Newport into another Boston or even Providence. There are big cities up and down the Eastern Seaboard, but few places have the combined charms of Newport.

HISTORY

Settled in 1639, Newport began as one of early Rhode Island's typically tolerant colonies, a haven for those disenchanted with the religious and political conformity and ultimately oppression in the Massachusetts colonies. With a strategic, sheltered harbor, however, it wasn't long before enterprising locals turned the young city into a corner of the infamous Triangle Trade with the West Indies and Africa. Much of Newport's early trading was slave-oriented—in fact, Newport surpassed even Charleston, South Carolina, during the early years in the number of slaves that passed through its port.

Rhode Island's ban of slavery in 1774 did little to slow Newport's merchants, who continued to trade in rum, molasses, indigo, and other wares. The blow to the city's economic clout, and also its colonist pride, came at the

NEWPORT UNDER SIEGE

Chafing under British taxes, Newporters harassed British ships on several occasions during the 1760s and 1770s. When the Revolution broke out, the British decided to make an example of the port city, sailing 9,000 English militia and Hessian mercenaries into Newport Harbor in 1776. Those sympathetic to the revolutionary efforts fled to other parts of New England. In a matter of months, the permanent population declined from about 9,200 to 5,000.

Newport became a base of operations for the British army, who turned churches and civic buildings into their barracks and stables and imposed martial law under a stuffed-shirt British commander, General Richard Prescott (who was generally despised even by his own troops).

A glimmer of hope appeared in the form of French commander Count D'Estaing, who sailed into the harbor in summer 1778 with a small but potent fleet of ships, but a huge storm caused them to run for shelter. Even as a colonial militia attacked from Portsmouth, D'Estaing retreated out to sea and then all the way back to Boston. The Portsmouth rebels were left unsupported; disheartened, they retreated farther inland, only to encounter an even larger group of British troops along the way. A skirmish ensued, during which the Americans had at least a small victory, killing quite a few of the British before escaping to safety.

It wasn't until October 1779, when the British decided to bolster their defenses in New York, that they left the city. The day after the British evacuation, American troops returned to reoccupy what was left of Newport, confiscating property and transferring it to American owners. On July 12, Newporters prepared for a new, friendlier occupation when French General Rochambeau arrived in the city with more than 5,000 troops and a massive bounty of provisions.

Perhaps the most glorious day in Newport's still-young history occurred on March 6, 1781, when the commander-in-chief of the Continental Army, General George Washington, arrived by ship in Newport Harbor, debarking at Long Wharf clad in a full French uniform as a show of solidarity. A huge crowd of locals greeted the commander, and an exhilarating military parade was held on what is now Washington Square. The following evening Rochambeau, Washington, and the many other dignitaries celebrated their cooperative war effort with a lavish ball held in the still-standing Colony House on the square.

beginning of the Revolutionary War, when British forces decided to occupy Newport. From 1776 to 1779 the city remained firmly under British control. Most of the population, which was sympathetic to the war for independence, fled Newport, decimating trade. Even as it started to recover after the war, the shipping embargo imposed on New England during the War of 1812 effectively sealed Newport's fate as nothing more than a small-time port city.

For much of the 19th century, shipbuilding, naval exploits, and trade continued to play some role in Newport's fortunes, but Newport's greatest commodity continued to be its marvelous location at the tip of Aquidneck Island. Wealthy factory owners, rail and shipping tycoons, and other captains of industry began summering in this town that rarely became as hot in the summer as other parts of the Northeast. By the middle of the 19th century, almost any family with a big name, from Edith Wharton to the Vanderbilts, had a summer "cottage" (read: mansion) in the area south and east of downtown on Ocean Drive or Bellevue Avenue. And those who didn't had friends to visit here and were thus still a part of the town's culture. Since then, everyone from President Kennedy to Billy Joel has had homes here.

The city's brief stint as a pleasure village took a hit during the Depression. As fortunes fell and a spirit of fiscal conservatism took hold through World War II, many of Newport's mansions fell empty and were sold and subdivided into

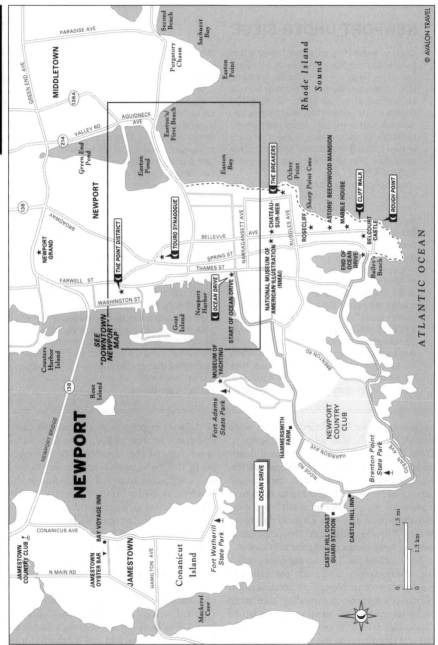

apartments, while others were shuttered completely. As weeklong summer vacations became increasingly popular with middle-class families after World War II, however, an increasing number of visitors began spending summers in Newport, and even more did so in the several motels just outside the city in Middletown.

Newport enjoyed a slow but steady resurgence from this point forward. Locals began to look around more and notice the city's incredible bounty of notable architecture, first by working toward the preservation of the city's grand "summer cottages." In 1967, tobacco heiress Doris Duke and others formed the Newport Restoration Foundation, which helped to preserve hundreds of important colonial houses. By the 1980s, one of Newport's oldest intact neighborhoods, the Point District, had become quite fashionable, its many 18th-century homes repainted and restored. For at least the past 30 years, Newport has enjoyed a reputation as a yachting hub, an increasingly upscale vacation destination, and a favorite place for touring magnificent homes.

PLANNING YOUR TIME

Newport is the most popular destination in the state, and you'll want to spend at least a weekend here to touch on the major sights and activities. It is possible, though less than ideal, to see Newport in one day by touring Ocean Drive, walking the waterfront, and taking in at least one mansion tour. But of all the communities in Rhode Island, this is one where you should try to dedicate at least two full days.

Newport is really two cities in one—there's the tightly laid out downtown with its narrow one-way streets and rows of buildings dating from colonial through Victorian times, and then there's the sweeping, wealthy peninsula that juts south and east of all this, where expensive homes on large plots of land dominate the landscape. One full day to tour each of these areas, along with a little time set aside for the beach or a sail, is an ideal way to spend a weekend.

The catch is that Newport can be crowded in summer and on weekends just about any time of year, and hotel rates are among the highest in New England, so consider staying nearby and making several daytrips into town. Moderately priced motels and hotels are in nearby Middletown, where it's also not hard to find reasonably priced eateries. Still, there's no way of getting around the fact that summer is a favorite time to visit but an awful time for parking, getting a table quickly at restaurants, and enjoying the city's many house-museums and attractions without enduring long lines. Consider visiting during shoulder seasons of May or September, or on a weekday, when you'll have much more elbow room for exploring.

Sights

DOWNTOWN AND THE HARBOR

While the mansions and beaches are Newport's biggest attractions, the downtown waterfront has and irresistible draw. It's difficult to say what holds the bigger appeal: gawking at the chorus line of blinding white yachts moored in the harbor, or admiring the crush of humanity that fills the cobblestone wharfs on summer afternoons. A good place to start is the **Newport Visitors Information Center** (23 America's Cup Ave., 800/976-5122, www.gonewport.com), which is unusually comprehensive and useful. It is right at the northern entrance to downtown, adjacent to the city's bus terminal and the centrally located Newport Marriott. It's an excellent place to begin your explorations of the city, and it has a large pay-parking lot and garage, making it a good spot to ditch your wheels. Newport's downtown and harbor area can be managed easily on foot, and you can take public transportation from the visitors center to other parts of the city, including Ocean Drive and the mansions down on Bellevue Avenue.

NEWPORT

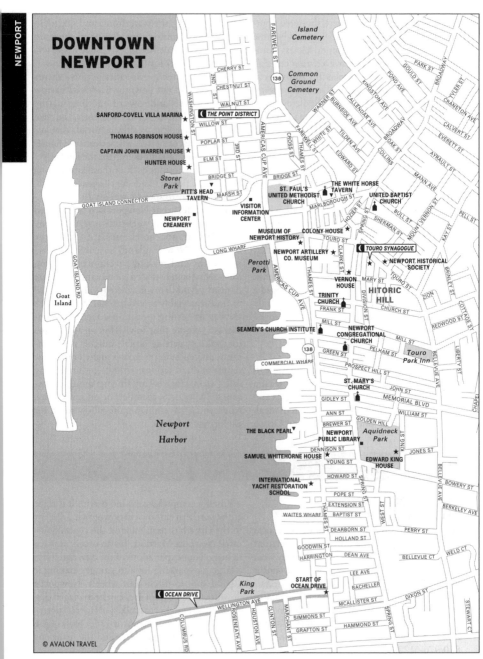

DOWNTOWN NEWPORT

Island Cemetery

Common Ground Cemetery

CHERRY ST
2ND ST
CHESTNUT ST
WALNUT ST
WILLOW ST
POPLAR ST
ELM ST
3RD ST
BRIDGE ST
MARSH ST

FAREWELL ST
138
WARNER ST
BURNSIDE AVE
CALLENDAR AVE
TILDEN AVE
EDWARD ST
COLLINS

WASHINGTON ST
AMERICA'S CUP AVE
THAMES ST
CROSS ST
FAREWELL ST
WHITE ST

PARK ST
GOULD ST
BROADWAY
POND AVE
KINGSTON AVE
BOAK ST
MANN AVE
BROADWAY
SHERMAN ST
SPRING ST
MOUNT VERNON ST

TYLER ST
CRANSTON AVE
CALVERT ST
EVERETT ST
AYRAULT ST
PELL ST
KAY ST
BRINLEY ST
COTTAGE ST

SANFORD-COVELL VILLA MARINA ★
THOMAS ROBINSON HOUSE ★
CAPTAIN JOHN WARREN HOUSE ★
HUNTER HOUSE ★

(THE POINT DISTRICT

Storer Park

GOAT ISLAND CONNECTOR

▼
PITT'S HEAD TAVERN
NEWPORT CREAMERY

VISITOR INFORMATION CENTER ■

ST. PAUL'S UNITED METHODIST CHURCH ♦
MARLBOROUGH ST
HOZIER ST

THE WHITE HORSE TAVERN ♦

UNITED BAPTIST CHURCH ♦
BULL ST

MUSEUM OF NEWPORT HISTORY
COLONY HOUSE ★
TOURO ST
CLARKE ST

(TOURO SYNAGOGUE
★
★ NEWPORT HISTORICAL SOCIETY

Long Wharf

NEWPORT ARTILLERY CO. MUSEUM ★

VERNON HOUSE ★
MARY ST
TOURO ST
ZION

Perotti Park

AMERICA'S CUP AVE

TRINITY CHURCH ♦
DIVISION ST
HITORIC HILL
CHURCH ST
REDWOOD ST

Goat Island

Goat Island

GOAT ISLAND RD

FRANK ST
MILL ST

SEAMEN'S CHURCH INSTITUTE ♦

NEWPORT CONGREGATIONAL CHURCH ♦
PELHAM ST
MILL ST

LIBERTY ST

138
GREEN ST
PROSPECT HILL ST
Touro Park Inn

COMMERCIAL WHARF

ST. MARY'S CHURCH ♦
GIDLEY ST
JOHN ST
MEMORIAL BLVD
WILLIAM ST

ANN ST
BREWER ST
GOLDEN HILL ST

Newport Harbor

THE BLACK PEARL ▼
NEWPORT PUBLIC LIBRARY ■
DENNISON ST
Aquidneck Park

KING ST
BELLEVUE AVE
CHAPEL

SAMUEL WHITEHORNE HOUSE ★
YOUNG ST

EDWARD KING HOUSE ★
JONES ST

INTERNATIONAL YACHT RESTORATION SCHOOL ★
HOWARD ST
POPE ST
SPRING ST
BOWERY ST

EXTENSION ST
BAPTIST ST
WEST ST
BERKELEY AVE

WAITES WHARF
THAMES ST
DEARBORN ST
HOLLAND ST
PERRY ST

GOODWIN ST
HARRINGTON
DEAN AVE
BELLEVUE CT
WELD CT

LEE AVE

(OCEAN DRIVE

King Park

START OF OCEAN DRIVE ★
BACHELLER ST
MCALLISTER ST
DIXON ST
SPRING ST
STEWART CT

WELLINGTON AVE
COLUMBUS RD
ROSENEATH AVE
HOUSTON AVE
CLINTON ST
MARCHANT ST
SIMMONS ST
GRAFTON ST
HAMMOND ST

© AVALON TRAVEL

NEWPORT

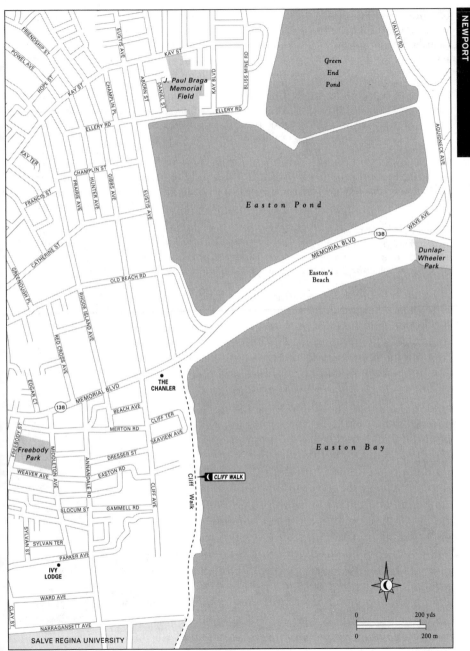

Green End Pond

J. Paul Braga Memorial Field

FRIENDSHIP ST
POWEL AVE
HOPE ST
KAY ST
EUSTIS AVE
KAY ST
ABOIN ST
DANIEL ST
CHAMPLIN PL
KAY BLVD
BLISS MINE RD
ELLERY RD
VALLEY RD

ELLERY RD
KAY TER
CHAMPLIN ST
PRAIRIE AVE
HUNTER AVE
GIBBS AVE
EUSTIS AVE
FRANCIS ST
CATHERINE ST
GREENOUGH PL
OLD BEACH RD
RHODE ISLAND AVE
RED CROSS AVE
EDGAR CT

Easton Pond

AQUIDNECK AVE
WAVE AVE
138
MEMORIAL BLVD
Dunlap-Wheeler Park

Easton's Beach

MEMORIAL BLVD
138
BEACH AVE
MERTON RD
CLIFF TER
SEAVIEW AVE
FREEBODY ST
Freebody Park
MIDDLETON AVE
ANNANDALE RD
DRESSER ST
WEAVER AVE
EASTON RD
CLIFF AVE
SLOCUM ST
GAMMELL RD
SYLVAN ST
SYLVAN TER
PARKER AVE
IVY LODGE
WARD AVE
CLAY ST
NARRAGANSETT AVE
SALVE REGINA UNIVERSITY

THE CHANLER

Cliff Walk

🐚 CLIFF WALK

Easton Bay

0   200 yds
0   200 m

◖ Touro Synagogue

Rhode Island's famous religious tolerance is symbolically—and beautifully—enshrined in Touro Synagogue (60 Touro St., 401/847-4794, www.tourosynagogue.org, 9:30 A.M.–4:30 P.M. Sun.–Wed. and Fri., 9:30 A.M.–7 P.M. Thurs. July–early Sept., 10 A.M.–2:30 P.M. Sun.–Fri. Sept.–Oct., $12 adults, $8 children under 13). Not only is it the oldest Jewish house of worship in the United States, it's also one of the most impressive 18th-century buildings in New England. Like so many historic buildings on the Eastern Seaboard, the synagogue's brochure brags that George Washington spent time here—in fact, it was here that he declared the new nation's position on religious freedom, pledging he would "give to bigotry no sanction, to persecution no assistance." If that connection helps draw visitors who might not otherwise venture into a synagogue, OK then, but Touro Synagogue should be on every visitor's short list of Newport attractions for its own historical, religious, and architectural significance.

In the mid-17th century, Sephardic Jews from Portugal and Spain caught wind of Roger Williams's Rhode Island colony and its unyielding tolerance of people of all religious persuasions. A small group of Jews arrived on Newport soil in the 1650s and formed a small congregation that met for decades in private homes and other temporary spaces. Eventually, the Newport Jews made plans to construct a synagogue, given a boost when one of the young nation's most prominent architects, Peter Harrison, volunteered to design it. The congregation, which chose the name Yeshaut Israel (Salvation of Israel), broke ground in 1759, roughly a century after the first Sephardi had arrived.

The design presented some unusual challenges for Harrison, who was forced to adapt his Georgian ideals to accommodate Sephardic traditions. Located on an inconspicuous side street, as custom dictated, the building stands diagonally on its plot so worshipers could face eastward in prayer towards Jerusalem. The exterior design is elegant but austere, and inside

Touro Synagogue features elaborate and symbolic architecture.

EARLY NEWPORT'S QUAKER AND JEWISH GROUPS

Newport's enviable strategic position and all of Rhode Island's religious and political tolerance were not lost on persecuted people elsewhere in the New World and in Europe. Quakers were among the earliest and most numerous settlers; a shipload of them arrived in 1657, and in a short time many of Newport's most prominent citizens joined the Friends movement, among them William Coddington and Governor William Brenton (for whom Brenton Point, at the southwest tip of the city, is named). While Rhode Island was founded by Baptists, the state's first two centuries saw the election of more Quakers than adherents of any other religion.

Quakers were feared and despised elsewhere in New England. In fact, Mary Dyer, a Quaker and the wife of the secretary of Rhode Island, was hanged in Boston in 1660 after having been warned not to proselytize.

The second-oldest Jewish congregation in the United States was established in Newport (the first was formed four years earlier in New York City). In 1658 a ship containing 15 Sephardic Jewish families arrived from Barbados (having come originally from Spain and Portugal) and immediately formed a small congregation that would be formally named Jeshuat Israel a century later. They worshiped in private homes for many years until 1763, when they built the Touro Synagogue, the oldest synagogue in the United States. Newport's Jews also established what many believe is the first Freemasons lodge in the New World. Jews also immigrated to Rhode Island during the colonial era from Curaçao and later from Portugal. New England's whaling industry was begun by Jacob Rodrigues Rivera, who fled Spain during the Inquisition in the 1740s.

Early Jews were among the first and most successful pioneers of Newport industry, and had the British not occupied the city during the Revolutionary War, they might very well have helped steer the city to unrivaled economic growth. Instead, industry died with British occupation, and most of the city's Jews fled to colonies loyal to the American Revolution.

there is a sumptuous chamber supported by 12 Ionic columns that represent the ancient tribes of Israel. These columns support an upper gallery, from which 12 Corinthian columns reach skyward to support a domed ceiling. One of the most notable features of the interior is the five huge brass candle chandeliers that were donated by prominent Newport merchants during the 1760s. On the east side of the room stands the Holy Ark, which contains the Torah—the scrolls are hand-printed and set on wood rollers. Above this, the Ten Commandments are painted in Hebrew.

Four years after construction began, on December 2, 1763, Reb Isaac Touro led the first service in the synagogue that today bears his name. Interestingly, many non-Jews attended this first service, which is amazing considering the complete intolerance that not only Jews but all non-Congregationalists faced in most of the neighboring New England colonies. Shortly thereafter, however, the British occupation of Newport resulted in a near-abandonment of the city by most of its Jewish population, and services were discontinued. The road back to the building began in the mid-1800s, when Touro's sons, wealthy merchants Abraham and Judah, left immense fortunes upon their deaths to care for the structure, which eventually reopened in 1883. It has continued to operate in the Sephardic tradition of worship ever since.

Except on Saturdays and Jewish holidays, Touro Synagogue is generally open for tours 10 A.M.–4 P.M. daily in summer, with shorter hours the rest of the year. You can easily walk from here up Touro Street to the congregation's burial ground, where Judah Touro, Aaron Lopez, and other prominent members of the community are buried.

Historic Hill

While Newport is best-known for the mansions constructed in the late 19th century, the town has historically significant buildings stretching back more than 200 years, many of which are clustered around the area west of the waterfront. Before setting foot in any of the mansions, culture and history buffs should take a detour to the **Museum of Newport History** (Thames St., at the bottom of Washington Sq., 401/841-8770 or 401/846-0813, www.newporthistorical.org, 10 A.M.–4:30 P.M. Tues.–Fri., by appointment Mon., shorter hours in winter, $4 adults, $2 children over 5), where the exhibits give a nice overview of the history of the city and southern Rhode Island. Housed in the historic Brick Market Place, the space is crammed with many artifacts that trace the city's history, including decorative pieces and artwork, vintage photos, and ship models. Other exhibits touch on the city's founding fathers, John Clarke and William Coddington, as well as on the indigenous Native Americans who lived here for many centuries and the diverse ethnic and religious makeup of Newport's earliest citizens, including Quakers, Jews, Portuguese, and African Americans.

May–mid-September a variety of guided walking tours (401/841-8770, www.newporthistorytours.org, $12 adults, $5 children under 12) that focus on the city's history leave from the museum. Themes include Jewish Newport, Colonial Newport, and pirate tours.

The **Newport Historical Society** (82 Touro St., 401/846-0813, www.newporthistorical.org, 9:30 A.M.–4:30 P.M. Mon.–Fri., 9:30 A.M.–noon Sat., free admission), home to Newport's historic **Seventh Day Baptist Meeting House,** the first home of the Seventh Day Baptists, is a rather simple building that dates to 1730, when it was designed by Richard Munday. It looks far more like a house than a place of worship. The Newport Historical Society, founded in 1854, bought the building in the 1880s and has used it as its headquarters ever since, although the actual offices and exhibit areas are in an addition behind the church.

The Historical Society also manages several other properties, both private homes and public buildings, that are well worth looking into. The most significant is **Colony House**

Trinity Church overlooks Queen Anne Square.

(Washington Sq., 11 A.M.–2:30 P.M. Thurs.–Sat. July–Aug., 11 A.M.–2:30 P.M. Sat. Sept.–Oct., or by appointment, $5 adults and seniors, $3 children), which dates to 1739. Here on May 4, 1776, the state assembly forswore its allegiance to the British crown, thus establishing Rhode Island as the young nation's first independent state exactly two months before the other 12 fell in line. It is the fourth-oldest existing building in the United States to have served as a state capitol, serving as one of the two Rhode Island State Houses until 1901, when the new State House in Providence opened. Architect Richard Munday, who's also responsible for the nearby Seventh Day Baptist Meeting House and Trinity Church, designed this Georgian-style building. Inside you'll find one of Rhode Islander Gilbert Stuart's famous portraits of George Washington.

Also in the vicinity of Washington Square is the 1846 **United Baptist Church, John Clarke Memorial** (30 Spring St., 401/847-3210, 8:30 A.M.–noon Mon.–Fri.), located to the north and east of Colony House. The congregation was established in Portsmouth in 1638 by pastor Dr. John Clarke, the very gentleman who obtained Rhode Island's Royal Charter in 1663 from King Charles II.

For background on the Revolutionary War's Battle of Newport as well as other conflicts, visit the **Newport Artillery Co. Museum** (23 Clarke St., 401/846-8488, www.newportartillery.org, 10 A.M.–4 P.M. Sat. or by appointment, free admission), which is housed in a cut-granite Greek revival building just south of Washington Square on Clarke Street. Military objects and artifacts from more than 100 nations fill these rooms, including 15 cannons spanning 150 years, one of them struck by Paul Revere in 1798. Other unique military artifacts include uniforms worn by former general and Secretary of State Colin Powell, the Vietnam War's General Westmoreland, and Egyptian president Anwar Sadat.

A little farther down Clarke Street at the intersection of Mary Street is **Vernon House** (46 Clarke St., 401/849-7300, www.newportrestoration.org), a fine colonial house with a hipped roof. It served as headquarters for Rochambeau, the commander of French expeditionary forces during the Revolutionary War, who assumed control of the house in 1780 after British forces ceded the city. In this building in early March 1781, he and George Washington reportedly planned the Continental Army's coup de grâce against the British at the Battle of Yorktown. The home is now managed by the Newport Restoration Foundation as a private residence, although it is open to scholars by special appointment.

Another notable historic home nearby is the Newport Historical Society's **Wanton-Lyman-Hazard House** (17 Broadway, 401/846-0813, www.newporthistorical.org, open for tours 11 A.M.–2:30 P.M. Thurs.–Sat. July–Aug., 11 A.M.–2:30 P.M. Sat. Sept.–Oct., or by appointment, $5 adults and seniors, $3 children under 12), which dates to 1675—it's one of the oldest restored houses in the state. The imposing house was built as the residence of wealthy sea captain Stephen Mumford, but the most famous owner was the former governor of Rhode Island (in 1741) Richard Ward, and the house takes its name from members of the family that occupied the house 1782–1911. Several additions were made to the house during its first 100 years, including the fine interior crown molding and wood paneling. The society has also worked with the Newport Garden Club to restore its gardens, which include an interpretive colonial herb garden.

Just around the corner, near the corner of Farewell and Marlborough Streets, the **Great Friends Meeting House** (401/846-0813, www.newporthistorical.org, 11 A.M.–2:30 P.M. Thurs.–Sat. July–Aug., 11 A.M.–2:30 P.M. Sat. Sept.–Oct., or by appointment, $4) was once the largest and most prominent building in Newport, visible to ships arriving in Newport Harbor from some way out. With parts dating back to 1699, it is the oldest surviving house of worship in town and was expanded continuously over the subsequent two centuries. Quakers used it as the setting for the New England Yearly Meetings. The Society of Friends was an important influence on Newport society during the 17th and 18th centuries, a time when the then-radical religion was harshly persecuted in other parts of the New World. Newport Quaker Nicholas Easton was elected governor of Rhode Island in 1672; he helped push through the young land's earliest known conscientious-objector law, which allowed any citizen to turn down military enlistment if his religion forbade him from fighting.

In addition to the single admission charge for each of its properties ($5 for adults), Newport Historical offers a package deal with admission to Colony House, Wanton-Lyman-Hazard House, and Great Friends Meeting House for $12.

Nearby is **St. Paul's United Methodist Church** (12 Marlborough St.), whose congregation dates to 1800. The church was built six years later, becoming the first Methodist church in the world with a steeple, a bell, and fixed pews. Having opened in 1687, the **White Horse Tavern** (26 Marlborough St., 401/849-3600, 11:30 A.M.–2:30 P.M. and 6–9 P.M.

Mon.–Fri., noon–3 P.M. and 6–9 P.M. Sat.–Sun.) is said to be the oldest extant tavern in the United States, and it still operates as a restaurant. During the state's early history, when Newport was the capital, members of the Rhode Island Assembly often convened in the tavern.

If you haven't yet tired of churches, one of the grandest in Newport is **Trinity Church** (1 Queen Anne Sq., 401/846-0660, www.trinitynewport.org, 10 A.M.–1 P.M. Mon.–Fri. May–mid-June, 10 A.M.–4 P.M. Mon.–Fri. mid-June–early July, 10 A.M.–4 P.M. daily early July–Aug., 10 A.M.–1 P.M. Mon.–Fri. Sept.–mid-Oct., 10 A.M.–4 P.M. Mon.–Fri. mid–late Oct., services 8 A.M. and 10 A.M. Sun. and noon Wed. year-round), dramatically overlooking leafy Queen Anne Square. The elegant building dates to 1726 and is modeled after the London churches designed by famed British architect Christopher Wren. With its lofty white spire, this dignified building is one of Newport's most recognizable and impressive structures. Definitely try to peek inside to see the only three-tiered, center-aisle, glass pulpit in the country. For the obligatory George Washington connection, take a look at pew number 81, in which the first president once worshiped. Tours are given every Sunday following the 10 A.M. Episcopal service.

Two blocks south on Spring Street is another of Newport's elegant places of worship, the **Newport Congregational Church** (73 Pelham St., 401/849-2238, www.newportcongregationalchurch.org, 9 A.M.–noon Mon.–Sat., services 10 A.M. Sun.). This 1880 structure is one of only two churches left standing in the United States with an interior designed entirely by noted architect John La Farge, who also perfected the technique for creating the opalescent glass used in the windows. On the interior walls are elaborate and colorful murals.

The Waterfront

Down the hill, more shops and restaurants line the eastern portion of Thames Street, while wharves jut into Newport Harbor across the street. These wharves now contain a mix of

a summer scene on a Newport wharf

© MICHAEL BLANDING

businesses, restaurants, and hotels. You might stop at the **Seamen's Church Institute** (18 Market Sq., just off Thames St., 401/847-4260, 6 A.M.–6 P.M. daily) to catch your breath and to admire this handsome building that has served the needs of seafarers for nearly a century. The building contains a small nondenominational chapel, a café, public restrooms with a coin laundry and showers, a library, and a small museum (with limited hours; call ahead). After merging with America's Cup Avenue to become a broad and busy road for a few blocks, Thames Street once again becomes a narrow one-way street with an easy and quaint pace past Commercial Wharf.

A block up Memorial Drive from the intersection with Thames Street is **St. Mary's Church** (Spring St. at Memorial Blvd., Mass 8 A.M., 9:30 A.M., and 11 A.M. Sun., 5 P.M. Sat., 7:30 A.M. Mon.–Fri.), which houses the oldest Catholic parish in the state, established in 1828. The present church dates to 1852 and is considered one of the finest examples of Gothic revival architecture on the Eastern Seaboard, but the building's real claim to fame is having served as the setting for the wedding of John F. Kennedy and Jacqueline Bouvier on September 12, 1953.

Just south and a block east of Thames Street is leafy Aquidneck Park, bounded by Spring, Golden Hill, King, and Bowery Streets. Adjoining the park is the imposing **Newport Public Library** (300 Spring St., 401/847-8720, www.newportlibraryri.org, 11 A.M.–8 P.M. Mon., 9 A.M.–8 P.M. Tues.–Thurs., 9 A.M.–6 P.M. Fri.–Sat.), a general-purpose facility that also has some impressive special collections on Newport history, U.S. history, cookbooks, African American studies, Chinese culture, and Chinese-language books. Also facing the park is the imposing **Edward King House** (35 King St., 401/846-7426), one of the finest examples of Italianate villa design in the United States. Designed by noted architect Richard Upjohn, it was the largest house in Newport when it was built in 1847 for China Trade merchant Edward King, presaging the elaborate Newport mansions that were to follow several decades later. Today the building is a seniors center. While there are no formal tours, visitors are welcome to look around at the opulent interior.

While Newport has many homes and museums from the colonial and Victorian periods, the only house-museum from the Federal period is the **Samuel Whitehorne House** (416 Thames St., 401/847-2448, 11 A.M.–3 P.M. Thurs.–Mon. May–Oct., $6 adults, free for children under 12), a few blocks down Thames Street. The property is overseen by the **Newport Restoration Foundation** (51 Touro St., 401/849-7300, www.newport-restoration.com), an organization founded by the late heiress Doris Duke, who assembled an incomparable collection of Federal and colonial pieces from Newport's top cabinetmakers. She placed much of the collection in this house, which dates to 1811 and originally belonged to one of Newport's most successful shipping merchants, Samuel Whitehorne, who earned his fortune in rum distilling, shipping, and—although it's not documented conclusively—the slave trade. The house has all the classic elements of Federal architecture: a symmetrical hipped roof, a lavish formal garden, and a circular entryway. Guided tours are offered at 10:30 A.M. and 3 P.M. Thursday–Monday in summer for $12 pp. A $30 combination ticket is available to tour both the Whitehorne House and Duke's former estate at Rough Point.

While Newport has more than its share of restored homes and public buildings, only here could there also be an organization dedicated to the restoration of nautical craft. The **International Yacht Restoration School** (449 Thames St., 401/848-5777, ext. 227, www.iyrs.org, 10 A.M.–5 P.M., Wed.–Mon., tours at 1 P.M., free) is a nonprofit organization whose mission is to teach the "skills, history, and science needed to construct, restore, and maintain classic watercraft." Regardless of your own knowledge and experience with classic boats, you might just stop in to check out the school's impressive collection of fine old boats, including the IYRS flagship, the *Coronet,* which has sailed around the world and hosted such luminaries as Alexander Graham Bell and the king of Hawaii. A trip here makes a great prelude to checking out the Museum of Yachting at Fort Adams; a free shuttle makes the trip between the two properties.

◖ THE POINT DISTRICT

The Point District, which has one of New England's finest concentrations of colonial architecture, extends from just north of the Newport Visitors Center north to the Newport Bridge. It's a thoroughly engaging neighborhood for a stroll, its narrow streets packed with colonial and later Victorian homes, most of them painted in traditional Newport blues, slates, brick reds, mustards, and creams.

A highlight of the neighborhood is **Hunter House** (54 Washington St., 401/847-1000, www.newportmansions.org, tours 10 A.M.–5 P.M. daily late June–late Sept., $25), which sits at the southwest edge of the Point District near the bridge to Goat Island. This 1748 slate-gray Georgian mansion contains a priceless collection of 18th-century furnishings, ceramics, silver, pewter, and ornately carved woodwork. While Hunter House is the only home here open to the public, it's worth taking the time to see the dozens of wonderfully preserved homes by strolling the dozen or so blocks up Washington Street along the waterfront about as far as the Newport Bridge, then back down 2nd Street, which runs parallel a block east.

Just a block east of Hunter House is the **Pitt's Head Tavern** (77 Bridge St.), which is actually not original to the neighborhood. This 1724 gambrel-roofed building was built on Washington Square but moved here in the mid-1960s. Back on Washington Street and north past Hunter House is a pair of distinctive buildings, the 1736 **Captain John Warren House** (62 Washington St.), notable for its elegant central fanlight front door, and the **Thomas Robinson House** (64 Washington St.), owned by generations of the same family for two centuries. Just a bit farther north is the **Sanford-Covell Villa Marina** (72 Washington St., 401/847-0206 or 866/916-0206), a towering Victorian mansion designed by leading 19th-cenutry architect William Ralph Emerson; it's now a bed-and-breakfast.

BROADWAY

An untouristy but increasingly hip neighborhood that begins on the eastern edge of downtown and extends northeast into Middletown, Broadway is everything that the rest of Newport is not: slightly countercultural, highly quirky, and offbeat. You can understand why some locals refer to it as the East Village of Newport. Broadway is a repository of thrift shops, trendy but inexpensive eateries, affable pubs, and piercing parlors—it's the city's nod to Wickenden Street in Providence, and a refreshing change of pace when you become tired of seeing hordes of tourists and neatly preened yachters.

◖ OCEAN DRIVE

One of the most famous scenic drives on the East Coast, 9.5-mile Ocean Drive is a roughly C-shaped route that begins at the lower end of downtown, on Wellington Avenue at the intersection with Thames Street. Ocean Drive isn't one road but rather the name of a well-marked route that connects several roads. At least half the fun of this journey, which can take from an hour to half a day, depending on how often you stop, is simply peering out the window at the stunning homes, sandy beaches, and ocean vistas.

Still right in town on Newport Harbor, you'll pass little **King Park** on your right as you drive west along Wellington Avenue; this is the city's small but pleasant in-town beach. About one mile farther along, you'll come to a National Historic Landmark and one of the most formidable coastal forts ever built in the United States, **Fort Adams** (Eisenhower House, Fort Adams State Park, 401/841-0707, www.fortadams.org, 10 A.M.–4 P.M. daily late May–mid-Oct., grounds admission free, fortification tours $10 adults, $5 youths 6–17, free for children under 6, $25 families). The fort served the region from the 1820s through World War II, occupying a grassy point opposite downtown Newport, about a mile across Newport Harbor. Today you can tour the bastions, officers quarters, the enclosed 6.25-acre parade, and the exterior dry moat that helped prevent the fort from ever being compromised by an enemy. Entrance to the main fortification is by guided tour only, but admission to the grounds is free.

Also located at Fort Adams State Park, the **Museum of Yachting** (Fort Adams State Park, 401/847-1018, www.moy.org, 10 A.M.–5 P.M. daily late May–Sept., $5 adults, free for students and children under 18) documents Newport's legacy as one of the world's great centers for boating. Exhibits include the impact of Newport's Gilded Age on the city's reputation as a yachting center as well as an America's Cup Gallery, where photos and records document the races since the 1930s. Different events are held throughout the year, including the Classic Yacht Regatta on Labor Day weekend and several smaller regattas and events.

On leaving the park, continue back onto Harrison Avenue. Although it's no longer open to the public, **Hammersmith Farm** (off Harrison Ave., next to Fort Adams State Park) is home to an 1887 mansion that is one of Newport's most fabled properties. The site of Jacqueline Bouvier and John F. Kennedy's wedding reception in 1953, it became the "summer White House" for the first family after Kennedy became president. Once open for tours, the house was sold for $8 million to a private owner in 1999.

A short distance farther along Harrison Avenue, make a right onto Ridge Road and follow it around, passing the elegant Ocean Cliff Hotel. This road meets with Castle Hill Avenue, from which a small lane leads to the **Castle Hill Coast Guard Station** (75 Ridge Rd., 401/846-3676, tours by appointment during daylight hours). Back on the main route, you'll finally reach Ocean Avenue, which runs right along the water with mostly contemporary and colonial-style beach homes on the inland side of the street.

Where Ocean Drive turns nearly 90 degrees around Brenton Point, you'll find a parking area for **Brenton Point State Park** (401/849-4562 May–Oct., 401/847-2400 year-round, www.riparks.com/brenton.htm), a rugged, rocky promontory overlooking the ocean. You can picnic here or stroll along the beach, and it's phenomenally popular for kite-flying.

Continue on Ocean Drive along the waterfront back toward Newport, passing the Newport Country Club, some private beaches, and several gorgeous homes that range from century-old Victorian castles to rather recently built compounds with lavish decking and many-gabled roofs. Officially, Ocean Drive ends at Coggeshall Avenue, where a left turn will bring you back into lower downtown, about two miles away. Make a right turn, however, and after following the road a short way, make a left onto Bellevue Avenue to begin a tour of the Newport mansions of the Gilded Age—in the reverse direction from most visitors, who approach the mansions from town.

◀ ROUGH POINT

Some people get rich for being famous; other are famous for being rich. Heiress Doris Duke—the title is practically part of her name—belongs to the latter category. In 1925, when she was just 12 years old, she inherited $100 million on the death of her father, a tobacco and electricity magnate. She led a colorful life, to say the least, traveling around the world, working as a foreign correspondent during World War II, and famously romancing a number of men, marrying and divorcing three of them. Today, her legacy is best seen in the field of historic preservation through her establishment of the Newport Restoration Foundation, which started the city's preservation boom in the 1960s. Since then, it has helped fully restore more than 80 threatened structures in Newport, including the mansion where Duke herself spent the summers, Rough Point (680 Bellevue Ave., 401/847-8344, www.newportrestoration.com, tours by appointment 9:45 A.M.–3:45 P.M. mid-May–early Nov., $25 adults, free for children under 13).

A grand mansion built in 1889 for Frederick W. Vanderbilt, the home occupies a rocky point overlooking the ocean. James B. Duke, Doris's father, bought the estate in 1922 but lived in it for just three years before his death. Inside, you'll find a collection of rare Ming vases and ceramics, plus original paintings by Renoir, Van Dyck, and portraitist Joshua Reynolds. There is also a phenomenal collection of furniture and antiquities, rare among Newport mansions.

Rough Point can be visited only by guided tour, which are offered regularly at the Gateway Visitors Center, or you can book online at www.newportrestoration.com; only a limited number of tickets are sold each day, so it's highly advisable to buy tickets online well in advance, especially on summer weekends. The upside is that the tours are limited to just 12 people, making for a more intimate experience.

A new exhibit explores the life of Doris Duke and her efforts to preserve Newport's homes. It's included with the cost of the tour, or visitors can visit it on its own (1–4 P.M. Thurs. and Sat., $5).

BELLEVUE AVENUE

Running parallel to Thames Street a few blocks east and up the hill from Newport Harbor, Bellevue Avenue had become a wealthy, exclusive retreat by the time of the Civil War. Each season, new arrivals built ever-larger summer cottages until development peaked around 1890–1914, generally referred to as Newport's Gilded Age. During these 25 years, unbelievably wealthy industrialists and high-society types built massive, fortresslike homes and threw parties that sometimes cost more than $250,000 a pop. Many of the grandest of these houses still stand today, operated as house-museums and open to the public—a legacy that Newport's self-important summer bigwigs would have deemed unacceptable.

As stunning as the mansions are, they are not the only sights along Bellevue Avenue. North of the intersection with Memorial Boulevard is the **Redwood Library** (50 Bellevue Ave., 401/847-0292, www.redwoodlibrary.org, 9:30 A.M.–5:30 P.M. Mon., Wed., and Fri.–Sat., 9:30 A.M.–8 P.M. Thurs., 1–5 P.M. Sun.), a neoclassical structure built in 1750 by one of the nation's first architects, Peter Harrison, and once frequented by Gilbert Stuart, William and Henry James, and Edith Wharton. Tours of the library are given at 10:30 A.M. Monday–Friday, but the public is welcome to visit anytime during regular library hours.

Just a block south and across the street is the **Newport Art Museum** (76 Bellevue Ave., 401/848-8200, www.newportartmuseum.org, 10 A.M.–5 P.M. Tues.–Sat., noon–5 P.M. Sun. May–Oct., 10 A.M.–4 P.M. Tues.–Sat., noon–4 P.M. Sun. Nov.–Apr., $10 adults, $8 seniors, $6 students, free for children under 5), which shows the works of mostly regional artists, running the gamut from American impressionism to modern sculpture. Much of the work is quite good, especially the evocative seascapes by members of the Provincetown or Gloucester schools of artists in the same league (if without quite the same artistry) as Winslow Homer. Colonial-era portraits line the stairway of the Griswold House, the older of the two buildings. Across a sculpture-studded field, the

The Newport Art Museum features the work of regional artists.

© MICHAEL BLANDING

Cushing House stages changing exhibits, some of them quite clever: A recent exhibition, for example, focused on Newport's connection to Japan, which was opened to U.S. trade in the 19th century by the city's own Commodore Matthew Perry; items on display included a full suit of samurai armor.

Across Bellevue Avenue and down Mill Street is the **Old Stone Mill,** which anchors Touro Park. Much controversy surrounds this structure, which many locals had believed was built by Vikings 1,000 years ago, until improved forensic research cast doubt on this explanation. Another story is that one of the city's earliest residents and Rhode Island's first governor, Benedict Arnold, built the structure sometime in the 18th century.

International Tennis Hall of Fame

Tennis may have originated in England, but in the United States its history passes through Newport. The first U.S. National Lawn Tennis Championship, later known as the U.S. Open, was played on the grass-lawn tennis courts of the Newport Casino in 1881. Now that hallowed ground has become the International Tennis Hall of Fame and Museum (194 Bellevue Ave., 401/849-3990 or 800/457-1144, www.tennisfame.org, 9:30 A.M.–5 P.M. daily, $11 admission includes court access). Just south of Memorial Boulevard, the museum contains about a dozen exhibit rooms displaying memorabilia of the game, including an Andy Warhol portrait of Chris Evert, the original 1874 tennis patent granted by the queen of England to Major Walter Clopton Wingfield, and a gallery celebrating tennis champions of the early 20th century. The museum is unusual in that it remains a working tennis facility that's open to the public for play; this is the only lawn tennis facility in the country that's not a private club. There's also quite an extensive gift shop as well as a restaurant overlooking the courts.

National Museum of American Illustration

Just a bit farther south is the National Museum of American Illustration (NMAI,

© MICHAEL BLANDING

the grass courts at the International Tennis Hall of Fame

THE GILDED AGE

Around 1850, real estate speculators began buying up the land south and east of downtown, and Bellevue Avenue was extended south toward the water. This development triggered the period of wealth in Newport that would come to be known as "The Gilded Age." Wealthy New Yorkers and Bostonians began building summer cottages in this new section of Newport, and each summer the newest structures dwarfed the previous ones both in size and opulence. Many Southerners also built homes in this increasingly exclusive summer colony. The value of land skyrocketed, and the boom continued through the late 1850s.

After a short-lived recession, civic leaders decided to throw a sumptuous party for summering bigwigs as well as the many past Newport residents who had not been back for some time. The ball was a huge success, and the tradition of summer entertaining continued to grow each subsequent year. Predictably, the Civil War interrupted Newport's growth as a resort, but as soon as it ended, grand summer life in Newport returned stronger than ever.

This time, the ranks of summer residents included visibly fewer Southerners and many more wealthy families from Boston, New York, and Philadelphia. Local society movers and shakers included Mrs. Nicholas Beach, who hosted well-attended dance balls; Ward McAllister, who popularized the tradition of sumptuous picnics; and Mrs. August Belmont, who threw over-the-top dinner parties. For several weeks every summer, these rituals of entertaining on the grandest scale were embedded in Newport's regimen, as the very wealthiest hosts sought to outdo one another.

Into the 1880s, the presence of Newport's superrich part-time residents began to pay off in the form of significant investments in infrastructure improvements. A city water system was inaugurated in 1881, and private telephone service came the following year. Electric trolley service, which ran from Commercial Wharf up over Bath Street (now Memorial Boulevard) to Easton's Beach, became a reality in 1889. Upper-class leisure activities also made inroads during these years, with the earliest national tennis matches commencing in 1881, followed by polo and then golf tournaments. The little city by the sea, virtually bereft of industry or commercial clout, became a powerhouse owing to its sterling reputation as a playground for the rich and famous.

The ostentation hit its peak beginning in the next decade. As recorded in the Works Progress Administration guidebook on Rhode Island, which was written in 1937, "probably America will never again see such lavish entertaining as took place at Newport during the summer seasons of the 'gilded years,' 1890-1914. Into six or seven weeks each season were crowded balls, dinners, and parties of every description.... Huge sums were

492 Bellevue Ave., 401/851-8949, www.americanillustration.org, 11 A.M.–4:30 P.M. Sat.–Sun. late May–early Sept. or by appointment year-round for a minimum of 8 visitors, $18 adults, $16 seniors, $12 children 5–12, free for children under 5), which is worth admiring from the outside and also interesting to tour, keeping in mind the limited hours of admission. This museum is housed in one of the grand mansions along Bellevue Avenue, the 1898 Vernon Court, which is modeled after a 17th-century château. John Merven Carrère and Thomas Hastings, also responsible for the New York Public Library and the Frick Collection, designed the mansion, noted for its marble Great Hall and its steep roof punctuated by nine tall chimneys. The museum was formed with a mission to preserve and present the nation's finest illustrated art—works commissioned to appear in magazines, books, advertisements, and other print products. The collection displays work by dozens of famous illustrators, among them Maxfield Parrish, Norman Rockwell, N. C. Wyeth, Charles Dana Gibson, Howard Chandler Christy, and many others. As you tour the mansion you'll also see a vast array of decorative arts and period furnishings.

spent in the prevailing spirit of rivalry. Mrs. Pembroke Jones set aside $300,000 at the beginning of every Newport season for entertaining, and some hostesses spent even more. Sometimes a single ball cost $100,000." Even by the outlandish standards of today, as evidenced by multimillion-dollar Hollywood weddings, the social excesses in Newport remain unmatched.

Looking back, it's hard to imagine that most of these very rich Newporters even derived much pleasure from their wealth or their social standing. The jockeying for favorable social position was a blood sport, and it's supposed that many an upper-class family in the United States avoided Newport altogether, unwilling or unable to compete in this major league of snobbery and self-aggrandizement.

Newport year-rounders, sneeringly called "footstools" by the elite, despised the summer "cottagers," all the while, in many cases, undertaking their lowliest chores. A slightly higher class of full-time residents made out rather well, running shops or offering services and gouging the summer-comers for all they could; they had absolutely no shame in attempting to live well off these unbelievably rich visitors. And there was almost no interplay between the summer visitors and the full-time Newporters – even streetcars were not allowed to travel along Bellevue and Ocean Avenues.

In the Gilded Age, Harry Lehr and Mrs. William Astor became the leading society players in Newport, more or less controlling every aspect of the social season, determining who could move in the city's most desirable circles and who should be kept down. The so-called "400," a social precursor of sorts to today's Forbes 500, were those individuals fortunate enough to attend the ball held each summer in the ballroom of the Astor home. The room accommodated 400, and so Harry Lehr and Mrs. Astor pored over the *Social Register* each year to arrive at a definitive guest list. To be on this list could easily legitimize a person's social standing; to be excluded from it could scar one's reputation irreparably.

The outrageous antics of Newport's society mavens gradually began to wear on those outside looking in, most significantly the press. The gossip writers of the time took great glee in reporting each and every excess, from the time that Harry Lehr and Mrs. Stuyvesant Fish held a party at which a diminutive trained monkey was booked as the guest of honor, to the infamous dog gala, when Lehr invited about 100 canines and their owners to a lavish sit-down meal where thousands of dollars were spent on food. The public reaction to these displays was finally such that the summer party-throwers began to exercise more restraint, but the over-the-top parties still continued for many years.

Salve Regina University

Just off the east side of Bellevue Avenue is the attractive campus of Salve Regina University (Ochre Point Ave., 401/847-6650, www.salve.edu). There are 18 historically significant buildings on the property, which is a few blocks east of Bellevue Cliff Walk. The school is heavily involved in preservation programs, sponsoring lectures and preservation events and working hard to preserve its many prominent structures. The most famous building on campus is perhaps **Ochre Court,** one of the city's earliest grand summer cottages, completed in 1892 with a design by Richard Morris Hunt.

Ochre Court was donated in 1947 to serve as the foundation of Salve Regina, and through the past few decades, several other summer cottages in the adjoining neighborhood have been donated to the school. Noted architects whose works are now part of the campus include H. H. Richardson, the father of Richardsonian Romanesque; Charles Eamer Kempe; and the firm of McKim, Mead, and White. Designers who have worked on these homes and grounds include Louis Comfort Tiffany and Frederick Law Olmsted. You can walk through the main floor of Ochre Court, which serves as the school's main administrative offices,

A BRIEF HISTORY OF TENNIS

Tennis is an extremely old game, with roots in 11th-century France, and also a rather modern game – its present form dates to around the 1870s, when many wealthy Brits installed courts at their country manors. Similarly, as a wealthy leisure class was emerging in the United States, especially in New England, interest in tennis increased there.

In 1874, British Major Walter Clopton Wingfield devised a new form of tennis that combined the centuries-old game, which is now generally referred to as "court tennis" or "real tennis," with some characteristics of badminton, which has Native American origins. This variation, called lawn tennis, is the true ancestor of the game we play today, while real tennis is a comparatively obscure game played in few places.

Just a few years after its introduction to high society in New York, the first men's tennis championship in the United States was held at the Newport Casino; a women's championship was added in 1887. International competitions began in 1900 with the Davis Cup, which started as a men's tourney between the United States and England, although tennis had already developed a strong following in Australia, France, Holland, and many other nations.

Although tennis was something of a blue-blooded country-club activity during its first half century, its popularity spread to the general public during, ironically, the Depression, when a number of federally funded New Deal programs led to the construction of tennis courts at public parks and schools.

Professional tennis, of course, has enjoyed an almost meteoric rise in popularity through the past three decades. One of the four major tournaments, the U.S. Open is the modern-day descendant of that first championship held in Newport in 1881. For about 35 years, the Newport Casino and its illustrious tournament served as the U.S. equivalent of Wimbledon, and it might still today if not for Newport's relative isolation from the Northeast's major population centers. In 1915, the U.S. Open was shifted from Newport to Long Island, New York.

Nevertheless, from 1915 onward an invitational tournament continued to be staged at Newport's grass court, and in 1954 the Newport Casino was converted into the home of the National Tennis Hall of Fame. Starting in 1976, the Newport Casino has hosted the Hall of Fame Tennis Championship (now sponsored by Campbell's Soup), the only pro tournament in the nation still played only on grass courts.

9 A.M.–4 P.M. Monday–Friday; there's no admission charge, but keep in mind that this isn't a formal house-museum with tour guides.

NEWPORT'S MANSIONS

Much has been written about Newport's vast marble halls, and not all of it positive. As the railroad and steel tycoons began constructing their ostentatious summer homes at the end of the 19th century, they symbolized a new Renaissance in American architecture. Finally, the New World would have palaces to rival those of the Old World—built not by kings but by captains of industry. And while they might give a nod to the classical forms of Europe in style, they implemented the most advanced technology—electric lighting, hot and cold running water—that American ingenuity could conjure. Within a few short years, however, as the excesses of the Gilded Age spawned a Progressive backlash, no less an authority than novelist Henry James derided the Newport cottages as "white elephants"—beautiful but useless symbols of excess. Some modern architects have continued to turn up their noses at the extravagant tastes of the robber barons of the day, who seemed to choose the most garish forms of decoration in their homes that they could find.

Even knowing that, however, there's nothing like the impact of walking into some of these homes, whose every element seems calculated to impress. The Astors, Vanderbilts, and other millionaires of the time literally spared no expense in constructing their masterpieces, lavishing the same care and attention on these architectural endeavors as they did in constructing their multimillion-dollar businesses. While the initial reaction of most visitors is one of sheer overwhelmed amazement, closer inspection reveals countless pleasures in the details. There's not a single sconce or column that's free of adornment—each wall panel, and in some cases each ceiling tile, is decorated with some family crest or symbol designed to bless the fortunes of its creator. Even the most cynical viewer of the selfishness of wealth has to feel some awe in the beauty of so many well-thought design elements coming together in a harmonious whole. Lovers of antiques and historic homes may feel they've died and gone to architectural heaven.

The **Preservation Society of Newport County** (401/847-1000, www.newportmansions.org) operates tours of most of the houses. Several different tour possibilities are available, including combination tickets that provide a discount.

Kingscote Mansion and the Isaac Bell House

The first mansion you find as you travel south down Bellevue Avenue is also historically one of the first to establish the trend of Newport as a summer vacation spot for the rich and powerful. Kingscote Mansion (Bowery Ave. at Bellevue Ave., 401/847-1000, www.newportmansions.org, 10 A.M.–4:30 P.M. daily late June–early Sept., $14 adults, $5 children 6–17, children under 6 free) was the brainchild of George Noble Jones, a wealthy Georgia plantation owner who wanted a grand seaside residence to escape the Southern heat during summer. He commissioned architect Richard Upjohn to build him a truly unique and modern residence—Upjohn's Gothic Revival cottage, all asymmetrical gables, dormers, and drip moldings, represented the cutting edge of English architecture at the time—a reaction against the staid classical forms of Greek

Revival that were otherwise in vogue. Today the home stands as one of the only examples of its style and size. Completed in 1841, Kingscote set the tone that other mansions were to follow over the next 75 years. One of its most impressive features, however, was added in 1881: the dining room by the architectural firm Mead, White, and McKim, a breathtaking hall with a cork ceiling and what is believed to be the earliest-ever installation of Tiffany stained glass windows, that manages to be grand and intimate at the same time.

Next door, Mead, White, and McKim went on to build the Isaac Bell House (Bellevue Ave., 401/847-1000, www.newportmansions.org, 10 A.M.–4:30 P.M. daily late June–early Sept., $14 adults, $5 children 6–17, children under 6 free), a demonstrably less imposing residence that nevertheless ranks among the nation's most impressive examples of shingle-style architecture. Completed in 1883, it is a quirky house even by Newport standards, with bamboo-style porch columns and an open floor plan inspired by the grand houses of Japan. Three narrow brick chimneys rise from the many-gabled roofline. A single ticket is good for both Kingscote and the Isaac Bell House.

The Elms

The first real eruption of grandeur on Bellevue Avenue is also one of the most appealing of Newport's mansions. The Elms (424 Bellevue Ave., 401/847-1000, www.newportmansions.org, 10 A.M.–5 P.M. daily early Apr.–mid-June, 10 A.M.–6 P.M. daily mid-June–early Sept., 10 A.M.–5 P.M. daily early Sept.–late Nov., 10 A.M.–4 P.M. daily late Nov.–Dec., $14 adults, $5 children 6–17, children under 6 free) is a near-perfect copy of an 18th-century French château, built for coal tycoon Edward J. Berwind in 1901. The grounds comprise 10 acres of landscaped parkland containing about 40 species of trees, plus dignified marble statuary and perfectly groomed shrubs. The interior, almost cozy compared to some mansions, abounds with gadgets as The Elms was among the earliest Newport homes to be lighted and

TOURING THE MANSIONS

Boasting over 15 historic properties and 80 acres of gardens and parks, Newport's collection of sprawling mansions can seem an overwhelming tour indeed. If you're intent on seeing as much of them as possible, consider the following tips.

Buy tickets ahead of time. The crowds in high season can be crushing, so take advantage of some of the online packages available through the **Preservation Society of Newport County** (424 Bellevue Ave., 401/847-1000, www.newportmansions.org), which manages most of the major mansions (one exception is Belcourt Castle). While individual mansions can be pricey, the fees for combination tickets can be quite economical. For example, a ticket to The Breakers is $19 for adults ($5 children 6-17); however, The Breakers and one other mansion is $24 ($5 children). If you are a mansion freak, a ticket to see any five mansions is only $31 ($10 children). So try to gauge your interest in the mansions realistically beforehand to benefit from these savings.

Tours are offered quite regularly at the largest mansions (approximately every 15 minutes during high season and every 30 minutes in spring). Times vary at many of the smaller mansions, but generally the wait time is no longer than 30 minutes. And because most tours are finished in under an hour and the mansions are within easy walking distance of one another (and transportation is provided in the form of natural-gas trolleys between the houses), it is quite reasonable to plan three mansion tours in one day. Some ambitious visitors opt to do four or five, but it should be noted that there are only so many gilded ceilings and marble hallways the human eye can gaze upon before they all start to blend together. To fully appreciate the level of grandeur and detail, it may be wisest to take in three tours per day, leaving time for a change of scenery – Newport's beaches, downtown, or parks. If you've got children, of course, you'll need to reduce that further to one or two mansions at most. (A good alternative, included in the combination ticket, is a tour of the Green Animals Topiary Garden in Portsmouth.)

Finally, take the time to invest in a good map or guide. The society produces probably the best map to the Cliff Walk and Bellevue Avenue, which includes a level of detail down to each individual building in the area, color-coded by type (private home, house museum, university building), along with step-by-step information about the Cliff Walk and the locations of bus and trolley stops. Many other publishers and organizations produce their own maps and guides to the area; they are readily available at local book shops and convenience stores.

The mansions are wheelchair accessible; baby strollers are not allowed, however.

run by electricity. Tours are self-guided with digital audio players, a format that allows you to walk through the house in 30–90 minutes, depending on how many specific topics you choose to hear about.

As sumptuous and stunning as the Venetian-style dining room, the grand ballroom, and the airy conservatory are, The Elms's most fascinating rooms are the service quarters and working areas. You'll have the chance to tour the incredibly well-organized kitchen and pantry, the laundry room, a coal tunnel, and the boiler room that heated the mansion. If this aspect of mansion life really interests you, consider taking one of The Elms's Behind-the-Scenes guided tours ($15 pp), which give a particularly detailed sense of the inner workings of the mansion told from the perspective of the 40 women and men who groomed the grounds, cleaned the rooms, and prepared the meals. It's recommended that you book Behind-the-Scenes tours at least 24 hours in advance, as space is limited.

Chepstow

Just north of the Salve Regina campus on Narragansett Avenue, Chepstow (401/847-1000, www.newportmansions.org,

10 A.M.–4:30 P.M. daily late June–early Sept., $14 adults, $5 children 6–17, children under 6 free) is another early Newport mansion. An Italianate villa designed by George Champlin Mason and completed in 1860, its exterior is harmonious if less grand than some of its cousins. The esteemed collection of Hudson River School paintings, however, is worth the price of admission. A descendant of Lewis Morris, a signatory of the Declaration of Independence, owned this cottage.

Château-sur-Mer

Continuing the taste for all things French following the Civil War, Château-sur-Mer (Bellevue Ave., 401/847-1000, www.newportmansions.org, 10 A.M.–5 P.M. daily early Apr.–mid-June, 10 A.M.–6 P.M. daily mid-June–early Sept., 10 A.M.–5 P.M. daily early Sept.–late Nov., 10 A.M.–4 P.M. daily late Nov.–Dec., $14 adults, $5 children 6–17, children under 6 free) might be considered the missing link between the large homes such as Kingscote and Chepstow and the true mansions like The Breakers and Rosecliff. It was first built in a blocky château style in 1852 for merchant and Far East importer William S. Wetmore. After he died, however, his children decided the home needed a makeover, commissioning architect Richard Morris Hunt to update it to a more modern style. Hunt transformed both interior and exterior into a grand ensemble of the most fashionable European designs. Before those pesky Vanderbilts moved to Newport in the 1890s, this massive home was the largest residence in Newport. The interior impresses immediately with a stairway out of *Gone with the Wind* and a morning room demonstrating intricate woodwork. Behind the house you can stroll through a colonial revival garden pavilion and a Victorian-inspired park with century-old copper beech trees and weeping willows.

The Breakers

Each of Newport's mansions is an undeniably overwhelming display of wealth, beauty, and

© MICHAEL BLANDING

The Breakers is the most sumptuous of Newport's mansions.

design, but even among such over-the-top grandeur, the most lavish of them all is The Breakers (44 Ochre Point Ave., 401/847-1000, www.newportmansions.org, 9 A.M.–5 P.M. daily Apr.–late June, 9 A.M.–6 P.M. daily late June–early Sept., 9 A.M.–5 P.M. daily early Sept.–Nov., 9 A.M.–4 P.M. daily late Nov.–Dec., $19 adults, $10 children 6–17, children under 6 free), completed in 1895 as the summer home of steamship and railroad giant Commodore Cornelius Vanderbilt II, the first among equals of "the 400," the nickname for the elite New York social circle that ran the country back in the day. Designed by an international dream team of architects, the house has no less than 70 rooms and is a dead ringer for Italy's most opulent 16th-century palazzos. Alas, Vanderbilt only enjoyed one summer of good health here— after a stroke in 1896, he died a few years later in 1899.

His children, however, more than enjoyed the estate, including the impressive 13-acre grounds, which overlook Cliff Walk and the Atlantic Ocean—it was the sound of the waves smashing against the rocks below that gave The Breakers its name. Inside, rooms are constructed with ample amounts of semiprecious stones, rare marble, baccarat crystal chandeliers, and even platinum leaf on the walls (platinum is the rarest and most expensive metal in the world for its ability not to tarnish). In the bathrooms, four faucets provide both hot and cold freshwater and saltwater, and the marble baths were so thick that servants had to fill and drain them several times with hot water before they'd hold enough heat. Then there is the 45-foot-high Great Hall, as grandiose a room as there ever was and the site of countless soirees during The Breakers's heyday. At some of them, it's said, guests slid down the polished banister on dining trays.

As at The Elms, the tour here is with an audio recording that is exceptionally well put together, allowing guests to journey through the house at their own pace—taking in a little or a lot of the detail along the way, or skipping rooms entirely if time is limited. As engaging as the audio tour may be, however, be sure to take the headphones off once or twice. It's easy to get into a herd mentality of drifting from one numbered station to another without properly taking in the scene around you. Touch the cold marble pillars, gaze up at the mosaics on the ceilings, and try to imagine what it must have been like to live surrounded by such wealth and opulence.

Before you leave, be sure to check out the **Breakers Stable** (Coggeshall Ave. and Bateman Ave.), designed by Richard Morris Hunt. It contains a collection of road coaches and other memorabilia from the Vanderbilt clan. It's a block west of Bellevue Avenue by way of Ruggles Avenue.

Rosecliff

More French influence is evident down the street at Rosecliff (548 Bellevue Ave., 401/847-1000, www.newportmansions.org, 10 A.M.–5 P.M. daily early Apr.–mid-June, 10 A.M.–6 P.M. daily mid-June–early Sept., 10 A.M.–5 P.M. daily early Sept.–late Nov., 10 A.M.–4 P.M. daily late Nov.–Dec., $14 adults, $5 children 6–17, children under 6 free), built by Stanford White in 1902 and inspired by the Grand Trianon section of the palace at Versailles, France. Originally commissioned by Theresa and Hermann Oelrichs, it has been featured in a handful of movies, including *The Great Gatsby* and *Amistad.*

As her husband increasingly preferred the more laid-back social life out West, the home became more and more the domain of "Tessie" Fair Oelrichs, a colorful silver heiress from Nevada who became the center of Newport society for many years. Luckily, Oelrichs knew how to throw a fete, and the house is remembered for having hosted a magic-themed party at which Harry Houdini entertained the guests, as well as many other outlandish events. A tour highlight is walking through the largest ballroom in Newport (and that's saying a lot in this city).

If the rest of the home lacks the luster of

COURTESY OF RHODE ISLAND TOURISM/IRA KERNS

Rosecliff's opulent exterior

Newport's grandest mansions, it's because many of the opulent furnishings from Oelrichs' day have been removed, giving some of the rooms a bit of an empty feeling. The colorful story of its mistress, however, more than makes up for it. Sadly, she subsequently experienced a complete mental breakdown, living in seclusion for several years before her death in 1926, supposedly reliving her storied parties with imaginary guests.

Astors' Beechwood Mansion

While none of the bigger and best-known mansions in the area are still owned by their original families, for many years one of them almost seemed to be: Astors' Beechwood (580 Bellevue Ave.) was long home to the Beechwood Theatre Company, which gave tours portraying the Astors, their friends, and their staff at the height of the Victorian era, becoming a steady favorite on the "cottage circuit." Alas, the mansion was sold for upward of $10 million in 2010, and the theater company disbanded. The current plans for the mansion are still under wraps, but it

seems it will no longer be open for tours, a shame given its place in Newport Gilded Age society. The facade of the building can still be admired from the outside.

When William Backhouse Astor Jr. purchased a modest summer cottage in 1881, he hired architect Richard Morris Hunt to do a complete renovation along the lines of an Italianate summer villa. It was his wife, Caroline Astor, who ran the house as well as most of Newport Society. Known as "The Mrs. Astor," she virtually created the exclusive New York social circle known as "the 400" and held court with an austere presence for the two months of the year she summered at Newport—culminating every year in her famous Summer Ball.

Marble House and Belcourt Castle

Another modest little Vanderbilt home is Marble House (596 Bellevue Ave., 401/847-1000, www.newportmansions.org, 10 A.M.–5 P.M. daily early Apr.–mid-June, 10 A.M.–6 P.M. daily mid-June–early Sept.,

10 A.M.–5 P.M. daily early Sept.–late Nov., 10 A.M.–4 P.M. daily late Nov.–Dec., $14 adults, $5 children 6–17, children under 6 free), built in 1892 by Richard Morris Hunt for Cornelius Vanderbilt's grandson once removed, William K. Vanderbilt, who commissioned the home as a present for his wife, Alva, for her 39th birthday (which makes you wonder what he gave her for her 40th). True to its name, it's now filled with nearly half a million cubic feet of marble and includes on its grounds a Chinese teahouse built by Alva overlooking the crashing waves of the Atlantic below. After The Breakers, this is one of Newport's most-visited house-museums—visitors can't seem to get enough of the stairwells, columns, and floors of Italian, American, and African marble.

You'll find about 2,000 works of art—paintings, sculptures, and antiquities—at Belcourt Castle (657 Bellevue Ave., 401/846-0669, www.belcourtcastle.com, regular tours noon–5 P.M. daily May–Oct., weekends Apr. and Nov., closed Dec.–Mar., specialty tours available at other times, $20 adults, $16 youth under 17 and seniors). This Louis XIII–style castle hosts afternoon teas and many special events. The home was built by the rather idiosyncratic Oliver Hazard Perry Belmont, who inherited untold millions as the heir to the Rothschild fortune. Built in 1894 by, you guessed it, Richard Morris Hunt, the 60-room cottage cost $3 million. Belmont kept a staff of about 40 servants and owned an ornate collection of rare armor, manuscripts, and art from more than 30 Asian and European nations.

Now on regular guided tours you can examine the mansion's superb collection of French antiquities and art, most pieces dating from Louis XI through the Napoleonic periods. Tours cover not only the history of Belcourt but also that of several European royal castles, some of whose treasures now adorn this grand mansion. Belcourt also has the inevitable ghosts, and you can learn more about them during the Wednesday and Thursday ghost tours. Unlike most Newport mansions,

Belcourt isn't run by the Preservation Society of Newport County, so a separate admission applies.

◖ CLIFF WALK

The two finest things Newport has to offer—its natural seaside beauty and the architectural relics of the Gilded Age—collide along the seaside Cliff Walk (www.cliffwalk.com), arguably one of the country's grandest strolls. Beginning at the western end of First Beach (also known as Easton's Beach), the 3.5-mile path runs between the rocky beach and many of the town's most impressive mansions. The area is a designated National Historic District and was deemed a National Recreational Trail in 1975, making it a double-whammy of natural and artificial glory. For many who walk it, the Cliff Walk is an opportunity to gaze at fancy estates and experience the same ocean views that mesmerized Newport's wealthy summer visitors at the turn of the 20th century. It is also a wonderful nature trail, abundant with opportunities for bird-watching and for admiring fields of wildflowers.

There are a number of access points along Cliff Walk, but none are near ample public parking except the beginning of the trail at Easton's Beach, so the other points are limited to pedestrians and cyclists. Sheppard Avenue, Webster Street, and Wetmore Avenue intersect the walk about midway and have some limited street parking, and Narragansett Avenue, about 0.5 miles into the walk, has the most parking of any intersecting streets. During the summer a bus runs up and down Bellevue Avenue, the main paved road that parallels the walk, and you can take the bus to any of the cross streets that lead to the walk.

Less than a mile into the walk, at the end of Narragansett Avenue, you'll come to the **40 Steps,** a sharply descending stone stairway that goes nearly to the sea below; from a small promontory at the base of the steps you can watch the waves smashing against the rocks. Soon after 40 Steps, the path meanders by

COURTESY OF NEWPORT COUNTY CONVENTION & VISITORS BUREAU

Newport's dramatic Cliff Walk

some of Newport's most famous mansions, including The Breakers, Rosecliff, Astor's Beechwood, and Marble House. Soon after, on the right and just above the path, you'll see the ornate red Chinese teahouse commissioned by Marble House's owner, Alva Vanderbilt. At this point the Cliff Walk cuts through a short tunnel before emerging again for another fairly well maintained stretch and then a second tunnel.

Once you emerge from this final tunnel, Cliff Walk becomes a scramble on the wild side, as it hugs the rocky shoreline by a series of large private homes. This span is aptly nicknamed **Rough Point,** and rather crude and ugly chain-link fences separate the path from the private properties. Northeasters and hurricanes have taken their toll on Cliff Walk's southern reaches, and in some places the seawall has been ripped out. It's all entirely passable, and it's generally not too steep or high, but you do want to wear sturdy shoes. As you cut around the southeastern

tip of the peninsula, you'll be able to see the Doris Duke estate, Rough Point, just off Bellevue where it bends from south to west.

As Cliff Walk turns west around the southeastern tip of Newport, you'll come to Ledge Road, a short dead-end that shoots south off Bellevue Avenue. At this point you might think that Cliff Walk comes to an end—indeed, a short walk up Ledge Road does lead you back to where buses pass along Bellevue Avenue. However, it's also entirely possible to climb along the jagged rocks, treading carefully, for a short distance around the southwestern tip of this small peninsula. After a little more than 0.25 miles of cutting your own trail, the official Cliff Walk resumes, now in a northerly direction along the western end of the peninsula. To your left, looking northwest, you'll see the exclusive **Bailey's Beach,** and before long you'll reach the eastern edge of this fabled stretch of sand.

For a detailed sense of the entire walk's history and highlights, the official website (www.

cliffwalk.com) has detailed maps and 360-degree panoramas of some of the most beautiful spots along the trail.

MIDDLETOWN

Part of Newport until 1743, Middletown (population 17,000) is a relatively sleepy town. There isn't a lot to do here except relax and admire the area's pristine beaches, historic homes, and natural scenery. If that's your idea of an ideal sojourn, you've come to the right place.

Like Newport, Middletown suffered at the hands of the Brits during the Revolutionary War. A fleet of 11 British ships landed in Middletown in December 1776 to begin their occupation of lower Aquidneck Island. They are said to have looted many private homes, and more than a quarter of the community's residents fled to the mainland.

These days, most visitors make their way here from Newport for the day for one of the beaches or bird-watching at the local bird sanctuary, or to take advantage of cheaper accommodations while touring Newport.

Sights

The Newport-Middletown border lies on the eastern end of Easton's Beach, otherwise known as First Beach. From there, Memorial Boulevard becomes Purgatory Road, passing by the campus of **St. George's School** (off Purgatory Road), a private seminary for boys that was founded in 1896. After passing St. George's, you can reach Second Beach by bearing left onto Paradise Road and then quickly right onto Hanging Rocks Road—you'll see parking on the right.

The parking lot nearest Newport at Second Beach is a short walk from **Purgatory Chasm,** a 160-foot-deep fissure in the cliffs that ranges 8–15 feet in width at the top and 2–20 feet at the bottom. There's a small parking area (maximum 30 minutes) at the short trail to the chasm itself. This narrow and perhaps overhyped geological feature, with a nice little wooden bridge over it, has been a curiosity for as long as anybody can remember. Still, it's fun to sit on the rocky

promontory and admire the view down over Second Beach. Second Beach also has a small campground that occupies an enviable spot between Sachuest Point and Gardiners Pond; camping facilities include RV hookups and restrooms.

From here, continue east along Sachuest Road to reach **Sachuest Point National Wildlife Refuge** (Sachuest Point Rd.), which has a visitors center that's good for trail maps and local information. The center sits on a small bluff that affords nice views back toward Newport. Looking up the hill to the north of Newport, you'll also see the Gothic towers of St. George's prep school. Anglers appreciate the miles of rocky shoreline; the preserve also has some good hiking.

Backtrack along Sachuest Road past Gardiners Pond, make a right onto Indian Avenue, and follow it to Third Beach Road, which leads to—you guessed it—**Third Beach.** A short distance up the hill along Third Beach Road is the entrance to the **Norman Bird Sanctuary** (583 Third Beach Rd., 401/846-2577, www.normanbirdsanctuary.org, 9 A.M.–5 P.M. daily, $6), which occupies a small hill overlooking Second and Third Beaches, Sachuest Point, and the ocean. The refuge encompasses over 300 acres of farm fields, meadows, woodlands, and rocky ridges. In addition to hiking trails, the sanctuary boasts a small museum inside a historic barn, with exhibits about beach ecology and Native American history as well as live snakes, rodents, and raptors found on the sanctuary. Various educational walks and programs geared toward experts and novices, adults and families are offered throughout the year. During the spring and fall migrations, bird walks are held at 8 A.M. Sunday. If you don't have a car, you can still get to the sanctuary during the summer months by taking the **Coyote Shuttle** ($5 round-trip), a bus that leaves from the Newport Gateway Visitors Center hourly to make the rounds of several Middletown attractions.

If you bear left after Second Beach instead of bearing right toward Third Beach, you'll

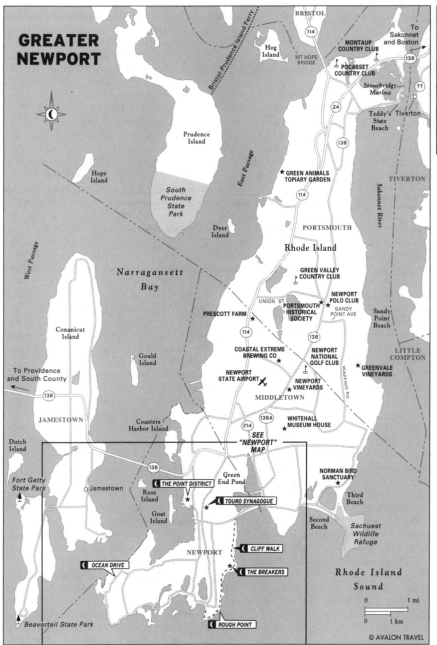

GREATER NEWPORT

BRISTOL

114

MT HOPE BRIDGE

Hog Island

To Sakonnet and Boston

138

MONTAUP COUNTRY CLUB

POCASSET COUNTRY CLUB

Stonebridge Marina

77

Bristol-Prudence Island Ferry

Prudence Island

East Passage

24

138

Teddy's Tiverton State Beach

★ GREEN ANIMALS TOPIARY GARDEN

TIVERTON

Hope Island

South Prudence State Park

Dyer Island

114

PORTSMOUTH

Rhode Island

Sakonnet River

West Passage

Narragansett Bay

GREEN VALLEY COUNTRY CLUB

NEWPORT POLO CLUB

Sandy Point Beach

Conanicut Island

UNION ST

PORTSMOUTH HISTORICAL SOCIETY ★

SANDY POINT AVE

PRESCOTT FARM ★

114

138

Sandy Point Beach

LITTLE COMPTON

Gould Island

To Providence and South County

138

COASTAL EXTREME BREWING CO ★

NEWPORT STATE AIRPORT ✈

NEWPORT NATIONAL GOLF CLUB

★ GREENVALE VINEYARDS

WAPPING RD

NEWPORT ★ VINEYARDS

JAMESTOWN

Coasters Harbor Island

MIDDLETOWN

214

138A

WHITEHALL ★ MUSEUM HOUSE

Dutch Island

SEE "NEWPORT" MAP

Green End Pond

NORMAN BIRD SANCTUARY

Fort Getty State Park

Jamestown

138

🏛 THE POINT DISTRICT ★

Third Beach

Rose Island

🏛 TOURO SYNAGOGUE ★

Goat Island

Second Beach

Sachuest Wildlife Refuge

NEWPORT

🏛 OCEAN DRIVE

🏛 CLIFF WALK

Rhode Island Sound

🏛 THE BREAKERS

Beavertail State Park

🏛 ROUGH POINT

0   1 mi

0   1 km

© AVALON TRAVEL

hit Indian Avenue, a rolling road lined with handsome, mostly early-20th-century homes that fringes the Sakonnet River. It's a beautiful stretch that's less fancy but also much less pretentious than Ocean Drive and Bellevue Avenue. Indian Avenue runs for about 2.5 miles before dead-ending; shortly before it ends, you can make a left turn onto Old Mill Lane and follow it a short way to Wapping Road, the main north-south route on Aquidneck Island.

From where Old Mill Lane intersects with Wapping Road, it's roughly one mile until you reach the right-hand turnoff for **Greenvale Vineyards** (582 Wapping Rd., 401/847-3777, www.greenvale.com, 10 A.M.–5 P.M. Mon.–Sat., noon–5 P.M. Sun.). Tastings at this attractive winery are held in a distinctive old gray building with a mansard roof. The breezes from the Sakonnet River keep things pretty cool even on hot summer days, making it a nice excursion in July and August. Back on Wapping Road, you can head north another mile or so until the road runs into Sandy Point Avenue; here a right turn leads down the hill to **Sandy Point Beach**, along the western shores of the Sakonnet River. This scenic beach is broad and flat and ideal for a picnic. In the other direction, Sandy Point Avenue runs west for about 0.5 miles until hitting East Main Road (Route 138).

Middletown may not have a Main Street, but it has two Main Roads—an East one and a West one, which run roughly parallel up the island from Newport. Both are accessible from downtown Newport by heading north on Marlborough Street from the Marriott, then north on Broadway from Washington Square. (Route 138 can also be reached by heading directly north up Memorial Blvd.)

Both routes also have attractions worth visiting. On West Main Road, a mile north from the intersection with Union Street, is the turn-off for Newport Restoration Society's third main property, **Prescott Farm** (2009 W. Main Rd., Middletown, 401/849-7300, www.newportrestoration.com, dawn–dusk daily year-round, free). This 40-acre farmstead, purchased by doyenne Doris Duke to preserve Aquidneck's farming history, makes an engaging alternative to the crowded mansions of Newport as well as a fascinating look at agrarian culture during Newport's colonial times. Among the attractions here is a 1730s guardhouse that contains notable Early American furnishings from the 17th century and an original 1812 windmill, still used today to grind grain, that spent time on several farms in the area after it was first built and installed in Warren.

Between West and East Main Streets is Newport State Airport; just north of it, take a turn onto Oliphant Avenue, one mile south of Prescott Farm or four miles north of downtown Newport, to find Rhode Island's only true microbrewery, **Coastal Extreme Brewing Co.** (307 Oliphant Lane, Middletown, 401/849-5232, www.newportstorm.com, noon–5 P.M. Wed.–Mon.), maker of the popular Newport Storm line of beers. In addition to its flagship Hurricane Amber Ale, the brewery produces Regenschauer Oktoberfest (available only in the fall), Blizzard Porter, Thunderhead Irish Red, and Maelstrom IPA. The visitors center is open every afternoon except Tuesday, and tours ($7), which include samples of several beers as well as a souvenir crystal beer glass, are given when there are enough visitors.

If you are still thirsty, the second of the area's wineries, **Newport Vineyards** (909 E. Main Rd., Rte. 138, Middletown, 401/848-5161, www.newportvineyards.com, 10 A.M.–5 P.M. Mon.–Sat., noon–5 P.M. Sun.), is a short drive away on East Main Street, just across from the airport. The winery produces several white and red varieties, including a riesling, a chardonnay, and a merlot, with tastings during opening hours and tours at 1 and 3 P.M. daily. As if that weren't enough, on the property you'll also find a toy store, a garden center, an art gallery, and a small restaurant; a farmers market is held on the grounds Saturday morning June–October.

Finally, 0.5 miles south of the winery just off Route 138, head east on Wyatt Road and south onto Berkeley Avenue by Middletown Cemetery to find an altogether different house-museum dedicated to noted Irish philosopher George Berkeley, who lived in Middletown 1729–1731 in the **Whitehall Museum House** (311 Berkeley Ave., 401/846-3116, http://whitehallmuseumhouse.org, 10 A.M.–4 P.M. Tues.–Sun., $5 adults, free for children under 15). It is a stately red saltbox that has been managed by the Rhode Island chapter of Colonial Dames since 1900 and is now furnished with period pieces (although none belonged to Berkeley himself). Berkeley was in Aquidneck on a 20,000-pound commission from the British parliament to found a college in Bermuda to educate the sons of colonists and Indians in the New World. A literary and ecclesiastical salon of sorts was begun here during Berkeley's time, and even though his commission fell through and he returned home after three years, he left behind the impetus for founding Brown and Columbia Universities. Later, when the University of California was looking for a name for a new town outside San Francisco where they were founding a school, they named it Berkeley in his honor.

PORTSMOUTH

Rounding out the tip of Aquidneck Island, north of Middletown, the town of Portsmouth (population 17,000) tends to get missed by many visitors to Newport, even though it claims to be nothing less than the "birthplace of American democracy." While that might seem like municipal hubris, it's actually not far off the mark: Founded in 1638 by religious heretics banished from Massachusetts Bay, including feminist preacher Anne Hutchinson, the town was the first to be ruled by its own members instead of the crown of England. A bronze tablet erected on a rock at Founders Brook memorializes the so-called Portsmouth Compact that founded the independent community.

The town played a minor part in the Revolutionary War as the site of the Battle of Rhode Island, which took place in August 1778 as a group of American troops led by General John Sullivan ventured by boat from Tiverton to Portsmouth, where they drove British forces back nearly to Newport. After the Revolutionary War, Portsmouth's early economy involved two things that Aquidneck Island has long excelled in: farming and

shipbuilding. Unusually in this part of the country, the town also did quite well with coal mining for a time—a large coal field on the western side of town produced large quantities of coal. Portsmouth today has its own rather modest summer colony, mostly along or just off Route 138, which runs down the eastern side of the town overlooking the Sakonnet River.

Sights

As with Middletown, Portsmouth attractions are divided between West and East Main Road. You can learn more about Portsmouth's impressive early history at the **Portsmouth Historical Society** (870 E. Main Rd., Rte. 138 at Union St., 401/683-9178, limited hours), which occupies the town's former Christian Union Church (circa 1865), 0.5 miles north of Sandy Point Avenue. Also on the grounds are the 1845 Portsmouth Town Hall and the Southernmost School, Rhode Island's oldest one-room schoolhouse, which dates to 1725.

From here it's a rather long but pleasant journey north on Route 138, which passes modern shopping centers along the way but is generally an appealing thoroughfare with several good views out over the Sakonnet River and toward the Sakonnet Peninsula. After about 4.5 miles, Route 138 bears right and becomes Park Avenue, which leads to an interesting, rather modest beach community called Island Park. Where Route 138 abruptly shifts to the left, stay on Park Avenue and continue straight for another mile to the Stonebridge Marina, on the right. You'll pass some fun little seafood eateries, the most famous being Flo's Clam Shack.

The marina marks the spot where a stone bridge across the Sakonnet River once connected Portsmouth to Tiverton, but the bridge was removed in 1956, leaving fishing piers on both shores—it's less than 200 yards between the ends of the piers. There's also a nice sandy beach by the marina. To the north, in the immediate distance, you'll see the massive new highway bridge, where Route 138/24 runs between Portsmouth and Tiverton.

From Stonebridge Marina, drive about 0.5 mile north and under the Route 138 overpass, making a left turn onto Hummocks Avenue. Follow it a short way south until it becomes Anthony Road; you're paralleling Route 138/24, which is on your left. When you reach Boyds Lane, turn right and head into the small village of Bristol Ferry, where a boat used to carry passengers across Narragansett Bay to the southern tip of Bristol. In 1927 the Mount Hope Bridge was constructed, carrying traffic along Route 114 across the bay. It is a narrow, graceful bridge, and from the top of its arch you'll enjoy great views out over the bay and Aquidneck Island.

From here, you can turn around and retrace your route back south along Route 114. Three miles south, turn right on Cory's Lane to arrive at the **Green Animals Topiary Garden** (380 Cory's Lane, 401/847-1000, www.newportmansions.org, 10 A.M.–6 P.M. daily Apr.–mid-Oct., $12 adults, $4.50 children 6–17), where humanity and shrubbery peacefully coexist in a menagerie of some 80 shrubs and trees sculpted into whimsical shapes, some of which have been intriguing visitors for almost a century. Among them are teddy bears, a giraffe, a unicorn, and an elephant. Also on the grounds is a small museum of Victorian toys, and there's an extensive gift shop of toys, garden items, and the like. Green Animals admission is included with the combination ticket for Hunter House and several Bellevue Avenue mansions.

JAMESTOWN

In the middle of Narragansett Bay between Newport and South County, the town of Jamestown occupies all of Conanicut Island, a cigar-shaped swatch of land with a smaller island off its southwestern tip. With a full-time population of 6,000, the island is not at all densely populated, although improved bridges have been built in recent decades and southern Rhode Island has expanded in general, making Jamestown a full-time home for more people.

It's a lovely island to explore, and Jamestown's tiny but picturesque downtown has several cute shops and a handful of notable eateries and accommodations. The leading attraction is the tremendous scenic beauty, and **Beavertail State Park** (Beavertail Rd., 401/423-9941 or 401/884-2010, www.riparks.com) covers 155 acres of pristine scrub and low woodland across a rocky point at the southern end of Conanicut Island. A loop road runs through much of the park and passes several scenic overlooks, including one that takes in Beavertail Lighthouse. The park is laced with hiking trails, and throughout the summer park naturalists lead a variety of walks.

Entertainment and Events

ARTS AND CULTURE

Considering Newport's glittering legacy of sophisticated and wealthy summer visitors along with its well-endowed visual arts scene, the city is relatively lacking when it comes to the performing arts.

One of the most popular entertainment venues is the **Newport Playhouse and Cabaret Restaurant** (102 Connell Hwy., near the foot of Newport Bridge, 401/848-PLAY—401/848-7529, www.newportplayhouse.com), which presents several generally light theatrical performances each year April–December. The show comes with a substantial buffet dinner, and the theater has a full liquor license. Different kinds of music concerts are sometimes held at the city's house-museums, churches, and at Salve Regina University's **Cecilia Hall** (in the Carey Mansion, Ruggles Ave., 401/341-2945). It's best to check with the **Newport County Convention and Visitors Bureau** (23 America's Cup Ave., next to the bus terminal, Newport, 401/849-8098 or 800/326-6030, www.gonewport.com) for details on what's happening where.

NIGHTLIFE

For a city of just 26,000, Newport does pack quite a punch when it comes to nightlife.

There's often live music at **Christie's** (351 Thames St., 401/847-5400), a fun gathering spot for schmoozing; the crowd tends to look as if they were fresh out of a J. Crew catalog. Below the Candy Store at Bannister's Wharf, the **Boom Boom Room** (1 Bannister's Wharf, 401/849-2900) draws a fairly mainstream and somewhat touristy crowd for dancing to DJ-spun Top 40 and disco hits. Upstairs in the bar at **Candy Store** (401/849-2900), yachting enthusiasts and Newport socialites trade gossip and cruise over wines by the glass and fancy cocktails. **Sabina Doyle's** (359 Thames St., 401/849-4466, http://fastour.com/sabina/) is a more centrally located Irish pub that's also quite fun. Over near the beaches, summer vacationers often congregate at **KJ's Pub** (61 Aquidneck Ave., 401/848-9991, http://kjsrestaurant.com), which serves decent seafood and burgers and often books live acoustic, blues, and other music.

Sing-alongs are a favorite pastime at the piano bar at **La Forge Casino Restaurant** (186 Bellevue Ave., 401/847-0418), which gets going on Friday and Saturday evenings. It tends to be a less chaotic alternative to the sometimes rowdy collegiate bars down along Thames Street. **Vincent's on the Pier** (10 W. Howard's Wharf, 401/847-3645, www.vincentsonthepier.com) presents very nice piano music, and nearly every table in this restaurant-bar overlooks Newport Harbor. The kitchen (lunch noon–3 P.M. daily, dinner 6–9:30 P.M. Sun.–Thurs., 6–10 P.M. Fri.–Sat.) turns out first-rate, upscale Mediterranean and new American cuisine. **Castaway's on Solar Wind** (28 Prospect Hill St., 401/849-9928) is Newport's small but festive gay nightspot, noted for its vintage antique bar. It's a classy little spot with a nice side bar that has a pool table.

Live Music and Clubs

Jazz lovers who couldn't be in town for the Newport Jazz Festival or just want a second show will find proper consolation at the **Newport Blues Cafe** (286 Thames St., 401/841-5510, www.newportblues.com). The restaurant-lounge showcases live music from acclaimed artists

seven nights a week. Progressive rock fans can catch indie acts—some big names, but mostly local—at **One Pelham East** (270 Thames St., 401/847-9460, www.thepelham.com). Usually packed on summer nights, it can be a comfortable spot to catch fall and winter acts.

The **Rhino Bar and Grille** (337 Thames St., 401/846-0707, www.therhinobar.com) is a mainstay for listening to live bands and dancing to DJ-spun techno, hip-hop, and dance tunes. The crowd is young and cruisy, generally on the make, and looking to have a good time. The grill serves better-than-average American food, pizzas, burgers, and grills, and there is a surprisingly sophisticated wine list.

FESTIVALS AND EVENTS
Summer

In early June, the **Schweppes Great Chowder Cook-off** (www.newportfestivals.com) is great fun. You can get a neat behind-the-fence look at many Newport properties on the **Secret Garden Tour** (www.secretgardentour.com), held in early June and then again in September.

Also in early June, look for the **Newport International Film Festival** (www.newportfilmfestival.com), a prestigious six-day festival of dozens of films that include features, special screenings, documentaries, and numerous shorts; there's usually a retrospective each year too. Many lectures, parties, and other events coincide with the film festival. At Rosecliff, the **Newport Flower Show** (www.newportmansions.org) is held at the end of June, filling tents with exotic plants and flower arrangements organized around a different theme each year. The **Snapple Sunset Music Festival** (www.newportfestivals.com), in late June–early July, brings national folk and rock acts to an intimate waterfront venue.

Newport's **Portuguese Cultural Festival** is held in early July in Touro Park, and features traditional Portuguese food along with music and folk dancing. A variety of venues hosts the **Newport Music Festival** (www.newportmusic.org), which has been going strong since the late 1960s. The event runs for roughly the last two weeks of July and presents about

NEWPORT JAZZ FESTIVAL

Every August, Newport's already impressive number of summer visitors swells by leaps and bounds thanks to one thing: the global draw of the renowned Newport Jazz Festival. Founded as the first outdoor jazz music festival by pianist George Wein and several Newport socialites in 1954, the festival is now a magnet for jazz fans for its mix of well-known performers and up-and-coming musicians. Over the decades, legends like Miles Davis, Duke Ellington, Billie Holiday, and Frank Sinatra have graced its stages.

Usually a three-day series of concerts and events, the festival packs in hundreds of performances, from organ trios and vocalists to Brazilian duos and big-band productions, on three primary stages. Performance schedules are always available ahead of time from the festival office (401/847-3700, www.jazzfestival55.com). Tickets are plentiful and can be bought in advance and by showing up in person. Regulars strongly recommend booking a hotel ahead of time, as the more desirable properties book up months in advance. There is also camping offered nearby in Melville Ponds Campground (401/682-2424) in Portsmouth.

Most of the festival's action takes place in Fort Adams State Park on Harrison Avenue, which has strict rules about what attendees may bring. When packing, bear in mind that they allow only one small handheld cooler per person; individual blankets must measure less than 8 by 10 feet; and only low-backed chairs (under 30 inches) are allowed, to ensure good viewing for those around you. No glass containers, alcohol, pets, bikes, or beach umbrellas are permitted. Children are welcome, and there are plenty of inexpensive kids' meals at the concession stands.

---

60 chamber-music and other classical concerts at some of the city's most famous mansions, including The Elms, The Breakers, Marble House, Salve Regina's Ochre Court, Rosecliff, and Belcourt Castle. Some of the concerts are held in ballrooms and indoor spaces, while others are presented under tent cover on the lush grounds. The **Newport Summer Comedy Series** (Newport Yachting Center, America's Cup Ave., www.newportcomedy.com) runs July–August and consists of a series of comedy shows held every Sunday night. The sponsors book mostly New England–based comedians, including several who have performed on late-night talk shows and have received awards at the prestigious Boston Comedy Festival.

Also in early July is the **Newport Kite Festival** (www.buyakite.com), with kite flying shows and demonstrations open to the public free of charge. Toward the end of the July the **Black Ships Festival** (401/847-7666, www.blackshipsfestival.com) celebrates the 1854 opening of U.S. trade with Japan by Newport's Commodore Matthew Perry. It is a citywide celebration of his trip and of Japanese culture. The International Tennis Hall of Fame hosts the **Campbell's Hall of Fame Tennis Championship** (www.tennisfame.org), a major draw on the Association of Tennis Professionals tour and the only grass-court professional tennis tourney in the country.

More music enjoyment is to be had at the **Apple and Eve Newport Folk Festival** (www.newportfolk.com). This three-day event, held at the sprawling, well-kept Fort Adams State Park in early August, is one of the nation's top folk festivals and has drawn dozens of major artists through the years; recent performers include Bob Dylan, Shawn Colvin, Arlo Guthrie, Dar Williams, and Bruce Cockburn. The following weekend in August, the hugely popular **Newport Jazz Festival** (401/848-5055, www.jazzfestival55.com) is also held at Fort Adams. Big international acts congregate here alongside promising up-and-comers to entertain jazz enthusiasts.

Fall

Over Labor Day weekend, the **Classic Yacht Regatta and Parade Day** (www.moy.org)

features about 100 vintage sailing vessels racing on Narragansett Bay; there's also a parade of ships. Around the same time is the ever-growing annual **Newport Waterfront Irish Festival** (401/846-1600, www.newportwaterfrontevents.com), which brings step-dancing, bagpipes, and Guinness to the waterfront. The city's many avid yachters make a point of visiting the annual **Newport International Boat Show** (www.newportexhibition.com). Later in September you can attend the **Tastes of Rhode Island Festival** (www.newportwaterfrontevents.com) and sample dishes offered by the state's top chefs. **Haunted Newport** (401/845-9123, www.hauntednewport.com) is held the last week in October and includes tours of area houses set up for the ghoulish holiday.

In early October, check out the **Norman Bird Sanctuary Harvest Fair** (www.normanbirdsanctuary.org), a 2-day celebration of fall with children's games, hayrides, and craft vendors. The city's **Fiesta Italiana,** in mid-October, celebrates Newport's Italian heritage with food, music, storytelling, and other family-oriented

events. Mid-October also features **International Oktoberfest** (www.newportwaterfrontevents. com), a traditional Bavarian festival with wurst and oompah bands, as well as the **Bowen's Wharf Seafood Festival** (www.bowenswharf. com), which offers lobster, stuffies, scallops, oysters, and other tasty dishes from local restaurants and fishermen, along with live Celtic music, folk songs, and sea shanties.

Winter and Spring

All through mid-November until Christmas, the holiday season sees the town's mansions decked out even more elaborately than usual; heavyweights such as Marble House and The Breakers are festively dressed in white lights and Christmas decorations for **Christmas at the Newport Mansions** (401/847-1000, www. newportmansions.org, late Nov.–early Jan., admission cost varies for different mansions). All through December is the annual **Christmas in Newport Celebration** (www.christmasinnewport.org), which fills the waterfront and historic districts with thousands of white lights

COURTESY OF NEWPORT COUNTY CONVENTION & VISITORS BUREAU

Newport's annual International Boat Show is a haven for yachters.

and Christmas music from live bands and choruses.

Newport tries hard to keep things lively through the colder months by throwing **12 Weeks of Winter** (www.gonewport.com) January–March. Each week has a different theme—popular ones include Cultural Arts Week; Mystery Week; Antiques and Collectibles Week; Black Heritage Week; the Kinsale, Ireland, Festival of Fine Food (Kinsale is Newport's sister city); and the Newport Winter Festival.

Come spring, every boat lover in New England heads for the **Spring Boat Show** (401/846-1115, www.newportspringboatshow.com, $5 adults, free for children under 12) in late May, the region's largest, to ogle the new and used vessels and to haggle at the stalls of the show's flea market, where everything from fishing line to used kayak paddles are for sale. Also in late May is the **Sail Newport Family Sailing Festival** (www.sailnewport.org), in which experienced sailors give free tours of the harbor, and **Fort Adams Day** (www.fortadams.org), which features kids' games, food, and tours of the fort.

Shopping

Newport can keep even the most dedicated shoppers content for days. In the downtown area, along Thames Street and the lanes and wharves just off it, you'll find dozens of mostly independent clothiers, jewelry shops, art galleries, and gift shops. Chain businesses have made some inroads, but for the most part you'll find a nice mix of stores that you won't find back home or even in other parts of Rhode Island.

Most of the house-museums along Bellevue Avenue have outstanding gift shops, and the proceeds help to keep these mansions running. Books on local and regional architecture and decorative arts, prints, and housewares are among the most common items you'll find in these shops.

Another Newport retail specialty is decorative and practical wares with a nautical bent, from the requisite ship's wheel and scrimshaw kitsch to high-quality maritime paintings and prints, sailing clothing and gear, and antique barometers, ships' clocks, and similar items. Quite a few local artists live in or near Newport and have their creations represented at galleries around town.

SHOPPING DISTRICTS

Several of the wharves in Newport function today as mini malls, many of them on the wharves jutting into the harbor. **Bannister's Wharf** (off Thames St., www.bannisterswharf.net)

has several fine shops. **Brahmin Handbags** (22 Bannister's Wharf, 401/849-5990, 10 A.M.–8 P.M. daily) is where to find high-quality handmade leather accessories that include prim and classic New England handbags to funky wallets that would be at home on the Riviera. Looking for something to wear out to dinner tonight? Turn to **Mandarine** (16 Bannister's Wharf, 401/848-9360, www.shopmandarine.com, 10 A.M.–6 P.M. Mon.–Sat., 10 A.M.–5 P.M. Sun.), which carries smart men's and women's sportswear and cocktail party–worthy gear. Pick up silk dresses, jewelry, suits, and accessories by designers from all over the globe.

Bowen's Wharf (Thames St. at America's Cup Ave., 401/849-2243, www.bowenswharf.com, 10 A.M.–10 P.M. Mon.–Sat., noon–7 P.M. Sun.) is a bit smaller than Bannister's Wharf but has an engaging mix of businesses, including Crabtree & Evelyn, Thomas Kinkade Galleries, and about 20 other shops, plus several restaurants, harbor tour companies, and galleries. Highlights include **Bellevue Beauty Walk** (2 Bowen's Wharf, 401/845-0800, www.bellevuebeautywalk.com, 10 A.M.–9 P.M. Mon.–Sat., noon–6 P.M. Sun.)—which stocks marquee lines such as Molton Brown, Paula Dorf, and Terax hair care—and **Michael Hayes** (204 Bellevue Ave., 401/846-3090, www.michaelhayesnewport.com, 10 A.M.–10 P.M. daily) for topnotch women's lines like Missoni and Roberto Cavalli

COURTESY OF NEWPORT COUNTY CONVENTION & VISITORS BUREAU

shopping on Bowen's Wharf

along with men's duds by Ermenegildo Zegna and Etro. **Thames Glass** (688 Thames St., 401/846-0576, 10 A.M.–6 P.M. Mon.–Sat., noon–5 P.M. Sun.) carries the handblown glasswork of Newport artist Matthew Buechner; you can take glassblowing lessons here too.

ARTS AND CRAFTS

There are many very good sources of nautical and marine art in town. One of the most extensive, **Arnold Art Store and Gallery** (210 Thames St., 401/847-2273, www.arnoldart.com, 9:30 A.M.–5:30 P.M. Mon.–Sat., noon–5 P.M. Sun.), fills three floors with original paintings and prints. Also highly acclaimed is **William Vareika Fine Arts** (212 Bellevue Ave., 401/849-6149, www.vareikafinearts.com, 10 A.M.–6 P.M. Mon.–Sat., 1–6 P.M. Sun., or by appointment), which carries exceptional American paintings, drawings, and watercolors from the past three centuries. **Blink Gallery** (89 Thames St., 401/847-4255, www.blinkgalleryusa.com, 10 A.M.–6 P.M. Mon.–Fri.) presents stunning contemporary photography with many scenes of Newport and other works

depicting scenes from all over the world. **Onne Van Der Wal** (1 Bannister's Wharf, 401/846-5556, www.vanderwal.com, 10 A.M.–5 P.M. Mon.–Fri., 10 A.M.–6 P.M. Sat., noon–5 P.M. Sun., or by appointment) is another superb photography gallery and an excellent place to pick up a memento of Newport.

Sheldon Fine Art (59 America's Cup Ave., 401/849-0030, www.sheldonfineart.com, 9 A.M.–9 P.M. daily) carries the works of several prominent artists, including John Mecray and John Phillip Hagen. **Spring Bull Studio and Gallery** (55 Bellevue Ave., 401/849-9166, www.springbullgallery.com, noon–5 P.M. daily) is a cooperative gallery of nearly 20 area artists. Contemporary jewelry and decorative arts are the specialty at **Suydam and Diepenbrock** (9 Bridge St., 401/848-9090). At **Cadeaux du Monde** (26 Mary St., 401/848-0550, www.cadeauxdumonde.com), you can browse folk art, textiles, clothing, and decorative arts from around the world, especially Latin America. **Roger King Fine Arts** (21 Bowen's Wharf, 401/847-4359, www.rkingfinearts.com, 10 A.M.–5 P.M. daily) carries an impressive selection of 19th- and 20th-century paintings, especially nautically themed works.

ANTIQUES, GIFTS, AND HOME FURNISHINGS

The **Griffon Shop** (76 Bellevue Ave., 401/848-8200, 10 A.M.–4 P.M. Tues.–Sat., 1–4 P.M. Sun.) carries a wide range of antiques, odds and ends, and original artwork by several local artists and craftspeople.

Another bric-a-brac emporium of solid repute is the **Eagle's Nest Antique Center** (3101 E. Main Rd., Rte. 138, Portsmouth, 401/683-3500, 11 A.M.–5 P.M. Mon.–Sat., noon–5 P.M. Sun.), a multiple-dealer space with more than 100 stalls representing every possible kind of antique, collectible, jewelry, and toy.

Karen Vaughan (148 Bellevue Ave., 401/848-2121, www.karenvaughanonline.com, 9 A.M.–5 P.M. Mon.–Fri.) carries a natty array of hip home furnishings and decorative arts. Furniture-maker Jeffrey Greene crafts fine 18th century–inspired designs at **The Ball and Claw** (55 America's Cup Ave., 401/848-5600, www.theballandclaw.com, 10:30 A.M.–6 P.M. Mon.–Thurs., 10:30 A.M.–7 P.M. Fri.–Sat., 11:30 A.M.–5:30 P.M. Sun.), which also carries porcelain, quilts, chandeliers, and lamps. For nearly a century, **J.T.'s Chandlery** (128 Spring St., 401/846-7256, www.jtschandlery.com, 10 A.M.–8 P.M. daily) has been a leading supplier of all things nautical; it's still a must for yachting and boating aficionados and a great source of gifts.

You can pick up reproduction home furnishings, gifts, and jewelry of Newport's Gilded Age at the **Museum Store** (Preservation Society of Newport, 1 Bannister's Wharf, 401/849-9900, www.newportmansions.org, 9 A.M.–10 P.M. daily). Before hitting the surf, hit the shelves and racks of **Helly Hansen** (154 Thames St., 877/666-8742, www.hellyengland.com, 9 A.M.–9 P.M. daily). The boating gear selection ranges from base layers to keep you warm on windy sails to fully waterproof parkas and snuggly soft shell jackets. Home to an excellent selection of stained-glass artwork, **Aardvark Antiques** (9 JT Connell Hwy., 401/849-7233, www.aardvarkantiques.com, 9 A.M.–5 P.M. Mon.–Sat., by appointment Sun.) is also where you'll find garden statues and fountains like nowhere else outside a Roman square: Giant gargoyles and ceramic fish squat next to structures festooned with mermaids and gods.

PICK-YOUR-OWN FARMS

Pick-your-own farms are more popular in other parts of the state, but **Sweet Berry Farm** (19 Third Beach Rd., Middletown, 401/847-3912, www.sweetberryfarmri.com, 8 A.M.–7 P.M. daily) is a great spot for this activity within a short drive of downtown Newport. In summer, go for strawberries and raspberries, then move on to cut flowers and vegetables as the months progress, and finally find pumpkins in the fall and Christmas trees in early winter.

Sports and Recreation

FIRST, SECOND, AND THIRD BEACHES

Along with the mansions, day-trippers from all over New England come to Newport for shopping, boating, and especially sunbathing. Newport and neighboring Middletown have been blessed with several largely undeveloped stretches of golden sand that are some of the most beautiful on the Atlantic Coast. The beach starts in Newport near the Middletown border with Easton's Beach (175 Memorial Blvd., 401/845-5810, www.cityofnewport.com/departments/economic-development/beach/home.cfm)—otherwise known as First Beach, which curves between Easton's Pond and the Atlantic below the Cliff Walk. In addition to its picturesque setting, the beach is particularly good for families, with a bathhouse, a full restaurant, and lots of activities going on all the time.

Easton's Beach, also known as First Beach

Children's programs are held early on Thursday evenings, and other activities geared for kids take place daily at a miniature amusement park at the Easton's Beach Rotunda, which includes the popular **Easton's Beach Carousel** (10 A.M.–8 P.M. Sat.–Sun. late May–mid-June, 10 A.M.–8 P.M. daily mid-June–early Sept., $1 per ride or $10 for 20). The city also recently introduced a new bumper-boat ride and waterslide (mid-June–early Sept., $5 unlimited rides), and a bouncy castle (5–8 P.M. Mon.–Thurs., $5).

Rounding out the experience is the miniature aquatic petting zoo at the **Save the Bay Exploration Center** (175 Memorial Blvd., 401/324-6020, www.savebay.org, 10 A.M.–4 P.M. daily late May–early Sept., $5, free for children under 3). The educational facility is filled with tanks of local marine life, and while it's not big enough to offer an entire day's worth of activities, it makes for a fun stop on the way to or from the neighboring beach.

Daily parking for nonresidents costs $15 on weekends, $20 on holidays, and $10 on weekdays. The parking lot holds about 600 cars and fills up fast in summer. If you're staying for longer than a week, it's worth considering a nonresident parking sticker good for the entire season (Memorial Day–Labor Day) for $80.

While First Beach may be where all the action is, quite a few locals actually consider Second Beach, also known as Sachuest Beach, as the best beach for sunning in all of Newport. A short distance east on Purgatory Road and Paradise Avenue, it's a three-mile-long crescent directly facing the Atlantic and sheltered by Eastern and Sachuest Points, making it ideal both for walkers and sun bunnies. Daily parking, plenty of which is available in several lots, costs $10 on weekdays and $20 on weekends—prices that clearly reflect the beach's immense popularity; nonresidents can also buy a season parking pass for $140.

Finally, traveling down Sachuest Point Road and then bearing left will bring you to Third Beach, the least popular but no less beautiful stretch of sand that faces northeast toward the Sakonnet River, which opens to the Atlantic just south of here. The river keeps the water even warmer than most Rhode Island beaches, making this an excellent spot for a dip. The beach is also much more secluded and quiet than First or Second Beaches, making it a nice spot for quiet contemplation away from the crowds. Parking fees are the same as Second Beach—$10 on weekdays and $20 on weekends.

OTHER BEACHES

Aquidneck Island has many other beaches, each with its own personality. The easiest to access from downtown Newport is **King Park** (Wellington Ave., 401/846-1398, free), right off Thames Street; it attracts swimmers, sunbathers, and picnickers, although it's small, and its harbor-side setting is not the most relaxing of vistas. A better view can be had just off of Ocean Drive on the edge of Newport Harbor at **Fort Adams State Park** (Harrison Ave., off Rte. 138, 401/847-2400, www.riparks.com/fortadams.htm, sunrise–sunset daily, free), which boasts 100-plus acres of manicured lawns, picnic spots, beaches, soccer fields, and boating and camping areas. Each year it's home to the area's folk and jazz festivals as well as a plenitude of private clambakes. Also on Ocean Drive, **Brenton Point State Park** has a medium-size parking area and a small pavilion with changing rooms. The beach is too rocky and rough for swimming, but it can be ideal for beachcombing and lying in the sun.

Perhaps the most intriguing beach in Newport is **Bailey's Beach,** which is really only accessible on foot, by bicycle, or by way of the Bellevue Avenue bus. In the late 19th century, Bailey's Beach became the ultraexclusive playground for Newport's wealthiest summer residents—over the years, however, enough people protested about the restricted access that city council intervened on their behalf. Much to the horror of local elitists, research into the original layout of Bellevue Avenue revealed that a good chunk of Bailey's Beach was in fact not legally private at all. A public easement was granted, finally giving the public access.

As you drive north along the eastern shore of Aquidneck Island, you'll come to a couple of other good beaches. **Sandy Point Beach** is a wide, peaceful expanse of sand along the Sakonnet River with picnic facilities, grills, and restrooms. Parking costs $10 on weekdays and $20 on weekends. **Teddy's State Beach,** near Stonebridge Marina off Point Road in the Island Park section of Portsmouth, offers a quiet crescent of pebbly sand beside the preserved section of Old Stone Bridge, with picnic tables and good spots for angling. Admission is $7 on weekdays and $10 on weekends.

BICYCLING

Newport and the rest of Aquidneck Island are prime territory for bicycling enthusiasts. Any of the walking or driving routes described in this chapter are excellent for two-wheeling, as is all of Conanicut Island and Jamestown, especially in and around Beavertail State Park. You can rent bicycles in Newport at **Ten Speed Spokes** (18 Elm St., 401/847-5609, www.tenspeedspokes.com, 10 A.M.–6 P.M. Mon.–Fri., 10 A.M.–5 P.M. Sat., noon–5 P.M. Sun.).

BOATING

Newport is one of North America's great sailing and yachting hubs. There are several full-service marinas in town, including **Bannister's Wharf** (off Thames St. in Newport Harbor, 401/846-4500, www.bannisterswharf.net/bann-mrna.htm), a relatively small facility in the heart of downtown Newport with gas, diesel, ice, electricity, showers, laundry, and a phone.

Look to **Adventure Watersports** (142 Long Wharf, 401/849-4820, 9 A.M.–6 P.M. daily) for rentals of personal watercraft, outboard motorboats, kayaks, sailboats, and dinghies. The company also customizes boat tours, fishing trips, and charters. At Fort Adams State Park, **Sail Newport** (60 Fort Adams Dr., 401/846-1983 or 401/849-8385, www.sailnewport.org, office 9 A.M.–5 P.M. daily year-round, dock office 8:30 A.M.–8:30 P.M. daily late May–early Sept.) rents 19–22-foot sailboats and provides professional instruction for all ages.

A great all-around resource for boat charters

of all kinds is the **Newport Yacht Charter Association** (28 Church St., 401/849-3340, www.newportcharters.com), a member-based organization of brokers who can help you choose the right vessel for you or your group to charter. These brokers work with about two dozen vessels that specialize in sailing, motor yachting, and sportfishing, and the boats vary from 155-foot schooners that can accommodate 80 passengers to 36-foot sailboats that can handle up to 15. Rates vary from $25–75 pp for a two-hour sunset sail to several thousand dollars for a weeklong charter.

Sea kayaking is a very popular activity along Newport's winding shoreline and up and down the Sakonnet River—there are hundreds of inlets and quite a few islands to explore within reasonable paddling distance of Newport and the surrounding towns. The best sources for rentals include downtown Newport's **Adventure Watersports** (142 Long Wharf, 401/849-4820, 9 A.M.–6 P.M. daily) and **Newport Kayak Company** (18 Elm St., 401/849-7404).

FISHING

From spring through fall, Newport is one of the Eastern Seaboard's premier destinations for saltwater fishing—you'll see surf casters up and down the beaches from Newport north along the Sakonnet River and all the way around Aquidneck Island, vying for Narragansett Bay's stripers, bluefish, and bonito. Fishing from a boat in greater Newport's waters provides access to many more species, among them mahimahi, tarpon, trigger fish, Atlantic mackerel, flounder, and swordfish. There are about eight freshwater ponds on the island that are stocked with bass and trout, including Easton's Pond, which is just beyond Easton's Beach on the Newport-Middletown border.

You can rent equipment and buy bait at a number of locations, including **Zeek's Bait and Tackle** (194 North Rd., Jamestown, 401/423-1170, 9 A.M.–7 P.M. Mon.–Fri., 7 A.M.–7 P.M. Sat.–Sun.). The **Saltwater Edge Fly-Fishing Company** (561 Thames St., 401/842-0062 or 866/793-6733, www.saltwateredge.com, 10 A.M.–6 P.M. Mon.–Fri., 9 A.M.–5 P.M. Sat., 11 A.M.–4 P.M. Sun.) is your one-stop shop for information and tackle for surf casting or boat fishing in saltwater; you can also hire guides here.

There are no deep-sea fishing charters available from Newport—you'd have to head over to South County's Port of Galilee to find the nearest one.

GAMING

If you're in the mood to take a chance, **Newport Grand** (150 Admiral Kalbfus Rd., 401/849-5000, www.newportgrand.com, 10 A.M.–1 A.M. Sun.–Thurs., 10 A.M.–2 A.M. Fri.–Sat. and holidays) is the place to try your hand at slot machines or bet on simulcast greyhound and thoroughbred racing and Florida jai alai. There's also a restaurant and bar.

GOLF

There are a few public golf courses in the area, the most popular and dramatic being the new **Newport National Golf Club** (324 Mitchell's Lane, Middletown, 401/848-9690, www.newportnational.com, $55–150), which has quickly become one of the top destination golf courses in New England. Another good course is **Montaup Country Club** (500 Anthony Rd., Portsmouth, 401/683-0955, www.montaupcc.com, $37–47). Another option is **Green Valley** (371 Union St., Portsmouth, 401/847-9543, www.greenvalleyccofri.com, $28–68); both have 18 holes. Across Newport Bridge is **Jamestown Country Club** (245 Conanicus Ave., Jamestown, 401/423-9930, $18–19), a nine-holer.

ICE-SKATING

At the **Born Family Skating Center** (Newport Yachting Center, 401/846-3018, www.skatenewport.com), a spacious outdoor rink on the city's waterfront, you can glide across the ice for $7 per three-hour session ($5 for seniors and children); rentals are available, as are lessons for all ability levels. A Zamboni grooms the ice hourly.

POLO

Polo has been an important rite of Newport's summer social season since the 1880s. At the **Newport Polo Club** (Glen Farm, Rte. 138, Middletown, 6 miles north of downtown Newport between Union St. and Sandy Point Ave., 401/846-0200, www.newportinternationalpolo.com), visitors can watch matches on Saturdays June–September. These contests pit international teams from the United States and several other countries against one another. Matches start at 5 P.M. June–August and 4 P.M. in September; admission is $10. Part of the tradition is setting up "tailgate" picnics on the grounds—this is one of Newport's, and even New England's, most unusual weekly summer events.

SCUBA DIVING

For the very reason that the waters around Newport and Aquidneck Island have proven treacherous to ship's captains for centuries, scuba divers love this part of Rhode Island. Lurking beneath the surface are countless coral reefs, ledges, and interesting—though potentially dangerous—formations, and there are plenty of sunken ships in these parts. For information on rentals, local laws and restrictions, and advice, contact **Newport Diving Center** (550 Thames St., 401/847-9293, www.newportdivingcenter.com, 10 A.M.–6 P.M. Mon.–Wed. and Fri., 9 A.M.–5 P.M. Sat., 9 A.M.–4 P.M. Sun.), which also offers charter diving excursions.

TENNIS

The **International Tennis Hall of Fame** (194 Bellevue Ave., 401/849-3990 or 800/457-1144, www.tennisfame.org) is the only place in the United States where any two travelers can drop in and play lawn tennis. Access to the "royal" court is included with admission to the museum ($8). There are 13 grass courts open May–October.

In mid-July, the Hall of Fame hosts the **Campbell's Hall of Fame Tennis Championship** (401/849-3990, www.tennisfame.org), which draws top players from the Association of Tennis Professionals tour for the only grass-court professional tennis tourney in the nation. This is also when the Hall of Fame holds its annual induction ceremony; 2010, for instance, saw the entry of doubles stars Todd Woodbridge, Mark Woodforde, Gigi Fernández, and Natasha Zvereva, mixed doubles champion Owen Davidson, and wheelchair tennis creators Brad Parks and Derek Hardwick.

Accommodations

Newport's summer population booms, and it's always a good idea to plan as early as possible when you're thinking of visiting. Rooms sell out especially quickly for key summer events—the folk festival, the jazz festival, the Newport Music Festival, and so on. At other times, you can almost always find a spot at one of the motels or hotels in Middletown or Portsmouth, or you can even base your operations in South County, a 20–30-minute drive from Newport over a pair of long bridges that span the Narragansett.

That being said, Newport has the greatest variety of hotel accommodations in the state, including dozens of inns and B&Bs. There are relatively few larger hotels in Newport, and those are very expensive, especially during the summer. If you're looking for mid- to low-end chain properties, try Middletown, a short drive away. Just over the Newport border along Route 138A in Middletown you'll also find a variety of ocean-side inns, motels, and hotels offering a wide range of rates. Newport proper has relatively few oceanfront accommodations, although several properties downtown overlook the harbor. If you want to be within walking distance of hotels, shops, and nightlife, downtown Newport is your best option—but keep in mind that you'll pay for this privilege.

TIME-SHARING IN NEWPORT

One option worth considering before you decide among the many hotels and inns in the area is a luxury time-share company called **Fairfield Resorts** (800/251-8736, www.fairfieldresorts.com). It owns a number of resorts throughout the country, including four right in the city of Newport, and two more across the bay in Jamestown, the **Bay Voyage Inn** (150 Conanicus Ave., Jamestown, 401/423-2100) and **Newport Overlook** (150 Bayview Dr., Jamestown, 401/423-1886). If you're seeking seclusion and a stunning setting with great views back toward Newport, both are great picks. In Newport, **Long Wharf Resort** (115 Long Wharf, Newport, 401/847-7800) is one of the nicest luxury condo resorts in the Northeast, and its location on the harbor, just a block off Thames Street, makes it a highly sought-after destination. A smaller property nearly next door, the **Inn on Long Wharf** (5 Washington St., Newport, 401/847-7800) is also home to the very nice Long Wharf Steakhouse. **Inn on the Harbor** (359 Thames St., Newport, 401/849-6789) and **Newport Onshore** (405 Thames St., Newport, 401/849-1500) are additional options farther down Thames Street.

There are big advantages to choosing any of these six properties over a conventional hotel or inn, especially if you visit Newport often or are traveling with a family or group of friends. First, the locations and settings are top-notch. The units themselves are in large, rambling shingle buildings – in Newport they're mostly 4-5-story apartment buildings, while the Jamestown structures spread out more and feel house-like. There are studio, one-bedroom, two-bedroom, and three-bedroom properties available, and each property has a full slate of amenities, including pools, spas, exercise rooms, children's playgrounds, and the like. The units themselves are furnished with tasteful, upscale contemporary resort furniture, and all have kitchens; the majority of them have water views, depending on the property, of course. These are not historic buildings, and some critics complain they lack character.

But they do make a lot of sense for the right traveler.

Fairfield Resorts is in the business of selling shares of ownership in vacation resorts, not merely renting out hotel rooms. This is something you need to keep in mind before you consider staying at one of these properties. Time-share schemes came under a lot of criticism in the 1980s and 1990s because they often proved highly inflexible or impractical, and in some cases their owners were shady at best. Fairfield Resorts is a legitimate and reputable company, but you will be hit with sales pitches if you stay at one of these properties, and that can be irksome for people uninterested in actually buying into the time-share premise.

If you simply want to vacation in one of the six condos described here, you can expect to find rates of about $150-350 per night May-October for a one-bedroom unit, up to $400-650 for a three-bedroom unit. Off-season, the rates drop by as much as 50 percent. You generally get the best deals at these places by booking via one of the major online travel websites, such as Expedia (www.expedia.com) or Orbitz (www.orbitz.com).

However, if you're willing to attend a 90-minute open-house presentation on buying a time-share condo, you can work out a very nice two-night vacation at one of the condo properties. This depends on availability, of course, and requires a reservation. If you actually buy a time-share in Newport, you're eligible to swap a week of your time there for a week at one of the other Fairfield Resorts properties in New Orleans, San Antonio, numerous cities in Florida, coastal Georgia, and South Carolina, St. Thomas (Virgin Islands), Branson (Missouri), Ocean City (Maryland), Williamsburg (Virginia), the Berkshires, Nashville, the Wisconsin Dells, Durango (Colorado), Sedona and Flagstaff (Arizona), Palm Springs, Las Vegas, and many other places. Read the terms and program descriptions carefully, and you may just find that Fairfield Resorts works for you; either way, it's worth considering as a vacation alternative.

There are a few reservations services in Newport that are useful if you're having trouble finding a room on your own. These companies can sometimes work out better rates with area inns and hotels than are available to the general public. **Bed and Breakfast Newport** (401/846-5408 or 800/800-8765, www.bbnewport.com) has more than 350 options, and there's also **Bed and Breakfast of Rhode Island** (401/849-1298 or 800/828-0000, www.visitnewport.com/bedandbreakfast).

DOWNTOWN
$100-150

Comfortable and centrally located, the **Chestnut Inn** (99 Third St., Newport, 401/847-6949, www.newportchestnutinn.com, $125–175) is a year-round Victorian bed-and-breakfast with several air-conditioned double rooms. The front porch makes a relaxing spot for breakfast before a day of sightseeing, boating, or touring mansions.

Once the summer home of a well-to-do Boston doctor, **The Ivy Lodge** (12 Clay St., Newport, 401/849-6865, www.ivylodge.com, $119–319) near Bellevue Avenue is a charming and refined stay at rates that can be quite good value considering the amenities offered. Dominated by a 33-foot gothic entryway, the house is filled with antiques—and many rooms come with fireplaces, DVD players, and whirlpool tubs. Daily teatime and breakfast are included, and if the savory bread pudding is on offer, don't refuse.

The Old Beach Inn (19 Old Beach Rd., 401/849-3479 or 888/303-5033, www.oldbeachinn.com, $135–275) is a thoroughly renovated Victorian home with exquisitely decorated rooms. A wealthy doctor built this elegant house in 1879. Guest rooms, named for garden plants and flowers, are in both the main house and a mansard-roofed carriage house that dates to the 1850s. The decor is over-the-top Victorian—the Rose Room has a lavish four-poster bed with a floral canopy, for example. Guests have use of a pantry stocked with tea- and coffee-making supplies plus snacks and bottled water. There's a gazebo out back surrounded by gardens, a brick patio, and wrought-iron patio furniture and Adirondack chairs. Continental breakfast is included. The inn is just a couple of blocks east of Bellevue Avenue at Touro Park, an easy walk to Easton's Beach.

Attwater Villa (22 Liberty St., 401/846-7444 or 800/392-3717, www.attwatervilla.com, $119–149), just off Bellevue Avenue, is one of the more distinctive-looking B&Bs in Newport—it was built in 1910 as a Bavarian restaurant called the Hof-Brau, which became a hoity-toity tearoom during Prohibition. The building was restored and converted into a European-style guesthouse in the 1980s. Rooms vary a great deal in size and layout, from standard units with queen-size beds to suites and apartments. The common areas are lovely, including an airy sunroom done in French country style and a very private sundeck. There's air-conditioning and a phone in every room. An expansive continental breakfast buffet is included, served in an attractive room with hunter-green walls and floral draperies.

A real gem with decent rates, considering the location near Aquidneck Park on a lovely stretch of Spring Street, is the **Samuel Durfee House** (352 Spring St., 401/847-1652 or 877/696-2374, www.samueldurfeehouse.com, $109–145), with five spacious and neatly decorated guest rooms done with mostly Federal antiques that match the home's 1803 construction; modern in-room touches include CD players, but the guest rooms do not have phones or TVs. One room has a beautiful mantel carved by Robert Adam; another has Chinese Chippendale twin beds and Asian rugs. An impressive full breakfast—a specialty is Portuguese sweet-bread French toast—is served in the stately parlor or, when weather permits, on the shaded back patio. The setting is marvelous, quiet and away from the noise of Thames Street yet an easy walk to several good restaurants.

Inn on Bellevue (30 Bellevue Ave., 401/848-6242 or 800/718-1446, www.innonbellevue.com, $50–135) is one of Newport's great bargains, with a terrific location and small but funky rooms with a smattering of antiques. The least expensive rooms, which are tiny and share a bath, start at just $50 on summer weekdays. Other units have whirlpool tubs. This creaky old inn is right at the upper end of Bellevue Avenue near where it meets Touro Street—you just can't find rooms this cheap in Newport in this location. As you might expect, the staff and the clientele tend to be young, outgoing, somewhat artsy, and very laid-back.

The colonial revival **Kitt Shepley House 1932** (23 Division St., 401/848-0607 or 877/362-8664, www.kittshepleyhouse.com, $99–140) is a reasonably priced 1930s B&B in the Historic Hill section of downtown. There are just two guest rooms in this cozy, easygoing inn, one of them a full suite with French provincial decor and a tile bathroom with a whirlpool tub, the other a standard room with a brass bed and hand-painted furniture.

$150-250

The **Cliffside Inn** (2 Seaview Ave., 401/847-1811 or 800/845-1811, www.cliffsideinn.com, $170–220), not to be confused with the more conspicuous Cliff Walk Manor nearby on Memorial Boulevard, is one of the city's most distinctive inns. The Second Empire mansion was built in 1880 as the summer retreat of Maryland's governor Thomas Swann; it briefly served as the campus for St. George's School at the turn of the 20th century before the Turner family of Philadelphia bought it in 1907. Daughter Beatrice Turner lived here for about 40 years, posthumously becoming one of Newport's best-known artists—her works are famous in part because they were mostly discovered only after her death in 1948, when executors of her estate found the house crammed with about 3,000 paintings, about a third of them self-portraits—alas, all but about 100 of these were destroyed by her executors. The inn has 13 guest rooms as well as three rooms in a more contemporary cottage across from the inn's front lawn and gardens. The cottage building has *three* fireplaces in each of its three suites, and there are a total of 17 fireplaces in the main mansion. Of the 100 surviving

Turner works, virtually every one can be seen at this inn—some are originals and others are high-quality reproductions; you'll find them in guest rooms and common areas. The antiques that fill this property have far more character than usual hotel pieces—the Cliffside is noted for its valuable collection of Victorian beds and many other fine collectibles. The guest rooms are also notable for their elaborate and often huge bathrooms, most of which have whirlpool baths, and four even have working fireplaces—the ultimate romantic touch. Afternoon tea and quite a stunning formal breakfast complete the experience of staying at this wonderful, luxurious small hotel.

The mansard-roofed **Pilgrim House Inn** (123 Spring St., 401/846-0040 or 800/525-8373, www.pilgrimhouseinn.com, $175–255) is an informal spot along a charming stretch of upper Spring Street. This 1809 inn with gingerbread trim has 10 guest rooms with a smattering of antiques. Overall the mood is very casual and low-key; rooms have rose carpeting, and some have sleigh beds. There are no TVs or phones in the rooms; it's more a place to get a good night's sleep than to hang out. The best feature is the third-floor sundeck, which offers terrific harbor and downtown views. Continental breakfast is included.

Inns of Newport (401/848-5300 or 800/524-1386, www.innsofnewport.com, $210–260) is a consortium of five lavish that define luxury in Newport, and the convenient and prestigious location is a huge draw—along Spring Street, just a block from the harbor, on a quiet street just in from busy Memorial Boulevard. Dozens of restaurants and shops are within an easy stroll. At the **Wynstone** (232 Spring St.), each of the five rooms has a TV and video player, CD player, feather bed, fireplace, and two-person whirlpool tub. The decorating is exquisite and evocative of the city's Gilded Age. Museum-quality antiques fill the rooms, as do custom-made fabrics and window treatments along with elegant paintings and tapestries. The bathrooms have marble tubs and vanities, separate marble showers, terrycloth robes, and high-quality sound systems.

A full breakfast is served fireside in your guest room each morning. The similarly luxurious **Clarkeston** (28 Clarke St.) is two blocks from the water—this exquisitely preserved 1705 colonial captures the charm of early Newport, with wide-plank floorboards and vintage antiques, but the house was restored top to bottom in 1993 and now contains guest rooms with such modern touches as whirlpool tubs and air-conditioning. The sleigh and canopy beds are supremely romantic. Across the street, the 12-room **Cleveland House** (27 Clarke St.) has a Victorian ambience that's more appropriate to its late-19th-century construction. The 300-year-old **Admiral Farragut Inn** (31 Clarke St.) lives up to the elegant standards of this fine hotel group; its rooms contain Shaker-style four-poster beds and brightly painted and stenciled chests and armoires. A full breakfast is served in the authentic colonial keeping room. Lastly, the **Elm Street Inn** (36 Elm St.) is a favorite with families because several of its suites sleep four.

A stunning boutique property in the heart of downtown, the **Mill Street Inn** (75 Mill St., 401/849-9500 or 800/392-1316, www.millstreetinn.com, $145–230) occupies a 19th-century mill whose high ceilings, exposed brick walls and wood beams, and warm character have been nicely preserved. There are 23 suites, some with private decks that look out over downtown and the harbor; the upper-level townhouse suites have two floors. Continental breakfast, afternoon tea, and parking are included.

Another first-rate pick is the handsome **Adele Turner Inn** (93 Pelham St., 401/847-1811 or 800/845-1811, www.adeleturnerinn.com, $180–270). The 13 guest rooms in this stately 1855 sea captain's mansion are filled with Victorian antiques and working fireplaces along with such modern amenities as TVs with video players (there's a large selection of videos and books on loan in the library), private phones, and in some rooms, two-person whirlpool tubs. There are fabulous views of the harbor, just two blocks away, from the expansive rooftop sundeck. It's especially romantic to sit up here at night, looking down over quaint 1st Street, the nation's first gas-lighted street. Full breakfast is served buffet style; afternoon tea is also served daily.

One of the most conveniently situated small downtown properties, the **Black Duck Inn** (29 Pelham St., 401/847-4400, www.blackduckinn.com, $210–240) looks across Thames Street toward myriad shops and restaurants of Bowen's Wharf—within a 15-minute walk are countless more opportunities to browse and nosh. The inn takes its name from an infamous rum-running ship that smuggled bootleg liquor into Newport Harbor during the late 1920s. The interior is on the frilly side, with floral fabrics and wallpaper borders. Most rooms have queen-size beds, and there's a two-bedroom suite that's nice for families or friends traveling together. Some units have hot tubs.

An elaborate, almost decadent Edwardian mansion oozing with character and run by friendly innkeepers Dennis Blair and Grant Edmondson, the ◖ **Hydrangea House Inn** (16 Bellevue Ave., 401/846-4435 or 800/945-4667, www.hydrangeahouse.com, $160–229) sits near the beginning of Bellevue Avenue, just up the hill from the harbor front. The house was built in 1876, and the lavish details of that period have been colorfully preserved. Among the more enticing units among the nine spacious guest rooms and suites, the Hydrangea Suite has a king-size canopy bed, a marble bath, a double whirlpool tub with its own fireplace, Oriental rugs, a steam shower, and cable TV with a video player—it's hard to think of a good reason ever to leave your room when you're surrounded by such plush amenities. Guests are treated to afternoon tea, chocolate-chip cookies before bed, and a full breakfast that's superior to most—eggs, raspberry pancakes, and home-baked breads are among the offerings.

The enthusiastic innkeepers who run **La Farge Perry House** (24 Kay St., 401/847-2223 or 877/736-1100, www.lafargeperry.com, $210–270) have done a great job balancing a homey ambience with striking decor and furnishings. There are five spacious suites, including the John La Farge, which contains convincing reproductions of paintings by the distinguished artist and former owner, for whom the inn is named. Bathed in whites and pale blues, the Honeymoon Suite has a bathroom with a double whirlpool tub. The dining-room walls are painted with a mural of Newport from the turn of the 20th century, and deep armchairs and comfy seating fill the common areas. Depending on the season, iced tea or sherry is served during the afternoon in the formal parlor. The bright, sunny house is especially impressive when decked out with holiday decorations in December.

For an opportunity to stay in one of the Point District's most delightful waterfront homes, consider the **Sarah Kendall House** (47 Washington St., 401/846-7976 or 800/758-9578, www.sarahkendallhouse.com, $190–245), an 1871 Second Empire house with a high green turret and a porch full of comfy wicker chairs and lounges overlooking the harbor and Newport Bridge. Historic Hunter House is just a couple of doors down, and the location so near the southern end of the Point District puts many shops and eateries within a very easy stroll. The guest rooms have polished hardwood floors and four-poster beds, and are furnished with a tasteful restraint that's not always so apparent in Victorian mansions. Many units have working fireplaces. From the sitting room, lodged in the third-floor turret, terrific views are to be had of the water and Goat Island. Afternoon tea and full breakfast are provided.

Over $250

The ne plus ultra of small luxury hotels, **€ The Chanler** (117 Memorial Blvd., 401/847-1300, www.thechanler.com, $309–1,399) feels a lot like sleeping in your own private mansion—except, of course, for the other guests. Not that you'll really notice them; you'll be too busy taking in the sumptuous decor (each room sports a different theme, from English Tudor to Martha's Vineyard), lounging in your private whirlpool tub, and gazing at the views of the ocean. Don't miss the "beach butler" service,

wherein a tuxedoed staff member drives you to and from a semi-private beach and sets you up with chairs, an umbrella, a customized beach picnic, and reading materials.

A sister property of the famed Cliffside Inn, the **€ Abigail Stoneman Inn** (102 Touro St., 401/845-1811, www.abigailstonemaninn.com, $290–700) occupies a grand Renaissance-style 1866 mansion on one of the city's most prominent streets. Named for the woman who is credited with being Newport's first female entrepreneur and innkeeper, this inn—like Cliffside and the company's other property, the Adele Turner—is a slightly kooky and completely sumptuous hostelry. Among the unusual draws: original drawings by William Makepeace Thackeray, Victorian author of *Vanity Fair*; a bath menu of about 30 soaps, salts, and oils from many different nations; a pillow menu of about 20 types, from UltraFoam Deluxe to magnetic buckwheat hull to tri-down; a tea menu featuring about 45 fine blends; and a free water "pub" that features 25 kinds of bottled H_2O, including good old Perrier and Fiji Island artesian well water. The location is steps from Touro Synagogue and an easy walk from the harbor and Bellevue Avenue. There are just five ornate bedchambers, all with high ceilings, TVs, video players, CD players, huge whirlpool tubs or steam showers, and decor from different eras. In the Vanity Fair suite, the furnishings date to 1865–1900, while the hip Above and Beyond contains pieces dating to about 1947–1975. This guest room is truly a showstopper—a six-room, third-floor suite with a magnificent paneled library, a media center with its own fireplace, a kitchen-dining room, and many other breathtaking features. There may not be a more memorable and romantic accommodation in Rhode Island than this suite, which rents for around $650–700 per night.

Vanderbilt Hall (41 Mary St., 401/846-6200 or 888/VAN-HALL—888/826-4255, www.vanderbilthall.com, $340–600) was built by the Vanderbilt family in 1909 as a gift to the citizens of Newport. After being used as the Newport Men's Social Club and later as headquarters for

Doris Duke's Newport Restoration Foundation, it was turned into a luxury hotel in 1997. Today it ranks among the most regal accommodations in Rhode Island, and even if you don't stay here, consider attending one of the famously decadent afternoon teas (tea is free for hotel guests). There are just 50 guest rooms, all of them decorated individually and many with unusual touches such as romantic sleeping lofts reached by spiral staircases. The Old World billiards room is a favorite spot to sip brandy and smoke a cigar, or play hearts with a few friends in the card room. There's also a clubby, white-glove restaurant open to the public—you'll want to dress nicely. There's nothing hip or trendy about this hotel, but if you want to feel like one of Newport's elite summer visitors of a century ago, Vanderbilt Hall is an excellent place to stay.

A favorite of families or groups of friends seeking luxurious harbor-side accommodations that has full kitchens and plenty of legroom, the **Newport Bay Club and Hotel** (337 Thames St., 401/849-8600, www.newportbayclub.com, $395–450) may lack the history of some of the city's colonial and Victorian inns; on the other hand, it outshines the majority of them in terms of both amenities and water views. All things considered, the rates aren't bad either, starting at $359 on summer weekends but with deep discounts for midweek stays, and staggered rates that drop to just $129 on some winter weekends. For this you get a unit that sleeps at least four (the one-bedroom suites have pull-out sofas) and as many as six, a marble bathroom with a whirlpool tub, a kitchenette with a microwave (a few have stovetops), and a nice-size living room with a dining area. Many units overlook the water, and city-side rooms have great views of the activity along Thames Street. The bi-level two-bedroom townhouses have private decks on each floor. Furnishings are contemporary and attractive, if not much more memorable than what you'd find at a typical upscale chain property. Continental breakfast is included.

One of Newport's undisputed class acts, the **Francis Malbone House** (392 Thames St., 401/846-0392 or 800/846-0392, www.

malbone.com, $289–360) occupies a ravishing 1760 shipping merchant's mansion across the street from the harbor. This grand house, built by Peter Harrison (who also built the Rosewood Library and Touro Synagogue), contains 18 exquisitely furnished rooms with fine crown molding, period window treatments and fabrics, four-poster beds, Oriental rugs, and delicate colonial furniture. The walls are painted in bold colors. Many rooms have hot tubs and fireplaces. Afternoon tea and full breakfast are included in the rates. The staff is highly personable and well-trained, and yet the inn retains a surprisingly informal air. The owners also run the adjacent Benjamin Mason House, a 1750 stunner with a guest suite and guest room.

Although its name suggests a doddering old seaside hotel with rickety floors and warped-glass windows, the **Harborside Inn** (Christie's Landing, Thames St., 401/846-6600 or 800/427-9444, www.historicinnsofnewport.com, $290–350) is actually a rather new construction at Christie's Landing, smack in the heart of the city's festive waterfront. This deluxe all-suites property has spacious units with refrigerators, wet bars, sleeping lofts, and balconies. The same management company has several other inns in Newport, including the Yankee Peddler Inn on Touro Street, the Jailhouse Inn on Marlborough Street, and the Newport Gateway Hotel on West Main Road in Middletown. It's a disparate group of properties with a wide range of rates.

The **Hotel Viking** (1 Bellevue Ave., 401/847-3300 or 800/556-7126, www.hotelviking.com, $240–355) feels a little too formal for an increasingly more casual town. Nevertheless, the massive top-to-bottom restoration in 2000 greatly improved the general appearance of this hulking historic hotel, which has a neat location equidistant from Broadway's hip eateries, Bellevue Avenue's mansions, and Spring Street's antiques shops. The 237 guest rooms, while nicely maintained, are rather dull, and a kitschy early-1960s addition to the hotel spoils its overall appearance. Public areas retain the glamour of yore, but somehow the Viking's overall effect is unintentionally retro. The hotel was built in 1926 and was one of New England's premier addresses for many years—it was commissioned by the owners of Bellevue Avenue's summer "cottages" as a place to put up guests and visitors. Furnishings are reproduction Queen Anne and Chippendale, but the rooms have all the modern trappings you'd expect of a luxury full-service hotel: TVs with in-room movies, climate control, hair dryers, irons and ironing boards, and phones with data ports. There's also a pool, a health club, and a sauna as well as a lavish spa, which is perhaps the highlight of the property. The hotel's Bellevue Bar and Grille serves steaks, seafood, and other favorites. The rooftop bar is great fun, affording terrific views of downtown and the harbor—it's a fine place to meet up with friends or take a date.

The **Hyatt Regency Newport** (1 Goat Island, 401/851-1234 or 800/233-1234, www. newport.hyatt.com, $310–580) is a pricey but superbly maintained option that occupies a terrific spot on Goat Island, with outstanding views back toward downtown and of the Point District in one direction and the Newport Bridge and Jamestown in the other. The staff here is extremely well-trained and professional, and the facilities and rooms are top-notch, but make sure you're going to use all these features before you spend the money to stay here. These facilities include a full-service spa with massage, facials, and treatments, plus an exercise room, a tennis court, indoor and outdoor pools, two restaurants, and lots of meeting space—it's a popular site for conventions. If you're angling for luxury, book one of the bi-level loft suites that have private balconies overlooking the water.

The **Newport Marriott** (25 America's Cup Ave., 401/849-1000 or 888/634-4498, www. newportmarriott.com, $240–475) is a grand luxury hotel on the edge of downtown. Some rooms open onto a bright atrium and others face downtown or the harbor. It's very attractively furnished, but this is still a large (319-room) chain hotel, and it doesn't exactly ooze with character. Amenities abound, including an indoor pool, outdoor deck, and an extensive full health club with racquetball courts. There are also scads of meeting rooms; indeed, the Marriott is often packed with conventioneers.

ELSEWHERE IN NEWPORT
Over $250

The **Inn at Newport Beach** (Memorial Blvd., 401/846-0310 or 800/655-1778, www.innatnb. com, $300–420) is the best of the First Beach–area properties—it's just across the street from the water and sand, and the staff is polite and well trained. The guest rooms are decorated with attractive, upscale colonial-style furnishings, satiny striped wallpaper, and the usual amenities, including cable TV, phones, and air-conditioning. Rooms are generally smaller than at newer properties in town, but they're no less attractive—and the rates are fair. There are 50 units, some of them suites with elegant sitting areas and others with two bedrooms. Rates vary considerably depending on room size and availability, but even in summer—during weekdays—you can sometimes find accommodations here for as little as $109 nightly. Included in the price is a substantial continental breakfast. There's also a decent restaurant on the premises.

The extraordinarily sumptuous **C Castle Hill Inn** (590 Ocean Dr., 401/849-3800 or 888/466-1355, www.castlehillinn.com, $420–745) enjoys one of Newport's most enchanting settings, perched on a grassy promontory jutting into the ocean with outstanding views of Narragansett Bay. The small Castle Hill Lighthouse (circa 1890) warns ships from the rocks nearby. Accommodations are in the main Agassiz Mansion and three distinguished outbuildings. In the main building, the 1874 summer home of Harvard marine biologist Alexander Agassiz, there are 10 rooms, most of them quite large and all with well-chosen antiques—the sorts of pieces you might expect to find decorating one of the summer cottages along Bellevue Avenue. Typical features include bay views, CD players, custom marble whirlpool tubs, Oriental rugs, gas fireplaces, pitched ceilings, and stately beds with goose-down comforters and imported damask linens. It's easy to understand why these are some of the priciest rooms in Rhode Island, and yet the Castle Hill measures up where some other luxury properties don't. A small Gothic chalet-style building, once Agissiz's laboratory, now contains two handsome suites; about 100 yards from the mansion, down directly facing the water, are Castle Hill's eight more contemporary beach-house rooms; these lack the historic ambience of other units but are no less plush. Additionally, they contain galley kitchens, French doors opening onto water-view decks, full entertainment centers with video players, and double whirlpool cast-iron tubs. If it's seclusion by the sea rather than Old World style that you're seeking, these units make a superb choice. Lastly, just to the side of the mansion, a row of similarly contemporary harbor cottages sit on a short cliff over the water and also measure up to the rest of the property's very high standards. An interesting bit of literary history: Thornton Wilder was a frequent guest of the Agassiz family and based parts of his book *Theophilus North* here.

MIDDLETOWN, PORTSMOUTH, AND JAMESTOWN
$50-100

Middletown isn't so agrarian these days, but the **Country Goose** (563 Green End Ave., Middletown, 401/849-5384 or 877/254-6673, www.countrygoosebnb.com, $79–110) feels and looks as if it could be a farmhouse in the sticks, aside from its location on a slightly busy road. It's just a short way east of Agincourt, also an easy drive or even bike ride into downtown Newport or to the beaches. This striking white 1898 house with gingerbread trim sits on a large lawn with mature shade trees and colorful gardens. Guest rooms have high ceilings and contain a mix of family heirlooms and newer pieces; some rooms have shared baths.

The 155-room **Howard Johnson Inn** (351 W. Main Rd., Middletown, 401/849-2000 or 800/654-2000, www.newporthojo.com, $90–120) has an indoor pool, sauna, and hot tub, refrigerators and microwaves in some units,

and tennis courts; there's an Applebee's restaurant next door. Some pets are welcome.

The **Sea Whale** (150 Aquidneck Ave., 401/846-7071 or 888/257-4096, www.seawhale.com, $65–110) looks a bit dreary from the exterior, but this 16-unit motel faces directly onto Easton's Pond (white chaise longues sit out back on the lawn overlooking the water). Rooms are basic but well kept, and those on the upper level have balconies; all of them face the pond and have cable TV, refrigerators, hair dryers, phones (with free local calls), and plenty of parking. It's a 10-minute walk to Easton's Beach, and you really can't beat the price for this location.

With among the lowest rates of any chain motel in the area, the **Travelodge Middletown** (1185 W. Main Rd., Middletown, 401/849-4700 or 800/862-2006, www.travelodge.com, $85–95), is a basic no-frills property with simple rooms—perfect if you're not going to spend much time back at the hotel.

$100-150

Perched on Narragansett Bay, the **Bay Voyage Inn** (150 Conanicus Ave., Jamestown, 401/423-2100, www.bayvoyageinn.com, $103–191) is more resort than inn. With 32 suites (including kitchenettes and parlor areas), the Victorian-style building is also home to a pool, indoor whirlpools, a fitness center, and a recreation director to help arrange sailing, fishing, or biking excursions in the area.

The owners of the Howard Johnson also operate the excellent **Hampton Inn and Suites** (317 W. Main Rd., 401/848-6555 or 800/426-7866, www.newporthamptoninn.com, $89–129), which has consistently received awards for being one of the best-run hotels in the popular chain. The 95-room property, which opened in 2004, has an indoor pool, a fitness room, a business center, a tennis court, and free wireless Internet. The 24 suites have refrigerators, microwaves, coffeemakers, and separate living areas.

The nicely maintained **Newport Courtyard Marriott** (9 Commerce Dr., Middletown, 401/849-8000 or 888/686-5067, www.

courtyard.com, $95–110) is another reliable chain property a few miles north of downtown Newport. There are 130 rooms and 10 suites, plus an indoor-outdoor pool, a hot tub, a small gym, and a laundry room; continental breakfast is included.

Rhea's Inn by the Sea (42 Aquidneck Ave., Middletown, 401/849-3548, www.rheasinn. com, $89–123) occupies a three-story cedar-shake building that's just a five-minute stroll from Easton's Beach. Although it's in the style of the old beach houses of yore, Rhea's is contemporary through and through, and all the motel-style furnishings feel new. There are nine rooms with private baths, air-conditioning, cable TV, and phones—all the basics. Two of the rooms have separate living areas, and some have whirlpool tubs; there's a common area on each floor. This is a reliable, economical option, and there's a second branch of Rhea's inland on Route 114 (401/841-0808 or 800/474-1194).

The three-story, clapboard **Quality Inn & Suites Atlantic Beach Hotel** (34 Wave Ave., Middletown, 401/847-5330, www.qualityinn. com, $149–299) is an attractive hotel with an inviting warm color scheme and an appealingly beachy look. The ocean is practically across the street, and many rooms have views. Although it's technically outside of Newport, this attractive hotel is just steps from the town line, and it's extremely close to area beaches. Among the units, there are 43 minisuites with two phones, large work desks, microwaves, refrigerators, and coffeemakers, plus separate sitting areas. The staff can be a little rushed and cursory.

The **Seabreeze Inn** (147 Aquidneck Ave., Middletown, 401/849-1211 or 877/227-8400, www.theseabreezeinn.com, $145–285) is a small Mediterranean-style hotel with a small restaurant on the premises. The seven rooms have floral-upholstered bedding, marble-floor bathrooms, the usual amenities (cable TV, air-conditioning, free local calls), plus decks, some of which overlook the ocean and others Easton's Pond. A full breakfast is included. The owners also rent two apartments (a one-bedroom and a two-bedroom), as well as a three-bedroom house. It's an attractive place, not fancy, but the decor is cheerier than some of the more prosaic motels along this stretch.

Food

For many years, until quite recently, it was difficult to find innovative cuisine in Newport. That's not to say that there weren't plenty of terrific restaurants, but fairly traditional seafood places, steak and chops houses, and natty old dining rooms serving haute continental and French cuisine were the rule. In the early 1990s, a few restaurants started experimenting with more interesting fare, and in the past few years several places serving highly creative regional American and globally influenced cooking have opened. Of course, it's still easy to get a traditional fried clam dinner or a juicy steak in Newport, but now there are also quite a few creative alternatives.

The island has the usual gamut of chain eateries, both regional and national, although few of these are found in downtown Newport. If you want IHOP, Newport Creamery, Burger King, Taco Bell, KFC, and their ilk, venture out along Route 138 just north of town to the intersection of Route 114.

Keep in mind that the vast majority of Newport's high-end formal restaurants have taverns or pubs attached that serve less-pricey food and demand much less fancy attire. Note that in the off-season, restaurants in Newport—and especially in the neighboring towns and on Block Island—greatly reduce their hours. Call ahead to check which meals are currently offered.

NEWPORT
Upscale

Even hard-core vegetarians have a hard time leaving Newport without craving seafood, what with shellfish and lobster shacks at almost every turn. Those who heed the call will fare quite nicely at **The Mooring** (Sayer's Wharf, 401/846-2260, www.mooringrestaurant.com, 11:30 A.M.–9 P.M. Sun.–Thurs., 11:30 A.M.–10 P.M. Fri.–Sat., $12–44), particularly if they're able to nab a table with a view of the harbor and sunset. No one's breaking the culinary sound barrier in the kitchen, but it's a great place to dig into a plate of fresh fried clams or seafood pie—or sample the impressively lengthy wine list.

The globally inspired, luxury-laden New England dishes that fly from the kitchen at **The Spiced Pear** (in the Chanler Hotel, 117 Memorial Blvd., 401/847-2244, www.spicedpear.com, 7:30–10:30 A.M. and 11:30 A.M.–2:30 P.M. daily, 6–9 P.M. Sun.–Thurs., 6–9:30 P.M. Fri.–Sat., $27–43) make such an impression that you could hear a fork drop throughout the elegant dining room as they're served. The butter-poached lobster with Israeli couscous is a must-try, and the fondue for two (with melted white chocolate and Godiva liqueur) alone is worth the hefty bill.

One of the city's definitive dress-up spots, **Le Bistro** (41 Historic Bowen's Wharf, 401/849-7778, 5–9 P.M. daily, $20–34) specializes in rich seafood, choice Angus steaks, and other rather elaborate continental grills. It has won countless culinary and wine awards, and the views of Newport Harbor make it a favorite place for special occasions. Service is superb, refined, and always impeccable.

Refined, traditional French food is served at the slightly formal and inviting **Restaurant Bouchard** (505 Thames St., 401/846-0123, www.restaurantbouchard.com, 5:30–9 P.M. Wed.–Mon., $19–29), which occupies the ground floor of a small B&B. Fine china and crystal along with deft service set the tone for such rarefied French fare as sliced tender lamb with red wine and a hint of curry sauce, roasted duck with currants, sautéed chicken breast with a creamy morel mushroom sauce, and wild mushroom ravioli with a walnut oil–balsamic vinaigrette.

The **Castle Hill Inn** (590 Ocean Ave., 401/849-3800, www.castlehillinn.com, lunch 11:30 A.M.–3 P.M., dinner 5:45–9 P.M. daily, $25–40), apart from having one of the most dramatic locations in the city, serves stellar regional American fare. A typical course is the starter of pulled-pork tamales with aged cheddar, smoked papaya salsa, and New Mexico red chili puree, followed by skillet-roasted spiced pork medallions with fried-potato wedges, braised summer greens, Gorgonzola aioli, and sweet-and-sour peach glaze. A favorite finisher is the Godiva chocolate soufflé with caramel crème anglaise, sugared berries, and biscotti. There are several dining rooms, all with large windows, and from many tables you'll enjoy a view over Narragansett Bay. After dark, when water views aren't such a draw, you might opt to dine in the main Castle Hill Room, which once served as the formal drawing room of this magnificent mansion by the sea.

Flash back to the 1950s and you'll appreciate the appeal of **La Forge Casino Restaurant** (186 Bellevue Ave., 401/847-0418, www.laforgenewport.com, 11:30 A.M.–9:30 P.M. daily, $17–29, in the pub $7–14), a supper club kind of spot known for its classic continental fare. To really live it up, order the chateaubriand for two with wine, a complete meal for about $50 that includes flame-grilled center-cut beef tenderloin carved tableside with a baked stuffed potato, stuffed tomato Florentine, fresh vegetables, and béarnaise sauce, plus a half-liter of house wine. With all the new eateries cropping up throughout the state serving trendy and sometimes bizarre fusions of this and that, it's refreshing to see a restaurant that refuses to depart from ancient (by culinary standards) traditions. This is an appropriate style of cuisine for the restaurant at the vaunted Newport Casino, one of McKim, Mead, and White's most distinguished works of architecture. The casino also has a much less formal Irish pub, where you can sample oysters Kinsale (baked in the half shell with blue cheese and potato stuffing), club sandwiches, fish-and-chips, and the like.

Clarke Cooke House (Bannister's Wharf, 401/849-2900, www.bannistersnewport.com/clarke_cooke_house.html, 6–9:30 P.M.

Mon.–Thurs., 6–10:30 P.M. Fri.–Sun.) consists of two restaurants: The Porch ($23–30) is the more formal of the two, set high overlooking Newport Harbor; down at wharf level, the Candy Store ($9–23) is much more casual both in cuisine and style (in summer there's also a sushi bar serving a wide range of rolls and *nigiri*). Some locals have grumbled in recent years that The Porch is resting on its laurels, but the kitchen seems to have responded to these complaints and heavily revamped its menu. Today's French-inspired menu might offer pan-seared breast of squab with a roasted-corn pancake, foie gras, and black mission figs in a phyllo pastry, followed by roast rack of lamb with caramelized onions, potato-turnip gratin, and a minted tarragon glaze. Down in the Candy Store, which is open for lunch, Sunday brunch, and dinner, signature dishes include steak au poivre with a brandy-madeira brown sauce and Mediterranean fish stew, but you can also order simpler burgers, light pastas, and creative salads.

22 Bowen's Wine Bar and Grille (22 Bowen's Wharf, 401/841-8884, www.22bowens.com, lunch 11:30 A.M.–3:30 P.M. daily, dinner 5–10:30 P.M. Sun.–Thurs., 5–11 P.M. Fri.–Sat., $24–47) is a hot spot that offers a new take on the old seafood-and-chops theme, serving easily the best steaks in town. You can also order fresh seafood from the excellent raw bar. This is a pricey place, but the city's many young movers and shakers seem all too willing to pay for 24-ounce porterhouse steaks, grilled tuna steaks, and broiled lobster. Each entrée comes with a choice of sauce, which could include green-peppercorn mustard, Maytag blue-cheese butter, shallot-and-dill butter, horseradish cream, and several others. Additional house specialties include broiled scallops with shallots, lemon, parsley, sherry, and seasoned bread crumbs; and grilled pork tenderloin with apricot-sausage stuffing and rosemary-garlic *jus*. The dining room, with its pitched ceiling and timber beams, has rows of tall windows overlooking the harbor.

The **Newport Dinner Train** (departs from 19 America's Cup Ave., 401/841-8700 or 800/398-7427, www.newportdinnertrain.com, hours vary) presents a number of theme excursions, including wine-tasting and murder mysteries. On Saturday mornings, kids are invited for a tour on the Musical Magical Train, a 90-minute journey with sing-alongs, games, and entertainment by a musician. Dinner rides last 2.5 hours and run along 22 miles of track, looking out at Narragansett Bay most of the way. Both lunch and dinner rides are available, and the food is better than you might expect, given the logistics of preparing high-quality cuisine aboard a train. The menu is limited to just 3–4 entrée choices: Baby back ribs (which are excellent), sesame-crusted salmon, and chicken Vanderbilt (layered with spinach, sun-dried tomatoes, and provolone) are typical, and there's always a vegetarian option too. You really don't make one of these journeys for the culinary experience as much as to relax and take in the phenomenal views. Prices vary according to the theme, but a typical dinner ride runs $55–65 pp; package deals that include overnight accommodations at Middletown's Ramada Inn are also available.

Creative but Casual

Bar culture had to begin somewhere in this country, and **The White Horse Tavern** (26 Marlborough St., 401/849-3600, www.whitehorsetavern.us, 11:30 A.M.–2:30 P.M. and 5:30–10 P.M. Mon.–Sat., noon–3 P.M. and 5:30–10 P.M. Sun., $29–48) may just be where it started. Opened in 1687 by the father of a pirate, the tavern features clapboard walls and huge ceiling beams typical of 17th-century architecture, but its menu, including grilled bruschetta and maple-glazed salmon, is surprisingly here-and-now.

Loud and jovial, the candlelit tavern area is the place to be in **The Black Pearl** (Bannisters Wharf, 401/846-5264, www.blackpearlnewport.com, lunch and dinner daily, $8–30)—the neighboring more formal dining room is notoriously overpriced for similar fare. Here's the spot to order up a bowl of the killer chowder (loaded with dill) and get your lobster fix; the 2.5-pounders come boiled and unadorned except with butter and a lemon wedge.

The White Horse Tavern opened in 1687.

Equally fun though with a very different vibe is **Christie's** (351 Thames St., 401/846-8018, noon–11 P.M. Sun.–Thurs., 10 A.M.–11 P.M. Fri.–Sat., $12–23), a funky and trendy restaurant overlooking the harbor. A snazzy crowd piles into the whimsically decorated dining room, complete with swing seats and communal tables, for tasty lobster quesadillas, oyster sliders, juicy burgers, and all manner of specialty cocktails; the pomargarita is a perennial favorite. Later in the evening on weekends, dancing takes over the bar area, which fills with a crowd that defines casual chic.

Since new owners took over the **Canfield House** (5 Memorial Blvd., 401/847-0416, www.canfieldhousenewport.com, 5–9 P.M. Tues.–Fri. and Sun., 5–10 P.M. Sat., $16–24), the restaurant has greatly improved. It's an elegantly faded Second Empire yellow house near the Tennis Hall of Fame. The restaurant's Patio Pub is a nice spot for a drink. Try the flatiron steak with maple-peppercorn demi-glace, braised pork shank with white beans and carrot-raisin slaw, or simple stream mussels in lemon-herb broth.

Always bustling **Yesterday's and The Place**

(28 Washington Sq., 401/847-0116, www.yesterdaysandtheplace.com, 11 A.M.–9 P.M. Sun.–Thurs., 11:30 A.M.–10 P.M. Fri. and Sat., dining room $22–30, pub $6–13) sounds, smells, and looks like a festive tavern—the main room is filled with revelers, has a long bar and a tile floor, and is usually noisy nearly to a fault. But off to one side you'll find a smaller wine bar and dining room called The Place that turns out pricey but first-rate globally inspired fare such as a Thai lobster "martini" with a vermicelli-noodle stir, seafood Napoleon with a coconut-lemongrass broth, and rack of lamb with a pecan-mustard crust with fennel and apples. Although the fancier part is refined, nowhere at Yesterday's will you encounter attitude or stuffiness—and plenty of folks dine in the more formal section and guzzle in the other. The food in the pub, though simple, is also commendable; try the house salad with apple, walnuts, and feta over seasonal greens, or the grilled yellowfin sandwich with wasabi mayo and sliced fresh tomatoes.

Cafe Zelda (528 Thames St., 401/849-4002, www.cafezelda.com, dinner 5–9 P.M.

daily, $15–22) has two identities—on one side it's an informal and always packed pub; on the other side you'll find a dark, romantic, and festive space that's more appropriate for a full meal. You can order from the same menu on either side. The food has improved greatly in recent years, with specialties that include balsamic-roasted half chicken with herb gnocchi and filet mignon with port wine Gorgonzola. Either space can get loud, which makes it a pretty fun spot to hang out with friends; there's also a significant wine cellar.

A trendy yet understated seafood place on Lower Thames, **Scales and Shells Restaurant and Raw Bar** (527 Thames St., 401/846-FISH—401/846-3474, www.scalesandshells.com, 6–10 p.m. Mon.–Thurs., 6–11 p.m. Fri.–Sat., 4–10 p.m. Sun., $12–25) prepares fresh fish and shellfish in an austere yet handsome dining room—just a few mounted fish on the walls decorate this airy room with hardwood floors. The simply prepared, outstanding fish can be ordered mesquite-grilled, broiled, or with a couple of other straightforward treatments; monkfish, bluefish, and tuna are among the possibilities. Also consider the clam pizza. The lobster *fra diavolo* for two is a signature dish and a favorite.

One of Newport's true standout dining experiences, ◖ **Asterisk** (599 Thames St., 401/841-8833, 4–10 p.m. daily, $20–31) occupies an old service station on Lower Thames—the pair of glass garage doors now act as enormous windows for the front of the dining room. Exposed air ducts, an unfinished floor, and an open kitchen create the feeling of a little food theater, where the entertainment lies as much in watching the chefs at work as it does in dining on their always delicious creations. The food is not overly complicated or stylized, just good, and the menu always offers plenty of specials. House specialties include a lobster salad starter that can easily work as a meal, rare tuna with a green peppercorn sauce, crispy duck with stir-fried rice and a ginger-lemon-soy glaze, and classic *moules et frites* (mussels steamed and served with fries, Belgian style). There's a long bar on the left where you can dine or sip cocktails or

wines by the glass (the wine list is extensive). Asterisk is self-assured without being stuffy and handsome without feeling formal. The crowd is good-looking and chatty, and you'll feel at ease here whether dressed to the nines or clad in jeans and a tucked-in shirt. There's live jazz on weekend evenings.

Puerini's Restaurant (24 Memorial Blvd. W., 401/847-5506, www.puerinisrestaurant.com, 5–9 p.m. Mon.–Thurs., 5–10 p.m. Fri.–Sat., $13–20) is a great local spot for outstanding Italian food, with both classic and innovative preparations that use the freshest ingredients—consider homemade linguine with hot sausages and fresh tomato sauce or lasagna layered with spinach pasta, fresh veggies, and several kinds of cheese. This attractive space is a short distance from busy Thames Street. Reservations are not accepted, which can translate to a wait on weekends.

Another locals' favorite for Italian, **Sardella's** (30 Memorial Blvd. W., 401/849-6312, 5–10 p.m. Mon.–Thurs., 5–11 p.m. Fri.–Sat., 4–10 p.m. Sun., $14–18) is right next to Puerini's and favors a more southern Italian menu. Chicken marsala, eggplant parmigiana, grilled New York steak with roasted-garlic butter, pasta Bolognese, and gnocchi with sweet Italian sausage, cherry peppers, and plum tomatoes are recommended dishes. In warm weather there's dining on the patio overlooking the garden.

With a stylish young chef who describes herself as a "Gen-X Martha Stewart," the eclectic fare at ◖ **Salvation Cafe** (140 Broadway, 401/847-2620, www.salvationcafe.com, 5–10 p.m. Sun.–Thurs., 5–11 p.m. Fri.–Sat., $7–16) verges on pan-Asian and sometimes dazzles, sometimes comforts, but always piques one's curiosity; the appetizers are especially fun. Consider the sweet-potato shrimp cakes with a coconut-lime dipping sauce, the pumpkin ravioli tossed in cinnamon sage butter and freshly shaved Asiago, or the Kama Sutra Platter of pork vindaloo, chickpea masala, cucumber *raita,* and garlic naan. Cocktails are also recommended. This is truly Newport's oddest, hippest, and happiest little bistro—an eclectic fun house that draws a hip young crowd and

clams

is decked in feather boas, a giant retro Gulf gas station sign, lime-green walls, a gilt-framed painting of a pink flamingo, and all sorts of other curiosities.

Another of Broadway's wonderfully offbeat restaurants, **Tucker's Bistro** (150 Broadway, 401/846-3449, www.tuckersbistro.com, 6–10 P.M. daily, $17–24) has a pair of narrow dining rooms with ruby-red walls, elaborate chandeliers of several shapes and sizes, gilt mirrors, and—from the tableware to the water glasses—mismatched everything. It feels like a Victorian salon; oil paintings, which are for sale, line the walls; and soft music, varying from Billie Holiday to Verdi operas, plays in the background. The decadent, flavorful food matches the ambience. You might sample orange-ancho-glazed pork chops or shepherd's pie layered with sweet corn and mashed potatoes; Thai shrimp nachos are an arresting appetizer; or knock back a stein of Newport Storm beer while noshing on steamed mussels on a cold winter evening. Homemade Bailey's is another specialty of the bar. For dessert, consider white chocolate, dried cherry, and pecan bread pudding.

One of Broadway's hottest spots for both dining and socializing is **Pop** (162 Broadway, 401/846-8456, 5 P.M.–1 A.M. daily, $5–19), a swank lounge with mod furnishings and a terrific menu of small plates and tapas. Vidalia onion and ricotta ravioli, Black Angus and lamb burgers, vanilla gelato with candied figs, and grilled salmon BLTs with yellow tomatoes are standouts. Plenty of devotees come simply for the ambience, glowing fireplace, and sophisticated cocktails.

Pizza, Pasta, Seafood, and Pub Grub

If you're craving barbecue, head to the **Smokehouse Cafe** (at the Mooring, Sayer's Wharf, 401/848-9800, 11:30 A.M.–10 P.M. Mon.–Thurs., 11:30 A.M.–11 P.M. Fri.–Sat., noon–10 P.M. Sun., $7–22), which serves a delicious smoked Cajun catfish sandwich and another piled high with jerk calamari steak. Other specialties include St. Louis–style pork ribs, jumbo Gulf shrimp with a

chili marinade, and grilled salmon with sesame-ginger sauce. The smoked corn and crab chowder is another favorite. The dining rooms overlook the harbor, and there's an expansive waterfront patio too.

Rhode Island Quahog Co. (220 Thames St., 401/848-2330, 11:30 A.M.–10 P.M. Sun.–Thurs., 11:30 A.M.–11 P.M. Fri.–Sat., $12–24) operates with a gimmicky theme, serving just about anything you can imagine with clams in it; if you stick to these dishes, you'll probably come away with a pretty decent meal. Portions are enormous, so you won't leave hungry. Steamers, clam cakes, chowder, baked cod, and all the usual seafood standards are offered, plus some inventive specials such as pan-seared red snapper with lobster and guava sauces. The cavernous dining room with cream walls and royal-blue napery is also the site of live music on many nights; in warm weather, grab a seat on the attractive tiled terrace overlooking the activity of Thames Street.

A favorite summer hangout of college students as well as quite a few visitors, the **Red Parrot** (348 Thames St., 401/847-3800, www.redparrotrestaurant.com, 11:30 A.M.–10 P.M. Sun.–Thurs., 11:30 A.M.–11 P.M. Fri.–Sat., $7–17) is a rambling restaurant with large open windows that face out over Thames Street and across the way to Perry Mill Market—ceiling fans whir overhead as friends fill up on booze and comfort food. Specialties include Jamaican jerk chicken, Oreo mud pie, lobster pizzas, mussels, fajitas, and big colorful frozen drinks that fall on the brash side. There's nothing especially subtle about this place, but there's no denying that it's good fun.

It looks, feels, and actually smells like one of those Old World Italian restaurants on Federal Hill in Providence, and sure enough, **Ristorante Lucia** (190B Thames St., 401/847-6355, noon–10 P.M. daily, $9–13) turns out some of the best pies you'll ever taste. This simple BYOB space, as popular for takeout as for dining in, prepares a superb white pizza with mascarpone, mozzarella, fontina, provolone, onion, and roasted sweet peppers, plus a memorable eggplant parmigiana version. The real house specialty, however, is the artery-clogging *crescentina,* a stuffed and fried pizza with Northern Italian lineage. Order it stuffed with pepperoni and provolone, or perhaps with Romano beans, a spicy tomato sauce, and herbs. There's also a wide range of pastas, salads, and Italian grills available.

Brick Alley Pub and Restaurant (140 Thames St., 401/849-6334, 11:30 A.M.–10 P.M. Sun.–Thurs., 11:30 A.M.–10:30 P.M. Fri.–Sat., $6–16) has long been a reliable, if usually quite crowded, standby for tasty comfort fare. The long menu includes Cajun catfish, broiled chicken and artichoke sandwiches, bacon burgers, spinach fettuccine, and sole Veracruz. The staff is friendly and fun, and the crowd is lively and loud: This is not a place for a quiet evening.

Ethnic Fare

Sushi fanatics converge on **Sumo Sushi** (198 Thames St., 401/848-2307, www.sumosushinewport.com, 11:30 A.M.–10:30 P.M. daily, $10–25) for exquisite Japanese food plus several Korean dishes and stews. Korean barbecue is one classic dish, as is spicy kimchi stew with beef, pork, vegetables, and tofu. Several Japanese teriyaki grills are also offered. From the sushi side of the menu, maki rolls include spicy scallop, salmon skin and cucumber, pickled radish, and more than a dozen others. The sedate, warmly furnished dining room is a calm alternative to some of Thames Street's busier restaurants.

For simple, hefty Mexican fare, drop by **Freaky Burrito** (16 Broadway, 401/847-7276, 11 A.M.–9:30 P.M. Mon.–Sat., 3–9:30 P.M. Sun., $4–8), a simple but attractive taqueria that serves up delicious quesadillas, burritos, and the like, all packed with both traditional Mexican and American ingredients.

Quick Bites

The local chain **Newport Creamery** (181 Bellevue Ave., 401/846-6332; 208 W. Main Rd., Middletown, 401/846-2767, www.newportcreamery.com, hours vary, $4–8) is often compared with the larger Massachusetts-based Friendly's Ice Cream chain. It's a cheap and cheerful option for light diner-style food, including seasoned French fries, club sandwiches, turkey-and-Swiss melts, burgers, chicken fajita wraps, fried clam dinners, and an extensive selection of breakfast foods. Of course, the big draw is ice cream—there's a long dessert menu of sundaes and awful-awfuls, those thick shakes that Rhode Islanders seem completely addicted to.

Down-home **Charlie's Good Egg** (12 Broadway, 401/849-7817, 10 A.M.–4 P.M. daily, under $8) is a downright downcast diner that serves excellent breakfast food that includes about 10 kinds of pancakes such as chocolate chip, banana, and raisin. Omelets as well as several kinds of French toast are specialties, and sandwiches and pastas are served later in the day. The no-frills space is packed with old photos and mismatched furnishings that seem to have been culled from garage sales.

You might not expect one of Newport's best-kept secrets to be a restaurant at the Hyatt Regency, but ◖ **Pineapples on the Bay** (Hyatt Regency Newport, Goat Island, 401/851-1234, 11 A.M.–10 P.M. daily late May–mid-Sept., $7–13) has a terrific setting by the pool and looking out over the Newport Bridge and Narragansett Bay, a great spot at sunset. Hotel guests often eat here, of course, but not a lot of nonguests know about it. The food is fresh and interesting—mostly creative seafood, sandwiches, and the like, and dining is at teak patio tables. It's the perfect spot to sip a fruity drink and enjoy the breezes off the water.

Taste Buds (406 Thames St., 401/846-1577, 11 A.M.–8 P.M. Mon.–Sat., noon–6 P.M. Sun., under $5) is a simple storefront café on Thames Street offering a wide and varied selection of coffees and teas, plus Italian ices, pastries, and cookies. More substantial fare includes spicy tuna sandwiches, hummus platters, and Brie and sun-dried tomato sandwiches. There are just a few tables, but this is also a good take-out option.

Java Joints

An elegant storefront space on Lower Thames, the **Steaming Bean** (515 Thames St., 401/849-5255) is hung with framed artwork and has a dining room of pretty blond-wood tables and chairs, plus a wide selection of magazines to

NEWPORT

peruse. It's Newport's favorite yuppie haunt for coffees and snacks.

Say what you will about the franchising of America, the **Starbucks** (212 Thames St., 401/841-5899, 5 A.M.–10 P.M. Sun.–Thurs., 5 A.M.–11 P.M. Fri.–Sat.) on Thames Street is a lovely inviting space with a particularly comfy seating loft overlooking the action down below.

With stainless steel tables, white-vinyl chairs, exposed air ducts, and a postindustrial feel, **Jack and Josie's** (111 Broadway, 401/851-6900, 10 A.M.–6 P.M. daily, $5–9) brings a touch of big-city cool to Newport's increasingly trendy Broadway area. The kitchen produces excellent lighter fare, including salmon BLTs, citrus-chicken salad, portobello and roasted red pepper paninis, great smoothies, and a wide range of teas and desserts. There's an Internet and computer station on one side of the room and free high-speed Wi-Fi throughout the place. A few discreetly placed flat-screen TVs show sporting events and videos. This is a terrific spot simply to hang out and read the paper or to grab a quick tasty meal.

Gourmet Goods and Picnic Supplies

Here's an option that's great fun if you're staying someplace with a kitchen, dining area, or patio, or if you're planning an outing on a boat or to a nearby park or beach: **McGrath Clambakes** (401/847-7743, www.riclambake. com) delivers lavish summer meals to your location hot and ready to serve. Included in each meal is a one-pound lobster, steamed clams, corn on the cob, butter and broth, mussels, baked potatoes, and Portuguese sausages. The minimum is 10 people per meal, and 24 hours' advance reservation is required.

Portabella (136 Broadway, 401/847-8200, 8:30 A.M.–5 P.M. Mon.–Sat., 11 A.M.–4 P.M. Sun.) sells delicious prepared Italian foods, octopus salad, lasagna, homemade sauces, gourmet groceries, artisanal breads, and dozens of cheeses. There are plenty of tables and chairs inside as well as seasonal outdoor seating.

Another terrific source of delectable gourmet prepared foods and groceries is the **Market Newport Gourmet** (43 Memorial Blvd., 401/848-2600). A short sampling of goodies regularly available here includes white-bean salad, bay scallops wrapped in bacon, designer sandwiches, and many kinds of casseroles and grills. Chocolates, vinegars, jams, cheeses, exotic produce, and smoked meats are also sold.

Head to **Harvest Natural Foods** (1 Casino Terrace, off Bellevue Ave., 401/846-8137, 11 A.M.–8 P.M. Mon.–Sat., 9 A.M.–7 P.M. Sun.) for organic and natural groceries, deli fare, and prepared salads and soups.

MIDDLETOWN, PORTSMOUTH, AND JAMESTOWN
Upscale

Offering among the best views of any restaurant in the area, the **Bay Voyage Inn** (150 Conanicus Ave., Jamestown, 401/423-2100, hours vary so call ahead, $22–34) is worth the drive or ferry ride from Newport, mainly so you can sit in the elegant dining room and gaze back across Narragansett Bay toward the city. Sunday brunch is an especially popular occasion at this historic inn that's part of the ubiquitous Eastern Resorts time-share company. Creative world-beat cooking is the hallmark of the kitchen—you might start with pan-seared ostrich fillet served with a potato-and-goat-cheese galette, sample an entrée of seared monkfish sautéed with a citrus risotto, wild mushrooms, and asparagus, and finish with a dried-cranberry demi-glace. Everything on the menu is wonderfully fresh. The dress code requires a jacket.

Little Jamestown also has one of the best regional Italian restaurants around with **Trattoria Simpatico** (13 Narragansett Ave., Jamestown, 401/423-3731, noon–10 P.M. Sun.–Thurs., 9 A.M.–11 P.M. Fri.–Sat., $18–32). Among the stellar starters is a velvety lobster bisque with fresh blue crab, sweet corn, and a goat cheese crostini. Jumbo pan-seared sea scallops with a pineapple-soy miso broth, steamed black rice, and sautéed julienne vegetables shows the chef's skill with both healthful and globally inspired dishes. In fact, the Italian menu borrows heavily from the U.S. Southwest, Asia, and Latin America. Corn-crusted halibut with double-corn polenta, black bean salsa, and grilled jalapeño and tomato jam is another terrific dish. Traditionalists can still find a delicious linguine with shrimp in white wine. There's live jazz many nights, and in summer you can dine alfresco beside the lush gardens.

The **Sea Fare Inn** (3352 E. Main Rd., Rte. 138, Portsmouth, 401/683-0577, 5–10 P.M. daily, $18–32) is a bit off the beaten path from Newport, but it's worth the trip for what many consider the best seafood on Aquidneck Island. Inside this stately white 1880s house fronted by elaborate gardens and a neatly trimmed lawn, dining rooms abound with Oriental rugs, white-linen tablecloths, fine crystal, and fireplaces.

Creative but Casual

Oyster lovers find bliss at the friendly and bare-bones **Jamestown Oyster Bar** (22 Narragansett Ave., Jamestown, 401/423-3380, 11:30 A.M.–9:30 P.M. Sun.–Thurs., 11:30 A.M.–10 P.M. Fri.–Sat., $7–18). The pub-meets-bistro ambience is the place to slurp bivalves fresh from local waters.

The **15 Point Road Restaurant** (15 Point Rd., Portsmouth, 401/683-3138, www.restaurant.com/microsite.asp?rid=336272, 5–9 P.M. Tues.–Thurs., 5–10 P.M. Fri.–Sat., 4–9 P.M. Sun., $14–22) is a dapper cottage right by the beach at Stonebridge Marina in the Island Park section of Portsmouth. Popular with northern Aquidneck Island locals and folks on the Sakonnet Peninsula, 15 Point Road is also a great option for Newporters seeking creative, deftly prepared cooking without the crowds and high prices of Thames Street. First and foremost, this handsome little dining room is a neighborhood restaurant, and the staff is easygoing and friendly, always willing to explain a particular preparation or ingredient. Seafood is a major player here—the Block Island scallops over a nest of angel-hair pasta in a light garlic–white wine sauce are terrific. The kitchen also turns out a tender and delicious beef Wellington and a rich lobster casserole baked in sherry and cream and topped with puff pastry.

Steaks, Seafood, Pizza, and Pub Grub

A casual longtime favorite in Jamestown, **Chopmist Charlie's** (40 Narragansett Ave., Jamestown, 401/423-1020, www.chopmistcharlies.com, 11:30 A.M.–9 P.M. daily, $11–17) serves lunch and dinner, specializing in local seafood. Fairly straightforward and always fresh stuffies, calamari, shrimp steamed in beer, scampi, and seafood au gratin are doled out in generous portions.

Right on the Newport-Middletown border, **Johnny's Atlantic Beach Club** (55 Purgatory Rd., Middletown, 401/847-2750, 11 A.M.–10 P.M. daily, $14–22) is a spacious eatery whose greatest attribute is its fine views over Easton's Beach and the ocean, enjoyed from an enormous patio or a similarly large dining room. The menu presents a fairly standard variety of somewhat upscale seafood dishes, including grilled yellowfin tuna, baked scrod, and lobster salad; rack of lamb Grand Marnier is popular among the nonfish fare.

A reasonably priced and dependable option in Middletown, the **Glass Onion** (909 E. Main Rd., Rte. 138, Middletown, 401/848-5153, 10 A.M.–9 P.M. daily, $10 and up) serves a nice range of American food, much of it with oniony themes: French onion soup, onion omelets, and the ubiquitous (if dreaded) fried onion blossom. Pastas and grills round out this menu that's especially strong on seafood. The dining room is rustic and warmly decorated, with two large fireplaces, hanging greenery, and tall ceilings.

Ethnic Fare

There's above-average sushi to be found at **Sea Shai** (747 Aquidneck Ave., Middletown, 401/849-5180; Long Wharf Mall, Newport, 401/841-0051, www.seashai.com, 11:30 A.M.–2:30 P.M. and 5–10 P.M. daily, $8–22), known for feather-light tempura, fresh sashimi, and decent Korean dishes such as classic *bulgogi* (sliced barbecue beef).

Tricia's Tropi-Grille and Oasis Lounge (14 Narragansett Ave., 401/423-1490, www.triciastropigrille.com, 4–9 P.M. daily, $12–18) occupies a cozy light-yellow clapboard house along Jamestown's main drag. The best spot to eat is out on the large side patio. This terrific restaurant specializes in Caribbean and Asian fare such as coconut batter-fried calamari with garlic and tomatoes, Thai curry sea scallops, and sesame-chicken peanut salad.

Ching Tao (268 W. Main Rd., Rte. 114, Middletown, 401/849-2112, 11:30 A.M.–9:30 P.M. Mon.–Fri., 11:30 A.M.–10:30 P.M. Sat.–Sun., $6–14) serves good if somewhat predictable Chinese food. Specialties include asparagus with pork ginger sauce, hot-and-spicy crispy tofu and seafood in a sizzling red wine sauce, and mango chicken in a white-wine reduction.

Quick Bites

In Jamestown, bright and sunny **Slice of Heaven** (32 Narragansett Ave., Jamestown, 401/423-9866, 6 A.M.–5 P.M. Mon.–Thurs., 6 A.M.–9 P.M. Fri.–Sun., $5–9), a friendly little bakery-café, packs them in for weekend brunch and breakfast served all day—try the panini sandwiches and wraps, lemon-ginger muffins, Grand Marnier French toast stuffed with berries

and fresh whipped cream, and terrific mozzarella salad. There's great people-watching from the deck out front.

A cute diner with a couple of U-shaped counters, red vinyl booths, and nautical photos on walls, **Reidy's** (3351 E. Main Rd., Portsmouth, 401/683-9802, 6 A.M.–8 P.M. Mon.–Sat., 6 A.M.–6 P.M. Sun., under $8) is a local gathering spot, especially for breakfast, served all day. The kitchen serves fairly typical diner fare plus some Greek and Portuguese specialties. Consider the excellent kale soup, veal parmigiana, tapioca pudding, clam cakes, stuffies, and homemade muffins.

Gourmet Goods and Picnic Supplies

Foodies should not miss the **Aquidneck Growers' Market** (909 E. Main St., Middletown, 401/848-0099, 9 A.M.–1 P.M. Sat. mid-June–late Sept.), held on the grounds of the Newport Vineyards and Winery. You can find both organic and conventional produce, fruits, flowers, wine, baked goods, breads, jams and jellies, sauces, cheeses, and other delicious foods.

Information and Services

VISITOR INFORMATION

Pamphlets, brochures, and visitor information are available from the **Newport County Convention and Visitors Bureau** (23 America's Cup Ave., next to the bus terminal, 401/849-8098 or 800/976-5122, www.gonewport.com), which also provides packages with discounted rates on lodging and restaurants and has a switchboard for last-minute hotel availability.

The area's major hospital is **Newport Hospital** (11 Friendship St., Newport, 401/846-6400, www.lifespan.org/newport). Local pharmacies include **Rite Aid** (268 Bellevue Ave., Newport, 401/846-1631, www.riteaid.com) and **CVS** (181 Bellevue Ave, Newport, 401/846-7800, www.cvs.com). A handful of banks are found on Thames Street, and several ATMs are located on Thames

Street and on Bellevue Avenue, as well as at the bus station and in convenience stores. Free **Internet access** is available in several local cafés, including **Jack and Josie's** (111 Broadway St., Newport, 401/851-6900, www.jackandjosies.com), and for guests only at the majority of hotels in town. Fax and shipping services are offered at **The UPS Store** (270 Bellevue Ave., Newport, 401/848-7600, www.theupsstore.com).

MEDIA

Most locals read the ***Providence Journal*** or the ***Boston Globe*** as their daily news source. Newport's local newspapers are the ***Newport Daily News*** (www.newportdailynews.com) and ***Newport This Week,*** which is mainly an arts and entertainment weekly.

Getting There and Around

BUSES

From T. F. Green Airport, **Cozy Cab** (401/846-2500 or 800/846-1502, www.cozytrans.com) runs a shuttle-bus service to Newport; the cost is about $20 each way.

Peter Pan Bus Lines (401/751-8800 or 888/751-8800, www.peterpanbus.com) offers service from Boston's Logan Airport via Boston several times daily; the cost is about $60 round-trip (about $50 round-trip if you're coming from Boston rather than from the airport). The ride takes about 90 minutes, not counting the short trip from Logan to Boston's South Station. Peter Pan also makes a run from Newport to New York City, connecting through Providence; the fare is about $100 round-trip.

The **Rhode Island Transportation Authority (RIPTA)** (401/781-9400, www.ripta.com) has bus service from T. F. Green Airport to Newport, and also from Newport to Providence and to the University of Rhode Island in Kingston. Buses arrive in Newport at the station attached to the Newport Visitors Center on America's Cup Avenue, in the middle of downtown and within walking distance to many hotels and businesses.

Within Newport, RIPTA operates local bus and trolley services that run among downtown, the outlying shopping centers, the mansions on Bellevue Avenue, and Cliff Walk and Easton's Beach. The fare is $1.75 one-way, $5 for an individual day pass, or $20 for a seven-day pass. You can park at the garage adjacent to the Gateway Information Center for just $2 for the entire day if you present the cashier with a parking ticket validated by RIPTA.

If you are heading to the sites in Middletown, consider taking the **Coyote Shuttle** (401/846-7090, www.newportvineyards.com), which leaves the Gateway Visitors Center every hour on the hour during summer, heading out to Norman Bird Sanctuary, Newport Vineyards, and other attractions for a $5 round-trip charge.

DRIVING AND PARKING

Several car-rental companies maintain offices in Newport, including **Enterprise** (70 West Main Rd., Middletown, 401/849-3939 or 800/325-8007, www.enterprise.com) and **Hertz** (400 Airport Access Rd., Middletown, 401/846-1645 or 800/654-3131, www.hertz.com).

Driving times to Newport from major cities are: from Providence, 45 minutes–1 hour; from Boston, 90 minutes–2 hours; from Cape Cod's Bourne Bridge, 1 hour–75 minutes; from Hartford, about two hours; from New York City, about three hours. Add at least 30 minutes to these times during busy periods, including most summer weekends.

Parking in Newport is not terribly difficult after Columbus Day through about Memorial Day, but the 3–4 months of summer can be a nightmare. Much of the angst, however, seems to come from locals and regulars who are so accustomed to finding ample parking in the off-season that they kick and scream when they can't find free or metered spots on the street during the warmer months. If you can stomach paying $15–20 for a parking space in summer, you won't have much trouble finding one. There are several large municipal and private garages around town, and you can park at the garage adjacent to the Gateway Information Center for just $2 for the entire day if you present the cashier with a parking ticket validated by RIPTA, the local bus and trolley company.

TAXIS

You can definitely get by in Newport without a car, using a cab for the few longer trips that might come up, and relying on sightseeing tour buses for trips out around Ocean Drive and to various outlying attractions. Local cab companies include **Cozy Cab** (401/846-2500 or 800/846-1502, www.cozytrans.com), **Rainbow Cab** (401/849-1333), and **Orange Cab** (401/841-0030, www.newportcabs.com).

FERRY SERVICE

To Providence: The high-speed **Newport-Providence Ferry** (401/453-6800, www.nefastferry.com) runs from Providence to Newport several times daily mid-May–mid-October. The fare is $7 one-way, and the trip takes just over an hour. In Providence the ferries dock at Point Street Landing, and in Newport at Perrotti Park, near Long Wharf and very close to the bus station.

To Block Island: This service is provided July–early September by **Interstate Navigation** (401/783-4613 or 866/783-7340, www.blockislandferry.com). Ferries leave Newport daily at 9:15 A.M. and return daily from Block Island at 4:45 P.M.; the sail time is about two hours. The one-way fare is $10.85 for adults ($15.75 round-trip, but only for same-day passage), $10.35/$14.75 for seniors, $4.90/$7.90 for children 5–11, and $3.05 each way for bicycles. The terminal is at Fort Adams State Park on Harrison Avenue; inexpensive water taxis run passengers back and forth between Fort Adams and downtown Newport.

To Jamestown: Even if you have a car, it's quite practical and pleasant to travel between Newport and Jamestown via the **Jamestown-Newport Ferry** (401/423-9900, www.jamestownnewportferry.com). From Jamestown, the boat leaves several times a day for Newport's Bowen's Wharf, right off Thames Street; it crosses to Goat Island, then back to Bowen's Wharf, and then returns to Jamestown, where it is based. The earliest boat leaves Jamestown at about 10 A.M., and the last one returns at about 10 P.M.

During the morning and afternoon runs, the ferry from Jamestown makes an added stop at the 16-acre wildlife refuge of Rose Island, which also includes a lighthouse and an old military outpost named Fort Hamilton. The landing fee, if you'd like to explore it, is $3 pp ($2 if you present your ferry ticket). From Rose Island, the boat continues to Fort Adams, where you're also free to get out and wander around, and then continues to Bowen's Wharf and Goat Island.

Fares vary according to the itinerary but range from $5 (from Bowen's Wharf to Goat Island or Fort Adams) to $16.50 (for a round-trip cross-bay ticket).

Around Newport and Aquidneck Island: There are a handful of launch services, including **Conanicut Marine Service** (401/423-1556, www.jamestownnewportferry.com), **Goat Island Marina** (401/849-5655, www.newportexperience.com/GoatIslandMarina.php), and **Oldport Marine Services** (401/847-9109, www.oldportmarine.com). These leave from Newport Harbor and can be chartered to a variety of destinations, including Fort Adams and Goat Island.

TOURS
By Boat

Oldport Marine Services (Sayer's Wharf, 401/847-9109, www.oldportmarine.com) offers cruises along Narragansett Bay and through Newport Harbor on the MV *Amazing Grace.* These hour-long narrated tours ($15 adults, $12 seniors, $5 children) are offered daily mid-May–mid-October.

Sightsailing of Newport (32 Bowen's Wharf, 401/849-3333 or 800/709-SAIL—800/709-7245, www.sightsailing.com) gives daily narrated tours aboard sailboats of three different sizes that generally last 75–90 minutes.

Classic Cruises of Newport (Christie's Landing, 401/847-0298, www.cruisenewport.com) has daily cruises from Bannister's Wharf. These include the 72-foot schooner *Madeleine,* the high-speed Prohibition-era *Rumrunner II,* and the *Arabella,* a 155-foot sailing cruise yacht that makes three-night excursions out to Martha's Vineyard, Nantucket, and elsewhere in the Northeast. Fares range $18–25 pp.

Narrated tours of Newport Harbor are given aboard the *Flyer* (401/848-2100 or 800/TO-FLYER—800/863-5937, www.flyercatamaran.com), a 57-foot catamaran with a large sundeck and room for more than 65 passengers; amenities include a full cocktail bar and a shaded seating area. This is a beautiful ship and a great way to experience Newport's glorious waters. The boat departs from Newport four times daily May–October. Rates are $30 pp for most sails, $35 pp for the sunset runs.

Leaving from Bowen's Wharf, the schooner *Adirondack II* (401/847-0000, www.sail-newport.com) also makes five 1.5-hour sightseeing trips around Newport Harbor, Fort Adams, and area lighthouses each day. Rates range from $27 adults, $22 children for a morning cruise to $35 adults, $30 children for a sunset cruise. It is also available for private charters.

There are several other sailing charters in town as well. **America's Cup Charters** (401/846-9886, www.americascupcharters.com) offers daily sunset cruises aboard actual America's Cup–winning yachts. These tours sail around Narragansett Bay.

On Foot

Newport Historical Society Walking Tours (401/846-0813, www.newporthistorical.org) offers extremely interesting walks through the city; these leave from the Museum of Newport History at Brick Market on Friday and Saturday May–October. The appeal of **Native Newporter** (401/662-1407, www.nativenewportertours.com) is right in the name—the owner-operated company comprises guides that reach back over three generations of Newport history. They present several forthright and factual Newport tours ($25–45) replete with an insider's knowledge of the city that can include one mansion tour. The best value, however, may be the group's special "Mansion Madness" tour ($95), which includes admission to *every* major mansion for one day of sightseeing. There's no set time limit, so the only limit to how many marble staircases and gilded chandeliers you can see is your own stamina and stomach for displays of conspicuous consumption.

Kids especially enjoy **Ghost Tours of Newport** (401/841-8600 or 866/334-4678, www.ghostsofnewport.com), which leave from the Newport Marriott. These lantern-led strolls show the dark and creepy side of the city. A newer addition are **Dead Man's Tales** (401/952-6601, www.deadmanstalesri.com), a group of costumed actors that lead "pirate tours" of Newport. Tours leave from Bowen Wharf several times during the day and once at night.

Last but not least, and not exactly on foot, the Segway tours given by **Segway of Newport** (438 Thames St., 401/619-4010, www.segwayofnewport.com) have proven to be an immensely popular way to explore the city. The only downside is that tours are a bit pricey at $75 pp for a complete circuit around Ocean Drive or a trip up Bellevue to gawk at the mansions. A better deal may be to rent one of the store's electric bicycles for $50 for up to four hours or $75 for the day; nonelectric ($15) and folding bicycles ($25) are also available.

By Bus

Viking Tours of Newport (Gateway Visitors Center, 401/847-6921, www.vikingtoursnewport.com) provides narrated trolley tours of the city that include Ocean Drive and the mansions along Bellevue Avenue. A standard tour is $24 pp; package deals that include tours of one or more of the mansions are also available.

By Train

People sometimes get confused about the sightseeing trains that depart from Newport's vintage rail depot (19 America's Cup Ave.). The **Newport Dinner Train** (401/841-8700 or 800/398-7427, www.newportdinnertrain.com) is a separately owned company from the other excursion train that uses these tracks, the **Old Colony Railroad** (401/849-0546, www.ocnrr.com). On either train you'll enjoy a breathtaking journey over tracks used for passenger service for roughly a century from the 1860s; they wend for five miles along the shore of Narragansett Bay, well beyond the Newport Naval Base, and then five miles back. The Old Colony tours are given in vintage rail cars that are about 100 years old; tours last about 80 minutes and cost $8 for adults.

By Air

The most thrilling way to see Newport is by jumping on a birdie with **Bird's Eye View Helicopters** (401/843-TOUR—401/843-8687, www.birdseyeviewhelicopters.com), which offers surprisingly affordable trips through the sky above Aquidneck. For a different perspective on Newport's mansions, a fly-by over The Elms, The Breakers, Rosecliff, and Marble House is only $59 pp with a two-person minimum ($49 pp with three people). Other tours, including buzzing a few lighthouses, range $89–129 pp. And if you'd like to take the stick yourself, you can sign up for a half-day "Introduction to Flight" class—a private lesson in helicoptering that culminates in a flight over Newport with you at the controls.

THE EAST BAY AND SAKONNET

The peninsular towns of Barrington, Warren, and Bristol dangle jaggedly off the mainland like stalactites, fringed on various sides by Narragansett and Mount Hope Bays and the Seekonk, Warren, and Barrington Rivers. All told, the three towns share about 20 miles of shoreline throughout Bristol County, meaning that strollers, inline skaters, cyclists, and joggers find ample and alluring scenery for roaming, and boaters and sailboarders consider this part of the state ideal. Best of all, the entire region lies sheltered from—but completely accessible to—the Atlantic Ocean.

There's relatively little to see and do in mostly residential Barrington, an attractive but fairly quiet bedroom community just 10 miles from Providence, but bustling Warren and courtly Bristol have a considerable number of attractions, restaurants, and shops—easily enough to keep visitors busy for a long weekend or more.

A short drive southeast, Sakonnet hugs the Massachusetts mainland on one side and the Sakonnet River, an extension of Narragansett Bay, on the other. Close to Newport and the towns of Bristol County, as well as busy Massachusetts cities such as Fall River and New Bedford, Sakonnet nevertheless enjoys an easygoing, downright sleepy pace. It encompasses two small towns: Tiverton up north along the river and Little Compton fronting the ocean.

PLANNING YOUR TIME

You can easily do either the East Bay or the Sakonnet Peninsula as a day trip from

HIGHLIGHTS

LOOK FOR ◖ TO FIND RECOMMENDED
SIGHTS, ACTIVITIES, DINING, AND LODGING.

◖ **Herreshoff Marine Museum:** There's no better way familiarize yourself with Rhode Island's rich sailing and boatbuilding history than with a tour of this fascinating place (page 91).

◖ **Blithewold Mansion and Arboretum:** Right up there with the most lavish summer cottages found in Newport, Blithewold ranks among the most impressive house-museums in the state (page 92).

◖ **Warren's Historic District:** This colonial shipbuilding center contains dozens of restored 18th- and 19th-century buildings, a great tour for history buffs who don't want to deal with excessive crowds (page 94).

◖ **East Bay Bike Path:** Among the state's several fine bike paths, this 14.5-mile asphalt path is the most scenic, stretching from Providence down through the East Bay and offering wonderful bay views along much of the way. It's also popular with walkers, runners, and inline skaters (page 97).

◖ **Sakonnet Vineyards:** In peaceful and rural Little Compton, this 50-acre vineyard and tasting room produces the top wines in the state (page 105).

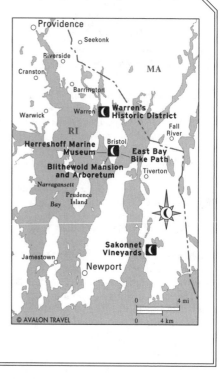

© AVALON TRAVEL

Providence or Newport—although it's recommended that you don't try to do both in a day. The appeal of these regions is less in ticking off sites than it is in rambling along streets filled with colonial homes and antiques stores or driving down country lanes lined with stone walls. If you truly want to fall into the slow pace of life here, an overnight or two is a nice respite on a harried vacation.

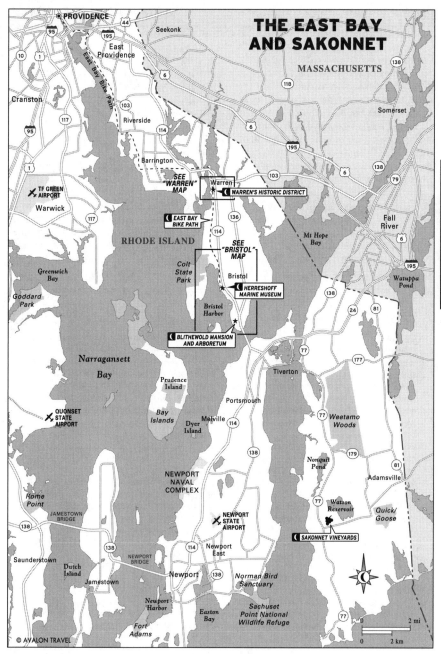

THE EAST BAY AND SAKONNET

MASSACHUSETTS

PROVIDENCE

Seekonk

East Providence

Cranston

Riverside

Barrington

SEE "WARREN" MAP

Warren

WARREN'S HISTORIC DISTRICT

TF GREEN AIRPORT

Warwick

EAST BAY BIKE PATH

RHODE ISLAND

Fall River

Mt Hope Bay

SEE "BRISTOL" MAP

Colt State Park

Bristol

HERRESHOFF MARINE MUSEUM

Greenwich Bay

Goddard Park

Bristol Harbor

BLITHEWOLD MANSION AND ARBORETUM

Watuppa Pond

Narragansett Bay

Prudence Island

Bay Islands

Dyer Island

Melville

Tiverton

Weetamo Woods

Portsmouth

Nonquit Pond

QUONSET STATE AIRPORT

NEWPORT NAVAL COMPLEX

Adamsville

Rome Point

JAMESTOWN BRIDGE

Watson Reservoir

Quick/Goose

Saunderstown

NEWPORT STATE AIRPORT

Dutch Island

NEWPORT BRIDGE

Newport East

SAKONNET VINEYARDS

Jamestown

Newport

Norman Bird Sanctuary

Newport Harbor

Easton Bay

Sachuest Point National Wildlife Refuge

Fort Adams

© AVALON TRAVEL

0   2 mi

0   2 km

Somerset

East Bay Bike Path

The East Bay

The East Bay comprises a narrow swath of land that extends in a southeasterly direction from Providence down toward Aquidneck Island, where Newport is, and the Sakonnet Peninsula. To the east lies the Massachusetts border, and to the west is Narragansett Bay. Although it's a small area with just three towns—Barrington, Warren, and Bristol—the East Bay has its own distinct identity and is by no means simply a suburban extension of metropolitan Providence.

This is an area rich in museums, parks, B&Bs, and restaurants, especially in the courtly town of Bristol, the southernmost of the East Bay communities. At the north end, just below East Providence, the town of Barrington is a pretty suburb that's worth taking the time to drive through but lacks much in the way of actual diversions and businesses. In the middle, however, plan to spend a little time exploring Warren, a semi-industrial town with a rich shipbuilding heritage. It has steadily gentrified in recent years and contains one of the most impressive historic districts of any small town in Rhode Island.

BRISTOL

If there was a runoff for all-American town, Bristol would be a finalist. The main street is festooned with flags left waving after the city's annual Fourth of July parade, the oldest in the country. The street itself is a vibrant vision of what main streets once looked like before malls, with boutiques and storefront cafés interspersed with solid granite buildings and picturesque colonial homes. Few communities

---

PRUDENCE ISLAND

One of the state's strangest little places, Prudence Island – which is about six miles long by a mile wide – lies just a few miles southwest of Bristol in the middle of Narragansett Bay. Technically it is within the town limits of Portsmouth, just to the east. It was entirely wooded until the Revolutionary War, when the British used it as a source of lumber. Despite being the third largest island in Rhode Island after Aquidneck and Conanicut, the island now has fewer than 100 year-round residents, including just a few summer homes and a small convenience store to pass for civilization.

Of course, that makes it a nature-lover's dream, with the densest white-tailed deer herd in New England, as well as wading birds such as great blue herons. It's an ideal spot for beachcombing, hikes, and taking advantage of nature lectures and strolls, which are sponsored by the **Audubon Society of Rhode Island** (401/949-5454, www.asri.org).

Near the boat docks at the southern end of the island and a four-mile bike ride or hike from the ferry landing, the **Narragansett Bay**

National Estuarine Research Reserve (S. Reserve Dr., 401/683-6780, www.nbnerr.org, 11 A.M.-3 P.M. Fri.-Mon., and by appointment), encompasses many acres of salt marsh, tidal flats and pools, forest, and even a historic farm site. Birding is a favorite activity at the reserve, where you'll also find a butterfly garden and several nature trails. A mile's walk from the boat docks is the 25-foot-high **Prudence Island Light** (www.lighthouse.cc/prudence), which stands sentinel on the island's east side.

While this is a great place for exploring, keep in mind that deer ticks are a major problem on the island – take necessary precautions when exploring, especially in wooded areas. No bridges connect the island to the mainland or Aquidneck. Transportation is by the **Prudence Island Ferry** (Church St. Wharf at Thames St., Bristol, 401/253-9808, www.prudenceferry.com), which runs several boats from Bristol sunrise-sunset daily. You can also dock your own vessel at the southern tip of Prudence Island. Unfortunately, camping is not permitted.

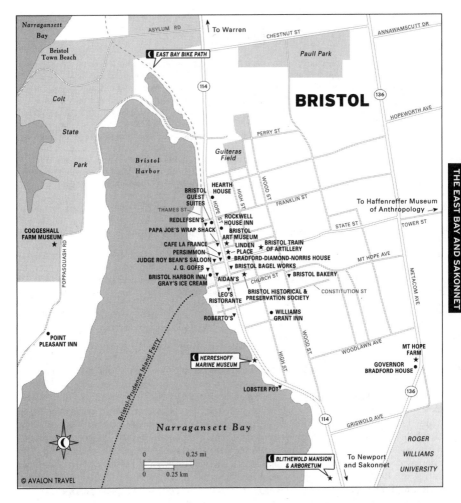

in Rhode Island so balance the aesthetic of colonial Americana with the unprepossessing charm of a small and friendly village.

From such quaint environs, you'd hardly believe Bristol's contentious history. In the 17th century the land served as the primary encampment of the Wampanoags, the Indians led by King Philip who staged the largest prerevolutionary Native American uprising. After Philip was defeated, the colonists who founded Bristol named it after one of Great Britain's greatest

seaports, deriving a good bit of their commercial success in the infamous slave trade. After that ignominious start, Bristol was pummeled during the Revolutionary War. On October 7, 1775, the British sailed several war ships into the town harbor and began an intense bombing campaign that damaged many buildings. A far worse attack occurred three years later, when about 600 British soldiers and Hessian mercenaries marched through the town and burned virtually every structure.

SLAVERY IN RHODE ISLAND

During the colonial era, ships from all over the state, especially in Newport and Providence, trafficked heavily in human misery and injustice, a highly profitable endeavor that involved shipping rum (produced locally in distilleries set up near Bristol's wharves) to Africa, where it was traded for slaves. The ships then continued back across the Atlantic to the West Indies (and later to Charleston, South Carolina), where the Africans were unloaded in exchange for a variety of goods, including the molasses used to manufacture more rum. The terms of each cargo proved extremely favorable to the Rhode Islanders, and throughout the 18th century fancy mansions went up all around the better neighborhoods of Providence, Newport, and Bristol.

To give an idea of the state's contribution to this ignominious period in U.S. history, consider that 1804-1808 approximately 8,500 of the 40,000 slaves brought through Charles-ton, South Carolina, were delivered on Rhode Island-registered ships; of these, about 4,000 came through on boats registered in Bristol, 3,500 on Newport boats, 600 on Providence boats, and about 300 on Warren boats. Also, while 59 of the 202 slave ships that docked in Charleston during this period were officially registered in Rhode Island, it's believed that a great many more were manned by Rhode Islanders but for various reasons registered elsewhere – so these numbers don't fully reflect the tremendous degree to which the Ocean State profited from the slave trade. In total, historians believe that about half the slaves brought to North America came on Rhode Island ships. In 1808, slave importation was banned in the United States; slave-trading had already been banned in Rhode Island in 1774, and owning slaves had been declared illegal in the state in 1784.

While never as well-to-do as Newport, Bristol's heyday as a shipping center after the Revolution led to many fine Victorian mansions and gardens being built on the outskirts of town. After slavery was outlawed, Bristol continued to rake in steep revenues on shipping and trade well into the mid-19th century, with ships sailing in and out of Bristol Harbor to China, the Mediterranean, northern Europe, the northwest coast of Africa, and the Caribbean. After shipping declined, several industries picked up during the 19th century, including wool- and cotton-milling, sugar refining, rubber refining, and the Burnside Rifle Company, which was established in 1849 by none other than Colonel Ambrose E. Burnside (whose famous facial hair gave him the nickname "Sideburns," the now-common term for this style). Finally, the town's legacy as a shipbuilding community was restored by the Herreshoff Manufacturing Company, which opened in 1863 in the factory space of the old rifle company, and became famous for creating the racing ships that helped the United States win the America's Cup sailing race year after year.

Industry led to an influx of Portuguese and Italian immigrants, many of whose descendants still influence Bristol's character—you'll find ample evidence of this heritage on local menus that include linguica sausage or puttanesca seafood dishes. Today the majority of residents are commuters from Providence and even Newport. The town is not really suburban in character or appearance, however, as it retains an organic small-town spirit with a clutch of restored, finely crafted historic homes. You'll see carved lintels, toothlike dentil molding, glazed sidelights and fanlights, and pedimented windows and dormers on buildings up and down Hope Street.

Also known as Route 114, Hope Street is one of those slice-of-Americana thoroughfares that looks nearly flawless enough to be a movie set. Shops and eateries line the west side of the street, grand colonial and Victorian mansions the other, and mature shade trees run along both. Restaurants range from upscale bistros to wiener joints and pizza parlors. It's a family town: a place where kids ride their bikes downtown, locals push strollers, and teens loiter harmlessly on park benches in a way that you can't help but envy.

South of Downtown

At the southern tip of Bristol, the narrow Mount Hope Bridge arches steeply and gracefully over Narragansett Bay, connecting the mainland with Aquidneck Island (a left turn onto Route 24/138 leads to the Sakonnet towns of Tiverton and Little Compton, while a right turn onto Route 114 leads to Newport). When it was built in 1929, this $4 million structure with a main span of 1,200 feet was the 13th-longest suspension bridge in the world and the longest in New England. The road rises to 135 feet over the water below, and the two bridge towers are 284 feet tall.

Just across the bridge, **Mount Hope Farm** (250 Metacom Ave., 401/254-1745, www.mounthopefarm.com) dates to 1745 and is open mostly as an event facility for retreats, weddings, and such. The area is owned by a private trust that allows public access, and respectful pedestrians and bicyclists are free to explore the more than 200 acres of greenery, gardens, and trails overlooking Mount Hope Bay. (Bicyclists must stay on trails; cars are prohibited.) There's also an inn, the Governor Bradford House, built by Isaac Royall, a royalist, before the revolution in 1745. It later passed to William Bradford, who actually wasn't governor but deputy governor of Rhode Island and later a U.S. senator. The interior of the home has been restored to the colonial period; tours are given around Christmastime (noon–4 P.M. Wed.–Sat. Dec.).

To get a full sense of the agrarian life that also characterized this part of the state during much of the past few centuries, pay a visit to the **Coggeshall Farm Museum** (Poppasquash Rd., off Rte. 114, 401/253-9062, http://coggeshallfarm.org, 10 A.M.–4 P.M. Tues.–Sun., $5 adults, $3 children under 16), which sits on 40 rolling acres overlooking Mill Gut Inlet, a sheltered expanse of Narragansett Bay. It's a princely property for a stroll, made more interesting by the vintage and reproduction-antique farming tools and the yards of livestock.

Throughout the year, docents conduct tours, lectures, and demonstrations, often in the farm's outbuildings (which include a blacksmith shop and a fieldstone springhouse).

Set on a 28-acre wildlife refuge on Narragansett Bay, the kid-popular **Audubon Society of Rhode Island's Environmental Education Center** (1401 Hope St., Rte. 114, 401/245-7500, www.asri.org, 9 A.M.–5 P.M. daily May–Sept., 9 A.M.–5 P.M. Mon.–Sat., noon–5 P.M. Sun. Oct.–Apr., $6 adults, $4 children 4–12, free for children under 4) contains the largest aquarium in the state along with well-executed 3-D natural history dioramas, marine-life touch tanks, and other provocative hands-on exhibits. This is an excellent resource for conservation education, but more importantly—to kids at least—the center is great fun. Nowhere else in Rhode Island can you walk inside a 33-foot-tall life-size right whale.

◖ Herreshoff Marine Museum

You can get an intimate sense of Rhode Island's unique bond with the ocean at one of the state's best attractions, the Herreshoff Marine Museum (1 Burnside St., 401/253-5000, www.herreshoff.org, 10 A.M.–5 P.M. daily May–Oct., $8). Herreshoff has long been famous as one of the world's most respected and longest-running manufacturers of ships. Brothers John Brown Herreshoff and Nathanael Greene Herreshoff, both named for legendary figures in Rhode Island history, founded the boat maker in 1863. John, famous for his photographic memory and keen sense of detail, laid out the plans for the craft, and Nathanael handled the execution. In its first year, Herreshoff produced nine sailboats, and it wasn't long before the company had taken over the old Burnside Rifle plant and produced several successful defenders of the America's Cup (beginning with the *Vigilant* in 1893), plus powerful steamers, sumptuous but sleek yachts, and other fine craft.

Inside the museum's extensive exhibit hall you can admire about 45 Herreshoff boats as well as dozens of fine ship models and other historic memorabilia. Cruises are taken regularly aboard the 56-foot *Belisarius,* a vintage yawl that was Nathanael Herreshoff's final design—you'll usually see the boat tied up in the bay outside the museum. There's also a Discovery Center, geared for kids and families, where staff conduct workshops on sailing and boat construction.

C Blithewold Mansion and Arboretum

Visitors to Rhode Island typically flock to Newport to tour the greatest homes of the Gilded Age, but serious mansion-goers should make a point of seeing Bristol's spectacular—and somewhat underrated—Blithewold Mansion and Arboretum (101 Ferry Rd., 401/253-2707, www.blithewold.org, $10). It's as famous for its lush 33-acre grounds as for the 17th century–style English manor house, which was built in 1908. Noted New York landscape architect John DeWolf laid out the grounds, which include 200 varieties of trees and more than 2,000 woody plants. A prize among these is a towering 90-foot giant sequoia, said to be the largest of its kind east of the Rocky Mountains. Inside the house's stone-and-stucco walls you can tour 45 rooms decorated mostly with pieces from the original family's impressive collection. The grounds are open 10 A.M.–5 P.M. daily, and the mansion and gift shop are open 10 A.M.–4 P.M. Wednesday–Saturday, 10 A.M.–3 P.M. Sunday April–October.

Downtown

Just off Hope Street, the **Bristol Historical and Preservation Society** (48 Court St., 401/253-7223) overflows with photographs, letters, deeds, reports, and other historical artifacts spanning the town's several centuries. The displays are set in the 1828 jail, which was constructed with the granite ballast of incoming Bristol ships. The society is open 1–5 P.M. Wednesday and Friday afternoon and 2–5 P.M. the first Sunday of each month, or by appointment; donations are encouraged.

Nearby, you can visit by appointment the **Bristol Train of Artillery** (135 State St., 401/253-2928, http://web.mac.com/

the Blithewold Mansion and its famous gardens

sageanne123/Bristol_Train_of_Artillery), which has been running strong since its formation on February 12, 1776. Today the BTA houses a small museum filled with vintage, often rare, military weapons and memorabilia, sabers, shoulder arms, and so on, some of which date back to the BTA's inception.

Linden Place

The name Samuel Colt is more associated these days with Connecticut; in Hartford you'll find the Colt factory village and former estate. However, Colt's more famous nephew, Samuel P. Colt, has roots in Bristol in the grand if garish 1810 mansion, now a museum, called Linden Place (500 Hope St., 401/253-0390, www.lindenplace.org, 10 A.M.–4 P.M. Tues.–Sat. early May–early Oct., $5), where his magnate grandfather, General George DeWolf, lived. The mansion, in classical revival style with major Victorian and Greek Revival alterations, eventually passed to Colt, who founded the U.S. Rubber Company (now Uniroyal) and the Industrial Trust Company (now Fleet Bank).

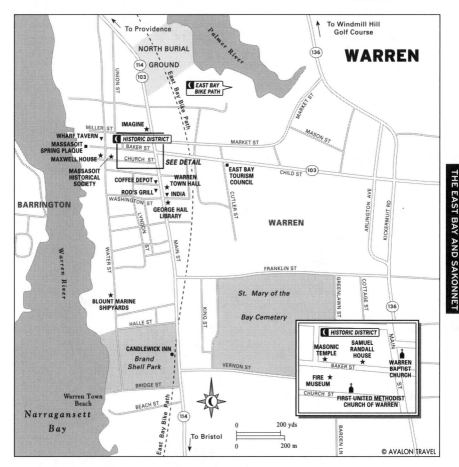

© AVALON TRAVEL

Hollywood has connections to Linden Place as well: The matriarch of the famous Barrymore acting dynasty, Ethel Barrymore, lived here at one time, and parts of the mansion played a role in the 1974 film adaptation of *The Great Gatsby*. The mansion contains decadent furnishings from the period, outbuildings that date as far back as the 1750s, an elaborate ballroom from 1902, an 1820s carriage house, and neatly manicured grounds set with dramatic sculptures.

Occupying the ballroom, the small **Bristol Art Museum** (entrance on Wardwell St., off Hope St., 401/253-2095, www.bristolart-museum.org, 1–4 P.M. daily) hosts local and national art exhibits throughout the year, with hours that change depending on the exhibition.

WARREN

At 6.2 square miles, making it the smallest town in the smallest county in the smallest state, Warren has continued to grow in popularity in recent years among professionals, educators, and artists. A mix of great historic buildings and affordable homes (compared with Newport or Boston) has helped encourage an emerging arts scene. Nevertheless, Warren is less quaint and upscale than Bristol. It's an eclectic and economically diverse community with an unpretentious, easygoing vibe.

Originally part of the southern fringes of the Massachusetts town Swansea, Warren officially became part of Rhode Island in 1747 and developed rapidly into a shipbuilding and commercial center. During the Revolutionary War, the Redcoats targeted the community, along with Bristol to the south, for its contributions to the Continental Navy. In May of 1778, raiding troops burned some 75 boats as well as a large portion of the town's buildings. It took many years to recover fully from the war, but eventually Warren returned to its shipbuilding prominence and produced some of the 19th century's finest vessels.

The town turned to textile manufacturing in the mid-1800s; the mills lured workers from different parts of the world, and Warren's—and the East Bay's—blue-blood personality changed with the significant immigration of Italians, Portuguese, and Irish. In the 20th century, Warren was also known briefly as the "oyster capital of the world" due to the famed Warren Oyster Company. Pollution and a 1938 hurricane took its toll on production, trade dried up, and the company finally shut down in the 1950s. Since then, Warren has slowly shifted from manufacturing to tourism.

Despite that shift, quite a few homes and commercial structures in town have yet to be touched by the magic wand of restoration. For many visitors and residents, Warren's lack of precious chain shops and high-profile eateries is refreshing compared to the glut of visitors in Newport and even neighboring Bristol. But there's quite a good bit to keep you busy here, especially if you're into shopping for antiques.

◖ Historic District

In the center of town you'll find the 1844 **Warren Baptist Church** (407 Main St., 401/245-3669, by appointment); Hessian and British soldiers burned the original church in 1776. Nearby is the 1844 **First United Methodist Church of Warren** (25 Church St., 401/247-9702, service 10:30 A.M. Sun.), whose 160-foot spire and clock tower defines the

town's skyline. From the churchyard extends Warren's simple but appealing town common, which is fronted by several of the community's most striking old homes. You can easily combine your antiques browsing with a tour of prominent sites, or just wander the streets around the intersection of Main Street (Route 114) and Child Street (Route 103).

Baker Street has a couple of noteworthy buildings, including the hulking building at 39 Baker Street, the oldest continuously operated **Masonic Temple** in the country; it was built in 1799 with timbers from sunken British war ships. Other notable structures nearby include the 1890 copper-domed **Warren Town Hall** (1 Main St.) and the Romanesque **George Hail Library** (530 Main St., 401/245-7686, 10 A.M.–8 P.M. Mon.–Thurs., 10 A.M.–5 P.M. Fri.–Sat.), built in 1889 and completely restored in the early 1980s. This structure also contains the **Charles W. Greene Museum** (2–4 P.M. Wed. or by appointment, free), where you can examine a fascinating collection of artifacts from North and South American indigenous people, including beads, farming implements, and currency.

Across from the Masonic Temple, the **Warren Fire Museum** (38 Baker St., 401/245-7600, www.townofwarren-ri.gov, by appointment, free) contains the documents and ephemera of the Narragansett Steam Co. No. 3. The building, a mid-19th-century fire barn, also contains the company's earliest fire engine, the hand-pumped, wooden-axle Little Hero, which dates to 1802. Adjacent to the fire museum in an 1860s carriage house, you'll find the **Federal Blues Museum and Armory** (42 Baker St., 401/368-5120, www.federalblues.com, by appointment), which is being restored but can be toured by making an appointment with Captain Edgar Hebert, the former commander of the unit, who now overseas historical sites up and down the eastern seaboard. The Federal Blues served as the town's militia during the Revolutionary War, and the museum contains military artifacts that include a fully restored 6,000-pound bronze French cannon used in the 1778 Battle of Rhode Island in Portsmouth.

Down the street stands one of the most impressive Federal buildings in the East Bay, the three-story **Samuel Randall House** (31 Baker St.), a home originally built by a wealthy sea merchant as a wedding present for his daughter. Purchased by the Warren Preservation Society (401/245-0397, www.preservewarren.org), which has its headquarters on the first floor, the home has been meticulously restored, with repairs made to the clapboards and windows and 100 new hand-carved corbels installed below the roofline. The rest of the interior has been renovated into five apartment buildings.

From this part of Main Street, you can take any intersecting street west a few blocks down toward the water to see Warren's bustling little dock, where oyster houses and boatyards thrive as they have for centuries. Views are especially good from the outdoor decks of the Wharf Tavern restaurant. These blocks cover what was once woodland and swamp settled by the Wampanoags under Massasoit and later his son King Philip. A bronze plaque at the foot of Baker Street marks the spot of **Massasoit Spring,** where King Philip presided over his people. You can learn more about Wampanoag history at **Maxwell House** (59 Church St., 401/245-0392, www.massasoithistorical.org, 10 A.M.–2 P.M. Sat., free), operated by the Massasoit Historical Association. Inside the 1750s Georgian colonial a multitude of documents and exhibits concerning Warren's past are on display, including two beehive ovens and a mix of colonial and Victorian furnishings; hearth cooking demonstrations and other food programs are offered from time to time.

Warren's maritime tradition continues today at the **Blount Marine Shipyards** (Gate 4, 461 Water St., 800/556-7450, www.blountsmallshipadventures.com), home to Blount Small Ship Adventures, a family-owned fleet of small ships that offers cruises around North America and the Caribbean. President Nancy Blount runs the company in memory of her father, Luther, who was instrumental in helping the town buy and preserve its downtown waterfront as open space.

BARRINGTON

Like Warren and Bristol to the south, Barrington has made a name for itself through the years in shipbuilding and fishing, although it was perhaps best known for many years as a major producer of bricks. Many of Barrington's oldest and most attractive homes lie in the Nayatt Point section of town, which you reach by following Route 114 about six miles south from I-195, then turning right onto Route 103 North. A little more than a mile north, make a left onto Washington Road and follow it south a couple of miles to get to the heart of Nayatt Point. During the early part of the 20th century, Barrington became popular as a summer destination among wealthy urbanites. It was more low-key than Newport but with some of the same panache; you can still see some of their enormous "summer cottages" along the water. To continue to Warren, follow Nayatt Road east past the Rhode Island Country Club, away from Nayatt Point, and make a left onto Rumstick Road, which takes you to Route 103/114.

Barrington has no major attractions, although **Tyler Point Cemetery** (Tyler Point Rd., off Route 114) makes for an interesting excursion, especially if you're a fan of Revolutionary War history. On this site a local patriot killed a Hessian soldier on his way from the burning of Warren. The graveyard is on the small spit of land between the Barrington and Warren Rivers, easily visited on your way down Route 103/114 to Warren.

ENTERTAINMENT AND EVENTS

While the East Bay isn't a major center of nightlife, Bristol does have several pubs that are especially lively on weekends, most of them near the waterfront and popular with a mix of students from nearby Roger Williams University, yuppies, blue-collar factory workers and fishers, and visitors. Favorites include **J. G. Goff's** (251 Thames St., Bristol, 401/253-4523), **Judge Roy Bean's** (1 State St., Bristol, 401/253-7526), and **Gillary's** (198 Thames St., 401/253-2012, 1 P.M.–3 A.M. Mon.–Wed., 1 P.M.–midnight

Thurs.–Sun.), by the waterfront. Gillary's quite often has live music, plus open mike and karaoke on some nights. Barbecue is served on the outdoor patio on summer weekends. **Jersey Lillie's** (1 State St., 401/253-7526, noon–11 P.M.) draws a college crowd for imported British drafts served at an authentic Victorian-era bar. The town of Bristol sponsors **Concerts on the Common** with classical performers on Thursday July–Labor Day.

Warren is home to one of the state's most respected regional performance spaces, the **2nd Story Theatre** (28 Market St., 401/247-4200, www.2ndstorytheatre.com), which presents several plays throughout its season, September–May; works in the past have varied from avant-garde works to classics such as *The Importance of Being Earnest* and *Picnic.* This first-rate company routinely draws theater fans from Newport, Providence, and even farther afield. The theater occupies the upper floor of a 1914 building that originally served as a community and social center for Warren's large early-20th-century population of French-Canadian textile workers.

Festivals and Events

No town in America has been celebrating the **Fourth of July** longer than Bristol, a community that ushers in this patriotic holiday with nearly fanatical fervor—notice as you stroll up Hope Street that even the fire hydrants are painted red, white, and blue. Nobody takes the parade through town lightly, and true devotees have been known to stake out space along the route as early as 4 A.M. the day of the big event. In mid-August, the Prudence Island Community Center hosts an annual **Firemen's Fair,** with food, an auction, and other festivities that include a bugle corps competition, a grand ball, a teenage beauty pageant, an old-time "orange crate derby" race, and—of course—fireworks on the harbor.

In mid-July, Rhode Island's favorite bivalve is feted at the **Warren Quahog Festival** (Burrs' Hill Park, S. Water St., Warren, 401/410-0045, www.warrenbartingtonrotary.org), which features chowders, cakes, and stuffies as well as

displays by the many artists who have taken up residence in town.

Off Route 114 in Warren, Burr's Hill Park hosts an annual **Bandshell Concert Series** throughout the summer; it's free and features live music and dramatic performances. A similar series, **Concerts on the Common,** is held in Bristol. In mid-September, the annual **Harvest Fair** (Coggeshall Farm Museum, Poppasquash Rd., off Rte. 114, Bristol) offers a weekend of pony rides, live music, hay-bale tosses and other farming fun, a jonnycake and sausage breakfast, children's games, and crafts demonstrations. Earlier in the month, similarly family-oriented festivities mark Warren's annual **Mum Festival** (Frerich's Farms, 43 Kinnicutt Ave., Warren), which is also a great place to buy chrysanthemums.

SHOPPING
Bristol

Hope Street is lined with cute boutiques and craft stores. **Green River Silver** (297 Hope St., 401/253-5005, www.greenriversilver.com, 10 A.M.–6 P.M. daily) has hundreds of different styles of sterling silver jewelry. **Boo Bracken & Co's Montage** (361 Hope St., 401/253-8614, noon–11 P.M. daily) is a fabulous shop bursting with Victorian-style hats and eclectic crafts. A stone's throw away in a striking yellow colonial house, **Alfred's Gifts and Antiques** (331 Hope St., 401/253-3465, 10 A.M.–5 P.M. Tues.–Sat., noon–5 P.M. Sun.) is one of Bristol's shopping highlights. There are several showrooms with an extensive selection of expensive and low-priced items, including Christmas decorations and home accessories. Nearby, **Kate and Co.** (301 Hope St., 401/253-3117, 10:30 A.M.–6 P.M. Mon.–Fri., 10 A.M.–6 P.M. Sat., noon–5 P.M. Sun.) is a similarly inviting boutique with gourmet foods, gifts, accessories, and clothing—a nice mix of goods with a country bent. **Robin Jenkins Antiques** (278 Hope St., 401/254-8958, 11 A.M.–5 P.M. Wed.–Sat., 1–5 P.M. Sun. but hours vary, call ahead) specializes in country pieces, painted tables and chairs, garden and architectural elements, and estate items; the selection is quite impressive.

The beautifully redeveloped waterfront complex Thames Street Landing (259 Thames St., opposite the foot of State St.) contains several fine shops in addition to the Bristol Harbor Inn. The **Claddagh Connection** (401/253-0000, 10:30 A.M.–6 P.M. Mon.–Sat., noon–5 P.M. Sun.) carries exquisite clothing, jewelry, and gifts imported from Ireland and Scotland; **Olde China Trader** (401/254-8954, 11 A.M.–5 P.M. Tues.–Sun.) stocks fine antique furniture, porcelain, and textiles from China.

Warren

Downtown Warren is honeycombed with antiques stores catering to every possible taste. One of the more unique is **Water Street Antiques** (147-149 Water St., 401/245-6440, noon–4 P.M. daily), which specializes in kitsch and retro lamps along with furniture that would seem at home in Josie and the Pussycats' pad. For period colonial, **The Meeting House** (47 Water St., 401/247-7043) has historic reproductions, old-fashioned candles, and light fixtures. Next to the Second Story Theatre, the nonprofit **IMAGO Gallery** (36 Market St., 401/245-3348, www.imagoartgallery.com, 4–8 P.M. Thurs., noon–8 P.M. Fri.–Sat.) shows a wide variety of works by local craftspeople and artists. You'll find photography, paintings, textiles, jewelry, ceramics, sculpture, and more. A huge three-story gift emporium that occupies what had been the Warren Antique Center, **Imagine** (5 Miller St., 401/245-4200, www.imaginegiftstores.com, 10:30 A.M.–5:30 P.M. Mon.–Sat., 10 A.M.–5 P.M. Sun.) keeps inveterate shoppers busy for hours with its extensive array of quirky goods. There are funky clothing and bedroom slippers, artful handmade jewelry, whimsical housewares and kitchen items, and gourmet knickknacks. Long home to luggage manufacturer Samsonite, Warren has a great bargain stop for luggage shoppers, the **Samsonite Factory Store** (95 Main St., 401/247-3302).

Warren's once notable antiques scene has diminished in recent years, but there are still several good shops concentrated in a small area, mostly around Main Street (Route 114) and Market Street, and then another section a couple of blocks west along Water Street, which runs parallel to Main Street. It's generally not hard to find a parking spot on or just off Main Street. Search for precious Staffordshire, Limoges, and other fine porcelain, crystal, and sterling at **Wren and Thistle Antiques** (19 Market St., 401/247-0631, http://wrenandthistlebandb.com, 11 A.M.–5 P.M. Mon.–Sat., 11 A.M.–4 P.M. Sun.), inside a 1910 telephone company building.

SPORTS AND RECREATION

One of the state's loveliest preserves and recreation areas, **Colt State Park** (off Hope St., 401/253-7482, www.riparks.com/colt.htm, sunrise–sunset daily, free) is a rolling waterside tract of about 470 acres with bike and walking trails (including a stretch of the East Bay Bike Path), numerous playing fields, fruit trees and flower gardens, and six picnic groves containing more than 400 picnic tables as well as an enchanting chapel-by-the-sea. Other facilities include a boat ramp, fishing areas, and grills; there is no beach and swimming is not permitted, however.

◖ East Bay Bike Path

The 14.5-mile East Bay Bike Path is a flat, 10-foot-wide, wonderfully scenic asphalt trail that hugs many sections of eastern Narragansett Bay from India Point Park in Providence to Colt State Park in Bristol. The path also welcomes joggers, strollers, inline skaters, and just about everyone with a yen for scenic rambles, provided they're not using motorized vehicles. The path, which follows the former Penn Central rail bed, covers a tremendously varied landscape from undeveloped waterfront to the lively commercial districts of Warren and Bristol. You can picnic at several spots along the way, and at several points on or just off the path you'll encounter places to stock up on snacks, deli sandwiches, and drinks. Bicyclists should keep to the right, others to the left. Dogs are permitted but must be on a leash (and you must pick up after them).

For any bike issues along the trail, you can stop at the small but friendly **Your Bike Shop** (51 Cole St., Warren, 401/245-9755, 10 A.M.–6:30 P.M. Tues. and Thurs.–Fri., 10 A.M.–5 P.M.

Wed. and Sat. Apr.–Oct., call for winter hours), located in Warren right off the bike path. The agile mechanics can fix a flat or other mechanical problem while you wait; the shop also sells maps and bike gear.

For rentals, head farther up the bike path to **East Providence Cycle** (414 Warren Ave., East Providence, 401/434-3838 or 800/235-BIKE—800/235-2453, www.eastprovidence-cycle.com, 9 A.M.–6 P.M. Mon., 9 A.M.–8 P.M. Tues.–Fri., 9 A.M.–5:30 P.M. Sat., 11 A.M.–5 P.M. Sun.), which has a second shop (111 Crescent View Ave., Riverside, 401/437-2453) farther south along the East Providence Bike Path. Rental rates run $25–50 for a full day.

The **Rhode Island Department of Transportation** (401/222-4203, ext. 4033, www.dot.state.ri.us/bikeri) produces a free booklet on bicycling titled *A Guide to Cycling in the Ocean State.* You can download the guide from the agency's website as a PDF file, or email or call for a print copy. The DOT website also has online bike maps, links to cycling organizations, and lots of other useful information. Additionally, the RIPTA buses that traverse the state are equipped with bike racks; the rack on the front of each bus holds up to two bicycles, and there is no additional fee to use them.

Beaches

The East Bay makes for an excellent beach outing, and while none of these towns front the ocean, they all have lovely spots for sunbathing, swimming, and playing in the summer sun. You'll find the most popular of the region's expanses at **Bristol Town Beach** (Colt Dr., off Rte. 114, 401/253-7000, www.bristolri.us/parks), a sprawling complex that includes athletic fields and tennis and basketball courts, where the beach is long and attractive. The **Warren Town Beach** (S. Water St., 401/245-0200, www.townofwarren-ri. gov), has parking for residents only; it's fairly easy to reach on foot from downtown, however, where there's metered parking and some public lots. It's also just off the East Bay Bike Path.

Fishing

There's great saltwater fishing in Mount Hope and Narragansett Bays and along the banks of the Warren and Sakonnet Rivers. Bluefish, snappers, scup, tautog, and flounder are among the most common catches. No license is required for saltwater fishing.

Golf

There are two short golf courses in the East Bay. The **Windmill Hill Golf Course** (35 Schoolhouse Rd., Warren, 401/245-1463 or 401/245-8979, 7 A.M.–1 hour before sunset daily, $14–23) has nine par-three holes ranging 118–220 yards. There's also a nice little restaurant open for breakfast, lunch, and early dinner daily. The **Bristol Golf Club** (95 Tupelo St., 401/253-9844, sunrise–sunset daily) is also just nine holes but plays a bit longer with a par of 36 (including one par 5) and a yardage of 2,273.

Sailing, Boating, and the Outdoors

As one of the world's great sailing hubs, it's not surprising that Bristol has an excellent school for this leisurely summer activity. The **East Bay Sailing Foundation** (401/253-0775, www.eastbaysailingfoundation.org) offers adult and youth sailing training on several kinds of sailboat. **Ocean State Adventures** (99 Poppasquash Rd., Bristol, 401/254-4000, www.kayakri. com) rents sea kayaks and leads nature tours and moonlight paddles in the bay.

There are also public boat launches throughout the East Bay, including the Town Beach, off Bay Road in Barrington; Haines Memorial Park, off Narragansett Avenue in Barrington; by the commercial fishing pier, off Water Street in Warren; at Bristol Narrows, off Narrows Road in Mount Hope Bay, which is off Route 136 in Bristol; at Colt State Park in Bristol; and at the foot of State Street, off Route 114 in downtown Bristol. The latter two launches are the most popular and scenic, and they put right into Bristol Harbor, from which you have good access to Narragansett Bay, the Sakonnet River, and the ocean.

You'll also find public marine facilities with water, electricity, and other amenities at the following marinas: **Ginalski's**

THE AMERICA'S CUP

In yachting circles, perhaps no competitive event carries more weight and prestige for its victor than the America's Cup race, which has been won a number of times by Rhode Island boats. Halsey C. Herreshoff of the America's Cup Hall of Fame in Bristol calls it the holy grail of yacht racing. The event was begun in 1851 as a companion to the Great London Exhibition, which sought to promote the world's many great technological successes, including those in transportation.

Held that year off the shores of the Isle of Wight, the competition of 1851 was called the All Nation's Race. In that event, a schooner called the *America*, helmed by John Cox Stevens of the New York Yacht Club, defeated a field of more than a dozen British ships to claim the prize.

For the next 130 years, a series of challenges were made on the trophy; the United States defended the America's Cup race continuously 1870–1983, disappointing challengers on no fewer than 25 occasions.

Rhode Island became famous for its ties with the America's Cup races starting in 1893, when the *Vigilant*, designed by Nathanael Green Herreshoff of the Herreshoff Manufacturing Company in Bristol, won the event. The next four competitions, in 1895, 1899, 1901, and 1903, were won again by Herreshoff boats; the most famous of these was the *Reliance*, which today serves as the logo for the Herreshoff Marine Museum. After a long break in the competition, Herreshoff produced the next America's Cup winner in 1920, the *Resolute*, and then two more ships that won in the 1930s and were helmed by magnate Harold S. Vanderbilt. For the first time in almost half a century, in 1937 the United States won the Cup with a ship that was not built at the Herreshoff boatyard, with a victory by the *Ranger*. The 1930 America's Cup event was the first of many that would be held off Newport, helping to ensure that city's reputation as the yachting capital of the world.

In 1983, in a race again held off Newport, the Americans were finally defeated by the *Australia II*, a ship owned by three-time challenger Alan Bond. Since then, the cup has bounced among American, Australian, New Zealand, and even Swiss champions. In 2010 the Americans won the 33rd America's Cup race off Valencia, Spain, in a 90-foot trimaran sponsored by American businessman Larry Ellison and German car company BMW.

THE EAST BAY AND SAKONNET

Boat Yard (6 Johnson St., Warren, 401/245-1940); **Stanley's Boat Yard** (17 Barton Ave., Barrington, 401/245-5090); **Bristol Marine** (99 Poppasquash Rd., Bristol, 401/253-2200, www.bristolmarine.com); and **Striper Marina** (26 Tyler Point Rd., Barrington, 401/245-6121). Striper Marina also offers full-day and half-day sportfishing charters on seven vessels.

Bird-watchers, hikers, and outdoors enthusiasts take to the nature trails at the **Osamequin Wildlife Sanctuary** (Rte. 114, Barrington, sunrise–sunset daily).

ACCOMMODATIONS

You'll find a smattering of B&Bs in Bristol and Warren, but it's also easy to explore the East Bay as a day trip from Providence or Newport, where there are many more lodging options. Also, just across the Massachusetts border in Seekonk, Swansea, and Fall River, you'll find a full range of chain hotels and motels.

$50-100

In Warren, the **Candlewick Inn** (775 Main St., Warren, 401/247-2425, www.candlewickinn. net) is, architecturally at least, something of a newcomer. This homey if modest clapboard bungalow was built in the early 1900s and retains the feel of that period, with polished wood floors, high ceilings, and scads of antiques and country quilts, many of them from previous generations of the innkeepers' families. There are just two rooms, one with twin beds that can be converted to a king and the other with one queen-size bed. Breakfast is a big event here. Well-tended gardens surround the house and are visible through several windows, and it's a short walk from the shops and restaurants of downtown Warren.

$100-150

In Warren, **Wren and Thistle Antiques** (19 Market St., Warren, 401/247-0631, http://wrenandthistlebandb.com, $120) rents an upscale, attractively furnished suite that can accommodate 1–2 guests (continental breakfast included). The B&B is set inside a 1910 telephone company building.

$150-250

Along Hope Street, steps from shopping and dining, is the **Rockwell House Inn** (610 Hope St., Bristol, 401/253-0040 or 800/815-0040, www.rockwellhouseinn.com, $219–279). The exquisitely restored Federal-style house dates to 1809, but various architectural elements and decorative details reflect the Greek Revival and Italianate influences of the subsequent decades. Rooms in this pink palace have high ceilings, high-quality period antiques, plush beds with soft linens, working fireplaces, and polished wood floors. Rockwell House is upscale and romantic but without the quaint-factor overkill prevalent in so many historic inns. A full breakfast is included.

In Bristol, the **Williams Grant Inn** (154 High St., Bristol, 401/253-4222 or 800/596-4222, www.wmgrantinn.com, $159–217) occupies a twin-chimney Federal-style colonial from 1808 that's right along Bristol's famous Fourth of July Parade route. The inn has many original features, including seven fireplaces (three of them in guest rooms) and two beehive ovens. Antiques and folk art fill the rooms. Accommodations are in five guest rooms, decorated with a mix of Victorian and colonial pieces, including blue-and-white porcelain lamps and dark-wood four-poster beds with floral quilts and throws. A full breakfast is served with specialties including blueberry-apple-cinnamon pancakes and bacon-and-egg pie. There's a peaceful fenced-in yard and patio out back.

The East Bay's largest and fanciest property, the 40-room **Bristol Harbor Inn** (259 Thames St., Bristol, 401/254-1444 or 866/254-1444, www.bristolharborinn.com, $155–249) was reconstructed along the scenic waterfront from a former bank and a rum distillery dating to about 1800. Guest rooms are simply decorated with understated nautical decor—but who needs wallpaper when you have a view of the harbor outside your window? Continental breakfast is served in the room where rum casks were once filled; wireless Internet is available throughout the hotel. On-site amenities include docking facilities, bike and boat rentals, and the excellent J. G. Goff's pub and restaurant. Many other excellent restaurants are within walking distance.

You can imagine yourself as lord of the manor at the **Governor Bradford House** (250 Metacom Ave./Rte. 136, Bristol, 401/254-9300, www.mounthopefarm.com, $175–250). Situated on Mount Hope Farm, a 200-acre preserve of fields, ponds, and woodlands, the house was once owned by an early Rhode Island governor and later by Rudolf Haffenreffer of Narragansett Brewing Company fame. And, of course, George Washington stayed here, in 1793 when he was an old man. Guest rooms are decorated with a designer's eye with canary or lime-green walls and grand four-poster beds; some guest rooms have working fireplaces.

Bristol Guest Suites (649 Hope St., Bristol, 401/396-9560, www.bristolguest-suites.com, $175) are three well-kept apartments that are great options for either weekend or weeklong stays. The three are The Sailor's Loft, a 500-square-foot studio overlooking Bristol Harbor; The Garden Loft, a small but airy one-bedroom; and The Harbor Loft. All have wireless Internet, queen beds plus a queen couch pullout, flat-screen televisions, and small but functional kitchen areas.

In the heart of downtown Bristol, few houses elicit more oohs and aahs than the **Bradford-Dimond-Norris House** (474 Hope St., Bristol, 401/253-6338 or 888/329-6338, $150–250), a decadent white wedding cake of a mansion run by the same owners as the Bristol Harbor Inn. The four guest rooms all have air-conditioning and modernized baths, but they're also replete with antiques, including four-poster canopy beds with white lacy linens, Oriental rugs, and country quilts.

Over $250

Perhaps the East Bay's most lavish and luxurious accommodations, the **Point Pleasant Inn** (333 Poppasquash Rd., Bristol, 401/253-0627 or 800/503-0627, www.pointpleasantinn.com, $350) sits on Poppasquash Point overlooking the sailboats of Narragansett Bay. The six sumptuously decorated guest rooms are over-the-top elegant, with rates to match the fine furnishings. All have deluxe bath amenities, bathrooms with both a tub and a stand-alone shower, hair dryers, fluffy bathrobes, and fine furnishings that include leather chairs, four-poster beds, antique mahogany tables and dressers, and noteworthy oil paintings. This 33-room mansion was built by a local business executive in 1940 and is run today like a small European-style hotel, with a solicitous staff that works hard to pamper guests. Facilities include a large in-ground pool with a slate deck, free use of bikes to take on the nearby bike path, a tennis court, croquet, an exercise room, an outdoor hot tub, a sauna, a music room, a billiards room, and an area for fishing in the bay.

FOOD

Considering the East Bay's small size and proximity to culinary powerhouses Providence and Newport, the peninsula has a surprisingly varied and polished dining scene. You'll find the best and brightest eateries in Bristol, most of them downtown along or near Hope Street. Less refined perhaps than Bristol, Warren's dining scene is extremely eclectic—and it's very easy to find a great meal here without spending a bundle of cash. Barrington has but a handful of casual eateries. If you're in the mood for fast-food or chain dining, cruise up and down Route 136.

Upscale

Channeling a Florentine trattoria, **Tuscan Tavern** (632 Metacom Ave., Warren, 401/247-

9200, www.tuscantavern.net, noon–9 P.M. daily, $6–25) serves Italian comfort food in cozy ambience. Some of the many pasta dishes have a New England spin, such as lobster ravioli with vodka cream sauce. A large brick oven churns out wood-grilled calzones.

A fixture overlooking Bristol Harbor since 1929, the **Lobster Pot** (119-121 Hope St., Rte. 114, Bristol, 401/253-9100, www.lobsterpotri. com, 11:30 A.M.–9 P.M. Mon.–Thurs., 11:30 A.M.–10 P.M. Fri.–Sun., $10–34) really must be experienced during daylight hours to be appreciated: Window-side tables put you directly on the water, and at dusk you can watch the sun slowly fall over the islands of Narragansett Bay. This is a spacious and somewhat dressy spot, though it is still casual, and service is excellent, especially considering it is one of the East Bay's more touristy venues. The menu varies from fairly simple and light bites (lobster salad sandwiches, Welsh rarebit with bacon served with a Caesar salad) to considerably more formal dinners—the usual surf-and-turf options, a decadently rich and delicious seafood casserole baked with butter and bread crumbs, blackened swordfish, and scallops Nantucket (baked with sherry and cheddar cheese). But the real pull here is the fresh-caught lobsters, which are available in several sizes boiled, broiled, grilled, or baked and stuffed "fisherman style" (with claws removed and filled with choice lobster meat and scallops). If money is no object, delve into the largest serving of the restaurant's eponymous crustacean—it is three pounds of pure joy, unless you're the lobster, of course.

A worthy reason for a foray into otherwise quiet Barrington, the **Tyler Point Grille** (32 Barton Ave., Barrington, 401/247-0017, www. tylerpointgrille.com, 4:30–9 P.M. Sun.–Thurs., 4:30–10 P.M. Fri.–Sat., $9–24) sits close to the confluence of the Barrington and Warren Rivers right by the East Bay Bike Path. It's a classic neighborhood restaurant with an upscale feel and sophisticated cuisine, along with some lighter options such as burgers and basic pasta pomodoro. It's also one of the nicer restaurants in the area to welcome children. Dining is in an airy room under a high ceiling with open views into the kitchen, where you might see

THE EAST BAY AND SAKONNET

chefs conjuring such tasty dishes as crab cakes with rémoulade sauce; gemelli pasta with veal sausage, asparagus, sun-dried tomatoes, and capers; and beef tenderloin with wild mushrooms, shallots, and a chianti wine reduction.

Creative but Casual

A dapper but small restaurant that opened in downtown Bristol in 2005, **Persimmon** (31 State St., Bristol, 401/254-7474, www.persimmonbristol.com, dinner from 5 P.M., $13–22) looks like a diner from the outside but is in fact a sophisticated bistro with a carefully planned wine list. Tables are tightly packed into the diminutive dining space and out on the sidewalk in warm weather, and the ever-changing menu lists a variety of enticing contemporary American dishes.

Bristol's fans of fine Italian fare adore **Roberto's** (301 Hope St., Bristol, 401/254-9732, 5–9 P.M. Mon.–Thurs., 5–9:30 P.M. Fri.–Sat., 5–8:30 P.M. Sun., $13–25). The preparation of the soft and silky polenta starter changes daily, and entrées such as cheese tortellini with prosciutto, snow peas, and yellow squash in a light pink cream sauce wow diners with superb execution and market-fresh ingredients. Beef eaters can savor the Black Angus New York steak with a mushroom madeira demi-glace. Roberto's is intimate, relaxed, and unprepossessing yet casually self-assured—the small dining room is staffed by a low-key, friendly bunch.

Redlefsen's (444 Thames St., Bristol, 401/254-1188, www.redlefsens.com, 11:30 A.M.–9 P.M. Mon.–Thurs., 11:30 A.M.–10 P.M. Fri.–Sat., 11:30 A.M.–8 P.M. Sun., $13–25), begun as a German restaurant, now offers a varied American and continental menu and is particularly noteworthy for its crab cakes and rotisserie chicken. A very nice weekend brunch is served. Other favorites from the kitchen include lightly breaded Wiener schnitzel sautéed and garnished with anchovy, lemons, and capers; and breast of chicken simmered in a sun-dried tomato and garlic cream sauce and finished with Gorgonzola cheese. On the menu, two wines are suggested with each entrée, a nice touch whether you're a seasoned veteran of wine-tasting or a novice curious to try new things.

Pizza and Pub Grub

With the most dramatic setting of any eatery in Bristol—even better than the Lobster Pot, although the latter has a more refined dining room—**J. G. Goff's** (251 Thames St., Bristol, 401/253-4523, 11 A.M.–10 P.M. Sat.–Thurs., 11 A.M.–11 P.M. Fri., $5–14) sits out on a dock at the end of State Street, attached to the handsome Bristol Harbor Inn. The entire second floor is a beautiful open-air deck with views of Prudence Island and clear down to Aquidneck. On the main level you can dine or rub shoulders with local college students, professionals, and visitors in a nautically themed pub-type room with ample seating (although it's tough to get a table on weekends). Happy hour draws a youngish, cruisy crowd, and there's live music many evenings. Casual American chow with an emphasis on seafood keeps everybody happy, but it's the ambience that makes J. G. Goff's a big winner.

A very true rendering of a genuine Irish pub, **Aidan's** (5 John St., Bristol, 401/254-1940, 11:30 A.M.–10 P.M. Mon.–Sat., 11:30 A.M.–9 P.M. Sun., bar 11:30 A.M.–1 A.M. daily, $6–14) makes a lovely diversion, whether killing time before boarding the ferry to Prudence Island, catching live music on a weekend evening, or hanging out with buddies over pints of stout and plates of hearty cooking. Friendly waiters and waitresses haul out heaping platters of burgers, fish-and-chips, bangers and mash, and pot pies. Across the street from Rockwell Waterfront Park, Aidan's has a handsome outdoor deck overlooking the bay.

The warmly furnished, old-fashioned **Judge Roy Bean's Saloon** (1 State St., Bristol, 401/253-7526, 4–9 P.M. daily, $6–13) is another atmospheric tavern with decent pub fare and a broad selection of imported ales, stouts, and porters. It's in the 1884 Holmes Block Building, a decadent three-story redbrick Victorian with a distinctive turret.

In Warren, dine on decent American and continental fare—lobster thermidor, broiled lamb chops—at the **Wharf Tavern** (215 Water St., Warren, 401/245-5043, 11 A.M.–9 P.M. Mon.–Thurs., 11 A.M.–midnight Fri.–Sat., 10 A.M.–1 P.M. Sun., $10–23), most famous for its wonderful views of the town's busy dock area and Narragansett Bay; it's especially memorable at sunset. The pub-like dining area has varnished woods, maritime memorabilia aplenty, and oil lamps on each table, and there's live entertainment on weekend evenings.

Ethnic Fare

The acclaimed Providence restaurant **India** (520 Main St., Warren, 401/245-4500, 11 A.M.–10 P.M. Mon.–Thurs., 11 A.M.–11 P.M. Fri.–Sat., $9–18) serves excellent Indian fare at its East Bay branch in downtown Warren. In addition to the usual standbys, India offers some unusual options, such as mussels steamed in garlic, lemon juice, and *chat* masala (tomato, cream, cardamom, fenugreek, and fresh cilantro); chicken in sweet-and-sour mango sauce; and fiery green-pea and chickpea *pulao* (with jalapeños, onions, cilantro, and mustard seed). It's one of the best eateries of this genre in New England—both for the food and the imaginative and bold decor. There's a trendy bar, Nirvana, above the restaurant.

Quick Bites

Just a block from the ferry to Prudence Island, **Leo's Ristorante** (365 Hope St., Bristol, 401/253-9300, 8 A.M.–9 P.M. Sun.–Thurs., 8 A.M.–10 P.M. Fri.–Sat., regular-size pies $8–12, sandwiches $4–7) opened in 1948 and is one of Bristol's most memorable dining traditions. The handsome old-fashioned storefront shop has high pressed-tin ceilings and ample sidewalk seating during the warmer months; it's a great spot for a light bite or a full meal after biking or strolling along Hope Street. The pizzas are exceptional and come with a variety of fine toppings, including broccoli rabe, chopped Portuguese sausage, and caramelized onions. A nice range of sandwiches is offered too, including a mouthwatering meatball sub. Beer and wine are served.

Bristol Bagel Works (420 Hope St., Bristol, 401/254-1390) is another appealing spot for lunch or a snack break. It is a sunny little café with blond-wood tables and Windsor chairs where you can nosh on a selection of about 15 kinds of bagels and spreads; traditional sandwiches are also offered. Right by the Bristol Harbor Inn is a branch of Tiverton's famous **Gray's Ice Cream** (259 Thames St., Bristol, 401/624-4500, 6:30 A.M.–9 P.M. daily summer, $2–6).

Always mentioned when locals start debating who serves the best New York System wieners in the state, **Rod's Grill** (6 Washington St., Warren, 401/245-9405, 6:30 A.M.–4 P.M. Mon., Wed., and Sat., 6:30 A.M.–7:30 P.M. Tues. and Thurs., 6:30 A.M.–6 P.M. Fri., $2–7) serves these juicy dogs with all the fixings along with a tantalizing array of short-order soups, sandwiches, and snackables. Rod's is open for breakfast and lunch only.

A small storefront selling wraps with exotic fillings, **Papa Joe's Wrap Shack** (567 Hope St., Bristol, 401/253-9911, www.papajoeswrapshack.com, noon–9 P.M. daily, $5–10) features varieties that include Mongolian beef and triple mushroom.

Java Joints

Break up an afternoon of strolling with refreshments at **Beehive Cafe** (10 Franklin St., Bristol, 401/396-9994, www.thebeehivecafe.com, 7 A.M.–6 P.M. Sun.–Wed., 7 A.M.–10 P.M. Thurs.–Sat., $4–7), an attractive café overlooking Independence Park and Bristol Harbor. Grab a table and chill out over smoothies, milk steamers (the chai is terrific), freshly made croissants, and fantastic chocolate cookies. The superfriendly staff will make you feel so at home that you may stay for the rest of the afternoon.

Downtown Warren's **Coffee Depot** (501 Main St., Warren, 401/608-2553, 6:30 A.M.–9 P.M. Mon.–Sat., 6:30 A.M.–8 P.M. Sun., $3–9) is a fun spot with funky atmosphere and a "living room" setting. The same owners also run the nearby health food shop, the Market at Cutler Mills (Child St. and North Cutler St., next to the East Bay Tourism Council offices).

Gourmet Goods and Picnic Supplies

In Bristol, pick up goodies for a picnic or light meal at **Bristol Bakery** (290 Wood St., Bristol, 401/254-8825, 6 A.M.–6:30 P.M., Mon.–Sat.,

6 A.M.–3 P.M. Sun., $6–8). It's a great place for fair-trade coffees and fine teas as well as hefty freshly made sandwiches on excellent breads (the cranberry walnut and marbled rye are local favorites).

INFORMATION AND SERVICES
Visitor Information
Pamphlets, brochures, and visitor information are available from the **East Bay Tourism Council** (16 Cutler St., P.O. Box 588, Warren, RI 02885, 401/245-0750 or 888/278-9948, www.eastbayritourism.com), whose offices occupy the restored Cutler Mills in downtown Warren. The town of Bristol runs a well-stocked **Visitor Center** in the basement of the town hall building (Burnside Bldg., 400 Hope St., Bristol, 401/253-7000, ext. 150, www.destinationbristol.com, noon–4 P.M. daily mid-May–Oct.); it has a full range of brochures as well as volunteers to answer questions about local attractions and to check availability for hotels and restaurants.

Media
The **East Bay Window** (401/253-6000, www.eastbayri.com) is a useful newspaper with tidal charts, features, and local tips. While it's geared toward locals, visitors will find it filled with useful information. The same publishers also produce the *Sakonnet Times*, *Warren Times-Gazette*, *Bristol Phoenix*, and *Barrington Times*.

GETTING THERE
Most visitors to the East Bay use a car to get around. Driving from Providence, it's a quick 12-mile, 20-minute trip down I-95 and Route 114 to Warren and 18 miles (25 minutes) to Bristol. From Newport, it's an equally quick 15-mile, 25-minute journey to Bristol and 20 miles (35 minutes) to Warren.

To reach the East Bay towns, you can also manage with **Rhode Island Transportation Authority (RIPTA) buses** (401/781-9400 or 800/244-0444, www.ripta.com), which pass through the busy town centers of Bristol and Warren and connect with Newport, Providence, and other large towns in the region. Buses from Providence to Bristol take 30 minutes and stop at the corner of Hope and State Streets. Fares are a reasonable $1.75 regardless of the distance.

GETTING AROUND
Within the towns, the central districts are small enough that you can see many of the key attractions on foot or by bicycle. There's ample street parking in Barrington, Warren, and Bristol, and there are municipal lots in Warren and Bristol.

Sakonnet

Originally named Pocasset by the Seaconnet Indians who lived here before selling the land to the Plymouth Colony in 1680, Tiverton and Little Compton to the south make up the Sakonnet Peninsula. It is not a true peninsula, since it shares a land border with Massachusetts to the east, but the area is nevertheless physically cut off from the rest of Rhode Island except by way of the Sakonnet Bridge (Route 24/138).

Sakonnet is the quiet corner of Rhode Island. Both Tiverton and Little Compton are small and pastoral with acres of flat farmland surrounded by trim stone walls and gray-shingled farmhouses that look as if they were airlifted from Nantucket. After exploring them both, it's amazing to consider that these two towns have a land area considerably larger than either Aquidneck Island (home to Newport, Portsmouth, and Middletown) or the East Bay towns of Barrington, Bristol, and Warren. In recent years suburbia has slowly crept into both towns, especially the northern reaches of Tiverton, but the two communities remain stubbornly bucolic. Little Compton has a large and close-knit summer community, many of the families having been regulars for generations. There are no miniature golf courses or amusements, however, just a handful of informal eateries, a yacht club, and a smattering of beach houses, most of them down quiet dirt lanes out of the public eye. Tourism isn't discouraged in these parts, but you won't find many places to stay or things to do, and that's just the way the locals and many visitors like it.

TIVERTON

Although Plymouth settlers bought the land that is now Tiverton in 1680, the town wasn't incorporated until 1694. No provisions for a church or school were made until 1746, shortly before the area, along with its East Bay neighbors to the north, were transferred to the Rhode Island colony.

During the Revolutionary War, however, the town's high bluffs overlooking the Sakonnet River and Aquidneck Island had tremendous strategic importance. From the town's shores, the Continental Army launched several raids on the British, who had settled comfortably in Newport and elsewhere on Aquidneck Island. Aside from the war, for its first 300 years Tiverton maintained a mostly agricultural existence with a smaller but still significant fishing industry.

Attractions are few, but shoppers will want to congregate around **Historic Tiverton Four Corners** (www.tivertonfourcorners.com), a village of mostly 18th-century houses full of boutiques, galleries, and cafés. It's at the junction of Routes 77 and 179, a few miles south of Route 24, the main road through the peninsula. Beachcombers should wander along **Grinnell's Beach** (Rte. 77), a narrow spit of sand where an old stone bridge used to cross the Sakonnet River before the towering Sakonnet Bridge replaced it. It's a scenic place to admire the river.

LITTLE COMPTON

Once the domain of the Seaconnet Indians, who were ruled in the late 1680s by a female chieftain named Awashonks, Little Compton is an enchanting town for bicycling and country driving. The town's history as a summer resort predates even the Civil War, making it one of New England's oldest retreats. Like Tiverton, it has also drawn heavily on fishing and agriculture to support itself. You can reach it most easily and scenically by driving south from Tiverton either on Route 77, on the west side of town, or Route 81, on the east side.

As you explore the west side of Little Compton by car or by bike, you can enjoy great views of the Sakonnet River and the many historic homes along Route 77. On your left, not long after crossing from Tiverton into Little Compton, you'll reach the **Wilbor House** (Rte. 77, 401/635-4035, tours 2–5 P.M. Wed.–Sun. mid-June–mid-Sept., free), a lovely old clapboard farmhouse with several restored outbuildings. Parts of the house date to the 1690s, but it has been added onto several times through the centuries. You can also picnic on the grounds.

◀ Sakonnet Vineyards

Still farther south along Route 77, Sakonnet Vineyards (162 W. Main St., Rte. 77, Little Compton, 800/919-4637, www.sakonnetwine. com, 10 A.M.–6 P.M. daily Memorial Day–Sept., 11 A.M.–5 P.M. daily Oct.–Memorial Day) has transcended New England's reputation for lackluster grapes to produce some exceptionally fine wines. Back when wine was a solely West Coast phenomenon, Susan and Earl Samson rolled the dice in Rhode Island, where they surmised the cool microclimate could support vines similar to those in France's Loire Valley. Founded in 1975, the vineyard has since been a smashing success—one of the first in New England and still among the best. Acres of grapevines produce several wines from the winery's signature vidal blanc grape, a French-American hybrid with floral aromas and fresh acidity. Also notable is the aromatic gewürztraminer. Sakonnet produces about 30,000 cases of wine each year, proving that it's far more than a boutique winery. Along with over the 50 acres of scenic vineyards, the

THE EAST BAY AND SAKONNET

© MICHAEL BLANDING

Sakonnet Vineyards produces some of the best wine in New England.

winery features tours, tastings, and an out-door café with a menu specially created for pairings.

Continuing South

South of Sakonnet Vineyards down Route 77, make a left on Meeting House Lane; at the end of this short road you'll come to **The Common,** perhaps the most enchanting little town green in Rhode Island. Almost entirely without commercial enterprise, the grassy plot stretches out beneath the towering spire of the United Congregational Church, most of it covered with gravestones, some of which date to the 1600s. Across from the church you'll find the legendary town commissary, the Commons Restaurant.

For even more quaint scenery, at the far end of the peninsula on Sakonnet Point is a collection of pleasingly ramshackle fishing villages with a strand of sandy beach just past the Sakonnet Yacht Club. Each summer the small harbor fills with sailboats and yachts and sunbathers crowd the local beach, but this vacation community remains sleepy and laid-back, looking much as it probably did a century ago. Some 600 yards offshore on an iron pier, **Sakonnet Point Light** (www.lighthouse. cc/sakonnet) is a majestic 66-foot-tall cylindrical tower still lit at night.

Adamsville

East of The Common is an even more backwater part of the peninsula named Adamsville. A brass plaque erected in 1925 sits at the center of the village, commemorating the Rhode Island Red, a type of chicken that was developed in Adamsville and revolutionized chicken farming, as it was the first both to lay eggs and provide meat.

On Main Street you'll find the 1788 **Gray's Store** (4 Main St., Adamsville, 401/635-4566, 6:30 A.M.–8 P.M. daily), reputedly the oldest continuously operating store in the United States. It still has the original soda fountain and penny-candy case along with a mini-museum of historical ephemera. A little farther east along Main Street (Route 179), just before the state border marker for Westport, Massachusetts, you'll pass a quirky old shop on your right called **Gray's Gristmill** (508/636-6075, www.graysgristmill.com, noon–4 P.M. Tues.–Sun.). Here you can buy authentic Gray's Old-Fashioned Rhode Island Johnny Cake Corn Meal as well as gifts, homemade jams, a few odd furnishings, and inexpensive bric-a-brac ranging from junk to some neat little finds.

To get to Adamsville from Little Compton Common, continue east along Simmons Road, make a left on East Main Street, and follow it north as it jogs up to Peckham Road. Make a fast right and then a left again onto Long Highway, make another quick right onto Colebrook Road, and follow it into Adamsville.

SHOPPING

In Tiverton, you'll find several fine shops at **Historic Tiverton Four Corners** (Rtes. 77 and 179, Tiverton, www.tivertonfourcorners.com), most of them inside the restored 18th- and 19th-century houses of the village's original residents. Among the highlights is the **Metal Works** (401/624-4400), which specializes in antique lanterns but can also custom-create all kinds of home furnishings and arts. At **Peter's Attic** (401/625-5912, 11 A.M.–5 P.M. Thurs.–Sat., noon–5 P.M. Sun.), you'll find three floors of fine country and colonial antiques. **Little Purls** (401/625-5990) carries a colorful and clever assortment of children's clothing and gifts, while **Sakonnet Purls** (888/624-9902, 10 A.M.–5 P.M. Tues.–Sat., noon–5 P.M. Sun.) offers one of the greatest assortments of yarn and needlework in southern New England.

Check out the fabulous array of hand-hooked rugs, throws and pillows, imported Italian and French pottery and ceramics, pine furniture, and stylish home accents at **Lou Lou's Decor** (104 Clock Tower Square Plaza, Tiverton, 401/624-8231, 10 A.M.–5 P.M. Thurs.–Sat., noon–5 P.M. Sun.).

Tucked into the back side of the Little Compton Commons, the **Commons Cottage Gallery** (7 South of Commons, Little Compton) has high-quality local art at reasonable prices. **Wilbur's General Store** (50 The

© MICHAEL BLANDING

Gray's Store is also home to a museum housing historical ephemera.

THE EAST BAY AND SAKONNET

Commons, Little Compton, 401/635-2356, 7:30 A.M.–7 P.M. Tues.–Sun.) is a reminder of life before Home Depot and Wal-Mart: a small shop stuffed with groceries, housewares, beach pails, hardware, and a deli counter with gourmet foodstuffs.

Just southwest of Adamsville Center, the **Old Stone Orchard** (33 Cold Brook Rd., Little Compton, 401/635-2663, 10 A.M.–5 P.M. Thurs.–Sun. fall only) has pumpkins, apples, and similar fall fare.

RECREATION

There aren't many formal venues for recreation in this region, but it's a wonderful place for many kinds of activities, especially bicycling on local roads. The terrain is relatively flat, and excellent views of the sea and rolling meadows are to be had in both towns, especially Little Compton.

You'll find excellent birding and hiking, as well as beachcombing, down at the southeastern tip of Little Compton at **Goosewing Beach Preserve** (off South Shore Rd., Little Compton, 401/331-7110, www.nature.org). There's a beach parking fee of $5 Memorial Day–Labor Day; at other times it's free. The Nature Conservancy oversees this pristine barrier beach and neighboring Quicksand Pond, and guided nature walks are given throughout the summer.

Fishing enthusiasts will find great opportunities for saltwater fishing from **Grinnell's Beach,** by the old Stone Bridge site off Route 77 in Tiverton, and also a bit farther south at Sapowet Point.

Hiking

In Tiverton, the **Emilie Ruecker Wildlife Refuge** (Seapowet Ave., Tiverton, 401/949-5454, www.asri.org) has some 50 acres of marsh environment crisscrossed by trails. Bird-watching blinds offer a chance to see snowy egrets, glossy ibis, and a breeding pair of ospreys.

Northwest of the Common in Little Compton on the way to Adamsville, you'll pass the turnoff for **Simmons Park,** a 400-acre plot laced with trails, shrub wetlands, a red maple swamp, and oak and American beech woodland. Here you can spot cottontail rabbits, foxes, mink, wood and mallard ducks, ospreys, and owls. Wild turkeys were released here in recent years and have become somewhat common. Note that this is also the town hunting grounds; all visitors must wear fluorescent orange when walking through the preserve during hunting season (Oct.–Feb.).

Beaches

The Sakonnet Peninsula has a number of attractive beaches with considerably smaller crowds than those in nearby Newport. **Grinnell's Beach** (Main Rd. at Old Stone Bridge) is a sandy crescent at the head of the Sakonnet River and is popular with surf fishers; it has a lifeguard, changing rooms, and restrooms. On the southeast tip of the peninsula, **Goosewing Beach Preserve** (off S. Shore Rd., Little Compton, 401/331-7110, www.nature. org, parking $5 Memorial Day–Labor Day) is a spectacular expanse of sandy barrier beach that narrowly divides the sea from a series of pristine coastal ponds.

ACCOMMODATIONS

Your options for spending the night, short of befriending a resident, are greatly limited in Tiverton and Little Compton. You'll find just two inns, both in Little Compton, and a few bed-and-breakfasts. Still, it's a short and easy drive to Sakonnet from Newport, Bristol, and Fall River, Massachusetts, all of which have ample lodging choices.

One dependable option is **Harmony Home Farm Inn** (465 Long Hwy., Little Compton, 401/635-2283, www.harmonyhomefarm.com, $130–175), where the rooms and cottages either have their own entrances and private porches or come with fully equipped kitchens.

Among the more unusual lodging options in Rhode Island is **Stone House Club** (122 Sakonnet Point Rd., 401/635-2222, www. stonehouseclub.com), technically a private club. The policy is that the accommodations and restaurant are intended for "members and their guests, primarily residents and folks who summer here, who find us to their liking." Most of the guests came to know the club through friends or associates who live in the area, but an introduction is not required. If you call and ask about staying, and you're comfortable with the terms, the Stone Club will book you a room (but first, you must agree to pay the $25 one-year membership fee). It's a great deal, considering the guest rooms here have rates beginning at just $60 or so for a shared bath and about $85 for a private bath (continental breakfast is included). The building dates to 1836, when the builder of Little Compton's first breakwater, at Sakonnet Point, constructed this stone house for his wife and 13 children. A narrow spiral staircase winds up to the guest rooms—those in the rear face out over a broad, neatly groomed lawn, an estuary, and the ocean. Furnishings are charmingly simple and even a little scruffy, as rooms have wood paneling, wood floors or rather dated carpeting, and cozy beds that in some cases take up two-thirds of the living space. The guest rooms range greatly in size and include a large suite that accommodates a family of five and has a kitchen; there are also several modest units with tight quarters. Because this is a private club, the hotel has a particularly friendly, low-key feel—not one of exclusivity, but rather common interest and appreciation of Little Compton and its antigrowth, preservation-minded ethic. Sakonnet Light is a short bike ride away, and this place has considerably more charm than the hundreds of comparably priced motels throughout coastal Rhode Island. There's a full-service restaurant (again, members only), which is useful if you're staying at the hotel. Dining is in a tap room and a formal dining room, and food varies from simple country tavern cooking to quite elaborate French and Pan-Asian specialties.

Intimate and romantic, **The Roost** (Rte. 77, Little Compton, 800/919-4637, www.sakonnetwine.com, $130–190) offers a peaceful, easygoing vibe. You'll feel miles and miles removed from the touristy fray of Newport and urban bustle of Providence at this three-room

B&B that occupies an old shingle farmhouse at Sakonnet Vineyards. Of course, oenophiles adore The Roost, as it puts them just steps from Sakonnet's tasting room, and the accommodations face out over the 45 rolling acres of neatly planted grape vines and beautifully manicured gardens. Guest rooms, all with private baths, have recently been updated with a neat mix of colonial and country furnishings; it's not fancy, but for the setting, The Roost represents a terrific deal.

FOOD

Although not as limited in dining possibilities as in places to stay, Sakonnet has but a few eateries. Quality and quirky ambience are hallmarks of dining in these parts—the restaurants are generally quite good and in some cases worth a trip from anywhere in the state.

Creative but Casual

The top pick in this area when it comes to special occasions, **Four Corners Grille** (3841 Main Rd., Tiverton, 401/624-1510, 11 A.M.–8:30 P.M. Mon.–Thurs., 11 A.M.–9 P.M. Fri., 8 A.M.–9 P.M. Sat., 8 A.M.–8:30 P.M. Sun., $6–17) is nothing fancy on the outside, but this neighborhood spot with cozy wooden booths, warm lighting, down-to-earth service, and limited parking excels in the food department, presenting a consistently excellent menu of regional American and Italian dishes at extremely fair prices. In season, try the soft-shell crab scampi. Other treats include shrimp Mozambique (a house specialty in which shrimp is served over pasta with hot peppers and a piquant sauce popular in Portuguese restaurants), herb-crusted grilled scrod with Maryland-style creole crab cakes, several kinds of burgers, tuna-steak sandwiches (with a lime-cilantro dressing), and seafood bisques.

The **Stone Bridge Restaurant** (1848 Main Rd., Tiverton, 401/625-5780, 11:30 A.M.–9 P.M. Sun.–Wed., 11:30 A.M.–10 P.M. Thurs.–Sat., $6–17) overlooks the boating activity along the Sakonnet River, sitting just across the street from the former bridge for which it's named. This is a locals' favorite, a good bet for unfussy yet surprisingly sophisticated Greek and Italian fare—the starter of mussels steamed in white wine with feta sits well on a chilly winter day. You can get traditional standbys—the usual mix of pastas, meatballs, steaks, and clam platters—but it's the more interesting Greek sausage with Greek salad or roast duck with a tangy-sweet black cherry sauce that deserve the greatest acclaim. If you're more in the mood for something light, there are many lighter options and sandwiches, available even at dinner.

Quick Bites

Gray's Ice Cream (16 East Rd., Tiverton, 401/624-4500, www.graysicecream.com, 6:30 A.M.–9 P.M. daily summer only) occupies a low-slung shingle building at Tiverton Four Corners. Since 1923 it has been making fans of frozen sweets happy with such homemade flavors as blueberry, coconut, maple walnut, peach brandy, and ginger. Swarms of devotees check in regularly to order their favorites and check on the new flavors added each season.

Near the Sakonnet River and overlooking Nanaquaket Pond, **Evelyn's Drive-In** (2335 Main Rd., Rte. 77, Tiverton, 401/624-3100, www.evelynsdrivein.com, 11:30 A.M.–8 P.M. daily, $2–9) delivers a somewhat more substantial variety of short-order goodies, from grilled tuna and swordfish to the usual lobster rolls, fried oysters, and chowders. It's perfect before an outing at the beach.

One of the Ocean State's great culinary institutions, **The Commons Lunch** (48 Commons, Little Compton, 401/635-4388, 6 A.M.–7 P.M. Sun.–Thurs., 6 A.M.–8 P.M. Fri.–Sat., $2–9) boasts an epic menu of diner-esque favorites, including massive but thin—almost crepe-like—jonnycakes. Breakfast is served all day, and the jonnycake special comes with two eggs, two cakes, and bacon. Stuffed seafood rolls are a favorite, and the quahog chowder is good but not quite worthy of its legendary status; old-timers seem to like the liverwurst sandwiches. Few desserts hit the spot better than the strawberry ice cream with freshly made strawberry sauce. This endearing little restaurant is named for the town common, which it

© MICHAEL BLANDING

Grab some jonnycakes at The Commons Lunch.

faces. The original building of this enormously popular gathering spot burned to the ground in 2004 and was subsequently reconstructed.

The Barn (15 Main Rd., Adamsville, 401/635-2985, $3–8) occupies an elegantly weathered 200-year-old clapboard barn. It's all about breakfast here—the place closes at noon on weekdays and 1 P.M. on weekends. More than a few foodies claim The Barn serves the best breakfasts in Rhode Island, and the lines on summer weekends are maddeningly long. A specialty is Eggs on the Bayou, poached eggs on English muffins with crab cakes and creole hollandaise sauce. If you have a sweet tooth, you can dig into raspberry-filled French toast with crème anglaise, toasted almonds, and fresh berries. Be sure to order a side of ostrich sausage.

Gourmet Goods and Picnic Supplies

In Tiverton Four Corners, you'll find a pair of shops stocked with fine foods, picnic supplies, and enchanted edibles. **Milk and Honey Bazaar** (3838 Main Rd., Tiverton, 401/624-

1974, http://milkandhoneybazaar.com, 10 A.M.–6 P.M. Mon.–Fri., 10 A.M.–5 P.M. Sat., noon–5 P.M. Sun.), in a cheerful cottage just north of the intersection, proffers white truffle oil, lavender honey, duck prosciutto, sea salt, pâtés, quince jam, and some of the most unusual and hard-to-find cheeses in southern New England. This shop is truly a gourmet find and well worth the drive from anywhere in the state. **The Provender** (Tiverton Four Corners, 401/624-8084) occupies the ground floor of a magnificent three-story Second Empire house crowned with a tall square cupola. There are long wooden benches on the wraparound porch, which is a lovely place to watch the world go by. In addition to selling imaginative, high-quality sandwiches and sweets, the Provender has fresh picnic supplies and a fine choice of goods for a bike ride. It sells olive oil, fancy mayonnaises, and sauces. The Virginia Lynch art gallery is attached.

INFORMATION AND SERVICES
Visitor Information
There's no formal visitors center on the Sakonnet Peninsula. For pamphlets, brochures, and visitor information, your best bet is the **Newport County Convention and Visitor's Bureau** (23 America's Cup Ave., Newport, 800/976-5122, www.gonewport.com).

GETTING AROUND
As in the East Bay towns, a car is the only viable way to get around Sakonnet. These are quiet little towns where parking is easy to find, usually off the street, except in summer by the beach in Little Compton.

THE EAST BAY AND SAKONNET

PROVIDENCE

The story of Providence's renaissance through the past two decades has been well documented in the media and by local boosters, but many people still have little sense of this hilly city of 175,000—the second-largest metropolis in New England. Travelers tend to focus on Rhode Island's coastal half; after all, it is the Ocean State. But Providence has grown into a distinctive and dynamic destination of its own. It's the state's culinary center as well as a hub for visual and performing arts. Providence possesses a larger and better-preserved district of colonial architecture than any other city in the United States. For many travelers, that is reason enough to spend time in Rhode Island, and as a destination, the city's rise in popularity has only just begun.

Beginning in the early 1980s, Providence invested many millions of dollars to reinvent its downtown, uncover and landscape the long-buried river system, and turn itself into a first-rate city. Plenty of U.S. cities have attempted the same sort of comeback in recent years, and few have done a better job than Providence, especially in terms of what the city now offers visitors. Starting with development of a fabulous arts district through sweeping tax incentives for artists and galleries, city hall helped develop a phenomenal restaurant scene by assisting in the financing of such ventures, dismantled a dreary downtown rail system, and uncovered and restored two long-forgotten rivers, transforming a muddled city center into a picturesque walking district that invites visitors to explore.

The downtown presence of major colleges and universities—Brown University, the Rhode

© MICHAEL BLANDING

HIGHLIGHTS

LOOK FOR ◖ TO FIND RECOMMENDED SIGHTS, ACTIVITIES, DINING, AND LODGING.

◖ **WaterPlace Park and Riverwalk:** The centerpiece of Providence's dramatic downtown renaissance, this four-acre park and river walk makes for a scenic stroll (page 118).

◖ **Culinary Arts Museum:** The largest collection of its kind in the world, this museum about all things culinary and food-related resides at the esteemed Johnson and Wales University. Check out the collection of more than 7,500 vintage cookbooks (page 122).

◖ **Federal Hill:** This bustling neighborhood just west of downtown might be the most dynamic Little Italy in the country, with dozens of first-rate restaurants, cafés, and gourmet food shops (page 123).

◖ **First Baptist Church in America:** Home to the first-ever Baptist congregation, established by city founder Roger Williams in 1638, this regal building dates to 1775 and is a marvel not only because of its rich history but also its architectural splendor (page 124).

◖ **John Brown House:** The highlight of Providence's most famous historic thoroughfare, Benefit Street, this three-story Georgian mansion dates to 1786 and abounds with fine colonial furnishings and decorative arts (page 126).

◖ **RISD Museum of Art:** Much more than your usual college art gallery, the RISD art

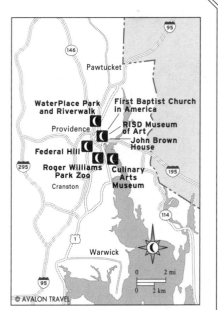

museum is a world-class museum offering an overview of visual art history dating back thousands of years (page 129).

◖ **Roger Williams Park Zoo:** It's worth venturing a bit off the beaten path to visit Providence's 430-acre oasis, notable for its fine gardens and greenery, first-rate zoo, and museum of natural history (page 134).

Island School of Design (RISD), Providence College, Johnson and Wales—accounts for the many offbeat and inexpensive shops and eateries, hip nightclubs, and stylish-looking 20-somethings slinking about. Densely populated, free-spirited, and progressively tolerant, Providence is one of the more politically liberal cities in the United States, and its most famous institution, Brown University, is one of the more politically liberal schools in the world. Many people think of Boston as left of center, which

by many measures it is, but Providence cultivates a significantly more freewheeling and bohemian arts, music, and political scene. It's less buttoned-down than its neighbor 50 miles to the north, and the high percentage of creative types (RISD is an arts school, and Johnson and Wales is famous for its culinary programs) infuses the city with an edgy, countercultural demeanor that you'd expect more of New York City or San Francisco than of a New England state capital.

PROVIDENCE

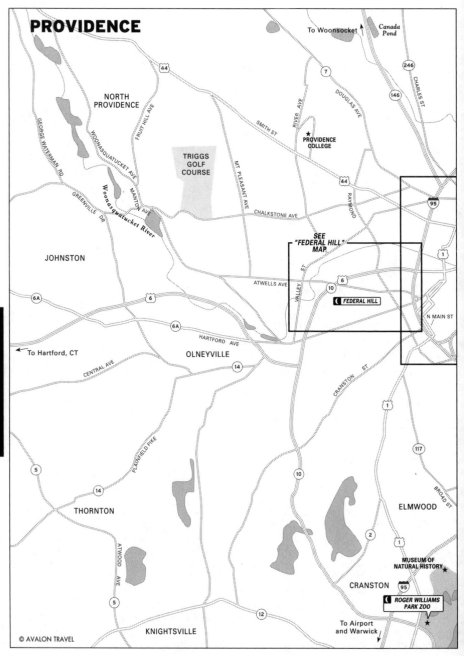

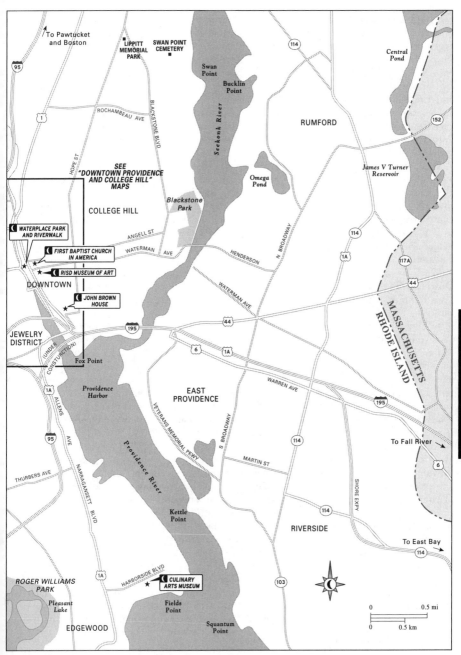

To Pawtucket
and Boston

95

1

LIPPITT
MEMORIAL
PARK

SWAN POINT
CEMETERY

Central
Pond

114

152

ROCHAMBEAU AVE

BLACKSTONE BLVD

HOPE ST

Swan
Point

Bucklin
Point

Seekonk River

RUMFORD

James V Turner
Reservoir

SEE
"DOWNTOWN PROVIDENCE
AND COLLEGE HILL"
MAPS

COLLEGE HILL

Blackstone
Park

Omega
Pond

114

1A

117A

WATERPLACE PARK
AND RIVERWALK

ANGELL ST

WATERMAN AVE

FIRST BAPTIST CHURCH
IN AMERICA

RISD MUSEUM OF ART

DOWNTOWN

N BROADWAY

HENDERSON

WATERMAN AVE

44

JOHN BROWN HOUSE

195

44

JEWELRY
DISTRICT

6

1A

Fox Point

(UNDER
CONSTRUCTION)

1A

ALLENS AVE

Providence
Harbor

EAST
PROVIDENCE

WARREN AVE

195

MASSACHUSETTS
RHODE ISLAND

To Fall River →

6

VETERANS MEMORIAL PKWY

S BROADWAY

114

THURBERS AVE

NARRAGANSETT BLVD

Providence River

MARTIN ST

SHORE EXPWY

Kettle
Point

114

To East Bay

114

ROGER WILLIAMS
PARK

1A

HARBORSIDE BLVD

CULINARY
ARTS MUSEUM

RIVERSIDE

103

Pleasant
Lake

Fields
Point

EDGEWOOD

Squantum
Point

0   0.5 mi

0   0.5 km

PROVIDENCE

ORIENTATION

Providence is separated into East Side and West Side by the Providence River, which flows through the middle of town. On the east, College Hill rises sharply to form almost a palisade, with Brown University and the Rhode Island School of Design anchoring its slopes. The south boundary of the East Side is Fox Point, a thriving Portuguese community that is also home to many students.

West of the river, a relatively flat network of curving streets forms downtown, also known as Downcity, a business district that also includes the city's major hotels and dining and cultural attractions. South of Downcity, the Jewelry District is a hip neighborhood of dance clubs, restaurants, and stores.

West of downtown, I-95 separates Downcity from the many mostly working-class residential neighborhoods that form the city's West Side. Finally, Olneyville (or just "Olney"), for years the main Hispanic enclave in Providence, has sucked up hipster cred from the Jewelry District and has an ever-changing circus of noise-rock bands, zine publishers, bicycle co-ops, and anarchist fairs among the former mill buildings.

PLANNING YOUR TIME

If you're visiting Rhode Island for the first time, especially if you're seeking a seaside vacation, you should probably think of Providence more as a day trip or at the most a weekend getaway than as the primary focus of your trip. You could see the best of the city's museums in one well-planned day. But if you're a shopper, a foodie, an aficionado of historic preservation, a theatergoer, a gallery hopper, or a live-music fan, you'll easily find plenty here to keep you busy for several days.

HISTORY

The history of Providence is closely linked to the history of Rhode Island. The city's founder, Roger Williams, an early proponent of the separation of church and state, was found guilty of heresy and banished from the colony of Massachusetts in 1636. He sought refuge among the southern Indian tribes, acquiring a written deed in 1638 from the chiefs of the Narragansett people, Canonicus and Miantonomoh.

The residents of Providence took particularly strong exception to financial demands leveled by the English crown on Rhode Island. In 1772 they burned the British tax ship the *Gaspée,* and three years later held their own tea party, modeled on Boston's, on March 2, 1775.

By 1820, Providence's population stood at about 12,000, having doubled since the Revolution—it was the seventh-largest city in the young republic. It remained a commercial powerhouse, in part because of the early industrial successes of the textile mills in Pawtucket. One rather unusual industry, jewelry manufacturing, remains a staple of the city's economy to this day. All kinds of costume jewelry and related products are still produced here. To support the factories, the city increasingly opened its doors to immigrants, mostly of Italian, Portuguese, French-Canadian, and Swedish descent, who formed ethnic enclaves throughout the city.

Providence endured a steady economic decline beginning with the Depression and lasting through World War II and well into the 1970s. The city had nowhere to go but up by the time a plucky and ambitious new mayor named Vincent "Buddy" A. Cianci Jr. took office, spurring a dramatic renaissance that has resulted in the dynamic city we see today. The city reclaimed its waterways by uncovering two rivers that had been paved over a century ago, and Venetian-inspired foot and auto bridges were built over the rivers. The Rhode Island Convention Center opened in 1993, and Providence Place Mall followed in 1999. The city bolstered such successes in the past decade with incentives to lure artists and restaurateurs to revitalize its downtown, a transformation that is still underway today.

ROGER WILLIAMS AND FRIENDS

You don't hear the phrase so much these days, but the greeting "What cheer, netop?" is supposedly what helped convince religious and political dissident Roger Williams to drop anchor at the confluence of the Woonasquatucket and Moshassuck Rivers. The year was 1636, and the place we now know as Providence.

"Netop" can be translated loosely to mean "friend." An amiable Native American spoke the greeting to a no-doubt dejected but determined Williams, who was paddling down the Seekonk River in search of a place to build a new settlement. After spending five years as an assistant minister, first in Salem, then in Plymouth, and then back in Salem, Williams had alienated himself from the Puritans for two reasons: First, he condemned the Puritans' unwillingness to split completely from the Anglican Church of England, a bold step the founders of the Massachusetts Bay and Plymouth Colonies could not bring themselves to take; and second, he believed that the colonies' governing bodies had no business whatsoever monitoring and controlling the religious beliefs and practices of its citizens. Essentially, Williams was an early proponents of the separation of church and state, and also a practitioner of unconditional religious tolerance.

His insistence on articulating these then-radical and seditious views eventually forced the hand of the Massachusetts Bay Colony powers, who convicted him for his contrary and dangerous beliefs in 1636 and made plans to deport him back to England. In February 1636, with arrest imminent, Williams and his wife, Mary, fled the colony, first spending time with the Wampanoag Native Americans between the Plymouth and Providence regions.

After making a brief stab at forming a settlement in East Providence, Williams sailed down the Seekonk River, where he heard the encouraging greeting from a Narragansett Indian, or so the story goes. He continued south and then west around India Point and turned north around Fox Point up the Great Salt (now Providence) River. Here Williams and five compatriots encountered a gurgling fresh spring, where they founded Providence.

© MICHAEL BLANDING

A statue of Roger Williams gazes at the Rhode Island State House.

Sights

THE STATE HOUSE AND RIVERWALK
The State House

A good place to begin a walk around the city is the grounds of Providence's white-marble-domed State House (bounded by Francis, Gaspee, and Smith Sts., 401/222-2357, http://sos.ri.gov/publicinfo/tours, 8:30 A.M.–4:30 P.M. Mon.–Fri., guided tours at 10 and 11 A.M. Mon.–Fri., free). Built in the late 1890s by McKim, Mead, and White, the leviathan work in white Georgia marble dominates grassy and hilly grounds of several acres. The enormous dome ranks among the largest freestanding domes in the world. Free tours of the interior last just under an hour but are not particularly impressive unless you are a big fan of government architecture. The tours do take in a replica of the famous Liberty Bell and one of the famous portraits of George Washington by Rhode Island artist Gilbert Stuart.

◖ WaterPlace Park and Riverwalk

South of the State House, the imposing facade of Providence Place Mall and the four-acre WaterPlace Park and Riverwalk anchor the city's much-touted renaissance. Once a large tidal basin, the area was filled in 1892 by the Providence and Worcester Railroad and laid over with rail lines and yards. You'd never believe the area's industrial past today: A newly created pond now lies approximately where the northern end of the basin once did, and various entertainment events, mostly rock and pop music, are presented at an adjacent outdoor amphitheater.

One of the more unusual ways to take in the revitalized riverfront is by gondola. Contact **LaGondola** (WaterPlace Park, next to Citizens Plaza, 401/421-8877, www.gondolari.com, 5–11 P.M. Sun.–Thurs., 5 P.M.–midnight Fri.–Sat., $79–159 for 2 people) for a ride aboard one of its Venetian-style gondolas. The 45-minute ride runs the length of the landscaped Riverwalk. You supply the beverages, alcoholic or not, and up to six people, and the gondolier will serenade you with schmaltzy but endearing love songs. It's a good idea to make reservations, especially on weekend evenings. The fare is about $159 for the first two people and $15 for each additional passenger in your group for a private boat. It's still possible to ride without reservations—just show up at the landing by Citizens Plaza, and if the gondola is available, you're free to book a 15–20-minute excursion; the price for this shorter trip is $40 pp. It's customary to tip your gondolier 15–20 percent.

About 10 evenings per year, generally Saturdays May–October, **Waterfire Providence** (401/272-3111, www.waterfire.org) dazzles spectators who come to marvel at the more than 100 bonfires set in cauldrons on pylons along the rivers. The fires, which burn from sunset to midnight, seem to dance

LaGondola brings a taste of Venice to downtown Providence.

COURTESY OF PROVIDENCE WARWICK CVB

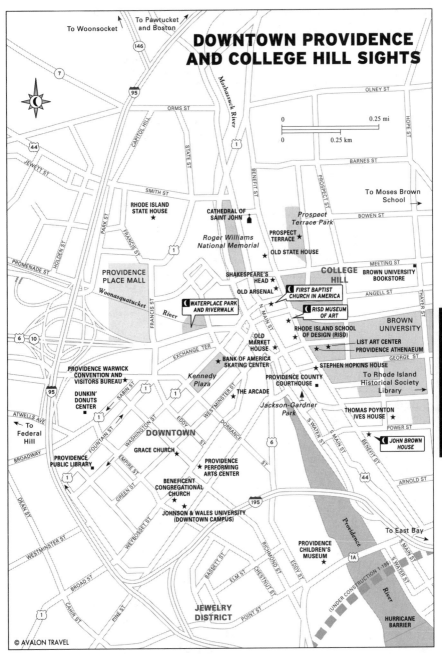

DOWNTOWN PROVIDENCE AND COLLEGE HILL SIGHTS

To Woonsocket

To Pawtucket and Boston

146

7

95

MDshassuck River

OLNEY ST

HOPE ST

ORMS ST

1

0   0.25 mi

0   0.25 km

44

JEWETT ST

CAPITOL HILL

STATE ST

BARNES ST

PARK ST

SMITH ST

BENEFIT ST

PROSPECT ST

To Moses Brown School

BOWEN ST

HOLDEN ST

FRANCIS ST

RHODE ISLAND STATE HOUSE ★

CATHEDRAL OF SAINT JOHN ◼

Roger Williams National Memorial

Prospect Terrace Park

PROSPECT TERRACE ★

MEETING ST

PROMENADE ST

PROVIDENCE PLACE MALL

Woonasquatucket

River

OLD STATE HOUSE ★

SHAKESPEARE'S HEAD ★

COLLEGE HILL

BROWN UNIVERSITY BOOKSTORE ■

ANGELL ST

THAYER ST

6 10

FRANCIS ST

(WATERPLACE PARK AND RIVERWALK

OLD ARSENAL ★

N MAIN ST

(FIRST BAPTIST CHURCH IN AMERICA

(RISD MUSEUM OF ART

BROWN UNIVERSITY

EXCHANGE TER

OLD MARKET HOUSE ★

RHODE ISLAND SCHOOL OF DESIGN (RISD) ★

LIST ART CENTER ★
PROVIDENCE ATHENAEUM ★

GEORGE ST

95

PROVIDENCE WARWICK CONVENTION AND VISITORS BUREAU ★

BANK OF AMERICA SKATING CENTER ★

Kennedy Plaza

STEPHEN HOPKINS HOUSE ★

PROVIDENCE COUNTY COURTHOUSE ■

To Rhode Island Historical Society Library →

SABIN ST

1

1

DUNKIN' DONUTS CENTER ■

THE ARCADE ★

Jackson-Gardner Park

S WATER ST

S MAIN ST

BENEFIT ST

THOMAS POYNTON IVES HOUSE ★

POWER ST

ATWELLS AVE

← To Federal Hill

WASHINGTON ST

WESTMINSTER ST

DORRANCE ST

6

(JOHN BROWN HOUSE

BROADWAY

FOUNTAIN ST

EDDY ST

DOWNTOWN

PROVIDENCE PERFORMING ARTS CENTER ★

ARNOLD ST

1

PROVIDENCE PUBLIC LIBRARY ■

EMPIRE ST

GRACE CHURCH ★

DEAN ST

GREEN ST

BENEFICENT CONGREGATIONAL CHURCH ★

195

JOHNSON & WALES UNIVERSITY (DOWNTOWN CAMPUS) ★

Providence

River

To East Bay

WEYBOSSET ST

WESTMINSTER ST

BASSETT ST

ELM ST

RICHMOND ST

CHESTNUT ST

EDDY ST

PROVIDENCE CHILDREN'S MUSEUM ★

1A

S MAIN ST

S WATER ST

BROAD ST

PINE ST

POINT ST

JEWELRY DISTRICT

(UNDER CONSTRUCTION I-195)

HURRICANE BARRIER

CADIR ST

1

© AVALON TRAVEL

PROVIDENCE

BUDDY CIANCI AND THE PROVIDENCE RENAISSANCE

As infamous as he is famous, Providence legend Buddy Cianci was one of the longest-serving mayors of a major U.S. city and first Italian American mayor of Providence. He's also one of the country's most controversial (and yet popular) political figures, inspiring everything from outrage to fascination – and even a high-profile documentary film about his life, released in 2006.

There's no question that a good deal of the credit for the city's so-called renaissance, as Cianci himself often referred to it, goes to this Huey Long–like mayor, who was convicted in 2002 of one "racketeering conspiracy charge accusing him of masterminding a criminal scheme that took bribes for favors, including tax breaks, jobs, and sweetheart deals on city-owned land," according to the *Providence Journal*. It was the culmination of an investigation into city officials that the FBI called Operation Plunder Dome. Given the conviction, Cianci decided not to run for another term.

Whatever their politics, just about everybody in Providence has a serious opinion on Cianci, the guy *Boston Magazine* described as a "born politician who could schmooze Satan." The colorful, controversial, stocky politico has had his hand – or his strong arm, some might say – in Providence politics since his dark-horse election to the mayor's office in 1974. Given Providence's relative prominence vis-à-vis the rest of the state, Cianci has obtained power and attention that seem more fitting of a state governor than a city leader.

At a time when Providence and virtually every other Northeastern city with working-class roots was down in the dumps, Cianci largely spearheaded an effort to recover downtown from the throes of urban blight and turn the city into a bona fide tourism and business destination. When a lot of people thought the idea was crazy, he believed that Providence could compete with Boston and even New York City for tourism dollars and corporations – and on some level, he succeeded.

Many things have helped Providence to recover, and Cianci is only responsible for some of them, but you really can't help but admire the genius of certain moves, such as offering low-interest city financing to restaurateurs to

above the water's surface, the flames choreographed by artist and creator Barnaby Evans to the sounds of classical and evocative world-beat music. The aroma of burning cedar, oak, and pine lends a distinct ambience to this ritual. Written descriptions of this highly unusual multimedia presentation are inadequate—try to check this one out in person.

DOWNTOWN

The part of Providence that most resembles the downtown of any Northeastern city lies just south of the WaterPlace Park area, bounded on the east by the Providence River, on the west by I-95, and on the south by the remains of the old I-195. Nicknamed **Downcity,** it is less a formal neighborhood than an urban core of commerce and business, though some arts and cultural attractions are included in

the mix. The northern and eastern fringes of the neighborhood have experienced the wave of the city's gentrification, especially the commercial area that borders WaterPlace Park. The area is anchored by the Providence Convention Center, the adjacent Westin Providence hotel, and across the street the Courtyard by Marriott hotel. Next to that, the former train station and nearby buildings now contain restaurants and offices.

Kennedy Plaza

Immediately south of the train station, across from Exchange Place, a grassy park faces **Providence City Hall** and extends across Kennedy Plaza, home to the city's bus terminal, the hub through which virtually every bus in Rhode Island seems to pass. Here too is the **Bank of America Skating Center** (2 Kennedy

lure them into the city and out of the wealthier suburbs. In the age of eating out, this trend has helped bring droves of suburbanites and visitors into the city, helping to infuse new blood into once-dowdy areas and to support a slew of related businesses such as hotels, art galleries, and nightclubs.

With the crude enthusiasm and gusto of a used-car salesman, and with plenty of bravado, determination, and innovation, he largely accomplished his aims. But there is a troubling side to this charmingly raffish character. Not only was Cianci convicted of racketeering, he has watched as one city political crony after another has gone down on corruption and bribery charges.

More infamously, in 1984 Cianci himself was convicted of violent crime. It was no white-collar tax dodge or sweetheart deal; he was arrested and pleaded no contest to kidnapping and then beating up his estranged wife's boyfriend with a fire log and burning him with a lighted cigarette. The loveable emperor of Rogue's Island, as the Ocean State is sometimes mockingly called, clearly revealed his unpleasant side.

He spent the term of his five-year suspended sentence as the host of a radio talk show, which drew fantastically high ratings. In 1991 Cianci ran for mayor again and won, this time capturing 97 percent of the vote – astounding when you consider he was a convicted felon and a Republican in a mostly Democratic and liberal state (although on most social issues, Cianci has a thoroughly progressive record). True to form, Cianci apparently went right back to his shady ways.

After his latest conviction in 2002 for racketeering, Cianci was sentenced to five years and four months in prison. He resigned as mayor a few days later and began serving his sentence at Elkton Federal Correctional Institution in Ohio, but of course, that wasn't the end of the story. Released in 2007, Cianci promptly returned to the airwaves with both a radio show and a job as special commentator on WLNE, TV channel 6, where he can be seen every weekday at 4 P.M. in a segment called "Buddy TV." He was later named chief political analyst for the station, disproving F. Scott Fitzgerald's famous maxim that there are "no second acts in American lives."

Plaza, 401/331-5544, ext. 5, www.kennedy-plaza.org/skating-information, 10 A.M.–10 P.M. Mon.–Fri., 11 A.M.–10 P.M. Sat.–Sun., adults $6, children $3), which contains a rink and offers ice skate and roller skate rentals. Kennedy Plaza underwent a major revitalization that saw the bus stands transformed into a new state-of-the-art transportation center. Various efforts have been made to bring the area to life, from farmer's markets to weekend festivals during the warmer months. In truth, however, beyond the skating center there's not a huge amount to see or do here. On the southwest corner of Kennedy Plaza, at Dorrance and Washington Streets, note the grand Providence Biltmore Hotel, built in 1922. A plaque on the facade shows the high-water mark reached during the devastating hurricane of 1938, which ravaged all of southern New England.

Extending south from Kennedy Plaza are a network of mostly one-way streets. The main east–west ones are Washington, Westminster, Weybosset, and Pine, and the main north–south ones are Dorrance, Eddy, Mathewson, and Empire. Visitors should see this neighborhood during the day, not because it's unsafe at night but because there's little to see or do after dark. The neighborhood's main draw is its wealth of fine 19th-century and early-20th-century commercial architecture, although quite a bit of it, especially on the floors above street level, has been vacant for years.

Along Weybosset Street

As you walk south through Downcity, consider strolling on Weybosset Street. Among other things, the street is home to perhaps the most distinguished architectural gem in downtown

Providence, **The Arcade** (65 Weybosset St., 401/598-1199), which dates to 1828 and is the oldest indoor shopping center in the nation. This magnificent example of Greek Revival architecture, designed by James C. Bucklin and Russell Warren, is made of granite and rests under a dramatic glass skylighted roof, its two entrances fronted by a dozen 13-ton Ionic columns. Once home to a variety of stores, the structure was closed in 2008 when its owners began an $8 million renovation; its future remains uncertain.

Farther down Weybosset Street to the southwest is the **Beneficent Congregational Church** (300 Weybosset St., 401/331-9844, www.beneficentchurch.org), an 1809 structure that is the oldest building in this neighborhood. It is notable for its massive gilded dome, which was added in 1836. Only slightly newer but quite famous because of its design by church architect Richard Upjohn, **Grace Church** (175 Mathewson St., 401/331-3225, www.gracechurchprovidence.org, 9 A.M.–1 P.M. daily) is a Gothic Victorian of somber brownstone presided over by an octagonal spire; its chimes resound throughout downtown.

In addition to the architecture in this neighborhood, another attraction is the **Providence Public Library** (150 Empire St., 401/455-8000 or 401/455-8090, www.provlib.org, 1–9 P.M. Mon.–Thurs., 12:30–5:30 P.M. Fri.–Sat., 1–5 P.M. Sun.), which has an art gallery with rotating exhibits.

Just around the corner from the library you'll find the always daring **AS220** art space (115 Empire St., 401/831-9327, www.as220.org, 1–6 P.M. Wed.–Fri., noon–4 P.M. Sat., free), plus the downtown campus of **Johnson and Wales University** (Weybosset and Empire Sts., 401/598-1000, www.jwu.edu). Begun by Gertrude Johnson and Mary Wales as a business-education school in 1914, Johnson and Wales has become a world leader in its technology, hospitality, and culinary arts programs; there are additional campuses in Miami; Charleston, South Carolina; Denver; Norfolk, Virginia; and Gothenburg, Sweden. Television chef Emeril Lagasse, who grew up just over the border in Fall River, Massachusetts, is among the most famous alumni.

◖ Culinary Arts Museum

If you're something of a foodie—or even just like to eat—don't miss the Culinary Arts Museum (315 Harborside Blvd., 401/598-2805, www.culinary.org, 10 A.M.–5 P.M. Tues.–Sun., $7 adults, $2 children) at the Johnson and Wales Harborside campus. The world's largest culinary archive, it contains every imaginable bit of food minutia, including an exhaustive and fascinating cookbook collection, some dating from the 1500s. Exhibits trace different types of food and how, when, and where they became popular over time, and the museum sheds light on the evolution of kitchen gadgetry and equipment and how restaurants have changed through the years. An excellent exhibit traces the history of diners in the United States—a history that has its roots right in Providence. Other exhibits include a re-creation of a classic New England tavern; rare tableware from presidential state dinners; and the Pantheon of Chefs, with display cases devoted to many of the world's kitchen greats, including many items owned by beloved chef Julia Child. Note that the archives are south of the downtown campus, a short drive away on the Providence-Cranston border, but this is one museum that's well worth going out of your way for; just don't come on an empty stomach.

JEWELRY DISTRICT

Fairly quiet during the day, the Jewelry District comes alive at night as a dynamic district of nightclubs and a handful of eateries. What may eventually make this neighborhood even more significant is the tentatively planned multiple-museum complex at Heritage Harbor, which has been postponed indefinitely. The complex was being developed inside a neoclassical turn-of-the-20th-century power plant on the Providence River at Eddy and Point Streets that had been donated to the city by the Narragansett Electric Company. The structure is within walking distance of downtown and the East Side, which is across the river and easily reached via a short bridge.

For the foreseeable future, Heritage Harbor has one attraction that's open, the **Providence Children's Museum** (100 South St., 401/273-5437, www.childrenmuseum.org, 9 A.M.–6 P.M. daily summer, 9 A.M.–6 P.M. other seasons, $5), which moved from Pawtucket in 1997. This engaging hands-on museum offers a range of cool exhibits, including a children's garden that takes visitors through a touch-friendly tour of trees, shrubs, and plants native to Rhode Island; a fun house of mirrors with a walk-through kaleidoscope; a miniature animal hospital sponsored by the Providence Animal Rescue League; and an toddler-oriented area called Littlewoods, in which participants can scamper through simulated caves and climb trees.

Just a short drive south of here via Allens Avenue is one of the city's newest attractions, the **Juliett 484 Russian Sub Museum** (Collier Point Park, off Allens Ave., 401/823-4200, www.juliett484.org, 10 A.M.–6 P.M. Sat.–Sun., $8). The museum is an actual former Soviet nuclear cruise-missile submarine, built in 1965, that patrolled the oceans for three decades before starring in the Hollywood thriller *K-19: The Widowmaker* with Harrison Ford and Liam Neeson.

◖ FEDERAL HILL

Go ahead, make those jokes about crime bosses and imagine characters from *The Sopranos* or a Mario Puzo novel sauntering along Atwells Avenue, the main drag of Providence's own Little Italy, Federal Hill. Just keep the jokes quiet, and don't spend a lot of time staring at guys who fit the image of a modern-day mob boss. Maybe there's a mafia presence here these days, maybe there isn't; unquestionably there have been mob-related busts here in the past. What you will find along Atwells Avenue, and also surrounding the charming neighborhood hub **De Pasquale Square,** are terrific restaurants and food shops that seem right out of a Roman streetscape. Years ago, local filmmaker Michael Corrente brought a bit of fame to the

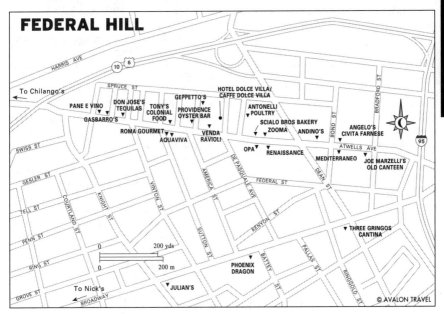

neighborhood by shooting the movie *Federal Hill* here.

The neighborhood begins just west of where Atwells Avenue crosses I-95, and you'll know you've found it the second you pass under the lighted **Federal Hill Arch,** from which an Italian pinecone hangs as a symbol of welcome. For about 15 blocks you'll find shops and eateries offering various delectables, not to mention dry-goods stores and a few random tattoo parlors. This is one stroll on which you probably won't burn any net calories.

ALONG THE RIVERFRONT

The city's East Side is divided from downtown by the Moshassuck River north of about Thomas Street, and then the Providence River south of that. While it is dominated by College Hill, several attractions line the waterfront just across the river. You can get a real sense of modern Providence's humble origins by visiting the site of the original natural springs where Roger Williams established a settlement, now the **Roger Williams National Memorial** (282 N. Main St., 401/521-7266, www.nps.gov/rowi, dawn–dusk daily). This 4.5-acre plot and the visitors center (9 A.M.–4:30 P.M. daily, free) dates from 1730, making it one of the oldest structures in the city; it's easily accessible from downtown hotels and lies just a few blocks east of the State House via Smith Street, at the lower slope of College Hill.

Outside the visitors center in the park, the **Bernon Grove** of trees and plantings commemorates the life of Gabriel Bernon, a French Huguenot who fled persecution in Europe in the 17th century for Providence, where he helped found the Cathedral of St. John (just across the street from the park). Marking what is believed to be the exact spot where the natural springs once flowed, the **Hahn Memorial** is a shapely sculpture named for the first Jewish citizen of Providence to hold elected office.

Just across from the Roger Williams National Memorial stands an elegant example of Georgian ecclesiastical architecture, the Episcopal **Cathedral of St. John** (271 N. Main St., 410/331-4662, www.cathedralofstjohn.

org), which also contains a number of Gothic elements, from tall lancet windows to a Gothic belfry. John Holden Greene designed the church in 1810, but the congregation dates back much earlier, when Gabriel Bernon established King's Chapel here with Nathaniel Brown. The adjoining cemetery contains graves of many of the city's early luminaries.

Those unfortunate enough to be found guilty of serious crimes in colonial Rhode Island were pilloried nearby, at the southwest corner of North Main and Haymarket Streets. The pillory stood until 1837, long after this form of punishment had ended. The home of Roger Williams stood behind what is now 235 North Main Street, nearly overlooking the spring where the state's founder decided to establish the city of Providence in 1636. The site of the city's first mill was at the corner of North Main and Mill Streets, where John Smith founded it in 1646.

The Providence Preservation Society has headquarters at the distinctive three-story wooden building known as **Shakespeare's Head** (21 Meeting St., 401/831-7440, www.ppsri.org). The 1772 house has enjoyed a colorful history, having served originally as the print shop for the city's first newspaper, the *Providence Gazette and Country Journal,* and then as the city's post office. Postmaster John Carter, who had been appointed by U.S. Postmaster-General Benjamin Franklin, not only oversaw the mail; he also sold books and writing materials. A sign depicting the head of William Shakespeare once hung outside the front door to advertise the shop. The Preservation Society tends a delightful restored colonial herb and flower garden (open to the public) behind the house; it has examples of flora commonly grown during the colonial period, including such flowering lovelies as Carolina silverbell, herbaceous peonies, foxglove, and wisteria.

◖ First Baptist Church in America

It may lack the height of the downtown skyscrapers, but the First Baptist Church in

America (75 N. Main St., 401/454-3418, www. fbcia.org) nevertheless effects a more dramatic influence on the city's skyline than any other building. Roger Williams established this parish in 1638, making it the nation's first such congregation. Interestingly, within just a few years, Williams parted ways with the Baptist Church, unable to reconcile his membership of any "earthly church" with his own devout beliefs in the New Testament. In 1700, member Pardon Tillinghast, who built the city's first wharf, constructed a meetinghouse for the congregation—at his own expense—along North Main Street. This structure was succeeded by a larger church in 1726, and in 1775 by the present Baptist church, whose triple-tiered spire rises to 185 feet.

A glimpse inside reveals the remarkable craftsmanship of the times, the five-bay vaulted ceiling rising majestically above rows of wooden pews. Pause to wonder exactly how the builders were able to hoist the church bell, which was cast in London and weighs 2.5 tons, to the belfry. Other notable elements include a massive crystal chandelier built in Ireland and brought over in 1792, and an elaborate E. and G. G. Hook organ that was installed in 1834. If you can time it right, visit during one of the congregation's many wonderful organ concerts.

Around North Main Street

The **Providence Art Club** (11 Thomas St., 401/331-1114, www.providenceartclub.org, noon–4 p.m. Mon.–Fri., 2–4 p.m. Sat.–Sun., or by appointment, free) occupies a pair of late-18th-century houses right around the corner from the First Baptist Church. Here you can visit the free galleries, which present rotating exhibitions of club members' works—this is a popular stop on the monthly Providence Gallery Night.

Thomas Street ranks among the city's most charming, offering historic residential architecture on a steep grade. A couple of doors over from the Providence Art Club, the half-timbered **Fleur-de-Lys Building** (7 Thomas St.) was the home of prominent Rhode Island

painter Sidney R. Burleigh until his death in 1929. Edmund R. Willson created the medieval-inspired structure, which has housed artists' studios since Burleigh's death. The **Deacon Edward Taylor House** (9 Thomas St.) dates to 1790 and was the residence of the deacon of the First Congregational Church for many years. The building is noteworthy for its steep-pitched roof.

Just down the hill from Brown University, directly on the Providence River, you'll find the beautifully preserved 1773 **Old Market House** (in Market Sq.), built as the city's agora, where farmers from outlying areas met to sell their goods in town. French soldiers were quartered in the building during the Revolutionary War. The building was designed by Joseph Brown and Stephen Hopkins.

An odd sight along North Main Street, right at Waterman Street, is the mouth of a large road tunnel that runs under College Hill and opens onto Thayer Street. The only way to pass through it is to take a bus across the East Side. The North Main Street entrance to the tunnel marks the spot where Roger Williams traditionally gathered townspeople for meetings and discussions on local government.

College Street marks the transition from North to South Main Street. South Main contains a curious mix of historic residences, funky and increasingly swanky restaurants and a few shops, vintage redbrick commercial structures, and new offices. Structures worth noting as you stroll along include the 1774 **Joseph Brown House** (50 S. Main St.), the home of one of the four famous Brown siblings. Joseph Brown took to architecture and designed this staunch redbrick city home with a widow's walk on the roof; he also designed the First Baptist Church and the Old Market House. Note the **Old Stone Bank** (86 S. Main St.), former home of the Providence Institution for Savings, which was the city's first savings bank and one of the country's oldest. The imposing gilt-domed neoclassical building dates to 1898. The private **Cooke House** (112 S. Main St.) is named for resident Benoni Cooke, grandson of Governor Nicholas Cooke. The Federal mansion dates to the 1820s and is considered one of John Holden Greene's finest residential architectural accomplishments.

Jackson-Gardner Park

Around the Westminster and Pine blocks of South Main Street is Jackson-Gardner Park, a small landscaped patch with benches shaded by tall oak trees and the inspiring 75-foot-tall World War Monument. The park is named for F. Ellis Jackson, who in 1933 built the **Providence County Courthouse** (30 S. Main St.) across the way, and Henry B. Gardner, a naval officer of note in World War II. The formidable eight-story neoclassical structure, built of red brick and limestone, covers a full city block. A four-stage square tower crowned by a cupola stands sentry over the vast structure, notable for its stepped, flanking gabled wings. Few buildings on the East Side command more respect, both architecturally and practically speaking, than the courthouse.

COLLEGE HILL

Rising precipitously to the east just past the river is College Hill, home to both Brown University and the Rhode Island School of Design and the heart of Providence's dynamic profusion of colonial and 19th-century architecture.

The city's "Mile of History," Benefit Street, runs parallel to North and South Main Streets just a block east but in most places many feet higher in elevation. During Providence's heyday as a colonial shipping center, and then throughout the 19th century's industrial periods, wealthy city residents built their homes along or just off Benefit Street, which remained fashionable well into the early 20th century. After World War II, however, and coinciding with the so-called "white flight" to the suburbs that affected most large U.S. cities, many of the old homes along Benefit Street were boarded up, and others were subdivided into boarding houses and cheap apartments. During the city's renaissance, which began in earnest in the late 1970s, the Providence Preservation Society began to restore Benefit Street house by house.

Walking through the neighborhood today, it's hard to believe that it was ever blighted—all told, you'll find about 200 buildings that date to the 18th and 19th centuries along Benefit Street, which is strung with vintage gas lamps and lined by brick sidewalks.

Providence Preservation Society Heritage Tours (21 Meeting St., 401/831-7440, www.ppsri.org), offers both guided and self-guided walking tours of the neighborhood. At certain times during the year, the general public gets a glimpse inside some of these exceptional examples of homes built in the colonial era through Victorian times, and sometimes into the elaborate gardens that surround them. In June, you can attend the **Festival of Historic Houses,** a two-day event of house and garden tours along Benefit Street. Then in December, come for the **Holiday Festival of Historic Homes** (401/831-8587), a Benefit Street ramble that includes carolers and street performers in period garb along with tours of several of the neighborhood's most prominent homes.

One of the first you'll come to as you walk north from Transit or James Streets is the immense **Nightingale-Brown House** (357 Benefit St., 401/863-1177, www.brown.edu/Research/JNBC, 8 A.M.–4 P.M. Mon.–Fri. summer, 8:30 A.M.–5 P.M. Mon.–Fri. other seasons, free). Colonel Joseph Nightingale built the enormous square hip-roofed house in 1792, Brown University founder Nicholas Brown bought the house in 1814, and his son John Carter Brown amassed an unrivaled collection of artifacts and documents here that traced the New World's early history. (This collection is now housed at the library at Brown University that bears his name.) The house remained in the Brown family into the 1980s and is now, appropriately enough, part of Brown University.

◀ John Brown House

Arguably the most imposing of the neighborhood's many impressive homes is the Rhode Island Historical Society's John Brown House (52 Power St., 401/273-7507, www.rihs.org,

1–4 P.M. Tues.–Fri., 10 A.M.–4 P.M. Sat. Apr.–Nov., 10 A.M.–4 P.M. Fri.–Sat. Jan.–Mar., $8 adults, $4 children). The sixth U.S. president, John Quincy Adams, described this as "the most magnificent and elegant private mansion I have seen on this continent." Exquisitely restored and furnished top to bottom, it still looks swanky today—few American house-museums from this period rival it. Inside you'll find a first-rate assemblage of colonial furnishings and decorative arts.

John Brown, a fabulously successful merchant and one of the masterminds of the *Gaspée* incident, began construction on the three-story Georgian mansion in 1786. For many decades during the building's first century, attending a party at the Brown House was obligatory for society types and academics. In 1941 the house was bequeathed to the Rhode Island Historical Society, which set about reproducing the interior's original colors and French wallpaper. Furnishings include many created by local artisans William Clagget, a clockmaker, and Goddard-Townsend, a Newport firm that specialized in high-quality colonial wood furnishings.

Other Historic Houses

Note the private **Thomas Poynton Ives House** (66 Power St.), one of the city's most important and impressive colonial mansions. The Georgian colonial dates to 1811 and is notable for its finely crafted rail running along the roofline and semicircular portico, which was added in the 1880s. Another noteworthy private home, the **Edward Carrington House** (66 Williams St.), demonstrates the shift around the early 1810s from Georgian colonial to Federal architecture (also called the Adam style). The three-story brick mansion was built in 1811, and the final story was added shortly after the original construction. With heavy stone corner quoins and lovely elliptical fanlights above the front door, it stayed in the Carrington family well into the 20th century.

Governor, U.S. senator, and Civil War general Ambrose Burnside may be best-known for lending his nickname to what we commonly call sideburns. The Rhode Island native, who wore a prominent pair of them, lived for many years at the now-private 1850s redbrick Victorian at 314 Benefit Street, between Power and Charlesfield Streets, a dramatic edifice with wrought ironwork around it.

Undoubtedly the most kindly street intersection you'll ever come upon, the corner of Benefit and Benevolent Streets is the site of John Holden Greene's **First Unitarian Church** (1 Benevolent St., 401/421-7970, www.firstunitarianprov.org), a structure with a tall steeple and magnificent classical revival detailing known for housing the largest bell ever cast by Paul Revere's foundry.

A particularly fine example of a mid-18th-century colonial home, the **Stephen Hopkins House** (Benefit St. and Hopkins St., 401/421-0694, www.stephenhopkins.org, 1–4 P.M. Fri.–Sat. May–Oct., free) was home to noted colonial governor Stephen Hopkins during his 10 terms at the helm of Rhode Island. Exhibits and artifacts in the house document his life and times as a signatory of the Declaration of Independence and Brown University's first chancellor. On warm days, be sure to stroll out back through the museum's exquisite parterre garden.

Providence Athenaeum

Among the oldest libraries in North America, the Providence Athenaeum (251 Benefit St., 401/421-6970, www.providenceathenaeum.org, 9 A.M.–7 P.M. Mon.–Thurs., 9 A.M.–5 P.M. Fri.–Sat., 1–5 P.M. Sun. Sept.–May, 9 A.M.–7 P.M. Mon.–Thurs., 9 A.M.–5 P.M. Fri., 9 A.M.–noon Sat. June–Aug., free), dates to 1753 and contains such rare and fascinating works as the seven volumes of the original double elephant folio edition of John J. Audubon's *Birds of America*. Rare works by Robert Burns, an early-19th-century study of Egypt commissioned by Napoleon titled *Description de l'Égypte*, and several books from 14th-century Europe are additional highlights of the Rare Books Collection.

The Athenaeum was established in 1831 and moved into this majestic Greek Revival structure in 1838. In the late 1840s Edgar Allan Poe and Sarah Whitman spent many an hour discussing literature and admiring one another's works in the Athenaeum's corridors. In addition to priceless original literary volumes and a comprehensive modern collection that can be viewed by any visitor (and taken out on loan by members), the Athenaeum houses several rare artworks, including *The Hours,* a famous painting by Newport-born miniature painter Edward G. Malbone.

Other Sights Along Benefit Street

A distinct departure from the many fine residences along Benefit Street, the formidable concrete **Old Arsenal** (176 Benefit St.) was designed in 1840 by James Bucklin, the same architect who designed downtown's Arcade and the nearby Providence Athenaeum. Behind the imposing Gothic Revival facade of white stucco with a giant green wooden door that looks like something out of "Jack and the Beanstalk" it housed troops during both the Dorr Rebellion and the Civil War.

Until the construction of the present-day State House near Providence Place Mall, Rhode Island's General Assembly met at the **Old State House** (150 Benefit St., 401/277-2678, www.rihphc.state.ri.us, 8:30 A.M.–4:30 P.M. Mon.–Fri.), the surprisingly humble-looking brick-and-sandstone structure dating to 1762 (its wooden predecessor burned down in 1758). From its first days, it served not only as the political center but also the social and commercial heart of the colony: In a juxtaposition of politics and commerce, the first floor was an open goods market while politicians assembled upstairs to debate and pass laws. On May 4, 1776, the young assembly passed what is considered the first declaration of independence in the United States, the Rhode Island Independence Act. Surprisingly, the state used this humble building as its capitol until 1900, when the current grand building was constructed.

A short distance up Benefit at stands a lavish private home known as the **Sullivan Dorr House** (109 Benefit St.), one of the city's most admired early-19th-century structures. The three-story mansion, built by Sullivan Dorr with fortunes accrued through overseas trade, contains a magnificent Palladian window whose design is loosely modeled on that of the English villa owned by the poet Alexander Pope. Sullivan Dorr's son Thomas's noble aim of universal suffrage inspired the infamous uprising in 1842 now known as the Dorr Rebellion.

In the 1790 colonial house at 88 Benefit Street, now a private home, lived the object of Edgar Allan Poe's affection. She was a young widow named Sarah Helen Whitman, and the poet dedicated the famous works "To Helen" and "Annabel Lee" to her. Poe had corresponded with Whitman, herself a poet, for a few years and finally met her when he came to lecture at the Franklin Lyceum. The two became immediately and seriously smitten with one another, but Whitman objected to Poe's habitual carousing and boozing—ultimately, she broke off their engagement and left him because of his inability to distance himself from the bottle. Shortly thereafter, the penniless and drunken Poe died in Baltimore.

Farther up College Hill at the intersection of Congdon and Bowen Streets is perhaps the most romantic outdoor space in the city, lofty **Prospect Terrace,** a grassy rectangle with a wrought-iron fence that's perched high above downtown and the State Capitol grounds. It's also the burial site of Roger Williams, whose image is carved in granite above his grave. Surrounding the park are more of the neighborhood's comely houses, and it's a relatively short walk southeast to Brown University's commercial strip along Thayer Street, meaning you could walk off your dinner and woo your sweetheart with a few blocks' stroll to the park.

RHODE ISLAND SCHOOL OF DESIGN (RISD)

The campus of the prestigious RISD occupies many of the blocks along Benefit Street from College to Waterman Streets; there are also buildings down the hill along Main Street and up a block on Prospect Street. The school

© MICHAEL BLANDING

opened with a very practical vocational aim: to train students in the ways of textile arts and design as well as in related fields represented in Providence, such as jewelry design and manufacture and machine works and design. Through the years, the school has gained considerable prestige not only for its applied design courses but for training some of the nation's leaders in fine and graphic arts, interior design, costume-making, and the like. An artsy buzz permeates the campus and nearby streets, and no doubt it has helped to influence the similarly alternative tone of neighboring Brown University, which is perhaps the most countercultural of the Ivy League schools.

Keep an eye out for signs marking RISD's Office of Admissions, which occupies a brilliant Italianate edifice called the **Woods-Gerry Mansion** (62 Prospect St., 401/454-6141, 10 A.M.–4 P.M. Mon.–Tues. and Fri.–Sat., 2–5 P.M. Sun., free). The building contains galleries with rotating art exhibits, and in back you can walk through a small sculpture garden.

◀ RISD Museum of Art

Be sure to stop by the RISD Museum of Art

(224 Benefit St., 401/454-6500, www.risd.edu/museum.cfm, 10 A.M.–5 P.M. Tues.–Sun., $10 adults, $3 children). As RISD is a school, the museum here offers a true survey of works from around the world and spanning many centuries. The collection varies widely, with several works by Monet gracing the French impressionist area and an excellent collection of mostly 18th- and 19th-century American artists such as Frank Benson, Thomas Cole, Winslow Homer, and John Singer Sargent. Rotating exhibitions vary considerably but in recent years have included such lofty themes as *Subject to Change: Art and Design in the Twentieth Century* and *The Figure: Contemporary Works from the Collection.* Guided tours (free with admission) are given Friday at 12:15 P.M.

BROWN UNIVERSITY

Few educational institutions can claim a greater degree of recognition, both nationally and internationally, than Brown University, whose stately—if somber—campus dominates the upper slope of the East Side's College Hill.

The seventh college founded in what became the United States, Brown began in 1764 in the East Bay community of Warren with the name Rhode Island College under the guidance of Reverend James Manning. Despite its Baptist leanings, an early edict related to the school's operations was that "into this Liberal and Catholic Institution shall never be admitted any Religious Tests but on the Contrary all the Members Hereof shall forever enjoy full free Absolute and uninterrupted Liberty of Conscience."

In 1770 a permanent location for the college was established on the east side of Providence on eight acres of what is now College Hill. It wasn't until 1804 that Brown University assumed its present name, in appreciation of the enormous $5,000 gift that merchant Nicholas Brown bestowed on it. Brown enjoys a reputation for being a flashy jet-set school of hipsters and dilettantes—depending on your point of view, a welcome relief to the overly tweedy Ivy League rivals Harvard and Yale, or an obnoxious celebration of narcissistic self-expression.

PROVIDENCE

WHO WAS JOSHUA CARBERRY?

Brown University has matriculated a great many prominent students, from famous writers and performers to illustrious business leaders and politicians. Perhaps the most distinguished alumnus and former professor you'll hear mentioned at Brown is Josiah S. Carberry. A vast trove of records exists dating to the late 1920s, noting that Carberry, a professor of psychoceramics (the study of cracked pots), has given important lectures, published valuable scholarly essays, and altogether changed the course of Brown's academic history. He has been listed in the cast of university plays, served as the subject of more than a few newspaper articles (including one by the *New York Times* that described him as "The World's Greatest Traveler" in 1974), and even been awarded the Ig Noble Prize (a playful take on the Nobel Prize) for, according to an article by a Brown University archivist, being a "bold explorer and eclectic seeker of knowledge, for his pioneering work in the field of psychoceramics."

Perhaps the most amazing thing about Josiah "Joshua" Carberry is that no such person actually exists. Indeed, it appears that Carberry was dreamed up as a hoax, some say by an actual professor at Brown, John Spaeth. Carberry's history is traced to a notice on a bulletin board in 1929 that read: "On Thursday evening at 8:15 in Sayles Hall J. S. Carberry will give a lecture on Archaic Greek Architectural Revetments in Connection with Ionian Philology." This minor event gradually snowballed to the point that Carberry became larger than life. He was cited as having a wife, a daughter, and a clumsy research assistant. In 1955 an unnamed person sent a donation of about $100 to Brown with the instructions that it be used to form the Josiah S. Carberry Fund. A stipulation is that every Friday the 13th, change be collected in brown jugs to bolster the fund. So the next time you hear somebody cite the considerable credentials of Joshua Carberry, think fondly of his legend – and consider how soon it is until the next Friday the 13th, your next opportunity to contribute to the Carberry fund.

Inarguably, Brown fosters a deeply liberal and somewhat countercultural collective philosophy, where avant-garde arts and studies of on-the-edge literary and social theories thrive. Since 2000, Brown has been helmed by Ruth Simmons, the first African American to become president of an Ivy League school.

Campus Buildings

On Brown's central hub, the **Main Green,** you can admire the elegant Georgian architecture of the original **University Hall.** But the university's picturesque hilltop campus incorporates nearly every popular civic architectural style of the past two centuries. Colonial and then Greek Revival architecture (note James C. Bucklin's 1835 **Manning Hall** and also the 1840 **Rhode Island Hall**) dominates the style of those buildings created until the late 1880s, when the aesthetic shifted to accommodate the Victorian movement. A new spate of building during the 1960s and 1970s produced more modern structures such as the **List Art Building,** where you'll find the **David Winton Bell Gallery** (List Art Center, 64 College St., 401/863-2932, www.brown.edu, 11 A.M.–4 P.M. Mon.–Fri., 1–4 P.M. Sat.–Sun., free), showing both contemporary and historic exhibitions.

Another building worth visiting is the **John Hay Library** (Prospect St. and College St., 401/863-2146, http://dl.lib.brown.edu/libweb/about/hay, 9 A.M.–5 P.M. Mon.–Fri., free) which dates to 1910 and serves as the repository for Brown University's rare collections. These include a substantial trove of manuscripts attributed to Abraham Lincoln, the correspondence of early horror writer H. P. Lovecraft, and many items from the life of Napoleon, among other ephemera. History buffs should visit the neoclassical 1904 **John Carter Brown Library** (George St. and Brown

St., 401/863-2725, www.brown.edu/Facilities/ John_Carter_Brown_Library, 8:30 A.M.–5 P.M. Mon.–Fri., 9 A.M.–noon Sat., free), whose collection of artifacts and documents pertaining to the history of the New World from the days of Columbus until the American Revolution is among the world's most important.

Brown's commercial college strip centers on **Thayer Street,** from about Bowen Street south to Waterman Street. Even in summer, when relatively few students are on campus, Thayer Street remains lively, cerebral, and youthful—there are coffeehouses, sandwiches shops, ethnic restaurants, bookstores, a few school buildings, and a decidedly countercultural buzz that befits the entertainment district nearest Brown; plenty of students from nearby RISD also hang out in these parts. When school's in session, expect to fight many Maynard Keynes–debating trust-funders for the alfresco tables.

FOX POINT AND INDIA POINT PARK

You'll find another corridor of artsy, student-frequented shops, eateries, and fair-trade cafés along the slightly less trafficked **Wickenden Street,** which runs east-west across Fox Point, at the southern end of College Hill fronting Providence Harbor. India Point, at the southeastern tip of this neighborhood, has for many years been the center of the city's Portuguese community, and because of its fine restaurants and shops it draws folks from all over. The crowd along Wickenden Street is less exclusively identified with Brown University—you'll find just as many RISD students as well as other teens and young adults from around the city.

Eighteen-acre India Point Park, accessible either from Exit 3 off I-195 or by heading south on Gano Street or South Main Street from Wickenden Street, provides the city's only frontage on Narragansett Bay, right at the bay's head where it meets the Seekonk and Providence Rivers. The northern terminus of the East Bay Bike Path, the park has a small network of paved trails suitable for biking or strolling, plus meadows ideal for tossing a ball or Frisbee.

At the west end of the neighborhood, South Water Street runs south along the east bank of the Providence River. There's a small park at the end and parking along the street, and from here you look down the river and see the hulking gates of the city's Hurricane Barrier, built in 1961–1966. Beyond it is the soaring arched truss of the bridge that carries the new "Iway"—the recently relocated I-195—over the bay. On the opposite side of the Providence River, via Globe Street, which is off Allens Avenue, you can get a closer look at the Hurricane Barrier, a roughly 700-foot-long structure whose massive doors are kept open except when the city is threatened by major storms; to date this has been only a handful of occasions.

NORTH AND EAST OF COLLEGE HILL

The lower slopes of College Hill to the north and east cover a substantial area, and while safe and pleasant, it is more difficult to cover on foot than College Hill, Wickenden Street, and downtown. You might consider driving or taking a bus to Blackstone Boulevard or Blackstone Park and then walking, or consider riding a bike through this area—it's one of the few neighborhoods within Providence city limits that's highly conducive to cycling.

North of the intersection with Wickenden Street, Hope Street has several cool shops and eateries, plus some fine old homes. A few blocks north of Wickenden Street is the **Rhode Island Historical Society Library** (121 Hope St., 401/273-8107, www.rihs.org, 10 A.M.–5 P.M. Wed.–Fri., free), worth a stop if you have even a casual interest in genealogy or early state history. Documents pertaining to Rhode Island, including all manner of birth, death, and marriage records, date as far back as the days of Roger Williams. There are also prints, paintings, photos, and other historical items. The society sponsors 90-minute city walking tours July–mid-October with a focus on history, the waterfront, architecture, art, and similar topics.

A few more blocks up Hope Street, note the decadent **Governor Henry Lippitt House Museum** (199 Hope St., 401/453-0688, www.preserveri.org, tours 11 A.M.–2 P.M. Fri. or by appointment, $10). A sterling example of a high-style Italianate Victorian mansion from the 1860s, the building reveals the fine craftsmanship of the day with ornately carved Renaissance revival woodwork, meticulous stencil work, and myriad faux finishes. Even if you have little interest in interior design and restoration, the Lippitt Museum is a must-see. Many of the furnishings in the house belonged to Lippitt family members, and the museum periodically throws events, teas, and dinners that offer an intimate glimpse into life in this house during the Victorian era.

Another block north, at Lloyd Avenue, you'll pass by the prestigious **Moses Brown School** (250 Lloyd Ave., 401/831-7350, www.moses-brown.org), a Quaker prep school notable for its tree-shaded lawns and fine old buildings that has been here since 1784. You can visit the **Krause Gallery** (Jenks Center, Friends Hall, www.mosesbrown.org/krausegallery, 8 A.M.–4 P.M. Mon.–Fri., free), which shows the works of noted local and national sculptors, painters, and photographers.

Farther down Angell Street, past the enormous Brown University Athletic Complex, is a short strip of shops and a handful of cheap eateries, including the engaging **Books on the Square** (471 Angell St., 401/331-9097, www. booksq.com) which has a lively café and is a great place for a break or book shopping. This tiny commercial district, **Wayland Square,** serves the many residential blocks nearby, home to young professionals, students, and faculty of Brown, RISD, and the city's other universities.

Blackstone Boulevard

Farther east down Angell Street past Butler Avenue is the hilly 40-acre **Blackstone Park,** a grassy, tree-shaded park ideal for a stroll. It has a couple of ponds and several walking paths, plus some nice spots for a picnic. The mostly upper-middle-class residential neighborhood surrounding the park contains many fine stucco, wood-frame, and redbrick homes from the early part of the 20th century, all with neat gardens and perfectly manicured lawns.

From the northern end of Blackstone Park, west down Irving Avenue is the southern end of Blackstone Boulevard, a broad tree-lined avenue with a wide grassy median that's usually abuzz with joggers, walkers, inline skaters, and cyclists. A little more than a mile north on Blackstone Boulevard, on the right, is the entrance to the gracious 210-acre **Swan Point Cemetery** (585 Blackstone Blvd., 401/272-1314, http://swanpointcemetery.com), laid out in 1875. This is one of the country's foremost garden cemeteries, and visitors are encouraged to bicycle (slowly), walk, or drive the grounds, which are laced with beautiful gardens. Among the famous Rhode Islanders buried here are horror writer H. P. Lovecraft and Civil War general Ambrose Burnside.

A short distance north along Blackstone Boulevard is **Lippitt Memorial Park,** a pretty little slice of greenery with a grand old central fountain and ample seating. The jogging path up the median of Blackstone Boulevard terminates where Hope Street becomes East Avenue, almost suspiciously across the street from **Maximillian's Ice Cream Cafe** (1074 Hope St., 401/273-7230). At this point you're a short walk from Providence's northeastern border with Pawtucket—this is a part of Providence many visitors never see, and yet it's extremely charming and diverse. Yuppies, families, gays and lesbians, and students and academics have settled here, taking advantage of the low-key and quiet pace still close to bustling downtown.

CRANSTON STREET ARMORY

Much of the rest of Providence—the neighborhoods south, west, and northwest of downtown—is dominated by lower-income residential neighborhoods and industry. One particularly fascinating site just southwest of downtown is the Cranston Street Armory (125 Dexter St.), a massive 1907 yellow-brick and granite building that housed the Rhode Island

National Guard for many years but is now threatened with demolition. This centerpiece of the gradually gentrifying West Broadway neighborhood is on the National Trust for Historic Preservation's list of most endangered structures. Much talk has centered on turning the building into a state-of-the-art performing arts center; so far, however, it has been rehabilitated piecemeal as state funds allow, including transforming some of the towers into office space for government agencies. This neighborhood has enormous potential, with many striking, but often dilapidated, Victorian homes, including many examples of Second Empire and Greek Revival styles.

ROGER WILLIAMS PARK

You'll want to drive or take the bus the roughly four miles south of downtown to reach the city's largest and most treasured urban oasis, 430-acre Roger Williams Park (Elmwood Ave., 401/785-3510, grounds 9 A.M.–9 P.M. daily), the home of Roger Williams Park Zoo. Visitors can bike, skate, or walk nearly 10 miles of paved roads (open to auto traffic, but only at low speeds, and there's usually ample room for all people and vehicles to maneuver). Unpaved trails also meander into the verdant greenery around the 10 lakes (many where you can rent small boats). The great-great-granddaughter of Roger Williams, Betsey Williams, donated the land for this park in the 1870s, and it retains its splendid Victorian layout, created by designer Horace W. S. Cleveland in 1878. The look and ambience borrows heavily from the most famous of 19th-century park designers, Frederick Law Olmsted.

One of the most architecturally significant structures in the park, the imposing redbrick colonial revival **casino** dates to 1896. It has impressive views from its veranda over the restored music bandstand and Roosevelt Lake. With a ballroom crowned by 20-foot ceilings and ornate plaster friezes and trim, it is a fine example of the park's success in restoration and a favorite place for weddings and parties. Surrounding the casino and extending throughout several parts of the park are lovely rose and flower gardens as well as a Japanese garden. The **Charles H. Smith Greenhouses** (11 A.M.–5 P.M. daily), which date to 1937, house cactus, rain forest, and herb gardens.

You can catch live music events at the **Benedict Temple to Music,** an amphitheater. Kids enjoy the reproduction vintage carousel at **Carousel Village** (11 A.M.–5 P.M. daily), which also has a miniature golf course, bumper boats, and other rides and amusements. You can also visit the **Betsey Williams Cottage** (1–4 P.M. Sun. mid-Apr.–mid-June and mid-Sept.–Oct.), a small history museum that preserves the legacy of the city's founding family.

Museum of Natural History

Roger Williams Park is home to the Museum of Natural History (401/785-9457, www.providenceri.com/museum, 10 A.M.–5 P.M. daily, museum $2, museum and planetarium $3), which contains a planetarium and more than 250,000 objects and artifacts collected during the past two centuries—at any given time, just 2 percent of the museum's holdings are on display. These include preserved mollusk shells, birds, mammals, rocks, minerals, and—a particular strength—fossils from the region's coal age. The museum displays cultural artifacts, mostly from North America, including baskets, textiles, tools, and carvings—but with significant representation from Africa, Oceana, and other parts of the world. Rotating exhibits are held every few months; a recent example is *Life of Stars: From Nebula to Supernova.* This grandiose but intriguing château-esque building dates to 1895 and was built by the firm Martin and Hall. The state's only museum of natural history, the museum has an impressive collection, but the overall feel and appearance of the place seems to be from another era—it's not a dynamic museum. Considerably more stimulating is the attached **Cormack Planetarium,** where a dazzling computerized star projector offers a memorable lesson in astronomy. The 35-minute shows are presented at 2 P.M. Saturday–Sunday November–June and at 2 P.M. daily July–October.

PROVIDENCE

Roger Williams Park Zoo

The Roger Williams Park Zoo (1000 Elmwood Ave., 401/785-3510, www.rogerwilliamsparkzoo.org, 9 A.M.–4 P.M. daily year-round, $12 adults, $6 children) has more than 1,000 animals of more than 165 species. It's the third-oldest zoo in the nation, and, believe it or not, has been ranked among the nation's 10 best. It's currently in the midst of an ambitious restoration plan called "New Zoo" to make it even better. The Fabric of Africa habitat, which has elephants, Masai giraffes, zebras, and cheetahs, was expanded and renovated in 2008 to include new interpretive signage, more space for the animals, and a new viewing deck to get close to the animals. As of 2010, work was shifting to the North America habitat, where the polar bear exhibit is being expanded to eight times its previous size, along with new habitats for bald eagles and seals.

Other animals on display here include playful lemurs in the Madagascar habitat; moon bears and snow leopards along the Marco Polo Trail; and monkeys, sloths, and snakes inhabiting the Tropical America exhibit, a recreated rain forest accessed by a swaying rope bridge. Smaller but still very popular exhibits include the African Fishing Village, a farmyard petting zoo, the Natural Wetlands Trail, and the educational zoo laboratory.

Entertainment and Events

NIGHTLIFE

Students, students, students…need anybody say more? They're everywhere you look, and they've created a vibrant market for pulsing nightclubs, swanky lounges, and singles joints. Providence also has the usual dive bars, with regular joes quaffing Bud tall boys, smoking Marlboro Lights, shooting pool, sucking down buffalo wings, and watching *Monday Night Football*. But for a relatively small city, it also has a surprising number of high-profile, sophisticated, and in some cases snobby boîtes. Actual velvet ropes are the exception rather than the rule, but a number of bars in this town set up invisible velvet ropes—if you don't fit the look or the style, you may feel rather left out.

Downcity and in the adjoining Jewelry District are the greatest concentration of the city's nightspots, including big and brawny dance clubs that simmer with the libidos of drunken college kids and revelers from the suburbs along with cool live-music clubs drawing the latest and strangest alternative rock and jazz acts. Providence also has a thriving gay scene, with several extremely popular clubs that pull in patrons from all over southern New England along with the many lesbian and gay students in town.

Hangouts

For pre- or postdinner drinks with a special someone, consider the Westin Providence's plush **Fleming's Steakhouse and Wine Bar** (1 W. Exchange St., 401/598-8000). Even if you're not a fan of hotel bars, you might give this upscale, inviting bar a chance—it's close to everything downtown, and the menu of fine wines and drinks is impressive. Keep in mind that it's also a favorite of cigar smokers.

Monet Dance Lounge (115 Harris Ave., 401/351-4848) is a classy alternative to the bump and grind of club life. Both indoor and outdoor space allows plenty of room to dance, and VIP sections give you star-worthy treatment.

Blake's Tavern (122 Washington St., 401/274-1230, www.blakestavern.com, 11 A.M.–1 A.M. daily) draws the after-work set for cocktails and tasty bar fare—wings, nachos, and the like. **AS220** (115 Empire St., 401/861-9190) features an eclectic mix of entertainment, from poetry slams to comedy shows, with a crowd that's just as diverse. **Liquid Lounge** (165 Angell St., 401/454-3434, 11:30 A.M.–1 A.M. Sun.–Thurs., 11:30 A.M.–2 A.M. Fri.–Sat.) is a sexy pickup spot off Thayer Street with a mostly Brown University crowd of arty countercultural types. Working professionals head straight from work to the **Tunnel Bar** (1 Cookson Pl., 401/421-4646), with a modern, cosmopolitan attitude that gets younger through the night. Among the several Irish pubs in the city, **Muldowney's** (103 Empire St., 401/831-6202, 10 A.M.–1 A.M. Mon.–Thurs., 10 A.M.–2 A.M. Fri.–Sat., noon–1 A.M. Sun.) scores significant crowds because of its proximity to AS220.

Suave and romantic **L'Elizabeth** (285 S. Main St., 401/861-1974, 11 A.M.–1 A.M. daily) is a sit-down bar pouring international coffees, single malts, cognacs, and similar after-dinner treats in a lavish drawing room of armchairs and sofas; soft jazz is piped in, and a handful of desserts are offered, including a delicious white-chocolate cheesecake. In the Jewelry District, young and old convene for jukebox tunes and Pabst Blue Ribbon at **Nick-a-Nee's** (75 South St., 401/861-7290, 3 P.M.–1 A.M. Sun.–Thurs., 3 P.M.–2 A.M. Fri.–Sat.), which hosts pool tournaments on Tuesday and Saturday nights.

At Providence Place Mall, you'll find a 40,000-square-foot branch of the national shrine to grown-ups who refuse to grow up: **Dave and Buster's** (401/270-4555, www.daveandbusters.com, 11:30 A.M.–midnight Sun.–Wed., 11:30 A.M.–1 A.M. Thurs.–Sat.) pulses with the sounds of high-tech video games and similar amusements; there's a huge bar, the crowd likes to party, and they party late. At **Snookers** (53 Ashburton St., 401/351-7665, www.snookersri.com, 11:30 A.M.–1 A.M. Sun.–Thurs., 11:30 A.M.–2 A.M. Fri.–Sat.), shoot pool to your heart's content—this sprawling place has many tables.

Live Music and Clubs

The city's main venue for major touring music acts is the **Dunkin' Donuts Center** (1 LaSalle Sq., at Broadway and Atwells Ave., 401/331-6700), in the western end of downtown. Down toward Fox Point, **Fish Co.** (515 S. Water St., 401/841-5510) pulls in a mix of local and nationally known alternative and rock music acts, playing mostly to a collegiate crowd. It's also a big draw for happy hour earlier in the evening.

At **Club Hell** (73 Richmond St., 401/351-1977), you'll find the city's Goth scene, where the pierced black-eyeliner set convenes to hang out. The sceney Federal Hill restaurant **Mediterreaneo** (134 Atwells Ave., 401/331-7760, www.mediterraneocaffe.com, 11:30 A.M.–9 P.M. daily) also has a dressy and rather exclusive nightclub where you'll hear mostly a Latin beat—that is, if you're able to get in; it's a very cliquey place. In the Jewelry District, the **Hi-Hat** (3 Davol Sq., 401/453-6500, www.thehihat.com, 4 P.M.–1 A.M. Tues.–Thurs., 4 P.M.–2 A.M. Fri., 5 P.M.–2 A.M. Sat.) offers live jazz, R&B, Latin, blues, and other cool beats in an attractive, urbane space.

Downtown, **Lupo's Heartbreak Hotel** (239 Westminster St., 401/331-LUPO—401/331-5876) is one of the top music venues in the city, booking rock, folk, country, and blues. **Ultra** (172 Pine St., 401/454-LIVE—401/454-5483) is one of the hottest spots in town for hip-hop beats, boasting the ultimate dance party complete with platforms and VIP tables. Look to **Safari Lounge** (103 Eddy St., no phone) for the latest underground, thrash, and punk acts.

Suburbanites and college students from schools throughout Rhode Island make the drive into the city to cut loose at **Jerky's** (71 Richmond St., 401/621-2244) for a night of cheap food, drinks, and pool. A bit of a dive bar, this is the place to go if you would rather wear jeans and flannel. If you're more the clubbing type, try **Art Bar** (171 Chestnut St., 401/272-0177, www.artbarprovidenceri.com/1.html), the original 25-and-over party spot for locals and vacationers alike. Music varies from past favorites to current hits, and Saturday all-request nights guarantee something for everyone.

Gay and Lesbian

Girlspot (150 Point St., 401/751-7166) is a terrific women's club that has a large dance floor, lots of nooks for sitting and talking, and friendly staff. A handsome bi-level space close to the bevy of straight and wild discos on Richmond Street, **Mirabar** (35 Richmond St.,

401/331-6761) is the definitive men's stand-and-model bar with a small dance floor and a cozier cocktail bar with a pool table upstairs. It tends to draw a fairly young and professional crowd.

Dark Lady (124 Snow St., 401/274-6620), on a desolate side street on the edge of downtown, is an appropriately shady location for a hard-core cruisy disco and hangout popular with leather men and other butch types.

THE ARTS

Providence enjoys a highly developed and richly endowed performing arts scene, with a slew of

---

GALLERY-HOPPING IN PROVIDENCE

Providence has an impressive fine arts scene, with galleries throughout downtown and College Hill. Among the better-known downtown venues is one at the historic Arcade: **Center-City Contemporary Arts** (65 Weybosset St., 401/521-2990), which focuses primarily on the works of Rhode Island artists. Also worth checking out is the **Stanley Weiss Collection** (292 Westminster St., 401/272-3200, www.stanleyweiss.com), known throughout the Northeast for its phenomenal selection of museum-quality antiques and silver jewelry and accessories. One of the most innovative and popular spaces in the city is **AS220** (115 Empire St., 401/831-9327), which is also a very nice restaurant and a place to listen to readings and live music. The **Rhode Island Foundation Gallery** (1 Union Station, off Exchange Terr., 401/274-4564, www.rifoundation.org), a former cafeteria in the old Union Station, shows rotating art exhibits. The Rhode Island Foundation is a center for philanthropy that acts as a liaison between donors and recipients in the public and private sectors in education, health care, and the arts. Works shown in the gallery focus heavily on local artists in all media.

On the East Side, a handful of galleries cluster around the Fox Point neighborhood, notably the **Peaceable Kingdom** (116 Ives St., 401/351-3472), where you'll find carved masks and figurines, lavish textiles, and paintings from around the world. Farther west on Wickenden Street you'll find **JRS Fine Art** (218 Wickenden St., 401/331-4380), which represents a number of reputable painters and potters, and **Picture This** (158 Wickenden St., 401/273-7263, www.picturethisgalleries.com), a respected frame and print shop. Down by

India Point is **Bert Gallery** (540 S. Water St., 401/751-2628), whose paintings are mostly by notable 19th-early-20th-century Rhode Island artists (it's an excellent place to get a lesson in local art history). Finally, there are two spots near RISD and Brown: the **David Charles Gallery** (263 S. Main St., 401/421-6764), which has fine maritime art, beautiful framed photos of the Providence skyline, and numerous depictions of noted New England landmarks; and the historic **Providence Art Club** (11 Thomas St., 401/331-1114). This is the country's second-oldest art club – it occupies the 1790 Obadiah Brown House, where members still carry out the tradition of munching on jonnycakes in the vintage dining rooms.

The third Thursday of every month 5-9 P.M., the city sponsors a free **Gallery Night** (401/751-2628, www.gallerynight.info). you can ride one of three trolleys, which depart from Citizens Bank (1 Citizens Plaza), on a historic loop through downtown and the East Side, stopping at about 25 art galleries and museums. On hand to mingle with visitors at most of these events are local artists and gallery owners. Each of the three trolleys plies a different route – one through the East Side, one through the West Side, and one making the entire loop. On board, volunteer guides from the Providence Preservation Society offer commentary on the sights and neighborhoods along the way. Sakonnet Vineyards donates free wine (and other refreshments are also provided), and there's live music at some venues. Keep in mind that Rhode Island has lifted sales tax on all galleries within Providence's downtown arts district – which means you'll find some very good art buys in these parts.

theaters that range from big-time showcases of pre-Broadway shows and national touring acts to inexpensive avant-garde local workshops that will challenge your sensibilities. It's a good destination for people who like to take chances—there's no shortage of educated and progressive, even a bit jaded, audiences. Not an evening passes in Providence without the opportunity to watch some out-there abstract dance piece, catch an obscure foreign film at one of the art cinemas, or see a courageous new dramatic work by the next wunderkind in the city's theater scene.

You can look to the city's colleges for a wide range of dance, theater, music, and other arts performances, with **Rhode Island College** (600 Mt. Pleasant Ave., www.ric.edu/perf_arts) offering some of the best works. It's always worth checking its website to see what's playing and where; visit the school's Bannister Gallery for rotating art exhibits. On the city's West Side, this school doesn't always get the same attention as some of Providence's larger educational institutions, but its arts program is notable.

Also check to see what's happening at **Providence College** (401/865-2218, www.providence.edu), whose Blackfriars Theatre produces some first-rate plays. At **Brown University** (www.brown.edu), the acclaimed music department presents concerts in a wide range of disciplines, from chamber music to jazz. Plays and other performing arts are scheduled regularly at the school's **Dill Performing Arts Center** (77 Waterman St., 401/863-2838).

Theater

The **Providence Performing Arts Center** (220 Weybosset St., 401/421-2787, www.ppacri.org) ranks among New England's top venues for concerts, children's theater, and Broadway-style musical comedies—plus ballet, opera, and classical music. Throughout the year, top recording stars and a smattering of comedians such as Diana Krall, David Sedaris, and the swoon-inducing Jonas Brothers perform here. In recent years Broadway and national-touring musicals have included *The Scarlet Pimpernel, Godspell,* and *Annie,* while

© MICHAEL BLANDING

AS220 offers a peek into Providence's diverse arts scene.

PROVIDENCE

Cinderella and *Sesame Street Live* have graced the children's stage.

One of the city's most innovative venues for all kinds of arts, **AS220** (115 Empire St., 401/831-9327, www.as220.org) has cultivated a following for undiscovered and experimental works. It occupies a large space with numerous artists-in-residence, and it's the home of various local theater groups, including the edgy **Perishable Theatre** (95 Empire St., 401/331-2695, www.perishable.org), which produces cutting-edge plays.

Another major key to the gentrification of the once-seedy Westminster Street area, the **Providence Black Repertory Company** (276 Westminster St., 401/351-0353, www.blackrep.org) formed in 1996 to help promote and celebrate the theatrical contributions of black dramatists, actors, and other performers. In addition to staging plays, this acclaimed theater hosts open-mike nights, discussions, readings, and music.

The Tony Award–winning **Trinity Repertory Company** (201 Washington St., 401/351-4242, www.trinityrep.com) presents seven classic and contemporary plays annually with a season running September–June. They also put on an annual holiday production of *A Christmas Carol*.

Music and Dance

The **Rhode Island Philharmonic** (667 Waterman Ave., East Providence, 401/242-7070, www.ri-philharmonic.org) has been a cultural mainstay in Providence since 1945, pulling in notable guest conductors from time to time, plus artists such as Debbie Reynolds and Marvin Hamlisch. The Philharmonic presents a classical series, three fully staged operas, a pop series, and several family-oriented pieces. The Lincoln-based modern-dance rep company **Fusionworks** (401/946-0607, www.fusionworksdance.org) performs at venues throughout the state and elsewhere in the Northeast.

Film

Try to catch a movie at the **Avon Cinema** (260 Thayer St., 401/421-0020, www.avoncinema.com), which shows both popular and art movies (and serves Häagen-Dazs), with midnight screenings some nights. Another art house is the **Cable Car Cinema** (204 S. Main St., 401/272-3970, www.cablecarcinema.com). At Providence Place Mall you'll find the 16-screen **Providence Place Cinemas 16** (800/315-4000) and the **IMAX theater** (www.imax.com), which shows larger-than-life features on a six-story screen with a mind-blowing (perhaps ear-splitting) 12,000-watt surround-sound system.

FESTIVALS AND EVENTS
Summer

In mid-June, one of Providence's most vibrant ethnic communities throws an **Annual Cape Verdean Independence Day Celebration** (India Point Park, 401/222-4133), which gives attendees a chance to sample authentic Cape Verdean foods, observe arts and crafts exhibits, and listen to music and storytelling. Also in June, Providence's dynamic gay and lesbian community celebrates **RI Pride Fest** (401/467-2130, www.prideri.com) at

Station Park, just opposite Providence Place Mall. In early August, foodies descend on the **Best of Rhode Island Party** (Rhode Island Convention Center, 401/781-1611), during which more than 80 winners of *Rhode Island Monthly* magazine's "best of" food awards dole out portions of the grub that made them so popular. Begun in 1997, the **Rhode Island International Film Festival** (various locations in Providence and neighboring towns, 401/861-4445, www.rifilmfest.org) has grown into a highly prestigious event showing more than 265 films; it's held every August.

Fall

In the middle of September, about 30 of the city's ethnic communities gather for the **Annual Rhode Island Heritage Festival** (Roger Williams National Memorial, North Main St., 401/222-4133, www.preservation.ri.gov/heritage) to share traditional song and dance, arts and crafts demonstrations, and foods. In early November, bring out your inner decorator at the **Annual Fine Furnishings–Providence** (Rhode Island Convention Center, 401/816-0963, www.finefurnishingsshow.com), which focuses mostly on the handcrafted furnishings and decorative arts of New England artisans. You'll find a nice range of both traditional and contemporary wares in all price ranges.

Winter and Spring

Like many U.S. cities, Providence ushers in the new year with **Bright Night** (various sites downtown, 401/351-2596, www.brightnight.org), with family-oriented theater, music, art, and dance performances. Yachting and sailing enthusiasts gear up for the coming season in mid-January at the **Providence Boat Show** (Rhode Island Convention Center and Dunkin' Donuts Center, 401/846-1115, www.providenceboatshow.com), where dealers show off the latest sailboats, powerboats, and equipment. A week later at the same venue, you can hunt for cars at the **Northeast International Auto Show** (Rhode Island Convention Center, 717/671-4300, www.motortrendautoshows.com/providence). In mid-February, the convention center hosts the **Rhode Island Spring Flower and Garden Show** (401/272-0980, www.flowershow.com). Later in February the convention center is the site first of the **RV and Camping Show** (401/458-6000); a week later the **Southeastern New England Home Show** (401/438-7400, www.ribahomeshow.com); and in early February the **Rhode Island Pet Show and the International Cat Association (TICA) Cat Show** (800/955-7469, www.jenksproductions.com). One of the most popular events at the convention center is the **Business Expo** (401/521-5000), which comes in late April and hosts about 400 exhibitors and dozens of professional development workshops.

Shopping

For several reasons, Providence offers an uncharacteristically good selection of unusual shops along with the chains you'd find anywhere. First, a nice thing about the city's Gaps, Victoria's Secrets, and other chains: The vast majority are contained within one of the best-designed and best-situated urban shopping malls you'll ever find, Providence Place. This mammoth structure anchors downtown and overlooks the brilliantly landscaped riverfront, and it's close to several hotels and within walking distance of the universities. There are several good restaurants on the ground floor, plus a top-level food court that's better than most, as well as a movie theater and IMAX. If malls are often guilty of sucking the life out of cities and forcing people out to bland suburban retail compounds that could be anywhere, Providence Place at least draws people to the heart of downtown. That being said, independent-shop owners have had a tough go of it for the past few years, and many around the city have closed, especially on the East Side. There's some concern that the presence of Providence Place Mall and the emergence of so many chain businesses elsewhere have cost a number of indies too many customers for them to make a successful go of it.

Beyond the mall, Providence has a number of funky and hip design shops, galleries, art-supply stores, indie book and record shops, vintage clothiers, and home-furnishings and gift boutiques. These are geared as much toward visitors as they are to the city's artists, students, academics, and hipsters. Providence lures creative types, and these very people often end up opening offbeat and innovative businesses. And while this isn't necessarily an ideal city for bargain hunters, commercial rents are much, much lower than in Boston, New York City, Block Island, or Cape Cod. You'll often find decent deals on antiques and art, and at the student-oriented spots you'll have no trouble homing in on discount threads, used books and CDs, and low-priced bric-a-brac.

PROVIDENCE PLACE MALL

Opened in 1999, Providence Place Mall (1 Providence Pl., 401/270-1000, www.providenceplace.com, 10 A.M.–9 P.M. Mon.–Sat., noon–6 P.M. Sun.) is an immense four-story atrium mall with a 16-screen Showcase Cinema multiplex and an IMAX theater along with a fairly standard upscale mix of apparel, home-furnishing, and other chain shops. The top-floor 700-seat food court is unusually good, with Ben and Jerry's, Johnny Rockets, Subway, Japanese and sushi that's excellent by mall standards, Italian, and Chinese eateries. The ground level is lined with sit-down restaurants that are mostly upscale-looking if not genuinely expensive; most of them are jam-packed on weekend evenings. The mall has been successful in drawing visitors from the burbs, but some question how much it has drawn people into the city—you can exit I-95 directly into the mall parking garages, barely touching city surface streets. On the other hand, the mall is within walking distance of the riverfront, State House, convention center, and even College Hill—especially on warm days, plenty of shoppers wander out and explore the city. Major shops include Filene's, Lord and Taylor, and Nordstrom (which draws plenty of bargain-hunters from Massachusetts, which strangely enough lacks a Nordstrom). You'll also find chain shops such as Abercrombie and Fitch, Aveda, J. Jill, Restoration Hardware, Bed Bath & Beyond, Brooks Brothers, J. Crew, Lindt, Yankee Candle, Borders, Ann Taylor Loft, and all the myriad siblings in the ubiquitous Gap family—about 150 stores total.

DOWNTOWN

Apart from Providence Place Mall, downtown's most engaging retail spots are scattered about, in many cases down quiet little streets where you might not expect to find anything. If shopping is a sport to you, it's worth covering downtown block by block to discover its gems.

For unique scores, be sure to check out **Copacetic** (17 Peck St., 401/273-0470, www.copaceticjewelry.com, 10 A.M.–6 P.M. Mon.–Fri., 10 A.M.–4 P.M. Sat.), where you'll find a colorful array of clever, if at times surreal, jewelry, clocks, candlesticks, and other cool handcrafted accoutrements. RISD students and other arts-and-crafts aficionados frequent the **Jerry's Artarama** (14 Imperial Pl., 401/331-4530, 10 A.M.–6 P.M. Mon.–Sat., noon–4 P.M. Sun.), set in an imposing old knife factory that is also the site of CAV restaurant on a quiet side street in the Jewelry District.

Cellar Stories Bookstore (111 Mathewson St., 401/521-2665, www.cellarstories.com, 10 A.M.–6 P.M. Mon.–Sat.) is the largest used and antiquarian bookstore in the state, specializing not only in hard-to-find and out-of-print books but also magazines and periodicals.

Westminster Street is becoming a hotbed of design shops, among them **Homestyle Abode** (229 Westminster St., 401/277-1159), which carries cool housewares, gifts, home accessories, and furnishings; and **Design Within Reach** (210 Westminster St., 401/831-1452, www.dwr.com, 10 A.M.–6 P.M. Mon.–Sat., noon–5 P.M. Sun.), an interior design studio that carries wonderful furniture.

THE EAST SIDE

Several commercial strips are on the East Side, beginning at the base of College Hill along North and South Main Streets, and also in the Brown University retail corridor along Thayer Street. Wickenden Street, at the southern tip of the East Side, also makes for great window-shopping, and you'll find a small but lively district around Wayland Square, just east of Brown University and Hope Street.

Don't be alarmed by the unusually friendly staff of the fine men's clothier **Marc Allen** (200 S. Main St., 401/453-0025). This upscale shop has been a favorite for business and sports suits since the 1940s and still makes personalized service and superlative-quality clothing a priority.

With art students strolling around every corner, it's no surprise that Providence has some excellent sources for supplies, including most prominently the **RISD Store** (30 N. Main St., 401/454-6464, www.risdstore.com, 8:30 A.M.–7 P.M. Mon.–Fri., 10 A.M.–5 P.M. Sat.–Sun.), which also has one of the best selections of art books and periodicals in the city. It's fitting that Providence would have several exceptional jewelry stores—among the best known is **Martina and Company** (120 N. Main St., 401/351-0968, www.martina-company.com, 11 A.M.–6 P.M. Tues.–Wed. and Fri., 11 A.M.–7 P.M. Thurs., 10 A.M.–5 P.M. Sat.), a contemporary gallery that occupies a dramatic space. Meanwhile, edgy and cool but very wearable women's clothing are the draw at **Capucine** (359 S. Main St., 401/273-6622, noon–4 P.M. Mon., 11 A.M.–6 P.M. Tues.–Fri., 11 A.M.–5 P.M. Sat.), a magnet for style-conscious hipsters.

Wickenden Street has a few good antiques stores, including the whimsically named **This and That Shoppe** (236 Wickenden St., 401/861-1394), a multiple-dealer establishment with about 50 sellers. Most of the businesses along this funky stretch, including the scads of eateries, are set in wood-frame and brick Victorians and a few colonials. Just off Wickenden Street, **Rustigian Rugs** (1 Governor St., 401/751-5100, www.rustigianrugs.com, 10 A.M.–5:30 P.M. Mon.–Fri., 10 A.M.–5 P.M. Sat.) has an astounding selection of fine rugs, mostly from Far Eastern and Middle Eastern locales. Where there are college students, you can always find used CDs—among several shops in town, **Round Again Records** (278 Wickenden St., 401/351-6292, www.roundagainrecordsri. com, 11 A.M.–6 P.M. Mon.–Fri., 11 A.M.–5 P.M. Sat.) ranks among the best.

In trendy Wayland Square, check out **Books on the Square** (471 Angell St., 401/331-9097, www.booksq.com, 9 A.M.–9 P.M. Mon.–Sat., 10 A.M.–6 P.M. Sun.), which has a broad selection of fiction and nonfiction and is particularly strong on feminist, gay and lesbian, political, and children's books. You can sit in a comfy armchair and flip through books before buying them. **Comina** (201 Wayland Ave., 401/273-4522, www.comina.com, 10 A.M.–5:30 P.M. Mon.–Sat., noon–4 P.M. Sun.) is a delightful home-furnishings shop with emphasis on country British and French furnishings.

The comprehensive **Brown University Bookstore** (244 Thayer St., 401/863-3168, http://bookstore.brown.edu, 7:30 A.M.–8 P.M. Mon.–Fri., 10 A.M.–8 P.M. Sat., 10 A.M.–6 P.M. Sun.) also sells college sweatshirts and other logo items. Since you're in the jewelry capital of the nation, you might want to poke your head inside **Details** (277 Thayer St., 401/751-1870, 10:30 A.M.–7 P.M. daily), a top purveyor of both high-end and less pricey costume pieces of all kinds and styles. You'll find everything from handmade semiprecious beaded necklaces to crystal chandelier earrings. A funky local favorite, **Oop!** (220 Westminster St., 401/270-4366, www.oopstuff.com, 10 A.M.–7 P.M. Mon.–Sat., noon–5 P.M. Sun.) offers a cool range of home furnishings that includes a distinctive line of rustic furniture fashioned out of sticks along with gifts, objets d'art, toys, crafts, and jewelry, much of it made locally. The reputation is for fun, fairly inexpensive items, but Oop! sells some pricier antiques. The management has keen marketing sense, presenting all kinds of themed events, from free face-painting days to birthday parties celebrating stars such as Judy Garland and Mick Jagger. Despite the chain stores overtaking the neighborhood, there are still several excellent indie-owned eateries, boutiques, and shops, plus a great movie theater.

Up Hope Street, check out **Green River Silver Co.** (735 Hope St., 401/621-9092, www. greenriversilver.com, 10 A.M.–6 P.M. Mon.–Sat., 11 A.M.–4 P.M. Sun.), which custom-makes fine sterling-silver jewelry. **Studio Hop** (810 Hope St., 401/621-2262, 10 A.M.–6 P.M. Mon.–Sat., noon–5 P.M. Sun.) carries a wide and unusual range of gifts from all over the world, including Asian and Mediterranean skin care and beauty products, candles, framed photos and artwork, carved wooden bowls and utensils, and other hand-crafted items. The whimsical **Frog and Toad** (795 Hope St., 401/831-3434, 10 A.M.–6 P.M. Mon.–Sat., 11 A.M.–4 P.M. Sun.) stocks beaded jewelry, specialty soaps, funky imported furniture and crafts, and lush plants and topiaries.

PROVIDENCE

Sports and Recreation

By virtue of being such a hilly city, merely maneuvering around Providence on foot qualifies as a recreational pursuit. Beyond that, within the city limits you'll find a smattering of venues for sports and enjoying the outdoors, but with so many large parks and recreation areas within a 15-mile radius, many residents get their exercise elsewhere. In addition to the activities described below, keep in mind the city's many exceptional parks, including Roger Williams Park, India Point Park, and Blackstone Park.

BICYCLING, JOGGING, AND INLINE SKATING

There aren't any great spots for mountain biking within Providence city limits (although you'll find several good spots nearby), but the city does have some neat routes for conventional biking. Keep in mind that this is a busy city with narrow streets and a high volume of auto traffic, particularly on the East Side, and you'll have some very steep hills to contend with.

Joggers and inline skaters face some of the same issues but can enjoy one span that bikers will find less useful. Beginning either by the Capitol grounds or at nearby Providence Place Mall, you can enjoy a marvelous stroll along the restored riverfront, a two-mile loop if you take it all the way down to Bridge Street.

Within Providence, few roads seem better suited to cyclists, joggers, and inline skaters than wide, tree-lined Blackstone Boulevard, which runs about 1.5 miles from Hope Street south to Blackstone Park, past handsome old homes and the entrance to Swan Point Cemetery. You can make a nice triangular loop out of this area, using Blackstone Boulevard as one leg, Hope Street as the longer leg (it meets with Blackstone near the Pawtucket border), and any of the many cross streets closer to Brown University as the shorter leg.

From Providence you have access to the 14.5-mile **East Bay Bike Path** (www.eastbaybike-path.com), which begins at India Point Park. You can rent bikes at **Providence Bicycle** (725 Branch Ave., 401/331-6610, www.providence-bicycle.com, 9:30 A.M.–8 P.M. Mon.–Thurs., 9:30 A.M.–6 P.M. Fri. and Sun., closed Sat.), which is in northern Providence but worth the trip if you're a devotee of cycling.

BOATING, CANOEING, AND KAYAKING

Although not the boating hub that Newport, the East Bay, or South County are, Providence does have some access points that lead directly into Narragansett Bay, including some excellent areas for kayaking. Unfortunately, there are no kayak or canoe rentals in town; you'll have to venture down to South County or East Bay for those. You can take sailing classes geared to all levels of ability and experience at the **Community Boating Center** (109 India St., India Point Park, 401/454-7245, www.communityboat-ing.com, 9 A.M.–5 P.M. Mon.–Fri.), which

has a new boathouse and a fleet of about 50 boats.

GOLF

Donald Ross, known for designing municipal courses in cities throughout New England, laid out **Triggs Golf Course** (1533 Chalkstone Ave., 401/521-8460, http://triggs.us, 6:30 A.M.–dusk daily, $23 for 9 holes, $40 for 18 holes) in the 1930s. It's a relatively affordable, reasonably well-maintained course with cart and club rentals.

Goddard Park Beach Golf Course (at Goddard State Park, Ives Rd., 401/884-9834, 7:30 A.M.–7 P.M. daily, $12–14) is a nine-hole public course that's open mid-April–late November.

ICE-SKATING

A favorite spot in the winter (November–March) is the **Bank of America Skating Center** (Kennedy Plaza, Dorrance St. and Washington St., 401/331-5544, www.provi-denceskating.com), which has public skating several times daily. This outdoor rink, twice the size of the famous one in Rockefeller Center, anchors downtown Providence, right by the bus station and close to the Riverwalk—it's good fun as much for taking to the ice as it is for watching skaters on a brisk day. Late spring–early fall, the focus shifts to roller-skating. Year-round, lessons in both of these balancing arts are given; you can also rent equipment at the large pavilion and admission booth at the end of the rink, which has lockers, a pro shop, a snack bar, and some private party rooms that revelers sometimes rent for birthdays and special events.

SPECTATOR SPORTS

Providence itself has but one pro sports team, the **Providence Bruins** (401/273-5000, www.providencebruins.com), an American Hockey League farm club that's a feeder for the NHL's Boston Bruins. The season runs October–early April, and tickets cost $20–30. Games are held at the **Dunkin' Donuts Center** (1 LaSalle Sq., box office 401/331-6700).

With all the schools in Providence, you'd

think there would be more opportunities to catch live college sporting events, but few of these institutions have notable athletic programs. A major exception is **Providence College** (401/331-0700, http://friars.collegesports.com), whose Friars basketball team frequently ranks near the top of the Big East Basketball Conference. Games are held at the Dunkin' Donuts Center. The college's hockey team (401/865-2168) is also quite accomplished and plays at Schneider Arena (Admiral St. and Huxley St.).

Accommodations

When it comes to hotels, Providence is a seller's market. There simply aren't many properties given the city's size and rapidly growing popularity—the city has among the highest occupancy rates in the nation. Things are improving, however, as the Westin Providence recently expanded, and the upscale Marriott Renaissance chain recently renovated the elegant Masonic Temple, near Providence Place Mall and the Rhode Island State House, into a fine hotel. The city's hotels are uniformly excellent, most within walking distance of great shopping, dining, and culture. You'll also find several historic inns, from high-end luxury spots to a few that serve travelers on a somewhat limited budget. For truly affordable accommodations, however, you'll have to venture outside town to nearby Warwick or Pawtucket, or even as far as Woonsocket, Bristol, or across the border to Seekonk or Fall River, Massachusetts.

It's fairly easy to get in and out of Providence, so consider choosing a hotel in the outlying regions—after all, Rhode Island is a tiny state, so even communities in the Blackstone River Valley or the East Bay are relatively convenient for exploring the capital. Staying in one of these nearby areas might save you $50–100 per night for a room that's comparable to what you'll find in the city, depending on the time of year. Providence is a commercial, educational, and political hub—it hosts a fair number of conventions and can be especially busy on weekends during the school year and weekdays any time. Generally, the farther ahead you book a room, the better you'll do on the rate.

DOWNTOWN PROVIDENCE $100-150

The **Courtyard by Marriott Providence Downtown** (32 Exchange Terr., 401/272-1191 or 888/887-7955, www.courtyard.com, $139–199) closely resembles the historic tan-brick structures on Exchange Street beside it—aesthetically it's a marvelous property, and it couldn't be more conveniently situated. Predictably, the hotel has been phenomenally popular since it opened, with relatively reasonable rates for downtown but high for the Courtyard brand. The 216 guest rooms are large and airy, and many have unobstructed views of the State House, Providence Place Mall, and WaterPlace Park. All have free high-speed Internet access, two-line phones, and large work desks. Common amenities include a business center and library, an indoor pool with a hot tub, a fitness center, and a small café. It can get a little harried in the small lobby, but that's a minor quibble; it's an all-around excellent property.

The **(Providence Biltmore** (11 Dorrance St., 401/421-0700 or 800/294-7709, www.providencebiltmore.com, $149–189) dates to 1922 and is unquestionably the city's grande dame. Each of the 291 guest rooms is quite cushy, and 181 of them are suites with sitting areas. It has a full health club, a car-rental agency next door, and a very good restaurant (a branch of the acclaimed seafood chain McCormick and Schmick's), but it's the sense of history and the perfect location that draw most guests back again. The hotel is worth visiting just to admire the elaborate lobby with its soaring three-tiered atrium, vaulted

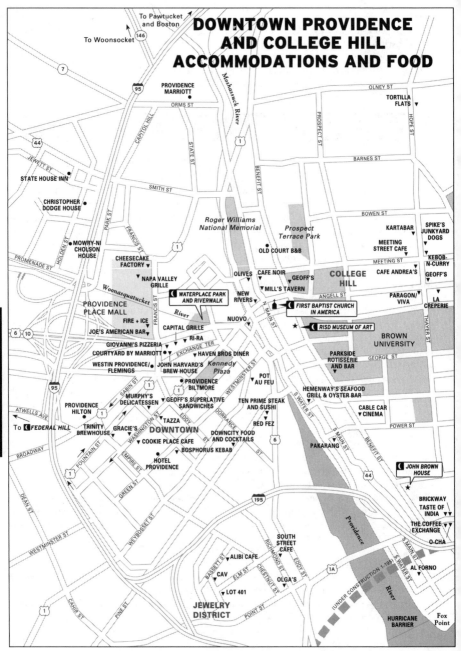

DOWNTOWN PROVIDENCE AND COLLEGE HILL ACCOMMODATIONS AND FOOD

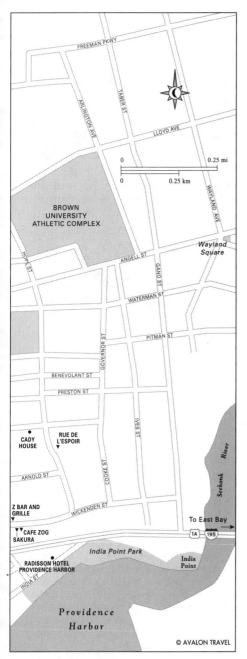

gilt ceiling, and gurgling fountains. At one time, the guest rooms had become somewhat less fabulous than the public areas, but an impressive and expensive $10 million rejuvenation in the early 2000s changed all that—accommodations are warm and atmospheric, with elegant bathroom fixtures, fine linens, and other cushy amenities. Fans of massage and facials should keep in mind that the Biltmore has a branch of the Red Door Spa.

Historic **Christopher Dodge House B&B** (11 W. Park St., 401/351-6111, www.providence-hotel.com, $130–180) occupies a gorgeously restored 1850s Italianate Victorian with a dignified redbrick facade, soaring pressed-tin ceilings, and beautifully crafted (and restored) original woodwork and plaster molding, tall windows, and polished wide-plank floors. The eight-room property offers a nice range of rooms, the higher-end units with kitchenettes and some with gas fireplaces; all have a mix of inviting reproduction American antiques and contemporary conveniences, such as reading chairs and desks. Full breakfast and off-street parking are included, guests can use the close-by Foundry Sports Medicine and Fitness Center, and all rooms have cable TV and in-room phones. This is an upscale but relaxed property where you'll receive personal but unobtrusive service.

The 274-room **Providence Hilton** (21 Atwells Ave., at Broadway, 401/831-3900, $139–179), formerly a Holiday Inn, has been completely updated and upgraded with new textiles in all the rooms along with a full fitness center, an indoor pool, and a whirlpool tub. Despite the upgrade, this property is in a loud and rather unattractive location at a busy intersection west of the convention center, just off I-95. You can walk to downtown attractions and Johnson and Wales, and Federal Hill is just a short walk in the other direction. Rates are lowest on weekends, and at busy times they go up significantly.

$150-250

One of the trendiest spots on the city's lodging

PROVIDENCE

scene, the boutiquey ◖ **Hotel Providence** (311 Westminster St., 401/861-8000 or 877/776-8430, www.thehotelprovidence.com $159–209) occupies a stunning late-19th-century building on formerly forlorn Westminster Street, now at the center of this downtown neighborhood's comeback. The 64 rooms and 16 suites are outfitted with tiger-maple furnishings, plush upholstered chairs and beddings (pillow-top beds, duvets and sheets with high thread counts), and original art by RISD Graduate School chair and acclaimed artist Nancy Friese. Each unit has a large work desk, a coffeemaker, a hair dryer, a shower with a rain showerhead, high-speed wireless Internet, dual phone lines with voicemail, a large TV, a CD player–clock radio, and top-quality bath amenities. This is a hip, design-themed hotel that has become a fashionable fixture of downtown Providence. It's very close to the Johnson and Wales downtown campus and all the bars and dining of the Jewelry District. The ground floor hosts one of the city's top restaurants, Aspire (formerly L'Epicureo).

Offering the only accommodations in the city's bustling Federal Hill neighborhood is the trendy ◖ **Hotel Dolce Villa** (63 De Pasquale Ave., 401/383-7031, www.dolcevillari.com, $169–309) on De Pasquale Square. Although this is a small operation with just 14 one- and two-bedroom suites, it's run like a full-service hotel, with a well-trained 24-hour staff and experienced management. A departure from the usual dark and heavy New England look, guest room decor feels distinctly contemporary, bright, and sleek, with stainless-steel appliances and white tile walls, white marble floors, linens, and modern furniture, including leather sofas; a few rooms have balconies overlooking the festive café culture in the square below. Every suite comes with a fully equipped kitchen, making this a true bargain—and a great nest to host dinner parties using ingredients from the fabulous food shops steps from the hotel. Other nice touches include DVD and CD players, flat-screen TVs, and, in the two-room suites, remote-control gas-burning fireplaces. Behind the main building, the hotel also rents out Villa Toscana, a spectacular VIP suite with two

© MICHAEL BLANDING

The Hotel Providence is a highlight of Westminster Street.

bathrooms, a living room, an impressive commercial kitchen, and plenty of room to entertain (rates start at $499 per night for the villa). This superb little gem is operated by the restaurant group that owns the excellent Caffe Dolce Vita and Geppetto's Pizzeria next door and the nearby Mediterraneo Caffe.

The **Providence Marriott** (1 Orms St., 401/272-2400 or 886/807-2171, www.marriott.com, $169–209) has a superbly trained and extremely warm staff, plush rooms with desks and armchairs with ottomans, upscale bath amenities, a very nice health club and indoor-outdoor pool, and a good restaurant with a summer outdoor pool deck and grill, the Bluefin Grille (401/553-0424). Parking is also included. It's a terrific property in every regard but for the fact that it's slightly north of downtown's attractions and restaurants—a 10-minute walk, which is unpleasant only if it's cold or wet outside. This 351-room hotel is just a short walk north of the State House, however, and it's right off I-95.

Over $250

One of the most distinctive and admired contemporary hotels in downtown Providence is the 364-room **Westin Providence** (1 W. Exchange St., 401/598-8000 or 800/937-8461, www.westinprovidence.com, $270–300), a dramatic neoclassical skyscraper with peaked gables and a redbrick facade. Interior elements carry out the elegant theme, from the massive glass-dome rotunda to public areas of marble, polished dark woods, and recessed lighting. Guest rooms mix reproduction French and British antiques with rich fabrics and wallpapers, and the oversized bathrooms boast plush fixtures and fancy soaps and shampoos. Units in a level of rooms called Westin's Guest Office contain business-oriented perks such as ergonomically designed seating and desks, in-room fax machines, printers, and copiers, and two-line speakerphones. The rooftop health club, located on the sixth floor under a cavernous glass dome, ranks among the top health club facilities at any hotel in New England. It's available for $10 per day for nonguests, but has no fee for anyone staying at any Providence hotel. The hotel also has two restaurants, Flemings and Agora, and three lounges that have an extensive selection of cognacs, wines, and aperitifs. Another plus is the central location, with enclosed elevated walkways that connect the hotel both to the Providence Convention Center and Providence Place Mall. The Westin may lack the tradition of the nearby Biltmore, but in every other regard it's comparable or better.

COLLEGE HILL AND THE WATERFRONT
$100-150

Radisson Hotel Providence Harbor (220 India St., 401/272-5577 or 800/395-7046, www.radisson.com, $149–179), with 136 rooms and an enviable location overlooking Providence Harbor, is a very good mid-priced chain property that enjoys equal popularity among leisure and business travelers. Its location, wedged between I-195 and an exit ramp, may sound off-putting, but you can't beat the convenience to India Point Park, the hip restaurants on Wickenden Street and down by Fox Point, and the campuses of Brown and RISD. Rooms themselves are fairly traditional and cookie-cutter, but they are clean and bright, half have water views, and for an extra $10–20 you can get one with a whirlpool bath. It has an exercise room with whirlpool, an outdoor pool whose terrace has water views, and a functional restaurant.

The **◖ Old Court B&B** (144 Benefit St., 401/751-2002, www.oldcourt.com, $145–215) has just about the most wonderful setting in Providence, in the heart of the historic Benefit Street neighborhood. Built as a rectory in 1863, it's beside the old Rhode Island courthouse and nearly across from the original state house. Guest rooms have truly museum-quality antiques, collectibles, and chandeliers mostly from the Victorian era and early 20th century, and they are themed after specific styles or mood-setting furnishings: One room has Chippendale pieces, another Eastlake Victorian antiques. The Stove Room is anchored by an antique stove original to the rectory. The rooms are refreshingly free of clutter and cloying tchotchkes, allowing the inn to strike a pleasing balance between a traditional B&B and a small luxury hotel. This is one of the priciest B&Bs in inland Rhode Island, but considering the lavish furnishings, delightfully scenic and convenient location, and modern amenities (phones, TVs, and private baths in every room), the Old Court represents a very smart value.

PROVIDENCE

Food

Providence had great restaurants well before Alice Waters and Wolfgang Puck began revolutionizing the way chefs approach cooking. The city has long been home to many ethnic groups with rich culinary traditions, including Italians, Portuguese, Latin Americans, and Asians. Providence's own Little Italy, on Federal Hill, ranks among the best in the world outside the big Italy. Indian and Thai restaurants flourished long before they became commonplace elsewhere, as did sushi. Seafood plays a vital role in local cuisine, and as an international port, Providence has always had access to exotic ingredients.

The city's arty element and throngs of students have created a desire, if not a need, for cheap and innovative foods—and don't forget, quite a few of those students and their professors are affiliated with the fabulous culinary arts program of Johnson and Wales University, home to the world's largest culinary archive.

As the trends of contemporary American cooking have evolved in recent years, from the garlic–mashed potato and sun-dried tomato phases of years gone by to today's obsession with kumquats, pomegranates, ostrich meat, and caramelized everything, Providence chefs have moved with the trends. The already exceptional seafood, Italian, Asian, and regional New England menus have been expanded and updated.

One of the more unusual ways to enjoy a bit of Rhode Island when you're miles away is to contact **Clambakes to Travel** (800/722-CLAM—800/722-2526, www.clambakeco.com), a Pawtucket-based company that will ship up to 16 authentic clambake meals anywhere in the continental United States. Each meal includes a 1.25-pound lobster, steamed clams, mussels, Portuguese *chouriço* sausage, corn on the cob, red bliss potatoes, and onions packed with rockweed inside a reusable pot. It's $123 for one meal but just $363 for six meals, which is a pretty reasonable price divvied up among a large group.

DOWNTOWN PROVIDENCE
Upscale

One of the most sought-after reservations for date-nighters, **New Rivers** (7 Steeple St., 401/751-0350, www.newriversrestaurant.com, 5–11 P.M. Mon.–Sat., $19–28) is an elegant, candlelit boîte housed in a 1793 warehouse originally built for iron merchants. The menu is as alluring as the atmosphere: The rabbit ravioli in sassafras *jus* with quail egg yolk and fava beans is a stunner, as is the grilled shoulder steak with peppercorn and coriander crust. Save room for the honey-drizzled Greek yogurt *panna cotta* in rhubarb consommé; you won't regret it.

A warm and romantic eatery in a quiet downtown alley, **Pot au Feu** (44 Custom House St., 401/273-8953, www.potaufeuri.com, 5–10:30 P.M. Sun.–Thurs., 5–11 P.M. Sat.–Sun., $16–23 in the bistro, $22–35 in the salon) is the city's seminal French restaurant. It opened in the early 1970s and has seemingly grown more popular each year. Depending on your mood or your budget, opt either for the classic bistro fare of the cozy basement space, where a classic bouillabaisse and a signature dessert of crème brûlée vie for your attention (dine here with a group of friends), or for the suave upstairs salon, which is good for celebrating a special occasion. Here try roast duckling, foie gras, and similarly rich French standbys.

The $25 prix fixe dinner menu is what pulls in value-loving gourmets to **Rue de L'Espoir** (99 Hope St., 401/751-8890, www.therue.com, 7:30 A.M.–10:30 P.M. Mon.–Fri and 8:30 A.M.–10:30 P.M. Sat.–Sun., $19–27). But it's the regular menu that they keep coming back for, with its specialties like delicate miso-glazed halibut and garlic-rubbed rib eyes.

Although it's a chain, the upscale **Capital Grille** (1 Union Station, 401/521-5600, 11:30 A.M.–11 P.M. daily, $25–45) feels distinctly local, a favorite haunt of politicos from the nearby State House and business execs from surrounding office buildings. The dry-aged porterhouse steaks are the main draw, plus broiled fresh lobster and obscenely large sides of baked potato, creamed spinach, and asparagus with hollandaise. The restaurant's interior has a dark, clubby feel, but that's part of the Capital Grille's gimmick. The entrance lies steps from Riverwalk and a very short distance from Providence Place Mall.

If you can pardon the mall location, the Providence branch of the upscale **Napa Valley Grille** (North Tower Entrance, Providence Place, 401/270-6272, 11:30 A.M.–9 P.M. daily, $17–33) works well as both an elegant setting for a special occasion and a spot for a tasty sampling of creative California-style cooking. Murals of the California wine country, wineglass chandeliers, and subdued amber lighting convey the theme, and the restaurant's wine list offers a nice balance of regional California wines. As for the menu, consider the crab-crusted Maine cod with zucchini noodles, Yukon gold potatoes, and orange-ginger sauce, or maple-walnut chicken breast with crème fraîche mashed potatoes, broccoli rabe, and a natural reduction.

Another of Providence's favorite power-lunch venues, **Nuovo** (1 Citizens Plaza, 401/421-2525, www.cafenuovo.com, 11 A.M.–10 P.M. Tues.–Sun., $24–40) presents an appropriately dazzling and extensive menu of rich and elaborate contemporary American dishes, including caramelized sea scallops, lamb-lobster ravioli, and a show-stopping Dover sole prepared at your table. The wine list reads like a who's who of top vintages. The restaurant occupies the ground floor of a fancy office tower at the confluence of the Moshassuck and Woonasquatucket Rivers—some seats are right on the river terrace.

Ten Prime Steak and Sushi (55 Pine St., 401/453-2333, www.tenprimesteakandsushi.com, 5–10 P.M. Mon., 11:30 A.M.–10 P.M. Tues.–Thurs., 11:30 A.M.–11 P.M. Fri., 5–11 P.M. Sat.–Sun., $20–40) has been a white-hot culinary star for a decade, serving tasty portions of Asian-inspired steaks and seafood. The sushi is artful and delicious, but not every item has an Asian spin—a formidable

veal chop, for instance, is served with portobello mushrooms and shaved Parmesan. As interesting as the food is, Ten Prime has been most successful because of its lavish decor, huge fancy martinis, extensive sake list, and sexy attitude. Drawbacks are the occasionally haughty, or in some cases just flaky, service as well as certain dishes that sound interesting but are executed unevenly.

Creative but Casual

The fashionable Downcity option that caters to a see-and-be-seen crowd but is nevertheless totally unpretentious, **Gracie's** (194 Washington St., 401/272-7811, graciesprovidence.com, 5 P.M.–close Tues.–Sat., $11–40) is one of the city's favorite "special occasion" spots, known for its sterling service, inviting contemporary dining room, and exceptionally creative and well-crafted food that relies heavily on organic ingredients. You could kick things off with the unusual confit of frogs' legs, baby fennel, and roasted garlic before trying the entrée of roasted lamb loin with rhubarb, sweet potato puree, and *min jus*. There's always a superb tasting menu offered each day.

The quirky hangout **CAV** (14 Imperial Pl., 401/751-9164, www.cavrestaurant.com, 11:30 A.M.–10 P.M. Mon.–Thurs., 11:30 A.M.–1 A.M. Fri., 10 A.M.–10 P.M. Sat., 10:30 A.M.–10 P.M. Sun., $15–32) occupies an old knife factory in the Jewelry District and offers coffee, antiques, and victuals—the first letters of these three words spell the restaurant's name. So you can drop in to sip espresso and nosh on fresh baked goods or hunker down for a substantial meal, all the while checking out the considerable selection of vintage furnishings and goods. The menu tends toward fresh pastas, but a number of innovatively prepared fish and meat grills, salads, and desserts show up. CAV has folk and jazz music many weekend evenings. This is a popular spot—book ahead when possible.

You're likely to see culinary students from nearby Johnson and Wales congregating at the art deco **Downcity Food and Cocktails** (50 Weybosset St., 401/331-9217, www.

PROVIDENCE

downcityfood.com, 11:30 A.M.–11 P.M. Mon.–Fri., 10 A.M.–11 P.M. Sat., 9 A.M.–11 P.M. Sun., $13–28), a stylish take on a traditional greasy spoon. The little cocktail bar has a following and is a favorite spot for an early drink; it's also a hot spot for brunch on Saturday and Sunday. Tasty dinner offerings include lobster-and-leek chowder with scallion-and-parsley crisps; roasted French rack of pork with apricot-guava glaze and mashed sweet and Idaho potatoes; and forest mushroom and port wine ravioletti with artichoke hearts, goat cheese, and arugula salad. There are great desserts too.

A quirky popular bistro serving mod-Californian cuisine, **Julian's** (318 Broadway, 401/861-1770, www.juliansprovidence.com, 9 A.M.–11 P.M. daily, $11–20) is a homey spot that offers uncomplicated, soul-warming fare that might include maple-walnut-pesto-crusted chicken breast with creamy potato salad and grilled pineapple, or ravioli with spinach, walnut, shallots, and goat cheese. The dining rooms are filled with unusual objects d'art and decorations. Breakfast is served all day—and the eggs Benedict Nova Scotia (with house-smoked salmon) is irresistible. At lunch, check out the long list of specialty sandwiches. BYOB.

The laid-back **Red Fez** (49 Peck St., 401/272-1212, lunch 11:30 A.M.–3:30 P.M. Tues.–Fri., dinner 5:30–10 P.M. Tues.–Thurs., 5:30–11 P.M. Fri.–Sat., $6–14) is a dark and intimate space that offers excellent light fare in the bar, including hefty and creative sandwiches, and more substantial dinners in a separate downstairs space, where you might sample orange-chipotle marinated pork tenderloin with seared kale and chipotle mashed sweet potatoes, or balsamic-glazed grilled salmon topped with tomato-caper relish served with grilled stuffed tomatoes and orzo-pesto salad.

Presenting healthful, creative, and truly eclectic cuisine that draws on Indian, Mediterranean, and East Asian ingredients and culinary traditions, **Lot 401** (44 Hospital St., 401/490-3980, from 5:30 P.M. Tues.–Sun., $18–28) definitely stretches when it comes to culinary innovation. Possibilities include Asian-braised pork bellies, or Atlantic cod with garlic, chives, flageolet beans, Chinese pork, and kale. This is a boisterous, see-and-be-seen place with a mod postindustrial aesthetic. It's in the Jewelry District and draws a young, fashionable crowd; the glitzy upstairs space becomes a swank night spot as the evening progresses.

Three Gringos CantinaMoJoe's (166 Broadway, 401/831-1183, 11 A.M.–9:30 P.M. daily, $8–18) is another of the cool Broadway spots. There's a great range of beers on tap and in bottles, and you can often catch cultural events here, including jewelry shows and art exhibits. It serves excellent grilled pizzas and other tasty comfort fare.

Pizza, Pasta, and Pub Grub

The loud, high-ceilinged **Cheesecake Factory** (94 Providence Pl., 401/270-4010, www.thecheesecakefactory.com, 11:30 A.M.–11 P.M. Mon.–Thurs., 11:30 A.M.–12:30 A.M. Fri.–Sat., 10 A.M.–11 P.M. Sun., $8–23) suffers a bit from crowds upon crowds (and that means obnoxiously long lines, especially on weekends), but the staff here takes it all in stride and remains consistently personable. If this seems like a lot of fuss for a national chain restaurant on the ground floor of a shopping mall, well, it is. Still, the many-paged menu suggests an amazing variety of foods, offering more appetizers than most restaurants have total items, plus pizzas, burgers, stir-fries, tacos, chicken and biscuits, pastas, seafood, steaks, and massive salads and sandwiches. Of course, plenty of people come simply for the cheesecake, which is available in about 35 varieties, from Dutch apple-caramel to lemon mousse.

Another of the popular chain eateries at Providence Place Mall, Boston-based **Joe's American Bar** (148 Providence Pl., 401/270-4737, www.joesamerican.com, 11 A.M.–11 P.M. Mon.–Thurs., 11 A.M.–midnight Fri.–Sat., 10 A.M.–10 P.M. Sun., $9–24) has a strong following for dependable—if rather predictable—comfort cooking favored by "regular joes" (and Janes): meat loaf flame-grilled with mashed potatoes and sautéed spinach, milk shakes, barbecued baby back ribs, and Cobb salads.

Vintage signs and memorabilia lend a festive air to **Ri-Ra** (50 Exchange Terr., 401/272-1953, www.rira.com, 11:30 A.M.–10 P.M. daily, $9–18), a dapper Irish eatery along Exchange Terrace. Try traditional standbys prepared with considerable flair, such as corned beef and cabbage, salmon boxty (charbroiled salmon with diced tomato, scallion, and cream cheese in a potato pancake with an Irish parsley sauce), and beef-and-Guinness stew—you'll find a smattering of vegetarian options as well. An oft-requested finale is Kelly's Cake, a dark-chocolate confection layered with Bailey's-chocolate mousse and coated with a milk-chocolate glaze. As you might guess, Ri-Ra is a hit with the after-work happy hour set.

Chicago-style pies are the specialty at the casual and kid-friendly **Giovanni's Pizzeria** (85 Richmond St., 401/621-8500, 11 A.M.–11 P.M. daily, $11–17). It's a favorite for the gooey, cheese-filled overstuffed calzones too.

An atmospheric subterranean haunt along Exchange Street, the **John Harvard's Brew House** (36 Exchange Terr., 401/274-BREW—401/274-2739, www.johnharvards.com, 11:30 A.M.–1 A.M. Sun.–Thurs., 11:30 A.M.–2 A.M. Fri.–Sat., $8–13) serves a fairly typical but reliable mix of pizzas, dinner salads, ale-battered fish-and-chips, hickory-smoked ribs, and more unusual foods such as baked crabmeat–stuffed cod over saffron rice with fresh corn, broccoli, and red pepper ragout.

Another favorite among fans of this genre, the **Trinity Brewhouse** (186 Fountain St., 401/453-BEER—401/453-2337, www.trinitybrewhouse.com, 11:30 A.M.–1 A.M. Mon.–Thurs., 11:30 A.M.–2 A.M. Fri., noon–2 A.M. Sat., noon–1 A.M. Sun., $8–22) brews several beers and serves an impressive range of snack foods and light entrées, including pulled-pork barbecue sandwiches and shepherd's pie. You'll find great burgers and also some veggie options such as falafel salad and margherita pizza.

Ethnic Fare

Look to **Bosphorus Kebab** (286 Westminster St., 401/454-3500, 11 A.M.–9 P.M. Fri.–Sat.,

11 A.M.–8 P.M. Sun., $3–7) for affordable and tasty Middle Eastern and Mediterranean victuals, including pizzas, salads, and freshly made soups.

Under the category of "eat-ertainment," **Fire and Ice** (48 Providence Pl., 401/270-4040, www.fire-ice.com, 11:30 A.M.–10 P.M. Mon.–Thurs., 11:30 A.M.–11 P.M. Fri.–Sat., 10 A.M.–10 P.M. Sun., dinner $17 all-you-can-eat, less for brunch and lunch) looks like a *Pee-wee's Playhouse* homage gone horribly awry, with dangling multicolored chandeliers and brilliantly hued furnishings of all shapes and sizes. Walk over to the various veggie, meat, and seafood stations, fill your bowl with whatever interests you (swordfish, pork, scallops, portobello mushrooms, leeks, or jalapeños), and then continue to a sauce station where again you get to pick (Jamaican jerk, rosemary, roasted corn and tomato, Thai basil cream, or a dozen others). Move on to a large grill, where you get to watch a chef cook your chosen ingredients. It's noisy and usually packed, but if the gimmick works for you, try it—there's no arguing that it's a great value for big eaters (return trips for extra helpings are included).

In the funky Broadway section, head to **Phoenix Dragon** (256 Broadway, 401/831-7555, www.phoenixdragonrestaurant.com, 11 A.M.–10 P.M. Mon.–Thurs., 11 A.M.–11 P.M. Fri.–Sat., 10:30 A.M.–9:30 P.M. Sun., $7–20) for commendable Chinese food. It's set on the ground floor of a stately redbrick Italianate Victorian with an attractive dining room. It's a classic menu of this genre, with so many options you wonder how the place could possibly stock all the ingredients, some of them rather unusual, on a regular basis. It's one of the best places in town for dim sum (most items are just $5–6), and the kitchen also turns out a very nice steamed half chicken with ginger and scallions. For something truly memorable (and pricey), consider the sliced Australia abalone with vegetables, or the braised sea cucumber with oyster sauce.

Quick Bites

For a memorable breakfast or lunch, don't miss

Nick's (500 Broadway, 401/421-0286, www.nicksonbroadway.com, breakfast and lunch 7 A.M.–3 P.M. Wed.–Sat., 8 A.M.–3 P.M. Sun., dinner 5:30–10 P.M. Wed.–Sat., breakfast and lunch $6–10, dinner $15–27), a tiny oasis of amazingly delicious cooking in the city's up-and-coming West Broadway section. It's basically a hole-in-the-wall, although it's bright and airy with massive plate-glass windows, helmed by one of the city's rising culinary stars, Derek Wagner. A typically tantalizing treat is the grilled sea scallops and shrimp with citrus, apples, frisée, and honey. You can create your own omelet at breakfast (choosing from memorable ingredients such as chèvre, capers, roasted red peppers, and caramelized onions), or perhaps dig into the buttermilk hotcakes with apple-cinnamon compote along with a side of smoked salmon.

In the Jewelry District, **Olga's Cup and Saucer** (103 Point St., 401/831-6666, http://olgascupandsaucer.blogspot.com, 7 A.M.–4 P.M. Mon.–Fri., 9 A.M.–2 P.M. Sat.–Sun., baked goods $2–6, lunch $8–10) produces delicious artisanal breads, apple-hazelnut pies, lemon-blueberry pudding, chocolate-almond marble cake, and coconut oat-crisp cookies. It's a cozy nook to enjoy a pastry, bagels, and coffee breakfast or break with friends.

Haven Bros. Diner (Kennedy Plaza, 401/861-7777, 5 P.M.–3 A.M. daily, $2–5) is another of the favorite late-night greasy spoons in town, famous for its hearty breakfast food. This loveably gruff hangout is actually a diner on wheels, which the owners park outside City Hall into the wee hours.

When you're jonesing for a solid sandwich—nothing more, nothing less—head straight to **Alibi CafeRue** (18 Bassett St., 401/273-2233, 11:30 A.M.–8:30 P.M. Mon.–Sat., closed Sun., $7–9) for first-rate lunches. It serves up clever world-beat takes on the standards: The "sea quest" is a delicious dill-laden tuna fish number, and the roast beef with Boursin is a long-time favorite of regulars.

Cookie Place Cafe (280 Washington St., 401/351-8789, www.cookieplace.org/cafe, 7 A.M.–11:30 P.M. Mon.–Fri., $2–5) serves a nice variety of sandwiches (the Cajun seafood salad and bacon cheeseburger are popular options), but it's best known for its addictive chocolate-chip cookies and other baked goodies such as Heath bar toffee crunch brownies and cinnamon rolls. And if chocolate isn't your thing, the lemon-butterscotch cookies are delicious. Cookie Place is a not-for-profit organization that offers supportive employment for people with psychiatric illnesses; it's closed weekends.

Since 1929, downtown office workers have relied on **Murphy's Delicatessen** (100 Fountain St., 401/621-8467, http://murphysdeliandbar.com, 11 A.M.–1 A.M. Mon.–Thurs., 11 A.M.–2 A.M. Fri., 8 A.M.–2 A.M. Sat., 9 A.M.–1 A.M. Sun., $4–15) for filling sandwiches. Favorites include the lobster salad roll; the artery-clogging corned beef, pastrami, salami, and Swiss; and Murphy's Reuben with Irish corned beef. Several burgers are offered as well as some veggie options.

Java Joints

A hot address in the cool Downcity area, **Tazza Caffe and Lounge** (250 Westminster St., 401/421-3300, www.tazzacaffe.com, 7 A.M.–11 P.M. Mon., 7 A.M.–midnight Tues., 7 A.M.–1 A.M. Wed.–Thurs., 7 A.M.–2 A.M. Fri., 8 A.M.–2 A.M. Sat., 8 A.M.–midnight Sun., $8–16) offers all kinds of live music and readings and serves coffee and wine. The food in this hip, arty space is great too—there are sandwiches, salads, and delicious desserts. It's one of the best spots for people-watching in the city, and valet parking is available.

Gourmet Goods and Picnic Supplies

Geoff's Superlative Sandwiches (217 Westminster St., 401/273-8885) sells a wonderful array of snacks, sandwiches, and gourmet prepared foods to eat in or take out. There are signature secret sauces in almost every sandwich—witness the "Providence Monthly" (grilled chicken, melted Muenster, avocado, and Shedd's sauce on a bun), or the "Celina" (hot turkey, coleslaw, melted Havarti, and *picante* sauce).

FEDERAL HILL
Italian

On Federal Hill, Providence has one of the most prominent Little Italy neighborhoods in the country. You could easily spend a week or so sampling the specialties of every delightful grocery, trattoria, pizza place, and food shop in the district.

An upscale favorite is the **Blue Grotto** (210 Atwells Ave., 401/272-9030, 11:30 A.M.–2 P.M. Mon.–Fri., noon–3 P.M. Sat., 5–10 P.M. Mon.–Thurs., 5–10:30 P.M. Fri., 4:30–10:30 P.M. Sat.; noon–9 P.M. Sun., $15–28), a dignified restaurant whose polite, tux-clad waiters glide about the somewhat formal dining room serving plates of gnocchi with a light basil-tomato sauce and fresh mozzarella, or lobster meat and littleneck clams in a spicy marinara over risotto.

Pane e Vino (365 Atwells Ave., 401/223-2230, www.panevino.com, 5–10 P.M. Mon.–Thurs., 5–11 P.M. Fri.–Sat., 4–9 P.M. Sun. $14–24) is upscale in feel more than in price. The high caliber of cooking is impressive, from a starter of littleneck clams with a garlic-tomato broth and cannellini beans to a main course of gnocchi with a rich port wine–wild boar sauce. Desserts here are excellent, and the wine list includes more than two dozen varieties by the glass.

Tavernlike █ **Mediterraneo Caffe** (134 Atwells Ave., 401/331-7760, www.mediterraneocaffe.com, 11:30 A.M.–9 P.M. Mon.–Thurs., 11:30 A.M.–10 P.M. Fri., 11:30 A.M.–1 A.M. Sat., 5–9 P.M. Sun., $14–22) is a loud and fun place with a youngish crowd. Tall French windows overlook the street, making it a prime spot to watch the world go by (everybody gravitates toward the sidewalk seating in summer). Don't think the glitzy ambience is merely a cover for so-so food: This kitchen knows what it's doing, presenting superb regional Italian fare such as a double-cut pork chops stuffed with spinach, prosciutto, and fresh mozzarella, and both straightforward and complicated pasta dishes such as fusilli with a pink vodka sauce of plum tomatoes, onions, pancetta, and heavy cream. Late at night, the place switches gears and becomes a euro-trendy dance club with an elitist velvet-rope door policy.

On reputation alone, **Angelo's Civita Farnese** (141 Atwells Ave., 401/621-8171, www.angelosonthehill.com, 11:30 A.M.–9 P.M. Mon.–Thurs., 11:30 A.M.–10 P.M. Fri.–Sat., noon–9 P.M. Sun., $4–9) could survive on any street in Providence, but here on Federal Hill it's a star among the cheaper eateries—expect heaping portions of traditional red-sauce fare in this boisterous place with communal seating. There's not much in the way of ambience, but it's fun—and former mayor Buddy Cianci loves it.

You can't miss the notably all-pink exterior of **Zooma Trattoria** (245 Atwells Ave., 401/383-2002, http://trattoriazooma.com, 11:30 A.M.–9:30 P.M. Sun.–Thurs., 11:30 A.M.–11 P.M. Fri.–Sat., $13–20), named for lyrics from the Louis Prima song "Angelina." The art-filled restaurant with high ceilings and elegant furnishings excels at creative regional Italian fare, from fresh pastas to fine grills. Save room for the luscious pear tart. There's also a first-rate wine list heavy on both Italian and North American vintages.

Geppetto's (57 De Pasquale Ave., 401/270-3003, www.geppettospizzeria.com, 11 A.M.–close daily, $6–14) is justly famous for its superb wood-fired pizzas, plus great salads, tender calamari, and a good selection of beer and wine. The restaurant doesn't have a regular closing time, but it's usually open late, with seating right on the busy square.

Try **Andino's** (171 Atwells Ave., 401/421-3715, 11 A.M.–1 A.M. daily, $10–24) for signature dishes such as chicken Andino (boneless chicken baked with artichoke hearts, sliced pepperoni, and sweet peppers in a white wine sauce); linguine with whole clams; and veal Zingarella (veal medallions sautéed with marinara sauce, roasted red peppers, sliced onions, and white mushrooms). **Joe Marzelli's Old Canteen** (120 Atwells Ave., 401/751-5544, http://theoldcanteen.com, noon–10 P.M. Wed.–Mon., closed Tues., $9–13) is an elegant white mansion made only slightly less elegant by its pulsing pink neon sign, a dependable middle-of-the-road option with reasonably priced fare. A memorable spot for desserts, especially on a warm summer evening, is **Caffe Dolce Vita**

PROVIDENCE

(59 De Pasquale Ave., 401/331-8240), a coffeehouse, pastry shop, and *gelateria* whose outdoor tables are shaded with umbrellas. Across the square, drop by **Antonelli Poultry** (62 De Pasquale Ave., 401/421-8739) for the freshest chicken around, not to mention pheasant, pigeon, rabbit, and farm-fresh eggs.

You can buy fantastic handmade ravioli in about 75 varieties at **Venda Ravioli** (275 Atwells Ave., 401/421-9105), one of the most inspired delis in any Italian neighborhood in the country; here you'll find fresh sausages, sauces, oils, vinegars, cheeses, and so on. A century-old wine and liquor shop, **Gasbarro's** (361 Atwells Ave., 401/421-4170) sells some wonderful Italian imports, including about 150 varieties of chianti and almost as many of grappa. **Tony's Colonial Food** (311 Atwells Ave., 401/621-8675) is a tempting *salumeria* with just about every kind of gourmet grocery imaginable. **Roma Gourmet** (310 Atwells Ave., 401/331-8620), across from Tony's, has imported cheese, olives, sauces, and pastas, as well as hot dishes ready for takeout. Family-owned since 1916, **Scialo Bros. Bakery** (257 Atwells Ave., 401/421-0986) fires up its brick ovens daily to produce delicious Italian bread, biscotti, cakes, and pastries.

Creative but Casual

Departures from traditional Italian fare are becoming more commonplace on the Hill: Shellfish devotees should consider **Providence Oyster Bar** (283 Atwells Ave., 401/272-8866, www.providenceoysterbar.com, 4–10 P.M. Mon.–Thurs. and Sat., noon–11 P.M. Fri., $16–28), which offers a great deal more than its name suggests—although the half dozen varieties of oyster on the half shell are always fresh. The rest of the menu offers a fairly typical array of seafood, including baked Chilean sea bass with a light citrus butter and platters of fried clams and scallops. An excellent oyster stew alone qualifies as a pretty substantial meal. The menu may suggest a bare-bones spot with butcher's paper on the tables, but in fact this chatter-filled eatery is warmly lighted with dark-wood trim and a handsome long bar.

Boisterous **Opa** (244 Atwells Ave., 401/351-8282, www.providencefederalhill.com/opa, 5 P.M.–1 A.M. Mon.–Thurs., 5 P.M.–2 A.M. Fri.–Sat., $13–23) offers a slight departure from the neighborhood's usual Italian standbys, presenting mostly Greek and Middle Eastern specialties. It's a cozy spot with just a handful of tables inside and a few more along the sidewalk. Drop by for hummus platters, mixed lamb and chicken grills, and some of the freshest and most bountiful salads in town.

Ethnic Fare

Federal Hill also has an excellent Mexican restaurant, **Don Jose's Tequilas** (351 Atwells Ave., 401/454-8951, www.donjoseteq.com, 3–10 P.M. Mon.–Wed., 11:30 A.M.–11 P.M. Thurs., 11:30 A.M.–1 A.M. Fri.–Sat., 11 A.M.–10 P.M. Sun., $14–22), with a mix of Americanized and quite authentic regional dishes. The little dining room is modest but cheerfully decorated, with small tables and black bentwood chairs; extremely friendly and helpful waitstaff deliver service with a smile along with platters of chiles rellenos stuffed with mashed potatoes and jack cheese, chicken quesadillas, swordfish burritos, and chips with a smoky chipotle salsa.

In a simple, nondescript house down the hill from Federal Hill, **Chilango's Taqueria** (447 Manton Ave., at Atwells Ave., 401/383-4877, 11 A.M.–9 P.M. Sun.–Thurs., 11 A.M.–10 P.M. Fri.–Sat., $5–10) is worth the drive for perhaps the most authentic down-home Mexican food in the state, plus a nice range of Mexican beers and tequilas. It's not fancy, but that's part of the fun.

COLLEGE HILL AND THE RIVERFRONT
Upscale

◖ **Al Forno** (577 S. Main St., 410/273-9760, www.alforno.com, 5–10 P.M. Tues.–Fri., 4–10 P.M. Sat., $16–32) occupies a squat warehouse near Fox Point with two-story-tall dining room windows that offer views of the ominous power plant across the Providence River and of the Hurricane Barrier. This restaurant put the neighborhood on the culinary map in 1980, and its reputation has raised the city's reputation as a dining destination—Al Forno's list of awards is almost unbelievable when you consider that it's not in one of the nation's larger cities. Among the high praise, the *International Herald Tribune* named it the world's best restaurant for casual dining. So what's all the fuss? Chef-owners (and married couple) Johanne Killeen and George Germon have made a study of northern Italian cuisine, which they prepare using—whenever appropriate—wood-burning ovens or open-flame grilling. Classic dishes include the clam roast with fiery hot sausage, tomatoes, endives, and mashed potatoes; and angel-hair noodles in fennel broth with roasted ocean catfish and peppery aioli. Pumpkin cod cake and avocado bruschetta is one of the more innovative starters. As you might guess, reservations are not easy to get—book well ahead if you can.

Waterman Grille (4 Richmond Sq., 401/521-9229, www.watermangrille.com, dinner 5–9 P.M. Mon.–Thurs., 5–10 P.M. Fri.–Sat., 5–8 P.M. Sun., brunch 10 A.M.–3 P.M. Sun., $18–29) has a less pricey pub menu in addition to more substantial fare. A lengthy list of creative martinis keeps trendsters happy. A big plus here is the location in a lovely old building on the Seekonk River. The art-filled dining room has floor-to-ceiling windows overlooking the water, so whether you come in the daytime or the evening, it's exceedingly romantic; weekend brunch is another great time to eat here. The menu emphasizes dishes like braised veal osso buco with garlic-mushroom demi-glace and celeriac mashed potatoes, or slow-roasted boneless duck with a Grand Marnier glaze and espresso sauce, praline–sweet potato hash, and sautéed and roasted vegetables.

Hemenway's Seafood Grill and Oyster Bar (121 S. Main St., 401/351-8570, www.hemenswayrestaurant.com, 11:30 A.M.–10 P.M. Mon.–Thurs., 11:30 A.M.–11 P.M. Fri.–Sat., noon–9 P.M. Sun., $17–35) is the place to go for fresh seafood. There's little pretentious or contrived about the food here—just fresh and simply prepared fish such as scampi over linguine,

fried shrimp dinners, broiled Florida grouper, baked scrod with seafood crumbs—just about every kind of fish imaginable. It's in an immense office building, but the nicest tables overlook the river. The oyster bar draws fans of the bivalve from all over the Northeast—14 varieties are served here.

Creative but Casual

Probably the most upscale and popular of the restaurants along Thayer Street, and still relatively affordable, is **Paragon/Viva** (234 Thayer St., 401/331-6200, www.paragonandviva.com, 11 A.M.–1 A.M. Sun.–Thurs., 11 A.M.–2 A.M. Fri.–Sat., $8–19), which occupies an airy street-corner space with funky hanging lamps and tall French door–style windows overlooking the varied pedestrian traffic. There's a lot of sidewalk seating in warm weather, and a sophisticated lounge with parquet floors and a large semicircular bar. People come here to drink as much as to nibble on tapas. If you don't look the part at this Brown University near-campus commissary, you may feel a bit out of place. The menu emphasizes creative pastas, pizzas, sandwiches, and fairly simple grills—good bets include the sea scallops with applewood smoked bacon, shallots, pinot grigio, and diced tomatoes; the lobster ravioli; the filet mignon with garlic butter; and the swordfish sandwich with a caper dill mayo.

One of several highly fashionable hangouts that have opened around Brown's campus in recent years, **Kartabar** (284 Thayer St., 401/331-8111, www.kartabar.com, 11 A.M.–1 A.M. Sun.–Thurs., 11 A.M.–2 A.M. Fri.–Sat., $10–20) is a martini lounge that has a second branch in Mexico. You might want to use a visit here as an excuse to show off those designer threads. The kitchen serves a vast array of low-maintenance comfort foods: burgers, grills, pastas, and the like, but it's more about the scene than the food.

Parkside Rotisserie and Bar (76 S. Main St., 401/331-0003, www.parksiderotisserie.com, 11:30 A.M.–10 P.M. Mon.–Thurs., 11:30 A.M.–11 P.M. Fri., 5–11 P.M. Sat., 4–9 P.M.

Sun., $15–32) is a terrific little neighborhood restaurant just across from Jackson-Gardner Park that draws a more adult and less sceney crowd than many of the restaurants this close to Brown and RISD. The staff is accommodating and fun. Inside this warmly lighted, long and narrow dining room, tables are set with crisp white napery and fringed by small wooden chairs or plush banquettes. The food is creative without going overboard, with an emphasis on pastas and rotisserie chicken as well as some excellent seafood grills. There's a nice selection of wines and beers.

Half lounge, half restaurant, **South Street Cafe** (54 South St., 401/454-5360, 11:30 A.M.–2 A.M. Tues.–Sat., closed Sun.–Mon., $13–22) rolls out a casual and solid grill menu in a somewhat noisy dining area. Some of the most popular offerings include *taquitos* and soft tacos, a roast beef sandwich with horseradish, and a hot pastrami on rye with powerful cheese.

Yuppies and students love to crowd the trendy bar at **◖ Rue de L'Espoir** (99 Hope St., 401/751-8890, www.therue.com, breakfast 7:30–11 A.M. Mon.–Fri., lunch 11:30 A.M.–5 P.M. Mon.–Fri., dinner 5–9 P.M. Sun.–Thurs., 5–10:30 P.M. Fri.–Sat., brunch 8:30 A.M.–2:30 P.M. Sat., 8:30 A.M.–3 P.M. Sun., $13–22) almost as much as they delight in supping here on sublime New American, Italian, and French fare—dishes include homemade ravioli filled with spinach, mushrooms, smoked Gouda, and ricotta. The restaurant maintains a friendly, low-attitude ambience. And as it's slightly off the beaten path for visitors, it has cultivated a strong following among locals since it opened back in 1976. It's a great all-around neighborhood eatery and a smart spot for brunch.

A snug and supertrendy café with exposed brick, tall gilt-frame mirrors, and walls covered with patrons' graffiti, **Café Noir** (125 N. Main St., 401/273-9090, www.cafenoirri.com, 5–10 P.M. Sun.–Thurs., 5–11 P.M. Fri.–Sat., $12–29) tends toward the outlandish, although it employs a waitstaff that can be snippy. The food combinations and preparations here can be overwrought—even outrageous—and not

always executed successfully, but usually you'll come away having enjoyed a memorable and tasty meal. Before you try any food, check out the sprightly and spunky drink list—the prickly pear margarita is a nice way to start things off. It's recommended that you order dessert first (lemon meringue tart with dried cherry compote and lemon confit is a popular option). Most patrons opt for the more expected (though unusual) starters such as five-spice duck confit spring rolls with pear jam, sautéed watercress, and duck demi-glace. A typically dazzling entrée of bacon-wrapped monkfish, sage-smoked flageolet beans, baby Russian kale, and zinfandel wine sauce appeared on a recent menu, but the kitchen is always toying around with new ideas.

Although it's less pretentious than Café Noir, **Z Bar and Grille** (244 Wickenden St., 401/831-1566, www.zbarandgrille.com, 11:30 A.M.–11 P.M. Sun.–Thurs., 11:30 A.M.–2 A.M. Fri.–Sat., $11–19) nevertheless strikes a sophisticated pose on the otherwise shabby-chic Wickenden Street restaurant row. Here you'll typically find a well-put-together crowd hobnobbing behind the long polished-wood bar or dining at tables in the loud but comfy dining room with exposed brick and air ducts. When the weather cooperates, you can escape the din on the lovely brick courtyard in back. Sup on creative pizzas, large salads, appetizers such as mushroom ravioli with shiitake mushroom and tasso cream, and entrées with a contemporary bent, such as filet mignon with garlic mashed potatoes and asparagus, or chicken, broccoli rabe, tomatoes, garlic, cannellini beans, and capers tossed over angel-hair pasta. Creative "Zangwiches" (groan) include oven-roasted turkey, cranberry sauce, and seasonal stuffing served on *lavash*.

An unassuming gem on the north side of Hope Street overlooking Lippitt Memorial Park, **Chez Pascal** (960 Hope St., 401/421-4422, www.chez-pascal.com, 5:30–9:30 P.M. Mon.–Thurs., 5:30–10:30 P.M. Fri.–Sat., $25–31) prepares stellar authentic French bistro fare: coquilles St.-Jacques; asparagus, hazelnut, and watercress salad with garlic flan and hazelnut oil; hanger steak with a shallot demi-glace; escargot in puff pastry with Roquefort; and baked goat cheese over baby spinach and sliced apples. You'll also find a first-rate vegetarian tasting menu. There's nothing gimmicky about either the ingredients or the preparation, and that's why loyalists love the place. Romantics appreciate the cute, dimly lighted dining room and unrushed pace.

Serving creative and superb contemporary American fare in a riotously loud but inviting dining room, **Mill's Tavern** (101 N. Main St., 401/272-3331, www.millstavernrestaurant.com, 5–10 P.M. Mon.–Thurs., 5–11 P.M. Fri.–Sat., 4–9 P.M. Sun., $18–29) earns tremendous acclaim. Dishes such as lobster and English pea risotto with vanilla mascarpone have helped this stately spot on increasingly trendy North Main Street develop into one of the city's top venues for celebrating a special occasion.

The former owners of Downcity Food and Cocktails opened a slick but low-key neighborhood hangout along the northern reaches of Hope Street in 2005; **Cook and Brown House** (959 Hope St., 401/273-7275, http://cookandbrown.com, dinner 5:30–9:30 P.M. Tues.–Wed. and Sun, 5:30–10 P.M. Thurs.–Sat., brunch 10 A.M.–2 P.M. Sat.–Sun., $8–25) is as enjoyable for an Angus burger with horseradish sauce and a pint of beer as for fancier fare such as spiced duck breast with a blackberry, lentils, and a port-wine reduction. Don't miss the hearty brunches, served on weekends, which are as much a hit here as they continue to be at Downcity Food. Lobster cakes and eggs with home fries star among the brunch faves.

Steaks, Seafood, Pizza, and Pub Grub

Olives (108 N. Main St., 401/751-1200, www.olivesrocks.com, 5 P.M.–1 A.M. Thurs., 5 P.M.–2 A.M. Fri.–Sat., $7–11) caters to a fashionable crowd of pre-nightclub crawlers and postwork revelers. The loud and lively tavern-like eatery with high pressed-tin ceilings and French doors opening onto North Main Street serves an eclectic menu of better-than-average comfort foods, including pasta pomodoro, sesame-orange salmon, and gourmet burgers.

Ethnic Fare

Another of the many eateries along South Main Street, **Pakarang** (303 S. Main St., 401/453-3660, www.pakarangrestaurant.com, lunch 11:30 A.M.–3 P.M. Tues.–Fri., noon–3 P.M. Sat., dinner 5–10 P.M. Sun.–Thurs., 5–10:30 P.M. Fri.–Sat., $11–18) is a reliable option for Thai; it's a lively, cleverly decorated spot with mounted fish "swimming" against a brick sea. House specialties include Choo Choo curry with snow peas, pineapple, peppers, zucchini, summer squash, and tomato; and sliced sautéed salmon with ginger, asparagus, onion, carrot, black mushrooms, red pepper, and scallions.

O-cha (221 Wickenden St., 401/421-4699, noon–10 P.M. daily, $5–16) is a cute little Asian eatery on the ground floor of a handsome old Wickenden Victorian—it's tiny but cozy with an almost familial-seeming staff that ranges from cheerful to gruff, and there's some outdoor seating on the side deck. The menu mixes Thai recipes (spicy duck topped with Thai herbs in wine sauce, beef with coconut curry, pad thai) with traditional Japanese sushi.

On the college strip, **Kebob-n-Curry** (261 Thayer St., 401/273-8844, www.kabobandcurry.com, 11 A.M.–10:30 P.M. Mon.–Thurs., 11 A.M.–11 P.M. Fri.–Sat., 11:30 A.M.–10 P.M. Sun., $7–14) presents an ambitious menu of Indian specialties, from the usual tikka masala and vindaloo to less predictable creations such as lamb chops marinated in mint and white wine or chunks of cod baked with cumin.

Taste of India (230 Wickenden St., 401/421-4355, www.tasteofindiaprovri.com, lunch 11:30 A.M.–2:30 P.M. Mon.–Fri., noon–3 P.M. Sat.–Sun., dinner 5–10 P.M. Mon.–Sat., 5–9:30 P.M. Sun., $11–17) is one of the very best bets in town for fine Indian cooking. Soft pink walls brighten an otherwise plain dining room, but this restaurant is recommended for its exceptionally fresh and well-seasoned food. The menu runs a fairly traditional course, with the usual tandoori, meat with spiced spinach, naan and *kulcha* Indian breads, *pakora* deep-fried vegetables, and the like.

India (1060 Hope St., 401/421-2600, www.indiarestaurant.com, 11 A.M.–10 P.M. Sun.–Thurs., 11 A.M.–11 P.M. Fri.–Sat., $9–16) brings excellent Indian fare to the northeast side of town. In addition to the standbys, India offers some unusual options like *papri chat,* an Indian take on nachos, with chickpeas, onions, cilantro, yogurt, and tamarind chutney; seafood in sweet-and-sour mango and cashew sauce; and swordfish kabobs. It is one of the best eateries of this genre in the state for it's food as well as for the imaginative and bold decor, with bright paintings, hanging Oriental rugs, and elegant light fixtures.

A Thayer Street mainstay since the 1960s, casual yet snazzy **Andreas Restaurant** (268 Thayer St., 401/331-7879, www.andreasri.com, 11 A.M.–1 A.M. Mon.–Fri., 9 A.M.–2 A.M. Sat.–Sun., $7–20) is a lively, always crowded Greek restaurant with a smartly furnished dining room and big windows overlooking the street. You can grab a lamb burger or grilled calamari appetizer, or opt for something more substantial, such as flame-broiled salmon with olive oil or pastitsio casserole topped with béchamel sauce. There's also a nice wine list.

A departure from the slick contemporary interior of so many Japanese restaurants, **Sakura** (231 Wickenden St., 401/331-6861, www.eat-inri.com/sakura, 11 A.M.–11 P.M. daily, $9–15) almost feels a bit cluttered (in a good way), set inside a grand old rambling wood-frame house with creaky wide-plank floors. Sushi rolls include dragon *maki* with eel, cucumber, rice, and avocado; and a crispy *kirin maki* that's lightly fried and filled with tuna, salmon, and whitefish. Entrée favorites include barbecued beef rolled with scallions, tuna teriyaki, and several tasty *udon* and soba noodle dishes.

Up near the Pawtucket border at the north end of Blackstone Boulevard, **Ran Zan Japanese Restaurant** (1084 Hope St., 401/276-7574, www.ranzan.net, lunch 11:30 A.M.–2:30 P.M. Tues.–Fri. and Sun., dinner 5–9:30 P.M. Tues.–Thurs., 5–10 P.M.

Fri.–Sat., 5–9 P.M. Sun., $9–18) is a hole-in-the-wall with a young and accommodating staff and a low-key ambience that replicates the experience of eating over at a friend's house (assuming you have a friend who cooks very good Japanese food and prepares fresh sushi). Pork *katsu,* shrimp *yakisoba,* snow crab–asparagus rolls, and various sushi combos are offered at quite reasonable prices.

Tortilla Flats (355 Hope St., 401/751-6777, www.tortillaflatsri.com, 11:30 A.M.–1 A.M. Mon.–Thurs., 11:30 A.M.–2 A.M. Fri.–Sat., 1 P.M.–1 A.M. Sun., $8–14) serves pretty tasty Mexican food, including a house specialty called the cactus flower, a tortilla basket stuffed with lettuce, tomato, cheese, guacamole, and olives, topped with grilled steak or chicken breast. It's no better or more authentic than most Mexican restaurants in Providence, but it has a pleasant ambience and serves consistently fresh food.

Quick Bites

Geoff's (163 Benefit St., 401/751-2248, www.geoffsonline.com, 10 A.M.–9 P.M. daily, $4–6), your source for hefty sandwiches along Thayer Street, suffers from indifferent service and a dull little dining room. But you eat here for the amazing sandwiches: try the Chicken George, with chicken salad, bacon, melted Swiss, hot spinach, tomato, onion, and Russian dressing; or the Mike Schwartz, with tuna, hot pastrami, Muenster, Russian dressing, lettuce, and tomato. More prosaic varieties are also offered, but it's the massive and elaborate creations that have earned Geoff's its sterling reputation.

La Creperie (82 Fones Alley, 401/751-5536, www.creperieprov.com, 10 A.M.–midnight Mon.–Thurs., 10 A.M.–2 A.M. Fri., 9 A.M.–2 A.M. Sat., 9 A.M.–midnight Sun., $3–6) is a tiny spot down an alley off Thayer Street, but this homey little place serves very good sweet and savory crepes, and it stays open very late (one wonders how, as so few people walk by it). Fresh fruit smoothies are another house specialty.

Of all the quasi-fast-food eateries along Thayer Street, **Spike's Junkyard Dogs** (485

COURTESY OF PROVIDENCE WARWICK CVB

The Coffee Exchange on Wickenden Street

Branch Ave., 401/861-6888, www.spikesjunk-yarddogs.com, 11 A.M.–11 P.M. Mon.–Thurs., 11 A.M.–1:30 A.M. Fri.–Sat., noon–10 P.M. Sun., $2–6) most deserves the chance to harden your arteries—the dogs here are exquisite, especially the chili-and-cheddar dog. They also serve subs.

Just off Thayer Street, the **Meeting Street Cafe** (220 Meeting St., 401/273-1066, www.meetingstreetcafe.com, 8 A.M.–11 P.M. daily, $3–7) serves immensely satisfying scones, pastries, pies, cookies, and light breakfast and lunch fare.

A hit with students from nearby RISD and Brown, **Cable Car Cinema** (204 S. Main St., 401/272-3970, www.cablecarcinema.com, 8 A.M.–11 P.M. Mon.–Fri., 9 A.M.–11 P.M. Sat.–Sun., $4–8) is known as much for its cheap and cheerful dining as for its art-film theater. White-tuna and other sandwiches, homemade soups, bagels and spreads, fresh-baked cookies, coffees, and all sorts of sweets are served in this quaint café with the black-and-white-striped awning.

Sun-filled **Brickway** (234 Wickenden St., 401/751-2477, 7 A.M.–3 P.M. Mon.–Fri., 8 A.M.–3 P.M. Sat.–Sun., $4–8), which has an inviting little brick terrace, is a casual spot with outstanding breakfasts and lunches in heart of Wickenden's dining area. About 10 kinds of pancakes and French toast are offered, including chocolate-chip and Caribbean, with pineapple, banana, and kiwi, plus great omelets and other egg dishes. Lunch options include curried chicken and pasta salad, veggie burgers and hamburgers, and hot and cold sandwiches.

Up at the northern end of Blackstone Boulevard and lovely Lippitt Memorial Park, **Three Sisters** (1074 Hope St., 401/273-7230, www.threesistersri.com, 6:30 A.M.–9 P.M. Mon.–Thurs., 6:30 A.M.–10 P.M. Fri., 8 A.M.–10 P.M. Sat., 8 A.M.–9 P.M. Sun., $3–7) is a good spot for snacking. This dark and cozy little parlor has frozen treats of many, many flavors, plus wraps, BLTs, soups, and other savories.

Java Joints

The Coffee Exchange (207 Wickenden St., 401/273-1198, www.sustainablecoffee.com, 6:30 A.M.–11 P.M. daily, under $4) occupies an attractive Second Empire Victorian house on Wickenden Street filled with bric-a-brac and coffee-related goods. There's also an attractive patio. The coffeehouse donates a share of its take to needy workers, many of them children, who struggle to make a scant living employed on coffee farms in poor countries.

Cafe Zog (239 Wickenden St., 401/421-2213, 7:30 A.M.–11 P.M. daily, $3–6) serves healthful salads, prepared foods, and *chai* teas to patrons tucked in around closely spaced tables and watching the world stroll by on Wickenden Street. Zog offers what might be one of the best bargains in the city: A few bucks gets you an omelet with your choice of numerous fillings and a nice bagel with cream cheese or butter.

Gourmet Goods and Picnic Supplies

For years, indigent college students have been

PROVIDENCE

spending what little money they have on the delectable baked goods at **729 Hope Street** (729 Hope St., 401/273-7290), a bakery and gourmet food shop. White-chocolate Cage Cake is the house specialty, and coffees and sandwiches are available.

A fabulous café and bakery with floor-to-ceiling windows and a sunny patio out on the side, **◖ Seven Stars** (820 Hope St., 401/521-2200, www.sevenstarsbakery.com, 6:30 A.M.–6 P.M. Mon.–Fri., 7 A.M.–6 P.M. Sat.–Sun., $2–7) serves delicious ginger biscuits, individual-size lemon cakes, olive bread, gooey chocolate brownies, and ham-and-cheese calzones, and it has a delightful garden patio that's great for sipping espresso.

In Fox Point, fans of Portuguese cooking shouldn't miss either the **Taunton Ave. Bakery** (208 Taunton Ave., 401/434-3450, 5 A.M.–7:30 P.M. Mon.–Fri., 5 A.M.–7 P.M. Sun.), famous for its Portuguese sweet bread,

or the **Friends Market** (126 Brook St., 401/861-0345, 9 A.M.–5:30 P.M. daily), which carries imported delicacies from the mother country.

OLNEYVILLE AND ENVIRONS

Well west of downtown in the Olneyville neighborhood, **Wes's Rib House** (38 Dike St., 401/421-9090, www.wesribhouse. com, 11:30 A.M.–2 A.M. Mon.–Thurs., 11:30 A.M.–4 A.M. Fri.–Sat., noon–2 A.M. Sun., $6–16) is a down-home Missouri-style barbecue spot that's worth the trip. Savor the Show Me platter (comes with your choice of four meats plus coleslaw, barbecue beans, and cornbread), or try the individual ribs, chicken, beef, and other plates. Well south of downtown, the **Portuguese American Market** (896 Allens Ave., 401/941-4480, 8 A.M.–5 P.M. daily) is the place to stock up on fava beans, linguica, salt cod, and fresh-baked sweetbreads.

Information and Services

VISITOR INFORMATION

For maps, updates on the city's events, and any other visitor information, call or stop by the **Providence Warwick Convention and Visitors Bureau** (1 W. Exchange St., 401/274-1636, www.pwcvb.com). You can also stop by the **Providence Visitors Center** (1 Sabin St., 401/751-1177), another vast repository of brochures and information, located inside the Rhode Island Convention Center.

Some major hospitals include: **Kent Hospital** (455 Toll Gate Rd., Warwick, 401/737-7000 or 888/455-KENT—888/455-5368, www. kentri.org), **Memorial Hospital of Rhode Island** (111 Brewster St., Pawtucket, 401/729-2000, www.mhri.org), **Mirium Hospital** (164 Summit Ave., Providence, 401/793-2500, www.lifespan.org/partners), **Rhode Island Hospital** (593 Eddy St., Providence, 401/444-4000, www.lifespan.org/partners/rih), **Our Lady of Fatima Hospital** (200 High Service

Ave., North Providence, 401/456-3000), **St. Joseph Hospital for Specialty Care** (Peace St., Providence, 401/456-3000, www.saint-josephri.com), **South County Hospital** (100 Kenyon Ave., Wakefield, 401/782-8000, www. schospital.com), and **Westerly Hospital** (Wells St., Westerly, 401/596-6000, www.westerly-hospital.com).

You'll find pharmacies, many of them open until 9 or 10 P.M., throughout the city; the leading chain is CVS (www.cvs.com). Pharmacies open 24 hours include **East Providence CVS** (640 Warren Ave., East Providence, 401/438-2272) and **North Providence CVS** (1919 Mineral Spring Ave., North Providence, 401/353-2501).

Banks are found all over the downtown area, in the college neighborhoods, and in areas frequented by tourists, and ATMs are scattered throughout the city.

Internet is available for free in libraries and

for a small fee (usually a few dollars per hour) in cafés and at **FedEx Office** (100 Westminster St., 401/331-1990), which also provides faxing and shipping services. Free Wi-Fi is offered at **Coffee Connection** (207 Wickenden St.), Cuban Revolution (50 Aborn St.), and other locations around town.

MEDIA

The city's (and the region's) daily newspaper is the **Providence Journal** (401/277-7700, www.projo.com). The paper has an outstanding and highly informative website with information on local dining, arts, music, travel, and kids-oriented activities, and it has recently been recognized for its breaking news coverage online. An excellent resource for metro Providence arts, dining, shopping, clubbing, and similar such diversions is the decidedly left-of-center **Providence Phoenix** alternative newsweekly (401/273-6397, www.thephoenix.com). Also look to the lively and free **Providence Monthly** (www.providenceonline.com, 401/521-0023), a glossy magazine, for great features on the city along with first-rate dining, shopping, and nightlife coverage.

Grab the free monthly **Federal Hill Gazette** (401/521-2701) for the scoop on one of the city's liveliest neighborhoods.

Other area papers include the twice-weekly **Warwick Beacon** (401/732-3100, www.warwickonline.com) and the **Kent County Daily Times** (401/821-7400, www.ricentral.com). **Southern Rhode Island Newspapers** (401/789-9744, www.ricentral.com) publishes several local weeklies, including *The Chariho Times* (Wyoming), *The Coventry Courier, The East Greenwich Pendulum,* and *The Standard Times.*

TOURS

Providence River Boat Co. (575 S. Water St., 401/580-BOAT—401/580-2628) offers water-taxi service, sightseeing cruises, and charter tours of the Providence waterfront and out into Narragansett Bay. **Conway Tours/Gray Line Rhode Island** (10 Nate Whipple Hwy., Cumberland, 401/658-3400 or 800/888-4661, www.conwaytours.com) runs all kinds of bus and boat tours of the region, including daily trips to Connecticut's Foxwoods Casino from Providence and cruises on Providence harbor.

Getting There and Around

GETTING THERE
By Air

Providence's international airport **T. F. Green Airport** (2000 Post Rd., Warwick, 888/268-7222 or 401/691-2471, www.pvdairport.com) is located south of the city and has regular flights from many U.S. and Canadian cities by Air Canada, Delta, US Airways, and other carriers.

By Bus

The **Rhode Island Public Transit Authority (RIPTA)** (401/781-9400 or 800/244-0444, www.ripta.com) runs frequent buses from T. F. Green to downtown for a fare of $1.75 one-way. In addition, **Peter Pan Bus Lines** (800/343-9999, www.peterpanbus.com) runs buses to Providence from throughout New

England, stopping at 1 Peter Pan Way (north of town, off exit 25 from I-95) and downtown (1 Kennedy Plaza). **Greyhound** (800/231-2222, www.greyhound.com) also connects to Providence from many U.S. cities, also stopping at 1 Kennedy Plaza.

By Train

It's fairly easy to get to Providence by train aboard **Amtrak** (800/872-7245, www.amtrak.com). Trains stop in Providence on their way from Washington D.C. (6 hours), New York (3.5 hours), and Boston (40 minutes).

GETTING AROUND
Buses

Bus travel is inexpensive and relatively

PROVIDENCE

convenient throughout the state on the **Rhode Island Transportation Authority (RIPTA) buses** (401/781-9400, www.ripta.com). Kennedy Plaza, in the heart of downtown, is the nexus for bus routes all over Rhode Island. Fares start at just $1.75 for any ride within a mile of downtown (transfers are an additional $0.50). Have some coins with you, as exact change is required. There are student discounts as well as monthly passes. Buses generally run 5:30 A.M.–midnight, and the Providence Visitors Center and the Convention and Visitors Bureau distribute free maps that detail popular routes.

In addition, both locals and visitors have taken a shine to the city's pleasant and inexpensive **LINK trolley.** The Green Line runs from Fox Point up through College Hill, past Thayer Street, and then west across downtown and over to colorful Federal Hill. The Gold line runs from the State House south through downtown and the Jewelry District, with a stop at the Providence ferry landing, terminating in the Southside at Blackstone. The fare is $1.75 for any ride on the system, and monthly and 10-ride discount passes are offered. LINK trolleys make their appointed stops every 20 minutes, on the Green Line 6:30 A.M.–9 P.M. Monday–Friday, 8 A.M.–6:30 P.M. Saturday, 11 A.M.–6:30 P.M. Sunday, and on the Gold Line 6:30 A.M.–7 P.M. Monday–Friday, 8:30 A.M.–6:30 P.M. Saturday, 11 A.M.–6:30 P.M. Sunday.

Driving and Parking

The pace of driving in Providence is less chaotic than in Boston, but this is still a Type A kind of place: People drive fast and use their horns. One-way, narrow, and crooked streets proliferate and can be confusing and frustrating (although they are charming to walk). Overall, if you're fairly used to driving and parking in urban environments, Providence is reasonably navigable.

Parking garages abound downtown but can be rather expensive. A smart strategy is to park at the 5,000-space, nine-level Providence Place Mall, which is within easy walking distance of most downtown attractions and is extremely economical, but only if you get your parking ticket validated at a shop in the mall. You don't have to buy anything pricey to get the validation—any store or eatery there can stamp your ticket.

Providence is a relatively safe city, and you don't often hear of car theft or break-ins, but it certainly can and does happen. You'll save a lot of money opting for street parking over garage or supervised-lot parking, but you also open yourself up to the risk of theft.

Taxis

People don't generally hail cabs on the street in Providence, but you can find them at major hotels and occasionally outside clubs at night. For trips to the airport or coming home late from a bar or restaurant, call ahead to **AA 24 Hour Taxi** (401/521-4200) and **American Cab** (401/487-2111). The fare is $2.50 per mile.

OUTSIDE PROVIDENCE

It's an old joke in Rhode Island, since the state is so small, that everyone except those who live in the capital can simply describe their residence as "outside Providence." There is, however, a distinct corner of the northwestern part of the state that is more aptly called Greater Providence as opposed to, say, the East Bay or South County. While it may not have a cohesive identity as such, the roughly square section of Rhode Island that encompasses some dozen towns and cities accounts for nearly half the area of the state. Within those boundaries are both some of the state's largest cities and its quietest townships. And while there may not be as many formal attractions as in other parts of the state, there are still several top-flight museums and a bevy of recreational opportunities in wild landscapes of forest, river, and wetlands.

The most appealing part of this region for visitors is the area directly north of Providence known as the Blackstone River Valley. This small corner of the smallest state has had an outsized influence on the history of the nation as a whole. It was here in the early 1800s in cities like Pawtucket and Woonsocket that industrious entrepreneurs began harnessing the power of the Blackstone River to create the nation's first textile mills. The factories were so successful at reducing labor and generating wealth that they were soon replicated throughout the Northeast, spurring the American industrial revolution that established the United States as a true world power within a generation. Much of this industrial history has been preserved in several museums as well as old mill buildings throughout the region that have

COURTESY OF PROVIDENCE WARWICK CVB

HIGHLIGHTS

LOOK FOR ◖ TO FIND RECOMMENDED SIGHTS, ACTIVITIES, DINING, AND LODGING.

◖ **Slater Mill:** This beautifully preserved complex contains important late-colonial factory buildings and machinery that figured prominently in the American industrial revolution (page 167).

◖ **Slater Park:** A crazy quilt of ball fields, picnic sites, and historic sites, anchored by the famous 1895 Looff Carousel (page 170).

◖ **Museum of Work and Culture:** In the otherwise prosaic little city of Woonsocket, a 20-minute drive northwest of Providence, this museum run by the Rhode Island Historical Society illuminates the ordinary and extraordinary lives of the thousands of mostly immigrant mill and factory workers who made the state what it is today (page 173).

◖ **PawSox:** A favorite Rhode Island tradition is a night at the ball game, where the Red Sox's future stars are born (page 178).

◖ **Kayaking the Blackstone:** Not your ordinary kayaking experience, the rushing Blackstone offers a different view on Rhode Island's industrial past (page 178).

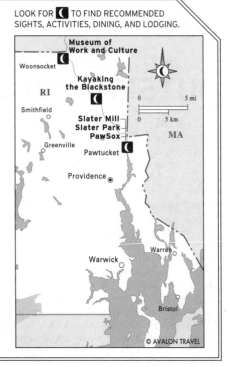

been converted into condos, offices, and art studios.

To the west, the river valley merges with Rhode Island's "quiet corner," a half-dozen towns that have resisted development of any kind to remain a bucolic vision of what New England looked like 100 years ago. You won't find any megamalls or amusement parks here—in fact, you won't find many hotels or restaurants either. But you will find miles of backcountry roads lined with stone walls, orchards, farm stands, and historic homes. This area comes alive especially during foliage season, when colorful red maples and yellow beeches frame postcard-ready small-town tableaux.

By contrast, the coastal area south of Providence along Narragansett Bay is home to the urbanization of Rhode Island's two largest cities after Providence—Cranston and Warwick. Unlike the capital, they have decidedly not gone through a renaissance. They remain gritty, working-class cities that offer a glimpse of the real lives of many Rhode Islanders without pretense. While there are no formal attractions for visitors in either city, Warwick has some pretty neighborhoods on the bay worth driving through, as well as some pretty beaches that are the closest place to Providence to sunbathe or take a dip.

PLANNING YOUR TIME

Truth be told, the Outside Providence area is better-suited to day trips than overnight stays. After your second or third day in Providence, it is almost mandatory to take a drive north to see the industrial towns of Pawtucket and Woonsocket. You can visit both towns in an afternoon, but it's more enjoyable to make an entire day of it, taking time at the historic sites,

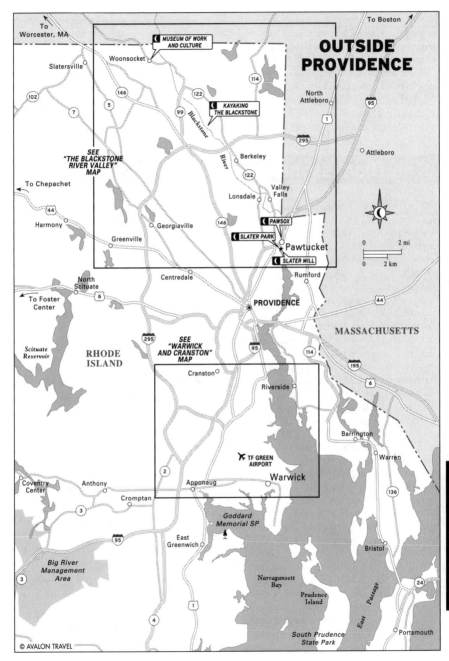

stopping at an ethnic restaurant for lunch, picnicking in Slater Park, or taking in a night game by the PawSox—the Boston Red Sox's minor league team.

If the outdoors are more your thing, there are plenty of opportunities for hiking, kayaking, and canoeing along the river as well as in the natural preserves in the far northwest corner of the state. You can take as little or as long as you want to view the bucolic towns of the "quiet corner"—although during foliage season, you could plan at least half a day to drive the back roads, perhaps passing through on your way to South County. Alternately, pass through Cranston and Warwick on your way south for a drive around historic neighborhoods or for clam cakes and people-watching on the waterfront.

The Blackstone River Valley

The part of Greater Providence with the most distinct cultural and historic identity is the Blackstone River Valley, which begins just north of Providence in Pawtucket and extends north to Woonsocket, encompassing a swath of nearby communities. In this area you can get a sense of how the nation shifted from being an agrarian land of farmers, independent artisans, and skilled craftspeople to a full-fledged industrial powerhouse. Shortly after the War of Independence, complete mill communities—with worker housing, community halls and churches, and massive mill buildings—sprang up all along the Blackstone River and its tributaries, from Pawtucket north through Woonsocket and across the Massachusetts border to Worcester, nearly 50 miles away.

In the course of its 46 miles the Blackstone River plummets about 450 feet—a rate of 10 feet per mile, more than the Colorado River drops as it passes through the Grand Canyon. As early as 1665, settlers began damming sections of the river, harnessing the energy of the powerful flow to run mills. By the late 19th century, the once crystal-clear Blackstone had become one of the hardest-working, most heavily dammed, and most polluted rivers in North America. In 1986 Congress designated the river as the John H. Chafee Blackstone River Valley National Heritage Corridor, and since that time major efforts have been made to clean it up and preserve both its pristine and industrial elements. Although Pawtucket and Woonsocket are bustling, if rather small, cities, the Blackstone River Valley nevertheless has a surprising number of areas with low population density and an almost rural character.

PAWTUCKET

Pawtucket (population 72,000) is a classic river town, its eastern and western boundaries formed by the Ten Mile and Moshassuck Rivers. The river for which it's most famous, however, is the Blackstone, which cuts through

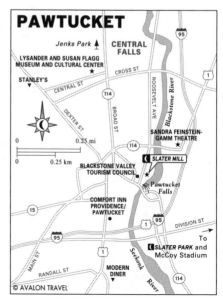

the center of the city. In colonial times the Blackstone River was the border between Rhode Island and Massachusetts. In 1874 the communities on both sides of the river formed one community that incorporated in 1885 as the city of Pawtucket. Since then, it has remained a densely packed little downtown of crooked and narrow side streets mostly emanating from the main drags, Main and Broad Streets and East Avenue.

The city has always had a hard-nosed, working-class personality, but at the same time it's without much urban blight and decay. Modest double-decker and triple-decker tenement housing proliferates in many neighborhoods, and large numbers of Italians, Portuguese, Puerto Ricans, and African Americans—along with smaller factions of myriad other ethnicities—make up the population. More recently, young professionals have moved in to take advantage of cheap real estate and proximity to Boston; it's only a matter of time before it blossoms with more sophisticated dining, shopping, and nightlife options.

◖ Slater Mill

For all intents and purposes, the American industrial revolution started at Slater Mill (Main St. and Roosevelt Ave., 401/725-8638, www. slatermill.org, 11 A.M.–3 P.M. Sat.–Sun. Mar.–Apr., 10 A.M.–4 P.M. Tues.–Sun. May–Oct., group tours by appointment Nov.–Feb., $12 adults, $8.50 children), a collection of mill buildings now preserved as a historic site along the Blackstone River. Young English immigrant Samuel Slater took a job in Ezekiel Carpenter's clothing shop, and by recalling the exact blueprints for water-powered textile machinery in his native country, developed the nation's first such textile factory. A 10,000-square-foot visitors center across from the mill provides orientation with an 18-minute video offering a stark view of mill life in Rhode Island.

The 5.5-acre site has several buildings, including the three-story **Wilkenson House,** built in 1810 on the site of an old metal works, which contains a full machine shop on the ground floor and a re-creation of the mill's massive waterwheel in the basement. During

COURTESY OF SLATER MILL

the machine shop at Slater Mill

the tour, you watch a nine-ton wooden waterwheel turn and spread the power through the building, the gears turning a series of pulleys that in turn power individual tools and machines. About 20 woodworkers and metalworkers worked in the Wilkenson House's first-floor machine shop. During the tour a guide demonstrates exactly how a drill is powered by the millrace.

Perhaps the most striking of the site's structures, the **Old Slater Mill** is a sturdy 1793 wooden structure commissioned by William Almy, Obadiah Brown, and Samuel Slater and built by local Pawtucket laborers. Sunlight streams through the building's many soaring windows. Within just a few months of its construction, the factory had turned out the first cotton yarn produced in the New World. Inside, you'll find a few original machines from the period and many more authentic replicas that provide a clear sense of how these factories operated in the early days. Many of the machines were either designed or modified by Samuel Slater himself. At one end of the building a small museum store sells penny candy and small gifts, including work by local artisans and fiber artists as well as a selection of books on industrial history and textile crafts.

Moved here in 1962, having been spared destruction when I-95 was built through Pawtucket, the 1758 **Sylvanus Brown** house, a nicely restored gambrel-roof colonial, is also part of the tour. Demonstrations of flax-weaving are often given inside—a garden of flax was installed behind the house in 2000. (The golden-colored debris left after flax has been combed through a large metal hackle is called tow, hence the term *towheaded* to describe a blond-haired child.) Millwright Sylvanus Brown ran the house as a carpenter's shop during the late 1700s. It has been fully restored to its original appearance.

The massive dam that runs across the Blackstone River from the Old Slater Mill dates to 1792. Running from above the dam and under the Old Slater Mill to the front of Wilkinson Mill, **Slater's Trench** (also known as the Great Flume) siphoned water from the

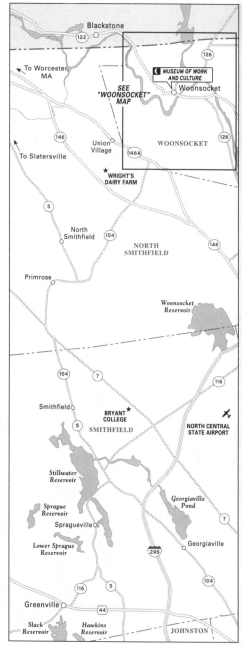

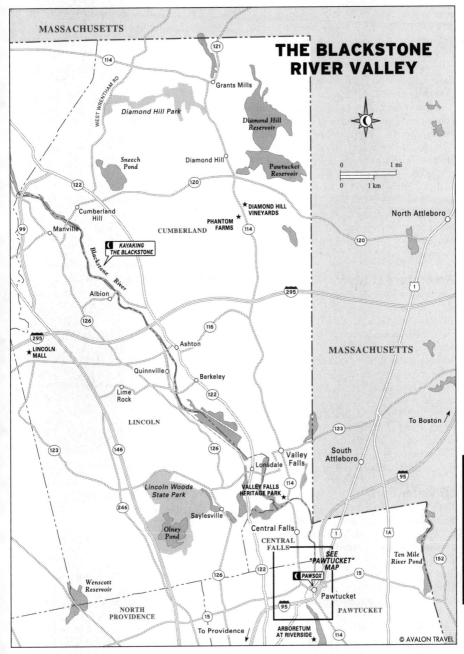

THE BLACKSTONE RIVER VALLEY

MASSACHUSETTS

WEST WRENTHAM RD

Grants Mills

Diamond Hill Park

Diamond Hill Reservoir

Sneech Pond

Diamond Hill

Pawtucket Reservoir

0   1 mi

0   1 km

North Attleboro

Cumberland Hill

Manville

CUMBERLAND

PHANTOM FARMS

★ DIAMOND HILL VINEYARDS

Blackstone River

☾ KAYAKING THE BLACKSTONE

Albion

★ LINCOLN MALL

Ashton

MASSACHUSETTS

Quinnville

Berkeley

Lime Rock

LINCOLN

To Boston

South Attleboro

Valley Falls

Lincoln Woods State Park

Lonsdale

VALLEY FALLS HERITAGE PARK ★

Saylesville

Olney Pond

Central Falls

CENTRAL FALLS

SEE "PAWTUCKET" MAP

Ten Mile River Pond

Wenscott Reservoir

NORTH PROVIDENCE

☾ PAWSOX

Pawtucket

PAWTUCKET

To Providence

ARBORETUM AT RIVERSIDE ★

© AVALON TRAVEL

OUTSIDE PROVIDENCE

river to power the machinery of the two mills. The water continued into **Sargeant's Trench,** which sent the water below the falls and back into the river.

Crashing down below the Main Street Bridge, Pawtucket Falls were a natural formation improved by artificial damming in 1718. These days the falls are faced in brick, and they continue to provide power to the Blackstone Valley Electric Company just downstream. The double-arch, cut-stone **Main Street Bridge,** from which you can get great views of the entire Slater Mill Historic Site, dates to 1858, but a bridge has stood at this point since 1714. Ezekiel Carpenter's original clothing shop stood on the southwest corner of the Main Street bridge and the river; it's where Samuel Slater first worked when he arrived in Pawtucket.

Arboretum at Riverside

Another noteworthy sight in Pawtucket is the Arboretum at Riverside (724 Pleasant St., 10 A.M.–2 P.M. Tues.–Sun., $5), where you can explore 80 acres of beautifully landscaped pathways and gardens along the Seekonk River, into which the Blackstone flows below Pawtucket Falls. Among the varieties of trees you're apt to find while strolling here are black oak, eastern red cedar, ginkgo, wild black cherry, big-tooth aspen, and white ash. Shrubs from as far away as Japan and central Asia thrive here, plus impressive stands of azaleas and rhododendrons. The arboretum is tended organically, using only natural fertilizers and pesticides.

◖ Slater Park

In the northeastern section of town, near the Massachusetts border, lies Slater Park (401/728-0500, ext. 252), which has entrances on both Newport Avenue (Rte. 1A) and Armistice Boulevard (Rte. 15). There are 18 picnic sites plus tennis courts, ball fields, gardens, and other diversions to while away a pleasant afternoon. Chief among them is a **Looff Carousel** (401/728-0500, ext. 316, 11 A.M.–5 P.M. Sat.–Sun. Apr.–June and Sept.–Oct., 11 A.M.–5 P.M. daily July–Aug., $0.25), which dates to 1895.

Charles I. D. Looff ranks among the earliest and most distinguished designers of carousels, and Slater Park's ride contains 50 whimsical characters.

The park is home to the historic **Daggett House** (401/722-6931, group tours 2–5 P.M. Sat.–Sun. June–Sept., $2 pp), the oldest extant house in the city, furnished in the period style with fine antiques, vintage pewter, and Revolutionary War–era china. Eight generations of Daggetts lived in the house through the years. The house is only open for groups of 15–20 people, but you can still admire the exterior.

Art aficionados might want to check out the **Rhode Island Watercolor Society Gallery** (in the park's J. C. Potter Casino, 401/726-1876, www.riws.org, 10 A.M.–4 P.M. Tues.–Sat., 1–5 P.M. Sun., free).

EAST PROVIDENCE

From downtown Pawtucket, drive south four miles along Route 114 to the center of this semi-industrial suburb just over the I-195 bridge from Providence. The town is often thought of as little more than an extension of Providence, a reputation it has had since it was founded in 1862. In reality East Providence has become a small industrial city like Pawtucket, its neighbor to the north, producing baking powder, refining petroleum, and engaging in other light industry. The city contains a few notable sites, especially toward the north part of town.

From Route 114, bear left onto Route 114A and make a right turn onto Hunt Mills Road. Just a few yards from the Massachusetts border, the **East Providence Historical Society** (Hunt Mills Rd., Rumford, 401/438-1750, http://ephist.org, 1–4 P.M. the second Sun. of every month, $3) makes its home in the Georgian-style John Hunt House in the historic Hunt Mills neighborhood of Rumford, a village within East Providence. The five-bay, center-chimney colonial was constructed in 1750 and then added to significantly in 1790. Inside, it is furnished as an upper-class country house of the day would have been; you'll find a varied collection of memorabilia, tools, documents, and photographs, most of them donated by residents through the years, that paint a picture of East Providence's history. Every couple of years changing exhibits are installed.

The historical society also manages the **Philip Walker House** (432 Massasoit Ave.), the oldest extant house in the city and the second oldest in Rhode Island, dating to 1676. A typical three-bay house with a central chimney, the structure was burned during King Philip's War but was rebuilt three years later. It remains an excellent example of very early colonial architecture and is worth a drive-by for anyone interested in the period. It is not currently open to visitors, but some furniture and other artifacts from the house are displayed in a special room in the society's Hunt House headquarters.

South from downtown East Providence along the waterfront is Crescent Park (take Rte. 103 S. and bear right onto Bullocks Point Ave.). Kids and any adult with fond childhood memories of carousels will get a kick out of the **Charles I. D. Looff Carousel** (700 Bullocks Point Ave., 401/435-7518, $1). This wooden 1895 structure has long been recognized as one of Looff's most beautiful and ornate designs. On it there are 62 figures carved of wood and four chariots. Beveled mirrors, faceted glass, and twinkling lights add further sparkle to the clanging contraption that rotates to the sounds of Wurlitzer organ music. The hours vary through the year, but you should be able to ride noon–7 P.M. on weekends from about Easter through Columbus Day. Call if you're visiting on a weekday, as it's sometimes open all week in summer. There's a small food concession where you can snack on clam cakes, chowder, and other traditional short-order favorites.

Central Falls

Little Central Falls lies just a mile north of downtown Pawtucket along Route 114. It's just a mile square, making it the smallest community in the nation's smallest state. The town began its foray into industrialization

with the foundation of a chocolate factory in 1790; for many years this area was called simply Chocolate Mill. Later, in the 19th century, gold and silver electrolytic extraction as well as textile businesses appeared. In the center of the village, a couple of blocks north of Central Street, is four-acre **Jenks Park** (Broad St., Rte. 114, 401/727-7480), home of the four-faced 1904 Cogswell Clock Tower atop Dexter's Ledge, which the Indians used as a watchtower during King Philip's War. Central Falls holds concerts here on Sunday during the summer, when you can also climb the tower and take in excellent views of the valley. At any time of day, you'll find walking trails ideal for a light stroll.

A short walk southwest of the park is the **Lysander and Susan Flagg Museum and Cultural Center** (209 Central St., 401/727-7440, www.cflibrary.org/flaggmuseum.htm, by appointment, free). This stately colonial revival home contains maps, newspapers, paintings, and photos relevant to the city's history as well as a collection of locally produced textiles. If you are interested in the collection, call ahead, as it is open only by appointment.

Cumberland and Lincoln

Cumberland offers a quieter and more rural vision of the Blackstone River Valley. Extensive mineral deposits, mostly iron and copper, provided early revenue for the town, but today Cumberland prospers with revenues from light manufacturing and retail. In Valley Falls, an old mill community in the southwest section of Cumberland, you can visit the **Valley Falls Heritage Park** (45 Broad St., Cumberland, 401/334-9996, free). This self-guided historic trail occupies the site of the former Valley Falls Company, which produced great amounts of textiles from the 1810s through the 1930s. There is no formal museum or guided tours, but a network of paths, ramps, and bridges traverses the property, and interpretive signs describe how different parts of the mill functioned.

From here, it's a five-mile drive north on Route 114 to reach family-owned **Diamond**

Hill Vineyards (3145 Diamond Hill Rd., Cumberland, 401/333-2751 or 800/752-1505, www.favorlabel.com, tours and tastings noon–5 P.M. Thurs.–Sat., 11 A.M.–3 P.M. Sun.). Since 1976, the winery has been producing acclaimed pinot noir along with traditional New England wines made with blueberries, peaches, and apples. You can tour the grounds and winery, which are anchored by an 18th-century farmhouse. Also nearby, just 3.5 miles farther north, is **Diamond Hill Park,** on Route 114, which offers very nice views of the Rhode Island and southern Massachusetts countryside from its summit.

Named in 1871 for the 16th U.S. president, Lincoln was once the home of Narragansett Indians and later the settler William Blackstone, for whom the river is named. At **Blackstone State Park** in the Quinnville section of Lincoln, you can learn about the riverboats that plied the Blackstone Canal as well as other forms of transportation in the valley at the **Captain Wilbur Kelly House Transportation Museum** (Lower River Rd., 401/333-0295, 9 A.M.–4:30 P.M. daily Apr.–Oct.).

WOONSOCKET

Barely a blip on the radar screen during Rhode Island's first 200 years, Woonsocket (population 43,000) developed during the mid-19th century into one of the nation's great hubs of woolen manufacture. The industry thrived well into the 1940s before succumbing to increased costs and competition from cheaper labor in the South. Today the city celebrates its labor history and strong French-Canadian heritage with the Museum of Work and Culture, one of the most fascinating and well-executed museums in the Northeast. Apart from it and the city's abundance of nicely preserved mill buildings, there are relatively few formal attractions here, but Woonsocket does offer visitors a glimpse of an industrial community relatively little changed in the past century.

Woonsocket may take its name from the Native American word *nisowosaket,* which translates roughly as "thunder mist," but there's some debate as to the legitimacy of this derivation. As trade among southern New England's major metropolitan areas began to flourish in the early 1800s, Woonsocket's star began to rise, first as a major stopover on the stage road from Hartford to Boston. The fast-flowing Blackstone River and its numerous tributaries provided power for dozens of Woonsocket mills during the city's peak years of production. Sluiceways branched out from the rivers and ran alongside streets and rail tracks, over viaducts, and into the basements of factory buildings. After an especially acute industrial boom after the Civil War, Woonsocket found itself with more factories than it could fill with workers. It welcomed workers from Quebec in Canada and then from many other countries.

You can still hear a French-Canadian accent in these parts, although distinctive intonations and words fade a little with each generation. Walk around downtown and the residential neighborhoods surrounding it and you'll see African Americans, Asians, Portuguese, Latin Americans, French Canadians, and people of many other ethnicities. The city abounds with grand, often formidable stone-and-redbrick industrial architecture, the framework of a once-vibrant factory town. Along many streets you'll pass imposing stick, Queen Anne, and gingerbread Victorian houses, most of them subdivided, as well as hundreds of southern New England's trademark triple-decker houses.

Market Square

You can get a real sense of the city's industrial heritage around Market Square, which overlooks Woonsocket Falls and lies within steps of numerous old factory buildings. Because of horrendous floods through the years, mechanical flood barriers were installed in 1955 by the Army Corps of Engineers—these now diminish the view of the 30-foot falls as they appeared before their energy was first harnessed. But as they rush below the Main Street Bridge, they still make quite a racket and produce a cool mist. Across the bridge, you'll see the turbine building where the Blackstone Electric Company's Thunder Mist Plant produces

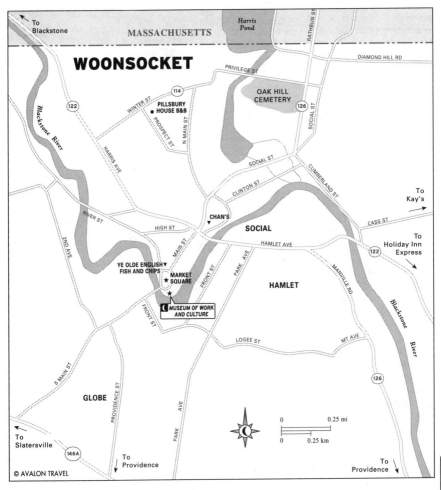

hydroelectric power. The falls produce more than 7 million kilowatt-hours of electricity per year. You can also see one of the old yarn mills just off Market Square. The names of many shops and on the sides of buildings display the city's French-Canadian ties.

◖ Museum of Work and Culture

The Rhode Island Historical Society's Museum of Work and Culture (42 S. Main St., 401/769-9675, www.rihs.org, 9:30 A.M.–4 P.M. Tues.–Fri., 10 A.M.–5 P.M. Sat., 1–4 P.M. Sun., $7)

anchors Market Square and provides a wonderfully vivid glimpse into the industrial history of Woonsocket and southern New England. The curators have beautifully designed imaginative, interactive exhibits that capture the spirit and reveal the hardships of the city's history.

Specifically, the museum traces the history of Woonsocket's French-Canadian immigration. You can get a very good sense of this insular community, its proud labor history, and its ardent preservation of customs and language. Among other things, exhibits recreate a 1920s textile mill shop, a farmhouse in rural Quebec, and a circa-1900 Catholic church. One of the better exhibits takes you into a triple-decker—these three-story tenements were mostly built from the 1890s to about 1930 and are notable for their stacked three-story exterior porches; they're a common sight throughout urban Rhode Island and in many other parts of New England.

The museum tour ends with a presentation inside a recreated 1930s Independent Textile Union Hall. The ITU was founded in Woonsocket in 1931 by Joseph Schmetz, a Belgian worker and socialist; it preceded the AFL-CIO and at its peak had a membership as large as 18,000, representing every craft and industry. Many of the tapes and interactive exhibits are narrated by older town residents who lived through the city's labor strife of the early 20th century. You can read some of the touching letters immigrants sent back to their families in rural Quebec. In one important respect, the Museum of Work and Culture succeeds where many of the famous mansions and historical societies elsewhere in the state fail: It actually talks with its visitors rather than merely showing them static displays or reeling off facts.

Bernon Street

Running east from Market Square, Bernon Street brings you alongside **River Island Park,** where a walking path traces one of the old trenches that carried water from the falls to factories decades ago. This is the heart of **Old Woonsocket Falls Village;** downriver a bit (a left from Bernon St. onto Front St.) is **Old Bernon Village,** home to several fine old cotton mills. Over the Court Street Bridge, you can take in a very nice view of the old Bernon Mills.

The Providence and Worcester rail bridge, supported by the original 1847 stone pillars, crosses the Woonsocket River downstream from the Court Street Bridge. At Depot Square is the 1882 **Worcester Railroad Depot** (1 Depot Sq., 401/762-0250, www.nps.gov/blac, 8 A.M.–7 P.M. Mon.–Fri., free) which replaced

*an exhibit at the **Museum of Work and Culture***

COURTESY OF RHODE ISLAND HISTORICAL SOCIETY

the wooden original, lost in a fire. Trains no longer stop here (although two freight trains pass by nightly), but the impressive station functions as the headquarters of the Blackstone River Valley National Heritage Corridor Commission. Inside are exhibits and documents about the Blackstone River Valley; park rangers can answer questions about the area's history.

Some of industrial Rhode Island's most notable commercial buildings line Woonsocket's Main Street, including the imposing **City Hall** (169 Main St.), where Abraham Lincoln once spoke. It was built in 1856 and added on to in 1891. Several vintage early-20th-century buildings line the street nearby. Some of these have been restored, and others have not, but there is great potential for full restoration. Many of the city's mills now house light industry and service-oriented companies.

North Smithfield

Just west of Woonsocket, North Smithfield, a rural community during its earliest years, incorporated in 1871, when it had become an

THE FRENCH CANADIANS OF WOONSOCKET

By the 1870s, the bustling mill town of Woonsocket had virtually no unemployment and an almost desperate need for new workers. Many factory owners had become nervous about hiring more American workers, as they were starting to speak up angrily about the mills' brutal working conditions. The population in nearby rural Quebec, Canada, depended largely on farming, but the area had a short growing season, meaning they accepted the long hours and poor living conditions of the mill towns without much complaint. The intensely close-knit French Canadians mingled little with workers from other backgrounds, which weakened the solidarity of Woonsocket's factory employees. Many Irish, Scottish, and English immigrants also came to work Woonsocket's mills during these years, but if they complained too much about their jobs, they could easily be replaced by more French Canadians.

Most French Canadian workers in Woonsocket were from small Quebec towns, but large numbers also came from Quebec City and Trois-Rivières. One of the largest French-Canadian populations thrived in Woonsocket, despite the local Yankees and many other immigrants who continued to disparage them for accepting work for the lowest wages and filling most of the jobs.

Their insularity kept their community cohesive for many generations. The social hub of close-knit French Canadian Woonsocket was the appropriately named neighborhood of Social. By 1940 people of French Canadian descent made up 75 percent of the overall population of Woonsocket, and the majority of residents spoke with one another in French. Until 1942 the city produced *La Tribune*, a French-language newspaper, and radio station WOON (then WWON) broadcast in French into the mid-1960s. Still today on some local radio stations you can hear programs spoken in the Quebecois French dialect.

The city celebrates its heritage in other ways: A handful of restaurants serve authentic French Canadian fare such as *poutine*, French fries with hot chicken gravy and cheese, and *ragout de pattes*, fresh pork hocks browned with flour and served with vegetables.

industrial stronghold like the rest of the region. Its historic mill towns include **Union Village** (southwest of the Woonsocket border off Rte. 146A, just 1.5 miles north of the intersection of Rtes. 146A and 104), which contains a number of fine old homes and makes for a pretty drive—most of the oldest buildings date to the 1790s and early 1800s.

From Union Village, continue northwest along Route 146A for about two miles, and turn left onto Green Street to reach historic **Slatersville,** the first planned industrial community in the country. Along with nearby Forestdale, once a mostly Polish and Portuguese factory hub that produced everything from scythes to flannel blankets, it was among the most prolific mill villages of the day. Slatersville was a continuation of the region's "great experiment" in mill industrialization.

The Slater mill complex in Pawtucket required no construction of housing and village buildings because it sat in the middle of an already established urban enclave, but Slatersville was created in a then-rural area west of Woonsocket. John Slater, the younger brother of Samuel, had come to the United States in 1803; Samuel hired him to scout out a site along a strong source of water power that would be suitable for the creation of a full-fledged mill village. He chose to build around a small existing settlement, then known as Buffum's Mills, and in 1807 they opened a mill. They also built a village of worker housing, which today remains remarkably intact. This charming little mill village offers a glimpse of the blueprint for so many villages around New England.

From Slatersville, take Main Street west to Route 102, which leads southwest into Burrillville.

OUTSIDE PROVIDENCE

Burrillville

Established in 1730 and incorporated as a town in 1806, Burrillville today is geographically one of the largest towns in the state, occupying about 55 square miles and comprising several old mill communities. By the 1850s, Burrillville was the state's most prolific producer of wool goods. Production peaked around the turn of the 20th century and then declined steadily through the next few decades. Most of the mills had packed up and moved south by the 1960s, and today these little vestiges of industrial life look rather dated and even deserted. The town is also a center of recreational activity thanks to its several lakes and nature preserves. As in Woonsocket and North Smithfield, Burrillville is home to many people of French-Canadian origin.

Some of the abandoned mills are interesting just to look at. In **Harrisville**, for instance, you'll drive by the old Stillwater Worsted Mills, which at the time of its construction was the largest concrete building in the country. Now the site is slowly being renovated into a modern mixed-use complex by the town, which recently opened a new library here and is working to bring a condo complex beneath the old clock tower. Even in its half-desolate state, you can stand here imagining the bustle of this village when hundreds of workers lived and toiled here.

Burrillville's mills are famous for having clothed a huge chunk of the Union Army during the Civil War and dressing U.S. soldiers during both World Wars. Quite a few buildings in Providence were made with granite quarried from Burrillville. It's one of the better towns in Rhode Island for leaf-peeping in the fall.

Smithfield

Not to be confused with North Smithfield, Smithfield (population 20,000)—which was settled as a Quaker enclave—lies just to the south and is its own incorporated entity. It also has a few small mill villages, but it's more a middle-class bedroom community for Providence commuters as well as home to **Bryant College** (1150 Douglas Pike,

401/232-6000 or 800/622-7001, www.bryant. edu), known to football fans as the summer training camp for the New England Patriots. Although the town developed heavily during the industrial revolution as a textiles center, it has always had strong agrarian roots and a reputation for apple farming; quite a few apple orchards still exist today. More recently, big-name corporate concerns have built modern offices in Smithfield, the largest being Fidelity Investments.

ENTERTAINMENT AND EVENTS
Performing Arts

The **Sandra Feinstein-Gamm Theatre** (172 Exchange St., Pawtucket, 401/723-4266, www.gammtheatre.org) presents five plays per year, including works by up-and-coming playwrights as well as established icons such as Tom Stoppard, Anton Chekhov, and Shakespeare. Recently restored in Woonsocket is the magnificent 1926 **Stadium Theatre Performing Arts Centre** (28 Monument Sq., Main St., Woonsocket, 401/762-4545, www.stadiumtheatre.com), which seats 1,100 and hosts live music, ballet and dance, children's theater, and cabaret. The success of this space has been a great boon to the region.

The **Blackstone River Theatre** (549 Broad St., Cumberland, 401/725-9272, www.riverfolk.org) is a nonprofit cultural center that presents music, dance, and folk arts, usually in the traditions of the many different ethnic groups that have settled in the Blackstone River Valley. Many presentations are geared toward children. The theater occupies a vintage former Masonic Lodge that had been slated for demolition until the theater company took it over in 1996.

Although based in Pawtucket, the **All Children's Theatre** (255 Main St., Suite 201, Pawtucket, 401/728-1222, www.act-inri.org) produces works at several locales, including the Vartan Gregorian School (455 Wickenden St., Providence), the Boys and Girls Club of Pawtucket Arts Center (210 Main St., Pawtucket), and other locales in Barrington,

East Greenwich, and Kingston. This outstanding company formed in 1987 to produce fine theater for, by, and with young people.

Nightlife

In Woonsocket, it's hard to find a more unusual and entertaining venue than **Chan's** (267 Main St., Woonsocket, 401/765-1900, www.chanseggrollsandjazz.com, 11:30 A.M.–10 P.M. Mon.–Wed., 11:30 A.M.–10:30 P.M. Thurs. and Sat., 11:30 A.M.–12:30 A.M. Fri. and Sun., $5–14), which brings in a great variety of jazz bands and musicians, especially on weekdays. Head to East Providence to tickle your funny bone at the **Comedy Connection** (39 Warren Ave., East Providence, 401/438-8383, www.ricomedyconnection.com), which features a steady roster of humorists and comics.

Events

Culture vultures should check out the **Pawtucket Arts Festival** (401/724-5200, www.pawtucketartsfestival.org), which runs from the last weekend in August to the last weekend in September at various places around Pawtucket. The first weekend's festivities are mostly around Slater Mill, and the second weekend around Slater Park. Eat a French-Canadian meat pie as you browse wood carvings, photography exhibitions, and more.

In Woonsocket, **Autumnfest** takes hold in early October at World War II Memorial Park (Social St., Woonsocket, 401/762-6400), with four days of live music and entertainment, amusement rides, fireworks, a Columbus Day parade, and foods of all kinds.

Befitting a region rife with arts and crafts galleries, the **Scituate Art Festival** (www.scituateartsfestival.org) attracts more than 100,000 enthusiasts every Columbus Day weekend to the 200 stalls set up along the Village Green and the several handsome streets that emanate from the main drag, Route 116. Come to enjoy the live music and great food.

Through most of December, you can attend the **Winter Wonderland at Slater Park** (Armistice Blvd., Pawtucket, 401/726-3185, www.pawtucketwinterwonderland.org), a miniature winter village set up on the park grounds. It includes live entertainment, clowns, snacks, and hayrides at the Looff Carousel. In early May, a similar day of festivities kicks off the spring opening of the Looff Carousel. On Christmas Eve, Slatersville comes alive with holiday lights and luminarias for an evening stroll through this picturesque village.

In mid-May, head to Woonsocket's lively River Island Park, at Market Square, for the **Annual Riverfest and Friends of the Blackstone Canoe/Kayak Race** (401/334-5003, www.blackstoneriver.org). The 4.2-mile race runs from downtown Woonsocket to Mannville, and the park hosts food stalls, live music, and crafts.

SHOPPING

A longtime favorite destination in Cumberland, **Phantom Farms** (2920 Diamond Hill Rd., 401/333-2240, 6:30 A.M.–6:30 P.M. Mon.–Fri., 7 A.M.–6 P.M. Sat.–Sun.) has a greenhouse gift shop and offers pick-your-own veggies, pumpkins, apples, and other fruits seasonally, along with fresh-baked pies, apple crisp, candied apples, and other gourmet goodies. During the holidays, it's also a great source of Christmas trees, wreaths, and other decorations, and there are Easter egg hunts and other family-oriented events in the spring. There's also a playground for kids.

In North Smithfield, **Wright's Dairy Farm and Bakery** (200 Woonsocket Hill Rd., 401/767-3014 or 877/227-9734, www.wrightsdairyfarm.com, 8 A.M.–7 P.M. Mon.–Sat., 8 A.M.–4 P.M. Sun.) is a working farm where you can view cow-milking daily and buy fresh milk, whipping cream, cream-filled pastries, and baked goods from the on-site shop. In the early 1970s they started a bakery, which has supplemented the farm's income and sells a vast range of cakes, cookies, and sweets (try the coconut cream pie or shortbread cookies).

It's only appropriate that Pawtucket would have one of the better fabric shops in the state. **Lorraine Mills Fabrics** (593 Mineral Springs Ave., 401/722-9500, 10 A.M.–6 P.M. Mon.–Sat., noon–5 P.M. Sun.) offers thousands of bolts of

OUTSIDE PROVIDENCE

fabric and is set inside a historic brick mill building. Knitters and darners will also want to check out the **Yarn Outlet** (225 Conant St., Pawtucket, 401/722-5600, www.theyarnoutlet.com, 9 A.M.–4:30 P.M. Mon.–Fri.), which has needles, books, yarns, and fabrics.

In the Greenville section of Smithfield, the **Greenville Antique Center** (711 Putnam Pike, U.S. 44, 401/949-4999, 10 A.M.–5 P.M. Fri.–Mon. and Wed., 10 A.M.–7 P.M. Thurs.) displays the wares of about 140 dealers, offering everything from furniture, toys, china, and glassware to vintage prints and paintings.

A 10–15-minute drive northeast of Woonsocket or Providence, **Wrentham Village Premium Outlets** (U.S. 1 at I-495, Wrentham, MA, 508/384-0600, www.premiumoutlets.com/Wrentham, 10 A.M.–9 P.M. Mon.–Sat., 10 A.M.–6 P.M. Sun.) includes about 170 branches of major-name stores, among them Banana Republic, Barneys New York, Bebe, Brooks Brothers, Burberry, Calvin Klein, Coach, DKNY Jeans, Ferragamo, Gap, Guess, Hugo Boss, J. Crew, J. Jill, Kenneth Cole, Nautica, Nike, Perry Ellis, Ralph Lauren, Sony, Timberland, and Williams-Sonoma.

SPORTS AND RECREATION
◖ PawSox

New Englanders root for the Boston Red Sox, but Rhode Islanders get behind their scrappy PawSox (McCoy Stadium, 1 Columbus Ave., Pawtucket, 401/724-7300, www.pawsox.com) with particular fervor. For a fraction of what they're charging up in Beantown, you can score great seats for a game of this Triple-A farm team that has been home to the rising stars Jason Varitek, Roger Clemens, Wade Boggs, Nomar Garciaparra, and countless others. The regular season runs April–early September, and you can also hear the games on the radio at 790 AM.

◖ Kayaking the Blackstone

The same powerful current that ran the mills also makes the Blackstone River a great spot for kayaking and, especially in spring when the river rises, white-water rafting. The Blackstone is a complex waterway for paddlers; you'll encounter dams, which require portaging, and unmarked spillways that can greatly alter the river's water level. Rangers at the **Blackstone River Valley National Heritage Corridor** (1 Depot Sq., 401/762-0250, www.nps.gov/blac, 8 A.M.–4:30 P.M. Mon.–Fri.) offer a great deal of information on how to make the most of canoeing and kayaking as well as how to do so safely. You can also learn a great deal about the river's history, and the flora and fauna encountered along it.

Before boating on the river, visit the website of the United States Geological Survey monitoring station (http://waterdata.usgs.gov), which is in Northbridge, Massachusetts. From here you can get a good indication of whether the flow is safe.

To familiarize the public with the Blackstone River, the National Heritage Corridor and the Rhode Island Canoe and Kayak Association have created the **Blackstone Valley Paddle Club** (401/762-0440, www.ricka.org), which offers rentals on the first and third Tuesday of every month. The club offers kayak and canoe lessons and organized excursions led by park rangers, and also advice and information on taking to the river in these parts. You can also participate in water-quality monitoring projects, river and canal clean-ups, and other activities that promote the health of this valuable resource. Guided paddles are typically given through the summer at 6:30 P.M. on Tuesday and Wednesday. Putting-in points along the river change each week, so call ahead for details. On Saturdays, you can come by for lessons or to improve your kayaking and canoeing skills.

Bicycling, Jogging, and Inline Skating

The **Blackstone River Bikeway** follows parts of the Blackstone River and the old Blackstone Canal—it runs from Pawtucket 17 miles north to Woonsocket but will someday connect all the way to Worcester. Another connection is currently in the works to hook up with the East Bay path in order to create a continuous route of more than 30 miles of biking within the state. You can access it at several points, and you can park your car at lots in Lincoln (at both ends of Front Street, along the river) and at Blackstone State Park at the end of Lower River Road. It's a hit among bikers, inline skaters, joggers, and strollers. You'll pass by some of the great old mills of the region, as well as vast meadows and some fairly mundane suburban stretches.

You can also rent bikes in East Providence at **East Providence Cycle** (414 Warren Ave., 401/434-3838, www.eastprovidencecycle.com, 9 A.M.–6 P.M. Mon., 9 A.M.–8 P.M. Tues.–Fri., 9 A.M.–5:30 P.M. Sat., 11 A.M.–5 P.M. Sun.). Rental rates in the area run $25–50 for a full day.

Northwest of Providence in Lincoln, a favorite spot in the area for strolling, jogging, swimming, and having fun is **Lincoln Woods State Park** (2 Manchester Print Works Lane, off Rte. 123, 401/723-7892, www.riparks.com), also known as Lincoln Woods Reservation. Established in 1909 on Abraham Lincoln's birthday, the heavily wooded, gently rolling 627-acre park surrounds Olney Pond, which is popular for swimming, trout-fishing, and—when weather permits—ice-skating. Other features include playing fields, a snack bar, picnic tables and shelters, fireplaces, a bathhouse with changing rooms and showers, and a boat ramp.

ACCOMMODATIONS
$50-100
Just off I-95, the **Comfort Inn Providence/Pawtucket** (2 George St., Pawtucket, 401/723-6700 or 877/424-6423, www.comfortinn.com, $99–175) has standard rooms in a typical midrise building; amenities include an outdoor pool, guest laundry, and continental breakfast. Attached is the Ground Round Restaurant.

A gorgeous Second Empire Victorian with a green mansard roof, the **Pillsbury House B&B** (341 Prospect St., Woonsocket, 401/766-7983 or 800/205-4112, www.pillsburyhouse.com, $95–135) is one of the most appealing inns in northern Rhode Island and one of the better values in the state. The 1870s house with a big leafy yard sits along one of Woonsocket's most prestigious streets, lined with large homes that were once the domain of mill owners. It's an easy walk from downtown. Rooms are spacious and bright with mostly Victorian antiques that include ornate chandeliers, plush beds made up with either country quilts or fine white linens, and myriad antiques, and most of the rooms have soaring 10-foot ceilings and period wallpapers.

$100-150
Woonsocket is home to the well-maintained **Holiday Inn Express** (194 Fortin Dr., 401/769-5000 or 800/315-2621, www.hiexpress.com, $117–149), which has a convenient downtown location. This clean and efficiently run 88-room property has an indoor pool, a whirlpool, and a health club; there are also 16 suites.

In Smithfield, the **Quality Inn** (355 Rte. 116, Smithfield, 401/232-2400, www.qualityinn.com, $109–189) is another inexpensive, low-frills property. It has 117 rooms and an outdoor heated pool; rates include continental breakfast.

One of the better chain properties in the region, the 84-unit **Holiday Inn Express** (1010 Douglas Pike, Rte. 7, Smithfield, 401/231-6300 or 800/315-2621, www.hiexpress.com, $100–139) has business services, a gym, and rooms with microwaves and refrigerators. Every morning there's complimentary coffee in the lobby.

$150-250
Certainly one of the most distinctive accommodations in New England, the English-built **Samuel Slater Canal Boat B&B** (Central Falls, 401/724-2200 or 800/454-2882, www.bedandbreakfastblackstone.com) was brought to Central Falls in 2000; the 40-foot boat offers a look back into the era when canals drove the economy in this region, about 1828–1848. The boat can be chartered by up to 12 passengers for tours along the river, or up to four can

use the boat as an overnight B&B. Amenities include a TV and DVD player, a phone, and a full galley with a microwave; breakfast is delivered to your door in the morning.

FOOD

The region is dominated by fairly simple and affordable restaurants that emphasize steak, pastas, and the region's famous "family chicken dinners." With such a diversity of ethnicities in the region, you'll also find several fine purveyors of authentic Portuguese, Italian, and French-Canadian food.

Upscale

It's one of the few restaurants in northern Rhode Island that could be called dressy, but even at **Bella** (1992 Victory Sq., Burrillville, 401/568-6996, www.bellarestaurantandbanquet.com, 4–9 p.m. Tues.–Thurs., 11:30 a.m.–9 p.m. Fri., 4–10 p.m. Sat., noon–8 p.m. Sun., $9–24) you can get by with casual attire. The spacious dining room of this Italian restaurant looks and feels like a banquet hall—the ambience is not especially distinctive, but it's pleasant nonetheless. The menu has great variety, and specialties include grilled New York sirloin steak brushed with rosemary-infused oil and grilled marinated chicken over a tossed field greens with balsamic vinegar. Pastas, of course, are a great option: Homemade lasagna and gnocchi are favorites, and you can mix and match several types of pasta with about 15 kinds of sauce (red or white clam, vodka, primavera, and so on).

Pizza and Pub Grub

Justly famous for introducing northern Rhode Islanders to the communal concept of "family chicken dinners," **Wright's Farm Restaurant** (84 Inman Rd., Nasonville, 401/769-2856, www.wrightsfarm.com, 4–9 p.m. Thurs.–Fri., noon–9:30 p.m. Sat., noon–8 p.m. Sun., $8–14) presents family-style meals—the heaping platters of chicken, green salad, fries, rolls, and pasta sides can feed armies. The concept is so simple, so all-American: all-you-can-possibly-stuff-down-your-throat dinners that bring legions of family members and friends together in a homey ambience. It's a huge place, with banquet seating for 1,600 patrons, plus a gift and toy shop that sells house-made specialties such as Italian dressing, barbecue sauce, fudge, and pasta sauce. It has become increasingly famous every year since it opened in 1972. It's

KENYON'S GRIST MILL

Rhode Islanders love their jonnycakes, and probably the most famous purveyor of the main ingredient of jonnycake batter, stone-ground cornmeal, is **Kenyon's Grist Mill** (21 Glen Rock Rd., just off Rte. 138, five miles east of I-95 exit 3, West Kingston, 401/783-4054 or 800/753-6966, www.kenyonsgristmill.com). The Kenyon Corn Meal Company has been milling grist since the early 1700s, and the current operations are in a charmingly raffish clapboard building with peeling red paint that dates to 1886. It looks about like it must have more than a century ago, and the staff still grinds the meal the traditional way, using a massive granite millstone – it's great fun for visitors to watch the staff make the meal using a process that's remarkably similar to that which the indigenous people of New England did for centuries before Europeans arrived.

The mill employs ancient techniques but often comes up with new meals and grains, which it grinds without any preservatives or additives. So whether you're an amateur baker or a real pro, or you just want to try making jonnycakes at home, this is the definitive source for meals and flours. Some favorite Kenyon's Grist Mill products, in addition to jonnycake meal, include buckwheat flour, scotch oat flour, buttermilk-honey pancake mix, quince jam, cinnamon apple jelly, whole quinoa, Rhode Island flint corn, Indian pudding, and local honey.

a pretty amazing operation—75 ovens work away in the kitchen.

Another excellent chicken-dinner purveyor in northern Rhode Island is **Village Haven** (90 School St., Forestdale, 401/762-4242, www.thevillagehaven.com, 4–8:30 P.M. Wed.–Thurs., 4–9 P.M. Fri.–Sat., noon–8 P.M. Sun., $8–14), which scores high marks for its down-home American cooking such as prime beef and baked stuffed jumbo shrimp. The cinnamon buns are the stuff of legend. It's a very lively spot, with friendly staff and dependable food.

At **Ye Olde English Fish and Chips** (Market Sq., Woonsocket, 401/762-3637, 10 A.M.–8 P.M. daily, $2–7), you can grab your food and eat it on a bench overlooking the Blackstone River and falls, or eat in the casual sit-down dining room. This place has been serving fresh seafood since 1922, and its proximity to the Rhode Island Museum of Work and Culture makes it a hit with visitors. Of course, fish-and-chips are the menu favorite, but you might also try a fish burger, stuffed quahogs, baked scallops, baked stuffed shrimp, or Manhattan-style clam chowder.

Set in a grove of towering pine trees in North Smithfield, the aptly named **Pines Restaurant** (1204 Pound Hill Rd., 401/766-2122, www.thepinesrestaurant.com, 4:30–8:30 P.M. Thurs., 4–9 P.M. Fri.–Sat., noon–8 P.M. Sun., $7–16) is another favorite for family-style chicken as well as traditional American standbys such as lobster, prime rib, baked haddock, king crab legs, and chops. It's family-un and tends to draw a local crowd.

Slatersville's best dining option is **Pinelli's Cucina** (900 Victory Hwy., 401/767-2444, www.pinellimarrarestaurants.com, 11:30 A.M.–10 P.M. daily, $14–21), where you might sample both classic and contemporary Italian fare, such as scampi over capellini, veal topped with prosciutto and mozzarella with a mushroom marsala sauce, and grilled Italian pork chops with sautéed vinegar peppers and Tuscan potato wedges.

In Cumberland, **Tuck's** (2352 Mendon Rd., 401/658-0450, 11 A.M.–11 P.M. Mon.–Sat.,

3–8 P.M. Sun., $6–13) is a reliable option for burgers, salads, chicken wraps, homemade soups, fish-and-chips, and other tavern fare. The bar also serves 12 kinds of beers on tap, making it a favorite watering hole for locals. There's a popular outdoor deck too.

Ethnic Fare

Somewhat Americanized but plenty of fun is **Chan's** (267 Main St., Woonsocket, 401/765-1900, www.chanseggrollsandjazz.com, 11:30 A.M.–10 P.M. Mon.–Wed., 11:30 A.M.–10:30 P.M. Thurs. and Sat., 11:30 A.M.–12:30 A.M. Fri. and Sun., $5–14), an elaborate, almost campy Chinese restaurant that since 1905 has been noted perhaps more for its live entertainment than anything else. It's well regarded enough that people will drive 30 minutes or more to check out the scene here, sample the tasty Szechuan fare, and listen to the line-up of hip jazz greats and other musicians. The menu is encyclopedic, with nods to just about every Chinese culinary tradition you can think of. Specialties include roast pork egg foo yong, beef sautéed with pickled ginger, egg drop soup, lobster with fried rice, and the inevitable Tahitian Delight (fresh sea scallops and tender chicken stir-fried in a light sauce with straw mushrooms, broccoli, carrot slices, and water chestnuts on a bed of pan-fried noodles).

At the Lincoln Mall, **Asia Grille** (off Route 146 and I-295, 401/334-3200, www.asiagrille.com, 11 A.M.–9:30 P.M. Sun.–Thurs., 11 A.M.–10:30 A.M. Fri.–Sun., $5–15) serves a well-prepared if fairly standard range of Chinese and other pan-Asian specialties, such as hot-and-sour soup, shrimp with almonds, and General Tso's chicken. It's an attractive spot with hanging Chinese prints, tapestries, and regional artwork.

East Providence has one of the state's several outstanding Portuguese restaurants, **Madeira** (288 Warren Ave., 401/431-1322, www.madeirarestaurant.com, 11:30 A.M.–10 P.M. Mon.–Thurs., 11:30 A.M.–11 P.M. Fri.–Sat., noon–10 P.M. Sun., $10–21), a classy spot with a highly solicitous staff. Here you can try

OUTSIDE PROVIDENCE

flame-grilled Portuguese sausage; kale, chorizo, and potato soup; fillet of scrod topped with the restaurant's secret Madeira sauce; paella Valencia; and boiled dried codfish served with boiled potatoes, chickpeas, and hard-boiled egg. Everything is cooked to order, which means you'll often have to wait 30–40 minutes for your dinner, but it's worth the wait for such authentic fare. Vegetarian entrées are available on request.

Quick Bites

In Woonsocket, drop by **Kay's** (1013 Cass Ave., 401/762-9675, $3–10) for superb sandwiches and like fare—the huge steak sandwich is a specialty, and there is a fine lobster roll. The kitchen serves till midnight.

Modern Diner (364 East Ave., Pawtucket, 401/726-8390, 6 A.M.–3 P.M. Mon.–Sat., under $7), a crimson-and-cream Sterling Streamliner steel railroad-car diner attached to a Victorian house, serves excellent home-style food. It's a short drive from Slater Mill, and breakfast is served all day. Plenty of the state's diner aficionados rank this place among the best around. Cranberry-almond pancakes are a highlight, but you'll find a full slate of typical diner favorites. It's not open for dinner and accepts cash only.

For several decades, devotees of burgers and fries have been cramming into **Stanley's** (535 Dexter Ave., Central Falls, 401/726-9689, www.stanleyshamburgers.com, 11 A.M.–8 P.M. Mon.–Thurs., 11 A.M.–9 P.M. Fri.–Sat., $3–7); the patties here are freshly made and wonderful, grilled with several toppings (cheddar, mushrooms, onions); the French fries are prepared with just the right crispness.

Horton's Seafood (809 Broadway, East Providence, 401/434-3116, 11 A.M.–8 P.M. Wed.–Thurs., 10 A.M.–9 P.M. Fri., 11 A.M.–8 P.M. Sat., $4–11) serves tasty lobster rolls that can be admired for both their heft and lack of filler. In summer you can dine on the screened-in porch.

Get ice cream kicks at **Sunshine Creamery** (305 N. Broadway, East Providence, 401/431-2828, noon–10 P.M. Sun.–Thurs., noon–11 P.M.

Fri.–Sat., $2–5), which dishes out nearly 40 flavors of the sweet, frozen treat.

Ice Cream Machine (4288 Diamond Hill Rd., Cumberland, 401/333-5053, www.icecreampie.com, 11 A.M.–10 P.M. daily Apr.–Oct., under $4) is one of the top homemade ice cream shops in the state, also known for its ice-cream pies.

Technically in Pawtucket but literally a few steps from the Providence border is a prosaic shopping center that has several delicious options for cheap eats. The top picks are **Rasoi** (727 East Ave., Pawtucket, 401/728-5500, www.rasoi-restaurant.com, 11:30 A.M.–10:30 P.M. Mon.–Sat., 11:30 A.M.–9:30 P.M. Sun., $6–14), a brightly colored, good-quality Indian eatery with fast service and an eclectic, tasty menu. The kitchen focuses on coastal Indian regions, where boiling and steaming are preferred to frying, so dishes are flavorful but also healthful. Next door is an attractive little veggie eatery called **Garden Grille** (727 East Ave., Pawtucket, 401/726-2826, www.gardengrillecafe.com, 10 A.M.–9:30 P.M. Mon.–Sat., 11 A.M.–8 P.M. Sun., $3–8), with a full juice bar, healthful goat cheese and arugula salads, fresh sandwiches, and all manner of great food. Also check out **Ronzio Pizza and Subs** (727 East Ave., 401/722-5530, 11 A.M.–10 P.M. Sun.–Thurs., 11 A.M.–11 P.M. Fri.–Sat., $9–17)—a locally owned chain of pretty good pizzerias, known for its Florentine chicken pizza (with plenty of spinach), steak arrabiata pizza, and two-foot calzones.

INFORMATION AND SERVICES
Visitor Information

Pamphlets, brochures, and visitor information are available on the towns north and northwest of Providence from the **Blackstone Valley Tourism Council** (175 Main St., Pawtucket, 401/724-2200 or 800/454-2882, www.tour-blackstone.com).

Tours

One interesting way to explore the region is on

one of the cruises offered on the **Blackstone Valley Explorer** (175 Main St., Pawtucket, 401/724-2200, www.rivertourblackstone.com, $10 adults, $8 children), a 49-passenger riverboat with a canopy roof that runs up and down the Blackstone River June–mid-October. Several kinds of excursions are offered, departing from Central Falls and Woonsocket. Some of these are available only to groups and students, so it's best to call ahead for details. These tours give a particularly strong sense of the mix of rural and wildlife-inhabited lands that exist side-by-side with the great old mill villages of the past two centuries.

Another possibility is the **Conway Gray Line** (10 Nate Whipple Hwy., Cumberland, 401/658-3400 or 800/888-4661, www.conwaytours.com), which offers narrated van tours of the valley that pass by attractions both in Providence and Slater Mill as well as the many industrial sites of the area. The same company also operates a 33-passenger vintage-style trolley that can be chartered for tours; call for schedule information.

The most intriguing tour option is a tour on the *Samuel Slater* **Canal Boat** (401/724-2200 or 800/454-2882, www.tourblackstone.com/canal.htm), a bright red-and-green vintage canal boat. Built in Cambridgeshire, England, it can be chartered for tours along the Blackstone River and can also be booked as a bed-and-breakfast. It has seating for 12 and overnight accommodations for up to four guests. Charter rates are quite reasonable if you have a large group—it's $190 for the first 90 minutes and $75 each additional hour. Also offered are onboard clambakes, which cost $85 for two, $155 for four.

GETTING THERE AND AROUND

As for the surrounding area, the Blackstone River Valley is easy to get around by car, although you can take the bus to several places, among them Pawtucket and Woonsocket. It's fairly easy to get to Slater Mill from Providence using public transportation—Bus 99 is your best bet; it runs regularly between Kennedy Plaza in Providence and downtown Pawtucket. If you're driving, note that I-295 cuts across the southeastern half of the Blackstone River Valley as it loops from I-95 south of Providence back up to I-95 north of it in Attleboro, Massachusetts. From Providence, Route 146 is a quick limited-access highway northwest to Woonsocket.

Warwick and Cranston

On the opposite side of Providence from the Blackstone River Valley, Rhode Island's most densely populated suburbs, Warwick and Cranston, lie immediately south of the capital and contain high concentrations of indoor and strip malls, chain restaurants and motels, and busy roads lined with traffic lights. Warwick is also home to T. F. Green Airport, New England's third-busiest. Although it's crowded and in many places prosaic, this patch of middle-class upper-middle-class bedroom communities is not without charm. Both towns lie along Narragansett Bay and have several interesting and historic residential neighborhoods near the water. In Warwick especially, you'll find several villages with their own personalities, histories, and walkable commercial districts. The towns also contain the nearest public beaches to Providence, and just south of Warwick, the all-American community of East Greenwich has a delightfully charming downtown with hip eateries and a smattering of cool boutiques.

WARWICK

It's almost incorrect to call Warwick a suburb—this full-fledged city is one of the state's most prominent communities, as it's home to Rhode Island's main airport and has

OUTSIDE PROVIDENCE

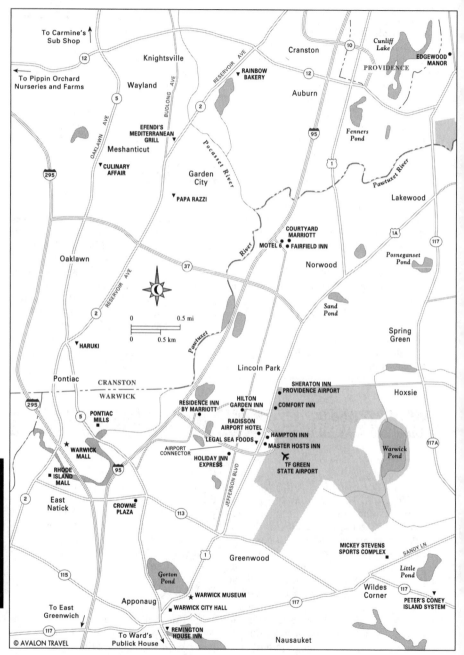

OUTSIDE PROVIDENCE

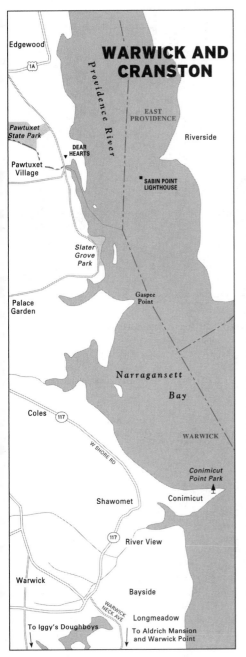

WARWICK AND CRANSTON

Edgewood

1A

East Providence

Riverside

Providence River

Pawtuxet State Park

Dear Hearts

Pawtuxet Village

Sabin Point Lighthouse

Slater Grove Park

Gaspee Point

Palace Garden

Narragansett Bay

Coles

117

W Shore Rd

Warwick

Conimicut Point Park

Shawomet

Conimicut

River View

117

Warwick

Bayside

Warwick Neck Ave

Longmeadow

To Iggy's Doughboys

To Aldrich Mansion and Warwick Point

a population of about 85,000 (second only to Providence). Like many of the state's communities, Warwick actually comprises a slew of small village centers rather than one coherent core. Through the early 20th century, textile mills engaged in dyeing, bleaching, and finishing employed many of Warwick's workers, but even a century ago many residents commuted to Providence and other nearby towns, and it has remained a bedroom community ever since.

Apponaug Village

The city's civic center is historic Apponaug Village, where you'll find the dramatic 1894 **Warwick City Hall** (3275 Post Rd., U.S. 1, 401/738-2000, www.warwickri.gov), crowned with an imposing six-story clock tower. Practically next door, the **Warwick Museum of Art** (3259 Post Rd., U.S. 1, 401/737-0010, www.warwickmuseum.org, noon–4 p.m. Tues.–Sat., free), which was built in 1912 as the Kentish Artillery Armory, presents exceptionally interesting and well-curated rotating art and some history exhibits throughout the year. There are more than 30 buildings of historic or architectural distinction in the village; you can learn more about them by obtaining the free *Walking Tour of Historic Apponaug Village* booklet distributed by the Warwick Convention and Visitors Bureau, which produces a similar booklet on Pawtuxet Village.

Pawtuxet Village

Pawtuxet is Warwick's oldest village and contains a number of fine old colonial homes, most of them along Narragansett Avenue and the roads that intersect it. From Pawtuxet (not to be confused with Pawtucket, another city north of Providence) a party of local patriots attacked the grounded British revenue schooner *Gaspée,* one of several early acts of defiance against the crown in New England that ultimately led to the American Revolution. Since 1966 Pawtuxet has hosted the annual *Gaspée* Days celebration (401/781-1772, www.gaspee.org), held in late June,

COURTESY OF PROVIDENCE WARWICK CVB

Pawtuxet is Warwick's oldest village.

which features, among other events, a parade, a road race, fireworks, and a symbolic burning of the *Gaspée* in effigy.

Conimicut Village

An early fishing enclave that developed into a fashionable summer colony around the late 19th century, Conimicut Village has gradually become a laid-back, upper-middle-class suburb of attractive homes, many dating to the early part of the 20th century. There's great strolling along the bay and by Conimicut Park and Lighthouse, which pokes out into the Narragansett Bay and overlooks Patience and Prudence Islands. During Labor Day weekend, 30,000 people attend the Conimicut Festival, a lively crafts and food event. Just offshore from the village, **Conimicut Lighthouse** sits along a rocky ledge by Conimicut Point Park. You can't visit this 1868 structure, but it cuts a dashing figure in the bay. In 1960 the lighthouse was changed from kerosene to electric power—it was the last lighthouse in the nation to convert to electricity. In 2004 the city of Warwick acquired the lighthouse and is currently working

on restoring the interior with a grant from the national Department of Transportation, with the goal of eventually opening the building for tours.

Warwick has another impressive lighthouse at the tip of Warwick Neck. This 51-foot cast-iron tower was built in 1932 and was the last traditional lighthouse constructed in Rhode Island. It's now operated by the Coast Guard. Warwick Neck is one of the city's fanciest neighborhoods, the appropriate setting for one of the state's most imposing estates, even compared with those in Newport, the **Aldrich Mansion** (836 Warwick Neck Ave., 401/739-6850, www.aldrichmansion.com). This 75-acre estate on Narragansett Bay was the home of one of Rhode Island's greatest political figures, Senator Nelson W. Aldrich. On this estate, John D. Rockefeller Jr. married Aldrich's daughter, Abby, setting up one of the nation's more formidable political-industrial dynasties. The couple's son, Nelson Rockefeller, later served as vice president of the United States. It took more than 200 craftspeople more than 15 years to build this lavish 70-room mansion, which was completed in 1912. Today the mansion is rented out for weddings, business meetings, and other functions—it contains a fine collection of art, and all the original detailed woodwork has been carefully restored. The house starred alongside Brad Pitt in the 1998 film *Meet Joe Black*.

Potowomut

To reach one of the most interesting parts of Warwick, you have to get out of town. Potowomut occupies a peninsula south of Warwick proper on the shoreline of East Greenwich. You reach it by driving south of U.S. 1 through downtown East Greenwich, then make a left onto Forge Road, and another left onto Ives Road. Most of this land was used for raising cattle during colonial times, and Revolutionary War hero Nathanael Greene was born on the peninsula. At the tip of the peninsula is a small residential neighborhood with a mix of new and old homes, many of them overlooking the bay.

The big draw here is **Goddard Memorial State Park** (Ives Rd., 401/884-2010, free), the site of an ambitious tree-growing project undertaken by the late-19th-century owner of this land, Henry Russell, and continued by the subsequent owner, Colonel William Goddard. Today you can stroll or ride horseback through the park on many trails, admiring the fruits of their labors. There's also a fine beach along Greenwich Bay, numerous playing fields, bridle trails, picnic areas, changing facilities, and a nine-hole golf course. Concerts are given during the warmer months in the park's restored carousel pavilion, next to the beach.

CRANSTON

Cranston lies immediately southwest of Providence and is easily reached via I-95 or Route 10. The area was settled in 1638 by associates of Roger Williams, including William Harris, Zachariah Rhodes, and William Arnold (the progenitor of the traitorous Revolutionary War general Benedict Arnold). Harris waged a battle with Williams, asserting that his township was not under the jurisdiction of Providence. The land was then known as Pawtuxet, and in 1754 this and the adjacent settlements joined to form the town of Cranston (named for Samuel Cranston, governor of Rhode Island 1698–1727). It thrived as a textile-manufacturing center during the 19th and early 20th centuries.

ENTERTAINMENT AND EVENTS
Nightlife

Folks in Warwick and Cranston tend to have cocktails at restaurants with good bars attached, including **20 Water Street** (20 Water St., East Greenwich, 401/885-3703, www.twentywaterstreet.com), **Remington House Inn** (3376 Post Rd., Apponaug Village, 401/736-8388, www.theremingtonhouseinn.com), **Ward's Publick House** (3854 Post Rd., Warwick, 401/884-7008, www.wardspublickhouse.com), and **Legal Sea Foods** (2099 Post Rd., Warwick, 401/SEAFOOD—401/732-3663, www.legalseafoods.com). The local outlet of bar-restaurants chain **Chelo's Waterfront Bar and Grille** (2225 Post Rd., Warwick, 401/737-7299, www.chelos.com) overlooks the bay. Head to **Copperfield's** (1551 Warwick Ave., Warwick, 401/738-7936) to shoot pool, watch a game on TV, belt out karaoke tunes, play darts, or listen to live bands—it's a large and popular hangout, sort of an adult's Chuck E. Cheese, with 10 pool tables and about a dozen large-screen TVs. There's often live folk, R&B, and rock at the **Harp and Shamrock** (557 Warwick Ave., 401/467-8998), a friendly, traditional Irish pub.

Events

Warwick's most celebrated event, *Gaspée Days* (401/781-1772), takes place toward the end of May and lasts well into June in Pawtuxet Village, in celebration of one of the American Revolution's earliest acts of defiance. Events include a huge arts and crafts fair, a gala ball in period colonial costume, a children's costume contest, a parade, and a mock battle reenactment.

In August, Rhode Island celebrates the region's French and French-Canadian heritage with **Pawtuxet Valley Franco-American Heritage Festival** (Majestic Park and Gazebo, Main St., West Warwick, 401/822-1232, www.franco-americanheritagefestival.org), with storytelling, regional cuisines, living-history exhibits, and live music.

SHOPPING

Warwick is a shopping hub for the state, although you won't necessarily find a huge number of independent stores. Still, if you're looking for the nearest outpost of your favorite chain, drive along Route 2, where you'll find Best Buy, Home Depot, Sam's Club, Sports Authority, T. J. Maxx, Barnes and Noble, Pier 1 Imports, Toys R Us, K-Mart, Newbury Comics, Staples, Petco, Bed Bath and Beyond, and a Christmas Tree Shop, among more than 200 others. Also along Route 2 are two large if fairly run-of-the-mill indoor shopping malls: the mid- to upscale **Warwick Mall** (400 Bald Hill Rd., Warwick, 401/739-7500, www.warwickmall.com, 10 A.M.–9 P.M. Mon.–Sat., 11 A.M.–6 P.M. Sun.), which is home to the nation's largest Old Navy as well as branches of JCPenney, Macy's, Ann Taylor, Lane Bryant, Nine West, Zales, and the Disney Store; and the even more bland **Rhode Island Mall** (Rtes. 2 and 113, Warwick, 401/828-7651, 9:30 A.M.–9:30 P.M. Mon.–Sat., noon–6 P.M. Sun.), whose anchors include Sears, Kohl's, and Wal-Mart.

In Cranston, **Garden City Center** (Rte. 2, Cranston, 401/942-2800, www.gardencitycenter.com, 10 A.M.–9 P.M. Mon.–Sat., noon–6 P.M. Sun.) is an open-air shopping center with more than 70 upscale shops, including both local and chain operations. Good picks here include Banana Republic, Chico's, Crabtree and Evelyn, Eddie Bauer, Eastern Mountain Sports, J. Jill, Talbots, Victoria's Secret, and Williams-Sonoma.

Fans of antiques shopping should check out Warwick's **Antique Haven** (30 Post Rd., Warwick, 401/785-0327, 11:30 A.M.–5 P.M. daily) in historic Pawtuxet Village. Since 1910, the famed shop **Axelrod** (663 Killingly St., Johnston, 401/421-4833 or 888/429-3576) has been crafting fine musical instruments.

ANTIQUING

The towns in western Rhode Island tend to be fairly rural, with few formal attractions and shopping districts, but two charming exceptions have developed through the years: North Scituate and Chepachet. Both of these small historic villages contain a number of well-preserved 18th and 19th-century buildings, and both have become quite well known for their first-rate antiques shopping.

In the center of North Scituate village you'll find a nice range of antiques shops, including **J&M Hobbies** (180 Danielson Pike, North Scituate, 401/647-7778), a delightful nostalgic shop with vintage model railroad equipment, die-cast toy cars, crafts, puzzles, rockets, and other paraphernalia that may take you back to your childhood. **Village Antiques** (143 Danielson Pike, at Rte. 116, North Scituate, 401/647-7780) specializes in furnishings and decorative and fine arts from the mid-19th-

mid-20th centuries, from Victorian to arts and crafts to art deco.

In Chepachet, you can take classes at **Holidaze Stained Glass** (6B Money Hill Rd., Chepachet, 401/568-5140, www.holidazestainedglass.com), a studio where art and gifts in stained glass are sold and custom-made. **Magnolias and Memories** (171 Danielson Pike, Chepachet, 401/647-3335) occupies a fading Greek revival house and is piled high with collectibles, crafts, and country gifts. Almost everybody who visits Chepachet makes it a point to stop by the **Brown and Hopkins General Store** (1179 Putnam Pike, U.S. 44, Chepachet, 401/568-4830), which opened in 1809 and is alleged to be the oldest continuously operating store in the nation. It's a good place to buy local foods and gourmet items, baskets and pottery, fine upholstered furniture and antiques, and Christmas decorations (displayed year-round).

ACCOMMODATIONS
$50-100

Next to Hampton Inn at the airport, the **Best Western** (2138 Post Rd., Warwick, 401/737-7400 or 800/251-1962, www.bwprovidence. com, $50) has 103 units, including a few suites with wet bars and refrigerators. The property's slogan, "luxury for less," is a bit optimistic, but the rooms are pleasantly decorated as far as economy chains go, and the staff is consistently helpful and friendly.

Just three miles north of the airport are the region's two least-expensive chain properties, the **Motel 6** (20 Jefferson Blvd., Warwick, 401/467-9800 or 800/466-8356, www.motel6.com, $50-72) and the **La Quinta Inn** (36 Jefferson Blvd., Warwick, 401/941-6600 or 800/753-3757, www. lq.com, $95-119). Both are perfectly fine if you just need a cheap clean bed for the night.

One of the better and newer options, the **Courtyard Marriott Providence-Warwick** (55 Jefferson Park Rd., 401/467-6900 or 800/321-2211, www.courtyard.com, $99-179) has attractive, airy rooms and some nice perks, such as free high-speed Internet and a very good continental breakfast. It also has a pool, an exercise room, and larger rooms with whirlpool tubs or separate living areas with kitchenettes; some rooms have balconies. It's just three miles north of the airport—easy driving distance from downtown Providence.

$100-150

Best among the lower-priced properties in these parts, the **Holiday Inn Express** (901 Jefferson Blvd., Warwick, 401/736-5000 or 800/315-2621, www.hiexpress.com, $117-169) is just off the Post Road, west of the airport. There are 147 guest rooms, including 31 suites, plus full business services, an indoor pool, a small gym, and a hot tub.

The **Hilton Garden Inn** (1 Thurber St., Warwick, 401/734-9600 or 877/782-9444, www.hiltongardeninn.com, $118-139) is the newest hotel option in the Warwick area.

A couple of properties in town are better suited to longer-term guests (usually business travelers, but these can also be good choices for families

and leisure travelers). The **Residence Inn by Marriott** (500 Kilvert St., Warwick, 401/737-7100 or 800/331-3131, www.residenceinn.com, $109-209) is 0.5 miles west of the airport, just off I-95. In West Warwick, **SpringHill Suites by Marriott** (14 J. P. Murphy Hwy., 401/822-1244 or 888/287-9400, www.springhillsuites. com, $129-149) also caters to long-term stays. Each unit has separate sleeping, eating, and working areas as well as a sleeper sofa. Other amenities include in-room refrigerators, microwaves, coffeemakers, and wet bars, plus there's an on-site exercise room and indoor pool.

In Cranston, the 18-room **Edgewood Manor** (232 Norwood Ave., 401/781-0099 or 800/882-3285, www.providence-lodging.com, $129-269) is a grand early 1900s Greek Revival mansion with five beautifully crafted fireplaces and ornate architectural detailing. Guest rooms and suites carry out the building's lavish theme, with plush linens, Oriental rugs, four-poster beds, neatly framed paintings and prints, paneled walls, and high-style Victorian antiques.

$150-250

The only upscale chain property that's not directly facing the airport, the **Crowne Plaza** (801 Greenwich Ave., Warwick, 401/732-6000 or 800/227-6963, www.crowneplaza.com, $150-200) sits two miles southwest, near I-95's exit 12, on an attractively landscaped 80-acre plot. The bulk of the clientele are business travelers, who appreciate the many amenities, including free shuttle service to the airport, a popular wine bar with 24 wines served by the glass, an indoor pool and fitness center, a full business center, and a sauna and whirlpool. The facilities are in tip-top shape, the rooms large and well-equipped, and the staff friendly if not necessarily more efficient than the employees at most of the less pricey chain properties by the airport. Weekend packages are sometimes offered with certain meals are included. The restaurant presents a lavish Sunday brunch on holidays that's well attended by both guests and nonguests.

The Crowne Plaza's most obvious competitor, the 207-room **Sheraton Providence Airport** (1850 Post Rd., Warwick, 401/738-4000 or

800/325-3535, www.sheraton.com) occupies a rather dated-looking building within view of the airport and offers rates generally about 10 percent to 25 percent lower than the Crowne Plaza. Rest assured that once you're past the drab exterior you'll find a brightly furnished and well-managed contemporary property with about 200 nicely proportioned guest rooms, a restaurant, a fitness center, and an indoor pool. Sheraton has put quite a lot of money into this place in recent years, and its efforts show.

Rates at the **Hampton Inn and Suites** (2100 Post Rd., Warwick, 401/739-8888 or 800/426-7866, www.hamptoninn.com) run about the same as the others along this stretch but sometimes creep a bit higher. Considering this and the beautifully kept guest rooms and public spaces, this is an excellent choice, whether you just need a night close to the airport or a good base for visiting the entire region. Rooms are homey, with high-quality furnishings, and a fireplace warms a lobby lounge that feels comfortable for reading or relaxing, unlike many hotel lobbies. Amenities include an indoor pool, continental breakfast, a gym, a whirlpool, a business center, a game room, two-line phones, and coffeemakers.

Along the same stretch, the **Comfort Inn** (1940 Post Rd., Warwick, 401/732-0470 or 877/424-6423, www.comfortinn.com) sits right next to Bertucci's Pizza and Atwood Grill (casual American food) but has few other distinguishing features. Considering its rates are typically no lower than the Hampton Inn's, it should be considered a last choice. Nothing is especially wrong with it, but the decor, staff, and amenities are just so-so. Some rooms have whirlpool baths.

Nearly across the street from the airport entrance, the **Radisson Airport Hotel** (2081 Post Rd., Warwick, 401/739-3000 or 800/395-7046, www.radisson.com) has rates that are comparable to or sometimes even better than its competitors. It nearly adjoins Legal Seafoods and also has its own decent restaurant, and about 40 suites have whirlpool baths and wet bars. There's also a business center. It's a fairly ordinary-looking building, but the big plus is that the hotel is staffed by young and enthusiastic students from the Johnson and Wales's hospitality program, which means you can usually count on highly responsive and cheerful service as well as clean rooms.

SPORTS AND RECREATION

The **Mickey Stevens Sports Complex** (975 Sandy Lane, 401/738-2000, ext. 6800) is Warwick's recreation facility, with a public ice- and inline skating rink (401/738-2000, ext. 6810), a one-mile walking and jogging path, basketball courts, eight lighted tennis courts, three baseball diamonds, and two volleyball courts, plus a public swimming pool (401/738-2000, ext. 6809).

Beaches

Warwick has the best beaches in Greater Providence, including **Goddard Memorial State Park** (1095 Ives Rd., 401/884-2010 or 401/884-9620 in season, www.riparks.org) and 126-acre **Warwick City Park** (401/738-2000), which has a saltwater beach, changing facilities, bike paths, hiking, and ball fields. It's said, although not verified, that the very first clambake was held here in the late 1800s. Sheltered **Oakland Beach** (401/738-2000) at the southern tip of Oakland Avenue off Route 117 is a smaller swath of sand that's near several restaurants and bars; there's also a restored carousel, a big hit with kids.

Boating

Warwick is interior Rhode Island's boating capital, with more marinas, moorings, and slips than any other city in the state. Some of the larger marinas include **Apponaug Harbor Marina** (17 Arnold's Neck Dr., 401/739-5005), with 204 slips and 30 moorings; **Brewer Yacht Club** (100 Folly Landing, 401/884-0544), with 240 slips and 10 moorings; **C-Lark Marina** (252 Second Point Rd., 401/739-3871), with 350 slips; **Greenwich Bay Marina** (1 Masthead Dr., 401/884-1810), with 320 moorings; and **Norton's Shipyard** (foot of Division St., 401/884-8828), with 160 slips and 160 moorings.

Biking

The **Cranston Bike Path** offers 5.5 miles of

COURTESY OF PROVIDENCE WARWICK CVB

a beach in Warwick

pancake-flat terrain along a former railway bed. Parking is on the Cranston-Warwick border just off Pontiac Avenue (below I-295).

Golf

A windswept, fairly level course that runs fairly long, **Cranston Country Club** (69 Burlingame Rd., 401/826-1683, www.cranstoncc.com, 6 A.M.–dusk daily, $39 for 18 holes, $27 for 9 holes Mon.–Thurs., $45 for 18 holes, $27 for 9 holes Fri.–Sun.) is known for its sizable greens that demand skillful putting.

FOOD

Warwick has dozens of restaurants, many of them chains, and many of these lie along the busy Route 2 retail strip. Along here you'll find Pizzeria Uno, Red Lobster, Olive Garden, Lone Star Steakhouse, and Friday's, among many others. Warwick, Cranston, and East Greenwich are somewhat upscale suburbs, so quite a few notable chefs have opened restaurants in this area in recent years, especially in East Greenwich's quaint downtown.

Upscale

One of the better-known dining options in these parts, the **Post Office Cafe** (11 Main St., East Greenwich, 401/885-4444, www.pinellimarrarestaurants.com, 4:30–9:30 P.M. Tues.–Thurs., 4:30–10:30 P.M. Fri.–Sat., $14–24) actually occupies the town's original circa-1930 post office. It's a bright high-ceilinged space with friendly, refined service and excellent contemporary Italian fare. The same owners operate the Grille on Main, Pinelli's, and several other great Rhode Island restaurants. You might start with sautéed calamari with fire-roasted peppers and served with a champagne-garlic-butter sauce. The Post Office *frutti di mare* has a loyal following, as does the slow-simmered wild-mushroom risotto with truffle oil. There's also an impressive wine list. This place fills up fast on weekends; book well ahead.

Excellent Mediterranean and Greek fare is served at **Efendi's Mediterranean Grill** (1255 Reservoir Ave., Cranston, 401/943-8800, www.efendisbarandgrill.com, 11 A.M.–9 P.M. daily, $11–19), a laid-back restaurant with sophisticated cooking that rises above its casual

OUTSIDE PROVIDENCE

environs. Specialties include rack of lamb confit with fresh-herb red wine sauce; Turkish *izgara kofte* (ground beef with spices and vegetables served with *tzatziki*); and seafood kebabs. Pita sandwiches are offered at lunch, and the Sunday brunch draws a sizable crowd for a mix of traditional breakfast fare and more savory grills and egg creations.

Arguably the best all-around dining option in the West Bay region is a meal at **Table 28** (28 Water St., East Greenwich, 401/885-1170, www.table28.com, 5:30–9 P.M. daily, $17–32), worth the drive from anywhere in the state. The kitchen takes relatively simple staples of contemporary American cuisine and presents them artfully with unusual ingredients. For instance, there's a terrific starter of crispy calamari paired with charred jalapeño-tomato sauce and roasted garlic-lemon aioli. Top main dishes include plantain-crusted fried snapper with shiitake stir-fried rice, baby bok choy, and mango chutney, and butter-basted lobster risotto with sun-dried tomatoes, *gremolata,* and crispy shallots. Save room for the signature chocolate pudding.

Creative but Casual

The **Grille on Main** (50 Main St., East Greenwich, 401/885-2200, www.pinellimarrarestaurants.com, 11:30 A.M.–10 P.M. Sun.–Tues., 11:30 A.M.–11 P.M. Wed.–Thurs., 11:30 A.M.–midnight Fri.–Sat., $8–16) is a swanky little eatery on this pretty village's dapper Main Street. Singles appreciate the long and comfy wooden bar, where you can also order from the food menu. Tables in front look out through a bow-front window over the busy sidewalk. The urbane dining room, with lavender trim and tightly spaced wooden tables, is noisy and fun. The menu changes often, and highlights include focaccia stuffed with mozzarella, vine-ripened tomatoes, fresh basil, and garlic; an excellent Buffalo chicken salad; and more substantial dishes such as oven-baked haddock topped with Ritz cracker crumbs and a citrus vinaigrette, or blackened Cajun chicken Alfredo pasta. Burgers and creative pizzas are also offered, plus lavish desserts.

The owners of the popular Chardonnay's restaurant just over the border in Seekonk, Massachusetts, operate the similarly excellent **Meritage** (5454 Post Rd., 401/884-1255, www.meritageri.com, 4:30–10 P.M. Sun.–Wed., 4:30–11 P.M. Thurs.–Sat., $12–26) in East Greenwich. This spacious, lively place is known for its eclectic menu, which offers everything from sushi to designer pizzas to creative pastas to artful grills. The pan-seared sesame tuna steak served rare with wasabi aioli is a favorite, but don't overlook the hearty pork medallions gratiné with Dijon mustard, brown sugar, and port wine, finished with Gorgonzola. Note that there's also a branch of Chardonnay's, which features the same menu, in Seekonk at 393 Taunton Ave., 508/336-0967.

The famous Boston fish house **Legal Sea Foods** (2099 Post Rd., Warwick, 401/SEA-FOOD—401/732-3663, www.legalseafoods.com, 11:30 A.M.–10 P.M. Mon.–Thurs., 11:30 A.M.–10:30 P.M. Fri., noon–9 P.M. Sat.–Sun., $11–27) has a popular branch across the street from T. F. Green Airport, and even with Rhode Island's many considerable seafood eateries, Legal draws plenty of kudos. Eat either on the casual deck, where you can watch planes taking off and landing, or in the clubby, masculine interior. Favorite starters include blackened sashimi tuna, bluefish pâté, marinated grilled calamari with white beans and grilled onions, and the restaurant's trademark clam chowder. Lobsters are the most popular entrée offering, but you'll find a large selection of grilled and fried fish platters.

A smart and contemporary space with light-wood furnishings, matte-green walls, and a couple of booths, **Culinary Affair** (650 Oaklawn Ave., Cranston, 401/944-4555, 11 A.M.–3 P.M. Mon., 11 A.M.–9 P.M. Tues.–Sat., $6–18) serves both unusual and rather expected American and Italian dishes. Grilled squid over couscous with baby greens and an orange vinaigrette makes a tempting starter. Tasty entrées include penne with grilled shrimp and plum tomatoes in a cracked pepper–Dijon sauce, or veal paillard grilled with broccoli rabe and carrot mashed potatoes.

You'll find superb, creative Italian fare at

Cafe Fresco (301 Main St., East Greenwich, 401/398-0027, www.cafefrescori.com, 5 P.M.–close daily, $12–24), a snazzy, high-ceilinged space with tall windows and banquette seating. A raw bar turns out oysters, littlenecks, and a house specialty called Oyster Fresco, topped with raspberry vinaigrette, sour cream, and caviar. Top-flight starters are bruschetta topped with shredded Black Angus beef and a creamy shallot sauce, and seared-tuna sashimi over mixed baby greens, while memorable main dishes include portobello risotto; shrimp *fra diavolo*; and clams and sausage with tomatoes, onions, and garlic over mashed potatoes.

Pizza, Pasta, and Pub Grub

In Cranston, head to **Papa Razzi** (Garden City Center, 1 Paparazzi Way, 401/942-2900, www.paparazzitrattoria.com, 11:30 A.M.–10 P.M. Mon.–Thurs., 11:30 A.M.–11 P.M. Fri.–Sat., 11:30 A.M.–9 P.M. Sun., pizzas $10–11, entrées $12–26) for pizzas and pastas. This is a classic trattoria with a couple of twists: On Monday nights opera classics are performed, and on weekends there's a fantastic brunch. Stars from the kitchen include slow-roasted lemon-garlic chicken with wilted greens and roasted potatoes, a terrific rendition of spaghetti Bolognese (with pancetta, ground veal, mushrooms, and a light tomato-cream sauce), and the pizza topped with prosciutto, mozzarella, arugula, and balsamic tomatoes.

In historic Apponaug Village, the **Remington House Inn** (3376 Post Rd., Apponaug Village, 401/736-8388, www.theremingtonhouseinn.com, 4–10 P.M. Sun.–Thurs., 4–11 P.M. Fri.–Sat., $15–18) is a charming colonial inn marred only slightly by its very busy location. Inside you'll find an inviting spot with hanging brass pots, a dark timber ceiling, and a redbrick fireplace that glows all winter long. There aren't a lot of surprises on the American-Italian menu, but portions are large and the food is well-prepared. You might sample chicken sautéed with roasted red peppers, garlic, onion, tomato, and fresh herbs tossed with bowtie pasta in a mascarpone-cream sauce; or lamb tenderloin charbroiled and finished with a merlot sauce. Clams Remington is a worthy appetizer for the Ocean State—the tender bivalves come sautéed with Portuguese *chourico* sausage, fresh tomatoes, garlic, and onion. There are many draft beers offered, and there's an impressive wine list.

Ward's Publick House (3854 Post Rd., Warwick, 401/884-7008, www.wardspublickhouse.com, 4 P.M.–close daily, $8–12) fits the bill if you're craving decent pub fare and a pint of imported draught beer (Harp, Guinness, Tetley's, Speckled Hen, and Murphy's are all on tap). For sustenance, try the stir-fried veggies, traditional Irish bangers and mash, shepherd's pie, or blackened salmon. There's traditional Irish music many evenings. Whether for a meal or for drinks, this is a festive and atmospheric hangout with warm pub decor.

In East Greenwich, yuppies and yachting types flock to **20 Water Street** (20 Water St., East Greenwich, 401/885-3703, www.twentywaterstreet.com, 11:30 A.M.–close daily, $15–23 in the dining room, $9–15 in the tavern and on deck), a festive waterside bar and eatery with a lovely deck overlooking the many sailboats and fishing trawlers on Narragansett Bay—it looks out toward Goddard Park. The dining room, decked with hardwood floors, Windsor chairs, and dark-wood paneled walls, presents a somewhat upscale menu of seafood favorites, such as clams casino, seafood casserole with a sherry-wine lemon butter, and rack of lamb with garlic and rosemary. More casual fare is served on the deck and in the tavern, including grilled swordfish steak, lobster rolls, and Caesar salad. By most accounts, the tavern fare is both better tasting and a better value.

Chelo's Waterfront Bar and Grille (2225 Post Rd., Warwick, 401/737-7299, www.chelos.com, 11:30 A.M.–10:30 P.M. Mon.–Thurs., 11:30 A.M.–11:30 P.M. Fri.–Sat., noon–10 P.M. Sun., $7–15) overlooks the bay and serves casual seafood and American fare.

Ethnic Fare

Providence takes the prize in Rhode Island when it comes to ethnic fine cuisine, but the burbs have caught up fast in recent years. Take the **Cucina Mista** (455 S. Main St., East Greenwich,

401/398-2900, www.cucinamista.com dinner daily, year-round, $10–18), which serves commendable pastas and creative salads, grilled meats, and a remarkably flavorful risotto.

You can get your sushi fix at **Haruki** (1210 Oaklawn Ave., Cranston, 401/463-8338, www.harukisushi.com, lunch 11:30 A.M.–2:30 P.M. Mon.–Fri., noon–3 P.M. Sat., dinner 5–9:30 P.M. Mon.–Thurs., 5–10 P.M. Fri.–Sat., 4:30–9:30 P.M. Sun., $9–17); you'll seldom dine alone at this phenomenally popular spot on busy Oaklawn Avenue inside a bright, beautiful dining room with varnished wood trim and elegant Japanese murals. There's an extensive and reasonably priced sushi menu—unusual options include the yellowtail and scallion rolls, sea urchin, and spicy codfish roe. Specialties from the grill vary from crispy fried catfish with wasabi and light pepper-onion sauce to scallops teriyaki and honey-barbecued pork ribs.

Quick Bites

Iggy's Doughboys (889 Oakland Beach Ave., Warwick, 401/737-9459, www.iggysdoughboys. com, 11 A.M.–10 P.M. Sun.–Thurs., 11 A.M.–11 P.M. Fri.–Sun. summer, 11 A.M.–7 P.M. Sun.–Thurs., 11 A.M.–8 P.M. Fri.–Sat. winter, $3–9) might just serve the best clam cakes in the state—it's certainly fun to test them out against the many reputable competitors around Rhode Island. The original Iggy's opened in 1924 and has withstood hurricanes and recessions; the view, out toward Newport Bridge, Jamestown, and across to the East Bay, is outstanding—you'll actually feel as though you're down by the ocean. Standard fare includes chowder, stuffies, fried scallops, the famous Iggy Burger with sautéed peppers and onions, tuna grinders, meatball subs, and chicken wings. Iggy's also specializes in greasy little fried doughboys, which are dusted liberally with powdered sugar; a half dozen costs just $2.95. The website has coupons discounting several items on the menu.

You'll find a nice selection of tasty sub sandwiches at **Carmine's Sub Shop** (310 Atwood Ave., Cranston, 401/942-9600, 9 A.M.–7 P.M. daily, under $5). Fillings include veal steak, meatballs, and a wide and tempting array of cold cuts. Pick up a couple (or a few…or a plateful) of New York wieners at **Peter's Coney Island System** (2298 West Shore Rd., Warwick, 401/732-6499, under $4), one of the legions of exceptional purveyors of these addictive treats scattered around the state.

A meager burger stand when Jigger Lindberg opened it in 1918, **Jigger's Diner** (145 Main St., East Greenwich, 401/884-5388, 6 A.M.–2 P.M. Mon.–Fri., 6 A.M.–1 P.M. Sat.–Sun., $5–11) serves some of Rhode Island's best diner fare, from the trademark gingerbread pancakes to more prosaic dishes such as eggs and bacon. This may not be fancy food, but it's definitely not your typical greasy-spoon cooking either—presentation verges on elaborate, with fresh and inventive ingredients, such as the sandwich of fresh mozzarella, pesto, and vine-ripened tomatoes; or pan-roasted cod topped with salsa fresca (a dinner entrée served Fridays only, when the restaurant also allows patrons to bring their own wine or beer). The fries are hand-cut and homemade, as is the breakfast sausage. It's one of the oldest restaurants in town and is housed in a little railroad car with a blue facade along the ranks of pretty shops in East Greenwich.

Head to **Sweet Temptations** (450 Main St., East Greenwich, 401/884-2404) for freshly made cakes and sweets as well as deli sandwiches and light breakfast fare that use the bakery's exceptional fresh breads. **Dear Hearts** (2214 Broad St., Cranston, 401/272-2000, ext. 1, www.dearhearts.com, 10 A.M.–10 P.M. daily) doles out about 50 varieties of delicious homemade ice cream.

Java Joints

Grab a light lunch, pastries and baked goods, or a cup of espresso at **SimonSays Cafe** (96 Main St., 401/884-1965, 6:30 A.M.–6 P.M. daily), a fun little coffeehouse in downtown East Greenwich.

Gourmet Goods and Picnic Supplies

Home of the intriguing and strangely satisfying stuffed pickle, **Pickles Gourmet Deli** (135

Frenchtown Rd., East Greenwich, 401/884-1828, www.picklescustomcatering.com, 9 A.M.–3 P.M. Mon.–Sat., $3–8) also serves about 30 kinds of breakfast and lunch sandwiches, plus homemade quiche and stuffed eggplant tortes.

Rhode Island Monthly magazine once had a bunch of second-grade schoolkids in Barrington taste-test cookies from a few of the state's most reputable bakeries. **Rainbow Bakery** (800 Reservoir Ave., Cranston, 401/944-8180, www.rainbowbakeryri.com, 7 A.M.–5 P.M. Tues.–Fri., 7 A.M.–2 P.M. Sat., 7 A.M.–1 P.M. Sun.) took the prize for the best chocolate-chip cookies; it's hard to argue with such a reputable panel of experts.

VISITOR INFORMATION

Pamphlets, brochures, and visitor information are available from the **Providence Warwick Convention and Visitors Bureau** (144 Westminster St., 401/456-0200, www.goprovidence.com). You can also get information on the Warwick and Cranston area from the **Warwick Tourism Office** (Warwick City Hall, 3275 Post Rd., 401/738-2000, ext. 6402, www.visitwarwickri.com).

Points West

The largely rural and sparsely populated towns of western Rhode Island, like those just across the border in eastern Connecticut, have relatively few attractions and notable sights. You will find a handful of enchanting small villages characterized mostly by rolling woodland, obsolete but often handsome mills, and fast-growing tracts of suburban housing. There are very few accommodations in these parts, and extremely limited public transportation. But it is an ideal region for relaxing country drives, bike rides, or moderately hilly strolls.

GLOCESTER

One of the state's largest towns, Glocester comprises about 56 square miles, even more than its large neighbor to the north, Burrillville. It was once part of Providence, which occupied most of northern Rhode Island until the 1730s. Coal mining, potash making, iron forging, marble quarrying, felt-hat making, and cottonseed oil manufacture were among the eclectic industries this town supported, along with farming, which remains to a small extent today. The town has just under 10,000 residents, making the population density among the lowest in the state.

CHEPACHET

From Providence, U.S. 44 cuts west up through Glocester and into its most notable village, Chepachet, which lies at the crossing of Routes 100/102 and U.S. 44. This pretty village embodies the sleepy pace of northwestern Rhode Island while also defying the stereotype that there's little to see or do in these parts. Main

COURTESY OF BLACKSTONE VALLEY TOURISM COUNCIL

Cherry Valley Herb Farm in Glocester

OUTSIDE PROVIDENCE

Street abounds with antiques and other unusual shops, and you can get a brief lesson in state history by visiting the bronze plaque marking the site of the 1842 Dorr Rebellion, an event that threw Rhode Island politics into chaos.

In Chepachet you can also visit the **Job Armstrong Store** (1181 Main St., U.S. 44, 401/568-8967, www.glocesterheritagesociety. org, 11 A.M.–2 P.M. Thurs. and Sat. Apr.–Dec., by appointment only Jan.–Mar., free), which was the largest of 13 dry-goods stores in this village in the early 1800s. Today it has been converted into a living-history museum, where you can watch crafts, spinning, quilting, and rug-hooking demonstrations. It's also the headquarters of the Glocester Heritage Society and a visitors center with information on the area's few local attractions.

Just south of Chepachet you'll find **Sprague Farm** (Pine Orchard Rd., 401/588-9124, www. glocesterlandtrust.org), a 291-acre site administered by the Glocester Land Trust and containing mature evergreens, striped maples, and Atlantic white cedars. There are also flower gardens and shrubs as well as several stone bridges of note.

SCITUATE AND FOSTER

From Providence, U.S. 6 eventually leads west into Scituate and then on to the Connecticut border via Foster. It's a fairly nondescript drive through these parts aside from a stop in the town's administrative center, North Scituate, an endearingly unfussy village of mostly white clapboard colonial houses. North Scituate is entirely ingenious—unsullied by development and still totally free of banal attempts at gentrification. There's nothing cutesy here, just a few historic buildings that always seem to need a fresh coat of paint.

One of Scituate's best-known features is six-mile-long Scituate Reservoir, a narrow waterway that terminates at the immense 3,200-foot-long Scituate Dam. The state created the reservoir in the 1920s by relocating about 1,600 residents of seven villages—Kent, South Scituate, Ashland, Richmond, Rockland, Saundersville, and Ponganset—and flooding the entire basin.

It's now the state's largest body of fresh water and provides water for about two of every three Rhode Island households. You can drive around parts of the 60-mile shoreline, but recreational activity—including fishing, boating, and hiking—is strictly forbidden.

Still farther west, Little Foster Center is the civic hub of the large but sparsely populated town of Foster. By Rhode Island standards it's quite hilly and rugged, its slopes feeding into the Moosup and Ponaganset Rivers. Anchoring this village is the **Foster Town House** (180 Howard Hill Rd., 401/392-9200, www.townoffoster. com, 8:30 A.M.–5:30 P.M. Mon.–Thurs., free). This 1796 two-story building was built and used as a Baptist church until the 1840s.

COVENTRY

You can follow Route 117 from the busy suburbs of Cranston and West Warwick to the quiet township of Coventry, at 62 square miles the second-largest town in the state. The village of Washington, the civic seat, was the site of mills specializing in lace, cotton, and wool during the 19th century.

In the Anthony section of town, just north of Washington, lived the famous colonial military statesman Nathanael Greene. Born to Quaker parents in 1752, the distinguished general lived in the **Nathanael Greene Homestead** (50 Taft St., 401/821-8630, 10 A.M.–5 P.M. Wed. and Sat., 1–5 P.M. Sun. Apr.–Oct., or by appointment, $5 adults, $2 children) from 1770 to 1776, after which it was owned by his brother, Jacob. The 2.5-story frame house has two chimneys and sits on a bluff by the south branch of the Pawtuxet River. Every room in the house contains a paneled fireplace and three double-hung windows; it has been a museum since it was restored in 1924 and contains furnishings and artifacts from the Greene family. It's believed that the cannon in front of the house was made at the Greene family forge in Potowomut.

SHOPPING

In a cavernous vintage red barn in Glocester, **Cherry Valley Herb Farm** (969 Snake Hill

Rd., Glocester, 401/568-8585, www.cherryvalleyherbfarm.com, by appointment only) sells a wide array of mostly country French collectibles, home furnishings, and garden accoutrements, plus gourmet jams and sauces and a long list of herbs and spices. Another nearby spot with both a year-round Christmas Shop and a wide array of toys, teddy bears, dolls, and gifts is **Johnson's Farm and Santa's Workshop** (33 Money Hill Rd., Glocester, 401/568-1693, 10 A.M.–6 P.M. Mon.–Fri., 10 A.M.–5 P.M. Sat.).

John and Cindy's Harvest Acres Farms (425 Kingstown Rd., South Kingstown, 401/789-8752, 10 A.M.–6 P.M. daily) is an extensive farmstead with fresh honey, maple syrup, sweet corn, tomatoes, mums, milk, eggs, fresh fruit and jams, and pumpkins. Pick fresh fruit, fall pumpkins and Indian corn, and other seasonal goods at **The Junction** (1194 Putnam Pike, Chepachet, 401/568-4619). Here you can also browse the extensive selection of garden statuary, candles, antique furnishings, plants, and flowers. Beginning in June, fresh strawberries, raspberries, sweet corn, pumpkins, and hay are the order of the day all summer long at **Salisbury Farm** (Rte. 14 at Plainfield Pike and Pippin Orchard Rd., Johnston, 401/942-9741, www.salisburyfarm.com, 7 A.M.–6 P.M. Fri.–Wed., 7 A.M.–8 P.M. Thurs.), which was founded in the 1800s and has been run by five generations of the Salisbury family. The farm also contains an intricate corn maze, the first of its kind in New England. About a mile of pathways cuts through four acres of corn rows—it's no easy feat finding your way out. In the fall, you can go on hayrides.

SPORTS AND RECREATION

In the towns west of Providence, beyond the immediate suburbs, you'll find copious opportunities for hiking, biking, fishing, and enjoying the outdoors. West of Warwick is the **Arcadia Management Area,** a 14,000-acre preserve that passes through Richmond, Hopkinton, and Exeter. It has two freshwater beaches along Beach Road (off Rte. 165) and also one at Browning Mill Pond (off Arcadia Rd.). You can pursue hunting, fishing, hiking, mountain biking, and horseback riding in the preserve.

Hiking

A half-hour drive west of Providence, an excellent spot for a ramble is Exeter's **Beach Pond,** which lies half in Rhode Island's Beach Pond State Forest and half in Voluntown, Connecticut's Pachaug State Forest (access is off Rte. 165, about 6 miles west of Rte. 3). From the parking area, head to marked trails of varying lengths that climb through hemlock and birch forest, around the north shore of the pond, and through some quite steep valleys. An additional network of trails meanders south of the pond, nearly as far as Route 138. These blazed trails cross several scenic stream beds and wooded glens. The pond is also a popular spot for fishing and boating. This is one of several popular hiking areas off Route 165, which cuts through some of the state's prettiest and least populated terrain. Other hikes to consider are the Mt. Tom, Bald Hill, and Stepstone Falls trails.

ACCOMMODATIONS
$50-100

Best Western West Greenwich Inn (101 Nooseneck Hill Rd., West Greenwich, 401/397-5494 or 800/528-1234, www.bestwestern.com, $69–99) is one of the best lodging options in these parts. The 56-room hotel tends to have rates comparable to the less desirable nearby Super 8. It's on attractive wooded grounds but has no restaurant.

$100-150

There's a top-notch **Hampton Inn** (850 Centre of New England Blvd., Coventry, 401/823-4041 or 800/426-7866, www.hamptoninn.com, $100–139) in Coventry, just off I-95 exit 7, close to West Warwick and East Greenwich. It has all the usual perks of Hampton Inns, including a nice fitness center, pool, and hot tub, and some king studio suites, which have kitchenettes, living rooms, and whirlpool tubs.

OUTSIDE PROVIDENCE

FOOD
Creative but Casual
A relative newcomer in inviting Harmony, **Chester's** (102 Putnam Pike, U.S. 44, 401/949-1846, Harmony, 11 A.M.–1 A.M. daily, $7–13) doles out respectable portions of comfort foods, many of the dishes with nouvelle tendencies, including veal saltimbocca, chicken sautéed with sun-dried tomatoes, mushrooms, and pasta with a pink cream sauce, and scallops Nantucket baked with bacon and cheddar. Burgers are a big hit, as is the fried calamari. A fieldstone fireplace warms the dining room.

Pizza, Pasta, and Pub Grub
Gentlemen Farmer Restaurant (845 Providence St., West Warwick, 401/615-7777, www.genltemenfarmerrestaurant.com, 6 A.M.–8 P.M. daily, $3–11) is a delightful little stone-and-timber pizzeria and diner where locals hang out and the waitresses call you "hon." There's a long and varied menu, and portions are huge and well-priced, with about 20 kinds of grinder, a variety of pizzas, seafood platters, bacon burgers, hot dogs, Greek salads, barbecued pork sandwiches, and hearty breakfast fare. Most of this stuff will give your arteries a good hardening, but it's tasty cooking.

The **Tavern on Main** (1157 Putnam Pike, Chepachet, 401/710-9788, www.tavernonmainri.com, 4–9 P.M. Wed.–Thurs., 11:30 A.M.–9:30 P.M. Fri.–Sat., 11:30 A.M.–8:30 P.M. Sun., $11–22) serves mostly traditional American dishes (prime rib, steak, seafood casseroles, and pizzas) plus some kicky ethnic takes such as teriyaki-marinated steak tips and chicken marsala. Ask the friendly staff about the tavern ghost, and you'll get an earful about alleged sightings; they host ghost dinners on Wednesday nights.

Quick Bites
You can't miss **Cindy's Diner** (46 Hartford Ave., North Scituate, 401/934-2449, 6 A.M.–8 P.M. Sat.–Thurs., 6 A.M.–9 P.M. Fri., under $8) with its glittering pink, blue, and yellow neon sign. It's a big hit with the breakfast crowd. **Shady Acres Restaurant and Dairy Bar** (164 Danielson Pike, Foster, 401/647-7019, 6 A.M.–8 P.M. daily, under $6) is a typical roadside short-order eatery with a long menu of delicious home-baked pies and ice creams. Burgers and fried seafood are also offered, and breakfast is served early. If you find yourself hungry out near Arcadia Management Area, there's always the **Middle of Nowhere Diner** (222 Nooseneck Hill Rd., U.S. 3, Exeter, 401/397-8855, 5 A.M.–8:30 P.M. daily, under $6), a simple clapboard eatery with tasty short-order cooking, including fantastic omelets.

SOUTH COUNTY

Technically, there is no such thing as what Rhode Islanders call South County. It is really Washington County, which comprises 11 townships, and part of southern Kent County. More specifically, when people talk about South County they are mostly referring to the shore towns, beginning with Westerly to the west, extending east through Charlestown and South Kingstown to Narragansett and north along Narragansett Bay to North Kingstown.

This is where Rhode Island's nickname, the Ocean State, really becomes evident, with sandy beaches and barrier islands along a 30-mile coastline. It's also the part of the state that most appeals to families and summertime shore-goers. Sure, Newport may be more famous, but it's also largely an adult city with an upscale reputation. South County is Rhode Island's kid-friendly, teen-popular beach retreat with scads of low-key motels and inns, some of them owned by the same families for nearly a century. You'll find a few snazzy boutiques here and there, and the occasional luxurious bed-and-breakfast or swank bistro. But for the most part, this is the place to tuck into clam fritters at an in-the-rough seafood shanty, ride Jet-Skis, or surf cast into a salt pond.

For all its youthful buzz, South County is for the most part happily old-fashioned and uncluttered by strip-mall excess. Nowhere do high-rise hotels and massive condo communities exist, and where high-density beach housing has been allowed, it's mostly tasteful and unflashy in the traditional New England

COURTESY OF SOUTH COUNTY TOURISM

HIGHLIGHTS

LOOK FOR ◖ TO FIND RECOMMENDED SIGHTS, ACTIVITIES, DINING, AND LODGING.

◖ **Watch Hill:** This quintessential Victorian village abounds with funky shops and dining options in all price ranges, and there's lovely strolling along the town beaches as well as the chance to visit historic Watch Hill Lighthouse (page 203).

◖ **Misquamicut Beach:** The definitive family getaway, chock-full of miniature golf courses, ice-cream stands, seafood shacks, and relatively affordable motels and beach cottages (page 205).

◖ **South County Museum:** You'll find more than 20,000 tools, photographs, documents, and artifacts tracing the rich past of the Narragansett area at this living-history museum that occupies a onetime farm (page 224).

◖ **Gilbert Stuart Museum:** For a glimpse into the life of colonial America's foremost portraitist, visit this estate of Gilbert Stuart, whose depiction of George Washington graces the $1 bill. The scenic grounds and gardens here are part of the draw (page 225).

◖ **Wickford:** The charming waterfront village of Wickford contains about 40 distinctive boutiques, virtually all of them independent, including fine art galleries, gourmet food shops, and urbane clothiers (page 227).

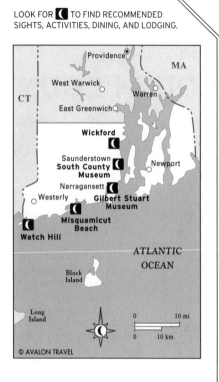

style. Watch Hill, in Westerly, looks like the set of an old movie, its dainty harbor and petite shopping district without a single neon sign or modern chain shop. Punctuating the shoreline are vast tracts of protected wilderness preserves and sheltered saltwater ponds.

While beachfront fun is a major attraction of South County, that's not all there is to do here. The old ports of Galilee and, across the river, Jerusalem, rank among the nation's leading fishing communities. These are charming but rough-and-tumble working ports that make for a fascinating visit, although there are no formal attractions—just a few low-frills restaurants serving superfresh seafood. Galilee is also the main port from which ferries run

back and forth to Block Island. Up the coast on Narragansett Bay, in North Kingstown, the village of Wickford is one of the best-preserved colonial villages of its size anywhere in the region—you'll find scores of handsome 18th- and 19th-century homes here in this quaint hamlet that's also famous for shopping. Peace Dale, the site of the country's first power loom, still contains a number of handsome granite and brick buildings from its heyday as a textile mill town, and nearby Kingston is dominated by the many stately buildings of the University of Rhode Island. A final inland gem worth a look is Westerly, which has a lovely walkable downtown replete with dignified civic buildings, a few inviting boutiques and antiques

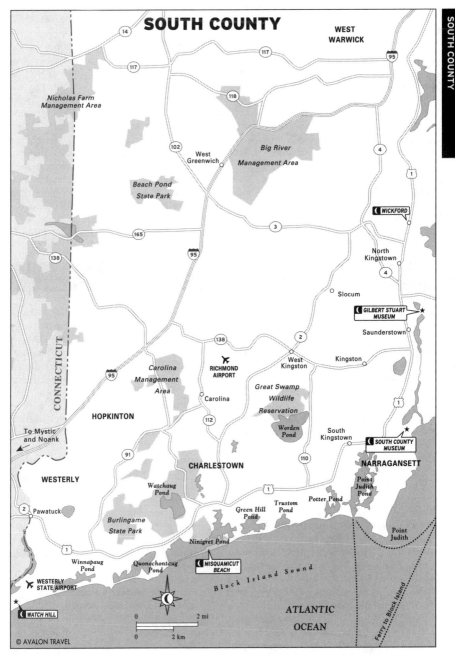

shops, and a leafy green park that's perfect for a stroll or picnic.

PLANNING YOUR TIME

As South County is Rhode Island's definitive family destination, and also a great area for hiking, beachcombing, sailing, golfing, and other outdoorsy pursuits, you might want to make this your base if you're traveling with kids or pursuing sporting and recreational activities. Watch Hill is a particularly good beach for the little tykes, who will love to take a whirl on the antique carousel. Older kids and teens will prefer the action at Misquamicut Beach, as will young adults and couples. Many visitors to this part of the state, especially in summer, rent cottages or efficiencies for a week or more. From South County, you can easily explore other parts of the state on day trips or even overnighters.

Otherwise, South County is probably a part of the state that you can enjoy in a relatively short period. You'll find a smattering of sophisticated restaurants and shops in this area, especially in the browser's paradise of Wickford Village, and there are some bona fide historic attractions in the South County Museum and Gilbert Stuart Museum, but adults aiming for a romantic, adult-oriented, urbane getaway will find much more to their liking in Providence, Newport, Block Island, and even the East Bay. Plan no more than an overnight—and as little as a few hours— if your interests do not include the realm of family and outdoors attractions.

Westerly to Charlestown

WESTERLY

Named for its location on the far end of the Rhode Island coast, Westerly is one of those rare towns where the past and the present seem in perfect harmony. The downtown area is as picturesque as they come, with solid granite buildings from the 19th and early 20th centuries built with stones from nearby granite quarries. The granite made the little town rich, and its residents gained a rich appreciation for the arts, a tradition that carries on to the present day.

As with most Rhode Island municipalities, the town of Westerly is a large area that takes in several small villages, among them Westerly proper, Watch Hill, Misquamicut, Weekapaug, and Bradford. Hopkinton and Ashaway lie just northeast. Most visitors spend their time in Watch Hill, Misquamicut, and Weekapaug, three popular summer resort communities on the Atlantic Ocean.

When indigenous people lived on these lands, the whole coastal area in this part of Rhode Island and in Connecticut was called Misquamicut (which translates to "place for salmon fishing"). After settlers form Newport established Westerly in the mid-17th century, residents derived income mostly from farming, along with some shipbuilding. That changed in 1846, when the town's vast granite resources were discovered. Westerly's handsome red granite has since been used in the construction of thousands of buildings throughout southern New England and New York.

Of course, downtown Westerly is full of granite buildings from the late 19th and early 20th centuries, making it a pleasant and attractive walking area. Most of the town's civic buildings, as well as several of its largest and grandest homes, are on or near gracious **Wilcox Park** (bounded by High St., Broad St., Granite St., and Grove Ave.), a broad and rolling 18-acre green with mature shade trees, a duck pond, and several distinctive fountains and sculptures (look for one of *The Runaway Bunny* of storybook fame).

Probably the most imposing building by the park is the **Westerly Public Library** (44 Broad St., 401/596-2877, www.westerlylibrary. org, 9 A.M.–8 P.M. Mon.–Wed., 9 A.M.–6 P.M. Thurs.–Fri., 9 A.M.–4 P.M. Sat. year-round, also 9 A.M.–4 P.M. Sun. Oct.–May), a lavish brick and red granite structure with a red-tile roof accented with terra-cotta trim. It was built in 1894 as a memorial to local Civil War veterans and originally included a bowling alley, gymnasium, art gallery, and community space for the Grand Army of the Republic. Also note the very handsome U.S. Post Office at the corner of Broad and High Streets; constructed in 1914, this dramatic building with a broad white marble facade is decorated with fluted Doric columns.

The **Babcock-Smith House** (124 Granite St., 401/596-5704, www.babcock-smithhouse. com, 2–5 P.M. Sat. May–June and Sept.–Oct., 2–5 P.M. Fri.–Sat. July–Aug., $5) is Westerly's de facto local history museum; the 1734 early Georgian-style house was built for physician Dr. Joshua Babcock, later appointed the chief justice for Rhode Island. Inside you'll find a superb collection of 18th-century furnishings, varying from primitive pieces to an ornately wrought Federal sideboard and a towering highboy from Connecticut.

HOPKINTON AND RICHMOND

Just north of Westerly, Hopkinton and Richmond don't abound with formal attractions, but they do possess some of the state's best hiking, canoeing, fishing, and camping areas, as well as several excellent golf courses.

The town of Hopkinton comprises some 16 villages, three of them—Hopkinton City, Wyoming, and Carolina—designated National Historic Districts. Stroll through any of these small communities, and you'll see numerous examples of colonial and Victorian architecture.

Hope Valley is one of the more prominent little towns in western Rhode Island. In 1770 the village took hold when Hezekiah Carpenter built a dam here and used the power to build a sawmill, a gristmill, a fulling mill, and a carding plant.

Among Richmond's many villages, Shannock, Kenyon, and Woodville are quaint old mill communities, still with their clapboard and redbrick buildings. Shannock Village, with

its Shannock Mill Complex and Horseshoe Falls, is especially scenic—some of its buildings date back well into the 18th century.

◖ WATCH HILL

Rhode Islanders call the rocky point at the south end of Westerly one of the best-kept secrets in the state. And no wonder: The village of Watch Hill—named because it was used as a lookout position during the Revolutionary War—is a quaint resort community welcoming families and couples alike. At the turn of the 20th century, an enterprising local rented out rooms in the lighthouse at the top of the hill; grand old hotels followed, and high society, including Clark Gable, Douglas Fairbanks, and Henry Ford came to cool their heels by the sea. It still draws its fair share of vacationers and second-home owners, plus some workers from other parts of Rhode Island, as it's just a 45-minute commute to Providence and even closer to the many businesses in Warwick, Cranston, and eastern Kent County.

The commercial center of the village runs along Bay Street for about 400 yards and contains a mix of cafés, galleries, boutiques, and a handful of accommodations. It's a tight-knit little town with a friendly personality, and it's completely devoid of the modern development that characterizes South County's beach communities farther east. High above Bay Street, a parallel road called Bluff Avenue has the grandest of Watch Hill's summer homes. In some ways, Watch Hill feels like a little slice of Block Island clinging to the mainland.

The very tip of Watch Hill, a long hook of sand, juts into the water like a scythe and forms the boundary where the eastern end of Long Island Sound becomes the Atlantic. This watery location, which opens the town to constant ocean breezes, accounts for the fact that Watch Hill enjoys some of the coolest summer temperatures of any community in Rhode Island, and this in turn accounts for its popularity. It's just a 10–15-minute drive from here up Route 1A into Westerly's downtown, and yet the temperature on a summer day can be as much as 10 degrees cooler.

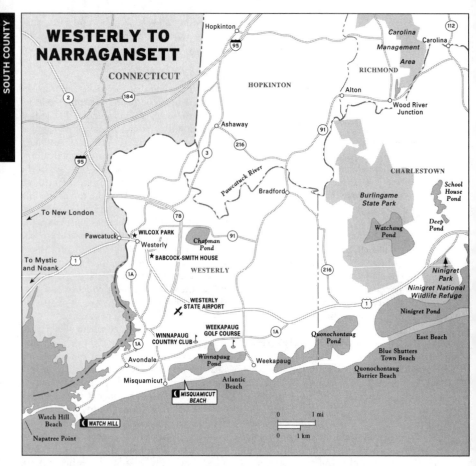

WESTERLY TO NARRAGANSETT

CONNECTICUT

Hopkinton

Carolina

Carolina

Carolina Management Area

RICHMOND

HOPKINTON

Alton

Wood River Junction

Ashaway

Bradford

Pawcatuck River

CHARLESTOWN

Burlingame State Park

School House Pond

Deep Pond

Watchaug Pond

Pawcatuck

WILCOX PARK

Westerly

Chapman Pond

BABCOCK-SMITH HOUSE

WESTERLY

To New London

To Mystic and Noank

Ninigret Park

Ninigret National Wildlife Refuge

Ninigret Pond

WESTERLY STATE AIRPORT

WEEKAPAUG GOLF COURSE

East Beach

Quonochontaug Pond

WINNAPAUG COUNTRY CLUB

Avondale

Winnapaug Pond

Weekapaug

Blue Shutters Town Beach

Quonochontaug Barrier Beach

Misquamicut

Atlantic Beach

MISQUAMICUT BEACH

0   1 mi

0   1 km

Watch Hill Beach

WATCH HILL

Napatree Point

The beach at Watch Hill is quite well known, at least among southern Rhode Islanders and others who live nearby—this long strand largely unblemished by development ranks among the prettiest beaches in southern New England. It's also one of the most popular with young kids because of the **Flying Horse Carousel** (Bay St., 401/348-6007, 11 A.M.–9 P.M. Mon.–Fri., 10 A.M.–9 P.M. Sat.–Sun., $1). Built in 1876, it is thought to be the oldest carousel in the country. The name comes from the fact that the wooden horses are suspended by metal chains, causing them to fly farther out the faster the carousel spins. While the carousel has been renovated many times over the years, the horses still have leather saddles and genuine horsehair manes. During the ride, kids can reach for the famous brass ring to win a free ride.

Jutting into Watch Hill's little harbor, on the mouth of the Pawcatuck River, is the private **Watch Hill Yacht Club,** which sits along a wharf. The **Watch Hill Lighthouse** (14 Lighthouse Rd., no phone, www.lighthouse. cc/watchhill, grounds 8 A.M.–8 P.M. daily, museum 1–3 P.M. Tues. and Thurs. July–Aug., free) lies just south of the village center, down

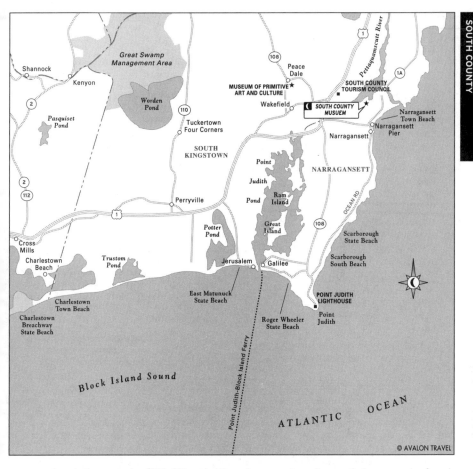

Great Swamp
Management Area

Shannock

Kenyon

Pasquiset
Pond

Worden
Pond

Tuckertown
Four Corners

SOUTH
KINGSTOWN

Peace
Dale

MUSEUM OF PRIMITIVE
ART AND CULTURE ★

Wakefield

SOUTH COUNTY
TOURISM COUNCIL

SOUTH COUNTY
MUSUEM ★

Narragansett
Town Beach

Narragansett
Pier

Narragansett

Point

Judith

Pond

Ram
Island

NARRAGANSETT

OCEAN RD.

Perryville

Potter
Pond

Great
Island

Scarborough
State Beach

Cross
Mills

Charlestown
Beach

Trustom
Pond

Jerusalem

Galilee

Scarborough
South Beach

POINT JUDITH
LIGHTHOUSE

Charlestown
Town Beach

East Matunuck
State Beach

Roger Wheeler
State Beach

Point
Judith

Charlestown
Breachway
State Beach

Point Judith-Block Island Ferry

Block Island Sound

ATLANTIC OCEAN

© AVALON TRAVEL

a sandy spit that extends off Bluff Avenue. For nearly 200 years Watch Hill has been known for its lighthouse, which was commissioned in 1806 and established the town. In 1879 a life-saving station was commissioned after a disaster in which two ships collided just offshore, claiming more than 70 lives. The unadorned granite tower isn't the prettiest lighthouse in the world, but its vantage point on the top of the hill is spectacular.

◖ MISQUAMICUT BEACH

Three miles east of Watch Hill on Route 1A is Misquamicut (mih-SKWAH-mih-cut), which

has a gracious three-mile-long stretch of sand. Unlike Watch Hill, Misquamicut was not settled until the very end of the 1800s, and it really only began to flourish as a resort community around 1910.

This community is a traditional shore strip of pastel-hued clapboard cottages, houses, and motels. The larger places facing the beach offer clear ocean views and guest rooms just steps from the surf; many have kitchenettes, and most have their own fairly predictable seafood and chops restaurants. There are no franchise restaurants or hotels in Misquamicut. Instead, you'll mostly find properties that have been

TO THE LIGHTHOUSE

It's fitting that a state nicknamed "The Ocean State" should have some of New England's prettiest and most historic lighthouses along its coastline. Rhode Island's waters are notoriously treacherous, with sunken reefs and narrow passages throughout Block Island Sound and Narragansett Bay. Twenty-one lighthouses still stand along the coastline, 13 of them in use today to guide ships. Of these, only a few are open to the public, but there's nothing to prevent you from exploring the grounds and snapping pictures to your heart's content:

- Beavertail Light (1749; Beavertail Point, Jamestown). Active 68-foot handsome gray-granite square tower with a museum inside, open during summer.

- Block Island North Light (1829; Sandy Point, Block Island). Active 51-foot octagonal brick tower; grounds are open daily, and a small museum inside is open during summer.

- Block Island Southeast Light (1875; Mohegan Bluffs, Block Island). Active 52-foot octagonal brick tower dramatically situated on

seaside bluffs; museum and tower are open to tours in summer.

- Bristol Ferry Light (1846; Ferry Rd., Portsmouth). Inactive 54-foot active cylindrical brick tower; grounds closed.

- Castle Hill Light (1890; Castle Hill Point, Newport). Active 40-foot granite tower; grounds open.

- Conanicut Island Light (1886; north end of Conanicut Island, Jamestown). Inactive two-story tower visible only from the water.

- Conimicut Shoal Light (1868; Providence River, Warwick). Active 58-foot white cylindrical tower, visible from Conimicut Point Park.

- Dutch Island Light (1826; Dutch Island, Jamestown). Active 56-foot cylindrical tower visible from Fort Getty Recreational Area in Jamestown.

- Hog Island Shoal Light (1886; Portsmouth). Active 60-foot cast-iron tower on a small island, visible from Prudence Island Ferry.

---

in the same family for generations, catering to successive generations of guests. Plenty of these hotel employees know their guests' names on sight, and vice versa. It's the sort of tight-knit community where kids grow up together as their families visit every summer.

North of the beach is a long salt pond, Winnapaug, popular for sailing, fishing, crabbing, and other activities because of its sheltered location. In the center of Misquamicut is the actual **Misquamicut State Beach** (257 Atlantic Ave., Westerly, 401/596-9097, www.riparks.com/misquamicut.htm), with a large and attractive beach pavilion, a big playground, changing rooms, and other facilities. This is a beautiful and well-kept stretch of sand. The section of the community just east of the state beach is more honky-tonk and less pristine, but it is an excellent place to bring the kids, with go-kart tracks,

miniature golf courses, snack bars, and video arcades. Farther east along Atlantic Avenue is Dunn's Beach, a long swath of summer houses punctuated by just a few businesses.

WEEKAPAUG

As you follow Atlantic Avenue along the beach it eventually crosses a small stream that feeds into Winnapaug Pond; bear right over the bridge and you'll enter the more upscale and secluded summer resort of Weekapaug. The shore here is rocky and a bit more dramatic, and except for a couple of hotels it's without the commercial development of Misquamicut. Weekapaug has its own large salt pond, Quonochontaug, with a quiet and undeveloped barrier beach that has a boat launch and a very popular fishing area. It's also a great spot for a hike along the sand, but keep in mind that parking is limited.

- Ida Lewis Rock Light (1854; off Wellington Ave., Newport). Inactive 13-foot granite tower.

- Nayatt Point Light (1828; Nayatt Point, Barrington). Inactive 25-foot tower; closed, but visible from Nayatt Road.

- Newport Harbor Light (1824; Goat Island, Newport). Active 35-foot tower accessible from Hyatt Regency Hotel; tower closed.

- Plum Beach Light (1897; Narragansett Bay, North Kingstown). Active 53-foot red-and-white "sparkplug" tower on a small island, visible from the Jamestown Bridge.

- Point Judith Light (1810; end of Rte. 108, Narragansett). Active 51-foot octagonal tower, one of the most picturesque in the state; grounds are open daily.

- Pomham Rocks Light (1871; Willett Ave., East Providence). An unusual 40-foot octagonal tower atop a Second Empire Victorian house on a small island in the Providence River. Site closed, but visible from East Bay Bike Path.

- Poplar Point Light (1831; Wickford Harbor, North Kingstown). Inactive 45-foot octagonal tower; visible from Sauga Point.

- Prudence Island (Sandy Point) Light (1852; Sandy Point, Prudence Island). Active 30-foot octagonal tower has an unusual "birdcage" lantern on top; grounds open.

- Rose Island Light (1870; Newport). Active 35-foot octagonal tower; site accessible by ferry during summer.

- Sakonnet Light (1884; Little Compton). Active 66-foot cylindrical tower located on an island off Sakonnet Point, accessible only by boat.

- Warwick Light (1827; Warwick Neck Rd., Warwick). Active 51-foot active cylindrical tower with a red roof; site closed.

- Watch Hill Light (1808; Lighthouse Rd., Watch Hill). Active 45-foot square granite tower with white cylindrical top; the tower is closed, but grounds are open, as is a small museum in the keeper's house during summer.

CHARLESTOWN

East of Westerly is the large rural town of Charlestown, one of Rhode Island's great recreation hubs, with outstanding beaches as well as several extensive tracts of undeveloped and preserved land. If there's an outdoor activity that interests you, except perhaps mountain-climbing, there's a fairly good chance you'll find a venue for it here along with new friends to pursue it with. The town itself is dominated by two large parks. On the north side of the road, signs point the way to Burlingame State Park. On the south side of the road is a parcel divided into Ninigret National Wildlife Refuge and Ninigret Park. This land borders another of South County's big saltwater ponds, Ninigret Pond.

The town does have some development. Coming from the west, bear right on Route 1A to find one of the more unusual sights in Rhode

Island, or anywhere, really: the eclectic collection of shops, farmland, and animal exhibits known as the **Fantastic Umbrella Factory** (4820 Old Post Rd./Rte. 1A, Charlestown, 401/364-6616). When the back-to-the-land movement was in full swing during the 1960s, a small group of hippies took up residence in the backwoods of Charlestown, where they created a curiosity shop and flower nursery that has grown over the years into a veritable Wonka-esque fantasyland. Guinea fowl and emus prowl the grounds among shops selling African masks, rain sticks, and samurai swords, while a greenhouse full of Technicolor perennials dazzles the eye. It's a great place to buy flowers, to let the kids gawk at the animals, or just to wander around and explore.

From here, Route 1A briefly rejoins U.S. 1 before veering south toward the tiny village of

Cross Mills, an utterly charming and sleepy community that's home to Fort Ninigret, for years thought to have been a Niantic Indian fortification (today's historians believe it was built by Dutch settlers). Cross Mills is the site of a pair of corn mills, the small Charlestown Town Hall, and the old Indian Burial Ground. The Charlestown Historical Society has a 19th-century one-room schoolhouse on the grounds of the Cross Mills Library (4417 Old Post Rd., 401/364-6211, 1–8 P.M. Mon., 9 A.M.–1 P.M. Tues., 9 A.M.–6 P.M. Wed., 9 A.M.–8 P.M. Thurs., 1–6 P.M. Fri., 9 A.M.–3 P.M. Sat.). The school building has been faithfully restored and decorated with 19th-century furnishings, and is open for tours in the summer.

From the Old Post Road (Route 1A), just east of Cross Mills, turn right onto Matunuck School House Road to reach Charlestown Beach and, farther east, Grill Hill Beach; these areas are well marked. Eventually Matunuck School House Road dead-ends at Matunuck Beach Road; turn right to reach Matunuck Beach. This is a popular longtime family resort area packed with fairly modest cottages. You'll also find a few pubs and taverns at the beach, as well as the famous Matunuck Theatre-by-the-Sea.

From here, drive back up Matunuck Beach Road to U.S. 1, turn right, and go a short way to Succotash Road. A right turn leads down to the village of Jerusalem, which, with Galilee on the other side of the river that flows into Point Judith salt pond, forms the massive fishing port of Galilee. There are a few places to buy fresh seafood, and it's an interesting place to watch the boats chug in and out of the port.

ENTERTAINMENT AND EVENTS
Bars and Clubs
Ocean Mist Beach Bar (895A Matunuck Beach Rd., Matunuck, 401/782-3740, www.oceanmist.net, 11:30 A.M.–1 A.M. Mon.–Fri., 9 A.M.–1 A.M. Sat.–Sun.) has live music and draws a rowdy bunch of sunburned beachgoers on summer nights; it's within walking distance of East Matunuck State Beach.

Performing Arts
South County has a number of small theaters that present a great variety of dramatic and musical works. In Westerly, the professional **Granite Theatre** (1 Granite St., 401/596-2341, www.granitetheatre.com) stages about eight classic plays April–September and Thanksgiving–Christmas. The theater occupies a former church, a Greek Revival structure built in 1849 that lost its spire during the 1938 hurricane. The **Colonial Theatre** (Westerly, 401/596-7909, http://thecolonialtheater.org) hosts free Shakespeare in the Park productions at Wilcox Park each July.

Festivals and Events
Summer and fall are major event seasons in South County, especially for seafood, specifically quahogs, which are celebrated with great fervor. Spring has its share of engaging festivals too: Westerly hosts the **Rhode Island Scottish Highland Festival** (401/596-5849, www.riscot.org) each May, with an amateur Scottish athletics competition, a Highland dance festival, and live Scottish music along with numerous activities for kids. The **Virtu Art Festival** (Wilcox Park, Westerly, 401/732-7636) is a performing and visual arts festival on Memorial Day weekend.

In early August, the **Charlestown Seafood Festival** (401/364-4031) draws hundreds of chowder and quahog aficionados to Ninigret Park. Activities include helicopter tours and live mamba music; just about every type of seafood popular in the Ocean State is available, including raw oysters and clams, steamed lobsters, clam cakes, fish-and-chips, and fried whole-belly clams. Later in August, locals turn out in big numbers for **Washington County Fair** (Rte. 112, Richmond, 401/539-7042).

In early September, the **Rhythm Roots** festival (Ninigret Park, 888/855-6940, www.rhythmandroots.com) has quickly grown to become one of Rhode Island's top music festivals, an eclectic mix of Cajun and zydeco, bluegrass, folk, and rockabilly. It's a festive event, with excellent food stalls that have items from all over the world along with arts and crafts vendors.

Westerly hosts a large and popular **Columbus Day Parade** (401/596-7761) each October, and in early October the popular **Guy Fawkes Bonfire Night** (Misquamicut Beach, www.guyfawkesusa.com) celebrates the British holiday with an effigy burned in a raucous beachside bonfire. Throughout December, retail hub Wickford hosts the **Festival of Lights,** when the town is aglow with holiday lights and alive with holiday shopping.

SHOPPING
Westerly and Watch Hill
The **Book and Tackle Shop** (166 Main St., Westerly, 401/315-2424; also in summer at 7 Bay St., Watch Hill, 401/596-0700) specializes in vintage books, including some rare finds—there are more than 50,000 titles. Westerly also has several good antiques shops, among them **Homespun Cottage** (229 Post Rd., Westerly, 401/322-9800, 10 a.m.–5 p.m. daily), which boasts two floors of eclectic wares full of New England charm. At **Mary D's** (3 Commerce St., Westerly, 401/596-5653, 10 a.m.–5 p.m. Wed.–Mon.), you'll find stalls from several dealers selling an eclectic range of antiques. The **Black Duck Gallery** (25 Broad St., Westerly, 401/348-6500, 10 a.m.–5:30 p.m. Sun.–Fri., 10 a.m.–5 p.m. Sat.) carries all manner of wood-carved birds along with paintings and other fine art relating to animals of flight.

At **Mo Books and Art** (60 Bay St., Watch Hill, 401/348-0940), a curious little gallery-boutique, browse the out-of-print children's books as well as art and local photography shot and framed by owner Mo. **The Wise Owl Toys and Kites** (50 High St., Westerly, 401/348-9555, 10 a.m.–6 p.m. Mon.–Fri., 9:30 a.m.–5:30 p.m. Sat., 11:30 a.m.–5 p.m. Sun.) is a great spot for colorful games and toys, and there's no better kite-flying than in breezy Watch Hill. You can reward kids you've dragged into countless grown-up stores with a visit to the **Candy Box** (14 Fort Rd., Watch Hill, 401/596-3325, 10 a.m.–8 p.m. Mon.–Fri., 10 a.m.–9 p.m. Sat.–Sun.). **Comina** (117 Bay St., Watch Hill, 401/596-3218, 10 a.m.–5:30 p.m. Mon.–Sat., 11 a.m.–5 p.m. Sun.), which has several other locations in Connecticut and Rhode Island, carries imaginative home furnishings, collectibles, and gifts, including beautifully hand-crafted Mexican aluminum tableware. The **The Summer Place** (19 Bay St., Watch Hill, 401/596-6540, 10 a.m.–5 p.m. daily, but call ahead as hours vary) carries garden accessories, dried floral arrangements, framed art, small painted furnishings, and other elegant wares.

Richmond and Hope Valley
Richmond Antiques Center (320 Kingstown Rd., Wyoming, 401/539-2279, 10 a.m.–6 p.m. daily) is popular for its auctions, and there are two floors of dealers. The **Remnant Shop** (1081 Main St., Hope Valley, 401/539-2500) is an expansive redbrick building filled with high-quality fabrics in all patterns and textures. **Hack and Livery General Store** (1006 Main St., Hope Valley, 401/539-7033, 10 a.m.–5 p.m. daily) is a typically locals-oriented business in little Hope Valley. Inside you can shop for penny candy, gifts, odds and ends, pottery, and all sorts of interesting collectibles and one-of-a-kind items. **URE Outfitters** (1009 Main St., Hope Valley, 401/539-4050, daily), in a brick warehouse, is an excellent source of outdoors gear and clothing and is close to several of western Rhode Island's recreation areas.

Charlestown
The **Fantastic Umbrella Factory** (4820 Old Post Rd./Rte. 1A, 401/364-6616, 10 a.m.–5 p.m. Mon.–Fri., 10 a.m.–6 p.m. Sat.–Sun.) is just off U.S. 1, down the Old Post Road from Ninigret Park, and qualifies as a certifiable tourist attraction. At the whimsical complex you'll find shops, an art gallery, lavish gardens, a petting zoo, and a snack bar. Among the shops is Dave's Den, which sells incense, tapestries, oils, beaded curtains, Native American arts and crafts, and other odd goods. The main store carries a fairly bizarre assortment of collectibles culled from different parts of the world—kites, jewelry, soaps, greeting cards, mugs, toys, wood carvings, and paintings are among the goodies. At Small Axe Productions, craftspeople create handblown

SOUTH COUNTY AMUSEMENTS

As it's a tremendously popular family destination, South County has a wide assortment of amusement centers, miniature golf courses, driving ranges, and other activity parks geared toward the zillions of kids who visit, especially in summer (most of the places below are open spring–summer). Popular options include **Adventureland of Narragansett** (Point Judith Rd., Narragansett, 401/789-0030), which has batting cages, bumper boats, a go-kart track, and one of the county's best miniature golf courses; **Bay View Fun Park** (330 Atlantic Ave., Misquamicut, 401/322-0180), known for excellent miniature golf plus batting cages, bumper boats, and go-karts; and **Old Mountain Lanes** (756 Kingstown Rd., Wakefield, 401/783-5511), which is open year-round and has bumper bowling, billiards, a game room, and two restaurants. There's an inline and roller-skating rink at the **Narragansett**

Ocean Club (360 S. Pier Rd., Narragansett, 401/783-1711).

If you're visiting with kids, keep in mind that South County has a couple of YMCA summer camps that run weekly sessions. In Charlestown, **Camp Watchung** (401/596-2894) is open to boys and girls ages 4-14 and sits along 60 acres overlooking Watchung Pond; it offers a full slate of athletic and outdoors activities. A related half-day and full-day **Kiddie Kamp** (401/596-2894) in Westerly is geared toward kids ages three through kindergarten. Hope Valley's best kids' amusement is **Enchanted Forest** (Rte. 3, Hope Valley, 401/539-7711), a family activity center with boat rides, a roller coaster, a Ferris wheel, a batting cage, miniature golf, and recreated scenes from nursery tales. You can pick fresh berries here and pet tame animals in the petting zoo.

glassworks, stained glass, and stoneware pottery. You can also dine at the Spice of Life restaurant, which specializes in natural foods. The "factory" was founded in 1968, and it definitely still has a hippie sensibility.

At the **General Stanton Flea Market** (General Stanton Inn, 4115 Old Post Rd., off U.S. 1, 401/364-8888, www.generalstanton-inn.com, 8 A.M.–3:30 P.M. weekends and holidays May–Oct.), browse for a wide variety of wares, collectibles, furnishings, and odds and ends from more than 200 dealers. If you're looking for something a little more modern, try **Galapagos Boutique** (Rte. 1, 401/322-3000, www.shopgalapagos.com, 9 A.M.–6 P.M. daily), which stocks a variety of trend-conscious design pieces. At **Charlestown Village** (U.S. 1 at Rte. 2), you'll find a smattering of eclectic shops selling a variety of things like T-shirts, chocolates, and nautical ephemera.

SPORTS AND RECREATION

South County, both near the beach and inland, contains a vast cache of preserved, undeveloped land, especially in the town of

Charlestown. Near the shore is the **Ninigret National Wildlife Refuge** (50 Bend Rd., off U.S. 1, 401/364-9124, www.fws.gov/refuges), a broad rolling space that leads down to the shores of Ninigret Pond, one of several massive salt ponds in the region. The preserve has almost no facilities but has some excellent hiking trails, including a gentle 1.4-mile loop that ends at Grassy Point, where you can climb to an observation platform and gaze out over Ninigret Pond.

Adjacent to and east of the preserve and with an entrance off Route 1A, which is just off U.S. 1, **Ninigret Park** (401/364-1222) is the more activity-oriented section of the Ninigret lands. Facilities include athletic fields, public tennis courts, an impressive children's playground, a paved bike trail, hiking areas, fishing in Ninigret Pond and a small freshwater pond with a beach, and picnic groves. The **Frosty Drew Nature Center** (401/364-9508, www. frostydrew.org, 10 A.M.–1 P.M. Sat. July–Aug.) in the park contains exhibits on natural history and offers weeklong nature programs for kids 6–10 throughout the summer. Nature Center staff regularly give walks, talks, and other programs, usually on Saturday mornings in summer. Near the nature center is the **Frosty Drew Observatory** (401/596-7688), a nonprofit center that hosts many programs open to the public, usually on Friday nights. A retractable roof allows the observatory's powerful telescope to peer into the brilliant night sky. In summer the observatory is open after dark, and during the fall you can typically visit at about 6:30 P.M.

Beaches

It may not seem like a huge area, but South County has about 100 miles of shoreline, most of it accessible to the public, including some of the best stretches of sand in New England—especially along the secluded coast of Charlestown, a hidden gem that locals know but outsiders usually do not. As you move west to east in the county from the Connecticut border, you'll first come to the beaches of Watch Hill, which include **Watch Hill Beach** (off Route 1A, 401/596-7761 or 800/732-7636), with restrooms and a bathhouse on a pretty stretch of sand; the half mile of beach leads farther out to isolated **Napatree Point** (401/596-7761 or 800/732-7636), which juts into Long Island Sound. Parking at Watch Hill (there's none specifically for Napatree) costs $10 per day, and space is quite limited—for this reason you won't typically find swarms of people here. Napatree has a well-deserved reputation for bird-watching, as many migrating shorebirds frequent these sands at various times during the year.

Farther east, **Misquamicut State Beach** (257 Atlantic Ave., off Route 1A, 401/322-1026, www.riparks.com/misquamicut.htm) offers a half mile of very popular and heavily used beachfront—it's among the most developed in the state. The undertow here is slight, and the comparatively mild surf is ideal for swimming. In mellow Weekapaug, to the east, there's shore access at **Quonochontaug Beach** (off West Beach Rd.), which has very limited facilities but is overseen by lifeguards. A lot of people choose to swim in the eponymous salt pond that borders the beach; like Napatree, this is a fine place for bird-watching.

Check out a Friday night program at the Frosty Drew Observatory.

© MICHAEL BLANDING

A secluded and modest barrier beach with ocean on one side and the west end of Ninigret Pond on the other, **Blue Shutters Town Beach** (off East Beach Rd., off U.S. 1, 401/364-1206) has a few parking spaces, a snack bar, and changing facilities with showers. Remote **East Beach** is reached on foot by walking farther along the shore; this is an uncrowded and largely unsupervised area that's nice for swimming at your own risk. **Charlestown Town Beach** (off U.S. 1, 401/364-1208, parking $10) is a good bet for beating the crowds, although avid outdoorsy types love it for its big crashing waves (note the surfers) and wide beach (note the volleyball court). The beach has full changing facilities, restrooms, picnic areas, and lifeguards.

Boating and Sailing

For information on the more than 50 party boats that sail from South County, contact the **Rhode Island Party and Charter Boat Association** (401/737-5812, www.rifishing.com/charter.

htm). A full list of boats and contact information appears on the website along with links to websites for many individual boats.

Popular boat charters include **Night Heron Harbor and Nature Cruises** (401/783-7766), which offers trips that explore the great salt ponds of South County as well as snorkeling and diving tours and sunset cruises.

Near the Cross Mills section of Charlestown, **Ocean House Marina** (60 Town Dock Rd., off Post Rd./Rte. 1A, Charlestown, 866/981-4383, www.oceanhousemarina.com, 7:30 A.M.–4:30 P.M. Mon.–Fri., 8 A.M.–noon Sun.) was built as the town meetinghouse and later came to be run as a summer resort. Today it's a marina renting all types of boats along with a bait-and-tackle shop. It sits right on Ninigret's salt pond, from which you can reach Block Island Sound.

Canoeing and Kayaking

Freshwater boaters and anglers should check out the **Wood River,** the state's best trout-fishing stream—it meanders down through Exeter and Hope Valley, passing through the southwestern corner of the state before emptying into the Pawcatuck River in Westerly and flowing south to the ocean. If you tackle the full navigable length of the river, it'll take a good seven hours by canoe or kayak (the river is nearly 14 miles long). One of the most popular put-ins is off Route 165 in Exeter (follow it west from Rte. 3, just south of the I-95 overpass); head toward Beach Pond State Park until you reach the bridge over the Wood River. This upper stretch is relatively brisk but without any rapids.

Another popular access point is Hope Valley Road Landing, just off Route 3 in the village of Hope Valley. From here it's a quite smooth run for about six miles down to Alton Dam. This lower stretch is especially picturesque, the riverbanks lined with dense maple and oak woodland.

Another excellent spot for canoeing, kayaking, or fishing is **Great Swamp,** a dense swath of South County that are inaccessible except

RENTING A COTTAGE

Many visitors to South County rent cottages for multiple weeks at a time, or even for the entire summer. This option can be a great money-saver even if you're planning to visit only for a week, and it's definitely an economical and convenient way to go if you're visiting for longer. Weekly rentals typically begin and end on Saturday afternoon, although certain owners require Friday-to-Friday or even Sunday-to-Sunday agreements. Most rentals in South County and other shore areas in Rhode Island are available May–September, although some properties are available during the off-season.

Amenities and costs vary greatly depending on proximity to the beach, but here's a sampling of what you might expect to pay for certain properties around the area. On the high end, an upscale three-bedroom house on the ocean in Charlestown rents for $4,000 per week. In the midrange, a Watch Hill two-bedroom ocean-view condo one block from the beach goes for $1,700 per week. In the most affordable range, a two-bedroom house on a pond that's a mile or so from Misquamicut Beach rents for just $850 per week, while a two-bedroom house just a short walk from Green Hill Beach near Charlestown rents for $900 per week.

Most real-estate agents accept reservations on properties up to a year in advance, and the very best rentals get booked up quickly, often by January or February for the following summer. Nevertheless, don't despair if you find yourself interested in a vacation rental and it's already early August – with so many rentals on the market, you'll generally find something in your price range and with the amenities and location you're seeking. Once you make a reservation, you'll be asked to make a deposit, often as much as 50 percent down by mid-January–February (if you book later, 50 percent is usually re-by boat. The main route begins at the launch in West Kingston off Route 138, known as Taylor's Landing. From here you enter a very narrow stretch of the Chipuxet River and paddle south; after a while the trickle of water opens to a much wider and more stable stretch of river. After about three miles of fairly easy paddling you'll enter one of the larger freshwater bodies in the state, Worden's Pond. There are all sorts of opportunities for wildlife sightings on this trip. There's also a put-in and take-out area at the south end, off Worden's Pond Road.

The **Kayak Centre** (562 Charlestown Beach Rd., Charlestown, 401/364-8000 or 888/SEA-KAYAK—888/732-5292, www.kayakcentre. com, 9 A.M.–6 P.M. Mon.–Wed., 9 A.M.–7 P.M. Thurs., 9 A.M.–6 P.M. Fri.–Sat., 11 A.M.–5 P.M. Sun., from June 21) is an excellent resource, renting and selling kayaks and offering tours, lessons, and advice. Another place for kayak rentals and instruction is **Quaker Lane Bait and Tackle** (4019 Quaker Lane, North Kingstown, 401/294-9642, www.quaker-lanetackle.com, 5 A.M.–8 P.M. Mon.–Fri., 4:30 A.M.–8 P.M. Sat., 4:30 A.M.–7 P.M. Sun.).

Golf

South County is Rhode Island's golfing capital, and a handful of excellent courses have opened just in the last couple of decades, including some fairly new ones. Greens fees at South County courses are among the most reasonable you'll find in southern New England. Among the best in the area is **Winnapaug Country Club** (Shore Rd., Westerly, 401/596-1237, www.winnapaugcountryclub.com, $17–40), an attractive 18-hole course with very nice views of Winnapaug Pond. The layout was designed by acclaimed architect Donald Ross, and a nice little restaurant is open for lunch and dinner.

Water Sports and Parasailing

If you're a fan of boogie-boarding, head to East Beach in Westerly. The salt ponds behind the

quested within a week or two of making the reservation). Always read the fine print carefully, especially those clauses that apply to cancellations and transfers – and be prepared to lose the 50 percent deposit if you change your plans after April 1 or so. You may have some or all of this amount returned to you if the agency is able to rent the property during the period you had booked it, but even this policy varies among agencies.

Most rental agencies accept only cash, checks, or money orders – no credit cards – and most expect full final payment at check-in. You may also be asked to make a security or damage deposit. Agencies can be very strict about prohibiting house parties and excessive numbers of guests (student groups, frat brothers, and the like are frowned upon if not outright forbidden by some agencies). Check around if you want to bring your pet, as a few properties permit this by arrangement (and often request

an additional security deposit). Many units are nonsmoking.

Renting a cottage differs considerably from booking a room at a hotel. Housekeeping is not included, and renters are expected to take good care of the homes and leave them as clean as they found them (or forfeit the deposit).

Numerous real estate agents in South County specialize in beach rentals, among them **Charlestown Beach Real Estate** (401/364-6926 or 800/800-6926, www.riliving.com/02483), **Durkin Cottages Realty** (401/789-6659, www.durkincottages.com), **JBL Realty** (401/783-5183, www.jblrealty. com), **Lila Delman Real Estate** (401/789-6666, www.liladelman.com), **Properties Unlimited** (401/364-6700, www.propertiesunltd. com), **Stanton Realty** (401/596-2885, www. stantonrealty.com), and **Wallander Realty** (401/364-3616 or 888/RI-OCEAN – 888/746-2326, www.wallanderrealty.com).

barrier beaches along the South Coast shoreline are ideal for activities that are better in calm water, such as riding personal watercraft. An excellent spot is **Winnapaug Pond,** by Misquamicut State Beach; at **Purple Ape** (401/596-9518, www.purpleape.com) you can rent Jet Skis ($150 per hour) and paddle boats ($20 per hour) along with all the equipment and instruction you need.

Hiking

The western and northern parts of South County are more remote and less crowded, making them ideal for horseback riding, camping, and hiking. The 72-mile **North-South Trail** runs from the northern boundary of the state all the way through South County before ending at the coast. It enters lower Washington County near the junction of Routes 138 and 112, in Wyoming east of I-95 exit 3, and it terminates at Charlestown's Blue Shutters Town Beach. Highlights and good access points along the trail include Burlingame State Park, Indian Cedar Swamp, and the Carolina Management Area. The website http://outdoors.htmlplanet.com/nst/nst_map00.htm has a good detailed map of the trail as it runs through the state.

Some of the best area hikes are in Hope Valley around **Blue Pond, Long Pond,** and **Ell Pond.** Marked trails meander around these lakes and through groves of hemlock and clusters of rhododendrons. Long Pond makes for an especially nice hike—follow Route 138 west from Hope Valley and turn left at Rockville village onto Canonchet Road. After about a mile you'll come to a parking area for the Narragansett Trail, which leads west along the south shore of Long Pond. From the same parking area, a different trail cuts south toward Asheville Pond. The terrain in these parts is somewhat challenging, sometimes passing over steep rock ledges and leading to relatively high bluffs.

ACCOMMODATIONS

In some respects, South County is a throwback to another era when it comes to accommodations. Of the more than 100 options in the area, the vast majority are closer than a mile from the ocean. Almost none are chain properties, and very few offer the sort of upscale accommodations you'd find in Newport or Block Island. South County is a value-oriented community where family-run, comparatively simple hotels, motor lodges, and motels dominate the landscape. It's quite easy to find accommodations that sleep 4–8 guests with kitchen facilities and plenty of social- and activity-oriented amenities like playgrounds, expansive pools, shuffleboard courts, and boat launches. Especially in Misquamicut, you'll find several properties directly on the beach.

A drawback of sorts is that it's rather difficult to find seaside properties with character; the expectation is that visitors to South County aren't likely to spend a whole lot of time in their rooms. There are a couple of historic properties in Watch Hill, and you'll find a smattering of atmospheric inns both near the shore and inland. Also, while accommodations aren't fancy or super expensive, they're generally not bargain-basement cheap in summer, at least near the water. During July–August weekends it can be tough to find accommodations for less than $100. The most economical deals tend to be hotels that have efficiencies or cottages available by the week—these are especially economical if you're booking a unit that sleeps a few people.

$50-100

Along U.S. 1 near Westerly Airport, the family-run **Ambassador Motel** (201 Post Rd., Westerly, 401/322-7995, www.ambassadormotelri.com) is a cheap and cheerful little property that feels as if it's from another time. Friendly owners take good care of the place, and rates dip below $60 on weekdays and in the off-season and aren't much higher on summer weekends. There are nine guest rooms, all with cable TV, tiled bathrooms, phones, and air-conditioning.

A modern, immaculately kept low-rise hotel less than a mile north of Misquamicut's beaches and adjoining Weekapaug golf course,

COURTESY OF SOUTH COUNTY TOURISM

The Winnapaug Inn is affordable and relaxing.

the family-run [Winnapaug Inn (169 Shore Rd., Misquamicut, 401/348-8350 or 800/288-9906, www.winnapauginn.com, $89–179) is a terrific option if you're seeking moderately priced rooms and a low-key setting that's both greener and less chaotic than the beach properties. Some upper-level guest rooms do have distant ocean views, and many more look out over the fairways of the golf course; most have balconies. Guest rooms are spacious but simply furnished and come in a variety of sizes, including some fully-equipped townhouse units with kitchens. Some have whirlpool tubs, refrigerators, and wet bars. There is a large heated pool at one side as well as a shuffleboard court, and guests receive free passes to the beach and free breakfast. The owners also operate the excellent Venice Restaurant next door.

$100-150

At the comparatively quiet west end of Misquamicut Beach, still an easy walk or bike ride from the boardwalk and with glorious views of the ocean and plenty of beachfront,

the **Pleasant View Inn** (65 Atlantic Ave., Misquamicut, 401/348-8200 or 800/782-3224, www.pvinn.com, $125–165) is this community's largest hotel, with 112 rooms, many of them overlooking the ocean. Room rates depends on the view, size, and amenities, but all rooms have cable TV and most have private balconies; suites have microwaves, refrigerators, and wet bars. There's nothing at all fancy about the cookie-cutter chain-hotel-style decor, but the functional furnishings are generally well maintained and definitely appropriate for families. Another plus for kids are the extensive facilities, which include a heated outdoor pool, a sauna, and an exercise room; you can also rent video players for your room along with movies from the hotel's video library. The Pleasant View has a pair of restaurants, one more casual and serving lighter snacks, but neither of them is overly formal.

A six-room Second Empire farmhouse dating to the 1870s, **Langworthy Farm** (308 Shore Rd., Westerly, 401/322-7791 or 888/355-7083, www.langworthyfarm.com, $135–160) is an upscale bed-and-breakfast with four charming guest rooms and a pair of suites. In the Weekapaug section of Westerly, the inn has ocean views from some rooms. One suite has two full bedrooms, each with its own private bath. Some rooms have whirlpool tubs. The farm also has a small winery.

The **Breezeway Resort** (70 Winnapaug Rd., Misquamicut, 401/348-8953 or 800/462-8872, www.breezewayresort.com, $100–225) is an attractive family-oriented property with four acres of nicely manicured grounds with lush green lawns and Japanese maple trees and 48 superclean guest rooms. It's not on the beach, but the beach is just a short walk down the road. Amenities include in-room refrigerators, phones with data ports, and whirlpool tubs in some units; there are also bicycles for guest use, a large heated pool with a sprawling sun deck, a shuffleboard court, a small playground, and hammocks. The resort also runs Maria's restaurant, near the beach. In addition to standard guest rooms, you can book a suite in the nearby annex; several of these have kitchens. Villas that sleep four and have kitchens are rented by the week. Free continental breakfast features bagels delivered from the famous A&M Bakery in New York City. The entire resort is an excellent value.

A short walk from the beautiful beaches of Matunuck, the **(** **Admiral Dewey Inn** (668 Matunuck Beach Rd., Matunuck, 401/783-2090, www.admiraldeweyinn.com, $120–170) is a towering 1898 summer beach house whose upper floors afford exceptional views of the ocean and Block Island Sound. The inn opened as a boardinghouse back at the turn of the 20th century; these days you can expect somewhat fancier accommodations, but the 10 guest rooms are still happily uncluttered and informal, with hardwood floors, brass and carved-wood headboards and beds, and Victorian furnishings and wallpapers. Most rooms have private baths, and half offer ocean views. A buffet breakfast is set up in the dining room or, when weather permits, on the porch. Just across the street is Matunuck's Theatre-by-the-Sea.

On Route 1A near Winnapaug Pond and just a short drive from the ocean, the turn-of-the-last-century **(** **Grandview B&B** (212 Shore Rd., Misquamicut, 401/596-6384 or 800/447-6384, www.grandviewbandb.com, $105–130 year-round, 5-room suite $230) occupies a handsome white clapboard and stone house. The sun-filled house is furnished in tasteful and elegant pastels, white or floral bedspreads, wicker armchairs and rockers, and other well-chosen and understated furnishings. Some of the 11 guest rooms have private baths (some of these with showers but not tubs), while a few of the least expensive accommodations share baths. Everything is kept immaculately, and if you don't mind sharing a bath, these rooms are an excellent value.

$150-250

The **(** **Shelter Harbor Inn** (10 Wagner Rd., off U.S. 1, Weekapaug, 401/322-8883 or 800/468-8883, www.shelterharborinn.com, $178–258) is a grand old white inn down a long circular drive off a commercial-free stretch of U.S. 1. Adirondack chairs dot the beautifully manicured grounds. Inside is a creaky-floored warren of comfortable guest rooms and common areas, including a sunny bar and dining room, with working fireplaces throughout. There are nine guest rooms, some of which have fireplaces and private decks; the barn has been renovated to house 10 guest rooms, and a separate carriage house has four more, each with its own working fireplace. Lush terraced gardens surround the house, and public rooms include a library and a sun porch. Amenities include paddle tennis and croquet courts, a hot tub on the third-floor sundeck, and a private beach (which is a short drive away and has restricted parking; however, the inn provides either shuttle-bus service or beach parking passes)—this beautiful swath of sand extends for about two miles along the shores of Quonochontaug Pond and the ocean. You can borrow beach towels and pick up a box lunch to take with you. There's a fine restaurant on the premises that serves three meals a day and an excellent Sunday brunch; breakfast is free for inn guests. The massive, rambling inn was built in the late 19th century.

It's part of a 200-acre community that was originally a gathering place for musicians that came to be known as Musicolony. Streets are named for famous composers—Rossini, Verdi, Handel, Grieg, and so on.

Short of pitching a tent on the sand, you can't really sleep much closer to Scarborough State Beach than renting a room at the **Anchor Motel** (825 Ocean Rd., 401/792-8550, www.theanchormotel.com, $159–199), a 13-room motel with some of the best rates of any near-ocean property in South County. Rooms are basic but pleasant enough, especially if you're planning to spend most of your time out on the beach.

Charlestown Willows Resort (U.S. 1, Charlestown, 401/364-7727 or 800/842-2181, www.willowsresort.com, $150–175) is a small and attractive mustard-hued motel complex that faces Ninigret Pond. Opened in the early 1930s, it is family-run and has a simple good-natured atmosphere; there's nothing fancy about it, and the guest rooms are spotless. Efficiencies, rented by the week, have stoves, sinks, microwaves, and refrigerators; there is a large pool and a tennis court, a game room, shuffleboard, volleyball, two practice golf holes, and boat rentals. It nearly adjoins the Ninigret Wildlife Preserve, whose entrance and parking lots are just a short distance farther on Foster Cove on the right. You can also dock your boat right behind the motel. The adjoining Mariners Fare Restaurant serves fresh-caught seafood and occasionally presents traditional New England clambakes, prepared in a pit outside.

Andrea Hotel (89 Atlantic Ave., Misquamicut, 401/348-8788 or 888/318-5707, www.andreahotel.com, $195–270) is a good option for families and adults—it's right along the beach and has a lifeguard watching over the 300 feet of beachfront all summer. The amusement parks and video arcades of Misquamicut are within walking distance, but this is far enough west of all that to be relatively mellow for adults. This is one of the more popular hotels along the beach, owned for more than 50 years by the Colucci family. There's a large restaurant and bar, both

looking out at the sea, and the recreational facilities are extensive. The 25 rooms are pleasant, and all have received top-to-bottom overhauls in recent years; they all have decks, some overlooking the water, and some have individual climate-control. The restaurant serves sandwiches, burgers, seafood grills, and pub fare.

Paddy's Restaurant and Rentals (159 Atlantic Ave., Misquamicut, 401/596-2610, www.paddysbeach.com) is a smaller property with beautifully maintained guest rooms available nightly or weekly that are a cut above most along Misquamicut. Guest rooms have hardwood floors, fresh flowers, attractive light-wood furnishings, and very new and clean fixtures and bathrooms. Lifeguards patrol the beach out back, and the Misquamicut Boardwalk is just steps away. Paddy's also has a large and popular restaurant.

A stately gambrel-roofed house near both Misquamicut and Watch Hill is **The Villa** (190 Shore Rd., Misquamicut, 401/596-1054 or 800/722-9240, www.thevillaatwesterly.com, $245–275), down a short driveway where you'll find a beautifully landscaped circular drive and the grand entryway to this handsome house. The grounds have abundant flower gardens, and an in-ground pool sparkles out back. The Mediterranean-inspired house contains six guest suites, some with whirlpool tubs, fireplaces, and private terraces; all have refrigerators, coffeemakers, microwaves, TV and DVD players, and CD players. These are cushy, couples-oriented rooms that are perfect for special occasions; one has a skylight situated directly above its double whirlpool bath, while the master suite's double whirlpool bath faces the gas fireplace. Rooms all have big fluffy queen-size beds and lavish fabrics and bedding. In warm weather, breakfast is served on the lanai overlooking the pool and gardens.

The 1845 **Watch Hill Inn** (38 Bay St., Watch Hill, 401/348-6300 or 800/356-9314, www.watchhillinn.com, from $200 off-season, from $280 summer) contains all two-bedroom efficiency suites, some with fireplaces and terraces, booked only by the week. It is an excellent choice for longer stays, as all rooms have full kitchens. This inn has a perfect location in the heart of Watch Hill.

Over $250

A Victorian-inspired inn that actually dates to 1939, the **Weekapaug Inn** (25 Spray Rock Rd., Weekapaug, 401/322-0301, www.weekapaug-inn.com) was built to replace the original 1890s structure that succumbed to the tremendous hurricane of 1938. This long building, with a roofline punctuated by more than a dozen gables, overlooks pristine Quonochontaug Pond and the ocean just beyond that. Its refreshingly uncomplicated rooms are tidy and attractive, well-tended by the fourth generation of Buffum family innkeepers. However, you won't find TVs or phones in these rooms—guests who favor the Weekapaug are seeking the peace and quiet of the sea. Entertainment tends to revolve around playing board games in the lobby or taking in one of the many guest lectures or story-telling events frequently set up by the innkeepers. Outdoor amenities are many: shuffleboard, lawn bowling, croquet, bicycles, canoes, sailboats, and tennis courts. Children's activities, including arts and crafts and nature walks, are organized each day. This is an all-inclusive resort, so while rates begin at nearly $450 per double-occupancy room per night, they include three very good meals each day, plus all activities and facilities (children are charged about $150 pp per night). Alcohol is not sold in the dining room, but setups are provided and guests are welcome to bring their own. Credit cards are not accepted, smoking is allowed only outside, and men are asked to wear jackets at dinner each night. If the rules and simple attitudes seem off-putting, this may not be the best option for you—but the Weekapaug has a devoted following, and many first-timers leave completely sold on the inn's wholesome and uncomplicated take on vacationing.

Camping

Burlingame State Park (Sanctuary Rd., follow signs north from U.S. 1, Charlestown, check station 401/322-7994, camp store 401/322-2629, free) is an enormous reserve of about 2,100 acres with about 750 primitive campsites; you can stay as long as two weeks, and there are washing facilities and toilets near the sites. You'll also find a general store and excellent swimming. Other park facilities include a boat launch, ample covered and open picnic facilities, and fishing. Picnic sites cost $2 per day, and the group picnic shelters cost $35. As at all Rhode Island state parks, except the beaches, there's no day-use fee.

An easy drive from the ocean is **Whispering Pines Campground** (41 Saw Mill Rd., Hope Valley, 401/539-7011, www.whisperingpines-camping.com, $38–52 per night), which has 200 sites for tent and RV camping, some with water and electricity hookups, all with free Wi-Fi. Facilities include a sizeable swimming pool, mini-golf course, bocce and horseshoes, basketball and volleyball courts, athletic fields for softball and soccer, a game room, snack bar, and playground. You can also fish in a catch-and-release freshwater pond, which has a beach with complimentary canoes and paddleboats. The campground also has several well-outfitted cabins ($89 per night).

FOOD
Upscale

The **Shelter Harbor Inn** (10 Wagner Rd., off U.S. 1, Weekapaug, 401/322-8883 or 800/468-8883, www.shelterharborinn.com, 7:30 A.M.–10 P.M. daily, $15–27), a sun-filled, elegant dining room inside the historic inn of the same name, serves traditional American and continental fare. Specialties include crab-and-salmon cakes, horseradish-crusted scrod, cedar plank–grilled salmon, sautéed calf's liver, and tournedos of beef. The inn is also a popular spot for breakfast and lunch.

For lovers of Italian food, **Siena** (5600 Post Rd., East Greenwich, 401/885-8850, 5–10 P.M. Tues.–Thurs., 5–11 P.M. Fri., 4:30–11 P.M. Sat., 3–9 P.M. Sun., $18–34) offers award-winning traditional Tuscan cuisine. Consider starting off with a modern day Tuscan favorite, the Polpette Grande—a full pound of ground sirloin, veal, and pork topped with marinara and fresh ricotta. If you've got any appetite left, go for the classic, velvety tagliatelle alla Bolognese.

The **Seaside Grille** (38 Bay St., Watch Hill, 401/348-6300, 5 A.M.–9 P.M. daily June 25–Sept. 6, $18–35), at the Watch Hill Inn, is noted for its wonderful bay views, especially at sunset. You can dine in the rather upscale dining rooms or on the sunny veranda and patio decks. The kitchen serves fairly traditional seafood and American favorites, from grilled swordfish in olive oil with lemon-dill hollandaise sauce to golden neck clams sautéed with white wine, garlic, virgin olive oil, shallots, and fresh herbs.

Creative but Casual

Opened as a quaint lunch spot and ice-cream parlor in 1916, the 🄲 **Olympia Tea Room** (74 Bay St., Watch Hill, 401/348-8211, 11:30 A.M.–9 P.M. Mon.–Thurs., 11:30 A.M.–10 P.M. Fri.–Sat., noon–9 P.M. Sun., $10–24) has gradually evolved through the years into one of Watch Hill's most dynamic and inventive restaurants. The handsome dining room with a black-and-white checked floor, salmon-pink walls, and lazily whirring ceiling fans serves a wide range of regional American cuisine, from grilled Kansas City sirloin to littleneck clams with sausage simmered in marinara with linguine. Specials change often and have included Connecticut River shad roe pan-fried with butter and baked in cream, and a Watch Hill fried oyster po'boy with spicy red tartar sauce, vine-ripened tomatoes, and shaved red onion.

One of the largest dining rooms on the beach, **Paddy's** (159 Atlantic Ave., Misquamicut, 401/596-4350, call for hours, $14–25) serves surprisingly good and often creative food, especially considering the crowds that pile in on many summer weekends. Favorites include penne in pink vodka sauce with lightly fried calamari and Parmesan cheese; the "bucket" of mussels with a sweet-and-spicy Thai butter sauce and grilled focaccia; and pan-seared tuna served rare over mashed potatoes with a miso vinaigrette. The kitchen does a nice job balancing hearty and

Try the littleneck clams at the Olympia Tea Room.

uncomplicated favorites with some nicely inventive fare. The fine ocean views from the restaurant make this a romantic choice.

84 High Street (84 High St., Westerly, 401/596-7871, www.84highstreet.com, 11:30 A.M.–3 P.M. and 5–9 P.M. Mon.–Thurs., 11:30 A.M.–3 P.M. and 5–10 P.M. Fri., 9 A.M.–3 P.M. and 5–10 P.M. Sat., 9 A.M.–3 P.M. and 5–9 P.M. Sun., $12–20) is a small and snazzy restaurant that shows the work of prominent local artists on its walls. It's steps from Wilcox Park and right in the heart of Westerly's pretty downtown. The kitchen prepares relatively simple but contemporary regional American fare, including grilled lemon sole in a light cucumber sauce and grilled pork tenderloin finished with an applejack brandy cream sauce, plus several well-executed pastas. There's a large assortment of grilled pizzas, appetizers, and salads, which are also available at lunch, arguably the more popular meal here, when you'll also find a very long list of creative sandwiches.

Serving excellent food without pretense, **Up River Cafe** (37 Main St., 401/348-9700, www.theuprivercafe.net, 5–9 P.M. Tues.–Thurs., 5–10 P.M. Fri.–Sat., lounge 4 P.M.–late daily, $11–26) wows with its location in a refurbished mill overlooking the Pawcatuck River. Similarly, the San Francisco–trained chef-owners provide updated riffs on old classics, such as a Parisian-style Delmonico steak with potatoes au gratin and seared local scallops with lobster home fries. Save room for dessert, which includes nostalgia-heavy items such as root beer floats, ice-cream sundaes, and a butterscotch pudding to die for.

Smart decor, fresh ingredients, and cheerful service make **Maria's** (132 Atlantic Ave., Misquamicut, 401/596-6886, www.mariasseasidecafe.com, call for hours, $11–28) one of the most sophisticated options at Misquamicut, and it's just across the street from the beach. Excellent starters include jumbo shrimp sautéed with apricots and a Grand Marnier sauce or arugula salad with goat cheese crostini. Starters include a wide range of pastas, among them a very nice lobster *fra diavolo*, and grills

such as filet mignon Florentine and chicken balsamico. This is a more adult-oriented restaurant than most in Misquamicut, but there is a small children's menu.

Set to a Southwest theme with the barbecue sauce and saloon to back it up, **W. B. Cody's** (265 Post Rd., Westerly, 401/322-4070, noon–9 P.M. Sun.–Thurs., noon–10 P.M. Fri.–Sat., $11–22) has been a favorite for hearty American fare with a kick. Regulars appreciate the setting and the menu, which offers plenty of Southwest standbys—barbecue ribs, chicken fajitas, Black Angus burgers, and Cajun fries. The Buckaroo menu offers plenty of tasty options for the kids, who eat for free on Sunday.

Pizza, Pub Grub, and Seafood

Just once, experience the sheer vastness of **Nordic Lodge** (178 E. Pasquiset Tr., Charlestown, 401/783-4515, www.nordiclodge.com, 5–8:30 P.M. Fri., 4–8:30 P.M. Sat., 3–6:30 P.M. Sun.). It is famous for its dinner buffets, which cost a not-insignificant $65 pp but include unlimited access to heaping platters of more food than you can imagine. Favorites include nicely proportioned steamed lobsters, prime rib, broiled scallops, Asian pork ribs, filet mignon, shrimp cocktail, and dozens of massive cakes, pies, and other desserts. People drive here from miles around to experience this embarrassment of culinary riches. The restaurant sits in a remote wooded area overlooking a lovely pond. It's rather tricky to find this place, a good drive north of Charlestown's beaches; it's a good idea to call ahead for directions.

A spacious light-filled restaurant in a 1911 redbrick building at the center of downtown Westerly, **Pizza Place Pie and Suds** (43 Broad St., Westerly, 401/348-1803, 11:30 A.M.–9 P.M. daily, pies $10–16) serves some rather inventive pizzas despite its prosaic name. The scallops-and-bacon pie with chopped garlic, Parmesan cheese, and olive oil is a favorite, but don't overlook the perfectly simple and wonderful one with fresh spinach and Gorgonzola. Red and white pizzas are available, and the list of toppings is long and impressive. The menu also includes about six pastas and several tasty salads.

Dylan's Restaurant (2 Canal St., Westerly, 401/596-4075, 4–9 P.M. Sun.–Thurs., 4–10 P.M. Fri.–Sat., $12–19) is an old-fashioned steak and seafood place with a dark-wood interior, vintage photos, and friendly service. You might dine on shrimp Diane (sautéed jumbo shrimp with scallions, wild mushrooms, fresh basil, fish stock, a touch of cream, and fettuccine), veal marsala, or fried scallops.

The food at **Wilcox Tavern** (5153 Old Post Rd. at U.S. 1, Charlestown, 401/322-1829, from 4:30 P.M. Tues.–Sun., $12–20) tends toward the tried-and-true (standard renditions of veal, chops, chicken, and seafood), but devotees appreciate the tavern-esque feel of the dining rooms in this 1730 center-chimney house.

In an enormous building next to the Winnapaug Inn, which is run by the same owners, **Venice Restaurant** (165 Shore Rd., Misquamicut, 401/348-0055, from 4 P.M. daily, $12–23) ranks among South County's most popular Italian restaurants, both for dinner and for the lavish weekend brunch spreads. Veal is a house specialty, prepared several ways, but also consider the vegetarian portobello parmigiana, the grilled filet mignon with a burgundy-mushroom sauce, or the linguine with clam sauce. You won't find a lot of surprises on the menu, but nightly specials are sometimes a little more adventurous. The huge, warmly furnished dining room can get noisy, but otherwise it's a very nice restaurant.

Ethnic Fare

For reasonably authentic (by New England standards, anyway) Mexican fare, consider festive **Señor Flacos** (15 Canal St., Westerly, 401/315-2626, 4–8 P.M. Tues.–Thurs., 4–10 P.M. Fri.–Sat., 4–9 P.M. Sun., $7–15), a colorful little spot with commendable carne asada, seviche, fish tacos, and garlic shrimp with avocado cream sauce. Fresh ingredients and attractively presented dishes make this a winner.

Quick Bites

Spice of Life (Fantastic Umbrella Factory, 4820 Old Post Rd./Rte. 1A, just off U.S. 1, Charlestown, 401/364-6616, $5–14) has organic soups and salads, some south-of-the-border fare, ice cream and frozen yogurt, and even an organic espresso bar.

A popular short-order seafood place on the Post Road in Charlestown, the **Hitching Post** (5402 Post Rd./U.S. 1, Charlestown, 401/364-7495, 11:30 A.M.–8 P.M. daily, $5–13) is the sort of place where you order at the window and take your food back to devour in your car as you watch others do the same. The food here is simple and mouthwatering: burgers, clam rolls, Rhode Island clear-broth clam chowder, Italian ices, and Good Humor ice-cream products. You'll find a small outdoor dining area with picnic tables too.

◀ Fra's Italian Gourmet (Shore Rd. and Crandall Ave., Misquamicut, 401/596-2888, www.frasitaliangourmet.com, from 9 A.M. daily, $4–8, large pizzas $10–16) is an excellent source of freshly made sauces, pastas, and delicious prepared and packaged goods; the families who rent cottages in this area swear by this place. Specialties include the Calabria grinder (stuffed with mortadella, *genoa, capicola, sopressata,* provolone, lettuce, tomatoes, balsamic-marinated onions, and dressing), ricotta-stuffed shells, chicken-cutlet focaccia sandwiches, and fresh tomato-basil bruschetta. And if that's not enough, check out the selection of gourmet pizzas.

Bay Street Deli (112 Bay St., Watch Hill, 401/596-6606, 8 A.M.–8 P.M. daily, $2–16) serves superb Rhode Island clam chowder, lobster rolls, bagels, ice cream, muffins, pies and cakes, espressos, soups, and salads. You'll find a handful of sidewalk tables, but this is mostly a place to pick up takeout vittles.

By the Weekapaug fishing area and Dunn's Beach you can gorge on more short-order eats at **Seafood Haven Snack Bar** (688 Atlantic Ave., Weekapaug, at the Misquamicut/Weekapaug Breechway, 401/322-0330, open daily but call for hours, $6–20), a two-story white shanty with some indoor seating and several more outside tables. Clam cakes are the house specialty, a claim made by many fish restaurants in South County, but they really are delicious here. Also consider the twin lobsters served with drawn butter, rich home-style chili with melted cheese, three kinds of clam chowder, chicken teriyaki, Stonington scallops, and mussels in marinara sauce. The owners also run a fish market (10 A.M.–6 P.M. daily) next door; you can buy complete clam-bakes from the market or order the similar Shore Dinner combo in the restaurant.

St. Clair Annex (141 Bay St., Watch Hill, 401/348-8407, 8 A.M.–8 P.M. daily, ice cream 8 A.M.–9:30 P.M. daily, $3–11) is a favorite option for ice cream, fried seafood, grinders, and other casual fare. It has been open since the 1880s.

A homey little bakery that champions the local pastry delicacy known as the Bismarck, **West's Bakery** (995 Main St., Hope Valley, 401/539-2451, 6 A.M.–3 P.M. Thurs.–Sat., 6 A.M.–1 P.M. Sun.) lies right in the heart of Hope Valley and also serves tasty grinders and excellent ice cream (the "peanut buttah!" parfait is a memorable treat).

Java Joints

An enjoyable Westerly coffee hangout that also doubles as a wine bar is **Perks and Corks** (62 High St., Westerly, 401/596-1260, 11 A.M.–9 P.M. Mon.–Fri., 9 A.M.–9 P.M. Sat., 5–7 P.M. Sun., $2–12), a living room–style café with plush sofas and armchairs and a slightly bohemian buzz. You can also order bagels, fresh-baked breads, and yummy desserts to munch on, and fine wines, single-malt scotches, and martinis to sip, along with organic teas, lattes, and the like.

Bean Counter (2 Broad St., Westerly, 401/596-9999, 7 A.M.–8 P.M. Mon.–Sat., 8 A.M.–7 P.M. Sun., $3–8) is a friendly shop serving specialty coffee drinks and mouthwatering sandwiches in a convenient location.

Gourmet Goods and Picnic Supplies

In the tiny Avondale section of Westerly, very convenient to Watch Hill and Misquamicut, the **Cooked Goose** (92 Watch Hill Rd., Westerly, 401/348-9888, www.thecookedgoose.com,

7 A.M.–7 P.M. daily summer, 7 A.M.–3 P.M. daily Columbus Day–Memorial Day) is one of the best sources in the county for gourmet foods, both prepared and packaged. You can also pick up takeout sandwiches, breakfasts, and the like. Specialties include fresh H&H Bagels delivered from New York City, quiche (the selection changes daily), curried chicken salad, and gourmet sandwiches such as the Avondale (smoked turkey, Havarti cheese, and cranberry mayo on pumpernickel). Fresh-baked pies, Louisiana bread pudding, and lemon squares are among the dozens of desserts available each day.

If you've got kids in tow, definitely check out **Lickety Splits** (39 Kingstown Rd., Wyoming, 11 A.M.–10 P.M. Fri.–Wed., 11 A.M.–11 P.M. Thurs., 401/539-9047), a sweets shop and ice-cream stand with an extensive selection of goodies. It's on Route 138 just east of I-95, occupying a pair of gray clapboard cottages.

VISITOR INFORMATION

For information on Westerly, stop by the **Greater Westerly-Pawcatuck Chamber of Commerce** (1 Chamber Way, 401/496-7761 or 800/732-7636, www.westerlychamber.org), which runs a comprehensive visitors center off of Route 1. For Charleston, contact the **Charlestown Chamber of Commerce** (4945 Old Post Rd., 401/364-3878, www.charlestownrichamber.com).

Media

Get local news and entertainment information from the **Westerly Sun** (401/348-1000, www.thewesterlysun.com), published daily.

GETTING AROUND
Airports

Westerly Airport (U.S. 1 and Rte. 78, in Connecticut I-95 exit 92 from the south, in Rhode Island I-95 exit 1 from the north) is South County's regional air facility. It's primarily used by private planes and charters, and it's where you can catch flights on several airlines to Block Island. **New England Airlines** (800/243-2460, http://users.ids.net/flybi/nea), the regular airline between Westerly and

Block Island, can be booked for charters from Westerly to many other parts of the country. Of course, as for all of Rhode Island, Warwick's T. F. Green Airport is the main way to reach South County by air.

Buses

Rhode Island Public Transit Authority (RIPTA) (401/781-9400, www.ripta.com) runs several buses connecting South County with Providence, Newport, and other parts of the state.

Driving

I-95 skirts the upper half of South County and is the best way to reach the area from Connecticut

and points south, but the main road through lower South County is U.S. 1, a busy four-lane highway and a fairly quick route except on summer weekends and at rush hour. Route 1A is the more scenic route, running mostly parallel to U.S. 1 as it jogs along the coast, offering access to beaches and many of the quaint shoreline communities. Route 138 runs west–east through the county's midsection and then continues to Jamestown and Newport. For taxi service, contact **Wright's Taxi** (Westerly, 401/789-0400 or 401/596-8294).

Trains

Amtrak (800/872-7245, www.amtrak.com) stops in Westerly at 14 Railroad Avenue.

Narragansett to North Kingstown

Wedged between Charlestown and the bay that bears its name, this small community is the easternmost of South County's coastal resorts—it runs along the southeastern tip of the oceanfront and then up the western side of Narragansett Bay. The northern section of town, along the bay, is called Narragansett Pier. Sandy beaches line the shore along with large and stately summer homes, cottages, and smaller residences. Other than the fishing and boating business down at Galilee and Point Judith, Narragansett is almost entirely a tourist town, although plenty of folks also commute to Providence, just 30 miles north.

GALILEE AND POINT JUDITH

South of U.S. 1, Point Judith Road (Route 108) runs four miles to the turnoff for Galilee, a bustling port opposite Jerusalem. This whole area is more generally part of Point Judith, which is a tiny community in terms of population; it ranks fifth, however, on the East Coast and a formidable 17th in the nation among fishing ports, producing annual fishing revenues of $37 million. Approximately 250 boats call Point Judith home. You'll also find many of the area's summer homes, plus clam shacks, charter fishing

> ## SOUTH COUNTY VILLAGES
>
> To an out-of-towner, it may seem like South County delights in confusing travelers, as each of the major towns is divided into several villages with obscure Native American names or maddeningly similar sobriquets. A quick guide, then: North Kingstown contains the villages of Quonset Point, Saunderstown, and Wickford; Narragansett includes Galilee and Point Judith; South Kingstown encompasses Jerusalem, Kenyon, Kingston, Matunuck, Peace Dale, Wakefield, and West Kingston; Charlestown includes Cross Mills and Quonochontaug; and Westerly contains Avondale, Misquamicut, Watch Hill, and Weekapaug. Is all that clear?

operations, and some of the state's top beaches. From here you can book whale-watching tours and other excursion boats, and this is also where you catch the ferry to Block Island.

Back out on Route 108, the road leads a bit farther south, where a right turn onto Ocean Road leads to **Point Judith Lighthouse** (www.lighthouse.cc/pointjudith). Fans of lighthouses should explore the grounds of the 1857 structure, a 51-foot octagonal tower that is the third incarnation to be built on this spot; the original Point Judith Lighthouse went up about a half century earlier. The lighthouse itself, which underwent a major restoration in 2000, is not open to the public.

NARRAGANSETT

Ocean Road then becomes Route 108 and turns north following the shore. This five-mile road passes beautiful Scarborough State Beach and some very posh residential neighborhoods near the ocean before entering the village of Narragansett Pier, which came into its own as a Victorian resort where wealthy vacationers arrived in droves by steamship and train. Until it burned down in 1900, the draw of the neighborhood was the Narragansett Casino Resort, still famous as the location where clams casino was invented. Only the majestic arch of the **Towers** (35 Ocean Rd., 401/782-2597, www.thetowersri.com, noon–4 P.M.

year-round, free) survives in all of its turn-of-the-century elegance. Now the building hosts a small museum with old photographs as well as lectures, dances, and musical performances. Numerous beach cottages and quite a few shops and eateries also line the streets of Narragansett Pier.

◖ SOUTH COUNTY MUSEUM

Located on the estate of a former state governor, the South County Museum (Strathmore St., off Rte. 1A, 401/783-5400, www.southcountymuseum.org, 10 A.M.–4 P.M. Wed.–Sat., noon–4 P.M. Sun. July–Aug., 10 A.M.–4 P.M. Fri.–Sun., noon–4 P.M. Sun. May–June and Sept.–Oct., $5 adults, $4 seniors, $2 children 6–12, free for children under 6) offers an engaging and useful overview of a gentleman's farm, a carpenter's shop, a blacksmith shop, a general store, a one-room schoolhouse, and many other historic venues that you might find in colonial and then Victorian coastal Rhode Island—you'll find more than 20,000 period artifacts and implements spread among these

© MICHAEL BLANDING

Point Judith Lighthouse in the fog

exhibits. The museum organizes dozens of events, including apple pie–eating contests, fall harvest fairs, Victorian teas, and quilt shows. Displays here are geared largely to kids and families and include an exhibit on the railroads of South County. Many rotating exhibits are also shown. The museum sits on 175-acre Canonchet Farm, which dates to the 18th century and was once the home of Rhode Island governor William Sprague.

SAUNDERSTOWN

North of Narragansett Pier on Route 1A is the village of Saunderstown. Keep your eyes open as you pass **Historic South Ferry Road,** where you'll find the old South Ferry Church, the historic port and ferry landing, the World War I–era Fort Kearney, and a World War II POW camp. A short distance farther north is **Casey Farm** (2325 Boston Neck Rd./Rte. 1A, 401/295-1030, www.spnea.org/visit/homes/casey.htm, 9 A.M.–2 P.M. Sat. June–mid-Oct., $4 adults, $3 seniors, $2 students), which dates to 1750 and has beautiful ocean vistas over Narragansett Bay, was the site of several small battles during the Revolutionary War. Now this 300-acre working farm is a rare parcel that preserves the agrarian ways of colonial times in coastal New England—rare not only for Rhode Island but for the entire country. As a visitor you can tour what is run as a community-supported farm by the Society for the Preservation for New England Antiquities (SPNEA) and see how produce was grown organically in colonial times. Hiking trails lace the property. Special events throughout the summer and fall include hayrides, produce sales, and demonstrations.

◖ GILBERT STUART MUSEUM

Open up your wallet and chances are you'll find an example of the work of Gilbert Stuart, best known for his portrait of George Washington that graces the one-dollar bill. Stuart's life and work are encapsulated at the Gilbert Stuart Birthplace and Museum (815 Gilbert Stuart Rd., Saunderstown, 401/294-3001, www.gilbertstuartmuseum.com, 11 A.M.–4 P.M. Mon. and Thurs.–Sat., 12–4 P.M. Sun. early May–Sept., limited hours Oct., $6 adults, $3 children 6–12, free for children under 6), centered around the red gambrel-roofed colonial house where Stuart was born on December 3, 1755. He lived in the house only until he was seven, at which time his family moved to Newport; soon after, people began to notice his prowess as a painter.

The house has been preserved as it functioned—both as a home and a small colonial factory of sorts. Each room contains a corner fireplace, and many of the original woodworking and construction details are still intact, from the wooden door latches to the hand-blown windowpanes. Reproductions of Stuart's works hang throughout the house. In the common room you'll see a display of colonial cooking utensils and tools. Costumed docents are often on hand to demonstrate colonial activities, such as fulling wool and grinding meal.

The house occupies wonderfully scenic grounds near a pond and a stream; on the grounds is the restored gristmill in which two massive grinding stones made the cornmeal used in jonnycakes. There is an herb garden where plants commonly used in colonial times are grown, and a children's activity garden with educational and interactive outdoor exhibits.

WICKFORD AND NORTH KINGSTOWN

North Kingstown was once home to many thriving farms and plantations, several of which are still in operation or have now become museums. The town, however, has long since been overshadowed by its own village of Wickford, one of the most delightful you are ever likely to see. One of New England's best-kept secrets, Wickford has scads of beautifully preserved colonial houses and lies just minutes east of busy U.S. 1. The village center at Main Street and Brown Street is barely a crossroads, but it overflows with brick and clapboard buildings from the 18th and 19th centuries, all pleasantly weathered and peeling. Making them more attractive are the many boutiques and galleries that have taken root, making this the perfect place to forget about the modern world for an afternoon or a weekend.

Almost nothing about Wickford suggests the last half century, except perhaps the occasional jet rushing overhead from nearby T. F. Green Airport. It seems like a movie set for a film set many decades ago, and indeed, the town inspired the setting for John Updike's novel *The Witches of Eastwick*. Follow Main Street from the village's commercial district out to the town pier on Wickford Harbor, which opens to Narragansett Bay. Here you can walk alongside stacks of lobster traps, listen to the squawk of aggressive seagulls, breathe in the briny air, and look back over the dozens of masts in the harbor toward the colonial homes and businesses of town.

Just north of Wickford, don't expect to see battlements at **Smith's Castle** (55 Richard Smith Dr., off U.S. 1, just north of Wickford, 401/294-3521, www.smithscastle. org, noon–4 P.M. Thurs.–Mon. June–Aug., noon–4 P.M. Fri.–Sun. May and Sept.–Oct., or by appointment, grounds free, house $6 adults, $1 children 6–12, free for children under 6). In fact, the neatly restored mansion is the oldest surviving plantation house in the country. Its fascinating history mirrors the checkered history of Rhode Island; during the state's slave-trading heyday in the early 18th century, this manor was a slave-holding plantation, producing tobacco, grains, apples, and vegetables as well as sheep, cattle, and pigs. After slavery was outlawed, the plantation lay dormant for a century before functioning again as a small dairy in the early 20th century. You can now walk the grounds year-round, admiring the cove that looks across to Queens Island and strolling through the lush gardens.

North Kingstown's **Quonset Naval Air Base** (Quonset Point, off U.S. 1, 401/294-9540, www.theqam.org, 10 A.M.–3 P.M. daily, $7 adults, $6 seniors, $3 children under 12) is home to the Quonset Air Museum and the headquarters of the Rhode Island National Guard. Numerous aircraft can be viewed, including Douglas Skyhawks, Hellcat fighter

planes, and several helicopters. On open-cockpit days, the third Saturday of each month, you can climb inside many of the aircraft. The base hosts an air show each June, which features daredevil stunts by the Blue Angels.

ENTERTAINMENT AND EVENTS
Bars and Clubs

Other sources of live rock, reggae, and the like include **George's of Galilee** (Port of Galilee, Narragansett, 401/783-2306, www. georgesofgalilee.com, from 11:30 A.M.); the **Bon Vue** (1230 Ocean Rd., Narragansett, 401/789-0696, kitchen 11:30 A.M.–10 P.M. Mon.–Fri., 8 A.M.–10 P.M. Sat.–Sun., bar 11:30 A.M.–1 A.M. daily); the **Oak Hill Tavern** (565 Tower Hill Rd., North Kingstown, 401/294-3282, 11 A.M.–1 A.M. daily); and **Sandy's Lighthouse** (148 Atlantic Ave., Misquamicut, 401/596-1496, 11 A.M.–1 A.M. daily).

The bar at Misquamicut's **Paddy's Restaurant** (159 Atlantic Ave., Misquamicut, 401/596-4350, call for hours) is a popular spot all summer long, and here you can order all sorts of froufrou tropical drinks such as banana rumrunners and some vaguely hallucinatory-sounding concoctions, including one called Fish on Acid (a shooter containing Jägermeister, coconut rum, and pineapple juice). Paddy's hosts live bands throughout the summer and has fun theme nights, such as reggae Saturdays.

PJ's Pub (135 Boon St., Narragansett, 401/789-3200, 11 A.M.–1 A.M. daily) is located in the heart of the Historic District. Near the beach in Narragansett, **Charlie O's** (2 Sand Hill Cove Rd., 401/782-2002, 11:30 A.M.–1 A.M. daily) draws a convivial mix for shooting pool, watching sports on TV, and drinking.

Festivals and Events

Boating enthusiasts gather to watch the **Annual Blessing of the Fleet** (Galilee, 401/783-7121) each July. In mid-July, the sky fills with color during the **South County Hot Air Balloon**

Festival (401/783-1770, www.wakefieldrotary. com), which draws more than 20 hot-air balloons offering both tethered and untethered rides over the area for three full days. There are also concerts, crafts, a classic car display, kids' amusements and games, a petting zoo, a Revolutionary War reenactment, and lots more going on.

Every July, Wickford Village comes alive with the much anticipated **Wickford Art Festival** (401/294-6840, www.wickfordart. org), when hundreds of artists set up booths in the town center.

SHOPPING
Narragansett

Narragansett Pier Marketplace (Ocean Rd.) is a small collection of tourist shops, including the **Shell Boutique** (401/788-8046, 10 A.M.–9 P.M. daily summer, 10 A.M.–4 P.M. daily other seasons), which specializes in art and Native American gifts but also has an astounding selection of shells. There's a T-shirt shop in the market, a gift shop, and a wonderful ice-cream parlor called Nana's. Adjoining the market is the Coast Guard House restaurant.

◖ Wickford

Wickford has about 40 shops and boutiques, most of them independently owned. The vast majority are along West Main Street and Brown Street, Wickford's main drag. **Beauty and the Bath** (11 W. Main St., 401/294-3576, www.beautyandthebath.com, 10 A.M.–5 P.M. Mon.–Sat., noon–5 P.M. Sun.) sells upscale bath amenities, plush robes, soaps, gels, and shaving creams. At the **Grateful Heart** (17 W. Main St., 401/294-3981, www.gratefulheart. com, noon–5 P.M. Sun.–Mon., 10 A.M.–6 P.M. Tues.–Sat.), pick up New Age and other spiritual and holistic health–related books, incense, oils, crystals, and music. **Village Reflections** (5 W. Main St., 401/295-7802, 10 A.M.–6 P.M. Mon.–Thurs., 10 A.M.–8 P.M. Fri.–Sat., noon–6 P.M. Sun.) offers smart and stylish contemporary women's clothes and beautiful jewelry. Foodies flock to **Wickford Gourmet Kitchen and Table** (21 W. Main St., 401/295-

Wickford shops

8190) for intriguing food items, cookware, and table settings.

Studio Zwei (2 W. Main St., 401/295-5907 or 800/760-5907, by appointment only) has a remarkably extensive showing of local works, including Wickford sea- and landscapes. Owner Elsie Schaich Kilguss has taught and exhibited her works since 1980. **Nautical Impressions** (16 W. Main St., 401/295-5303, 10 A.M.–5 P.M. Mon.–Sat., noon–5 P.M. Sun.) sells appropriately sea-themed art and gifts.

Wilson's of Wickford (35 Brown St., 401/294-9514 or 800/371-9514, www.wilsonsofwickford.com, 10 A.M.–6 P.M. Mon.–Thurs. and Sat., 10 A.M.–8 P.M. Fri., 11:30 A.M.–5 P.M. Sun.) is a large department store selling casual yachting and beach wear with a country-club casual aesthetic. **J. W. Graham** (17 and 26 Brown St., 401/295-0757, 10 A.M.–8 P.M. Mon.–Sat., 11 A.M.–6 P.M. Sun.) has beautiful handcrafted glassware, lamps, home furnishings, and accessories with an emphasis on birds, fish, and the colors of the sea. The **Hour Glass** (15 W. Main St., 401/295-8724 or 800/585-8724) has a fairly amazing selection of timepieces, including ship's clocks and hourglasses; you'll also find kaleidoscopes, thermometers, sundials, and barometers. **Midnight Sun** (83–85 Brown St., 401/295-1601, 10 A.M.–6 P.M. Mon.–Sat., noon–6 P.M. Sun.) offers the exotic wares of South America, including hemp products, clothing, and jewelry, without the added travel time.

You can browse for art at the **Wickford Art Association Gallery** (36 Beach St., 401/294-6840, www.wickfordart.org, 11 A.M.–3 P.M. Tues.–Sat., noon–3 P.M. Sun.), a nonprofit cooperative with about 300 members. For information on the many other shops and businesses in Wickford, check out the website of the **Wickford Village Association** (www.wickfordvillage.org).

SPORTS AND RECREATION
Beaches
Narragansett is Rhode Island's beach-bumming capital, its crown jewel being **Roger Wheeler State Beach** (Sand Hill Cove Rd., off Rte. 108, Narragansett, 401/789-3563,

www.riparks.com/wheeler.htm), a typically packed swatch of golden sand at Point Judith with among the best facilities in the county, including an excellent playground, a picnic area, and a bathhouse. Just west of Roger Wheeler in Galilee is **Salty Brine State Beach** (254 Great Rd., Galilee, 401/789-8374, www.riparks.com/saltybrine.htm), a short span that's popular with area teens and young people. On the Narragansett Bay side of town, **Scarborough State (North) Beach** and **Scarborough South Beach** (both off Ocean Ave., Narragansett, 401/789-2324 or 401/782-1319, www.riparks.com/scarborough.htm) connect and provide a total of about 3,000 parking spaces and roughly a half-mile of sand. These are both hot spots for college students, and the crowds can get a bit rowdy from time to time. Farther up Ocean Avenue at Narragansett Pier is **Narragansett Town Beach,** a broad beach with shallow bathing, a full slate of facilities, and plenty of parking (although the state beaches have more parking).

Fishing
Home to the third-most-profitable fishing port in New England, Point Judith is nirvana for fishing enthusiasts. Several companies offer fishing charters, including **Frances Fleet** (33 State St., Galilee, 401/783-4988, www.francesfleet.com), which hosts a variety of trips, including cod-fishing excursions at sunrise, nighttime bluefish and striped bass runs, and tuna trips far out at sea. Other fishing boats include **Kerritim Charters** (401/364-0498, www.kerritimcharters.com), **C-Devil II Sportfishing** (401/364-9774, www.cdevilsportfishing.com), and **White Ghost Charters** (401/828-9465, www.whiteghostcharters.com).

Boating
Frances Fleet (33 State St., Galilee, 401/783-4988, www.francesfleet.com) also offers whale-watching cruises out of Narragansett, while the *Southland* Riverboat (401/783-2954, www.southlandcruises.com) offers tours on

an authentic riverboat that departs from State Pier in Galilee. The 11-mile narrated tour chugs along the South County shoreline and lower Narragansett Bay, past lighthouses and through prized fishing waters, passing about a dozen small islands and countless coves and peninsulas. This flat-bottom riverboat, built in Mississippi, holds about 150 passengers and has a full bar and snack area. Both standard sightseeing cruises and evening sunset sails are offered, with prices ranging $10–15 for adults, children roughly half that price. In Wickford, the Dutch sailing yacht the *Brandaris* (7 Main St., Wickford, 401/294-1481) helped evacuate troops from the shores of Dunkirk during World War II and is now available for sightseeing excursions. The 63-foot ship accommodates up to 30 guests.

ACCOMMODATIONS
$100-150

The Haddie Pierce House (146 Boston Neck Rd., Wickford, 401/294-7674 or 866/442-3343, www.haddiepierce.com, $140–160) is a traditional early-20th-century four-square clapboard home with five warmly furnished guest rooms, each with a private bath. Decor is heavy on frill; one room is named for and accented with stuffed teddy bears, another for the vintage dolls contained therein. More masculine is the Nautical Room, with blue and white curtains and bedspreads and framed nautical prints on the walls. Some rooms have whirlpool baths. The large common rooms are decked with elegant Victorian furniture. The inn is just a short walk from downtown Wickford.

One of the best economy motels in Rhode Island, the **Hamilton Village Inn** (642 Boston Neck Rd., North Kingstown, 401/295-0700, www.hamiltonvillageinn.com, $100–119) is a dapper white structure that sits along the road between Wickford village and the bridge to Jamestown—it's close to Casey Farm and the Gilbert Stuart Museum and not far from the beaches. Rooms are immaculate, and suites have fully equipped kitchens. This is a cut above some of the more dated motels in South

County—rooms have brand-new carpets and light-wood furnishings, and the kitchens and baths are modern and attractive. The grounds consist of nicely cared-for gardens and towering trees, and the diner-style on-site restaurant, Sea View Station, serves three meals a day.

A popular spot facing Narragansett Bay, the **C Ocean Rose Inn** (113 Ocean Ave., Narragansett Pier, 401/783-4704, www.oceanroseinn.com, $149–289) offers a mix of new and vintage Victorian accommodations. The main inn dates to 1901 and contains nine gorgeous Victorian-style guest rooms with polished hardwood floors, four-poster beds, and Oriental rugs; some have private decks and fireplaces, and all enjoy fabulous water views. There's also a long veranda with wicker chairs looking out over the water. A second, contemporary building contains 18 guest rooms, many of which also enjoy very nice water views—these accommodations have less character but are more practical for kids. All rooms in both buildings have private baths. The Turtle Soup restaurant, on the ground floor of the main inn, serves very good contemporary fare.

Just 1.5 miles south of Wickford village, **Crosswinds Farm** (800 Boston Neck Rd., North Kingstown, 401/339-7813, www.crosswindsbnb.com, $125–185) is a dapper 1850s farmhouse with a pair of homey guest rooms, each with a private bath. The owners will rent a third room, which shares a bath with one of the other rooms, but only when the guests of both units are traveling together and request this arrangement. Slanting ceilings, country furnishings, and heavy quilts create a cozy and warm feel in each room, and common areas contain a smattering of antiques—this is a low-key property that's ideal if you're seeking a peaceful and convenient location and are traveling on a moderate budget.

A simple and inexpensive option near historic Wickford, and also a good base for exploring metro Providence and even Newport, the **Budget Inn** (7825 Post Rd., North Kingstown, 401/294-4888, www.budget-inn.net, $125–195) is a one-story brick motel with clean rooms with phones, cable TV, and in some cases microwaves and refrigerators.

$150-250

A large clapboard hotel right on the bay in the heart of Narragansett Pier, the **Village Inn** (1 Beach St., Narragansett Pier, 401/783-6767 or 800/THE-PIER—800/843-7437, www.v-inn. com, $189–284) has 62 fairly large and contemporary rooms with typical chain hotel–style furnishings. The big reason to stay here is location: It's adjacent to the Towers at Narragansett Pier and within walking distance of the beach, many shops and restaurants, and the South County Museum. Pluses include whirlpool tubs in most rooms and a large indoor pool with a whirlpool, a full-service spa, and one of the county's best restaurants, Amalfi. There is also a lounge with a sundeck and two restaurants.

The Richards B&B (144 Gibson Ave., Narragansett, 401/789-7746, www.therichardsbnb.com, $150–200) is an imposing 8,500-square-foot stone mansion that was once the anchor of the 200-acre estate. No luxury or degree of craftsmanship was spared in constructing this stunning house, which even has a working elevator. There are four guest rooms, each with a working fireplace and a private bathroom; two suites have large sitting areas. The house is filled with museum-quality antiques and is situated on a lovely parcel with beautifully kept gardens—this is Narragansett's most photogenic inn. In each room you'll find a decanter of sherry awaiting you, and a full breakfast is served each morning.

An easy walk from Town Beach in Narragansett, the 1870s **Blueberry Cove Inn** (75 Kingstown Rd., Narragansett, 800/478-1426, www.blueberrycoveinn.com, $150–180) has seven warmly furnished guest rooms, including one suite with a whirlpool tub and fireplace. The white Victorian presides over well-trimmed lawns and gardens, and rooms are decked with luxurious Egyptian-cotton linens, canopy beds, TVs with video players, air-conditioning, and tasteful country furnishings. A lavish full breakfast is included. Ask about the decadent "chocolate weekends," when the innkeepers treat guests to two dozen rich chocolate treats.

FOOD
Upscale

Intimate **Basil's** (22 Kingstown Rd., Narragansett Pier, 401/789-3743, 5–10 P.M. daily, $16–29) is a tiny spot that's very romantic and a favorite for special occasions. Here you can sample excellent, straightforward French continental cuisine and order from an extensive wine list. There aren't a lot of surprises on this menu, but traditionalists never seem to tire of the expertly prepared frogs legs, duck à l'orange, steak au poivre, escargot, and crème brûlée.

Spain of Narragansett (1144 Ocean Rd., Narragansett, 401/783-9770, www.spainri. com, 4–10 P.M. Tues.–Thurs., 4–11 P.M. Fri.–Sat., 1–9 P.M. Sun., $11–23), while not fancy, is one of the more dramatic dining spaces in South County—its high-ceilinged dining room is anchored by a gurgling fountain. This isn't a tapas restaurant per se, but you will find a number of nicely prepared starters, from clams casino to garlic-smoked chorizo. Sole lightly egg-battered and pan-sautéed in a lemon chablis sauce and chicken Andaluza (stuffed with pine nuts, diced smoked ham, spinach, and manchego cheese, topped with fresh cilantro and tomatoes) are excellent entrées. Some dishes are available for two, such as paella Valenciana with shrimp, sea scallops, clams, mussels, chicken, and calamari with saffron rice and spices, or *solomillo al Jefe,* medallion of beef tenderloin served with artichoke hearts and mushrooms in a rioja wine, Dijon, and garlic sauce.

As ambience goes, **Rhode Island Quahog Company** (1065 Tower Hill Rd., North Kingstown, 401/294-2727, 11:30 A.M.–9 P.M. Mon.–Thurs., 11:30 A.M.–10 P.M. Fri.–Sat., $14–25) earns praise for its warmed-by-the-fire feel, inviting circa-1760 quarters, and casual—if predictable—pub fare, from pizzas and pasta to steaks and seafood. The menu is long, and the kitchen does turn out a smattering of more innovative dishes, such as grilled salmon with light raspberry sauce. There's also an excellent shelled and sautéed lobster served in a rich sherry cream. Tuesday night brings out plenty of longtime fans for the $9.95 stuffed shrimp and prime rib dinners, and early-bird specials are offered daily.

Creative but Casual

A decent spot for inspired yet reasonably priced American food, **☾ Turtle Soup** (113 Ocean Rd., Narragansett, 401/792-8683, 11:30 A.M.–11 P.M. daily, $11–20) occupies a distinctive twin-gabled Victorian beach hotel, the Ocean Rose Inn, with nice views across the street of the water—it's an elegant space but unfussy, as one would expect of a beach restaurant. The menu offers a nice range of options, including pork tenderloin with honey–Dijon mustard cream, and blackened tuna with avocado butter. Less expensive sandwiches (burgers, chicken clubs) are also available, and you can order from a nice selection of appetizers to create a good meal—pan-seared crab cakes with a smoked jalapeño rémoulade are a fave. Service is low-key and friendly.

The classy Mediterranean restaurant at Narragansett's Village Inn, **☾ Amalfi** (1 Beach St., Narragansett, 401/792-3999, www.amalfiofnarragansett.com, call for hours, $15–30) serves some of the most consistently wonderful food in the region, specializing in the cuisines of Spain, southern France, Italy, Greece, and Morocco. Notable dishes include an appetizer of bruschetta topped with black mussels and littleneck clams, and blue-crab cakes with lemon-basil aioli. Among the main courses, try the stellar grilled center-cut swordfish with roasted pepper–basil butter, or the pork shank osso buco with truffled macaroni and Parmesan cream. Amalfi's sunny dining room affords splendid water views, and in good weather you can dine on the breezy deck, breathing in the sea air.

Pizza, Pub Grub, and Seafood

An easygoing tavern serving a fairly typical compendium of steaks, chops, seafood, burgers, and bar munchies, **Charlie O's** (2 Sand Hill Cove Rd., Narragansett, 401/782-2002, 11:30 A.M.–1 A.M. daily, $5–16) is a reliable option, especially late at night, as the kitchen stays open until around midnight and sometimes later. The place is big with collegiate types, in part for its pool tables and sports-bar theme, and also because it's a short drive from the beach.

The **Coast Guard House** (40 Ocean Rd., Narragansett, 401/789-0700, lunch 11:30 A.M., dinner 4:30 P.M. Tues.–Sat., lunch 10 A.M.–2 P.M., dinner 4–9 P.M. Sun.) has spectacular views. This is a favorite spot for brunch, as it offers an immensely varied all-you-can-eat buffet with Belgian waffles, omelets, seafood Newburg, sausage, and so on. There's nothing especially gourmet about the food, but it's an enjoyable spot for an outing. The restaurant occupies a former lifesaving station that adjoins the towers of the old Narragansett Casino.

Ethnic Fare

Many locals swear by the spicy and subtly seasoned Szechuan and Mandarin cooking at **Ocean View Chinese Restaurant** (Mariner Sq., 140 Point Judith Rd., Narragansett, 401/783-9070, 5–10 P.M. daily, $9–15). House favorites include hot-and-sour tofu with brown rice and string beans with pork. Alas, the place lacks somewhat in service and ambience, but in a region with few Asian restaurants, it's a reliable pick.

A spicy twist on a traditional Irish pub, **Pancho O'Malley's** (Mariner Sq., 140 Point Judith Rd., Narragansett, 401/782-2299, 11:30 A.M.–1 A.M. daily, $6–14) serves a mix of Mexican and Irish dishes, margaritas, and Irish stouts. As you might guess, it's as popular as a drinking hole as it is for food, and the place especially rocks late on weekends. Earlier in the evening, it's a good choice for families.

Quick Bites

A cozy hole-in-the-wall that serves excellent breakfast and lunch fare, **Dad's Place** (142 Boon St., Narragansett, 401/783-6420, under $5) serves heavenly chorizo omelets, fluffy pancakes, and a wide range of sandwiches at lunchtime. Locals are crazy about **Crazy Burger Cafe & Juice Bar** (144 Boon St., Narragansett, 401/783-1810, www.crazyburger.com, 8 A.M.–8 P.M. Sun.–Thurs., 8 A.M.–9 P.M. Fri.–Sat., $4–11), a hopping joint serving pancakes and "breakfast pizzas" for cheap along with uniformly high-quality meat and veggie burgers. Flavors include "quirky Cajun" and "hummabouli."

The **Station House** (Rte. 138, West

Kingston, 401/783-0800, 7:30 A.M.–1:45 P.M. Mon. and Wed.–Fri., 8 A.M.–12:45 P.M. Sat.–Sun., closed Tues., $3–8) is just a couple of miles west of the University of Rhode Island campus, making it a good option in the western part of the state. This cheerful eatery serves a nice range of breakfast and lunch foods, including heavenly cinnamon buns, fluffy omelets, prodigious burgers, and a very nice Reuben sandwich.

The stainless steel **Tucker's Wickford Diner** (64 Brown St., Wickford, 401/294-9058, $3–9) is a retro greasy spoon with similarly delicious food. It generally opens at 4:30 or 5 A.M. and closes at 2 P.M. Meatball grinders, clam rolls, burgers, steak and eggs, corned-beef hash, fluffy banana pancakes, and fish-and-chips are among the more popular offerings.

Waterfront Grille (83 Brown St., Wickford, 401/294-1150, $4–10) is an excellent spot for breakfast, bagels, deli sandwiches, pastries, coffees, and early dinner (it's open until 8 P.M.). This casual storefront eatery has counter service and a simple but pleasant ambience with lots of hanging plants. The best feature is the small outdoor dining area overlooking the many sailboats and yachts in Wickford's harbor.

More than a few Rhode Islanders believe that █ Aunt Carrie's (1240 Ocean Rd., Narragansett, 401/783-7930, www.auntcarries ri.com, call for hours, $9–22) serves not only the best clam cakes and chowders in South County but the best in the state—maybe even in southern New England. This handsome little casual eatery on the bay in Point Judith, with an American flag hoisted high on a flagpole over the roof, looks directly over a tidal pond, the turf of a few graceful swans. There is ample outdoor and indoor seating, but its immense popularity results in lines most summer days—although a bring-your-own-booze policy makes the wait a little more pleasant for some patrons. After putting your name on the invariably long list for a table, you can wander around the attractive grounds or even hike down by the beach, which is nearby. The brightly painted dining room buzzes with chatter every night as satisfied customers gorge on fried lobsters

with drawn butter, whole-belly fried clams, and other fruits of the sea.

Iggy's Doughboys (1157 Point Judith Rd., Narragansett, 401/783-5608, http://iggysdoughboys.com, 11 A.M.–10 P.M. Sun.–Thurs., 11 A.M.–11 P.M.Fri.–Sat. summer, 11 A.M.–7 P.M. Sun.–Thurs., 11 A.M.–8 P.M. Fri.–Sat. other seasons, $3–11) might also serve the best clam cakes in the state—it's certainly fun to test them out against the many reputable competitors around Rhode Island. Standard fare includes chowder, stuffies, fried scallops, the famous Iggy Burger with sautéed peppers and onions, tuna grinders, meatball subs, and chicken wings. Iggy's also specializes in greasy little fried doughboys, which are dusted liberally with powdered sugar. Check the website for coupons discounting several items on the menu.

Gourmet Goods and Picnic Supplies

It's hard to find fresher seafood than at **Champlin's Seafood** (256 Great Island Rd., Galilee, 401/783-3152, 11 A.M.–9 P.M. daily), which overlooks the fishing fleet and harbor at this famous port. You can dine here on the open-air deck, or buy fresh fish from the retail market and cook it back at your rental. There's also a branch in Wickford (170 Main St., 401/295-4600).

INFORMATION AND SERVICES
Visitor Information

The **Narragansett Chamber of Commerce** (36 Ocean Rd., 401/783-7121, www.narragansettri.com/chamber) runs a visitors center in the Towers in Narragansett Pier. For info on Wickford and the rest of North Kingstown, contact **North Kingstown Chamber of Commerce** (8045 Post Rd., North Kingstown, 401/295-5566, www.northkingstown.com).

Media

This part of South County produces two newspapers: *The Standard-Times* (401/789-9744, www.ricentral.com) and the *Narragansett*

Times (401/789-9744, www.ricentral.com), which comes out twice weekly.

GETTING AROUND

U.S. 1 runs west–east near the shore to Narragansett and then north near the bay through North Kingstown. Route 4 cuts northwest from it and joins I-95 as the most direct route from South County to Providence and points north. For taxis, contact **Eagle Cab** (Narragansett, 401/783-0007 or 800/339-2970). You can also rent a car from **Enterprise** (6980 Post Rd., North Kingstown, 800/736-8222, www.enterprise.com).

South Kingstown and Wakefield

In keeping with Rhode Island's confusing place names, South Kingstown lies about six miles south of North Kingstown and includes the village of Kingston (not to be confused with Kingstown) and Wakefield (not to be confused with Wickford). Get a bird's-eye view of the territory at the **Wooden Observation Tower** (3481 Kingstown Rd., U.S. 1 and Rte. 138, dawn–dusk, free). The 100-foot-tall tower with an open-air observation deck sits on one of the county's higher points, MacSparran Hill, and affords stunning views of Narragansett Bay, Conanicut and Aquidneck Islands (and the bridges that connect them), and the South County shoreline.

KINGSTON AND THE UNIVERSITY OF RHODE ISLAND

West on Route 138, the county seat **Kingston** was formerly known as Little Rest, some say because during colonial times it was home to several taverns providing room and board. It's one of the state's most famous towns today because it's home to the **University of Rhode Island** (URI, www.uri.edu), founded in 1892 as Rhode Island College of Agriculture and Mechanic Arts. URI has a student body of about 11,000 undergrads and 3,000 graduate students. One notable facility on the campus is the **Thomas M. Ryan Center,** a 200,000-square-foot athletic arena that seats 9,000 and hosts major sporting events and big-name concerts.

The former athletic center, the Keaney Gymnasium, was converted into the **New England Basketball Hall of Fame** in 2002, part of the larger **International Scholar-Athlete Hall of Fame** (Feinstein Bldg., 3045 Kingstown Rd./Rte. 108, 401/874-2375, www. internationalsport.com, 10 A.M.–5 P.M. Mon.–Fri., 10 A.M.–3 P.M. Sat., free), a quirky museum on the campus that honors those who "exemplify the scholar-athlete ideal." Its egalitarian list of honorees includes Jackie Robinson, George H. W. Bush, and Plato.

The public is also welcome to visit the **URI Fine Arts Center Galleries** (105 Upper College Rd., 401/792-2775, www.uri.edu/artgalleries, free), which include the Main, Photography, and Corridor exhibit spaces. The hours for each vary, so it's best to phone ahead or visit the website.

Apart from URI, Kingston is notable for its small but pretty village of Federal and colonial buildings. Across from campus stands the **Pettaquamscutt Historical Society** (2636 Kingstown Rd./Rte. 138, 401/783-1328, www. pettaquamscutt.org, 1–4 P.M. Tues., Thurs., and Sat., suggested donation $5 adults, $3 seniors and students, free for children under 12). The dignified granite-block building dates to 1792, when it was built as the Washington County Jail; a cell block was added in 1858. The historical society took ownership in 1960, and today as a museum it contains household goods and tools from the period, vintage toys and clothing, Native American arrowheads, and other implements; you can also tour the old cell block, which looks much as it did when in use. The society also houses a genealogical library, and anyone is welcome to visit and conduct research.

Just down the street, the 1802 **Helme House** (2587 Kingstown Rd., 401/783-2195, www. southcountyart.org, 1–5 P.M. Wed.–Sun., free), one of the town's most stately Federal buildings, is headquarters to the South County Art Association. Art classes are given, and there's a small gallery with frequently changing exhibits. Also headquartered here is the esteemed Potter's Cooperative Gallery, which includes a number of local photographers, sculptors, painters, and potters.

The historical society is also restoring the **Hale House** (2625A Commodore Perry Hwy./Rte. 1, South Kingstown), the former summer home of Boston minister, abolitionist, and short-story author Edward Everett Hale. Little known today, he was a literary lion in the Civil War era, with broad influence on American thought and letters. (His best-known short story is 1863's "The Man Without a Country," which helped shore up Union resolve after President Lincoln's assassination in the middle of the war.) In 2008 the exterior of the home was stripped down to the original clapboards and painted red to the match its color in the 1890s, when it was known as the "Red House." Next will be a restoration of the interior, which will be open to visitors for tours.

Kingston has had two impressive courthouses through the years, and both still function in different capacities. The earlier is an immense 1775 structure that served on a rotating basis 1776–1791 as the Rhode Island State House, now the **Kingston Free Library** (2605 Kingstown Rd., 401/783-8254, 10 A.M.–6 P.M. Mon.–Tues., 10 A.M.–8 P.M. Wed., noon–8 P.M. Thurs., 10 A.M.–5 P.M. Fri.–Sat. Sept. 7–June 20, 10 A.M.–6 P.M. Mon.–Tues., 10 A.M.–8 P.M. Wed., noon–8 P.M. Thurs., 10 A.M.–5 P.M. Fri., 9 A.M.–noon Sat. June 21–Sept. 6). The building can be mistaken for a construction of the late 19th century; indeed, the mansard roof and central Gothic Revival tower were added in the 1890s, as was much of the ornamentation. The building has a beautiful interior, completely renovated in the 1990s.

Down the road is the second former courthouses, now the **Courthouse Center for the Arts** (3481 Kingstown Rd., 401/782-1018, www.courthousearts.org, 10 A.M.–4 P.M. Mon.–Fri., 10 A.M.–2 P.M. Sat., free), a tall and imposing granite structure built in 1896.

It houses art galleries and a shop selling locally produced arts and crafts, as well as classrooms for various visual and performing arts workshops. This is also the site of music concerts throughout the year.

Nearby is one of two Rhode Island train stations served by Amtrak, **Kingston Railroad Station** (1 Railroad Ave., off Kingstown Rd./Rte. 138, www.trainweb.org/kin, 6 A.M.–10:45 P.M. daily). This handsome clapboard building, which is on the National Register of Historic Places, was built in 1875 in the stick Victorian style with influences of a European chalet.

PEACE DALE

At the intersection of Routes 138 and 108, follow Route 108 south into Peace Dale, a prosperous old factory town that is now a bit quiet but which has some impressive stone factory buildings. The mill buildings once made up the Peace Dale Manufacturing Company, which began turning out fine woolens and shawls around 1800 and employed about 750 workers during the mill's heyday. Among the many impressive structures throughout the town, notable buildings include the **Peace Dale Public Library** (1057 Kingstown Rd., 401/789-1555, 9 A.M.–8 P.M. Mon.–Tues., 9 A.M.–6 P.M. Wed.–Thurs., 9 A.M.–5 P.M. Fri.–Sat. Sept. 7–June 20, 9 A.M.–8 P.M. Mon., 9 A.M.–6 P.M. Tues.–Thurs., 9 A.M.–5 P.M. Fri., 9 A.M.–1 P.M. Sat. June 21–Sept. 6), a majestic Richardsonian Romanesque building designed in 1891 by Frank W. Angell; the stone structure is notable for its huge chimneys, grand porte cochere, and conical turret. Inside what was originally an auditorium you can see a detailed reproduction of *Cantoria,* a work by Italian Renaissance sculptor Lucca della Robbia, carved into a plaster frieze. On the grounds of the library is *The Weaver,* a bronze relief sculpture executed by Lincoln Memorial sculptor Daniel Chester French in 1920.

Nearly across the street you'll find the **Museum of Primitive Art and Culture** (1058 Kingstown Rd., 401/783-5711, www.primitiveartmuseum.org, 10 A.M.–2 P.M. Wed., suggested donation $2), which originally contained the mill's post office, company store, and housing for mill workers. Today it's South County's oldest museum, containing a collection of archaeological and ethnological materials culled from all over the world, including pottery, weapons, tools, and blankets.

WAKEFIELD

Continue from Peace Dale down Route 108 into **Wakefield**, the administrative center of South Kingstown, home of the stately 1877 **South Kingstown Town Hall** (180 High St., 401/789-9331, www.southkingstownri.com, 8:30 A.M.–4:30 P.M. Mon.–Fri.). Here you'll find the usual array of prosaic shopping centers and strip malls, but follow Main Street west away from U.S. 1 into downtown and you'll find a more attractive stretch of mostly late Victorian and early-20th-century shop fronts and buildings. One notable structure is the **Campus Cinema** (297 Main St.), built as an opera house in the 1890s. The Saugatucket River passes through the center of town, and a number of businesses have opened here within the last decade in an attempt to revitalize the downtown area and make it a destination. The town has also working hard to develop a greenway along this historic river, once industrial and polluted. It is now lined by a walking path that is nice for strolling and bird-watching.

Wakefield lies just northwest of Narragansett and north of Charlestown; a short drive east or south will return you to U.S. 1.

ENTERTAINMENT AND EVENTS

South County has a lot going on in performing arts and nightclubbing, especially considering that the area is in no way urban, but much of this activity doesn't really start up until late spring and dies just as quickly by October. The one area institution that keeps South County lively during the colder months is URI, which presents musical and theatrical events throughout the school year and whose students keep several bars hopping year-round.

Bars and Clubs

There are dozens of mostly low-key taverns along the shore in South County, and a few spots inland in Westerly and Wakefield are popular with students of nearby URI. Especially in summer, the bars and taverns near the shore can get pretty wild, with a mix of summer-break college students, youngish visitors and vacationers, and gruff fishers, depending on the venue. Singles on the make will find plenty of cruisy hangouts, although South County has no specifically gay nightlife. In Misquamicut, where you'll find the greatest number of beach hotels and motels, much of the action takes places in bars at the resorts themselves. You can hear live music at a number of places, and sports pubs are also relatively common.

A favorite hangout for locals in Wakefield, **Casey's** (191 Old Tower Hill Rd., Wakefield, 401/789-9714, restaurant 11 A.M.–midnight daily, bar 11 A.M.–1 A.M. daily) is a spacious tavern that's a short drive from the beaches and serves a long menu of American, Mexican, and Italian fare. There's karaoke on Sunday and live music on Wednesday and Saturday. A hugely popular nightspot with college students and everybody else in South County with a yen for microbrews and imported liquors from all over the world, the **Mews Tavern** (456 Main St., Wakefield, 401/783-9370, 11 A.M.–1 A.M. daily) may just be the most crowded building in southern Rhode Island on weekends.

For bigger shows, the spanking new **Thomas M. Ryan Center** (1 Lincoln Almond Plaza, Kingston, 401/788-3200, www.theryancenter.com) hosts national performers like Bob Dylan and John Mayer in an 8,000-seat auditorium. Inside a Romanesque granite building, the **Courthouse Center for the Arts** (3481 Kingstown Rd., West Kingston, 401/782-1018, www.courthousearts.org) features indie films and community theater.

Performing Arts

Many of the arts events in South County revolve around URI, including the **University of Rhode Island Theatre** (Fine Arts Bldg., Kingston, 401/874-5843, www.uri.edu/artsci/

the), which presents four plays a year, including musicals and classic works. The **Music Department** (Fine Arts Bldg., 401/874-2431, www.uri.edu/artsci/mus) presents a wide range of works during the school year, including choral programs, classical concerts, and live jazz. The **South County Chamber Singers** (401/783-0943, www.sccsingers.org) perform at different venues around the area.

The **SC Players Children's Theatre** (401/783-6110) performs year-round and hosts a Children's Theatre Camp during the summer for kids ages 5–8, and then for ages 9–13.

Festivals and Events

In mid-June the **National Guard Air Show** (Quonset Air Museum, North Kingstown, 401/294-9540) features high-flying displays of several exciting planes, including fighter jets and bombers. Many planes are also exhibited on the ground and can be toured up close. In early October, head to the South County Museum in Narragansett for the annual **Octoberfest and Apple Pie Contest** (401/783-5400).

SHOPPING

Near URI, **Kingston Hill Store** (2528 Kingston Rd., Kingston, Rte. 138, Kingston, 401/792-8662, 10 A.M.–5 P.M. daily) is a fine source of rare and antiquarian books, with quite a few titles on Rhode Island history. A few miles west of URI, off Route 138, **Peter Pots Pottery** (494 Glen Rock Rd., West Kingston, 401/783-2350, 10 A.M.–4 P.M. Mon.–Sat., 1–4 P.M. Sun.) has been an acclaimed shop and gallery since the 1940s; it's a source of beautiful yet functional stoneware, including coffee mugs, table accessories, wine decanters, lamps, and pitchers. The showroom is set inside a circa-1700 stone mill.

Thomas Ladd Pottery (352 High St., Peace Dale, 401/782-0050, 9 A.M.–6 P.M. Tues.–Sat., or by appointment) is a nice little shop showing both contemporary and traditional styles in a quiet residential neighborhood.

Downtown Wakefield has a smattering of antiques shops and other independent stores and boutiques. The headquarters and outlet store of the noted mail-order company **Kenyon Consumer Products** (1425 Kingston Rd./Rte. 108, Peace Dale, 401/792-3705, www.kenyon-consumer.com, 10 A.M.–5 P.M. Mon.–Fri., 10 A.M.–6 P.M. Sat., noon–5 P.M. Sun. during the holiday season) is a top seller of discounted outdoor gear, clothing, and sporting goods. The **Purple Cow** (205 Main St., Wakefield, 401/789-2389, 10 A.M.–6 P.M. Mon.–Wed., 9 A.M.–8 P.M. Thurs.–Fri., 10 A.M.–6 P.M. Sat., noon–5 P.M. Sun.) is an offbeat gallery with custom-made clothing, jewelry, greeting cards, and other gifts. At **Zero Wampum** (161 Old Tower Hill Rd., Wakefield, 401/789-7172), you'll find a vast selection of clothing, household decor, cards, jewelry, and gifts. Wakefield's **Hera Gallery** (23 North Rd., 401/789-1488, www.heragallery.org, 1–5 P.M. Wed.–Fri.) is a nonprofit artist's cooperative filled with gifts, crafts, and knickknacks worth taking home.

Located in a former art deco gas station, **Glass Station** (318 Main St., Wakefield, 401/788-2500, www.ebenhortonglass.com, 10 A.M.–5 P.M. Tues.–Sat.)—get it?—is now the studio-gallery of glassblower Eben Horton, who creates vases inspired by ocean waves and whimsical glass fish. Inside an old dining car, **Kiddie Closet** (329 Main St., Wakefield, 401/783-8680, 10 A.M.–5 P.M. daily) is heaven to cash-strapped parents with rack after rack of sports clothing, strollers, books, and more. In the 19th-century historic home of a blacksmith, **Fayerweather House** (1859 Mooresfield Rd./Rte. 138, South Kingstown, 401/789-9072, www.fayerweatherhouse.8m.net, 10 A.M.–4 P.M. Tues.–Sat. mid-May–Dec.) is now a craft center selling hooked rugs, woven baskets, and other handmade items.

SPORTS AND RECREATION
Beaches

A rather narrow stretch of South Kingstown cuts down to the ocean between Charlestown and Narragansett; here you'll find a pair of excellent beaches. By far the most popular is **East Matunuck State Beach** (off 950

Succotash Rd., 401/789-8585), which has a 700-car parking lot, lifeguards, and full changing facilities. This half-mile beach is close to **South Kingstown Town Beach** (Matunuck Beach Rd., 401/789-9301, www.riparks.com/eastmatunuck.htm), which is just over 1,000 feet long but has sports facilities, grills and a picnic grove, changing rooms with hot showers, a playground, and other good stuff.

Bicycling

Taking advantage of South County's mostly flat topography is the impressive **William C. O'Neill Bike Path** (www.southcounty.com/bikepath), which runs six miles from Kingston Amtrak station, just off Route 138, to Route 108 in Wakefield near the Narragansett border. In late 2010 construction on the last phase of the path had started, to continue it another two miles to the South County Museum near Narragansett Pier. To keep up with the trail's status and learn more about sites along the way, visit the website.

You can also check for maps and more info on biking in Rhode Island on the website of the state Department of Transportation (www.dot.state.ri.us/bikeri).

Bikes can be rented at **Narragansett Bikes** (1153 Boston Neck Rd., Rte. 1A, Narragansett, 401/782-4444, http://nbxbikes.com, 10 A.M.–6 P.M. Mon.–Fri., 10 A.M.–5 P.M. Sat., noon–5 P.M. Sun.). Rates are around $25–35 per day, $100–120 per week.

Ice-Skating

At URI's Ryan Center, the snazzy **Boss Ice Arena** (1 Lincoln Almond Plaza, URI campus, Kingston, 401/788-3200, www.bossicearena.com, $6) is open to the public daily for skating and pickup games for ice hockey.

Tennis

The town of South Kingstown has public tennis courts at several of its town parks, including **Brousseau Park** (Succotash Rd.), **Old Mountain Field** (Kingstown Rd.), and **West Kingston Park** (Rte. 138). Call South Kingstown's recreation department (401/789-9301) for details.

Golf

A terrific short nine-holer is the new **Rose Hill Golf Club** (222 Rose Hill Rd., Wakefield, 401/788-1088, www.rosehillri.com, $13–20).

Fairly close to the URI campus, **Laurel Lane Golf Course** (309 Laurel Lane, West Kingston, 401/783-3844, www.laurellanecountryclub.com, $40–50) is a short but pleasant 18-hole course; it also has a lounge and snack bar. This is an exceptionally well-cared-for course, with beautiful greens and fairways.

ACCOMMODATIONS
$100-150

If you're looking to stay inland in the Wyoming and Hope Valley area, not far from the University of Rhode Island, consider the immaculate **Stagecoach House Inn** (1136 Main St., Wyoming, 401/539-9600 or 888/814-9600, www.stagecoachhouse.com, $129–199), a former 18th-century stagecoach inn. The hotel is just off I-95, overlooking a peaceful river, and all guest rooms—which are in a newer motor-lodge-style unit—have gas fireplaces and tubs with jets. Half a dozen golf courses are within a 10-minute drive. Continental breakfast included.

An imposing 26-room mansion with 14 airy, high-ceilinged guest rooms, many with fireplaces, **Eden Manor** (154 Post Rd., Wakefield, 401/792-8234 or 877/430-1613, www.edenmanorbandb.com, $125–175) exudes romance with its elegant antique furnishings, expansive common areas, and fragrant gardens; there's also complimentary wireless Internet. This is one of the more impressive accommodations in the South Kingstown area.

Set on a couple of acres crisscrossed by stone walls and dotted with flowering shrubs and leafy trees, **Sugarloaf Hill B&B** (607 Main St., Wakefield, 401/789-8715, www.sugarloafhillbandb.com, $110–155) contains four sunny guest rooms and a large suite with a skylight and its own private deck; one room has a fireplace. Two guest rooms have private baths, and another has a separate bathroom down the hall. The decor in the guest rooms and common spaces is eclectic and charming. Full breakfast is included, and it's a short walk into downtown Wakefield.

$150-250

One of only a handful of chain properties in South County, the **Holiday Inn South County** (3009 Tower Hill Rd./U.S. 1, at Rte. 138, 401/789-1051 or 877/805-9008, www. holiday-inn.com, $199–279) sits high on a hill by the Wooden Observation Tower on U.S. 1. It's representative of the chain, with pleasant if unremarkably furnished rooms. The location is extremely convenient to URI, as well as to South County beaches and Newport. The 107 rooms are spread over four floors, and there are a full-service restaurant, a lounge, business services, a pool, a pair of volleyball courts, and a fitness center. The hotel books up completely for many weekends during the school year—parents' weekend, homecoming, and others.

Camping

Inland a few miles but along a glorious freshwater body, **Worden's Pond Family Campground** (416A Worden's Pond Rd., Wakefield, 401/789-9113, www.worden-pondcampground.com, May–mid-Oct., $35 per night) is a 65-acre spread with about 200 campsites nestled in the woods. Amenities include showers, restrooms, fishing, swimming, and a playground. **Greenwood Hill Family Campground** (Newberry Lane, Hope Valley, 401/491-9121) occupies a pastoral, secluded setting surrounding a pond and field in quiet Hopeville. It has full RV hookups, a general store, and children's activities.

FOOD
Upscale

Meat lovers won't be disappointed by a night at **Crave Steakhouse** (333 Main St., Wakefield, 401/789-0914, www.craveseafoodsteak. com, 5–9 P.M. Wed.–Thurs., 5–10 P.M. Fri., 9 A.M.–2 P.M. and 5–10 P.M. Sat., 9 A.M.–2 P.M. and 4–9 P.M. Sun., $14–31); the kitchen grills and churns out admirable specimens of beef, lamb, and pork. Seafood is less spectacular, but the pasta dishes more than make up for it.

Creative but Casual

An attractive, somewhat upscale spot, **Pinelli's Cucina and Twist** (Rte. 108, South Kingstown, 401/789-5300, 4–9 P.M. Mon.–Wed., 4–10 P.M. Thurs., 4–11 P.M. Fri.–Sat., 4–9:30 P.M. Sun., $10–16) serves a nice mix of traditional and contemporary Italian favorites, including chicken portobello with herbs and white wine over linguine, penne with pink vodka sauce, and shrimp *fra diavolo*. Slightly more adventurous specials are served up at the nearby **◖ Cheeky Monkey Cafe** (21 Pier Marketplace, South Kingstown, 401/788-3111, www.cheekymonkeycafe.com, 5:30–10 P.M. Wed.–Sun., $18–32). True to its name, the spot is filled with cheeky appointments like faux leopard-skin carpeting and monkey motifs. The menu runs the gamut, from delicious calamari with spicy prosciutto and pepper sauce to sesame-seared tuna with lemongrass.

Kabuki (91 Old Tower Hill Rd., Wakefield, 401/788-0777, 11 A.M.–1 A.M. Mon.–Fri., noon–1 A.M. Sat.–Sun., $15) is a sophisticated Asian bistro, serving creative Japanese food, sushi, and a smattering of Thai and Vietnamese dishes. Try the Tuna Amazing; it lives up to its name.

A longtime favorite for seafood, **Hanson's Landing** (210 Salt Pond Rd., Wakefield, 401/782-0210, 11:30 A.M.–10 P.M. daily, $7–18) overlooks a marina just south of downtown Wakefield off U.S. 1. This is a casual pub with a nautical feel, but the food is a cut above what's typical of a casual eatery. You might start with the pear-walnut salad or steamed Prince Edward Island mussels before moving on to baked cod stuffed with lobster and topped with Mornay sauce. There are plenty of sandwiches too, from bacon-Swiss burgers to pesto-shrimp on French bread, and it's a fun spot to catch live music many evenings.

Pizza, Pub Grub, and Seafood

Few such lovely buildings were ever constructed for more mundane purposes than the **Pump House** (1464 Kingstown Rd., Rte. 108, Peace Dale, 401/789-4944, www. pumphouseri.com, 4–10 P.M. Mon.–Sat., noon–9 P.M. Sun., $8–19), which dates to 1888 and originally served as the pumping station for the water system that served Peace Dale, Wakefield, and Narragansett. Today the elegant stone building with a towering chimney contains this rather simple restaurant, a popular option for families, that serves traditional American food such as fish-and-chips, steaks, and chowders. There's also an extensive salad bar.

OK, so you might not think to eat dinner at a bowling alley, but **Camden's** (756 Kingstown Rd., Wakefield, 401/782-2328, 11 A.M.–10 P.M. Mon.–Sat., noon–10 P.M. Sun., $8–16) adjoins Old Mountain Lanes and serves a full range of no-surprises American fare, including prime rib, seafood chowders, fish-and-chips, and surf-and-turf plates. A coffee shop also serves three meals a day from 5:30 A.M.

The quintessential house of good cheer, **Mews Tavern** (456 Main St., Wakefield, 401/783-9370, 11 A.M.–1 A.M. daily, $7–16) serves outstanding burgers along with dozens of other hearty rib-sticking dishes: scallops carbonara, seafood pie pizzas (scallops, shrimp, crab, smoked salmon, and a blend of cheeses), stuffed portobellos, Cajun steaks, teriyaki chicken wings, and beef-and-bean burritos. Of course, plenty of people descend on this rambling faux log-cabin ski lodge in the center of downtown Wakefield for the huge liquor list, including 70 microbrews on tap, more than 200 single-malt scotches, and three dozen tequilas.

On the road to Jerusalem, **Cap'n Jack's** (706 Succotash Rd., Wakefield, 401/789-4556, 11 A.M.–8:45 P.M. Mon.–Fri., 11 A.M.–9 P.M. Sat.–Sun., $7–17) has been serving big portions of seafood and pasta since 1972—the cavernous restaurant is always packed, and nobody seems to mind the rather dull decor. What you come for is lobster bisque with a hint of sherry, broiled scallops in a lemon-butter sauce, shrimp *fra diavolo*, baked scrod with mussels, and a few nonfish items such as gnocchi with meatballs and chicken teriyaki. The restaurant

also makes its own pastries and desserts, which are just as hefty as the seafood platters. If you're renting a cottage or staying somewhere with a kitchen, Cap'n Jack's has a takeout counter.

Ethnic Fare

A great deli specializing in Middle Eastern and Lebanese food, **Pick Pockets** (230 Old Tower Hill Rd., Wakefield, 401/792-3360, 10 A.M.–9 P.M. Mon.–Fri., 10 A.M.–8 P.M. Sat., 11 A.M.–5 P.M. Sun., $4–10) stays open through the dinner hour each evening. It's a good place to pick up sandwich supplies and other goodies.

Gourmet Goods and Picnic Supplies

Stop by the **Bagel Bakery** (11 Main St., Wakefield, 401/783-9700, 6 A.M.–6 P.M. Mon.–Fri., 6 A.M.–5 P.M. Sat.–Sun., under $6) for fresh-baked goods, including 15 types of bagels accompanied by many kinds of cream-cheese spreads, plus deli and wrap sandwiches, breakfast fare, chais and lattes, and cookies.

Bringing the kids to **Sweenor's Chocolates** (21 Charles St., Wakefield, 401/783-4433, 9:30 A.M.–5:30 P.M. Mon.–Sat., noon–5 P.M. Sun.; Garden City Shopping Center, 140 Hillside Rd., Cranston, 401/942-2720, noon–5 P.M. Mon.–Fri., noon–6 P.M. Sat.–Sun.) ranks among South County's great shopping traditions. Family-owned for four generations, these shops sell 25 flavors of hard candy, an enormous variety of hand-dipped chocolates and confections, and cream and butter fudge of every permutation.

INFORMATION AND SERVICES
Visitor Information

For information on all of South County, contact the **South County Tourism Council** (4808 Tower Hill Rd./U.S. 1, Wakefield, 401/789-4422 or 800/548-4662, www. southcountyri.com). To learn more about South Kingstown, contact **South Kingstown Chamber of Commerce** (230 Old Tower Hill Rd., Wakefield, 401/783-2801, www.skchamber.com).

BLOCK ISLAND

The gray cliffs that rise from the waves of Block Island's north shore are conspicuously naked. If this were another island within such easy grasp of both Boston and New York, they would be capped with sprawling homes of moneyed summer folk. But only the green fringe of conservation land tops the cliffs of Clay Head, the first sight that you are likely to see of the island coming over on the ferry from Point Judith. It's a fitting introduction to an island that counts conservation land as almost half of its area, the result of a dogged campaign by island residents eager to preserve Block Island's sense of tranquility.

About 200 years passed before the European colonists on Block Island built a proper dock to accommodate mainland visitors. Perhaps they were staving off the inevitable. A little more than a century later, Block Island has been reluctantly colonized by the overflow of visitors from the Vineyard and the Hamptons, and the main street in Old Harbor can get crowded in summer. Every year, 15,000 visitors descend on the pear-shaped 6.5- by 3.5-mile isle in high season. Especially during the shoulder season, however, you can still find deserted beaches, quiet country roads, and dramatic vistas of clay and limestone that plummet 250 feet to the waves below.

The geological result of debris left in the wake of the last glacial recession, the island is strewn rather artfully with granite boulders, many of which are used to make up the miles of stone walls separating former sheep pastures and agricultural fields. Most ferries dock at Old Harbor, within a short walk of several fine beaches and the island's only significant concentration of hotels, restaurants, and businesses. New Harbor,

HIGHLIGHTS

LOOK FOR ◖ TO FIND RECOMMENDED SIGHTS, ACTIVITIES, DINING, AND LODGING.

◖ **Southeast Light:** Built in 1873, this Victorian-style lighthouse is one of the most photographed in New England. Any time of year, it's worth walking the grounds, and in summer you can actually climb the 50-foot staircase to the top for a ravishing view of Block Island and surrounding waters (page 244).

◖ **North Lighthouse:** Block Island's other beautiful lighthouse, at the northern tip of the island, requires an easy and scenic half-mile walk from the parking area and contains a small but interesting maritime museum (page 246).

◖ **Crescent Beach:** No visit to Block Island is complete without a visit to one of its pristine white-sand beaches; this two-mile stretch just north of Old Harbor is the prettiest and also has the most comprehensive facilities (page 249).

◖ **Sailing in Block Island Sound:** Block Island is one of the great yachting centers of the East Coast, and these waters are ideal for a sail, whether you rent a boat or bring your own (page 252).

◖ **Fishing in Block Island Sound:** If you've always dreamed of hauling in a prize bonito or mackerel, here's your chance. The fishing in Block Island Sound, whether surf casting from the beach or fishing from a private or charter boat, is outstanding year-round (page 253).

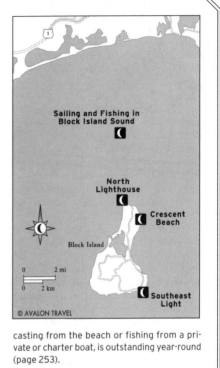

BLOCK ISLAND

---

a couple of miles away, welcomes just one ferry but is also a large marina with slips for hundreds of yachts and sailboats.

That's mostly what passes for civilization—which is just the way many returning guests like it. Once on island time, they lapse into a languid routine of sunbathing and leisurely bike rides, perhaps broken up with a hike or kayak paddle through conservation land. The overriding attitude is relaxed and even a bit funky, with the only sense of exclusivity the proud preservation of nature and wildlife—this is an island that's absent of airs or the crass commercialism that can so mar a small and highly desirable getaway. The ocean may keep battering it and developers may eye it with

avarice, but Block Island possesses an indefatigable resilience and the promise of uncommon natural beauty for decades to come.

HISTORY

Narragansett Indians occupied the island they called Manisses (MAN-iss-eez) for many centuries before Italian explorer Giovanni da Verrazano first sighted it. Reporting its character to be similar to the Greek island of Rhodes, he inadvertently inspired what would become the name of the entire state. The current and rather inelegant moniker traces to Dutchman Adriaen Block, who visited in 1614. About 50 years later, a group of 16 British colonial families bought and settled what was then a territory within Massachusetts.

From the beginning, Block Island's history has been one of hardship and violence. During its first century, pirates, privateers, and Frenchmen invaded the island regularly, robbing and terrorizing islanders at will. (It's still rumored that no less a seadog than Captain Kidd buried treasure on the north shore.) During the Revolutionary War, General George Washington had all of the islanders' livestock shipped to the mainland to keep it out of the hands of British ships. During the War of 1812, residents turned around and sold goods and produce to the enemy British.

Block Island's relative autonomy continued well into the 19th century, maintained by its treacherous waters and lack of a suitable harbor. In fact, it's estimated that about half of all the shipwrecks in New England have occurred off Block Island—the total is roughly 500. A true anchorage wasn't created until 1878, when Old Harbor was born. That spurred a frenzied tourism boom, when its fame as "Bermuda of the North" spurred the construction of leviathan wood-frame hotels with sweeping mansard roofs, towering turrets, and long wraparound porches. In 1900, New Harbor was finally established at nearby Great Salt Pond when engineers dredged a permanent channel connecting it to the sea.

Almost as soon as it became popular, however, its brief fame as a tourist destination plummeted, with tough years following the Depression and World War II. It wasn't until the renewed popularity of New England's coastal islands and a nationwide embrace of historic preservation took hold, beginning in the 1970s, that Block Island began drawing major summer crowds again.

PLANNING YOUR TIME

The local tourism board goes out of its way to promote the island as a year-round destination, and the effort is more than just a marketing ploy. Granted, few hotels and even fewer restaurants remain open through the colder winter months, but the island possesses a brooding, rugged beauty at this time, and lines are nonexistent.

Spring is a breathtakingly scenic season on Block Island, with even more devotees than fall. In part because of the absence of hardwood forest, there's less foliage drama in fall than in spring, when flower beds burst and beach shrubs and grasses turn emerald green. It is also prime season for bird-watching, when hundreds of species pass through on their way north to summer in Canada.

Last, and obviously not least, there's summer—*the* time to visit the island for the majority of visitors. Just about every business is open, and certain activities, such as **fishing** and **sailing,** are ideal. Of course, in summer you'll pay dearly for accommodations, especially on weekends, and meals, and you may endure long lines at the ferry. But there's no denying the infectious joy of summering on Block Island.

Sights

What few formal sightseeing opportunities you'll find here evoke Block Island's topsy-turvy history of duplicitous privateers, rogue pirates, and brave seafarers (great ill-gotten treasures allegedly lie under the island's dunes and hills, perhaps even one buried by the infamous Captain Kidd). It doesn't take long to make a quick drive of the island, which is only about 10 square miles. Even on a bike you can tour all of the major points of interest in one day.

OLD HARBOR

Most visitors begin their explorations of Block Island with a jaunt around Old Harbor—allowing minimal time for browsing shops, you can easily tour this charming waterfront commercial district in an hour or two. Businesses are concentrated along Water Street, which sweeps alongside the harbor-front; several lanes running perpendicular also contain a smattering of shops and eateries.

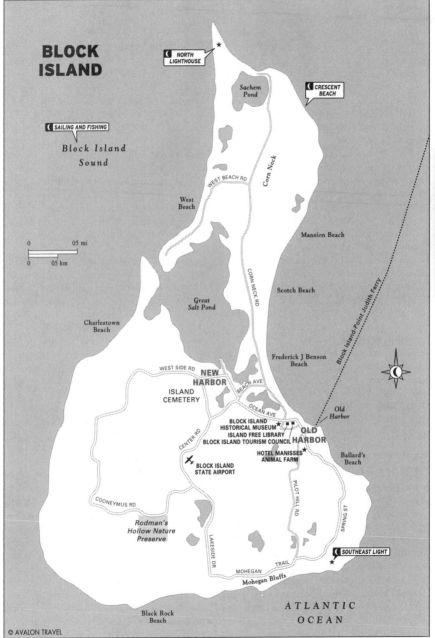

BLOCK ISLAND

BLOCK ISLAND

NORTH LIGHTHOUSE

CRESCENT BEACH

Sachem Pond

SAILING AND FISHING

Block Island Sound

Corn Neck

WEST BEACH RD

West Beach

Mansion Beach

CORN NECK RD

Scotch Beach

0   05 mi
0   05 km

Great Salt Pond

Charlestown Beach

Frederick J Benson Beach

WEST SIDE RD   **NEW HARBOR**

BEACH AVE

Block Island-Point Judith Ferry

ISLAND CEMETERY

OCEAN AVE

Old Harbor

BLOCK ISLAND HISTORICAL MUSEUM
ISLAND FREE LIBRARY
BLOCK ISLAND TOURISM COUNCIL

OLD HARBOR

CENTER RD

HOTEL MANISSES ANIMAL FARM

Ballard's Beach

BLOCK ISLAND STATE AIRPORT

PILOT HILL RD

COONEYMUS RD

SPRING ST

Rodman's Hollow Nature Preserve

LAKESIDE DR

MOHEGAN   TRAIL

SOUTHEAST LIGHT

Mohegan Bluffs

Black Rock Beach

ATLANTIC OCEAN

© AVALON TRAVEL

For centuries, there was no harbor at all at Block Island. The U.S. government finally installed two breakwaters here in the 1870s, and Old Harbor was developed with lightning speed. Today Old Harbor is a National Historic District, one of the best preserves of Victorian seaside architecture in the country. Outside of shopping, eating, and people-watching, there's little to see and do in Old Harbor—although keep the **Island Free Library** (401/466-3233) in mind as a useful resource. Most nights during the summer season, the library presents an early-evening story hour geared toward children—a very nice event given that Block Island has no explicitly kid-oriented attractions.

Walk south (left as you leave the ferry parking lot) and you'll come to just about the only major four-way intersection in Old Harbor, at Spring, Water, and High Streets. In the traffic island stands the **Statue of Rebecca,** a monumental fountain erected in 1896 by the Women's Christian Temperance Movement. Inspired by the biblical story of Rebecca at the well, the statue was intended to encourage islanders to stay away from alcohol, a lesson few heeded then or now.

At the very southern tip of Old Harbor stood the island's most famous and immense Victorian hotel, the Ocean View, which burned down in the 1960s. On the site now stands the **Ocean View Pavilion,** which looks out toward Crescent Beach and the ocean. It's a pretty spot for a stroll.

EXPLORING SOUTH FROM OLD HARBOR

South of Old Harbor on Spring Street is the distinctive **Hotel Manisses,** crowned by a squared-off central tower. Particularly if you have kids along, be sure to visit the next-door **Abrams' Animal Farm** (Spring St. and High St., 401/466-2421, www.blockislandresorts.com, dawn–dusk daily, free), an exotic animal farm with llamas, camels, Highland steers, and Zeke the zebu (a breed of cattle from India that is the oldest known), collected by the hotel's owner Justin Abrams. New animals are taking up residence here all the time—recent arrivals include a troop of ring-tailed lemurs and a giant tortoise named Tank.

⬤ Southeast Light

Perched way up on the cliffs of Mohegan Bluffs on the south shore of the island is the highest and most visible lighthouse on the New England coast, with a beam that can be seen 35 miles out to sea. The lighthouse (122 Mohegan Tr., 401/466-5009, www.lighthouse.cc/blockisoutheast, 10 A.M.–4 P.M. Sat.–Sun. late May–late June, 10 A.M.–4 P.M. daily late June–early Sept., 10 A.M.–4 P.M. Sat.–Sun. early Sept.–early Oct., free) looks more like a Gothic mansion than the traditional black-and-white tower. The brick keeper's house is attached to the structure, making the 52-foot structure look like a turret.

Part of the appeal for visitors is its history of migration. While the lighthouse was originally built 300 feet from the bluffs in 1878, erosion over time narrowed that gap to just 35 feet. In 1993 the Southeast Lighthouse Foundation spent more than $2 million to lift the entire structure on beams lubricated with Ivory soap and slide it back 300 feet from the edge. Inside, a small museum details the history of the structure and the move, supplemented by tours ($10 adults, $5 seniors and children 6–17, free for children under 6) every hour on the half-hour. At the rate the cliffs are receding, no doubt the museum will one day include exhibits about a second heroic move back from the edge.

Mohegan Bluffs to Rodman's Hollow

Just beyond the lighthouse is a small parking lot that marks the entrance to the nearly 200-foot-high Mohegan Bluffs, the stretch of delicate outcropping that extends below nearby Southeast Light. The expanse of steep, crumbly cliffs derives its name from an infamous battle that took place centuries ago between the Mohegan and the Manisses Indians. At Payne Overlook, just past the lighthouse, you can hike down wooden stairs to the beach where you'll encounter far fewer crowds than at Block Island's more central beaches.

You'll find an even more dramatic vista at Second Overlook, a few hundred yards past Payne Overlook. Few cyclists take the turn-off here, so you are likely to have the view all to yourself (although there is no beach access). On clear days you can see all the way to the tip of Long Island's Montauk Point.

Continue west along Mohegan Trail, which hugs the island's southern shore, making a right onto Lakeside Drive, then a left onto Cooneymus Road, and you'll soon come to unpaved Black Rock Road, which leads to the island's most famous nature preserve, Rodman's Hollow. All told, it's about three miles to get here from Southeast Light. The first property bought by Block Island Conservancy in the 1970s, this sunken glacial-outwash ravine has become an emblem of Block Island's crusade to preserve the island's natural spaces. A network of trails traverses the hollow and leads down the cliff to the sandy beach below. Among the trails there are some 40 different endangered species, most of the insect variety, as well as migratory birds looking for a rest on the Atlantic Flyway.

Near Rodman's Hollow, the **Smilin' Thru Greenway** is one of the more challenging hikes on the island. The trail is steep and rocky but offers some great views of the ocean. Take the trail into the greenway from the intersection of Lakeside Drive and Cooneymus Road. You can connect to Rodman's Hollow from the greenway via a signed trail at the southern section of the preserve.

West of Rodman's Hollow on West Side Road is the ancient **Island Cemetery,** where headstones mark the passing of many of Block Island's earliest families. Names such as Ball, Rose, Dodge, and Champlin appear on dozens of these markers, several of which date to the 1600s. It's a stunning location, with fine views north out over New Harbor and Great Salt Pond.

NEW HARBOR

The town's other concentration of civilization—or at least shops and restaurants—is the

yachts in New Harbor

smaller New Harbor, which is "new" only in the relative sense (it was developed in 1890s). Before this, Great Salt Pond had been a great freshwater pond, except when occasional storms breached the pond's land barrier and let in the ocean water. The breach was made permanent when a deep channel was dredged to open the new harbor. Today, especially in summer, you'll see upward of 1,500 boats moored on the one-square-mile pond.

Just inland, at the corner of Old Town Road and Ocean Avenue, you can tour the **Block Island Historical Museum** (Old Town Rd., New Harbor, 401/466-2481, blockhistory@ me.com, 10 A.M.–5 P.M. daily late June–early Sept., 10 A.M.–5 P.M. Sat.–Sun. Sept.–June, $5 adults, $3 seniors and students, free for youth and children under 16), where exhibits—both permanent and temporary—illustrate the island's fanciful and fascinating history, with particular emphasis on the primary industries, fishing and farming. There are also several rooms set up in the style of the island's heyday of Victorian tourism. This 1850s Second Empire building contains antiques donated by local families through the years. It's not a large museum, but it does well at explaining how Block Island developed into the community it is today.

NORTHERN BLOCK ISLAND

The town districts of Old and New Harbor are just under a mile apart. Between them you can head north on Corn Neck Road to tour the narrow, northern tip of Block Island.

◖ North Lighthouse

The reward for this 3-mile trip is a chance to visit the island's other great beacon, North Lighthouse (Sandy Point, north end of Corn Neck Rd., 401/466-3220, 10 A.M.–4 P.M. Sat.–Sun. June, 10 A.M.–4 P.M. daily July–Aug., 10 A.M.–4 P.M. Sat.–Sun. Sept., $2), which is 0.5 miles' walk up the beach from a small parking area. This granite beauty has stood guard above a boulder-strewn beach since 1867. It opened as a maritime museum in 1993 after many years of disuse and neglect. The exhibits inside detail the island's history of shipwrecks and dramatic rescues. A favorite time to walk along the pebbly beach to the lighthouse is at dusk, when the views of the sun setting over the horizon are magical.

In the parking area for the lighthouse, note **Settler's Rock monument,** which marks the spot where the island's first English settlers came ashore in 1661. It was placed by island residents in 1911 to mark the 250th anniversary of the colonization of the Block.

Entertainment and Events

This is not a major party island, even in high season, but you will find quite a few convivial hangouts frequented by young summer hotel employees and a fair share of islanders and visitors of all ages.

The most popular dance club is **Captain Nick's Rock-N-Roll Bar** (Ocean Ave., 401/466-5670), a rollicking spot that brings in live music, throws a lively disco night on Monday, and can drum up pretty substantial crowds on weekends. If you've spent much time in the Caribbean, you know the kind of place—overflowing with lots of kitschy pirate decor, skeletons, tiki masks, and nautical ephemera, along with plenty of

drink specials featuring Captain Morgan's rum. It tends to draw a boat-loving crowd of 30- and 40-somethings and up.

Another longtime favorite for live music is **McGovern's Yellow Kittens Tavern** (Corn Neck Rd., 401/466-5855), just around the corner, which brings in a mix of original and cover bands to perform for a somewhat younger crowd. In addition to the music, it features a pool table, darts, and video games. On the same block as Nick's, **Albion Pub** (Ocean Rd., 401/466-9990) also showcases live music as well as DJs on the weekends.

Day or night, **Ballard's Restaurant** (42

Water St., 401/466-2231, www.ballardsinn. com) on Ballard's Beach showcases live bands and singers on its beachside stage, while the beautiful people lounge and preen with cocktails and Coronas on the beach. This is definitely a see-and-be-seen crowd, drawing reinforcements yearly from the influx of young foreigners (many from Eastern Europe) who come to work in the restaurants and hotels, and the muscle-bound locals who man the fishing charters and boating tours on the nearby wharf. Finally, up the hill a short walk from Nick's, **Club Soda** (65 Connecticut Ave., 401/466-5397, www.clubsodabi.com) draws almost the polar opposite—an equally young but much more alternative crowd (think prominent tattoos, dreadlocks, and piercings) to its subterranean bar for grungy rock bands, karaoke, and cheap drinks.

In addition to the club venues, several of the larger hotels also offer entertaining places to hang out at night. The **Tap and Grille** (Water St., 401/466-2901, www.blockislandhotels. com) at the stately National Hotel offers great views over the harbor, complete with the satisfaction that comes with watching the crowds come off the ferry while you are already relaxing, drink in hand. Watch for weekly drink specials, such as a popular mojito night, along with half-price appetizers.

In **Victoria's Parlor** (Spring St., 401/466-5844, www.springhousehotel.com/victorias. htm), the decadent sitting room and lounge at the Spring House Hotel, you can order vintage port wines and cognacs among Oriental rugs and Victorian settees and armchairs. Similarly refined is the **Upstairs Parlor at the Hotel Manisses** (1 Spring St., 401/466-2421, www. blockislandresorts.com), a dark and clubby room decked in Victoriana and wicker where you can sip fine drinks and play chess.

The island also has a pair of movie theaters showing first-run films, the most interesting being the **Empire Theatre and Cafe** (Water St., 401/466-2555), a lavishly restored venue that offers live music many evenings in addition to movies. Beer and wine are served before most performances. The other option is **OceanWest Theatre** (Champlin's Resort, 401/466-2971, www.champlinsresort.com), which not only shows first-run movies at night but also runs a matinee for kids on rainy days.

FESTIVALS AND EVENTS

Block Island has a broad range of events and gatherings through most of the year. The summer season officially kicks off the first week in June with the **Taste of Block Island** weekend, featuring lots of food, drink, and entertainment specials at venues around the island. (A similar event closes the season in late September.) The **Fourth of July** is a hugely popular time on Block Island—celebrations include a grand parade through Old Harbor followed by a band concert at Nicholas Ball Park.

There are a number of races and athletic events on Block Island throughout the year, including early August's intensely challenging **Triathlon** (www.blockislandchamber.com). The Block Island Historical Society sponsors a well-attended and quite fascinating **House and Garden Tour** (401/466-2481, blockhistory@ me.com) each August, while in the middle of the month the **Block Island Art & Artisan Festival,** spanning two days, has become one of the island's most crowded and lively weekends.

In late September, antique cars parade past the Victorian hotels in the annual **BI Motoring Event.** Birders and naturalists flock to Block Island the first weekend in October for **Audubon Birding Weekend** (401/949-5454). And just when you think the island has all but shut down for the year, the weekend after Thanksgiving kicks off the **Annual Christmas Shopping Stroll,** during which several boutiques and shops display seasonal wares and gifts. That same weekend, there's a well-attended **Block Island Artist Guild Fair** held at Harbor Baptist Church.

The **Groundhog Day Census** is a fun way for islanders to gauge just how many residents are actually present on the island during the bleakest part of winter, early February. On the Saturday nearest Groundhog Day, everybody on Block Island registers with "census takers," at least some of whom are positioned at one of the few pubs on the island. In 2009

BLOCK ISLAND

the Groundhog Day Census recorded the highest tally in many years, 1,001. By the time the **St. Patrick's Day Celebration** comes and goes with some fanfare and a big party at McGovern's Yellow Kittens, Block Island's die-hards have generally sickened of the gray winter and seem eager for the spring thaw—even eager to welcome a new batch of visitors.

You can usually get the latest on upcoming events in the pages of the *Block Island Times* or by checking with the chamber of commerce.

Shopping

ART GALLERIES

There are a handful of art galleries on Block Island, a place where artists of all genres have been summering or living year-round for decades. **Greenaway Gallery** (Water St. at Fountain Sq., 401/466-5331, 10 A.M.–9 P.M. daily late May–early Sept., Sat.–Sun. early Sept.–mid-Oct.) ranks among the most respected; it is the domain of contemporary photographer and island resident Malcolm Greenaway.

Spring Street Gallery (Spring St., 401/466-5374, www.springstreetgallery.org, 10 A.M.–6 P.M. Mon.–Sat., 11 A.M.–7 P.M. Sun. late May–mid-Sept.) is an artists' co-op, with a wide range of media that includes prints, photography, jewelry, and textiles.

The best place to find a piece of the island to take home is **Island Gallery** (211 Water St., 401/466-2062, www.islandgalleryblockisland.com, 11 A.M.–5 P.M. Wed.–Mon. mid-June–early Sept.), located above the post office. It specializes in oil and watercolor paintings of local scenes by local artists in a rotating selection of two-week shows.

OTHER SHOPPING

Block Island Health and General Store (High St., 401/466-5825, 10 A.M.–6 P.M. daily year-round) is something of a cross between a massive pantry and an offbeat variety store, stocking everything from snack foods and holistic vitamins to appliances and toiletries; the store also has a fax service. You can rent TVs, video players, and movies here too.

Somewhat similar but with much more emphasis on gifts, beachwear, and touristy stuff, **Star Department Store** (Water St., 401/466-

5541, 8:30 A.M.–10 P.M. daily May–early Sept., 9 A.M.–5 P.M. daily early Sept.–Apr.) has a nice selection of men's and women's sportswear, T-shirts, sweats, and caps.

Buy film and develop pictures at the **Photo Dog** (National Hotel, Water St., 401/466-5858, www.biphotodog.com, 10 A.M.–10 P.M. daily May–Sept., call for off-season hours), which also sells frames, postcards, art, T-shirts, and a smattering of gifts.

Old Harbor has a pair of small but very nice bookstores. Up a hill by the post office and with the largest selection of books on the island, **Island Bound** (off High St., 401/466-8878, 10 A.M.–5:30 P.M. daily Apr.–May, 9 A.M.–9 P.M. daily June–Aug., 10 A.M.–5:30 P.M. daily Sept.–Oct., call for winter hours) has a good children's section, stationery, some local history books, and a nice general selection of paperbacks and hardcover titles.

The island's newer bookstore is **Beth's Books** (Corn Neck Rd., 401/466-2236, 9 A.M.–4 P.M. daily year-round). Located on Corn Neck Road across from Papa's Pizza, the spacious used bookshop is lovingly curated by Beth Gaffett Tengwall, who has a degree in library science and is daughter of the island's longtime librarian. Fiction, nonfiction, and children's books are all represented on the shelves.

The **Salty Dog** (226 Water St., 401/466-5254, 10 A.M.–9 P.M. Sun.–Thurs., 10 A.M.–10 P.M. Fri.–Sat. early May–early Sept., 10 A.M.–9 P.M. Thurs.–Sun. early Sept.–mid-Oct., call for hours in off-season) sells a mix of beachy items: towels and flip-flops, saltwater taffy, coolers, T-shirts, boogie boards, and casual beachwear.

Old Harbor abounds in gift stores and

antiques. **Lazy Fish** (235 Dodge St., 401/466-2990, 11 A.M.–4 P.M. Mon.–Tues. and Thurs.–Fri., 10 A.M.–5 P.M. Sat.–Sun. May–Oct.) sells affordable old furniture that has been attractively weathered by decades of salt and sun as well as vintage children's toys.

Whether you pray to Buddha, Kokopelli, or the Virgin of Guadalupe, you'll find inspiration at **East of the River Nile Trading Company** (Chapel St., 401/466-3152, www.eastoftherivernile.com, 10 A.M.–8 P.M. daily May–early Sept., 10 A.M.–5 P.M. daily early Sept.–mid-Oct.), which peddles exotic tchotchkes from around the world, including Nepalese engraved copper pots, Peruvian nativity scenes, Chinese porcelain, and more.

Up the hill, **234 Water** (Water St., 401/466-8600, www.234water.com, 9 A.M.–10 P.M. daily late May–early Sept., 10 A.M.–6 P.M. daily early Sept.–late May) sells trendy handbags with the Block Island outline and other upscale gifts and accessories that wouldn't seem out of place with, say, a Ralph Lauren or Burberry ensemble.

Inside a charming little house on Dodge Street,

Scarlet Begonia (401/466-5024, 9 A.M.–7 P.M. daily May–Oct., closed Nov.–Apr.) is a terrific trove of crafts and fine arts, much of it locally produced. Pottery, painting, table linens, decoupage lamps, and jewelry are among the distinctive wares.

If you're looking for some funky new threads to wear to the beach, **Archipelago** (Water St., 401/466-8920, 10 A.M.–10 P.M. daily) features clothing and accessories from Southeast Asia, along with its own line of custom-designed sarongs and bikinis from Bali.

For fancier occasions, **Carmen's Closet** (234 Weldon's Way, 401/316-0770, 10 A.M.–9 P.M. daily May–mid-Oct.) is a consignment store featuring unusual upscale clothing culled by owner Carmen Rodriguez from island closets and mainland boutiques.

A cut above the island's many T-shirt shops, high-quality men's clothes are on sale at **Mahoney's Clothier** (Water St., 401/466-8616 10 A.M.–5 P.M. Tues.–Fri., 10 A.M.–3 P.M. Sat. June–Oct.), which sells a popular line of polo shirts and silk ties with a Block Island logo.

Sports and Recreation

BEACHES

With 17 miles of beaches encircling the island, beachcombers and solitude-seekers need not worry about excessive crowds, even in the height of summer—it's usually possible to find at least a small stretch of beach that's nearly or entirely deserted. Keep in mind that only Benson and Ballard beaches are staffed by lifeguards, and riptides are a serious problem in the waters surrounding Block Island. Pay close attention to water and wind conditions before venturing into unfamiliar waters.

◖ Crescent Beach

The most famous but also most crowded swath of sand is two-mile Crescent Beach, which begins just north of the Surf Hotel and comprises a few distinct sections. The main one, within an easy walk of both Old and New Harbors, is

Frederick J. Benson Beach off Corn Neck Road—here you'll find a large parking lot with bike racks, changing facilities and showers, chair and umbrella rentals, and a small snack bar. You can also rent boogie boards and ocean kayaks. This town beach, formerly run by the state, tends to draw the bulk of day-trippers and other visitors, especially on weekends.

South of Benson Beach, practically in Old Harbor, you'll find the shallow pools of **Baby Beach,** where families often bring children. It's a short walk from many hotels, and the tidal pools are fun for picking up fiddler and hermit crabs, collecting seashells, and swimming or wading. On just about any summer day, this beach is loaded with preteens.

On the other side, 0.25 miles north of Benson, the somewhat more secluded **Scotch Beach** section tends to draw a lot of summer workers,

GREEN SPACES

To take a few steps on Block Island is to experience perhaps its most enduring pastime: hiking. This is by far the best way to appreciate the island's vast green spaces. Even simply walking along Block Island's roads is a relatively safe and quite scenic endeavor, particularly through the island's west side. More avid outdoorsy types will find trails that extend several miles, but the majority of the island's trails are easily navigated by people of all ages and abilities.

As you hike across Block Island in summer you'll stroll beside fragrant bayberry, blackberry, honeysuckle, and dense underbrush. While you're welcome to pick blackberries, leave all other flora and fauna as you find it. Interestingly, while Block Island claims quite a few endangered species, it is largely without mammalian wildlife, except deer and muskrats.

Bird-watching is a major activity along these trails. Ideal times for viewing are the spring and fall migrations, when you'll see hawks maneuvering across the moors and myriad wading birds along the shore. In September and October, the island teems with bird-watchers trying to get a look at the nearly 200 species that take advantage of Block Island's shoals, sheltered channels, beaches, sandbars, meadows, thickets of shrub, and light woodlands. Thermals rising from the ocean-side cliffs on the south side of the island attract kestrels, peregrines, and merlins. In salt marshes, look for herons and egrets. Quite a few species nest here permanently in winter; in summer you'll see mainly shore birds.

Block Island has about 25 miles of nature trails, quite a few of them linked through a comprehensive network called the **Greenway,** which is accessible at 11 points. The Greenway runs through the southern half of the island, and highlights include Nathan Mott Park, the Enchanted Forest, the Turnip Farm, and Rodman's Hollow.

The **Elizabeth Dickens Trail,** which winds through open meadows and along high bluffs, is popular with bird-watchers. Its namesake taught natural history, conservation, and ornithology on the island and was very involved in its preservation.

Another excellent walk for birders is **Clay Head Hill Trail.** You get to it from the east side of Corn Neck Road, where you'll see signs pointing the way to the parking area and trailhead – you reach it shortly before Corn Neck Road ends at the parking area for North Lighthouse. About 0.3 miles from the trailhead you'll come to a fork – make a right to descend to a lovely beach; make a left to rise to the bluffs and enter a famous section of the island known as the **Maze,** a vast and happily haphazard network of groomed walking paths – about 10 miles' worth – that run along and beside bluffs and hollows.

Of course, much of the best hiking on the island is along the windswept beaches. You can circumnavigate the entire island this way, except at the channel at New Harbor and the commercial district of Old Harbor. Allow about eight hours to make this grand tour; you can begin the walk from any beach.

Spot some birds on the Clay Head Hill Trail.

© MICHAEL BLANDING

© MICHAEL BLANDING

rock sculptures on a Block Island beach

local teens, avid volleyball players, and the like. It's less suitable for families than Benson. North of here, beautiful **Mansion Beach** forms the northern end of this stretch. It lies beneath the remains of a mansion that burned in a fire long ago. There's not much parking here—many visitors arrive by bike. It's a very scenic and romantic spot, perfect for a picnic or some relative peace and quiet and yet more accessible than some of the island's most tranquil beaches.

Other Beaches

A lively spot that gets rowdy at night, **Ballard's Beach,** at the southern tip of Old Harbor's commercial district, is right by Ballard's seafood restaurant, just beyond the harbor's southern breakwater. This attractive span is popular with young singles and couples: Waitstaff scurry about delivering beer and fruity drinks, revelers play volleyball, and rock bands entertain the crowds on summer afternoons. The surf can be pretty intense at times, although it's perfectly safe for adults with swimming experience.

A short drive or bike ride from Old Harbor, **West Beach** (West Beach Rd.), with parking just past the town transfer station, is a relatively peaceful beach that's ideal for a stroll, especially at sunset. From here you can hike up the entire western shore of the island, heading north to North Lighthouse. Part of this area is a bird sanctuary, so dogs are not permitted, and humans are asked to stay below the high-tide line and avoid disturbing the dunes and wildlife.

There are several other smaller and more secluded beaches around the island, many of them known only among locals and accessible primarily on foot or by bike. Favorites among these include **Black Rock Beach** and **Vail Beach,** both of which are accessible from Snake Hole Road on the south shore of the island. Vail is a pretty if rocky spot in the shadow of Mohegan Bluffs and has some rough surf. Black Rock takes its name from the large black rock offshore; it has a series of secluded coves perfect for hiking or quiet sunbathing. You'll want to take a bike here, as the road to the beach is more than a mile long and mopeds are forbidden. Given the seclusion of the area, some beachgoers may decide to make their excursion clothing-optional, although you didn't hear that from us.

© MICHAEL BLANDING

kayaking in Great Salt Pond

BICYCLING

Few places in the Northeast are more ideally suited to bicycling than Block Island, where curving country lanes pass rugged bluffs and magnificent vistas alongside sweeping pastures and meadows. There are about 40 miles of road, most with mild grades as no point on the island is higher than 250 feet; there are a handful of reasonably challenging hills and bluffs, however. There really aren't specific bike trails per se, but all of the island's roads are appropriate for cycling.

◖ SAILING IN BLOCK ISLAND SOUND

One of the yachting capitals of New England, Block Island has a couple of companies offering boat rentals. A popular and reliable business is **Sail Block Island** (Smuggler's Cove Marina, New Harbor, 401/466-7938, www. sailbi.com), from which you can rent sailboats ranging 15–30 feet in length. You can hire captains to take boats on tours, and it's also possible to take sailing lessons, either in groups or privately. Probably the most prolific source of boat

rentals of just about every kind is **Champlin's Marina** (401/466-7777 or 800/762-4541, www. champlinsresort.com), where you can take out pontoon boats, paddleboats, kayaks, bumper boats, and such. If you'd rather leave the sailing to someone else, book a cruise with **Passion for Sailing Charters** (401/741-1926 or 401/741-1290), which features several two-hour trips from New Harbor, a wine-and-cheese sunset cruise, and monthly full-moon sails.

CANOEING AND KAYAKING

Canoeing or kayaking is another great way to explore Block Island—take to Great Salt Pond, or venture out along the jagged coast. You can rent boats from **Pond and Beyond Kayak** (401/466-5105 or 401/578-2773, www.block-island.com/kayakbi), which also leads guided tours of Great Salt Pond (and yes, beyond) for $50 pp ages 12 and up. The organization also schedules special kayaking trips for kids on Saturday and Sunday morning and Monday afternoon as well as full-moon paddles for adults. You can also rent kayaks at the concession at Fred Benson Town Beach, Champlin's Marina, and **Water Sports** (401/466-2700), located at the entrance to New Harbor.

◖ FISHING IN BLOCK ISLAND SOUND

There's more than saltwater fishing in these parts—many of the ponds on Block Island teem with perch, bass, and pickerel; you'll need a license from town hall, however, to fish these waters. In September, bonito swim up and feed off the shores of Block Island, delighting anglers who like a challenge. June is prime time for reeling in bluefish. Right in New Harbor Channel you can catch fluke, mackerel, and flounder. One of the best ways to fish out here is surf casting from the beach, but there are also charters available for deep-sea fishing.

Whether you're looking for a fly-fishing or surf-casting guide or lessons, a charter, or general advice on where and how to cast a line on Block Island, look to **Block Island Fishworks** (401/742-3992, www.bifishworks.com) as a one-stop source of information and guidance. This company, run by Block Island's harbor master, does 4–8-hour charters on both large and small boats into some of southern New England's best fishing waters, which surround Block Island. It also offers both group and private fly-tying clinics and surf-casting lessons.

The oldest charter company on the island, **G. Willie Makit Charters** (401/466-5151, www.gwilliecharters.com) provides charters from Old Harbor on a 28-foot fishing boat captained by Bill Gould, who has been fishing the waters around Block Island for nearly 30 years. The specialty of G. Willie is bluefish during the day trips and striped bass for night excursions.

HORSEBACK RIDING

Rustic Rides (West Side Rd., 401/466-5060) provides many kinds of horseback excursions on Block Island, from pony rides geared toward families with kids to guided trail rides through some of the island's most magnificent preserves and open spaces.

WATER SPORTS

Surfing is not uncommon on Block Island, and it's a popular place for scuba and snorkeling. You can rent boogie boards at several locations, including the kiosk at Frederick J. Benson Beach. The island's main diving company, **Island Outfitters** (Ocean Ave., 401/466-5502), rents wetsuits, scuba gear, and snorkeling and spearfishing equipment.

One of the exciting ways to see the island is with **Block Island Parasail** (401/864-2472, www.blockislandparasail.com), which takes passengers high above the water with the help of a ginormous parachute sail for a true gull's-eye view of the Block. The company, based on Old Harbor dock near Ballard's Beach, also offers banana-boat rides on gigantic inflatable yellow rafts pulled through the waves—needless to say, it's not a dry experience.

BLOCK ISLAND

Accommodations

It isn't cheap to stay anywhere on Block Island, especially during high season, when room rates soar above $200–300 per night. Even during summer, however, you can often find specials (some advertised, some not), especially during midweek when demand is lower.

Reservation Services and House Rentals

The **Block Island Chamber of Commerce** (401/466-2474 or 800/383-BIRI—800/383-2474, www.blockislandchamber.com) runs a reservation service that is especially useful if you're trying to find out about last-minute availability.

Block Island Hotel Reservations (401/466-2605 or 800/825-6254, www.blockislandhotel.com) rents rooms at several hotels, inns, and private homes and also has entire houses and cottages available around

BLOCK ISLAND'S HOTEL SEASONS

About a dozen of the nearly 60 accommodations on Block Island stay open year-round, but sometimes only on weekends in winter. The larger hotels in town are open mostly from April or early May through late October, some open or close a month earlier or later, and a couple stay open only Memorial Day–Columbus Day.

In high season, July–August, virtually every accommodation has a two-night minimum on weekends, and many a four-night or even seven-night minimum. These policies are based on supply and demand – in a slow week, or if there's iffy weather, you may get lucky and find a place willing to book you in for just a night. Accommodations generally let the Block Island Chamber of Commerce know when there are last-minute availabilities or cancellations. So don't give up hope, even on a busy weekend, of finding a room on short notice – just keep in mind that your options may be limited.

Compared with Newport, Nantucket, the Hamptons, or many other upscale seaside resorts in the Northeast, Block Island does not have exorbitantly priced rooms. On a high-season weekend, you'll rarely see rooms with private baths renting for less than $100 nightly, but it's pretty easy to find them for under $150. Budget travelers who don't mind a room with a shared bath will find a substantial selection on Block Island – sometimes for even less than $100 per night on high-season weekends. On the other hand, rates at higher-end properties have been edging up during the past few years. It's now common to find rooms over $250 per night, and even over $350, that are far from luxurious. Location and the laws of supply and demand, rather than amenities, seem to dictate these higher prices.

Because so many of Block Island's visitors stay for four days or more during the high season, midweek rates generally don't fall by much – but it is realistic to expect a drop of 10-20 percent at most places. You should also have more luck booking a single-night stay or scoring a last-minute room during the week. During the spring and fall shoulder seasons, rates on weekends drop 20-40 percent compared with summer; they can fall 30-50 percent at the few properties open in winter. Off-season weekdays usually see even more dramatic rate reductions. And even in the high-season it's worth calling a property before deciding definitively that you can't afford it. On weekends with lower demand, for instance Memorial Day–Fourth of July or the last two weeks of August, hotels sometimes offer "specials" with substantial reductions on their high-season rates even if they are loath to drop their published rates overall.

---

the island. Many of the rentals can accommodate two to three couples.

In addition, hundreds of Block Island property owners rent out their homes for part or all of the summer, either on a weekly or multiple-week basis. In high season, expect to pay about $1,200–2,000 for a small and basic cottage that sleeps two to more than $5,000 per week for a mansion. Renting can be very economical, however, for groups of four or more—factor in money saved by preparing some of your meals at home and it can be a bargain. Real estate agents that specialize in rentals include **Ballard Hall Real Estate** (401/466-8883, www.blockislandproperty.com); **Block**

Island Realty (401/466-5887, www.birealty.com); **Sullivan Real Estate** (401/466-5521, www.sullivansalesandrentals.com); and **Phillips Real Estate** (401/466-8806, www.phillipsonbi.com).

$100-150

The quintessence of seaside simplicity, the **❰ Sea Breeze Inn** (Spring St., 401/466-2275 or 800/786-2276, www.blockisland.com/seabreeze, year-round, $130–290) is a delightful compound of weathered cottages on a hillside overlooking marshes and swan ponds, and beyond that the ocean. On the grounds you'll find aromatic and colorful perennial gardens and meadows carpeted with wildflowers. The 10 rooms are airy, uncluttered, and tastefully furnished with well-chosen country antiques.

It's hard to miss the distinctive **Gothic Inn** (Dodge St., 401/466-2918 or 800/944-8991, www.thegothicinn.com, mid-Apr.–late Oct., $135–195), decked with frilly verge board, sharp pointed gables, and striking finials. Set back from the road on a grassy lawn, the inn backs on Crescent Beach and is steps from Old Harbor restaurants and shops. Room decor is not fancy but is pleasant, with a clean, minimalist feel and Shaker-style furniture; from some windows you can enjoy views of the harbor. Also available are two-bedroom efficiency apartments, which are great for families and friends traveling together.

Another reasonably priced option conveniently situated on Dodge Street, the **Gables Inn** (Dodge St., 401/466-2213, www.gables-innblockisland.com, mid-Apr.–Nov., $125–210) is a compound of two attractive 1860s Victorian inns with many of their original details preserved, including pressed-tin ceilings, vintage floral wallpapers, Victorian rockers, and wicker chairs. The guest rooms in one of the houses, the Gables Inn, are definitely more romantic as they contain most of the antiques, but the more functionally furnished apartments and cottages in Gables II are ideal for longer stays, families, or guests who appreciate dining or cooking in. Among the common amenities are barbecue grills and picnic tables, a laundry room, and bike racks. This is one of the relatively few properties on the island that not only allows children but actively welcomes them; cribs and strollers are available by advance request. It's only a two-minute walk to Baby Beach, and the inn supplies beach chairs, umbrellas, coolers, and toys for you to take with you.

The **Harborside Inn** (Water St., 401/466-5504 or 800/825-6254, www.blockislandreservations.com, early May–late Oct., $130–230), along with the neighboring National Hotel, is one of the most recognizable buildings in Old Harbor—this wedding-cake-like inn faces the ferry landing. The Harborside is the smaller and somewhat quieter of the two inns, with small guest rooms but with high ceilings and large windows that let in plenty of light. All of the rooms were "renovated" in 2009, though in practice that means little more than that the walls and ceilings were repainted. Floors still creak, and mattresses remain lumpy box-springs, but you'll find few places in Block Island cheaper during the high season, especially so close to the ferry and downtown shops and restaurants.

An inn only since 1999, the dramatic Second Empire 🅒 **Hygeia House** (Beach Ave., 401/466-9616, http://thehygeiahouse.com, year-round, $125–295) has been meticulously restored by the great-grandson and family of the home's first owner, physician and hotelier Dr. John C. Champlin, whose doctor's bag and other artifacts are displayed in a glass case in the entryway. The 1883 home has 10 guest rooms, most of them suites and all with views of the ocean or Great Salt Pond and New Harbor, fully updated bathrooms, and well-chosen Victorian antiques that impart a characteristic yet uncluttered look. One of the guiding lights behind Block Island Poetry Project, innkeeper Lisa Starr has placed inspirational verses around the hotel along with books of poetry in each of the rooms to provide some contemplative gems during your stay.

Down a quiet country lane off High Street (almost behind the Atlantic Inn), about a 10-minute walk from Old Harbor, the **Rose Farm Inn** (Roslyn Rd., 401/466-2034, www.rosefarminn.com, mid-May–mid-Oct., $140–310) consists of two neighboring properties. The rambling 1890s Farm House contains 10 period-furnished guest rooms (eight with private baths and walk-in tile showers), a large southern-exposure sundeck, and a stone front porch. Across the lane, the gable-roofed Captain Rose House was built in 1993, and although some of the nine guest rooms here have double-whirlpool baths and a more modern feel, the decor, fabrics, and color schemes are authentically

Victorian. Second-floor units in the Captain Rose House are perhaps the most romantic, as they have dormer windows and decks overlooking the 20 acres of pastoral grounds—a working farm until the 1960s, the property now acts as something of an unofficial wildlife preserve. There's also a vacation cottage, the Meadowview Suite, which is generally rented out by the week.

$150-250

Considering its cheerful and friendly staff, breathtaking setting, and attractively furnished rooms, the **(Atlantic Inn** (High St., 401/466-5883 or 800/224-7422, www.atlanticinn.com, late Apr.–mid-Oct., $190–290) is one of the best choices on the island, perfectly balancing a grand setting with reasonable (if not bargain) room rates. This white three-story hotel with a dark gray mansard roof and 21 guest rooms sits high on a hill a short walk from town. The interior seems to be done on a more intimate scale than some of the other grand hotels but is still overflowing with character. The lobby can be dizzying, with flowered wallpaper, tasseled lamps, and peacock feathers evoking a high-Victorian atmosphere. Decor varies from room to room, but Victorian antiques abound.

Victorian Inns by the Sea (401/466-5891 or 800/992-7290, www.blockislandinns.com, year-round, $195–395) consists of two main inns and a handful of smaller cottages, all of them quite upscale and with great locations. The late 1800s Blue Dory on Dodge Street walks a nice balance between elegantly inviting and yet unstuffy and homey—from the back deck, a wooden doorway leads down the steps to the beach and crashing surf. The adjacent Waverly Cottage contains three large suites ideal for longer stays—each has either a wet bar or a kitchen, a living area, and a whirlpool tub. Around the corner, the Avonlea Inn is more spacious and airy, with a wraparound veranda overlooking the beach. Typical in all the units are floral bedspreads and wallpapers, iron or brass beds (many of them four-posters), and period tables, chairs, and other pieces.

You might not think to choose an accommodation on Block Island that's actually set inland with no water views at all, but the **Old Town Inn** (Old Town Rd., 401/466-5958, www.oldtowninnbi.com, late May–mid-Oct., $175–245) has plenty going for it. The building consists of an 1820s main section and a similar-style newer wing, which contain a total of 10 warmly appointed rooms with private baths and a tasteful mix of antiques and newer pieces. Although the inn doesn't overlook the water, it does enjoy a sylvan setting of meadows, gardens, and shade trees, far enough away from the summer crowds to have peace and quiet, but not too far from restaurants and shops to be inconvenient. Rates include quite a good full-breakfast buffet with daily changing specials as well as afternoon hors d'oeuvres.

A lavish contemporary property built in the Victorian style in 2002, **Payne's Harbor View Inn** (Beach Ave., 401/466-5758, www.paynesharborviewinn.com, year-round, $235–395) sits right beside Hygeia House, high on a hill with an outstanding view of both New Harbor and Block Island Sound. Rooms are spacious and outfitted with lovely, mostly Victorian antiques (including some impressively ornate beds), and all have whirlpool tubs; the fanciest units have two-person whirlpool tubs, and four have decks. A continental breakfast is served in a bright and appealing breakfast room, or you can eat out on the patio in back, enjoying the views.

Consisting of two inns and several smaller nearby cottages, the **(1661 Inn and Hotel Manisses** (1 Spring St., 401/466-2421 or 800/626-4773, www.blockislandresorts.com, year-round, $220–450) offers a distinctive and impressive range of historic accommodations, plus one of the island's finest restaurants. The pale-gray Hotel Manisses, though smaller than the other classic hotels on the island, has plenty of admirers with its five-story central tower and admirable scale. Each of the 17 guest rooms is named for a famous Block Island shipwreck; generally they are a bit darker and more elaborately decorated than rooms in some of the other large hotels. Across the street, the imposing white 1661 Inn, with nine guest rooms, and the nine guest rooms in its adjoining contemporary guesthouse offer a similarly plush experience, but with colonial instead of Victorian decor; four smaller units in the guesthouse share a bath and have considerably lower rates. Some rooms open onto a broad sundeck with stunning water views. The hotel also offers more privacy and quiet in several other cottages that range from quaint to modern, some with fireplaces and spa tubs. A lavish buffet breakfast, included in the rates (even for the cottages), is served daily in the 1661 Inn's breakfast room. Additional perks for all units include a guided island tour by van, a farm tour (Saturday only), late-afternoon wine and snacks, and a decanter of brandy in each room. When you factor in all the extras and the many types of accommodations, this well-operated resort can be considered a very good value.

Located on the main strip of Old Harbor within a short walk of the ferry, the **National Hotel** (Water St., 401/466-2901 or 800/225-2449, www.blockislandhotels.com, early May–late Oct., $230–340) presents a dashing profile and more comfortable interior than the neighboring Harborside. It was built in 1888 and has 45 guest rooms that have been handsomely updated in recent years, outfitted with phones, cable TV, hair dryers, and attractive modern bathrooms. Even so, this is still an old hotel and can be a bit musty at times; the interior isn't nearly as fancy as some of the similarly-priced Victorians up the hill. The sunny lobby and enormous veranda, however, makes this an excellent choice when you want to be in the heart of the action.

OVER $250

With its red mansard roof, striking cupola, and enviable setting on a bluff overlooking Old Harbor Point, few hotels on the Eastern Seaboard strike a more commanding and regal pose than the **C Spring House Hotel**

(Spring St., 401/466-5844 or 800/234-9263, www.springhousehotel.com, Apr.–Oct., $250–350), which opened in 1852 to considerable excitement and was rebuilt in 1870 in grand Second Empire style. Since then, celebrities like Mark Twain and Billy Joel have stayed here. This romantic hotel affords guests spectacular ocean views from many rooms. Despite the hotel's reputation as one of the most luxurious on the island, keep in mind this is still Block Island—don't expect the Ritz. The 40 guest rooms and suites in the main building are simply but attractively furnished with floral-print bedspreads, valances, and fabrics, pastel color schemes, and wicker dressers and nightstands; 10 similarly furnished additional guest rooms are next door in the Samuel Mott Building.

Champlin's Marina, Hotel, and Resort (New Harbor, 401/466-7777 or 800/762-4541, www.champlinsresort.com, May 15–Oct. 15, $265–335) isn't one of the island's old beauties, but it is the ideal accommodation as far as plenty of sailors and boaters are concerned. Set along a beautiful stretch of Great Salt Pond, this full-service resort offers both pleasant—if fairly ordinary-looking—hotel accommodations and a formidable marina that can accommodate about 250 boats. The hotel has 28 rooms, all with decks looking either onto the water or toward the island; many have convertible sofas and kitchenettes. There's a casual restaurant on-site and a rather campy lounge called the Tiki-Bar, where revelers nurse froufrou cocktails and shoot pool. Additional amenities include an in-ground pool, bike rentals, tennis courts, a children's playground, kayak rentals, a first-run movie theater, an ice-cream parlor, laundry facilities, a beach, and a bait-and-tackle shop.

CAMPING

Block Island has no campground, and in fact, camping is illegal throughout the island, except for a small tract of land owned by the Boy Scouts of America, on which only visiting scout troops may pitch tents.

Food

UPSCALE

The lavish dining room at the (C) **Hotel Manisses** (1 Spring St., 401/466-2421, www.blockislandresorts.com, 6–9:30 P.M. daily May–late Oct., $23–44) offers creative regional American fare, such as free-range chicken confit with blue-cheese béchamel and sweet chili glaze followed by pork roulade "three ways" with loin, prosciutto, pancetta, and sweet potato hush puppies, which may be the most daring—and richest—food you'll find on Block Island. Both á la carte and prix fixe menus are offered. The flower-filled dining room of this stately old hotel makes a sublime setting for such a fine meal.

Dining at the **Spring House Hotel** (Spring St., 401/466-5844, www.springhousehotel.com, 7:30–11 A.M. and noon–10 P.M. daily late June–Aug., reduced hours off-season, $22–36) is another of the island's more lavish experiences. The dining room presents consistently fine contemporary continental fare—past starters have included mussels in red curry broth with pineapple cinnamon basil and cilantro as well as softshell crab tempura with citrus and tarragon *gastrique*. Main courses such as lamb osso buco with saffron risotto and pine nut *gremolata*, or coriander-crusted swordfish with tomato confit, wilted greens, and Parmesan oil, look as good on the plate as they taste. The dining room, with white napery and Windsor chairs, overlooks the ocean.

Local opinions on the upmarket **Atlantic Inn** (High St., 401/466-5883, www.atlanticinn.com, 6–10 P.M. Thurs.–Sun. late May–mid–June, 6–10 P.M. daily late–June–Aug., 6–10 P.M. Thurs.–Sun. Sept.–mid-Oct., $21–30, $49 prix fixe) run hot to cold, as some think the food stupendous while others claim the kitchen is resting on its laurels and the service doesn't always live up to expectations. There's no arguing that the food is creative—typical offerings from the four-course menu include crispy Malaysian pork belly with kimchi, cilantro, and spicy Malay sauce followed by seared halibut cheeks with escargots and fiddleheads. The strawberry tiramisu is a memorable dessert.

CREATIVE BUT CASUAL

Consider yourself lucky if you're able to score a table at **Eli's** (456 Chapel St., 401/466-5230, www.elisblockisland.com, 6–9 P.M. Fri.–Sun. Mar.–Apr., 6–9 P.M. Wed.–Sun. June, 5:30–10 P.M. Fri.–Sat., 6–10 P.M. Sun.–Thurs. July–Aug., 6–9 P.M. Tues.–Sun. Sept., 6–9 P.M. Thurs.–Sun. Oct.–mid-Nov., $19–27), a hole-in-the-wall that locals speak of with solemn reverence. Executive chef Evan Wango's tastes run to rustic Italian cuisine, using simple fresh and local ingredients that pop with natural flavor. Recent entrée standouts include seared salmon with garlic potato puree and brown butter vinaigrette, and roasted lamb steak with lemon-couscous salad.

The **Mohegan Café & Brewery** (Water St., 401/466-5911, 10:30 A.M.–9 P.M. daily mid-Mar.–late May, 10:30 A.M.–10 P.M. daily late May–early Sept., 10:30 A.M.–9 P.M. daily early Sept.–Oct., $8–23), which overlooks Old Harbor, is always a great bet for tasty lunch and dinner fare—it's also one of the island's best nightlife choices, with live music late many evenings. The food spans the American culinary vernacular with some distinctive Asian and Southwestern influences. Good picks include the burgers, bay scallop seviche, Argentinean rib eye, and herb-roasted chicken with hoisin-rum barbecue sauce. The dining room is warmed by amber lighting and staffed by friendly young folks.

With a vantage over Old Harbor from its hilltop location, **Harry's Café b.i.** (Water St., in the Post Office Bldg., 401/466-5400, 11 A.M.–3:30 P.M. and 5–10 P.M. daily June–Sept., $9–24) serves up creative meals from scratch with Asian and Caribbean influences. Pad thai and curried mussels are crowd-pleasing favorites, while the blend of spices in its Jamaican jerk pork is a closely held island secret.

Right on Crescent Beach, attached to Yellow Kitten's nightclub, **◖ Winfield's Restaurant** (Corn Neck Rd., 401/466-5856, http://mysite. verizon.net/restkino, 6–10 P.M. daily late May–early Sept., 6–10 P.M. Wed.–Sun. early Sept.–mid-Oct., $18–28) offers an improbable menu of upscale French-Texan cuisine. If you don't think that's possible, sink your teeth into tournedos of beef smothered in piquant pimiento cheese or swordfish topped with flavorful smoked tomatillo salsa. A few bites and you'll be singing the praises of chef Berke Marye to the tune of "The Yellow Rose of Texas," as locals have learned to do.

Once just a burger joint better known for its drinks and homey nautical decor than for its culinary prowess, the **Beachhead** (Corn Neck Rd., 401/466-2249, www.thebeachhead.com, 11:30 A.M.–9:30 P.M. daily year-round, $9–29) revamped its kitchen a few years ago and now serves very good seafood and American favorites in a space overflowing with art by island artists. It's the only Block Island sit-down restaurant open daily year-round, making it a favorite of locals and visitors for hearty fare that includes fantastic blue-cheese burgers and inspired seafood nachos. Tasty crab cakes, outstanding chili, and seafood bouillabaisse are also recommended.

PIZZA AND PUB GRUB

G. R. Sharky's (Corn Neck Rd., 401/466-9900, 5:30–9 P.M. daily Apr.–June, 11:30 A.M.–3 P.M. and 5–9:30 P.M. daily July–Aug., 5:30–9 P.M. daily Sept.–Oct., $11–22) is very good for steaks, seafood grills, hefty salads, chicken fajitas, fish-and-chips, and other casual dishes. The dining room is bright, attractive, and airy, with high ceilings. The bar boasts potent martinis, and there's a pleasant patio.

The National Hotel's **Tap and Grille** (Water St., 401/466-2901, www.blockislandhotels. com, 11 A.M.–11 P.M. daily May–Oct., $10–33) is justly renowned as one of the island's most memorable milieus—seating is along the hotel's long and gracious covered veranda, which faces out onto Old Harbor and the daily parade of pedestrians strolling along Water Street. The

BLOCK ISLAND

© MICHAEL BLANDING

Finn's Seafood Restaurant and Fish Market, by Old Harbor Ferry

food is pretty decent, with steaks, pastas, and seafood the specialties. Devotees swear by the balsamic barbecued chicken breast, and the fish-and-chips also receives considerable praise.

You can get tasty short-order fare from **Papa's Pizzeria** (Corn Neck Rd., 401/466-9939, www.papaspizzeriabi.com, 11 A.M.–10 P.M. Sun.–Thurs., 11 A.M.–11 P.M. Fri.–Sat. mid-Apr.–mid-Oct., $3–21), including calzones, subs, salads, and sandwiches. This reputable parlor will deliver anywhere on the island.

Seafood devotees linger blissfully around the raw bar at **Finn's Seafood Restaurant and Fish Market** (by Old Harbor Ferry, 401/466-2473, www.finnsseafood.com, 11:30 A.M.–9:30 P.M. daily mid-June–Oct., $8–38), which also serves hefty lobster dinners, rich chowders and stews, and heaping fried-clam platters. The bustling setting, by the ferry and overlooking the fishing boats sailing in and out of Old Harbor, is engaging—especially the seating on the patio, which fills up quickly on warm days. For overflow, the restaurant also has a takeout window with additional seating (without waiters) on another patio upstairs overlooking the harbor.

Aldo's Restaurant and Pizzeria (130 Chapel St., 401/466-5871, www.aldosblockisland.com, 11 A.M.–10 P.M. daily late May–early–Sept., 11 A.M.–9 P.M. Tues.–Sun. early Sept.–Oct., $7–20), attached to a wonderful little bakery and ice-cream café, serves casual but reliable pastas, seafood grills, pizzas, and other Italian fare. Littleneck clams with drawn butter are an addictive specialty, and pastas such as penne á la vodka and seafood pesto (lobster, mussels, shrimp, scallops, and clams in a wine sauce over linguine) use fresh ingredients and Old World preparations.

Club Soda (Connecticut Ave., 401/466-5397, www.clubsodabi.com, 4 P.M.–1 A.M. daily year-round, $8–12), which has been a bar since the 1940s, occupies the basement of the Classic Highview Inn and is best known for serving delicious Southern barbecue. Other pub-like dishes include burgers, pizza, tangy Buffalo wings, and the like. By the bar you'll find a series of murals depicting local scenes painted by local artist George Wetherbee.

Upstairs from the club, the newer **Wetherbee's** (Connecticut Ave., 410/466-5900, www.wetherbeesbi.com, 5–9 P.M. Thurs.–Sun. early Sept.–late May, $17–23) serves family-friendly meals in the off-season, including blackened tuna, barbecue ribs, chicken Parmesan, and steak.

A cheap and easygoing sister of the esteemed Hotel Manisses, ◖ **The Oar** (New Harbor, 401/466-8820, www.blockislandresorts.com, 11 A.M.–9 P.M. daily mid-May–June, 11 A.M.–10:30 P.M. daily July–Aug., 11 A.M.–9 P.M. daily Sept.–mid-Oct., $5–23) has a wonderful deck and dining room overlooking the sailboats and yachts on Great Salt Pond—a spectacular place for watching the sunset. Inside, the large room is hung with dozens of oars provided to the marina by boaters from all over the world. The menu leans on the fruits of the sea, with lobster and blackened mahimahi rolls, peel-and-eat shrimp, grilled fish fillets, and the like. Southern fried chicken is also a specialty.

QUICK BITES

◖ **Bethany's Airport Diner** (Block Island Airport, Center Rd., 401/466-3100, 6 A.M.–8 P.M. daily mid-June–Oct., $4–9) is more than just a stopover for a light bite before or after a plane ride—plenty of locals swear by the hearty breakfast fare, which includes flapjacks and breakfast burritos. Tasty burgers, sandwiches, and chowders are served at lunch, and rotating specials are offered at dinner. Fun people-watching is reason enough to come here, and from many seats you can see the planes landing and taking off.

Another absolute favorite for breakfast is **Ernie's** (Water St., 6 A.M.–noon daily, $3–8), which has occupied a ramshackle white building near the ferry terminal since the early 1960s.

For daytime sustenance, drop by **Aldo's Bakery** (Weldon's Way, 401/466-2198, 7 A.M.–9 P.M. daily early–late May, 6 A.M.–11 P.M. daily late May–early Sept., 7 A.M.–9 P.M. daily early–late Sept., $4–8) for ice cream, muffins, Portuguese sweetbread, and designer coffees as well as the all-you-can-eat country-style breakfast buffet on weekend mornings. There's a row of outdoor tables and chairs in front, where on warm summer mornings locals nosh on eggs Benedict, French toast, and omelets (lots of fillings are available).

You can grab a light and refreshing meal at **Froozies** (back porch of the National Hotel, Dodge St., 401/466-2230, www.frooziesblockisland.com, 7:30 A.M.–3 P.M. daily early–late May, 7:30 A.M.–5 P.M. daily late May–early Sept., 7:30 A.M.–3 P.M. daily early–late Sept., $5–9), whose eponymous specialty is what most of us know as a smoothie—many flavors are available, including apple, pineapple, peach, and mango, or a mixture of any of the flavors. This is also one of the best lunch options for vegetarians, with many veggie and vegan sandwich offerings along with tasty veggie burgers.

At the other end of the culinary spectrum, the **Burger Bar at Mahogany Shoals** (Payne's Dock, New Harbor, 11 A.M.–10 P.M. daily May–Sept., $6–16) is a big name for a simple concept: juicy burgers, lobster rolls, tuna steak sandwiches, and shrimp sold at a dockside bar and consumed at outside tables among the moorings of New Harbor. On an island of high-priced eateries, it's a good way to grab a tasty meal on the cheap.

JAVA JOINTS

A snug coffeehouse around the corner from Water Street in Old Harbor, **Juice'n Java** (235 Dodge St., 401/466-5220, 6 A.M.–2 P.M. daily Apr.–May, 6 A.M.–6 P.M. daily June–Aug., 6 A.M.–2 P.M. daily Sept.–Oct.) is one of the island's favorite

social hubs, a place to meet with old friends or make new ones and to sample coffees, teas, and desserts from a vast list. More substantial fare— sandwiches, eggs, and more—are also available, along with the antioxidant acai bowl, complete with acai berries, bananas, and granola. Shelves of board games and books keep snackers and sippers entertained, and there's sometimes live jazz.

GOURMET GOODS AND PICNIC SUPPLIES

Relatively close to Benson Beach and New Harbor, the **Old Post Office Bagel Shop** (Corn Neck Rd. and Ocean Ave., 401/466-5959, $2–7) is far more ambitious than its name suggests, presenting a wide selection of fresh-baked breads along with the house-made bagels for which this sunny and cheerful café is named. Creative green and pasta salads, breakfast sandwiches, and healthful fruit cups complement the many types of bagels and spreads.

Just down the hill by the ferry terminal, **Finn's Fish Market** (401/466-2473) has the best selection of fresh creatures from the sea (in the tank, smoked, and filleted), including fresh-prepared Rhode Island clam chowder to go.

Get your food basics at **Block Island Depot** (Ocean Ave., 401/466-2949) and **Block Island Grocery** (Ocean Ave., 401/466-2949). **Red Bird Package Store** (Dodge St., 401/466-2441) has been the island's source of booze and beer since the end of Prohibition; it's open daily.

Information and Services

VISITOR INFORMATION

For visitor information, contact the **Block Island Tourism Council** (P.O. Box 356, Block Island, RI 02807, 401/466-5200 or 800/383-BIRI—800/383-2474, www.blockislandinfo.com). The council's offices double as the **Block Island Chamber of Commerce** (www.blockislandchamber.com), whose information center faces the Old Harbor ferry terminal. It's definitely worth popping in when you arrive on the island—brochures abound, including several

that offer discounts on bike rentals or meals at restaurants, and there's an ATM, a fax and copier, and lockers for rent—ideal if you're on a day trip. Staff can also tell you which hotels and inns on the island have vacancies. Next door to the chamber you'll find public restrooms; there are also restroom facilities at the fire-police station, the Island Free Library, and North Light.

A few practicalities to keep in mind: Block Island has a water shortage—the situation has been grave at times, and visitors are asked to make every possible effort to conserve water. Also, do your best not to overuse electricity—the local utility company powers the island with diesel generators, and Block Island's electric rates are said to be higher than in any other town in the United States.

MEDIA

The weekly **Block Island Times** (401/466-2222, www.blockislandtimes.com) is an indispensable resource for anybody planning a visit of even a few days. Both the print paper and the online edition contain updated ferry information, news about upcoming events, and frequent features on local history.

TOURS

Other than taking a taxi tour of the island, boating excursions are a great way to get a different perspective on Block Island's enchanting scenery. A favorite tour boat is the **Ruling Passion** (401/741-1290 or 401/741-1926), a 45-foot trimaran that sails out of the Boat Basin three times daily (morning, afternoon, and early evening). On the last cruise, wine and cheese is served during sunset. The boat can carry up to 29 passengers. A more upscale option is the smaller **sailing yacht Sophia** (917/721-0801, www.sailingwithsophia.com), a 42-foot yacht that limits itself to six people per trip. Two-hour sails start at $50 pp, with custom trips and overnights available.

Getting There and Around

One way or another, you're going to have to get on a boat or a plane to get to Block Island.

GETTING THERE
By Ferry from Point Judith

Most ferry travelers leave from Point Judith, the Narragansett fishing village just 10 miles or so from the northern tip of Block Island. This is the only point from which ferries sail during the off-season (early Sept.–early June), and it offers by far the greatest number of crossings.

Conventional service is provided by **Interstate Navigation** (401/783-7996 or 866/783-7996, www.blockislandferry.com). There's always at least one (and usually 2–3) sailings each day, even in winter (except for Christmas Day, when there is no service). In fall and spring, service increases to four times most days and six times on weekends; in summer there are 8–9 sailings per day. Departure times vary widely, so call ahead or check the website for details. The fare is $11 pp one-way ($18 round-trip, but only for same-day passage), $47 for cars one-way, and $3 for bicycles. The trip takes about an hour.

The fastest option is the **Island Hi-Speed**

Ferry (866/783-7996, www.blockisland-ferry.com), a fleet of high-tech, passenger-only catamarans that reach speeds of up to 33 knots—the trip from to Block Island takes just 30 minutes. In summer, the ferry runs six times daily; in fall and spring, service is cut to five times daily. You'll pay a little more for these boats, $19 each way for adults ($36 round-trip) and $3 for bikes, but plenty of visitors think the quick and comfy ride is worth the extra cost. Reservations are strongly recommended for these ships, and you can book either online or by phone. As with the traditional ferry, service is to Old Harbor.

Ferries depart Point Judith from Galilee State Pier, at the southern tip of the town of Narragansett. From points north, take I-95 to Route 4, follow this south to U.S. 1, and then exit in Narragansett at Route 108. From points south, follow I-95 to exit 92 in Connecticut, follow Route 2, turn right onto Route 78, and then follow U.S. 1 north to Route 108. From here, signs mark the way. There are numerous commercial parking lots within walking distance of the ferry, generally priced according to how close by they are. The closest lots are $10 per calendar day, meaning if you park at 6 P.M. one night and get back the following day at 10 A.M., you'll pay for two days. Driving times to Point Judith average an hour from New London, 50 minutes from Providence, and a little more than 90 minutes from Boston.

There are several ways to reach the ferry terminal without driving. You can take **Amtrak** (800/872-7245, www.amtrak.com) to Kingston station, a 12-mile, 20-minute ride by taxi from the terminal. Kingston station is about three hours by train from Manhattan and an hour from Boston. Cab companies serving the area include **Best Taxi** (401/781-0706 or 800/310-1127), **Eagle Cab** (800/339-2970), and **Wakefield Cab** (401/783-0007). The fare from the station to Point Judith is $30–40.

You can also get to Point Judith using **Rhode Island Public Transit Authority (RIPTA) buses** (800/244-0444, www.ripta.com). Buses run to the ferry terminal from Narragansett; you can use RIPTA to get to Narragansett from T. F. Green Airport in Warwick, downtown Providence, and other parts of the state. This option requires a bit of planning and generally isn't worth the bother unless you're familiar with Rhode Island and used to regional bus systems or traveling on a tight budget (in which case you might want to skip Block Island entirely).

If you're flying into T. F. Green Airport, which is served by many major U.S. airlines, you can always catch a cab to the ferry terminal—it is much easier than taking a RIPTA bus, but also much more expensive. Contact **Best Taxi** (401/781-0706 or 800/310-1127); the fare is about $60.

By Ferry from Newport

As with Point Judith, service from Newport is provided by **Interstate Navigation** (401/783-7996 or 866/783-7996, www.blockisland-ferry.com). Ferries leave from Newport at 9:15 A.M. daily and return from Block Island at 4:45 P.M. daily, July–early September only; the sail time is about two hours. The fare is $9 for adults one-way ($13 round-trip, but only for same-day passage), and $2.50 one-way for

bicycles. Discounts are available for children and seniors.

The terminal is at Fort Adams State Park on Harrison Avenue; inexpensive water taxis run passengers back and forth between Fort Adams and downtown Newport, where there are plenty of lots and garages with long-term parking. Driving time to Newport is about 90 minutes from the Cape Cod canal crossing, and a little under two hours from Boston. Using this service to reach Block Island makes the most sense if you're driving from Cape Cod or somewhere east of Newport. In all other cases, including traveling from Boston, the Point Judith ferries make more sense.

By Ferry from New London, Connecticut

Service from New London is via high-speed passenger-only catamarans operated by **Block Island Express** (860/444-4624, www.goblock-island.com). The trip takes just 70 minutes, and ferries arrive on Block Island at Old Harbor. Late May–mid-June and mid-September–mid-October, Block Island Express runs only Friday–Sunday (as well as the Monday after Memorial Day and the Monday after Columbus Day), four times per day. Mid-June–mid-September Block Island Express runs daily, with four daily runs Monday–Wednesday and five daily runs Thursday–Sunday. The fare is $24 pp one-way ($43 round-trip, but only for same-day passage), and $10 for bicycles. Discounts are available for children and seniors.

The New London ferry terminal is off Governor Winthrop Boulevard, just off I-95 (exit 84S from the south, exit 83 from the north)—follow signs from the exit. Long-term and short-term parking is available at the municipal **Water Street Parking Garage** (Atlantic St., just off Eugene O'Neill Dr., $6 per day Mon.–Thurs., $15 per day Fri.–Sun. and holidays). Depending on traffic, it takes 2.5–3 hours to reach New London from Manhattan, and about an hour from Hartford.

The terminal is also just steps from New London's train station, which is served by **Amtrak** (800/872-7245, www.amtrak.com), with service from many major cities, including Manhattan (about 2.5 hours), Hartford (about 3.5 hours, with a change in New Haven), and Washington, D.C. (6–7 hours).

Greyhound (800/231-2222, www.greyhound.com) has service to New London from many major cities, including Manhattan (3–4 hours), Hartford (2.5–3 hours), and Washington, D.C. (8–10 hours). The bus station is adjacent to the ferry terminal.

By Ferry from Long Island, New York

Viking Fleet (631/668-5700, www.vikingfleet.com) runs from Montauk, New York, at the eastern tip of Long Island's south fork, to Block Island late May–mid-October. Boats leave once daily from Montauk at 10 A.M., arriving at Block Island at 11 A.M. The return departure back to Montauk is at 5 P.M., arriving at 6 P.M. (one additional boat departs Montauk at 3:30 P.M. and Block Island at 11:30 A.M. Fri.–Mon. July–Aug.) The Montauk ferry arrives at Champlin's Marina in New Harbor rather than at the Old Harbor terminal. The adult fare is $40 one-way, $70 round-trip; for children 5–12 $40 one-way, $25 round-trip; $10 per bicycle or surfboard; automobiles are not carried.

Bringing Your Car

Cars can be brought over only on the ferries from New London and Point Judith. This can be a very tricky business, especially on weekends or virtually any day during summer. Unless you're hoping to obtain standby passage, make a reservation at least 4–5 months ahead for summer or holiday weekends; there's more flexibility on weekdays. On the day of passage, be at the ferry dock and check in at the ferry window at least one hour before departure—if you're late, you risk losing your reservation to those waiting on standby.

If you're traveling with your car off-season or you're flexible with time, consider going standby. In high season, standby is highly unreliable. Again, arrive at the terminal at least

an hour before departure (a few hours ahead if you're trying to cross at a busy time). Once at the departure lot, check in with the attendant; he or she'll give you a ticket that establishes your place in the line, and then you must remain with your vehicle if and until you're permitted to board (when it's not especially crowded, attendants sometimes let drivers leave their cars unattended for a bit). If you travel standby, you're not guaranteed return passage from Block Island—which means you may have to return at a different time or on a different day than you had hoped.

By Plane

Flying to Block Island may not be as expensive as you think, and the time it saves, to say nothing of avoiding potential ferry hassles, can make this option quite useful. The only regularly scheduled service is offered by **New England Airlines** (800/243-2460, www.block-island.com/nea) out of **Westerly Airport** (56 Airport Rd., Westerly, U.S. 1 and Rte. 78, I-95 exit 1 from the north, I-95 exit 92 in Connecticut from the south). Hourly 12-minute flights are offered 7:30 A.M.–5:30 P.M. daily to Block Island, and 8 A.M.–6 P.M. back to Westerly. In summer, service runs a bit later, and additional flights to Block Island are offered on Thursday–Friday night and back to Westerly on Monday morning. The fare is about $50 one-way, $90 round-trip; for children $40 one-way, $80 round-trip; discounts are also available for seniors. New England Airlines also offers charter service to Block Island from virtually any airport in the continental United States.

You can reach Westerly Airport by **Amtrak** (800/USA-RAIL—800/872-7245, www.amtrak.com). Amtrak trains stop in the town of Westerly, where you'll need to take a cab to the airport. Call **Eagle Cab** (800/339-2970); the fare is about $15. If you miss the last ferry, or if high winds or poor weather force cancellation of the ferry, it's a 20–25-minute drive from the ferry terminal in Galilee to the airport in Westerly, and a 35–40-minute drive from New London.

A few other charter airlines fly frequently in and out of Block Island, often to regional Northeastern airports. These include a reputable Block Island–based option, **Resort Air** (401/466-2000, www.resortaircharter.com). Also, in summer, **Action Airlines** (800/243-8623, www.actionairlines.com) flies out of Groton, Connecticut, a few minutes from New London's ferry terminal, which makes this a handy option if you miss your boat; Action also does charter flights to New York City and the Hamptons in eastern Long Island.

Block Island Airport sits atop a hill in the center of the southern half of the island. The 2,500-foot runway is lighted, and taxis usually greet regularly scheduled flights and can easily be phoned to meet charters. There's a funky little restaurant here, Bethany's Airport Diner, and both car and bike rentals are available in summer. It's a pretty 20-minute walk into town from the airport: turn right out of the entrance and walk down Center Road.

GETTING AROUND

You'll hear plenty of grumbling among islanders about the blight of mopeds—they are a frequent cause of accidents, and as a means of transportation they leave something to be desired. There aren't too many parts of the island that can't be managed on a bicycle, and in fact many roads to out-of-the-way beaches and trails are prohibited to mopeds. If you are staying for more than a few days or traveling with a large group, you're better off bringing a car over. Of course, islanders don't like visitors bringing their cars in high season, but politically correct or not, there's no question that a car is convenient, especially if you are lugging kids to and from the beach. If you're coming for fewer than four days, however, and staying anywhere within a 10-minute walk of Old Harbor or New Harbor, where 90 percent of the island's accommodations are, you really need nothing more than a good pair of walking shoes to

enjoy a vacation on Block Island. You can count on the island's fleet of taxis to take you on longer trips, when you have luggage or shopping bags, or when a group needs to get somewhere.

If you do rent a moped, keep to the side of the road, always rent a helmet, and do not travel on the island's dirt roads, where scars from wipeouts are a constant reminder of the dangers. Keep in mind that you cannot take mopeds out after dusk. There are about 170 mopeds for rent on the island, but you may encounter a few stares or glares from islanders who count themselves among the "no-peds" contingent.

There are no street numbers on Block Island. The little signs mounted on the fronts of most houses and buildings are "fire numbers," used by the police and fire departments to locate buildings quickly in the event of an emergency. They mean nothing otherwise—their sequence has nothing to do with their location.

Bike, Moped, and Car Rentals

Bike rentals are offered at several shops, with rates running $15–25 daily. Mopeds cost up to $100 daily. Many of these same agencies rent cars. Weekly rates are usually offered, and all of these agencies take MasterCard and Visa; some take American Express and Discover too. A quick tip: Before renting a bike or a moped, stop by a hotel or the chamber of commerce information booth, where you can frequently find flyers giving you $10 or 10 percent off the cost of a rental.

As you get off the ferry in Old Harbor, you'll find two rental agencies within steps of the terminal. **Island Moped and Bike** (Chapel St., behind the Harborside Inn, 401/466-2700) rents six-speed beach cruiser bikes, 21-speed mountain bikes, tandems and tag-alongs, mopeds, and all the standard safety equipment. Offering a similarly extensive selection of bikes and mopeds, **Old Harbor Bike Shop** (50 yards left of the ferry terminal as you disembark, 401/466-2029, www.oldharborbikeshop.com) also rents open-top Jeeps, vans, and other autos. With locations in New Harbor and at Block Island Airport, **Block Island Bike and Car Rental** (Ocean Ave., 401/466-2297) has bikes, cars, and vans for rent.

Taxis

You'll see taxis lined up in Old Harbor and New Harbor, and also at the airport, waiting for passengers on scheduled ferry and plane crossings. You can also hail cabs on the street: Hold out your right hand and wave as one passes, even if it looks full or doesn't appear to be slowing down. If the driver can take you, the cab will pull over. If not, he'll often hold up his CB and wave it to you, indicating that he's calling for another cab to come to get you.

Island cab drivers can be a font of information, and most of them offer hour-long tours of the island ($55 for 1–2 people, $10 more for each additional person, prices mandated by the town). For simple rides, cabs charge a flat fee and do not use meters. It's always quite reasonable, and fares are always displayed clearly in the cab. Fares are firm and set by the town; it's illegal to negotiate higher or lower fares. Cabs can be fined for taking too many passengers or for accepting passengers carrying open containers of alcohol.

If you need to phone a cab, try any of the following companies: **McGoverns' Cab** (401/862-6087); **O. J.'s Taxi** (401/741-0500), whose driver specializes in island history and photography tours; **Monica's Taxi** (401/742-0000); and **Mig's Rig Taxi** (401/480-0493 or 401/466-2892, www.migsrigtaxi.com), who is only bookable in advance and also gives interesting tours around the island.

BACKGROUND

The Land

A tiny state of just about 1,500 square miles (about the size of greater Houston), Rhode Island contains about 400 miles of shoreline, including inlets, rivers, estuaries, and bays. Nearly every inch of the state lies within 20 miles of the ocean or Narragansett Bay, which begins at the northern end of the state, first as the Seekonk River and then the Providence River, and a large chunk of the state is on the islands of Aquidneck, Conanicut, Prudence, Block, and a few others. And while Rhode Island has a very high population density, the state actually feels fairly rural and undeveloped in many places.

Despite the nearly constant proximity of water frontage, Rhode Island has a distinct inland region whose personality is much like that of the rest of interior southern New England. The southern end of the state, however, from Napatree Point in the extreme southwest to Point Judith to the east, is one long and scenic expanse of beautiful golden sand, punctuated only by the occasional inlet. Directly behind these beaches are long and deep salt ponds, created by occasional breaks in the beach that allowed saltwater to pour in and that have then been sealed by shifting sands. These salt ponds are sheltered havens for wildlife watching, water sports, and fishing.

At Point Judith, the endless string of

COURTESY OF NEWPORT COUNTY CONVENTION & VISITORS BUREAU

a Block Island beach

beaches gives way to the mouth of enormous Narragansett Bay. Beaches extend, off and on, up the western shore of the bay nearly to Providence. A little more than a mile across Narragansett Bay lies the long and narrow Conanicut Island and, another mile east of that, the considerably larger Aquidneck Island. About 10 miles due south of Point Judith, well away from the mainland, lies the summer resort community of Block Island. And another couple of miles east of Aquidneck is the final bit of Rhode Island's oceanfront, Sakonnet. Another five miles east and you're in Massachusetts.

The thin swath of land fringing the ocean from Napatree Point clear up around Narragansett Bay to Providence is characterized by its low elevation and sandy soil. The East Bay and Sakonnet areas are slightly higher in elevation and are composed mostly of sandstone and other rock that hasn't eroded to nearly the degree that the low coastal plain has through the eons. Most of Rhode Island, however, is characterized by rolling terrain with peaks rising occasionally to 700 or 800 feet—not terribly high compared with northern

New England or even the highest points in nearby northeastern Connecticut and central Massachusetts. But compared with other small states that fringe the Eastern Seaboard—New Jersey and Delaware, for example—Rhode Island is relatively hilly and offers a nice balance for anybody who loves to admire both the ocean and the hilly countryside.

GEOLOGY

Geologically speaking, Rhode Island offers a classic view of how glaciers form the land. Virtually every square foot of the state owes its general appearance to the encroachment and then recession of a massive glacial formation that ended just a split second ago in geological terms, around 8,000 B.C.

Except for a narrow strip of coastal plain near the ocean, the western two-thirds of Rhode Island sits atop very ancient igneous and metamorphic rock. The eastern third (where you'll find Providence and the Blackstone River Valley, the islands of Narragansett Bay, the East Bay towns, and the Sakonnet Peninsula) lies on younger and softer sedimentary rock. The land underlying Block Island and that little strip of coastal plain in South County, however, originally came from much farther north.

A block of ice perhaps a mile high drifted down from Canada as far south as the present tip of Rhode Island during the most recent ice age. This catastrophic action scarred the soil, lifting boulders, rocks, and sediment from northern New England and carrying them hundreds of miles south to the ocean. As the earth's temperature rose and the glacier on top of Rhode Island slowly melted, a stream of debris-laden water flowed downhill toward sea level, building up piles of rocks at the leading edge of the glacier—and forming the terminal moraine that underlies Block Island.

As the glacier continued to recede northward, it likely paused for a time, leaving another deposit of sand and debris called a recessional moraine. It now forms the narrow fringe of sandy coastal plain that lies along the shore.

While most of the land of Rhode Island was not deposited by glaciers, every inch of it was shaped by glacial movement. Before the ice age, this land would have stood many yards higher in elevation and would have looked much different from the way it does today. The land that has now been displaced by Narragansett Bay would have been soft rock and soil that gave way easily to the tremendous weight and pressure exerted by the massive glaciers—this soil was pushed out into the ocean by the glacier's steady and massive push.

The islands of Aquidneck, Conanicut, and Prudence, along with the jagged peninsulas that poke into the bay from Bristol, Warwick, and other Narragansett towns, resisted the glacial erosion more effectively. The earth here is chiefly composed of ancient igneous and metamorphic rock—it's not as hard and erosion-resistant as the western and northwestern interior sections of the state, and so it's not nearly as hilly. But these islands and peninsulas provided a substantial enough resistance to survive the ice age above sea level, while the glaciers carved out what is now the bay around them.

Throughout the state's interior, you'll see

THE NAME GAME

The genesis of how and why Rhode Island acquired its official name – technically known as Rhode Island and Providence Plantations – has never been definitively nailed down. The region has no particular history linking it to the Greek island of Rhodes, and it is quite clearly not an island. So how did it come to be known as Rhode Island?

The history of the name is a jumble of vague associations and mistaken identities, but it's believed that the name Rhode was first used to describe Block Island by 16th-century Italian explorer Giovanni da Verrazano, who wrote that it reminded him of the Greek island. In the next century, sailors passing by another small Narragansett Bay island, today known as Aquidneck, mistook it for the island Verrazano had identified, and started calling it Rhode Island. Later, as Providence developed, the entire region became known as Rhode Island and Providence Plantations.

Confused? No doubt the state's residents were too, which may be why they later shortened the state's name to simply Rhode Island. Legally, however, it remains Rhode Island and Providence Plantations – the longest name in all the United States, ironically held by its smallest state.

other evidence of glacial activity. Some of the state's many freshwater ponds and natural reservoirs were formed when a chunk of glacier broke off and melted, forming a so-called kettle pond. And everywhere you'll find boulders and rocks made up of granite, quartz, and other materials that were carried out this far by glacial activity.

The glacier is also partially responsible for eroding the softer soil that once covered much of western Rhode Island, revealing the harder igneous and metamorphic rock below the surface. Those rocks were formed by molten lava that pushed its way out from the earth's mantle and cooled beneath the surface over many millions of millennia. Where that surface has been eroded, jagged and sharp rocky ridges now rise out of the soil.

The mostly sedimentary rock that forms the eastern third of the state is rather new by geological standards, perhaps a couple of million years old. This rock was formed by deposits of mud, gravel, and sand over a lower bedrock of igneous and metamorphic rock, which over eons of shifting and faulting earth were compressed and in some cases pushed up to the earth's surface. Some of this muck compressed into coal, of which small deposits have been found in Portsmouth, Cranston, and other parts of Rhode Island through the years; these are among the easternmost coal deposits found on the North American continent.

CLIMATE

Compared with some other regions of New England, Rhode Island enjoys a fairly moderate climate, especially in the parts of the state that lie within 15 miles or so of the ocean and the bay (meaning most of the state). The presence of the Atlantic Ocean and Narragansett Bay keep temperatures a bit warmer in winter than inland, meaning that big snowstorms in Massachusetts often take the form of rain here. Conversely, in summer, hot weather is often cooled by sea breezes, especially out on Block Island and the southern tips of Westerly and Newport.

Its position on the Gulf Stream ensures rather unpredictable weather, especially during hurricane season (mid-summer through mid-fall), as ocean-driven winds often sweep across the entire state. Major damage-inducing storms rarely hit more than once every 5–10 years, however. The state has a long growing season by Northeastern standards, generally commencing in late April–early May and lasting through the better part of October (it's longer, obviously, along the coast).

Statewide, the average low temperature in January is about 29°F, and the average high in July is a comfortable 73°F. Annual precipitation (in both rain and snow) is averages about 42 inches per year and ranges anywhere from 25 to nearly 70 inches. The state, at least in

the northwestern hills, usually sees its first real snowfall in late November–early December, and the last one is in April. Rainfall tends to be consistent throughout the year, with 3–4 inches monthly (the lowest amounts are in summer, but passing and not infrequent late-afternoon and evening thunderstorms can dump significant amounts of rain).

ENVIRONMENTAL ISSUES

As nice as it is for wildlife watchers to be in such close proximity to fauna, it's also unfortunate because wild animals have become increasingly dependent on people and dangerously abundant in areas with heavy traffic and an environment that barely supports them. Where there is overpopulation, they are a nuisance in the eyes of many people—blamed for spreading Lyme disease, ravaging gardens and yards, and causing traffic accidents. Rhode Island does have some areas that are sparsely populated by people, especially the western and northwestern sections of the state—you'll even find a few designated hunting grounds. But anybody who drives on a daily basis in Rhode Island is sure to see deer leaping across the road, usually at night—sadly, many have been struck.

With all the talk these days of encroaching suburban sprawl—and it's true that this trend is one of the greatest threats facing the state in the 21st century—it's easy to forget that most of Rhode Island was already deforested by the early 1800s, when the state's economy was almost entirely agrarian.

Ironically, the region's woodlands were saved not so much by conservation efforts, which didn't develop in earnest until the 20th century, but by the industrial revolution. In places where the hilly, rocky terrain made fast and simple transportation routes difficult, or where a lack of rivers made hydropower impractical, the land was left largely to revert to woodland, and some areas were even reforested to increase the supply of lumber.

Despite this, the amount of undeveloped land has consistently diminished at a rapid rate since the late 19th century. In Rhode Island's countless river valleys, fields of crops gave way to magnificent mills and factories. Farms still thrive in a few parts of the state, but their number has decreased dramatically.

Rhode Island's regulatory economy has ensured that much of the area enjoys clean air and water, as efforts have been made to clean up the pollution of the mills and factories that boosted the economy in the 20th century. Isolated chemical factories and power plants continue to cause problems in some areas.

One of the most contentious ongoing issues in the region is the controversy over how to manage coastal fish and shellfish effectively. Rampant overfishing had decimated cod, flounder, and other groundfish species by the mid-1980s. At that point, the federal government seized fisheries all over New England in a bid to restore populations using quotas and periodic bans. While the effort has been successful at restoring some species, such as haddock, bluefish, and many species of shellfish, others still languish at severely reduced levels, with cod even less plentiful than in the 1980s. Along with the fish stocks, many people employed in the fishing industry have languished as well. Tensions between them and regulators have led to angry protests and outright flouting of quotas, as well as disputes over the numbers used by scientists and environmentalists to justify them. Currently the two sides are cooperating. While some areas of coastal Rhode Island—most notably, the port of Galilee in Narragansett—continue to thrive as fishing ports, they are nowhere near as vibrant as they once were.

Flora and Fauna

Much of Rhode Island's flora and fauna is typical of southern New England. The state is a haven for bird-watching, as the coast and Narragansett Bay are on a major migratory bird route. Several parks and preserves near the water have been established specifically for this purpose.

There's actually a misconception that the farther north you go in New England, the more likely you are to see wildlife. In fact, in Vermont, New Hampshire, and Maine, so much of the land is undeveloped that many animals steer clear of roads, villages, and people—they have the luxury of rarely having to leave their remote habitats, and they maintain a healthy fear of mankind. Rhode Island, however densely populated it may be, is actually an easy place to spot a variety of animals. The state is heavily wooded with quite a few parks and preserves, and yet it is also heavily developed. Wildlife and human life coexist in close proximity, and mammals in Rhode Island tend to be less afraid of people and better able to feed themselves by scavenging through backyards, compost heaps, and garbage cans.

TREES AND SHRUBS

About 50 species of tree are common to New England, but only a fraction are present in Rhode Island. The state is about 60 percent forested, with slightly more than 400,000 acres of woodland. Common conifers ("evergreens") throughout the state include the conical eastern red cedars, towering reddish-brown tamaracks, prickly blue spruces, white and red pines, hemlocks, and right along the shore in some spots, gnarled pitch pines.

While you don't hear as much about leaf-peeping in Rhode Island as you do in other New England states, Rhode Island's broadleaf trees put on a spectacular show each fall, especially in places with sugar, silver, and red maple trees—the red maple, also known as the swamp maple, is Rhode Island's state tree. The peak time for watching them burst with bright foliage is late October in most of the state and mid-October in the most northwestern and hilly areas. There are 11 species of oak in Rhode Island, and they can be quite brilliant in the fall—you're most likely to see white, scarlet, bear, swamp white, scrub, pin, post, chestnut, and black oak trees.

a butterfly at Bristol's Audubon Environmental Education Center

Some of the other tall Rhode Island broadleaf species include beech, birch (the pretty white birch are more prevalent in the north), dogwoods (which flower beautifully all spring), elms (although many of these perished from disease during the middle of the last century), holly, poplar, honey locust, hickory, and weeping willow.

Smaller broadleaf trees and shrubs that dot the landscape, many of which bloom with a riot of colors, include speckled alder, dogwood, sumac, pink azalea, rhododendron, multiflora and beach rose, northern bayberry, and pussy willow.

Hundreds of varieties of wildflowers bloom across the state, beginning most vibrantly in June and remaining vital well into early fall. Also look for beach plum, a shrub bearing hard plumlike fruit that is ubiquitous on the coast in Rhode Island and puts on quite a show with its pretty fuchsia flowers.

INVERTEBRATES

Coastal Rhode Island has long had a reputation for its abundance of shellfish, but during much of the 20th century pollution and overfishing combined to deplete or spoil the region as a source of seafood. Thankfully, immensely ambitious efforts to clean up the waters off Rhode Island, along with careful harvesting regulations, have restored the region's stock of these tasty creatures.

A great range of marine invertebrates are found off Rhode Island's shoreline, including a number of jellyfish and sea anemones, most of which are harmless, except for the large and extremely dangerous lion's mane jellyfish, which is more common in northern waters. Scour the beaches and rocks during low tide and you'll find marine mollusks of every ilk, from Atlantic dogwinkles and edible common periwinkles to large (up to six inches long) knobbed whelks that live in those pretty yellow-gray shells that kids are prone to hold to their ears in hopes of hearing the seashore. You'll also see tons of lively hermit crabs sidling along the beach line, living safely inside the mobile homes they've fashioned out of gastropod shells.

Tasty blue mussels cling to rocks and pilings. Bay scallops and Eastern oysters are found in shallow waters, as are clams. A true Rhode Islander knows how to identify clams—long thin razor clams, hard-shell Northern quahogs (which include the prized cherrystones and littlenecks, the latter often found minced in clam chowder and atop pizzas), Atlantic surf clams, and most deliciously, soft-shelled "steamer" clams. Also found in shallow waters among the rocks and mudflats are sea urchins (which are dangerous if stepped on), common green crabs, rock crabs, sand fiddlers, and the famously delicious blue crabs. Farther out, beginning in about 10 feet of water, sea scallops and lobsters make their homes, coming closest to the shore in summer.

Less engaging to most people are the many land invertebrates that slither and crawl around the state, and indeed some of these—ticks, mosquitoes, horseflies and deerflies, carpenter ants, yellow jackets, cockroaches, Japanese beetles—are a genuine nuisance. But on summer nights it's a comfort to fall asleep to the distinct chatter, trill, and staccato of the zillions of katydids and tree crickets. Spiders munch on most pests and rarely bother humans, as is true of the many beautiful dragonflies, butterflies, and ladybugs that swarm around flower beds.

BIRDS AND FISH

Given the Ocean State's coastal location, many islands, and extensive shoreline, Rhode Island is rich with sea creatures and birdlife, and fishing and bird-watching are among Rhode Islanders' favorite pastimes. Fairly close to shore in season (May to November) are bluefish and striped bass. Many other varieties of fish are found in deeper and farther reaches of the Atlantic. People sometimes overlook the fact that Rhode Island also has dozens of freshwater ponds, lakes, and rivers; inland species common in the state include trout (many ponds are stocked with them), bluegills, bass, and perch.

Rhode Island lies in the middle of a common migratory route for many species of North American birdlife. The state's coastal areas and many wildlife preserves contain a veritable who's who of the bird world, especially in spring as birds fly from warmer climes toward Canada, and in fall when they head south again. Large, dramatic species such as peregrine falcons and blue herons can be spotted throughout the year, while smaller species, including warblers, sparrows, and thrushes, congregate at beaches and other low-lying areas during the summer and fall.

REPTILES AND AMPHIBIANS

Thirteen species of snake live in Rhode Island, none of them poisonous. Rattlesnakes and copperheads, common to other parts of New England, are considered all but extinct here, although there may be some slithering around the western and northwestern hills. Note that many nonvenomous snakes resemble their venomous cousins; Eastern hognose snakes look like copperheads, for instance.

Turtles are the other type of reptile commonly found in Rhode Island, especially painted turtles, which are known to sunbathe in groups around rivers and swamps. Respect the space of the snapping turtle, whose sturdy jaws can leave you with a nasty bite. You won't see them very often, but they do love to swim and cavort in muddy-bottomed rivers and other bodies of water.

Among amphibians, newts and salamanders aren't easy to see, as they often blend in well with their surroundings, but the yellow-spotted and red varieties do stand out a bit. They tend to be found around creeks and live under rocks and logs, and they are most visible March–October during the day. Frogs are known for their often loud choruses on spring and summer nights when they seek out mates. Spring peepers, bullfrogs, and Woodhouse toads frequent ponds and swamps, while common American toads and wood frogs prefer yards, fields, and wooded areas. In spring, unfortunately, thousands of frogs and toads are hit by automobiles in areas where large numbers of them are moving toward popular breeding grounds.

MAMMALS

The mammals you're mostly likely to see around Rhode Island are white-tailed deer, raccoons, opossums, Eastern chipmunks, Eastern gray squirrels, and striped skunks. All of these species are common in secluded woodlands, developed suburbs, and even some urban areas, and most of them are not easily startled by the presence of human beings.

Skunks, opossums, and raccoons are primarily nocturnal, and if you see one during the day, you should keep your distance, especially if it's behaving erratically or aggressively; there's a chance it's carrying rabies. This disease can make an otherwise harmless animal bite at will, and if you come into physical contact with such a creature, you should immediately contact an emergency physician.

Less commonly sighted animals, which you have the best chance of seeing in state parks and preserves, include black bears (only rarely in northwestern Rhode Island), Eastern cottontail rabbits, woodchucks, beavers, meadow voles, coyotes (again mostly in the northern part of the state, but they are becoming increasingly common despite once being virtually extinct), gray and red foxes, fishers, mink, and river otters.

Whale-watching cruises operate off Rhode Island's coast—these dramatic sea mammals, once hunted to near-extinction, often inhabit the state's waters. Finback, humpback, and minke whales are sighted most often, as is the occasional school of bottlenose dolphins. Whales are most common spring–fall, with small numbers summering off the coast and the majority passing through in April–May on their way north and back south again in October–December during their migration to warmer waters.

Both harbor and gray seals, which have always been fairly common from Maine to Cape Cod, have made a recent comeback along Rhode Island's shoreline, primarily in Narragansett Bay.

History

BEFORE 1636

The land that is now Rhode Island was occupied by a handful of Algonquin Native American groups through much of the early part of the last millennium—Narragansetts, Niantics, Nipmucs, Pequots, and Wampanoags all lived here, and not always at peace with one another. The nations shared a common genealogical heritage and similar languages and other cultural traits, but they also observed their own distinct rituals, laws, and other practices. Even today, many Rhode Island place-names have Native American roots: Conanicut Island, for example, is named for Canonicus, a 17th-century leader of the Narragansetts; Pawtucket translates as "place with the waterfall"; and Sakonnet means "land of the wild goose."

Contrary to what some history books might have schoolkids believe, the colonists from England who arrived in the New World in the 1620s did not find an impenetrable wilderness but rather a network of Indian villages, staked-out fishing areas, and cleared and tilled fields. Even the forests were open and parklike, the result of frequent burnings to aid in hunting.

Among Rhode Island's indigenous people, women took on many of the most labor-intensive tasks, cultivating and harvesting the fields, tanning hides, and maintaining order at home. In warmer months the people settled in open fields, and with the coming of cold weather they moved to wooded valleys and other sheltered areas.

When Roger Williams and his followers settled in Rhode Island, the area was home to perhaps 20,000 Native Americans. Although Williams himself worked peacefully with the people he encountered near Providence, within 50 years the effects of European settlement almost wiped out the population. The settlers spread smallpox and other diseases that Europeans were immune to, but Native Americans were not; they systematically removed Native Americans from the best land, and eventually from all the land; they introduced alcohol, murdered many who fought to keep their land, and sold many more into slavery.

Before the first Europeans established a permanent settlement in Rhode Island, quite a few explorers passed near the shore or spent time on land, and some left accounts of their time here. A few early state histories asserted that the Vikings were Rhode Island's first European inhabitants, but it is now believed that those settlements were many miles north of present-day New England in Canada's Labrador. One early explorer to survey the coast appears to have been Portuguese navigator Miguel Corte-Real, who sailed through in 1511. The most celebrated explorer, however, is no doubt Giovanni da Verrazano, a Florentine sailing in the New World under the French flag; in 1524 he explored the waters around New York City (the Verrazano Narrows Bridge, which connects Brooklyn to Staten Island, is named for him) and up to Rhode Island. Dutch traders later explored the coast, among them Adriaen Block, for whom Block Island is named.

COLONIAL SETTLEMENT

The founder of modern Rhode Island's first permanent European settlement is Roger Williams, who arrived in what is now Providence in 1636. This happened a year after an odd and reclusive Anglican clergyman named William Blackstone (for whom the river and valley are named) established a camp in what is now Cumberland, but Blackstone lived alone, largely as a hermit, and no true community emerged in his wake. Williams arrived with the intention of establishing a settlement, and he did so quickly. More remarkably, he arrived after having been banished from the Massachusetts Bay Colony, where his beliefs in the separation of church and state, and that the Puritans should completely break their ties with the mother country's Anglican Church, greatly angered the colony's rigid and autocratic powers. Faced with an arrest warrant

and the threat of deportation, Williams gathered a handful of sympathizers and traveled to the confluence of the Woonasquatucket and Moshassuck Rivers.

He secured a tract of land there through negotiations with his Narragansett friend Canonicus, and within two years he had convinced a group of about a dozen other settlers to encamp at this new plantation he called Providence (in recognition of "God's providence" to Williams during his time of distress). Providence grew quickly and adopted a civil democratic form of government that tolerated all religious beliefs from the start. In 1639 he and a fellow resident of Providence baptized each other and then 10 others in founding what has become the modern-day Baptist Church of the United States. By 1640, Providence functioned as its own independent political entity, with a board of governors who conducted local business according to the will of the entire community.

Providence came to be the most influential of four independent communities that would eventually unify as the Rhode Island colony. Like Providence, Portsmouth, Newport, and Warwick were also formed by political dissidents from Massachusetts. John Clarke and William Coddington were banished from the Massachusetts Bay Colony in 1638 for publicly asserting their differences with Puritan governmental and religious authority. They came to Providence, consulted with Williams, and decided to settle in the northernmost section of Aquidneck Island. Later that year, their friend and political inspiration in Massachusetts, Anne Hutchinson, joined them at this new settlement, originally named Pocasset.

But Hutchinson, Clarke, and Coddington could not resolve their power ambitions, and in 1639 the latter two ultimately left with a small group of allies to form their own settlement, Newport, at the southern tip of the island. Pocasset came to be called Portsmouth. While Hutchinson and the Clarke-Coddington groups maintained some autonomy, they also recognized the strength in numbers, and in

THE FIVE INDIGENOUS TRIBES OF RHODE ISLAND

When Europeans first began to explore what is now Rhode Island in the 1500s, there were five indigenous groups living here: the Pequots, the Nipmucs, the Niantics, the Narragansetts, and the Wampanoags.

Among the five, the Pequots – who lived mostly in what is now southeastern Connecticut but also in southwestern Rhode Island – exercised the greatest degree of autonomy and defiance of the settlers. This warlike mentality quickly led to their near-extinction as colonists killed them and even turned friendlier tribes, such as the Narragansetts and the Connecticut Mohegans, against them.

In the 1630s the Pequots killed a pair of British merchants whom they encountered sailing up the Connecticut River on a trading mission. They further raised the ire of the settlers when they killed the respected explorer John Oldham off the coast of Block Island in 1636, an act that led to immediate reprisals in the form of burnings and raids by English troops. The Pequots continued to strike, attacking and murdering several Wethersfield families during the winter of 1636-1637 and unsuccessfully attempting to establish a warring pact with their neighbors, the formidable Narragansett Indians of nearby Aquidneck Island.

These tensions escalated the following spring into the great Pequot War of 1637, during which about 130 European settlers from the Connecticut River towns, along with 70 allied Mohegans, developed a plan to destroy their enemy. Believing it wise to approach from the least likely side, the group attacked from the east, sailing to Rhode Island's Narragansett Bay and marching west with a force of about 400 Narragansetts looking on.

The Pequots were concentrated in a pair of encampments near what is now Norwich, Connecticut, each of these a several-acre enclosure of a few dozen wigwams. The settlers, led by John Mason, struck the largest Pequot community at dawn and killed most of its inhabitants, burning the wigwams and shooting any who attempted to flee. The second Pequot encampment attempted to thwart the invasion but was easily driven to retreat. During the next two months, the remaining members of the severely crippled Pequot league moved west toward New York but were met in a massive swamp, which would later become Fairfield, by Mason and his battalion. Again most of the Indians were killed, with the remaining 180 Pequots taken hostage and brought to Hartford.

The Pequots could not have been conquered without the assistance of the Mohegans and the Narragansetts, with whom the English signed a treaty of friendship in 1637. But peace between the Native Americans and the English would last only a few decades, until King Philip's War.

The Nipmuc Indians lived principally in central Massachusetts but also occupied some land in Northern Rhode Island. Their fate after King Philip's War, in which they battled the colonists, is little documented, but it's believed that most survivors fled west into Canada, and those who remained joined with the few Indian groups that remained friendly to the colonists.

Rhode Island's Niantics, distinct from but related to the Niantics of southeastern Connecticut, lived in the southern part of mainland Rhode Island, where the sea borders modern-day Westerly and Charlestown. Their leader, Ninigret, managed to prolong their viability by keeping distance from the Native Americans who rebelled against the colonists. Ninigret met on several occasions with colonists, and he even refrained from participating in King Philip's War. This tribe of Narragansetts (as colonists increasingly came to call all Rhode Island Indians) continued to live on their land through the late 1800s. By that time, their numbers had dwindled, and eventually their final bits of land were taken from them.

Rhode Island's modern-day Narragansetts are mostly of Niantic descent, but they're joined by some who descend from the actual Narragansett nation, which was perhaps the largest tribe in Rhode Island during the 17th century. By the time of King Philip's War, there were 5,000 Narragansetts living throughout Rhode Island. Their larger numbers are explained in part by them not succumbing to the diseases that brought down the more powerful Wampanoags, who lived mostly in southeastern Massachusetts but also in part of eastern Rhode Island. As the Wampanoags declined, the Narragansetts took over their territory on the islands of what is now Narragansett Bay.

It was with Narragansett and Wampanoag leaders that Roger Williams socialized and negotiated a land treaty on his arrival in the 1630s. Canonicus was the sachem, or ruler, of the Narragansetts and would become a close friend of Williams until his death in 1647; Massasoit headed the Wampanoags, and Williams assisted in bringing some degree of peace between these two nations. He also made peace between the Native Americans of Rhode Island and the colonists of Massachusetts, who had arrested and banished Williams in the first place.

By the 1670s, the Narragansetts were led by a descendant of Canonicus named Canonchet. The leader of the Wampanoags, Philip, the son of Massasoit, sought to unify New England's many Native American groups in an ambitious and perhaps desperate attempt to overthrow the Puritan grip on the region. An Indian who was a Christian convert loyal to the settlers betrayed King Philip's intentions and was quickly killed by Philip's men. The settlers escalated the conflict by capturing and killing the people who had killed the informant, and so began King Philip's War, which would ultimately seal the fate of Native Americans in the northeastern United States.

The war was fought near the Rhode Island–Massachusetts border, where the Wampanoags occupied a fort at Mount Hope, today part of the Rhode Island community of Bristol. After several colonists in the town of Swansea were killed, thousands of colonial troops descended on Mount Hope. The Indians managed to destroy about a dozen colonial settlements and significantly damage another 40; in all, roughly half the English villages in New England during the 1670s were damaged. More than 800 colonists and about 3,000 Native Americans were killed. The Indians lost about 15 percent of their total population, while the colonists lost perhaps 1.5 percent.

In the end, although many colonists were killed, all of the region's Native Americans were ultimately contained. At the onset of the war, Canonchet and his Narragansetts adopted a neutral stance, but the colonists attacked the Narragansetts preemptively, and Canonchet then led several of the violent raids against the colonists, destroying houses in Providence and Warwick. King Philip spent time in northern New England attempting to unify other tribes into a greater resistance. Canonchet was captured and executed near Stonington, Connecticut, in 1676. Soon after, King Philip was captured and killed near Mount Hope. The last remaining Narragansett royal, Quaiapen, sister of Niantic leader Ninigret, died shortly thereafter in a battle at Warwick. By summer 1676, the Narragansetts had been broken and the Wampanoags decimated; Philip's surviving family members were sold into slavery. The end of King Philip's War signified the end of the Native American way of life in Rhode Island as it had existed before European settlement.

THE DORR REBELLION

Rhode Island governed according to its colonial charter, granted in 1663, for longer than any other Northern state. By the 1840s, the governing principles laid out in this document had become a poor fit for the state, especially given Rhode Island's rapid industrialization and growing immigration. What rankled many citizens was the antiquated criteria for voting rights – only men owning land worth $134 (a large amount in 1663, and still in 1840) were permitted to participate in the electoral process.

The unjust effect of these rules seemed particularly appalling given Rhode Island's track record on freedom of religion – and its vehement protests against taxation without representation during the American Revolution. Here, more than 60 years after the United States had secured independence, Rhode Island was letting a comparatively wealthy minority set policies and laws for the general population. Of course, the state legislature was made up chiefly of well-to-do landowners who knew that any concessions toward universal men's suffrage would severely diminish their power and influence. They fought to keep this enormous chunk of the population disenfranchised.

Thomas Dorr, a resident of the still-rural village of Chepachet in western Rhode Island, thought it was time for Rhode Island's lawmakers to recognize the changing times and extend full voting rights to all male residents, as neighboring states had done. Of course, women would not be empowered to vote in Rhode Island or in any U.S. state until well into the 20th century, so even with reform, half the adult population would continue to be excluded from the political process.

Interestingly, Dorr was from neither an immigrant nor an industrial background. Born in 1805 to a wealthy Rhode Island family, he became a successful lawyer and around 1840 began rallying for popular legal reforms to liberalize the state's voting laws. Dorr's People's Party, frustrated with the lack of headway they were able to make against the state's conservative incumbent legislators, called its own constitutional convention in October 1841 to amend the antiquated state constitution. During the convention, his party ratified what they called the People's Constitution. Of course, this entire process was outside the laws of Rhode Island, and the new constitution was not recognized by the sitting legislature, which overwhelmingly voted down the People's Party's attempts at reform.

In effect, Rhode Island suddenly found itself with competing legislatures, each acting in defiance of the other. The federal govern-

---

1640 agreed that the two communities would submit to joint rule, with Coddington as governor of this new "colony." A few years later the island then known as Aquidneck adopted the name accidentally assigned to it many years earlier—Rhodes—and in 1644 it officially took the name Rhode Island.

Warwick was settled in 1638 by yet another of the dissidents who originally came to Portsmouth, Samuel Gorton. An idealist and ideologue who made trouble everywhere he went, Gorton was banished first from Plymouth and then ultimately from Portsmouth, where he drew the ire of Hutchinson and her followers. He took up residence in Providence for a time, and then in 1645 moved with a small group to Pawtuxet, the original village of Warwick. He arranged a deal with the Narragansetts to transfer that land to the English crown, and a year later he sailed to England, where he enlisted the aid of an old friend, the earl of Warwick, to secure a royal guarantee of title from parliament. In honor of the earl's assistance, he named the settlement Warwick in 1648.

As the four individual settlements grew, Roger Williams began to recognize their vulnerability, especially given the proximity of the two colonies in Massachusetts that so despised them all and the growing colony to the

ment decided not to intervene and rather encouraged the dual governments to work things out. Matters worsened on April 18, 1842, when Dorr's party elected him the new governor of Rhode Island, while the original state government reelected incumbent Samuel H. King. By May, Thomas Dorr had rallied a team of supporters to stage a coup on the Providence Armory, in hopes of turning the military to his side and ultimately taking over the State House and other official state offices. Relatively few Dorrites took part in the mission on the armory, and Thomas Dorr and his followers were easily turned back. Several weeks later, Dorr decided to call his new government to assemble at Sprague's Tavern in Chepachet (which still operates today as a restaurant, the Stagecoach Tavern). Governor King sent the Rhode Island militia to silence this rebellion. Dorr's own small militia waited at Acote's Hill, about a quarter mile south of where present-day U.S. 44 crosses through Chepachet, but on realizing that King's troops were far greater in number and firepower, Dorr and his group retreated to the tavern.

King and his men marched to Sprague's Tavern, where they ordered the Dorrites out at gunpoint. During the standoff, more words were exchanged than bullets, although one of King's men did manage to fire a shot through the keyhole of the locked tavern, striking a Dorrite in the thigh.

After the standoff, Dorr fled the state. The appropriately named governor King took a rather autocratic approach to restoring order: He declared martial law and had Dorr arrested and charged with high treason. The rival government was completely shut down, and many of Dorr's followers were arrested.

Although disgraced by the state's official government, Thomas Dorr was hailed a hero by many, and the goals of the so-called Dorr Rebellion were eventually largely accomplished. Fearing a backlash and continued civic unrest, the conservative state legislature amended the constitution, dramatically liberalizing the requirements for voting rights. In 1843 Rhode Islanders took to the polls and approved the new Rhode Island constitution.

The rest of Dorr's life was quite sad, however. He was found guilty of treason in 1844 and harshly sentenced to hard labor for the rest of his life. Many Rhode Islanders and even some dignitaries rallied for his pardon, which was granted after he had served a year in prison. Still, Dorr was demoralized and physically weakened by this ordeal, and he died just a few years later.

west, Connecticut. In 1643 Williams sailed to England to secure a parliamentary grant that would guarantee all four communities a legal basis for existence; the grant, which he secured from the earl of Warwick in 1644, named the new colony "The Incorporation of Providence Plantations in the Narragansett Bay in New England." Originally the grant referred only to Providence, Portsmouth, and Newport; Warwick was admitted to this new union during the colony's first legislative session in 1647. That first session met in Portsmouth, and for a time subsequent sessions met in different cities, with Newporters typically serving as president of each session. At that time, Newport had the largest population (about 300), much more than Providence's 200 residents.

New towns were added to the Rhode Island colony through the rest of the 17th century, including Westerly in 1661, Block Island in 1664 (incorporated as the town of New Shoreham), Kings Towne in 1674 (it split into North Kingstown and South Kingstown in 1723), East Greenwich in 1677, and Jamestown (the town name for the island of Conanicut) in 1678. In Massachusetts during these years, the towns of Barrington, Little Compton, and Bristol were all formed; after a boundary dispute was resolved, these three communities became part of Rhode Island.

REVOLUTION

Even as it was consolidating itself as an independent entity, trouble was brewing with the original inhabitants of Narragansett Bay and would eventually boil over into the bloody conflict known as King Philip's War. Rhode Islanders are quick to point out that the war had its origins not in their state but in Massachusetts, even if most of it was fought in Rhode Island. Despite the good relations Roger Williams enjoyed with the Native Americans, the same could not be said of his neighbors to the north in Plymouth Colony. The colony's governor, William Bradford, originally got along well with the Wampanoag chief, Massasoit, but tensions began to simmer after the deaths of two leaders of settlers on the Rhode Island–Massachusetts border. Eventually colonists arrested Massasoit's son Alexander on spurious charges. During the march he was forced to make to Plymouth, he fell ill and died. Foreseeing the inevitable conflict, Massasoit's younger son, Metacomet, whom the colonists called Philip, launched a preemptive raid on the Massachusetts town of Swansea. The colonists counterattacked by invading the Wampanoag camp at Mount Hope in Bristol, forcing 1,500 Indians to escape across the river on rafts.

The war that followed drew together many of the Native Americans in New England in a last-gasp attempt to push back English expansion. Despite burning Providence and many other towns in the yearlong campaign, the Indians were defeated by their lack of supplies and treachery among infighting groups as much by the English arms. By the time peace was agreed on in 1676, Philip and more than 5,000 Indians had been killed, with many more sold into slavery; on the English side, 500 colonists had been killed. After the war, many Native Americans were permanently relocated to South County, near Charlestown, effectively ending autonomous Indian presence in the state. Eventually, of course, even those settlements were removed in the westward march of Europeans across America.

Despite the bloodiness of the war, it was not the only conflict that Rhode Islanders had to deal with. During much of the next century and beyond, there were an amazing number and variety of border disputes created by a legacy of conflicting land deeds and purchases from Native Americans as well as frequent claims on chunks of what is now Rhode Island by Massachusetts and Connecticut.

Within the first two decades of Rhode Island's formation, religious dissidents from around the world began to learn of the small colony's reputation for tolerance. Quakers arrived in the New World in 1657 with the hope of spreading the word through the colonies. Their proselytizing in Massachusetts was met with fiery resistance, to the point that one Quaker, Mary Dyer, was hanged in Boston in 1660 for attempting to make converts out of Puritans. But they were welcomed in Newport, many of whose residents actually joined the Society of Friends during the city's first several decades. Providence and Roger Williams were less enthusiastic about the Quakers, but consistent with their beliefs, they made no efforts to curtail this freedom of religion; Williams even engaged in a three-day debate with a Quaker spokesperson in 1671.

Jewish settlers from Holland came to Newport in 1658 and swiftly established the Jeshuat Israel congregation. The community thrived for more than a century, until Britain occupied Newport during the Revolutionary War. The settlement's Touro Synagogue, still in use, is the oldest in the United States.

A major shift in political power in England, the restoration of King Charles II in 1660, caused concern for the leaders of the young Rhode Island, so a group sailed to the mother country in 1663 and successfully secured a royal charter to supersede the parliamentary grant issued by the earl of Warwick in 1644. Interestingly, this charter—which fully asserted the religious tolerance of the state—remained in effect until 1843, well after the United States had secured independence from England.

Rhode Island developed a reputation as a rather ruthless little shipping powerhouse during the latter half of the 17th century.

Newport and other communities outfitted a number of privateering ships, mostly during the myriad colonial wars of that time—the Anglo-Dutch trade wars of the 1650s–1670s and the French and Indian Wars of the following century. Privateering, where private armed ships were enlisted to attack and capture enemy ships, was not even formally outlawed by the Rhode Island Assembly until the very end of the 17th century. Even then, illegal privateering, which is really just a nice way to say piracy, took place regularly at the hands of Rhode Island crews.

From the late 1600s onward, Rhode Island developed into one of the world's busiest trading hubs, establishing commercial ties with virtually every other colony and many other countries, including England, the Atlantic islands colonized by Portugal, western Africa, and the West Indies. Most colonists still made their living as farmers until well into the 18th century, but increasingly and especially in port communities such as Providence, Newport, Bristol, Westerly, Wickford, and Pawtuxet, many residents made their living in the merchant trade or related professions such as shipbuilding.

Slave-trading was easily the most lucrative form of commercial enterprise during this period, and Rhode Island raked in more money through this abhorrent practice than just about any other state. (Despite the colony's infamy as a slave-trading hub, in 1774 Rhode Island became the first state to ban slave trade; in 1784 the state outlawed owning slaves entirely.) A huge percentage of the New World's slave ships during the late 17th–late 18th centuries were registered to Rhode Island. Generally these ships sailed to Africa with rum and other goods in exchange for slaves, who were mostly brought to the West Indies or to South Carolina, where they were sold and distributed across the South. Many slaves were brought directly to Rhode Island and forced into domestic or agricultural service. From the West Indies, the ships brought molasses to Rhode Island, where it was distilled into the rum, which the ships carried to West Africa

to obtain more slaves. The process came to be known as the Triangle Trade.

With its prominent shipping interests, Rhode Island was one of the first New World colonies to object strenuously to the many trade regulations and taxes imposed by Britain through the mid-18th century. Some laws put limits on the manufacturing of goods in Rhode Island, forcing colonists to engage in expensive trade for such items, while other edicts placed onerous duties on molasses and other imported wares. Another practice that enraged the colonists was that of British ships whose "press gangs" randomly kidnapped Americans and forced them to enlist in the English navy. Whatever fame the Boston Tea Party may have as the opening blow of the Revolutionary War, in effect it merely followed in a tradition of vigilante attacks on British ships established by Rhode Islanders.

By 1765—eight years before the Sons of Liberty spilled their tea in Boston Harbor—resentment had turned to outright hostility in Rhode Island, and on one particular night in June, a posse of nearly 500 Newport men and boys cut loose a boat attached to a British ship that had been used for impressing colonists, dragged it to shore, and set it on fire. A few years later another band of Newporters destroyed a British revenue ship, the *Liberty,* and in 1772 perhaps the most notorious of these acts of insurrection further intensified anger between the British and the Rhode Island colonists: On a warm June evening a group from Providence sneaked out to the British revenue ship the *Gaspée* and set it on fire. This event galvanized support in Rhode Island for a full-scale war against the mother country—the *Gaspée* incident has been described by some as the colony's own Battle of Lexington. Rhode Island's governor at the time, Newport's Joseph Wanton, walked a political tightrope after the *Gaspée* incident, issuing a warrant for the arrest of the men who burned the ship but making little effort to capture them.

The Battle of Lexington in April 1775 stirred Rhode Island into a formal and fervent state of war. Within 24 hours of news of the Lexington and Concord battles reaching Rhode Island, the tiny colony put together a militia force of about 1,500. Governor Wanton, sympathetic to the colonial cause but skeptical that war would bring about positive change, declined to officially sanction military action. The assembly convened in October 1775, voted to depose Wanton, and immediately replaced him with Providence assemblyman Nicholas Cooke, who authorized Rhode Island's participation in the military campaign against Britain.

On May 4, 1776, the Rhode Island Assembly became the first colony in the New World to formally declare its independence from England—eight weeks before the Continental Congress in Philadelphia issued the unified Declaration of Independence. Rhode Island, therefore, can claim to be the oldest independent state in the United States, and legally, at least, could be considered an independent country for the brief two months before the rest of the states joined in. On July 18, 1776, the General Assembly convened and officially named its former colony the State of Rhode Island and Providence Plantations.

Rhode Island's shipping prowess became evident yet again during the Revolutionary War; Esek Hopkins, the brother of noted statesman and 1750s governor Stephen Hopkins, was the first commander-in-chief of the Continental Navy, and many in the colony served at sea during the campaign. Warwick son General Nathanael Greene successfully turned around the colonists' failing efforts in the South when he led his troops to victory over the British in March 1781 at Guilford Courthouse, northwest of Greensboro, North Carolina.

Meanwhile, Newport—which was occupied by British troops December 1776–October 1779, when colonists abandoned the city to provide reinforcements in New York City—played an important role toward the end of the war: It was here that General Rochambeau and his French troops encamped in March 1781 and where he conferred with General George Washington to plan out the sneaky and successful assault on

Yorktown. A detachment of the Rhode Island regiment, led by Captain Stephen Olney, also took part in the Yorktown battle.

The British occupation of Newport, however, proved devastating to that city, which had been well on its way to becoming one of the nation's most dynamic and important ports. The population of the city declined by nearly 50 percent after the war, in part because many Tory sympathizers had lived there during the British occupation—as the war drew to a close, they fled permanently to British North America, mostly Nova Scotia. In general, Rhode Island's economic prospects were gloomy for the first few decades after the war, and shipping trade was reduced to a trickle.

STATEHOOD AND THE INDUSTRIAL REVOLUTION

Although Rhode Island made the earliest declaration of independence of any colony, it also took the longest to agree to join the union, and existed essentially as an independent state 1776–1787. Almost wholly reliant on trade, its residents resented having to conform to trade restrictions and controls set by the entire union. The notion of joining with the other colonies struck at least some Rhode Islanders as no better than having to submit to British rule. The idea of having to funnel a share of state shipping revenues to the federal government, in the form of taxes, was totally unacceptable.

At the Constitutional Convention in Philadelphia in 1787, it was decided that Rhode Island would be made to join the Union—the colony itself sent no delegates to the convention in something of an act of protest. It was not until May 29, 1790—after much internal debate and external pressure from the newly formed U.S. Congress—that the state assembly convened in Newport and ratified the federal Constitution by an extremely close vote of 34 in favor, 32 against. At the time, the new state of Rhode Island comprised 30 towns and had a population of 70,000, nearly 10 times greater than in the previous century.

Rhode Islanders remained divided on a

number of issues facing the state and the young nation in the decades after the war, including whether to support Alexander Hamilton's Federalist agenda or Thomas Jefferson's Republican, pro-French stance. Sympathies were also split during the War of 1812, which hurt Rhode Island financially more than it did almost any other state because of its stifling effect on maritime trade. But one Rhode Island military star did make a name for himself during this war: South Kingstown's Oliver Hazard Perry, who commanded the victorious U.S. fleet during the Battle of Lake Erie in 1813. Having secured U.S. control of Lake Erie, Perry paved the way for General William Henry Harrison's short-lived invasion of Canada. Perry's younger brother, Matthew, earned fame by opening commercial trade with Japan in 1854. Bristol native General James De Wolf also contributed admirably against the British during the war.

While the state's shipping economy declined after the Revolution and its agricultural industry had been shrinking for the past century, Rhode Island was about to become a different kind of economic superpower. In early 1790s Pawtucket, Moses Brown—one of the Providence Brown brothers, after whom the university is named—financed a young textile worker from England, Samuel Slater, who had secretly traveled to the United States in hopes of profiting from his extensive knowledge of Britain's advanced mill technology (at this time it was illegal for British subjects to share their knowledge of technology with other nations). Slater almost single-handedly oversaw the formation of the U.S. textile industry, and in so doing played as important a role as anybody in sparking the American industrial revolution. Within a few years, several powerful and highly mechanized mills had sprung up in Pawtucket and neighboring towns of the Blackstone River Valley, a superb source of water power. Textile mills opened in Warwick, Coventry, and other cities within a few years. Twenty-five years after Slater designed the first water-powered textile mill in Pawtucket,

Rhode Island had about 25,000 workers employed in textile production, spinning about 30,000 bales of cotton annually into nearly 30 million yards of cloth. The boom continued through the 19th century, with capital expenditure in cotton textile production in Rhode Island rising from about $7 million in 1850 to more than $30 million in 1880.

Following on the heels of Rhode Island's cotton-textile milling success, the state developed into a leader in woolen and worsted production. By 1850 extensive worsted woolen mills ran in Cranston, North Kingstown, Hopkinton, Peace Dale, North Providence, Pawtucket, Woonsocket, and Providence. Innovations such as the carding machine, developed in Peace Dale by Rowland Hazard, and steam power, used in Providence at the Providence Woolen Manufacturing Company, further established the state's industrial preeminence. By 1890, Providence was second only to Philadelphia in woolen manufacturing.

MODERNIZATION AND INDUSTRY

Inventor George H. Corliss developed a proper steam engine for the Providence Dyeing, Bleaching, and Calendaring Company in 1848, and soon the Corliss Steam Engine was famous all over the world for saving time and labor. Eventually, Corliss became the largest steam engine producer in the country. Numerous related industries, especially machine-tool making, sprang up during the textile boom.

Another industry that expanded rapidly during the 19th century, especially in Providence, was the manufacture of jewelry, especially the costume variety. Seril and Nehemiah Dodge, brothers from Providence, had developed a cheap and fairly easy way to electrogild metal, thus enabling them to produce popular jewelry at extremely low prices. Nehemiah later expanded his business greatly, employing journeyman goldsmiths and silversmiths and apprentices to become the nation's first mass producer of discount jewelry.

One of the Dodge apprentices, Jabez

THE INDUSTRIAL REVOLUTION

After the Revolutionary War, Great Britain sought to cut its losses by preventing the export of technology and industrial innovation to the United States. Passengers on U.S.-bound ships were forbidden from taking with them blueprints, books, and materials containing the information that had made England an industrial superpower. Also prevented from leaving the country were workers with considerable experience in English factories.

Samuel Slater, a 21-year-old who had worked as a manager in England's technologically advanced Arkwright Mills, found a way around this policy. As the story goes, he snuck aboard a ship in attire and with baggage that gave no hint of his social and professional standing. He sailed to the United States, arriving first in New York, where he found few opportunities for employment. A newspaper ad placed by Moses Brown, of the famous Providence Brown family, caught Slater's attention, and he traveled to Pawtucket. Brown had sought an individual with experience in textile manufacture. With Slater's knowledge and Moses Brown's capital, Pawtucket quickly became the site of the nation's first textile factory. The new enterprise prospered beyond anybody's wildest expectations.

With the success of Slater's mills, investors quickly began pumping money into the region, building new cotton and wool mills as well as factories for tool manufacture, textile production, hat making, and shoemaking. The tremendous competition spurred constant innovation and technological improvement, and in this hothouse the United States came of age as an industrial nation. Farmers with ir-regular income based on the whims of nature were lured to these fast-growing mill villages with the promise of steady, albeit difficult, work. Mill owners ran their operations like fiefdoms, exploiting workers, hiring young children and women for some of the most difficult and dangerous jobs, creating inhumane working conditions, and controlling just about every aspect of the mill workers' lives. Workers were expected to attend church, remain sober, and buy all goods from a company store. Owners controlled housing, schools, roads, churches, and shops. The practice of employing and providing for entire families to work the mills came to be known as the Rhode Island system of manufacturing.

The child-labor practices of the day seem almost unbelievable in the 21st century. Mill workers were as young as six. In 1826, for instance, the superintendent of the Providence Thread Company was a 19-year-old man; he had 11 years of experience in the factory by that time. Children generally worked 12-14 hours per day, suffered frequent injury and illness, and being small and nimble, were often assigned the dangerous jobs that involved fast-moving machine parts. They were paid perhaps $1 per week.

Through the early 19th century, cotton mills and machine shops huffed and puffed along the banks of the river in tremendous numbers. In 1809 President Madison gave a great boost to the local textile industry when he wore a woolen suit manufactured in Pawtucket. Dr. Timothy Dwight, an early president of Yale College, detailed his travels in the young country in his diaries, in which he observed in 1810: "There is probably no spot in New England, of the same extent, in which the same quantity of variety [and] manufacturing business is carried on."

By 1815 there were 16 cotton mills in Rhode Island, Connecticut, and Massachusetts with 119,310 spindles (there were said to be about 350,000 spindles in the entire country at that time). The number of spindles in the nation grew to 1.5 million by 1830, and 2.3 million by 1840. By then, the leading cotton-manufacturing states were Massachusetts (278 mills, 666,000 spindles) and its much smaller neighbor, Rhode Island (209 mills, 519,000 spindles).

With the growth of factories all over northern Rhode Island and elsewhere in southern New England, transportation infrastructure improved rapidly and radically. A canal was opened in 1828 alongside the Blackstone River, and the Providence and Worcester Railroad followed in 1847, ending the canal business. Road improvements continued all the while.

SINCE 1900

Because it attracted families from all over Europe and the New World, the Rhode Island system of manufacturing encouraged tremendous diversity of ethnicity and religion, a mix unheard-of in Puritan New England before the industrial revolution. Rhode Island had already been a haven of religious freedom and practice, hosting New England's first significant communities of Quakers, Catholics, Baptists, and Jews. As mills ran out of local farmers to populate their mill villages, they began recruiting from afar. Through the decades, workers arrived from Ireland, Scotland, England, Germany, the Netherlands, Italy, Greece, Portugal, Ukraine, Sweden, Armenia, Poland, Lithuania, Finland, and Syria. And perhaps most prominently in northern Rhode Island, huge numbers of job-hungry French Canadians came to work in these enormous factories. In the middle of the 20th century, African Americans came to the region from the Southern states, as did Latin Americans and Asians.

By the 1940s, about 75 percent of Pawtucket's 75,000 residents were foreign-born. There were about 50 textile mills in Pawtucket, but these were outnumbered by about 60 general factories producing everything from machine parts to metal goods and jewelry.

The mills raised the bar worldwide for industrial productivity by the late 19th century as production soared to all-time highs. But by the early 20th century, cheaper labor, more land, and better water sources in the South began to cause industrial decline in New England. Labor problems caused disruption and closures, and mill owners began investing their capital in more hospitable parts of the country.

By the 1920s, the South accounted for half of the industrial output in the United States. The downward spiral of the Northeast translated to less capital, outmoded factories and machines, increasingly disgruntled workers, and more mill closures. Only about 10 percent of the textile mills in operation at the end of World War II remain open today. Many of the former mill villages of the Blackstone River Valley appear downtrodden and dispirited today, and quite a few of the old mills have been abandoned or demolished. However, a new interest in vintage mill architecture has resulted in restoration and retrofitting of at least some of the most important buildings in the valley.

Gorham, went from making silver spoons and selling them door-to-door to founding the now-famous Gorham Manufacturing Company in Providence. The early 19th century saw a rapid increase in production, with dozens of shops making jewelry and silverware by 1810. By 1880, Rhode Island led all U.S. states in the percentage of residents employed in jewelry manufacture.

Rhode Island didn't revise its constitution, which had been in place since the Royal Charter of 1663, until 1842, by which time a growing number of residents had begun to recognize the unfairness of a governing document that allowed only owners of more than $134 worth of land to vote. Slavery had been banned 60 years earlier, and sentiments favoring egalitarianism had been intensifying. The new constitution was therefore revised, after the constitutional crisis known as the Dorr War, to grant universal suffrage to all men in Rhode Island. Women remained without a voice, as they did throughout the United States, until 1920.

At the onset of the Civil War, Rhode Islanders actively supported the Union efforts, furnishing thousands of troops early on, the first regiment under the noted Colonel Ambrose E. Burnside (who later moved permanently to Rhode Island). The state governor at the time, William Sprague, served in the Battle of Bull Run. All told, 14 Rhode Island regiments went to battle during the Civil War, including an artillery regiment, the 14th, consisting entirely of African American men who aided valiantly in the defense of New Orleans. (Despite the immortalization of the Massachusetts 54th in the 1989 film *Glory,* the Rhode Island 14th actually suffered more casualties than any other African American regiment in the war.) Rhode Islanders participated in nearly every major battle—an interesting legacy for a state that profited from slavery for so many years.

Throughout the 19th century, as the state's industrial prowess grew, economic and technological advances followed. Gas lighting was introduced to the streets of Newport and Providence in the early 1900s, several state banks were chartered, steamboats connected Providence to Newport and then to many other locations, the Blackstone Canal was dug between Providence and Worcester, and railroad tracks linking Providence to Boston, southeastern Connecticut, and Worcester were laid between 1835 and 1847. In 1880 the state received telephone service, and around the end of the 19th century, Providence houses were illuminated with electricity. Also around this time, the present State House in Providence was constructed, with the first General Assembly convening there on New Year's Day 1901. Since that day, Providence has been the sole capital of Rhode Island—before then, it alternated with Newport.

Rhode Island's economy, and its intake of immigrant workers, grew precipitously after the Civil War. In addition to producing large quantities of textiles and jewelry, by the turn of the 20th century Rhode Island factories specialized in various types of metal manufacture (wire, hardware, stoves, fire extinguishers), rubber goods and footwear, paints, yacht and ship equipment, sewing machines, chemical and drug products, and baking powder. By 1900 the Providence-based manufacturer Brown and Sharp (it moved to North Kingstown in the 1960s) was the nation's largest producer of machine tools. There were about 150 machine shops and 250 costume-jewelry manufacturers in the state.

Conditions in factories were miserable, in some cases brutally inhuman, throughout the 19th century. In the early 19th century, men earned about $5 per week at mill jobs, women less than half that, and children a little over $1. A workweek consisted of six 12–14-hour days. Workers lived in tightly supervised mill villages—employers supplied the houses, schools, hospitals, churches, and shops; they effectively controlled every aspect of their employees' lives. And early on, at least, these villages were bleak and depressing.

A few mill owners, notably the Hazards of Peace Dale, made an effort to promote culture and education within their communities, but this was the exception rather than the rule. As early as 1836, the Children's Friends Society of Rhode Island was formed to rally on behalf of child workers' rights, and in 1840 a state law was passed requiring that children under 12 attend at least 12 months of schooling before beginning their "careers" in the mills.

Other unions formed gradually during the 19th century, as an increasing number of workers began to rebel against the horrid conditions. But mills simply imported foreign workers, who were less organized, less able to unionize, and more willing to accept harsh conditions. Immigration was mostly from French-speaking Canada, Ireland, Britain, Italy, Poland, and Portugal. It was not until 1909 that the state actually formed a board to oversee and regulate labor conditions in its factories, but even this organization had little success in improving working conditions until 1923, when the state Bureau of Labor was established. Strikes occurred regularly during the early 20th century, and some of these were intensely bitter and violent.

World War I, to which Rhode Island sent 29,000 troops (of which 600 perished), interrupted Rhode Island's steadily growing industrial power for a time. After World War I, as companies fled the increasingly strong labor unions of New England, Rhode Island began losing textile factories to the cheap labor of the South. But by the 1930s, even with the Depression in full swing and an increasing number of companies leaving the Northeast, Rhode Island had become the most highly industrialized state in the Union—more than half of the working population of 300,000 in 1930 was employed in manufacturing.

By 1940 the population of Rhode Island had grown to nearly 700,000. World War II interrupted everyday life here as it did all over the world; about 92,000 Rhode Islanders served in the war, and 2,157 were killed. The Ocean State, with its many factories, contributed tremendously to the war effort with the production of boots, knives, parachutes, munitions, and other supplies.

WORLD WAR II TO THE PRESENT

After the war, the advent of cheap suburban housing, a fast-growing and convenient interstate highway system, and a steady decline in urban industry inspired a rapid out-migration from Providence and other cities into neighboring towns. Even where jobs remained in the cities, at least for a while, workers no longer had to live near their places of employment. The 1950s marked the beginning of nearly four decades of wretched economic decline, high crime, and deterioration in Rhode Island's urban areas. Providence's 1950 population of about 250,000 dropped by 75,000 over the next 20 years. Economically, the state stagnated badly from the 1950s through the 1970s, and by the 1980s it had one of the least favorable climates for doing business in the country.

Suburbs such as Warwick, Cranston, Johnston, and North Kingstown blossomed over this period, and today as you drive through these communities you'll see thousands of suburban homes built between World War II and the 1970s, not to mention scads of shopping centers and a handful of large indoor shopping malls that also date to this period. In cities, urban renewal efforts led to the clearance of many so-called slums, including the destruction of some wonderful Victorian housing. But Providence, and Rhode Island in general, did a better job preserving its most important historic homes and neighborhoods than many other parts of New England. The Point District in Newport and College Hill in Providence, both of which fell into disrepair for a time, now rank among the most beautiful historic districts in the nation.

One industry that thrived in Rhode Island after World War II was the military—the U.S. Navy was the state's largest civilian employer during the 1950s and 1960s. The naval shipyard just outside Newport was responsible for building the nation's cruiser-destroyer fleet. But this industry crashed in 1974 when the Navy moved these operations to the South. Yet again, the relatively high operating costs and wages in New England sent business packing. Newport was left reeling, but the city rebounded by turning itself into a full-scale year-round destination. The tourism industry remains the most important in Newport today.

The tourism rebound of Newport and the general renaissance in Providence have been important factors in the great improvement in the state's image over the past two decades. There have also been failings, such as a slew of extremely embarrassing political scandals concerning bribery, extortion, misuse of funds, and other unethical misdeeds that shattered the public's faith in state and local government during the 1980s. But the reforms that grew out of these incidents ultimately helped to clean up government—at least to a degree.

Government

Rhode Islanders have long marched to their own drummer when it comes to politics. The colony was founded by Massachusetts Bay Colony dissidents who believed strongly in religious freedom and the separation of church and state. From the very beginning of the colony's settlement, there was tension between the southerners on Aquidneck Island and the northern residents of Providence.

The state operated under a Royal Charter issued in 1663 until well into the 19th century. Although this document proved antiquated and awkward by that time, it was replaced only in 1842 after a near civil war, the Dorr Rebellion.

Early on, Rhode Island was represented by a General Assembly comprising six men from each of the original towns. As new towns incorporated, the Assembly grew. Sessions were held at private homes until the first colony house was constructed in Newport in 1690, but for some time after that the assembly often met in homes in other parts of the state. Even the revised state constitution of 1842, which finally granted suffrage to all male adult Rhode Islanders, authorized that General Assembly meetings could convene in Newport, Providence, South Kingstown, Bristol, or East Greenwich. In 1854 the Assembly pared this list of towns to two, and from then until 1900 the legislature met alternately in Newport and Providence. It wasn't until 1900, when Providence had grown to become the state's hub of economics, education, and population, that it became the definitive state capital.

Until the 20th century, the General Assembly was made up of equal numbers of representatives from every town in the state. Eventually the law was changed so that the Senate's representation was based purely on population distribution. Currently, there are 75 state representatives and 38 state senators.

Before 1992 the governor of Rhode Island held office for a term of just two years, but this was extended to four years; the governor may serve a total of two full terms.

Rhode Island has two members in the U.S. House of Representatives in addition to its two U.S. senators.

POLITICAL PARTIES

Generally speaking, Rhode Island's popularly elected officials tend to be socially rather progressive; fiscally they're more varied but still pretty liberal. Like its neighbor Massachusetts, Rhode Island tends to vote overwhelmingly Democratic. Patrick J. Kennedy, son of Senator Ted Kennedy, decided not to seek reelection in 2010, which opened the state to the first truly contested congressional election in years. The vast majority of the state's elected Republicans have been considered moderate in relation to the national party as a whole.

For the smallest state, Rhode Island has one of the more impressive state houses.

Of course, many people think of the long-time mayor of Providence, Buddy Cianci, when they discuss Rhode Island politics—and indeed, he represents the best and worst of local politicians: forward-thinking, bold, and genuinely solicitous of the people he served while at the same time completely captive to political interests and prone to backroom dealing that both skirted and crossed the line of the law.

Economy

With its history of wealthy shipping magnates and ostentatious summer cottages, coupled with its legacy of industry and manufacturing, Rhode Island is a state with quite a few extremely wealthy citizens and a huge core of working-class wage earners. The median household income of $42,000 is about the national average, though far below the average for its New England neighbors, and indeed the state's positive and negative economic attributes tend to balance each other out.

There's something refreshingly down-to-earth about some of the state's old mill towns and interior highways. They remind you that Rhode Island is not simply a summertime playground of beachgoers and boaters. In fact, although Newport's Gilded Age in the early 1900s imbued the state with a reputation for privilege and excess, Rhode Island is mostly a place where middle-class, egalitarian values prevail, as they have since Roger Williams founded Providence Plantation as a haven for religious and political freedom in the early 1600s.

MANUFACTURING

The state's industrial clout continues to decline even today, but a rapid increase in the number of retail and service-oriented jobs has contributed to an overall economic boom not seen for many decades. Providence especially has benefited, and it has become a poster child for the urban renaissance that has swept across many American cities in the past 15 years or so.

Manufacturing jobs in Rhode Island still continue to disappear—between the economic censuses in 1997 and 2007, the number of state residents employed in manufacturing fell from 82,000 to 54,000, a decline of almost 35 percent, although it remains the state's second-most important economic sector. Other major areas include wholesale trade (22,000 workers); retail trade (51,000); health and social services (the leader with 82,000); accommodations and food services (45,000); professional, scientific, and technical services (23,000); finance and insurance (23,000); and construction (22,000). Rhode Island also continues to have a prolific commercial fishing industry.

In the manufacturing sector, the main business endeavors are primary metals, fabricated metals, machinery, and electrical equipment. Jewelry and silverware production remains a manufacturing force still larger than in any other state, and Rhode Island still has many people employed in textile production, even if the numbers are a small fraction of those a century ago.

TOURISM, EDUCATION, AND HEALTH CARE

As noted, 45,000 Rhode Islanders work in the accommodations and food services industry, with another 9,000 in arts, entertainment, and recreation, collectively known as tourism. After the Navy moved out of Newport in the 1970s, that city turned to tourism as its leading industry. Block Island also relies chiefly on tourism, although plenty of Block Islanders still make a living the way that they have for generations, in fishing. To a lesser extent, parts of South County—specifically the beach communities—are heavily dependent on tourism.

In recent years, with its vastly improved reputation, even Providence has come to depend heavily on tourism, a notion almost unthinkable during the city's darkest economic years in the 1960s and 1970s. Still, Providence has a way to go in building its tourism infrastructure to accommodate large numbers of visitors, and outside of the Northeast, many people remain unaware that the city has much to offer.

Rhode Island's other big service sectors are health and education. The former is especially significant in Providence and its suburbs, where there are many hospitals and health providers. Education, while only employing some 2,000 people, is still a big contributor to the economy in Providence and several other parts of the state. The University of Rhode Island, in Kingston, has the largest student enrollment in the state, while in Providence there are Brown University, Johnson and Wales, the Rhode Island School of Design, and Providence College. Other notable schools in Rhode Island include Bryant College in Smithfield, Salve Regina University in Newport, and Roger Williams University in Bristol.

People and Culture

Rhode Island is sometimes described as the nation's only city-state, a tempting designation given its diminutive size and high population density. Here again, there are some contradictions at work. On the one hand, most of Rhode Island is served by one metro bus system and one main newspaper. You can commute to Providence from virtually anywhere in the state, and Providence's mayor until 2002, Buddy Cianci, probably wielded as much statewide clout as any of the men who served as governor during his long tenure. In certain respects, the day-to-day events of Providence are the events of Rhode Island—and perhaps in no other state does a city wield so much influence.

On the other hand, only 171,000 Rhode Islanders actually live in Providence—that's barely more than 15 percent of the state's population. By comparison, about 25 percent of all

Nevadans live in Las Vegas, and more than 20 percent of all Illinois residents live in Chicago. Rhode Island was founded as a collection of distinct communities, all headed by dissidents and freethinkers who had become unwelcome in Puritan Massachusetts. The towns of Rhode Island continue to function with very much their own autonomy and individual spirit. Newport sees itself as entirely distinct from and independent of Providence, and it always will. A Block Islander would laugh aloud if accused of living in Greater Providence, even though the island lies just 40 miles from the state capital. Woonsocket is only 10 miles northwest of Providence, but these two cities have about as much to do with each another as Philadelphia and Pittsburgh—or so their residents might insist.

Although it's the smallest state in the Union, Rhode Island has more people living within its borders than Montana, Delaware, either of the Dakotas, Alaska, Vermont, or Wyoming. Roger Williams and the other early settlers hailed from England, and from the 1630s through the 1850s the population was largely white, of British descent, and Protestant. Within 50 years of European settlement in Rhode Island the Native American population had almost disappeared. The colony did possess a slightly more diverse population in the 1600s than other parts of New England: The founding doctrine protecting the worship of all religions contributed to an early influx of Quakers (most came from England) and Jews (mostly from Spain and Portugal). Catholics, mostly from France, began settling in Rhode Island in small numbers after the American Revolution, when locals became quite appreciative and fond of the French troops stationed in Newport under Rochambeau.

During the past 150 years, the industrialization of Rhode Island has led to other dramatic changes in demographics.

POPULATION

In the mid-19th century, Ireland's residents faced famine, poverty, and blight, and many moved to the young United States in search

LIBERIANS IN RHODE ISLAND

One of the more recent immigrant groups to make their presence known in the state has been Liberians, an ironic turn of events given that Liberia was established by freed slaves who returned to Africa after emancipation – and that Providence prospered hugely during colonial times through the slave trade. Modern-day Liberia has been ravaged economically and politically by a devastating civil war through the 1990s. In 1991 the U.S. State Department granted provisional immigration status to Liberian refugees, and since that time more than 4,000 of the roughly 10,000 people to receive this status have chosen to settle in Rhode Island.

of better opportunities. Along with a number of Scottish and English immigrants, they became the earliest foreigners to work in Rhode Island's factories.

By around 1850, Rhode Island's population included quite a few foreign-born citizens, particularly in the textile hubs of Pawtucket and Central Falls; about 97 percent of them hailed from Ireland, Scotland, Wales, and England. The next big wave of immigrants, from Quebec, first arrived during the Civil War to work in mills in northern Rhode Island, the vast majority of them settling in Woonsocket. They would remain a tight-knit and prolific force for many years, and even today there is a strong and vibrant French Canadian community in Woonsocket. As the mills have largely closed, however, many younger people from this area are moving elsewhere for better opportunities.

Perhaps the largest immigrant group to settle in Rhode Island are the Italians, and to this day Italian culture continues to be important in the social fabric of the state. The biggest wave of Italian immigration happened just as the French Canadian migration slowed, about 1900–1915, but they arrived in smaller

RHODE ISLAND ON THE SCREEN

Rhode Island has lobbied as hard as any state in New England to attract filmmakers, and the results have been impressive. Many notable movies have been set in the Ocean State in recent years, and the television show *Providence*, which aired 1999–2002, also did much to promote the capital city. The hit show, which starred Melina Kanakaredes, Mike Farrell, and Paula Cale, was filmed largely in Los Angeles, but the show shot a number of scenes each year on location in Providence and towns nearby – about twice each year the cast and crew traveled to Rhode Island to shoot on-site footage. Even former Providence mayor Vincent "Buddy" Cianci made a cameo on the show. The animated Fox TV show *Family Guy* is also set in Rhode Island and has even featured a fictitious Buddy Cianci High School. It was created by Seth MacFarlane, who studied animation at Providence's Rhode Island School of Design. Continuing the streak, the TV series *Brotherhood* aired on the cable network Showtime for three seasons 2006–2008 to critical acclaim, including a Peabody Award, even though it never grew outside of a cult audience. Filmed almost entirely on location in Providence, it dealt with familiar themes of an Irish-American politician and his brother, who happened to be a capo in the Irish mob. (The show was based on the Bulger brothers in Boston, who were also the subject of the Martin Scorsese movie *The Departed*.) Finally, one show that never aired but that we would have loved to see is *Waterfront*, a series about the mob-connected mayor of Providence, played by Joey Pantagliano, and a crusading attorney general played by Billy Baldwin. Although five episodes were filmed, CBS pulled the plug before it was ever aired.

Rhode Island's history as a filmmaking fave is rather recent, although a handful of classics were shot here. Newport, for instance, was the film locale for the 1956 Grace Kelly, Bing Crosby, and Frank Sinatra movie *High Society*. Newport, in fact, has been the location for a number of pictures, perhaps most notably the 1974 adaptation of F. Scott Fitzgerald's *The Great Gatsby*, starring Robert Redford, Mia Farrow, and Sam Waterston. The mansion scenes were shot at Rosecliff Mansion. Other Newport-filmed movies include *The Betsy* (1978, starring Laurence Olivier, Robert Duvall, and Katharine Ross), *True Lies* (1994, starring Arnold Schwarzenegger and Jamie Lee Curtis), *Thirteen Days* (2000, starring Kevin Costner), *Mr. North* (1988, starring Anthony Edwards, Robert Mitchum, and Lauren Bacall), *Heaven's Gate* (1980, starring Kris Kristofferson, Christopher Walken, and John Hurt), and *Amistad* (1997, starring Morgan Freeman, Nigel Hawthorne, and Anthony

numbers for many years after—the majority from Sicily, Naples, and other southern Italian regions. Today, Rhode Island's most pronounced Italian American communities are in Providence, especially the Federal Hill area, which has a Little Italy–style restaurant and shopping scene that's on par with any in the Northeast. There are other Italian enclaves in other parts of Providence, such as the North Side and Silver Lake, some of them dating to the early 1900s, and also large contingents in East Providence, Barrington, Bristol, and Westerly.

Other immigrant groups that have contributed to Rhode Island's eclectic population include Poles, who arrived in the greatest numbers 1895–1905 and settled heavily in Central Falls, Providence, Pawtucket, Cranston, Johnston, Warren, and Woonsocket; and Portuguese, especially those from the Azores, Madeiras, and Cape Verde island groups, who were recruited by the state's whaling industry in the 1850s and 1860s. As the whaling industry died out, many of the Portuguese settled in fishing communities, while others worked as farmers and both skilled and unskilled laborers. In smaller but still significant numbers, Swedes, Germans, Armenians, Greeks,

Hopkins). Scenes in *Amistad* were also shot in Pawtucket and Providence, including one at the Rhode Island State House.

One last Newport-filmed movie was *Me, Myself & Irene* (2000, starring Jim Carrey and Renée Zellweger), written and directed by perhaps Rhode Island's most famous movie-making team, brothers Bobby and Peter Farrelly. The Farrellys have become rather notorious for reinventing the "gross-out" genre with such ribald films as *There's Something About Mary* (1998, starring Ben Stiller, Matt Dillon, and Cameron Diaz), which was shot in part in Providence. And although they didn't direct it, the Farrelly brothers wrote and produced the Alec Baldwin and Shawn Hatosy movie *Outside Providence* (1999), which was indeed shot outside Providence, specifically in Woonsocket. *Me, Myself, & Irene* had filming locations in Jamestown, Galilee, and Narragansett.

Outside Providence was directed by another Rhode Island son, Pawtucket's Michael Corrente, who also directed *Federal Hill* (1995, starring Corrente himself), which traced the lives of five young men living in Providence's famed Little Italy. Corrente also directed the screen adaptation of David Mamet's *American Buffalo* (1996, starring Dustin Hoffman and Dennis Franz), which was filmed in Pawtucket. Corrente's movies offer an especially gritty and realistic look of urban Rhode Island.

Keep your eyes open while watching a few other Rhode Island-filmed movies, including *Mystic Pizza* (1988, starring Julia Roberts, Lili Taylor, and Annabeth Gish), which was shot mostly over the border in southeastern Connecticut but also had scenes in Watch Hill and Westerly; *Meet Joe Black* (1998, starring Brad Pitt and Anthony Hopkins), which was filmed in part at Warwick's Aldrich Mansion; *The Last Shot* (2004, starring Alec Baldwin, Matthew Broderick, Toni Collette, and Tony Shalhoub), a mob comedy set partly in Providence; *Reversal of Fortune* (1990, starring Jeremy Irons, Glenn Close, and Ron Silver), based on the true-crime book by lawyer Alan Dershowitz about the attempted-murder trial of Claus von Bulow – much of it was filmed in Newport; and *Wind* (1992, starring Matthew Modine, Jennifer Grey, and Cliff Robertson), which was shot in Jamestown. In more recent years, filming in Rhode Island has tapered off, but the state has served as primary location for the Steve Carrell vehicle *Dan In Real Life* (2007; look for a cameo by the Book and Tackle Shop in Watch Hill) and *Little Children* (2007), the critically acclaimed film starring Kate Winslet.

Incidentally, the film adaptation of John Updike's *The Witches of Eastwick* – a book said to have been based on Wickford, Rhode Island – was actually filmed mainly in Massachusetts.

Lithuanians, Finns, and Syrians settled in the Ocean State during the early 20th century.

DEMOGRAPHICS

Outside the big cities, Rhode Island is predominantly a state of Caucasians, chiefly of English, Irish, and Italian ancestry. Today about 85 percent of all Rhode Islanders identify themselves as white; 5 percent identify as African American, and 2 percent are Asian. About 9 percent of Rhode Islanders are of Hispanic or Latino origin.

As of the last census estimate in 2009, the state population stood at 1,053,209. The population has doubled since 1900 but has increased only slightly since 1970, when it stood at 950,000. As is true all over the Northeast, cities in Rhode Island have mostly lost population in the past half century, while suburban areas have seen tremendous growth. Providence, for instance, had a population of nearly 250,000 around the time of World War II, and the number dropped to just 160,000 in a matter of 25 years. In 1900 Providence was the 12th-largest city in the nation; today it ranks around 125th. Since 1990, however, Providence has seen a 7 percent increase in population to 171,000.

Towns just outside Providence have grown rapidly since the migration from the cities to the suburbs that began after World War II. The population has nearly quadrupled in Warwick, doubled in Cranston, tripled in Barrington and Johnston, and increased more than six times in North Kingstown.

Rhode Island was one of the few states in the country to lose population during the 1980s, so the recent stabilization of population is a welcome indicator that Rhode Island's economic future looks more promising. It appears the state's economy has bounced back somewhat since the recession of the early 1990s and has mostly weathered the more recent economic crisis. Of course, this is the second-most densely populated state in the Union, with just over 1,000 people per square mile; only New Jersey's density is higher, and not by much. Of Rhode Island's 39 towns, almost half have population densities greater than 1,000 per square mile, so it will probably never be a state that grows at an rapid rate—there simply isn't room to put a lot of new people.

On the other hand, if you're looking for a sparsely settled part of the state, fear not: Block Island, West Greenwich, and Foster all have fewer than 100 people per square mile (although Block Island is crowded in the summer with seasonal visitors). Little Compton, Exeter, Glocester, Hopkinton, Richmond, and Scituate have plenty of breathing room too.

RELIGION

Still true to the principles of its founder, Roger Williams, Rhode Island continues to embrace religious diversity. Interestingly, the largest religious group in the state, Catholicism, is the one that was actually least tolerated for the longest time, but the huge influx of Irish, Italian, and French Canadian immigrants between the 1850s and the 1930s, and the fact that Catholics often produced larger families than non-Catholics, have contributed to Rhode Island's overwhelmingly Catholic character.

Rhode Island was never a Puritan colony as Massachusetts was, so its village commons are rarely anchored by a Congregational church and cemetery. Nevertheless, there are large numbers of Protestants all over the state, the majority of them belonging to the Congregational Church. Various other Protestant sects and other Christian groups have congregations scattered throughout the state.

Ironically, although Rhode Island is home to the oldest synagogue in the United States, the Ocean State has a relatively small Jewish population, a legacy of their flight from their religious center in Newport during the Revolutionary War. Providence and other towns in the state do have Jewish congregations, and Providence—because of its strong ethnic diversity—also has mosques and other places of worship that serve the many non-Christians living in and around the city.

In keeping with Rhode Island's rather socially left-of-center reputation, fundamentalist and conservative Christians are in the minority in the state and among political candidates, who tend to vote progressively on controversial issues such as abortion, school prayer, gay rights, and school vouchers.

ESSENTIALS

Getting There

Rhode Island is tiny, crossed by a major interstate highway and railway tracks, served by New England's third-largest airport and within a two-hour drive of three other major ones, and easily reached from every major city in the Northeast. Few other states are more easily accessible from corner to corner than Rhode Island.

For general information on commuting, getting to and from Rhode Island, and getting around the state, contact the **Rhode Island Department of Transportation** (401/222-2481, www.dot.state.ri.us). Its website offers extensive information on numerous publications, traveler resources, road conditions, licenses and permits, upcoming roadwork and projects, legal notices, and construction bid notices.

BY AIR

Rhode Island is served by **T. F. Green Airport** (2000 Post Rd., Warwick, 888/268-7222 or 401/691-2471, www.pvdairport.com), which is eight miles south of downtown Providence off I-95 exit 13—it's a significant alternative to Boston's Logan Airport, as well as a pleasant, easy-to-use facility that readers of *Condé Nast Traveler* magazine have voted among the top airports in the world. It's served by seven airlines: Air Canada, Cape Air, Continental, Delta, Independence Air, United, and US

© MICHAEL BLANDING

DRIVING DISTANCES FROM PROVIDENCE

Albany, New York	185 miles		New Providence, Iowa	1,300 miles
Anchorage, Alaska	4,614 miles		New York City	180 miles
Atlanta	1,050 miles		Philadelphia	274 miles
Boston	50 miles		Portland, Maine	162 miles
Burlington, Vermont	267 miles		Providence, Utah	2,388 miles
Chicago	971 miles		Toronto	565 miles
Cleveland	640 miles		Washington, D.C.	407 miles
Concord, New Hampshire	119 miles		Westerly, Rhode Island	44 miles
Fort Providence, Northwest Territories, Canada	3,364 miles		Worcester, Massachusetts	39 miles
Hartford, Connecticut	73 miles			
Hyannis, Massachusetts	75 miles			
Mexico City	2,873 miles			
Miami	1,471 miles			
Montreal	361 miles			
Nashville, Tennessee	1,071 miles			
New Haven, Connecticut	102 miles			
Newport, Rhode Island	34 miles			

Interestingly, few state capitals are closer together than Providence and Hartford, but they are not directly connected by an interstate highway. You either have to drive down I-95 to the coast and then continue east to Route 9 in Connecticut or take another road combination.

Five cities that share Providence's approximate latitude: Salt Lake City; Beijing; Baku, Azerbaijan; Ankara, Turkey; and Madrid.

Three cities that share Rhode Island's approximate longitude: Quebec City, Canada; Santo Domingo, Dominican Republic; and Cuzco, Peru.

Airways have flights to numerous U.S. cities as well as the Caribbean and Canada. About 100 flights arrive at Green Airport daily, with an equal number of departures.

Green's recent expansion has resulted in lots of extra parking spaces; rates at the on-site garage range $15–26 per day (check out the airport's website for special-rate coupons). Just south of the airport, the long-term parking lot costs $11 per day and $55 per week. For the latest parking information, call 401/737-0694. There are also a number of commercial lots near the airport, several of which provide free shuttle service to and from the terminal.

Ground Transportation
Rhode Island Public Transit Authority (RIPTA) (401/781-9400 or 800/244-0444, www.ripta.com) provides frequent service daily from T. F. Green to downtown Providence (Bus 20, 35–45 minutes) and from T. F. Green to Newport (Bus 14, 1 hour). The fare is $1.75 one-way. **Airport Taxi and Limousine Service** (401/737-2868, www.airporttaxiri.com) serves

Warwick and neighboring communities and also provides regularly scheduled shuttle service from the airport to downtown Providence hotels, colleges, the convention center, and the train and bus stations. The cost is $11 pp to Providence for the shuttle; taxi rates vary by destination. **Cozy Cab/Newport Shuttle** (401/846-2500 or 800/846-1502, www.cozytrans.com) provides service from the airport to Newport for $25 pp.

Transportation from T. F. Green to South County, Newport, and some of the farther-away sections of Rhode Island is covered in detail in individual chapters of this book.

Prestige Limousine (2329 Post Rd., Warwick, 401/732-8600 or 800/220-5466, www.prestigelimo.com) offers all manner of ground transportation from T. F. Green Airport, including chauffeured limos and shuttle vans.

Car Rental

Major car rental agencies at T. F. Green Airport include **Alamo** (401/739-0696 or 888/826-6893, www.alamo.com), **Avis** (401/736-7500 or 800/230-4898, www.avis.com), **Budget** (401/739-8986 or 800/527-0700, www.budget.com), **Dollar-Thrifty** (401/739-8450 or 800/800-3665, www.dollar.com), **Enterprise** (401/732-5261 or 800/261-7331, www.enterprise.com), **Hertz** (401/738-7500 or 800/654-3131, www.hertz.com), and **National** (401/737-4800 or 888/826-6890, www.nationalcar.com).

BY BUS

If it has been a while since you traveled by bus, be prepared for a surprise: Onboard movies and other improvements can make the ride quite comfortable (and far less expensive than Amtrak). **Peter Pan Bus Lines** (800/343-9999, www.peterpanbus.com) runs from Rhode Island to a number of New England cities. Examples include an express run from Newport to Boston, which runs several times a day and takes about 90 minutes. The fare is around $25 round-trip. Service from Boston to Providence runs several times daily, takes

about an hour each way, and costs about $10 round-trip.

There's also bus service from Providence to Albany (New York), Falmouth (Massachusetts) on Cape Cod, Hartford (Connecticut), Hyannis (Massachusetts) on Cape Cod, Logan Airport in Boston, New Bedford (Massachusetts), Pittsfield (Massachusetts), Springfield (Massachusetts), the University of Connecticut in Storrs (Connecticut), Woods Hole (Massachusetts) on Cape Cod, and Worcester (Massachusetts). Newport also has service to New York City and Boston's Logan Airport.

Peter Pan bus terminals are in Newport (23 America's Cup Ave.), in the north end of Providence (1 Peter Pan Way, off I-95 exit 25), and downtown Providence (1 Kennedy Plaza). The stop used in Providence depends on the route, so check ahead.

You can find connections to a great many locations in New England and across the country from **Greyhound** (800/231-2222, www.greyhound.com), the largest national carrier. Stations are in Newport (23 America's Cup Ave.) and Providence (1 Kennedy Plaza) at the same locations as Peter Pan, but Greyhound's fares tend to be slightly higher; it can be worth it on the buses that offer free Wi-Fi.

BY TRAIN

Amtrak (800/872-7245, www.amtrak.com) runs trains through the state daily. This is a fairly hassle-free way to get here from Boston, New York City, Philadelphia, and other major metropolitan areas. The one Amtrak route in Rhode Island passes through on the way between Washington, D.C., and Boston, with stops at Providence, Kingston, and Westerly. From Boston it's about 40 minutes to Providence, another 10 minutes to Kingston, and another 20 minutes to Westerly. Many of the Amtrak runs are Acela express trains that stop at Providence but not Kingston or Westerly. From the south, train times (the shorter times are for the high-speed trains) to Providence are 6–7 hours from Washington, D.C.; 4.5–5 hours from Philadelphia; 3–3.5

hours from New York City; and 1.5–2 hours from New Haven.

Massachusetts Bay Transit Authority

The Massachusetts Bay Transit Authority (617/222-5000, for route and schedule information 617/222-3200, www.mbta.com), the nation's fourth-largest public transportation system, offers weekday commuter rail service between Boston's South Station and downtown Providence on the Attleboro/Stoughton line, with many stops in southeastern Massachusetts along the way. Trains depart Providence on weekdays about a dozen times daily 5 A.M.–about midnight; the ride takes about 70 minutes, and the fare is $7.75 one-way. The station is located at 100 Gaspee Street, just below the Rhode Island State House. Fewer trains run on weekends, generally 6 A.M.–11 P.M. Saturday and 11 A.M.–11 P.M. Sunday.

Getting Around

It's as easy to get around Rhode Island as it is to get to it. The well-maintained network of roads will get you anywhere in the state. For almost any destination it's also possible to rely on public transportation; for most of the state, that means the bus system, the Rhode Island Public Transportation Authority (RIPTA). For larger destinations (Providence, Newport, Westerly, Kingston) it's possible to rely on the train and larger bus carriers.

DRIVING

Rhode Island's main thoroughfare, I-95 is a convenient if rather dull road that runs from the southwestern corner of the state northeast through Providence before entering Massachusetts. A bypass highway, I-295, cuts around the west side of Providence, from Warwick nearly to Woonsocket and then east to Attleboro, Massachusetts. I-195 cuts east from Providence through the northern tip of the East Bay and into Massachusetts. These roads will get you where you need to go, but especially around Providence, they are prone to rush-hour traffic jams.

Route 146 is a convenient limited-access highway running northwest from Providence, and U.S. 6 is a similarly highway heading west from Providence, but both of these become regular four-lane roads once they're out of the metropolitan area. U.S. 6 and parallel U.S. 44 are generally fast roads with little commercial development that pass through the pretty wooded countryside of western Rhode Island; they're a smart way to get to Connecticut, even with the occasional traffic light. U.S. 1, the main shore road in South County, runs from Westerly east to Narragansett and then north to intersect with Route 4 in North Kingstown. Route 4 then leads back up to I-95. This route is generally fast, with some limited-access stretches. U.S. 1 north of North Kingstown is a slow, heavily developed road through Warwick, Cranston, Providence, and Pawtucket—it should be used only for local traffic, not as a way to get through the area quickly.

Top picks for scenery on other highways include Route 102 (from North Smithfield south to North Kingstown), Route 138 (from the Connecticut border at Exeter east to Newport and then northeast through Tiverton), Routes 77 and 81 (up and down the Sakonnet Peninsula), Route 122 (from Pawtucket through the Blackstone River Valley to Woonsocket), Route 94 (from Chepachet south through Foster), Route 14 (west from Providence over Scituate Reservoir through Kent to the Connecticut border), and Route 1A, which hugs the coast intermittently through South County, both along the ocean and then up beside Narragansett Bay.

MASS TRANSIT

Because Rhode Island is small, and a significant chunk of the state is urban, mass transit is quite useful and efficient, at least in terms of buses and, to a limited extent, ferryboats. There are no subways, commuter trains, or light-rail services in Rhode Island, although Amtrak makes stops in a few towns and the Massachusetts Bay Transit Authority (MBTA) provides commuter rail service connecting Providence with Boston's South Station.

It's quite possible and economically feasible to visit some parts of the state without using a car. If, for example, you're going to Block Island, Providence, Newport, parts of South County, and parts of the East Bay, you could get into town from Boston or New York City with a combination of bus, train, and (for Block Island) ferry, and then use a bus or cabs to get around locally—in some of these towns you can cover quite a bit of ground on foot. To make the most of western or northwestern Rhode Island, or the more remote coastal areas (Sakonnet, Jamestown, upper Aquidneck Island), you really need a car—it's also most practical to use one in Providence's suburbs, from Pawtucket to Woonsocket down to Warwick, although buses do serve all of these towns and are fine in a pinch.

For optimum convenience and freedom to explore, a car is your best bet for covering the state as a whole. Even Providence has a fair amount of street parking and plenty of garages. In summer, Newport is almost congested enough that a car defeats its purpose, but if you're planning to explore the outlying areas and your hotel or inn provides off-street parking, it's a good idea to bring one. Block Island, especially in summer, is best visited without a car. It's a small island with good public transportation, and it's excellent for biking; almost all accommodations are within walking distance of Old Harbor or New Harbor, where you'll find most of the island's shops and restaurants. If you're staying for a while, your accommodations offer off-street parking, or it's off-season, a car can make sense and give you a little more flexibility, but it's really not a necessity at any time of year. And everybody living on Block Island will be quite pleased if you arrive without a car that would to the already heinous traffic during the summer high season.

Intercity Buses

Rhode Island is small enough that much of the state is served by Providence's city bus system, operated by the **Rhode Island Public Transit Authority (RIPTA)** (401/781-9400, www. ripta.com). Most buses originate in Providence, but others start and end in other parts of the state. For example, you can use RIPTA buses to get from Newport to Providence or the University of Rhode Island in Kingston; from Bristol to Providence; from Providence to Burrillville; or from Coventry to Providence. The base fare is $1.75 per ride; charges increase as you travel through different zones. RIPTA's website is very useful in terms of plotting your exact trip.

Sports and Recreation

BIRD-WATCHING

From yuppies to senior citizens, families and singles, every kind of Rhode Islander seems to be taking up bird-watching these days, especially those folks who live around the coastal regions, with Block Island ranking among the best spots. Its popularity makes a lot of sense, as hobbies go, as it is not expensive and is highly educational. Best of all, birds are abundant in the state year-round, although which individual species can be seen depends on the season.

More than 400 species of birds live in Rhode Island. Much of the best birding is along the coast, where you'll see myriad waterfowl year-round and magnificent blue heron October–April. Peregrine falcons and hawks regularly fly around marshes and estuaries, and in August–September you'll see warblers and thrushes. A huge population of sparrows descends on coastal points during the fall. Owls are not easy to find, but they do live around the state.

For further information on specific species that live in Rhode Island, visit the website www.nenature.com/birds.htm, which has detailed information and photos of hundreds of birds common to Rhode Island and the rest of the Northeast.

The Rhode Island chapter of the **Audubon Society** (12 Sanderson Rd., Smithfield, 401/949-5454, www.asri.org) is also a useful resource. The society's website has helpful links for birders, including a bimonthly newsletter and information on recent sightings downloadable from its website. At the society's headquarters in Smithfield, the **Hathaway Library** houses a vast collection of books, publications, videos, and software related to birding in general and in Rhode Island specifically. You can also pick up books, tapes, and other birding materials at the two Audubon Society gift shops in the state, one at the headquarters and the other at the **Audubon Environmental Education Center** (1401 Hope St., Bristol, 401/245-7500).

The society owns or oversees about 9,500 acres of preserves throughout Rhode Island, several of them open to the public and excellent for bird-watching. **Kimball Wildlife Sanctuary** (off U.S. 1, adjacent to Burlingame State Park, Charlestown) is a 29-acre property with a 1.5-mile hiking trail through fields and forests. Another birding Valhalla is the **Emilie Ruecker Wildlife Refuge** (Seapowet Ave., just off Route 77, Tiverton), overlooking the Sakonnet River. The salt marshes here are a favorite spot for observing migrating birds during the fall and spring; there are blinds set up for watching and photographing the wildlife.

Another excellent spot is the **Headwaters of the Queen's River** (Henry Bowman Rd., reached via New London Turnpike and Rte. 102), a remote woodland that connects Fisherville Brook Refuge (owned by the Rhode Island Audubon Society) to the state-administered Big River Management Area. Walking along trails here, you're apt to see many kinds of forest interior birds, including hawks. Another excellent Nature Conservancy preserve for birdwatching is the **Francis C. Carter Memorial**

Reserve (Route 112, Charlestown), a large coastal preserve frequented in summer by species that include eastern towhee, scarlet tanager, and prairie warbler. Contact the Rhode Island chapter of the **Nature Conservancy** (159 Waterman St., Providence, 401/331-7110, www.nature.org) for directions to and descriptions of these and more than a dozen other pristine preserves around Rhode Island.

On Block Island, the Nature Conservancy works in partnership with several local organizations to preserve a huge section of the island from being developed—these preserves are among the state's most exceptional venues for bird-watching.

FISHING

Among the state's many great fishing holes and swift rivers, the Wood, Pawcatuck, Moosup, and Falls Rivers are among the best sources of troutfishing. A number of stocked ponds throughout the state are designated only for kids under 15. Stocked trout ponds are closed for fishing March 1–the second Saturday in April, which marks the beginning of trout-fishing season. For a complete list of trout-stocked ponds and rivers in Rhode Island, and for other details about fishing in the Ocean State, contact the **Division of Fish and Wildlife** (4808 Tower Hill Rd., Wakefield, 401/789-3094, www.dem.ri.gov/programs/bnatres/fishwild). The website also has links to all state fishing and hunting regulations, lists legal minimum sizes and possession rules, provides information on obtaining licenses, lists all of the state's freshwater and saltwater boat launches (and regulations concerning these launches), and provides tidal charts, lengths of fishing seasons, and scads of additional information.

Other common freshwater catches, some tasty and some usually thrown back, include banded sunfish, black crappie, bluegills, smallmouth and largemouth bass, and yellow perch. Largemouth bass and certain varieties of trout may also be found in brackish waters, and some species of anadromous fish (those that spawn in fresh water but live most of their lives in salt water) can be found, notably shad and herring, which were recently reintroduced to the

Blackstone River, where they had thrived before mills and dams rendered the waters inhospitable in the mid-19th century.

Along Rhode Island's shoreline, bluefish, sturgeon, striped bass, and cod are popular game fish, as are a variety of shellfish, including mussels, oysters, lobsters, crabs, and Rhode Island's most famous saltwater treasure, the quahog clam, which is found up and down the Eastern Seaboard but is especially prevalent in the Ocean State. The quahog (pronounced "CO-hog" in these parts but "KWAH-hog" in some other places), also known as a steamer, is a hard-shelled, vaguely round clam that can be found in many sizes; the little ones are typically called cherrystones, the midsize variety are littlenecks, and the largest ones are called—and are used to make—chowders (they're also used in clam cakes, fritters, and other delicacies). For a chance to fish for these and New England's many deep-sea species—such as haddock, black sea bass, bonito, mackerel, bluefin tuna, and swordfish—consider booking a trip on any of the state's many private fishing charter boats.

Recreational saltwater fishing does not require a license, except for shellfishing ($200 for the season or $11 for 14 days), and only for nonresidents—just be sure to observe all the rules on minimum-size limits. Recreational lobster fishing is permitted only for Rhode Island residents who buy a $40 license. Freshwater (and anadromous) fishing, if you're age 15 or older, requires a seasonal license, which costs $18 for residents, $35 nonresidents. Or, for just $16, out-of-state visitors can buy a three-day fishing license. These may be obtained at town halls and a number of bait-and-tackle shops. Fishing licenses expire on the last day of February each year, regardless of when you buy it. If you're fishing for trout, salmon, or char—or fishing in a catch-and-release or fly-fishing-only area—you must buy a trout conservation stamp along with your license for $5.50.

BOATING

Rhode Island loves boating, so much so that the purchase of boats (along with any equipment bought the same day) is tax-free. There are aquatic outfitters and tour providers throughout the state, with the most popular river sports (such as canoeing and kayaking) along the Wood River, the Seekonk River, sections of Narragansett Bay, and many of the salt ponds in Newport and South Counties. For information on boating safety and regulations throughout Rhode Island, visit www.boatsafe.com/Rhode_Island.

Contact the **Rhode Island Party and Charter Boat Association** (P.O. Box 3198, Narragansett, RI 02882, 401/737-5812, www.rifishing.com/charter.htm) for a full list of private fishing, sightseeing, and sailing charter boats in the state as well as links to many charter operators. Another good website, both for fishing and boating, is **Ocean State Angler** (www.oceanstateangler.com), which lists marinas, charters, bait-and-tackle shops, marine retail and rental operations, and countless additional resources for enjoying your time on Rhode Island's waters.

Many of the state's lakes and ponds allow boating, and there are marinas and launches strung along the shore from Westerly to Little Compton. For a complete list of public boat launches, contact the **Rhode Island Department of Environmental Management (DEM)** (401/222-6800, www.dem.ri.gov); the website has links to information on tidal charts, licensing information, and Rhode Island boating safety.

GOLFING

Rhode Island's number and variety of courses—from winding, relatively flat, and rather tight links to lush, narrow, and hilly woodland layouts—has increased rapidly through the years, especially in South County, which has become Rhode Island's golfing capital.

If you live or play regularly in Rhode Island, it makes sense to join the **Rhode Island Golf Association** (1 Button Hole Dr., Suite 2, Providence, 401/272-1350, www.rigalinks.org). The association's website lists dozens of member clubs, upcoming local tournaments, and many additional resources.

CAMPING

Rhode Island has two basic forms of camping: the more primitive tent-and-backpack activity that's offered at both commercial campgrounds as well as at the state-operated Fisherman's Memorial State Park Campground, the George Washington Management Area, and the Ninigret Conservation Area; and the somewhat cushier RV camping that's offered mostly at commercial sites but also at the state parks. There's also tent camping at three municipal facilities: **Fort Getty Recreation Area, Melville Ponds Campground,** and **Middletown Campground.**

The charge for camping sites at most state parks is $14 per night for residents, $20 for nonresidents. Additional fees apply for sites with water, electrical, and sewer hookups, and for use of septic dump stations. Some parks have camping cabins available. For details on which state parks have camping and accept reservations, contact the **Rhode Island Department of Environmental Management** (Parks and Recreation, 2321 Hartford Ave., Johnston, RI 02919, 401/222-2632, www.riparks.com).

There are private commercial campgrounds throughout the state, most of them in the rural western and northwestern areas. You can obtain a directory that lists a dozen of these by contacting the **Ocean State Campground Owners Association** (c/o Oak Embers Campground, 219 Escoheag Hill Rd., West Greenwich, RI 02817, 401/397-4042, www.ricampgrounds.com).

Popular camping areas include:

- **Burlingame State Park** (follow signs from Burlingame Picnic Area exit from U.S. 1, Charlestown, campground information 401/322-7337, park information 401/322-8910).

- **Charlestown Breachway** (follow signs from Charleston Breachway exit from U.S. 1, Charlestown, 401/364-7000, www.riparks.com).

- **East Beach** (Ninigret Conservation Area, E. Beach Rd., Charlestown, 401/322-0450, www.riparks.com).

- **Fisherman's State Park Campground** (1011 Point Judith Rd., Rte. 108, Narragansett, 401/789-8374, www.riparks.com).

- **Fort Getty Park** (Fort Getty Rd., Jamestown, 401/423-7211, www.jamestownri.net/parks/ftgetty.html).

- **George Washington Management Area** (2185 Putnam Pike, U.S. 44, West Gloucester, 401/568-6700 or 401/568-2013, www.riparks.com).

- **Melville Ponds Campground** (181 Bradford Ave., Portsmouth, 401/682-2424, www.portsmouthri.com/MelvilleCampground.htm).

- **Second Beach Family Campground** (474 Sachuest Rd., Middletown, 401/847-1993, www.middletownri.com).

Accommodations

Many destinations celebrate their peak seasons in the summer when the weather is the nicest; not so in the noncoastal areas of Rhode Island. Peak travel in Providence is in the fall, particularly in late September–October when the foliage is at its most dramatic and students are pouring into area colleges. Many hotels jack up their prices by a factor of two or even three during this brief crowded season. If leaf-peeping isn't your thing, you can save a lot of money by traveling in late August–early September when the summer humidity has dissipated but hotel prices haven't yet skyrocketed.

Of course, the opposite holds true for the state's many beach destinations; Newport in particular gets incredibly congested with beachgoers in the summer. Rhode Islanders make the most of the brief period of heat between Memorial Day and Labor Day, so do yourself a favor and schedule your beach vacation before or after these magical dates, when you'll beat both the crowds and high prices.

Along with the rest of the country, Rhode Island has seen a steady rise in the price of accommodations at all levels, making it difficult to find any bargains among the major-name hotels. Bed-and-breakfasts, especially in more rural areas, can be an attractive alternative; often run by couples or families, they can offer dirt-cheap prices without sacrificing amenities or homeness. Those who prefer the anonymity of a motel will find more bargains (though less consistency) in independent operations. Gone are the days when a Super 8 or Motel 6 offers a $39 double—$139 is more like it. By contrast, you can still find rooms in the $60–80 range at many smaller, family-run motels. If in doubt, don't be shy about asking to see a room before committing.

Tips for Travelers

TOURS AND TOUR OPERATORS

Bristol-based **Outside New England** (401/253-9039, www.outsidene.com) offers a slew of engaging and exciting trips throughout New England, including several based in Rhode Island. Activities on these outdoorsy adventures including hiking, cross-country skiing, biking, sea kayaking, and more, and all skill levels are accommodated.

STUDENT TRAVELERS

Providence is one of the most student-friendly big cities in the country, whether you're studying there or visiting. Especially along Thayer and Wickenden Streets in Providence, you'll find cafés, shops, and other businesses catering to and sometimes run by area students. You'll also find all kinds of resources and like-minded company at the libraries and student unions of Brown, the Rhode Island School of Design, the University of Rhode Island, and other schools across the state.

STA Travel Providence (220 Thayer St., Providence, 401/331-5810, www.statravel.com) caters to student travelers and is a great resource when you're looking for deals. Many Rhode Island museums and attractions offer student discounts; always bring your university or school ID card with you and ask, even if reduced prices or admissions aren't posted.

Note that oddly, there are no youth hostels in Rhode Island.

TRAVELERS WITH DISABILITIES

Rhode Island is on par with other Northeastern states in the degree to which establishments conform to the guidelines set by the Americans with Disabilities Act (ADA). With new hotels, larger and recently built restaurants, and most major attractions, you can expect to find wheelchair-accessible restrooms, entrance ramps, and other required amenities. But Rhode Island has many hole-in-the-wall cafés, historic house-museums with narrow staircases or uneven thresholds, tiny bed-and-breakfasts, and other buildings that are not easily accessible to people using wheelchairs. If you're traveling with a service animal, always call ahead and even consider getting written or faxed permission to bring one with you to a particular hotel or restaurant.

A useful resource is the **Society for the Advancement of Travel for the Handicapped** (212/447-7284, www.sath.org).

TRAVELING WITH CHILDREN

Rhode Island is an excellent, if not quite stellar, state for families and travelers with children. The only real drawback is that the most visited destination in the state, Newport, is more geared toward adults than children; many Newport inns and higher-end hotels tend to frown on children as guests, as do some of the rowdier or more sophisticated restaurants and bars.

Providence and the metropolitan region have

some terrific attractions that may be of more interest to kids than lavish Newport mansions, such as the Museum of Work and Culture in Woonsocket, Slater Historic Site in Pawtucket, and—of course—the Providence Children's Museum right downtown.

The hands-down capital of family travel in Rhode Island, however, is South County. From Watch Hill to Misquamicut to Narragansett, you'll find great beaches, miniature golf, amusement parks, events tailored toward kids, and family-friendly accommodations. Block Island is a little more sedate and less commercially kid-oriented, but it also has both hotels and cottage rentals that are perfect for families.

WOMEN TRAVELING ALONE

Rhode Island is generally a safe and progressive state when it comes to women traveling alone. Although Providence does have the same crime concerns that most major cities do, it's a fairly easy city to get around, and the handful of inns and bed-and-breakfasts are particularly popular with single female travelers. If you ever find yourself in any state of concern or crisis, contact the **Women's Center of Rhode Island** (401/861-2761, www.womenscenterri. org), which has a 24-hour hotline (401/861-2760) and emergency beds available at any time. The organization's mission is primarily to assist women (and children) coping with abusive situations or homelessness, but counselors here can assist women experiencing any kind of challenge.

SENIOR TRAVELERS

Rhode Island is less famous as a destination among senior travelers than Cape Cod or certain parts of coastal Maine that draw many visitors in their senior years, but it's definitely a place where travelers over 50 or even over 65 will not feel at all out of place. Depending on the attraction or hotel, you may qualify for certain age-related discounts—the thresholds can range from 50 to 65. It can also help if you're a member of **AARP** (888/OUR-AARP—888/687-2277, www.aarp.org). For a nominal annual membership fee, you'll receive all sorts of travel discounts as well as a newsletter that often touches on travel issues. **Elderhostel** (800/454-5768, www.elderhostel.org) organizes a wide variety of educationally oriented tours and vacations geared toward 55-and-over individuals or couples with one member in that age group.

GAY AND LESBIAN TRAVELERS

Close to such gay-popular vacation spots as Provincetown (Massachusetts), Fire Island (New York), Ogunquit (Maine), and Northampton (Massachusetts), and with several major cities with visible and vibrant gay neighborhoods, Rhode Island is a relatively progressive and accepting state when it comes to gay issues—it's in the region where four states (Massachusetts, Connecticut, Vermont, and New Hampshire) have legally recognized same-sex marriage, and oddly, Rhode Island itself allows gay marriages to be performed in the state even though it doesn't recognize them. As of late 2010, the state offered only limited domestic partnerships. Discrimination on the basis of sexual orientation is illegal (as it is on the basis of race, religion, gender, and age), and the vast majority of the restaurants, hotels, inns, and businesses in the state are quite accustomed to and comfortable with the presence of same-sex couples. As of late 2010, Providence was the largest city in the United States with an out mayor, David Cicilline.

While there are currently no gay newspapers in Rhode Island, you can find plenty of information online at the Web portal **EDGE Providence** (www.edgeprovidence.com), which offers news stories and entertainment listings for an LGBT audience. In Providence, you'll find bars and clubs with a specifically and predominantly gay clientele—on the whole, the city has a dynamic gay scene, and the Rhode Island School of Design, Brown, and Johnson and Wales all have active gay student groups. There's also one gay bar in Smithfield (the Loft), but no other bars in the state that specifically identify as gay. Newport, however, is a very gay-friendly city; a few of its inns have an especially gay following. For information on these and other gay-friendly businesses in the city, contact **Newport Out** (44 Catherine St., Newport, 401/849-9600, www.newportout.com). For information on Rhode Island's annual Pride festival, in mid-June by the State House in Providence, visit www.prideri.com.

Health and Safety

WILDLIFE ENCOUNTERS

Because it has relatively few truly wild areas, Rhode Island presents relatively few chances to encounter dangerous or menacing animals. Rabies is a relatively rare but persistent problem, occurring most often in skunks, opossums, raccoons, and other mostly nocturnal animals. The state is rarely visited by bears or other potentially dangerous mammals such as coyotes and moose. Watch out for ticks, however, and be alert to the recent spread of West Nile virus, carried by mosquitoes, throughout the United States. If you feel at all feverish or sick after having been nibbled on by mosquitoes and the condition persists, it's a good idea to consult with a physician.

LYME DISEASE

The close proximity of deer with human beings has contributed to a painfully debilitating disease named for the small Connecticut town, just 25 miles west of the Rhode Island border, where it was first diagnosed: Lyme disease. Symptoms, unfortunately, vary considerably from victim to victim, and one common problem is delayed diagnosis—the longer you go without treating the problem, the more likely you are to have severe effects.

In most cases, a victim of Lyme disease exhibits a red ring-shaped rash around the bite of a deer tick, somewhat resembling a little bull's-eye and appearing from a week to many weeks after the incident. Flulike symptoms often follow—fever, achy joints, and swelling. If left untreated for more than a couple of months, chronic arthritis or debilitation of the nervous system may set in. It is in no way a disease to be taken lightly.

Unfortunately, testing for Lyme disease is a sketchy business at best; in the absence of reliable blood tests, you should consult with your health care provider the moment you develop any of the symptoms outlined above—especially if you've been spending time in areas where ticks and deer are commonplace: wooded terrain, meadows, and coastal scrub.

Better yet, avoid getting bitten by ticks in the first place; when spending time in wooded areas, wear a long-sleeved shirt or jacket and long pants, and tuck your pant legs into your boots or socks. It's also a good idea to don light-colored clothing, as you'll have an easier time sighting ticks, which are dark. Remember that the more-common wood ticks do not carry the disease, and that deer ticks are extremely small, about the size of a pinhead.

HOSPITALS

Because of Rhode Island's high population density, you're never terribly far from a hospital when you're in the Ocean State. Some major hospitals include **Kent Hospital** (455 Toll Gate Rd., Warwick, 401/737-7000 or 888/455-KENT—888/455-5368, www.kentri.org), **Memorial Hospital of Rhode Island** (111 Brewster St., Pawtucket, 401/729-2000, www.mhri.org), **Mirium Hospital** (164 Summit Ave., Providence, 401/793-2500, www.lifespan.org/partners/tmh), **Newport Hospital** (11 Friendship St., Newport, 401/846-6400, www.lifespan.org/partners/nh), **Rhode Island Hospital** (593 Eddy St., Providence, 401/444-4000, www.lifespan.org/partners/rih), **Roger Williams Medical Center** (825 Chalkstone Ave., Providence, 401/456-2000, www.rwmc.com), **Our Lady of Fatima Hospital** (200 High Service Ave., North Providence, 401/456-3000), **St. Joseph Hospital for Specialty Care**

(Peace St., Providence, 401/456-3000, www.saintjosephri.com), **South County Hospital** (100 Kenyon Ave., Wakefield, 401/782-8000, www.schospital.com), and **Westerly Hospital** (Wells St., Westerly, 401/596-6000, www.westerlyhospital.com).

PHARMACIES

You'll find pharmacies, many of them open until 9–10 P.M., throughout Rhode Island, the only exceptions being the more remote towns in the western and northwestern part of the state and Sakonnet. The leading chain in Rhode Island is CVS (www.cvs.com). Pharmacies open 24 hours include **Cranston CVS** (681 Reservoir Ave., Cranston, 401/943-7186), **East Providence CVS** (640 Warren Ave., East Providence, 401/438-2272), **North Providence CVS** (1919 Mineral Spring Ave., North Providence, 401/353-2501), **Johnston CVS** (1400 Hartford Ave., Johnston, 401/861-0312), **Pawtucket CVS** (835 Newport Ave., 401/726-0724), **Woonsocket CVS** (1450 Park Ave., Woonsocket, 401/762-3174), **Wakefield CVS** (11 Main St., Wakefield, 401/783-3384), **Warwick CVS** (767 Warwick Ave., 401/467-7788), and **Westerly CVS** (150 Granite St., Westerly, 401/348-2070).

TRAVEL INSURANCE

Buying travel insurance makes sense if you've invested a great deal in a trip with prepaid accommodations, airfare, and other services, especially if you have any reason to be concerned about your ability to make the trip (if you have medical concerns, however, check the fine print regarding preexisting conditions). It's a good idea to buy insurance from a major provider, such as **Access America** (800/346-9265, www.etravelprotection.com) or **Travel Guard International** (800/826-1300, www.travelguard.com). Typically these policies can cover unexpected occurrences such as trip cancellations, interruptions, and delays, as well as medical expenses incurred during your travels.

CRIME

Crime is not a major problem in Rhode Island, although random acts of both serious violent crime and petty theft are about as common in the state's urban areas as they are in New York City or Boston. In other words, most crime occurs in the rougher parts of town, well away from tourist attractions and the heart of downtown. It's a good idea when walking in Providence, Pawtucket, Woonsocket, and to a lesser degree in the suburbs around them to keep your eyes forward and carry yourself discreetly, without displays of jewelry or cash. The crime rate has dropped sharply in every major city in the state, just as it has elsewhere in the Northeast, and virtually no community in Rhode Island is so dicey that you shouldn't feel safe driving around and walking on major thoroughfares.

In an emergency, dial 911.

Information and Services

MONEY

Banks are plentiful throughout Rhode Island, although they are fewer and farther between in rural areas, including Sakonnet and the western and northwestern parts of the state. There, finding a bank that's open can require looking around a bit. Most banks are open 9 A.M.–3 or 5 P.M. Monday–Friday and 9 A.M.–noon Saturday.

ATMs are abundant in Rhode Island; most of those found at banks are open 24 hours and accept a wide range of bank cards (typically Cirrus or Plus network cards) and credit cards. You'll also find ATMs in airports and at many bus and train stations, in many convenience stores and gas stations (especially larger ones that keep late hours), hotel lobbies, and increasingly in some bars and taverns. ATMs typically charge a fee ranging $2–4, the exception being when you're using a bank card issued by the same bank as the ATM.

Credit cards and, increasingly, bank cards are acceptable forms of payment at virtually all gas stations and hotels, many inns and bed-and-breakfasts (but not some of the small ones), most restaurants (except some inexpensive places, small cafés, diners, and the like), and most shops (except some small independent stores).

Currency Exchange

Rhode Island receives very few international visitors directly from their countries of origin—at T. F. Green Airport, foreign flights are handled only from Canada and a few Caribbean nations. Therefore, currency-exchange booths and services in the state are limited. It's best to make these exchanges in whatever city you fly into from your country of origin. Rhode Island is far enough from Canada that Canadian currency is not generally accepted in the state.

Costs

Compared with other parts of the United States, no part of Rhode Island could be called inexpensive. Newport, especially during the summer high season, has some of the highest hotel rates in the country, with rooms at top properties easily exceeding $300 nightly. However, if you search a bit or consider some of the chain properties out in neighboring Middletown, you can find rooms as low as $100 per night on summer weekends. Top restaurants are pricey in Newport, but you can also find a number of both independent and chain eateries with rates similar to those found just about anywhere in the Northeast—which is perhaps 10–20 percent more costly than the average in the United States. In the off-season, hotel rates in Newport drop a great deal, and the city can be a relatively affordable place to visit. Block Island has comparably priced accommodations and, relatively speaking, the most costly restaurants (and groceries) in Rhode Island. This is true for two reasons: The economy is seasonal, so businesses have to earn what they can during the summer high season; and every morsel of food, equipment, and material has to be ferried onto Block Island from the mainland, increasing wholesale costs, which are passed on to retail customers.

Providence can be quite costly owing to its relatively few hotel rooms and the city's increasing popularity, especially when area universities are in session. Room rates are still typically 25–40 percent less than for comparable accommodations in Newport or Boston, but this varies greatly when there are events in town. It's fairly easy to eat well in Providence without spending a bundle; in that sense, the city is actually quite a bit less costly than Boston or New York.

Cost-wise, accommodations in towns elsewhere in Rhode Island are similar to the rest of southern New England, with low-end chains charging as little as (but rarely less than) $80 nightly, and better-class properties charging as much as $200 per night.

Shopping in Rhode Island is not markedly pricier or cheaper than in other parts of New England, although you'll find some very upscale boutiques and galleries both in Newport and Block Island. Gas stations in Rhode Island charge about the same as in neighboring states, and often a bit less than in Connecticut.

COMMUNICATIONS AND MEDIA
Phones and Area Codes

For the time being, Rhode Island has just one area code, 401; when dialing within the state, it's unnecessary to use the area code.

Note when reading about establishments in this book, where there is one, the local telephone number precedes any toll-free number.

Pay phones are becoming increasingly rare with the widespread adoption of cell phones. When you can find them, they tend to be expensive, generally charging $1 for local calls, and they also add a surcharge for collect calls or for using a calling card. Most hotels charge a $1–2 surcharge for local calls, toll-free calls, or just about any other kind of call placed from their phones; long-distance rates can be outrageous at many hotels, and it's generally a good idea—if you don't already have a cell phone with an economical calling plan—to use your own calling card or buy a prepaid one. Calling cards are available at many convenience stores and gas stations at a wide range of prices. If you're a member of Costco, Sam's Club, or another wholesale discount store, consider buying one of the prepaid Sprint, MCI, or AT&T phone cards sold at these stores—often you can find cards that end up costing just $0.02–0.03 per minute.

Cell Phones

It's legal to jabber away on your cell phone while driving, although it's not necessarily a good idea; text messaging while driving, however, is illegal, and definitely not a good idea.

Internet Access

The best and most convenient place to check email and surf the Internet is the public library; there's one in virtually every Rhode Island town, although only those in larger communities tend to have public computers. Many libraries in the state have high-speed wireless connections you can access from your own wireless-enabled laptop. Libraries at Rhode Island's several universities and colleges are also open to the public, but their policies vary regarding computer use; some allow computer access only to students, faculty, and staff. Libraries generally allow you to use their computers for short periods of 15 minutes–1 hour.

A handful of cafés around the state have paid Internet stations, and literally thousands or them have high-speed wireless (Wi-Fi) hotspots, which range from free to several dollars per hour. You can always try **FedEx Office,** which has branches in Warwick (1020 Bald Hill Rd., 401/826-0808), Middletown (7 E. Main Rd., 401/848-0580), and Providence's East Side (236 Meeting St., 401/273-2830); all are open 24 hours. This is an excellent traveler's business and work resource, as it's also a place to make copies, buy some office supplies, use FedEx and other shipping services, and rent time on computers to surf the Internet, print copies, scan photos, and so on.

Finally, it is becoming more the norm than not for inns and hotels—even small ones—to provide Wi-Fi Internet access to guests. More and more this is free with you stay, although

some large chains still annoyingly charge fees of $10–15 per day.

Media

Rhode Island has about 20 newspapers, five TV stations, and nearly 40 radio stations. A few local magazines and periodicals cover individual regions within the state, some of them distributed free at visitors centers and in hotels.

The glossy magazine **Rhode Island Monthly** (401/649-4800, www.rimonthly.com) has good dining, arts, and events coverage. The **Providence Journal** (401/277-7300, www. projo.com) has an outstanding and highly informative website with information on local dining, arts, music, travel, kids-oriented activities, and more. An excellent resource for metro Providence arts, dining, shopping, clubbing, and similar diversions is the decidedly left-of-center alternative newsweekly **Providence Phoenix** (401/273-6397, www.thephoenix. com).

TIME ZONE

Rhode Island is entirely within the eastern standard time (EST) zone. Like most U.S. states and Canadian provinces, Rhode Island observes daylight saving time (EDT).

VISITOR INFORMATION

The statewide information bureau is the **Rhode Island Office of Tourism** (315 Iron Horse Way, Suite 101, Providence, RI 02908, 800/250-7384, www.visitrhodeisland.com), which runs a visitor information center on I-95 between exits 2 and 3 and can send you a free Rhode Island travel planner by mail.

In downtown Providence, a well-stocked info center run by the **Providence Warwick Convention & Visitors Bureau** (1 Sabin St., 401/751-1177, www.goprovidence.com) occupies the bottom floor of the downtown convention center.

In addition, there are a number of visitors centers throughout the state, some of which are unstaffed and others that are open only Memorial Day–Columbus Day.

RESOURCES

Suggested Reading

Rhode Island hasn't exactly been written about to death, but there are a number of useful and colorful books on the Ocean State. Most of those listed below focus exclusively on Rhode Island or at least southern New England, but bear in mind that a number of additional titles—general guidebooks, bed-and-breakfast guides, historical reviews—discuss the state as a component of its greater identity, New England.

For further information on other states in the Northeast, including Rhode Island's neighbors, check out the many Moon handbooks that cover the region. At present there are titles on Acadia National Park; Boston; Cape Cod, Martha's Vineyard, and Nantucket, Coastal Maine, Connecticut, Hudson River Valley, Maine, Massachusetts, New Hampshire, New York City, New York State, and Vermont. Also check out *Moon New England Hiking* and *Moon New England Biking,* both of which include many outdoor activities in Rhode Island.

You may recognize the "Images of America" series from Arcadia Publishing (888/313-2665, www.arcadiapublishing.com) by the trademark sepia covers of its hundreds of small soft-cover historic-photo essays on more than 1,000 communities across the country. These fascinating books each typically contain 200–250 early black-and-white photos of a particular region along with running commentary that is usually written by a local historian, librarian, or archivist from that area. The books cost $15–25, and at present there are dozens of titles on Rhode Island that cover nearly every township in the state, several smaller villages (Peace Dale, Wakefield, Watch Hill, and others), and an amazing variety of special topics, including *The History of Mass Transportation in Rhode Island, America's Cup, Italian-Americans in Rhode Island, Naval War College, Providence College Basketball,* and *Rhode Island's Mill Villages.*

DESCRIPTION AND TRAVEL

Lehnert, Tim. *Rhode Island 101: Everything You Wanted to Know about Rhode Island and Were Going to Ask Anyway.* Lunenburg, Nova Scotia: MacIntyre Purcell Publishing, 2010. A nice primer on everything from awful-awfuls to "The Call of Cthulhu" that will have you speaking like a native in no time.

McElholm, Jim. *The Rhode Island Coast: A Photographic Portrait.* Rockport, MA: Twin Lights Publishers, 2000. Grand coffee-table-style photography book with stunning images.

Smolan, Rick (editor). *Rhode Island 24/7.* New York: DK Adult, 2004. Part of DK's U.S. coffee-table series on every state, this book contains some remarkable images of the Ocean State.

Works Progress Administration. *Rhode Island—A Guide to the Smallest State.* Boston: Houghton Mifflin, 1937 (out of print). Arguably the best treatment of the state ever written is this dense and fascinating work compiled by the Works Progress Administration (WPA) Workers of the Federal Writers'

Project. Part of the amazingly well executed and thoroughly researched American Guide Series, the book is long out of print; many titles within this series have been picked up in recent years and reprinted by current publishing houses, but not yet Rhode Island. Your best hope of finding a copy of this wonderful tome is by scouring the racks of used bookstores or websites such as eBay. Depending on its condition and age, and whether it has its original cover and map, this guide should sell for $15–75.

MAPS AND ORIENTATION

There are a number of decent folding maps on Rhode Island, and if you contact the state tourism office (800/250-7384, www.visitri.com), you'll be sent the free annual *Rhode Island Travel Guide,* which contains a very good general state map, which can also be downloaded online.

American Maps (www.americanmap.com), available in most bookstores, make some of the best maps of the state, from full state atlases to pocket maps of several towns and cities.

Very precise maps of the state are published by Rand McNally, and the *Rand McNally Rhode Island Street Guide* (Skokie, IL: 2005) is the most comprehensive collection. The foldout maps *Rand McNally Connecticut/Rhode Island* and *Streets of Providence/Newport* are published annually and are more up-to-date, and they include excellent city coverage.

HISTORY

Conley, Patrick T. *Rhode Island's Founders: From Settlement to Statehood.* Charleston, SC: The History Press, 2010. A recent take on the brave and quirky iconoclasts Roger Williams, Anne Hutchinson, and others, written by the state's foremost historian.

Douglas-Lithgow, R. A. *Native American Place Names of Rhode Island.* Bedford, MA: Applewood Books, 2000. Provides the lore behind countless Rhode Island rivers, villages, lakes, and other features from the state's Native American history.

Eno, Paul F., and Glenn Laxton. *Rhode Island: A Genial History.* Woonsocket, RI: New River Press, 2005. This is a first-rate, readable history of the state's curious past.

Laxton, Glenn. *Hidden History of Rhode Island: Not-to-Be-Forgotten Tales of the Ocean State.* Charleston, SC: The History Press, 2007. An admittedly quirky grab bag of tales from Rhode Island history, this make an entertaining travel companion for those long bus and ferry rides.

Raven, Rory. *Wicked Conduct: The Minister, the Mill Girl, and the Murder that Captivated Old Rhode Island.* Charleston, SC: The History Press, 2009. A true crime history that reads like a novel, this book details an 1830s murder in Tiverton that reverberated throughout young America.

SPECIAL INTEREST

Allio, Mark R., and Mary Jane Begin. *R is for Rhode Island Red: A Rhode Island Alphabet.* Chelsea, MI: Sleeping Bear Press, 2005. An exquisitely illustrated picture book that provides a nice backdrop for young children as they tour the state.

Beaulieu, Linda. *The Providence and Rhode Island Cookbook: Big Recipes from the Smallest State.* Guilford, CT: Globe Pequot Press, 2005. In a great state for dining, this book by talented food writer and restaurant critic Linda Beaulieu is a must.

Brennan, John T. *Ghosts of Newport: Spirits, Scoundrels, Legends, and Lore.* Charleston, SC: The History Press, 2007. An engaging and, dare we say, "spirited" guide to the undead pirates, heiresses, and commoners that purportedly still crowd Newport's streets.

HIKING AND RECREATION

Kricher, John C., and Gordon Morrison. *Peterson Field Guide to Eastern Forests North America.* Boston: Houghton Mifflin, 1998. For more than 20 years, the best all-around guide on New England's geology, flora, and fauna.

Matheson, Christie. *Discover Rhode Island: AMC Guide to the Best Hiking, Biking, and Paddling.* Boston: Applachian Mountain Club Books, 2004. An excellent all-around guide to the outdoors by a longtime New England travel writer.

Mirsky, Steve. *Best Easy Day Hikes Rhode Island.* Guilford, CT: Globe Pequot Press, 2010. A wealth of ideas for short nature hikes in the state for those wanting to enjoy the outdoors without too much strain or stress. Also available in Kindle and iPhone editions.

Peterson, Roger Tory. *Peterson Field Guide to Birds of Eastern and Central North America.* New York: Houghton Mifflin Harcourt, 2010. The definitive guide for birders by the godfather of the hobby is newly updated in its sixth edition.

Samson, Bob. *Fishing Connecticut and Rhode Island: A Guide for Freshwater Anglers,* and *Fishing the Connecticut and Rhode Island Coasts.* Toronto: Burman Books, 2007 and 2003. Excellent guides to the state for fresh and salt-water anglers by an experienced outdoor writer.

Weber, Ken. *Weekend Walks in Rhode Island: 40 Trails for Hiking, Birding, & Nature Viewing* Woodstock, VT: Countryman Press, 2005. A good reading companion for avid strollers.

Wilson, Alex. *AMC River Guide: Massachusetts—Connecticut—Rhode Island.* Boston: Appalachian Mountain Club, 2006. The Appalachian Mountain Club publishes a favorite book of kayakers, rafters, canoeists, and fishing enthusiasts.

Internet Resources

Because Rhode Island is so small, it has relatively few regional websites, but several statewide ones go into great detail on every corner of the state. Furthermore, a number of national sites covering everything from transportation to the outdoors have specific Web pages on Rhode Island.

TOURISM AND GENERAL INFORMATION
The Providence Journal
www.projo.com
This website, produced by the state's most widely read newspaper, may be the most comprehensive and informative online resource in Rhode Island. On this site you'll find the same in-depth news coverage as in the daily *Journal* newspaper, and you can search for older stories. There are direct links to separate subsites covering dining, performing arts, and other areas. There's also a specific section just for travel and visitors that includes information on attractions, business travel, family travel, reservations, transportation, and more.

Rhode Island Monthly
www.rimonthly.com
This site contains stories, reviews, and information from the state's glossy lifestyle magazine *Rhode Island Monthly.* Included is a regularly updated events calendar and links to top picks in the magazine's annual "Best of Rhode Island" feature.

Citysearch
www.providence.citysearch.com
Excellent for scoping out the latest info on hot new restaurants, museum exhibitions, which movies are playing where, and where to find a great hotel. While the coverage is chiefly about Providence, you'll also find listings for the metro area, including Warwick, Cranston, Pawtucket, some of the Blackstone River Valley towns, and even towns just over the border in Massachusetts.

The Official State of Rhode Island Home Page
www.ri.gov

The official state website comes in handy when you're looking for detailed information on state and local politics, regional demographics, the state library, and local laws.

The Official State of Rhode Island Tourism Home Page
www.visitrhodeisland.com

The mother of all Rhode Island travel and tourism websites, it has links to the state's six regional tourism sites: Blackstone River Valley as well as northern and northwestern Rhode Island (www.tourblackstone.com), Block Island (www.blockislandinfo.com), East Bay (www.eastbayritourism.com), Newport, Aquidneck Island, and Sakonnet (www.gonewport.com), Providence (www.pwcvb.com), South County (www.southcountyri.com), and Warwick (www.visitwarwickri.com). Within each site you'll find a trove of links to regional attractions, dining, lodging, events, transportation, and other valuable information.

TRANSPORTATION

Several sites are very useful for exploring the different transportation possibilities in Rhode Island, including air, bus, train, and ferry options.

T. F. Green Airport
www.pvdairport.com

Find out about parking, airlines, check-in information, and arrivals and departures at the state's main airport.

Amtrak
www.amtrak.com

Home page for the national rail service, which has several stops in Rhode Island.

Peter Pan Bus Lines
www.peterpanbus.com

Details on interstate bus service to and from Rhode Island.

Rhode Island Public Transit Authority (RIPTA)
www.ripta.com

The site for Rhode Island's in-state bus line; it's an excellent, easy-to-use site with maps and schedules that show all of the bus routes throughout the state.

Block Island Ferry
www.blockislandferry.com

Find out about rates and schedules for the ferry that serves Block Island.

Rhode Island Department of Transportation
www.dot.ri.gov

Provides extensive information on numerous publications, traveler resources, road conditions, licenses and permits, upcoming roadwork and projects, legal notices, and construction bid notices.

SPORTS AND OUTDOORS
Rhode Island Department of Environmental Management (DEM)
www.dem.ri.gov

Among Rhode Island's top Internet resources for outdoors enthusiasts, the DEM home page provides information and policies pertaining to boating, hiking, going to the beach, and many other activities.

State of Rhode Island Division of Parks and Recreation
www.riparks.com

This site provides links to every property in the state park system and also has information on primitive camping at state parks.

Rhode Island Chapter of the Nature Conservancy
www.nature.org

Hikers might want to visit this site, which contains information about the Nature Conservancy's many Ocean State refuges and preserves.

Audubon Society
www.asri.org
Great site for birding, with specifics on the society's Rhode Island chapter.

Ocean State Campground Owners Association
www.ricampgrounds.com
Great for ideas about where to find a desirable commercial campground.

Rhode Island Division of Fish and Wildlife
www.state.ri.us/dem/programs/bnatres/fishwild
Covers rules, licenses, boat launches, and tidal charts.

Rhode Island Golf Association
www.rigalinks.org
Here golfers can learn all about the state's many public courses.

Rhode Island Party and Charter Boat Association
www.rifishing.com/charter.htm
Lists private fishing, sightseeing, and sailing charter boats throughout the state.

Index

List of Maps

Acknowledgments

First and foremost, a big thank you to our editors, Elizabeth Hansen and Leah Gordon, who patiently shepherded this book through the writing and editing process, and helped provide many suggestions and comments that improved it over the previous edition. Thanks also to copyeditor Christopher Church and everyone at Avalon Travel who helped make this book a success—Kevin McLain, Grace Fujimoto, Krissa Lagos, Albert Angulo, and Tabitha Lahr.

A special thanks to our tireless research assistants—Danielle Ossher, Natalee Ranii-Dropcho, and Maddy Schricker—who made countless calls and web searches to ferret out prices, hours, and addresses on our behalf.

A big thank you to as well to everyone around Rhode Island who helped us plan itineraries, gather information, check facts, track down photos, fill our bellies, or lay down our heads comfortably at night. A partial list of those we relied on includes: Alissa Bateman, Andrea Carneiro, Jaime Derbyshire, Jessica Dugan, Annie Everson, Myrna George, Marlene LeRoy, Laurie Maw, Michelle Munick, Andrian Paquette, Lorraine Provencher, Dinah Saglio, and Lisa Starr.

As always, this book is dedicated to the two smallest travelers in our family—our children, Zachary Martin and Cleo Simone—who bravely survived long hours chasing waves on the beaches and rigorous testing of Rhode Island's many ice cream parlors.